"Jesus was no stranger to trauma—from treating a woman who had just escaped stoning and another with an unhealed flow of blood to predicting trauma for the apostles and personally enduring the cross. Neither should we be, especially those of us in the helping professions. The themes of the Christian Scripture—pain, suffering, personal humiliation, resilience, hope, and meaning—are the themes dealt with by these esteemed authors. Heather and Fred Gingrich have assembled an all-star cast of Christian psychologists to inform about the up-to-the-minute science, healing, and faith of traumatology."

Everett L. Worthington Jr., author of *Forgiving and Reconciling*

"In light of the prevalence, complexity, and destructive impact of trauma, Christian counselors and other caregivers need quality resources to guide them. Thus I am very grateful for *Treating Trauma in Christian Counseling*. Heather and Fred Gingrich have strategized to cover a broad range of vital trauma care topics with precision and wisdom. I will highly recommend this to my students and to trauma care providers in our ministry."

Steven Tracy, professor of theology and ethics, Phoenix Seminary, founder and president, Mending the Soul Ministries

"*Treating Trauma in Christian Counseling*, edited by Heather and Fred Gingrich, is a comprehensive and substantial contribution to Christian perspectives and approaches in the treatment of trauma. The various authors cover a wide range of topics, including foundational perspectives, interpersonal contexts, complex trauma and dissociation, and global contexts. I highly recommend this very helpful book as essential reading for those involved in treating trauma."

Siang-Yang Tan, professor of psychology, Fuller Theological Seminary, author of *Counseling and Psychotherapy*

"*Treating Trauma in Christian Counseling* is a needed treatment, long overdue. Our present 'culture of trauma' craves identity without closure and protest without nurture. But Heather and Fred have skillfully pulled together an array of traumatic scenarios with an eye to integrating faith and trauma. This should be required reading for every missionary, pastor, counselor, and social worker who understands that 'we have this treasure in earthen vessels.' As a professor of the Bible and student of trauma, I look forward to even more integrative work among the disciplines in years to come."

Andrew J. Schmutzer, Bible professor, Moody Bible Institute, author of *Naming Our Abuse: God's Pathways to Healing for Male Survivors of Sexual Abuse*

TREATING

TRAUMA IN

CHRISTIAN

COUNSELING

EDITED BY

HEATHER DAVEDIUK GINGRICH

FRED C. GINGRICH

IVP Academic

An imprint of InterVarsity Press
Downers Grove, Illinois

InterVarsity Press
P.O. Box 1400, Downers Grove, IL 60515-1426
ivpress.com
email@ivpress.com

InterVarsity Press® is the book-publishing division of InterVarsity Christian Fellowship/USA®, a movement of students and faculty active on campus at hundreds of universities, colleges, and schools of nursing in the United States of America, and a member movement of the International Fellowship of Evangelical Students. For information about local and regional activities, visit intervarsity.org.

All Scripture quotations, unless otherwise indicated, are taken from The Holy Bible, New International Version®, NIV®. Copyright © 1973, 1978, 1984, 2011 by Biblica, Inc.™ Used by permission of Zondervan. All rights reserved worldwide. www. zondervan.com The "NIV" and "New International Version" are trademarks registered in the United States Patent and Trademark Office by Biblica, Inc.™

While any stories in this book are true, some names and identifying information may have been changed to protect the privacy of individuals.

Selected excerpts in chapter 14 are from Aten, J. D., O'Grady, K. A., Milstein, G., Boan, D., Smigelsky, M., Schruba, A., & Weaver, I. (2014). Providing spiritual and emotional care in response to disaster. In D. F. Walker, C. A. Courtois, & J. D. Aten (Eds.), Spiritually oriented psychotherapy for trauma (189-210). Washington, DC: American Psychological Association. Used with permission.

Cover design: Cindy Kiple
Interior design: Daniel van Loon
Images: cracked paper background: © ekychan/iStockphoto

ISBN 978-0-8308-2861-6 (print)
ISBN 978-0-8308-8912-9 (digital)

Printed in the United States of America ∞

Library of Congress Cataloging-in-Publication Data
A catalog record for this book is available from the Library of Congress.

P	26	25	24	23	22	21	20	19	18	17	16	15	14	13	12	11	10	9	8	7	6	5	4	3	2	1
Y	39	38	37	36	35	34	33	32	31	30	29	28	27	26	25	24	23	22	21	20	19	18	17			

To Rico, Lynette, and Janet

CONTENTS

INTRODUCTION

HEATHER DAVEDIUK GINGRICH
AND FRED C. GINGRICH

What drew you to this book? Perhaps your interest in trauma emerges from personal experience, and either you or people you care about deeply have suffered as a result of exposure to traumatic events. Or it may stem from genuine compassionate concern for those who suffer, even without such intimate knowledge of the topic. For others, the exploration of this aspect of human existence may be more academic, in the sense that trauma has become a major area of study in the disciplines of psychology, sociology, and related fields.

Whichever of the above categories best fits you, studying trauma is likely to have some degree of personal impact. The horror of entering into the worlds of those who are trauma survivors, even if only on paper, can often produce a resistance to thinking and learning about trauma, perhaps to the extent of denying its prevalence or severity. Alternately, it can lead to a desire to understand the complexities of why trauma happens, how people survive, and what is involved in recovery. Either way, you may find this book a difficult read as page after page and chapter after chapter describe the ways in which trauma survivors have been affected by the horrendous things they have experienced. So we recommend that you pace yourself as you read so that you can sit with the material and monitor your emotional reactions to it as you go along. Practicing good self-care (see chap. 4 for suggestions) is also a wise idea.

HOW BIG AN ISSUE IS TRAUMA?

It is big—unfortunately, too big. In some significant ways trauma provides the context of human experience. Following are a few research-based statistics on the ubiquity of traumatic experiences. Other authors in this volume have added prevalence rates with respect to their specific areas of focus.

The US Department of Justice (n.d.) reports the following:

- 9.3% of cases of maltreatment of children in 2012 were classified as sexual abuse (62,939 cases of child sexual abuse); however, approximately only 30% of sexual assault cases are reported to authorities.

- Approximately one in seven (13%) youth Internet users received unwanted sexual solicitations.

- About 20 million out of 112 million women (18%) in the United States have been raped during their lifetime.

- Research conducted by the Centers for Disease Control (CDC) estimates that approximately one in six boys and one in four girls are sexually abused before the age of 18.

- Approximately one in five female high school students report being physically and/or sexually abused by a dating partner.

Estimated Risk for Developing PTSD

- Rape: 49%
- Severe beating or physical assault: 31.9%
- Other sexual assault: 23.7%
- Serious accident or injury (for example, car or train accident): 16.8%
- Shooting or stabbing: 15.4%
- Sudden, unexpected death of family member or friend: 14.3%
- Child's life-threatening illness: 10.4%
- Witness to killing or serious injury: 7.3%
- Natural disaster: 3.8%

(Sidran Institute, n.d.)

The National Center for PTSD (2016) reports that "going through trauma is not rare. About 6 of every 10 men (or 60%) and 5 of every 10 women (or 50%) experience at least one trauma in their lives. Women are more likely to experience sexual assault and child sexual abuse. Men are more likely to experience accidents, physical assault, combat, disaster, or to witness death or injury." Furthermore, about 7%–8% of the population (about 10% of women and 4% of men) will develop posttraumatic stress disorder (PTSD) at some point in their lives. The rate of sexual assault within the military has been a national concern, with 23% of women reporting sexual assault while serving in the military.

The National Trauma Institute (2014) reports similar trauma statistics in a different way:

- Trauma is the number-one cause of death in the United States for people 1–46 years old.

- Trauma is the number-three cause of death in the United States overall.

- Each year, trauma accounts for 41 million emergency room visits and 2.3 million hospital admissions.

- Trauma injury accounts for 30% of all life years lost in the United States.

- The economic burden of trauma is more than $671 billion annually.

- Each year, more than 192,000 people lose their lives to trauma.

The United Nations Office for Disaster Risk Reduction (n.d.) reports the following economic and human impact of disasters worldwide (2004–2014):

- $1.4 trillion damage

- 1.7 billion people affected

- 0.7 million people killed

Most of these statistics focus on the US context. If the United States is one of the safer countries in the world in which to live, then rates are likely higher in most other countries (see Rhoades & Sar, 2005, for examples). In addition, the associations between trauma prevalence rates and challenging social conditions are high: lack of education, poverty, war, community violence, intrafamilial violence, natural and human-caused disasters, human rights violations, torture, and so on all contribute to the risk of trauma. A Christian mental health response is necessary.

WHY A BOOK SPECIFICALLY ON CHRISTIAN APPROACHES TO TREATING TRAUMA?

The field of traumatology has exploded in the past decade. The concept and language of trauma have entered the mainstream of not only the mental health fields but also the broader culture. As Christians, we believe in the power and relevance of the Bible to our current cultural context and our personal lives. Scripture and the resources of our faith, therefore, are directly relevant to the human experience of traumatic events. While this book is not primarily a theological or biblical treatise, we believe that Christian faith has direct application to understanding and responding to trauma through the overarching redemptive story of the Bible (creation, fall, redemption) and the long-affirmed power of the Jesus story (birth, life, death, and resurrection).

How exactly this plays out in the therapy room is the focus of this book. Chapter authors have examined the secular literature as it pertains to their topics, while also looking at what could be helpful adaptations or additions to treatment protocols for use by Christian counselors.

A BRIEF WORD ON SPIRITUALITY AND CHRISTIAN SPIRITUALITY

This book is a combined effort to introduce Christian reflections, trauma information, and counseling approaches to contribute to this literature and need. It is specifically geared to students and clinicians desiring to be involved in some way with responding to the intense suffering of people. We hope this book challenges Christians to continue to enter the dark world of human depravity and to bring the light and healing of Christ. As you read and explore the various chapters, it will become clear that we still have much to understand, learn, and do.

Beginning in chapter one and throughout the book, aspects of Christian spirituality are specifically addressed. Because we recognize that Christian spirituality encompasses a wide range of biblical and theological positions, we decided to provide a broad approach to how various Christian theologies and resources are related to the topic of trauma. We encourage you to keep this broader definition of spirituality in mind as you read. The appendix at the end of the book, described more fully in the first chapter, will be a valuable resource to any of you who are interested in the academic literature that addresses spirituality and trauma.

THE LANGUAGE AND THEMES OF THE BOOK

Having edited all of the chapters in this book, we are struck with a number of core ideas and themes that emerge. Despite the diversity of authors and topics, it is possible to identify a set of threads that are woven through the tapestry of the book. Here we briefly identify a number of them:

- *Pain*. This word tends to be used to describe physical discomfort but has broader applications as well.

- *Suffering*. Perhaps a more holistic concept than pain, suffering encompasses both physical pain, emotional distress, relational stress, life disruption, existential disorientation, and spiritual anguish.

> **"All the cruel and brutal things, even genocide, start with the humiliation of one individual."**
>
> *Kofi Annan of Ghana, Nobel Peace Prize laureate and former secretary general of the United Nations*

- *Humiliation*. This is a unique aspect of suffering that recently emerged in the trauma literature and speaks to a central feature of almost all trauma experience. Embarrassment is included, but so often a profoundly deeper experience of shame and humiliation accompanies trauma. We need to pay attention to this aspect of treating trauma. Spirituality becomes a critical resource in this regard (see Hartling & Lindner, 2016).

- *Resilience.* Why is it that the same potentially traumatic event has varying impacts on different individuals? How is it that some people bounce back fairly quickly while others are scarred for life? The relatively new literature on resilience to trauma offers some answers.

- *Posttraumatic growth.* It is not all bad news! A corrective emphasis in recent years rightly affirms that while trauma is devastating and can end life and livelihood, humans have a remarkable ability not only to survive and recover from trauma but also to continue to grow in the aftermath of trauma. It is easy enough to acknowledge that individuals, communities, and countries can be unalterably changed through the negative impact of trauma. While it may be very difficult in the midst of traumatic experiences to recognize the growth that can occur, traumatic experience can be likened to a forest fire that eradicates everything in its path, and yet, given a few years, the green begins to return and decades later has grown into a new forest. Growth cannot be divorced from trauma.

- *Hope.* Related to resiliency and posttraumatic growth is the human capacity to continue to hope in the face, the midst, and the aftereffects of trauma. Movies and novels are often predicated on this capacity for hope. The power of hope cannot be underestimated.

- *Meaning.* A final, related theme is that resilience, growth, and hope are not founded on wishful thinking and unbridled optimism; trauma can create meaning and purpose for life. Meaning is not always or even often apparent in the midst of trauma, but it is there to discover.

> **"To remain alive after such a traumatic event and to give meaning to life takes a lot of work. Surviving may not be that difficult, but to go back to fully living, after something like that, takes a lot of energy and commitment."**
>
> *Laura Dolci-Kanaan, in "Aid Worker Deaths: The Families Left Behind"*

In addition to the above themes, we recognize the wide variety of language used in the trauma literature in reference to unique, yet sometimes overlapping, aspects of trauma. Some of these are child abuse, sexual abuse, domestic violence, intimate partner abuse, community violence, school violence, medical trauma, ethnic trauma, societal trauma, human trafficking, commercial sexual exploitation, extreme and torturous experiences, persecution, torture, acute events, cumulative microtraumas, nonverbalized trauma, intergenerational transmission, and dislocation trauma.

Other terms within the field may be less familiar to readers. Following are some examples:

- *Traumatology* is the academic field that studies the various interdisciplinary aspects of trauma, a growing and immensely helpful perspective. Expertise in traumatology is a critical need in the mental health professions.

- *Complex trauma and dissociation.* The complex trauma literature has exploded in the past decade. The important distinction has been made between posttraumatic stress disorder (PTSD) without the dissociative subtype, which can be the result of even a single traumatic incident, and chronic relational trauma, which often begins in childhood and extends into and complicates adulthood. The latter is often referred to as *complex traumatic stress disorder*, or *complex PTSD*. This distinction does not appear in the *Diagnostic and Statistics Manual of Mental Disorders* (DSM-5) but has become generally accepted in the trauma field. Survivors of complex trauma could potentially fit criteria for numerous DSM-5 diagnoses, with PTSD (dissociative subtype) and dissociative disorders being relatively common. For dissociative identity disorder (DID) alone, a recent review of the international research literature has found that 1.1%–1.5 % of the general population meet criteria (Brand et al., 2016).

- *Integration* refers to the collaboration, coalescing, or coming together of what might be considered disparate parts or aspects of an issue. In this book integration can refer to the intersection of psychological and biblical/theological concepts and approaches—a significant goal of the book. However, it might also refer to the linking together of aspects of human experience. For instance, counseling can be seen as a process of facilitating the integration of fragmented aspects of self (e.g., emotions, cognitions, behavior, body, spirituality)—something commonly experienced by traumatized people. At the risk of confusing readers, integration can also refer to the mutual interaction between theories and concepts within various approaches to treatment. For instance, the theoretical integration between cognitive approaches and behavioral approaches to helping has resulted in what is commonly referred to as cognitive behavior therapy (CBT).

- *Theodicy and theology of suffering.* Theodicy refers to the centuries of philosophical and theological discussions regarding the origins and nature of evil. The phrase "theology of suffering" has recently become a focus among theologians and mental health professionals since the reality of trauma has not appeared to diminish in our postmodern world. Despite technology and economic prosperity, evil and suffering have not abated, and we need the biblical and theological resources of our faith to help us understand and respond.

DEFINITION OF TRAUMA

It is important to recognize the range of opinion in society regarding the relatively new language of trauma. Over the past 20 or so years, the concept of trauma has moved to center stage of the mental health field and has in many respects entered our everyday, household vocabulary. You will notice in the various chapters that authors use different language regarding trauma. They are each addressing different types and contexts of trauma, and they have different theoretical orientations. Some take a more academic approach focused on research and evidence-based practice. Others take a more descriptive or narrative approach, writing for a pastoral or ministry context. In addition, the various authors use different biblical stories and teaching passages from Scripture as they describe the theological dimensions and spiritual consequences of trauma as well as the faith-based resources that are at the disposal of Christian therapists doing trauma work. This is one of the advantages of an edited book: it represents perspectives from multiple authors.

The authors also have different examples of trauma in mind as they write, which reflects the reality that not all trauma is alike. In considering the book as a whole, there are both explicit and implicit variations in how authors interpret the concept of trauma and what constitutes a traumatic experience. While this may at times be unsettling to the reader in terms of the need for precision and accuracy, we have allowed authors to speak from their own understanding and contexts. This also reflects the differences within the broader trauma field.

English is a relatively rich language with regard to emotionally laden descriptions of human experience. The word *trauma* has many synonyms, and each cognate has nuances in denotative and connotative meaning. Take, for instance, words like *atrocity, cataclysm, ordeal,* or *tragedy* or less intense, more common words such as *disaster, distress,* or *unfortunate circumstances.* English has a plethora of words with overlapping meanings that range from mild to strong in intensity as well as having more positive or more negative emotional valence.

Language evolves over time as a society notices and then highlights different aspects of human experience. I (Fred) recently read a newspaper article by an essayist (Carter, 2016) about the use of the word *tragedy* to describe recent world events such as natural disasters or terrorism or any event with terrible, life-threatening consequences. The author wondered whether the word *tragedy* has lost its powerful meaning and has been "dulled by overuse." While the impact of a tsunami is indeed tragic, my favorite restaurant going bankrupt and closing hardly qualifies. Tragedies raise questions about life and death, about how the world functions, and ultimately about faith, God, suffering, and redemption.

Examples of Trauma Experiences that Risk the Development of PTSD

Anyone who has been victimized or has witnessed a violent act or who has been repeatedly exposed to life-threatening situations is at risk of developing PTSD. This includes survivors of the following:

- Domestic or intimate partner violence
- Rape or sexual assault or abuse
- Physical assault such as mugging or carjacking
- Other random acts of violence such as those that take place in public, in schools, or in the workplace
- Unexpected events in everyday life such as car accidents or fires
- Natural disasters such as tornadoes or earthquakes
- Major catastrophic events such as a plane crash or terrorist act
- Disasters caused by human error, such as industrial accidents

Also included are the following types of survivors:

- Children who are neglected or sexually, physically, or verbally abused, or adults who were abused as children
- Combat veterans or civilian victims of war
- Those diagnosed with a life-threatening illness or who have undergone invasive medical procedures
- Professionals who respond to victims in trauma situations, such as emergency medical service workers, police, firefighters, military, and search and rescue workers
- People who learn of the sudden unexpected death of a close friend or relative

(Sidran Institute, n.d.)

Sir Walter Scott profoundly argued that the world needs tragedy since it evokes "that strong instinctive and sympathetic curiosity, which tempts men [and women] to look into the bosoms of their fellow-creatures, and to seek, in the distresses or emotions of others, the parallel of their own passions" (as cited in Carter, 2016, p. D1). A "strong and sympathetic curiosity"—what a great way to describe our efforts to produce this book.

This book includes 18 chapters with a total of 37 authors, all of whom are drawn by such a curiosity—a deep, compelling desire to know and understand more about human experience and how God is intimately involved in human tragedy. This curiosity is strong, and for many of us it is closely connected to our life callings as mental health professionals. It is sympathetic since each of us, either through our own life journeys or through the stories of the many people we have journeyed with, has felt the pain and suffering of tragedies at the individual, family, community, national, and global levels.

But whereas the word *tragedy* is often used to refer to external events, the word *trauma*, the core concept of this book, in addition to describing the tragic external events of life, designates the internal, personal responses and shared responses to such experiences. It is this intrapsychic, subjective level that is the primary focus of this book. External events may be the precipitating cause of trauma, but as mental health professionals we are primarily interested in the intrapsychic and relational consequences of trauma.

Human history is the history of trauma. From war, natural and human disasters, family violence, and brutal atrocities to sexual exploitation, child abuse, and terrorism, throughout human history it is likely that more people have experienced trauma than those who have not. But thankfully, human history is also the history of resilience, posttraumatic growth, and human flourishing. Stories of people's lives recount both sides of tragic experiences.

But what is trauma? What constitutes a difficult set of circumstances versus a traumatic experience? To be blunt, trauma is not just a bad day. We remember reading to our young sons the story of the Muppets character Grover's "bad, awful day" (Dickson, 1986). It is a legitimate attempt to introduce children to the fact that bad things happen in life. Our days can involve experiences of rain, losing one's boot, and stepping in puddles, actually and figuratively. But to define trauma, as some authors have, as "anything that is less than nurturing" (Mellody, Miller, & Miller, 2003; Rosenthal, 2014), even if the complete definition adds "that changes your vision of yourself and your place in the world," is potentially to minimize the seriousness of trauma. This tendency to generalize the meaning of the concept beyond its usefulness can also be seen in book titles such as *The Trauma of Everyday Life* (Epstein, 2014). To be fair, Epstein's book has many helpful things to say about trauma, including its emphasis on the transformational potential of trauma to support human growth and development. Yes, traumas touch all of us—death, chronic illness, accidents, natural disasters—but these events in and of themselves do not constitute trauma; trauma must include the subjective experience of physical, emotional, or relational harm.

There probably is not much point in entering a detailed debate regarding which definitions are scientifically or theologically more correct, but suffice it to say that people who have experienced trauma generally know, at least at some level, that they have experienced a life event or series of life events that have hurt them—that have disrupted their ability to live life abundantly (Jn 10:10). The authors in this volume provide explicit or implied definitions in their chapters, but the focus of the book is not on definitions but on helping people overcome the impact of traumatic experiences. We know at some level that trauma is common in human experience and that it is often a shared human experience. Trauma is a painful disruption in personal, familial, or cultural/ethnic/national identity and involves a loss of assurance that the world is a safe place. At the same time, it is the experience of resilience, a vision of the indomitable human spirit that exists within the experience and survives trauma. Theologically, it is the affirmation of our creation in the image of a loving God and also the pervasive reality of sin. The trauma lens requires a new appreciation for the biblical themes of suffering, sin, redemption, resurrection, liberation, and hope. If Christianity is going to be relevant, it must address the issue of trauma and provide understanding and resources for living in the midst of a trauma-torn world.

As you read this book, it will be helpful to step back from concerns about what is and what is not trauma and acknowledge that, to a large degree, trauma is defined by the one experiencing it. While this could quickly dissolve into subjective meaninglessness, it keeps the focus on what might be helpful. It is clear from personal and therapeutic observation that people can experience horrific events and apparently have no negative longer-term consequences that would fit diagnostic criteria for acute stress disorder or PTSD. On the other hand, what to one person might be perceived as a negligible, unfortunate incident can be life altering to another individual.

HOW TO BENEFIT FROM THIS BOOK

We would like to make a few suggestions regarding how readers might benefit from this book.

For students. This book is a pretty thorough overview of the kinds of experiences and treatment methods that incorporate spirituality into our understanding and treatment of trauma. The chapters do not need to be read sequentially, but we have been intentional in trying to offer a flow to the topics. Of course, you will not remember the specifics of each chapter, but we do hope that you will become convinced of the value of including spirituality in your future trauma work. In all mental health contexts, you will encounter trauma, and having some familiarity with the spiritual dynamics of trauma will aid you in your future work.

For instructors/professors. We hope that the range of perspectives represented in the various chapters will provide rich fodder for critical analysis and emotional engagement with the topic. We believe this book may serve as a primary or secondary text in counseling, psychology, and social work courses specifically focused on trauma and abuse. However, since trauma is a significant contemporary lens in psychopathology, its use in a diagnosis course will offer a broader perspective on the etiology and treatment of mental disorders. The inclusion of a new trauma section and reorganization of trauma-related categories in DSM-5

(American Psychiatric Association, 2013) suggests that there is recognition of a growing awareness of the benefits of a metatheoretical trauma perspective in our understanding of diagnostic classification.

Of course, foundational courses on counseling and psychosocial interventions, as well as supervision for practicum or internship experiences, must address trauma since a significant number of clients will enter treatment with trauma either as a presenting problem or at least in the background of whatever brings the client to treatment. While not all topics in the book are equally represented in the clinical populations, this book may provide a valuable brief introduction to the kinds of trauma that present in practice.

For clinicians. In addition to providing a theoretical basis for trauma treatment and introducing specific interventions, this book offers a brief overview of the role of spirituality in treating a variety of trauma situations. We hope that individual chapters will serve as a starting point for information on treating a specific type of trauma, which can be pursued in more depth using the reference lists.

For researchers. As mentioned earlier, we were pleasantly surprised by the number of references we found that incorporate spirituality into some type of trauma treatment. The appendix, while not exhaustive, points to the fact that there is a fledgling research base in this area. However, a quick glance over the column identifying the type of research indicates that most of the publishing in this area is conceptual in nature and that little quantitative or qualitative research has been conducted. The appendix gives evidence of a strong need for empirical research on the integration of spirituality into our understanding and treatment of trauma.

PROS AND CONS OF EDITED BOOKS

We will end this introduction by sharing a few of our reflections on the advantages and disadvantages of an edited book:

- The book provides an introduction to the various types of trauma with a substantial overview of each of the topics. However, there are gaps because it is impossible in the space of a chapter to be exhaustive. Despite our editing, there is inconsistency in writing styles. We sought to maintain the uniqueness of the authors' perspectives and voices.

- The book is heavily referenced. Although this can be distracting at times, our goal is help readers in further research. We hope this volume encourages readers to delve further into the topic.

- Because every author wants to share his or her passion and knowledge regarding the topic, the chapters tend not to be light reading. After all, trauma is not a light topic, and these pages represent thousands of hours of clinical work, teaching, and consulting with hurting and wounded people.

- In academic projects it is sometimes easy to lose sight of the pain of the millions of people on this planet who are suffering; however, academic and narrative reflections together move us forward in the field.

On the basis these reflections, we think that the advantages of this being an edited book outweigh the disadvantages. We hope that others will extend and refine this work in the future. We also hope that, in reading, studying, and reflecting on the issues this book addresses, we will never lose our sensitivity to the suffering of the people in our own lives as well as the plight of billions of people throughout human history whom God loves and for whom Christ died and rose again.

A NOTE ON THE DEDICATION

An edited book with many authors could have multiple dedications, but we hope our coauthors will value the personal nature of this dedication in the midst of a large academic task. We (Heather and Fred) have been working on this project over a period of time that parallels the life of our three-year-old grandson, Rico. In our late fifties we are raising Rico, our beloved son's son. Rico is an absolute joy—a gift and a blessing. But we would not have survived the past few years if it were not for two other people who came alongside us. Lynette, Rico's Colorado "aunt," has been for him and for us the doting extended family we do not have close by. Janet, nanny extraordinaire, has tirelessly cared for Rico with stability and flexibility. What could have been a traumatic life event for Rico and us has been a wonderful experience of family in community—God's gift to us and the world. Thus we dedicate this book to Rico, Lynette, and Janet.

REFERENCES

American Psychiatric Association. (2013). *Diagnostic and statistics manual of mental disorders* (5th ed.). Washington, DC: Author.

Appleby, D. W., & Ohlschlager, G. (2013). *Transformative encounters: The intervention of God in Christian counseling and pastoral care.* Downers Grove, IL: InterVarsity Press.

Bade, M. K., & Cook, S. W. (2008). Functions of Christian prayer in the coping process. *Journal for the Scientific Study of Religion, 47*(1), 123-33.

Brand, B. L., Sar, V., Stavropoulos, P., Krüger, C., Korzekwa, M., Martínez-Taboas, A., & Middleton, W. (2016). Separating fact from fiction: An empirical examination of six myths about dissociative identity disorder. *Harvard Review of Psychiatry, 24*(4), 257-70. doi:10.1097/HRP.0000000000000100

Bänziger, S., Janssen, J., & Scheepers, P. (2008). Praying in a secularized society: An empirical study of praying practices and varieties. *International Journal for the Psychology of Religion, 18*(3), 256-65.

Benner, D. G. (1998). *Free at last.* Belleville, ON: Essence.

Campbell, E. (2015). Utilizing the Serenity Prayer to teach psychology students about stress management. *Journal of Psychology & Theology, 43*(1), 3-6.

Carter, S. L. (2016, July 24). It's no tragedy that "tragedy" is overused. *The Denver Post*, pp. D1, D6.

Chorpita, B. F. (2003). The frontier of evidence-based practice. In A. E. Kazdin & J. R. Weisz (Eds.), *Evidence-based psychotherapies for children and adolescents* (pp. 42-59). New York: Guilford Press.

Chorpita, B. F., Becker, K. D., & Daleiden, E. L. (2007). Understanding the common elements of evidence-based practice: Misconceptions and clinical examples. *Journal of the American Academy of Child and Adolescent Psychiatry, 46*(5), 647-52. doi:10.1097/chi.0b013e318033ff71

Chorpita, B. F., & Daleiden, E. L. (2010). Building evidence-based systems in children's mental health. In J. Weisz & A. Kazdin (Eds.), *Evidence-based psychotherapies for children and adolescents* (2nd ed., pp. 482-99). New York, NY: Guilford Press.

Chorpita, B. F., & Daleiden, E. L. (2013). Structuring the collaboration of science and service in pursuit of a shared vision. *Journal of Clinical Child & Adolescent Psychology, 43*(2), 323-38. doi:10.1080/15374416.2013.828297

Chorpita, B. F., & Daleiden, E. L. (2014). Doing more with what we know: Introduction to the special issue. *Journal of Clinical Child & Adolescent Psychology, 43*(2), 143-44. doi:10.1080/15374416.2013.869751

Dickson, A. H. (1986). *Grover's bad, awful day*. New York, NY: Goldencraft.

Epstein, M. (2014). *The trauma of everyday life*. New York, NY: Viking.

Frewen, P., & Lanius, R. (2015). *Healing the traumatized self: Consciousness, neuroscience, treatment*. New York, NY: Norton.

Girguis, S. (2016, March 12). *Incorporating meaning-making into trauma therapy: An integrative adaptation to evidence-based practice*. Seminar presented at the Christian Association of Psychological Studies, Pasadena, CA.

Hartling, L. M., & Lindner, E. G. (2016). Healing humiliation: From reaction to creative action. *Journal of Counseling & Development, 94*, 383-90. doi:10.1002/jcad.12096

Hathaway, W. L. (2009). Clinical use of explicit religious approaches: Christian role integration issues. *Journal of Psychology and Christianity, 28*(2), 105-22.

Hunter, L. A., & Yarhouse, M. A. (2009). Considerations and recommendations for the use of religiously-based interventions in a licensed setting. *Journal of Psychology and Christianity, 28*(2), 159-66.

Larsson, N. (2015). Aid worker deaths: The families left behind. *The Guardian*, August 19. Retrieved from www.theguardian.com/global-development-professionals-network/2015/aug/19/aid-worker-deaths-families-world-humanitarian-day.

Leach, J. (2016). Psychological factors in exceptional, extreme and torturous environments. *Extreme Physiology & Medicine, 5*(7). doi:10.1186/s13728-016-0048-y

Levine, P. (2010). *In an unspoken voice: How the body releases trauma and restores goodness.* Berkeley, CA: North Atlantic Books.

Levine, P. (2015). *Trauma and memory: Brain and body in a search for the living past: A practical guide for understanding and working with traumatic memory.* Berkeley, CA: North Atlantic Books.

McMinn, M. (1996). *Psychology, theology and spirituality in Christian counseling.* Wheaton, IL: Tyndale.

Mellody, P., Miller, A. W., & Miller J. K. (2003). *Facing codependence: What it is, where it comes from, how it sabotages our lives.* New York, NY: HarperCollins.

Moon, G. W., Bailey, J. W., Kwasny, J. C., & Willis, D. E. (1991). Training in the use of Christian disciplines as counseling techniques within religiously oriented graduate training programs. *Journal of Psychology and Christianity, 10*(2), 154-65.

National Trauma Institute (2014, February). Trauma statistics. Retrieved from http://nationaltraumainstitute.org/home/trauma_statistics.html

National Center for PTSD. (2016, October 3). How common is PTSD? Retrieved from www.ptsd.va.gov/public/PTSD-overview/basics/how-common-is-ptsd.asp

Oman, D., & Driskill, J. D. (2003). Holy name repetition as a spiritual exercise and therapeutic technique. *Journal of Psychology and Christianity, 22*(1), 5-19.

Plante, T. G. (2009). *Spiritual practices in psychotherapy.* Washington, DC: American Psychological Association.

Richards, P., & Bergin, A. (1997). *A spiritual strategy for counseling and psychotherapy.* Washington, DC: American Psychological Association.

Rosenthal, M. (2014, January 1). How to explain trauma to people who don't get it [Blog post]. Retrieved from www.healthyplace.com/blogs/traumaptsdblog/2014/01/01/feeling-misunderstood-how-to-explain-trauma-to-people-who-just-dont-get-it/

Rhoades, G. F., Jr., & Sar, V. (Eds.). (2005). *Trauma and dissociation in a cross-cultural perspective: Not just a North American phenomenon.* Binghamton, NY: Haworth Press.

Sidran Institute. (n.d.). Post traumatic stress disorder fact sheet. Retrieved from www.sidran.org/resources/for-survivors-and-loved-ones/post-traumatic-stress-disorder-fact-sheet/

Tan, S.-Y. (2011). Mindfulness and acceptance-based cognitive-behavioral therapies: Empirical evidence and clinical applications from a Christian perspective. *Journal of Psychology and Christianity, 30*(3), 243-49.

US Department of Justice. (n.d.). Raising awareness about sexual abuse: Facts and statistics. Retrieved from www.nsopw.gov/en-US/Education/FactsStatistics

United Nations Office for Disaster Risk Reduction. (n.d.). Disaster statistics. Retrieved from www.unisdr.org/we/inform/disaster-statistics

van der Kolk, B. A. (2015). *The body keeps the score: Brain, mind, and body in the healing of trauma.* New York, NY: Penguin.

Whittington, B. L., & Scher, S. J. (2010). Prayer and subjective well-being: An examination of six different types of prayer. *International Journal for the Psychology of Religion, 20*(1), 59-68.

Worthington, E. L., Jr., Johnson, E. L., Hook, J. N., & Aten, J. D. (Eds.). (2013). *Evidence-based practices for Christian counseling and psychotherapy.* Downers Grove, IL: IVP Academic.

PART ONE

FOUNDATIONAL

PERSPECTIVES

ON TRAUMA

THE CRUCIAL ROLE OF CHRISTIAN COUNSELING APPROACHES IN TRAUMA COUNSELING

FRED C. GINGRICH AND
HEATHER DAVEDIUK GINGRICH

For he has not despised or scorned
the suffering of the afflicted one;
he has not hidden his face from him
but has listened to his cry for help.

PSALM 22:24

So many are deeply wounded as a result of the trauma they have experienced. How can we even begin to meet the need? Where do we start? What do secular approaches have to offer, and where do they fall short? How are we as Christian counselors in a unique position to journey with survivors?

We have no definitive answers to these and similar questions. We will attempt, however, to address some overarching topics that we hope will give you a framework from which to approach your reading of the chapters that follow.

In this chapter we begin by addressing the question of the goal of trauma treatment. We go on to examine a specific model of trauma recovery, the 4-D model (Frewen & Lanius, 2015), describing and evaluating it. We then suggest that an expanded version of this model addresses some of its shortfalls. Our intention is to provide you with an idea of what recovery looks like, which will influence how you view further discussions on treatment as you read various chapters in this book.

The next section of the chapter looks at the area of research with respect to evidence-based practice for trauma treatments (EBTTs). It serves as an overview of the terminology and issues surrounding EBTTs and directs readers to helpful resources on the topic.

We then turn our attention to ethical issues surrounding trauma treatment and introduce the area of trauma and spirituality. Finally, we make some brief comments about the need for additional and ongoing effort to wrestle with our theology of suffering—the crux of what we as Christians have to offer.

WHAT IS THE GOAL OF TRAUMA TREATMENT?

The various chapters of this book imply a variety of ways of conceptualizing trauma and present a multitude of treatment approaches to trauma. Of course, to some degree the choice of trauma treatment utilized depends on the particular population, the background of the treatment provider, and a number of contextual factors. Obviously, treatment will be different if the client is a recent victim of a natural disaster rather than a sexual-abuse survivor of long-term, complex interpersonal trauma. Regardless of the type of trauma, though, the ultimate goal is healing.

But what are the hallmarks of healing? Is a decrease in posttraumatic symptoms such as intrusive reexperiencing in the form of flashbacks or nightmares what we mean by healing? Or is healing more than symptom reduction? Do trauma survivors need to have wrestled personally with the existential/spiritual questions related to how to make meaning out of suffering in order to be considered healed? But then again, none of us will be fully whole, that is, fully healed, this side of eternity. So perhaps the often-used metaphor of healing as a journey, a process, rather than as an end goal, would be most helpful when thinking about therapeutic work with trauma survivors. Successful termination of therapy, then, would come at the point in the journey at which the client determines they are healed "enough" for at least the time being.

A MODEL OF TRAUMA RECOVERY: THE 4-D MODEL

In our perusal of the literature, our attention was drawn to the 4-D model of a victim's sense of self as it relates to trauma and recovery (Frewen & Lanius, 2015). While not the only or necessarily even the best model of trauma therapy, it offers a clinically helpful conceptual framework to which we have added additional theoretical constructs including spirituality.

Description of the model. The model suggests that there is, ideally, movement happening for the client from a sense of identity emerging from a traumatized self to an identity of a recovered self. This movement fits with the idea of trauma healing as a journey that we alluded to above; it is a process, and our goal as clients and clinicians is to see some progression toward healing, although the movement may be quite different depending on numerous factors such as type of trauma, severity, and pretrauma adjustment.

The original four dimensions of the Frewen and Lanius (2015) model refer to time, body, thought, and emotion. Figure 1.1 illustrates the original model.

Figure 1.1. 4-D model sense of self from trauma to recovery (Frewen & Lanius, 2015, p. 304)

The dimensions and descriptions of movement from a sense of traumatized self to a sense of recovered self are as follows:

- *Time.* I am fixated/focused on the past—the trauma—and I am *moving toward* becoming more focused in the present.

- *Body.* At times I feel outside my body, that my body does not belong to me, and that things happened to my body, and I am *moving toward* a clearer sense of being my body and that it belongs to me, that my identity and body are integrated (cf. Levine, 2010, 2015; van der Kolk, 2015).

- *Thought.* Thoughts and voices or messages are intrusive and take control, and I am *moving toward* a sense of owning and being in control of my thoughts.

- *Emotion.* Either I can't feel anything, I don't know what I'm feeling, or I feel too much, and I am *moving toward* being able to feel and knowing what I'm feeling, and it is not overwhelming me.

Questions that arise from the model. We believe that these dimensions are a helpful starting place from which to assess trauma and healing from trauma. However, some questions arise from looking at these dimensions more carefully. Consider the following:

- To what degree does inclusion of the body as one of the four dimensions make sense? To begin with, the brain and nervous system are crucial parts of the body that recent research findings have shown to be deeply affected by trauma (see chap. 3). Additionally, if we are to be true to a biopsychosocial model of the person (McRay, Yarhouse, & Butman, 2016), we must take seriously the physically disorienting dimension of trauma in terms of somatoform symptoms, and even where the body is in place and time (i.e., with respect to symptoms of depersonalization and intrusive reexperiencing of physical symptoms that can be part of flashbacks). Trauma tends to disintegrate this biopsychospiritual connection, resulting in dissociated aspects of a sense of self and experience (Gingrich, 2013). Also, a strong argument can be made for a biblical anthropology that rests on our being created as an embodied, unified body-soul-spirit (Benner, 1998). Jesus' resurrection and ascension as an embodied person affirms that the body is essential to our existence. His body was tortured, and even after the resurrection he carried the signs in his body. Of course, the dimensions of thought and emotion are also essential to a biblical anthropology and to our understanding of what trauma destroys and what mental health in God's image looks like.

- To what degree does the movement from trauma to recovery involve an increased sense of an integrated self and individual identity, as well as identity within or as part of a group (e.g., familial, ethnic, religious)? We briefly looked at the separation of the physical sense of self from the other aspects of self in the discussion of the body in the bullet point above. We also alluded to disintegration of the psychological and spiritual aspects of self. However, the relational dimension of identity that is central in more group-oriented cultures is not addressed by the model. The broader sociopolitical and economic contexts of trauma also are often vastly underacknowledged. This would be particularly evident in disasters, war, and other mass casualty contexts.

- The dimensions of the model, considered in combination, point to some of the complexity of trauma symptoms. But the model does not take into account the differences in severity and life disruption that individuals may experience in response to trauma. Since behavioral symptoms are often most readily observed by others, what does a reduction in symptoms in the other dimensions look like? Change in behavioral symptoms such as compulsive, avoidant, or dissociated behavior, for example, are more easily seen, yet some of the emotional distress may actually be more disturbing for the client.

- Meaning making is a key component of the trauma healing process. This has been emphasized in Park's research (e.g., 2013; Slattery & Park, 2015). Has the survivor been able to make meaning of the suffering? How will the survivor's future be affected? What is the role of hope, and how do our current circumstances interact with the future trajectory of God's involvement with humanity (i.e., our "blessed hope," Titus 2:13; see also 1 Thess 4:13-18)?

- What is the place of spirituality in the emergence, continuity, and healing of the self? How crucial is it? How does it operate to facilitate healing? Where is God in the midst of the trauma narratives people tell? From our perspective, a model of trauma must consider spirituality as it interacts with all dimensions. For instance, with respect to the dimension of time, we suggest that faith, and particularly a biblical perspective, includes extensive attention to the history of God working in and through difficult situations over time. We believe, therefore, that whichever trauma model we adopt, we should consider spirituality as a key element of what is negatively affected as a result of trauma, along with taking into account the role of spirituality in how trauma negatively affects the whole person and the community and how healing from traumatic experiences can occur.

- Is the ultimate goal simply a recovered self, or is there something more that our spirituality has to offer? Specifically, while the literature (see appendix) refers extensively to coping, resilience, and posttraumatic growth, Christian faith provides hope that the biblical concept of shalom is a real possibility. Referring to biblical passages such as Isaiah 2:2-3 and 11:6-9, Wolterstorff (2013) argues that shalom, often translated as "peace," is a much richer concept: "But Shalom goes beyond peace, beyond the absence of hostility. Shalom is not just peace but *flourishing*, flourishing in all dimensions of our existence—in our relation to God, in our relation to our fellow human beings, in our relation to ourselves, in our relation to creation in general" (p. 114). Flourishing is more than basic recovery from trauma—it is the essence of what our Christian faith has to offer (see chap. 2 in this volume for a further discussion of this dimension).

OUR EXPANDED MODEL OF TRAUMA RECOVERY: A MULTIDIMENSIONAL MODEL

While no model can encompass all possible dimensions, we think that by adding the dimensions of behavior, relationships, identity, and spirituality, as well as the recovery aspects of coping, resilience, posttraumatic growth, and flourishing, the model is made more robust. Descriptions of these additional dimensions follow:

- *Behavior.* I don't always understand why I act the way I do, and I feel as though I don't have control over my actions, and I am *moving toward* having a better understanding of and sense of control over my actions.

- *Relationships.* I don't have healthy relationships; either I don't feel close to anyone and so experience emotional distance, or I feel swallowed up by the other person, or I'm terrified of being abandoned, or I feel continually victimized, and I am *moving toward* feeling connected without fear of abandonment or need to distance.

- *Spirituality.* I have no sense of purpose in my suffering; if God is even a consideration, either I don't believe in God or I believe in a God who is judgmental and punitive, and I am *moving toward* a sense of meaning that has resulted from my trauma; if I have a sense of relationship with God, there is more of a sense of connectedness to God without fear of reprisal.

- *Coping, resilience, posttraumatic growth, and flourishing.* My life is overwhelmingly negative, and I am *moving toward* finding healthy ways to cope, discovering strengths and capacities for resilience, actually growing as a result of the trauma, and even flourishing in life.

- *Identity.* My sense of self is diffuse; I don't feel as though I am an integrated whole, and I am *moving toward* having a sense of myself as an integrated whole; I know who I am.

EVIDENCE-BASED TRAUMA TREATMENTS (EBTTs)

As counselors we are ultimately interested in the arrow in figure 1.2. What can help us to help others move from a traumatized self to a recovered self? Below the arrow we have included three concepts that occur frequently in the trauma treatment literature, specifically coping, resilience, and posttraumatic growth. There are obvious overlaps in the definitions and treatment implications of these concepts, as can be readily seen by perusing the references in this section of the appendix at the end of the book. Without focusing on the subtleties in definitions, it is clear that trauma treatment will involve one or more of these processes. As counselors, whether we are helping clients to simply get through their week, assisting them to better cope with their circumstances and symptoms, facilitating their return to pretrauma functioning, or helping them to grow through this difficult experience, we want to implement treatments that are more likely to be effective than not.

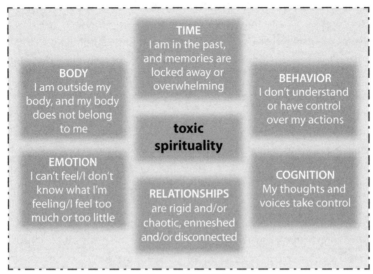

Traumatized Self

coping

resilience

posttraumatic growth

flourishing

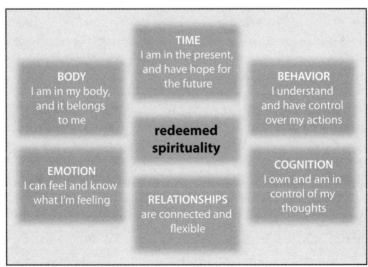

Recovered Self

Figure 1.2. Multidimensional model of self from trauma to recovery. Note: broken line represents diffuse identity; solid line represents integrated identity.

In the contemporary world of mental health treatment, there is rightly a concern that theorists, therapists, and those funding treatment programs (whether clients or institutions) subject their claims of understanding and of the effectiveness of treatments to research. Our creative programs and techniques, our wishful thinking, or even our hypotheses derived from rich clinical experience must be supported by scientific evidence. Christian counseling has not been quick to fully endorse this perspective since there is a pervasive belief that our faith operates beyond science and the power of God to effect real change should not be doubted. A helpful and convincing response to this issue is provided by Worthington (2010).

So a model such as we have described in figure 1.2 should be supported by research focusing on the key concepts in the model, and the treatment applications of such a model should be assessed as to their clinical effectiveness. This is beyond the scope of this book; however, it is essential to situate this book within the broader scientific community. Hence authors were instructed to heavily support their claims with research studies related to their topics. In addition, we will review in a cursory way the current state of the field regarding empirically supported trauma treatments.

The language of EBTTs and the research process. Researchers use various terms to describe different processes and levels of research support. "Research supported," "empirically supported," "evidence-based practice," "evidence-based treatments," and "empirically validated approaches or treatments" are examples. In general, the terms "evidence-based" and "empirically validated" refer to two levels of scientific support with the latter generally being seen as a more rigorous level of support. "Evidence-based" suggests that the concepts and interventions in a given approach are derived from research; that is, the ideas have research support. "Empirically validated" suggests that the particular strategy/program/intervention has been the subject of research to determine if it is effective.

As an example of research evidence building support for treatment effectiveness, in 2005 Bradley, Greene, Russ, Dutra, and Westen conducted a meta-analysis of 26 studies focused on the effectiveness of various psychotherapy approaches to the treatment of posttraumatic stress disorder (PTSD). The treatment approaches included 13 exposure-based therapies, five cognitive behavior therapy treatments other than exposure, nine approaches combining cognitive behavior therapy and exposure, 10 eye movement desensitization and reprocessing approaches, and seven other approaches.

The value of such research is that it begins to provide a rationale and scientific evidence to support the use of specific trauma treatment approaches. Specifically, for PTSD, Bradley et al. (2005) conclude that "on average, the brief psychotherapy approaches tested in the laboratory produce substantial improvements for patients with PTSD. Of patients who complete treatment, 67% no longer meet criteria for

PTSD" (p. 223). However, there are limitations in generalizing the results to all trauma patients. Bradley et al. noted that the majority of these studies were conducted in laboratory settings. The authors suggested examining what exclusion criteria were used (i.e., which types of patients were excluded and included in the studies), comorbidity (i.e., did patients fit criteria for more than one diagnosis?), the types of trauma studied, the specific criteria used to determine a successful treatment outcome, and whether follow-up data was obtained. Also, the research studies did not address the differences in the efficacy of specific treatments.

In response to the limitations of the above-mentioned studies, further research studies fine-tuned the evidence for various treatments. As the research builds the case, research summaries such as that by Cook and Stirman (2015) provide updates on the EBTT literature for PTSD. Over the years, these compilations of evidence for particular treatments encourage the refining of treatment approaches and comparisons of treatment efficacy and ultimately provide hope for those suffering.

This research process and emphasis on EBTTs in the field should lead Christians to conduct studies in the field of Christian trauma counseling. Worthington (2010) argues that this research process should not diminish the faith or belief of Christians in the authority of Scripture; good science will ultimately confirm our biblical and theological values.

In this book we will include both evidence-based and empirically validated trauma treatments under the rubric of EBTTs. Research on specific treatments in some areas of trauma (e.g., dissociative disorders, complex trauma, survivors of sex trafficking) is still in its infancy. Therefore, just because a particular treatment approach has not been identified as an EBTT does not necessarily mean that it will not be helpful or even the treatment of choice. For this reason we did not insist that chapter authors discuss only EBTTs. However, a few additional reflections on EBTTs are in order.

Common elements in EBTTs. Chorpita (2003, 2007, 2010, 2013, 2014) and his coauthors are some of the many researchers addressing the issues of common factors or elements in evidence-based treatment. While not specifically addressing trauma treatments, much of this research can be helpful in supporting trauma treatments and specific elements such as spirituality in treatment. We have summarized below what Girguis (2016) has identified as the common elements in EBTTs:

1. Psychoeducation: studying prevalence rates, normalizing trauma and trauma responses, educating people that physiological reactions to trauma are hardwired

2. Relaxation and coping: utilizing dialectical behavior therapy, acceptance and commitment therapy, and recent developments in cognitive behavior therapy, all of which emphasize the helpfulness of relaxation

3. Cognitive processing: recalling thoughts, behaviors, and affect related to memory; identifying misattributions and cognitive distortions

4. Exposure: eliciting memory, sitting with it, gradually acclimatizing while remembering

Critique/challenges of current EBTTs. We have a number of concerns regarding the current state of EBTTs.

1. Trauma is experienced by the whole person, and its impact is beyond simple exposure to a traumatic event. Trauma's effects are cognitive, emotional, physiological, spiritual, and communal.

2. The current EBTTs have a strong cognitive emphasis and tend to favor variations of cognitive restructuring as treatment methods. Emotionally focused, physiological interventions, memory processing, and alternative therapies such as expressive therapies (play therapy, somatic therapies, etc.) may be particularly helpful in accessing additional aspects of traumatic experience.

3. EBTTs appear to focus on the impact of trauma and pay little attention to the pretrauma functioning and mental health of the trauma victim. However, if, for instance, the victim's global meaning of life before the trauma consisted of significant cognitive distortions and tendencies to misattribution, treatment will need to tease out the trauma-caused mental health consequences from the individual's premorbid functioning. If a victim's use of spiritual resources prior to a trauma was dysfunctional, then how does this impact posttrauma growth?

4. The issue of therapist values in trauma treatment is particularly difficult since hearing trauma narratives is bound to result in intense countertransference responses within the therapist. The ethical dimension of trauma treatment needs to be explored in greater depth in the trauma treatment literature (see below).

Resources for further information on EBTTs. The following paragraphs describe sources of information related specifically to the research on trauma treatments. Some programs may include a spirituality component, but research findings are not detailed enough to support a claim that the inclusion of spirituality is empirically supported.

1. Division 12 (the Society of Clinical Psychology) of the American Psychological Association provides a list of research-supported psychological treatments categorized by disorder. For PTSD, Hajcak and Starr (2016) list seven treatment approaches with varying levels of research support:

   • Prolonged exposure (strong research support)

   • Present-centered therapy (strong research support)

- Cognitive processing therapy (strong research support)

- Seeking safety (for PTSD with comorbid substance use disorder, strong research support)

- Stress inoculation therapy (modest research support)

- Eye movement desensitization and reprocessing (strong research support, controversial)

- Psychological debriefing (no research support, potentially harmful)

2. The National Child Traumatic Stress Network (NCTSN; www.nctsn.org) lists 44 evidence-based interventions for children who have experienced trauma. They range from specific psychotherapy models for individuals, families, and groups to advocacy programs for specific populations. Some programs include cultural components, and some include training guidelines. Examples are child-parent psychotherapy (CPP) for families with children who are zero to five years old; parent-child interaction psychotherapy (PCIP); structured psychotherapy for adolescents responding to chronic stress (SPARCS); and trauma-focused cognitive-behavioral therapy (TF-CBT), which is probably the best-researched approach utilizing a version of exposure therapy (i.e., remembering a traumatic experience and pairing it with relaxation).

3. The California Evidence-Based Clearinghouse for Child Welfare (CEBC; www.cebc4cw.org) rates treatments for a wide variety of mental health problems for children, adolescents, and adults. For example, under the category "Trauma Treatment (Adult)," four therapies qualify as "well-supported by research evidence," two as "supported by research evidence," and five with "promising research evidence."

4. The Substance Abuse and Mental Health Services Administration (SAMHSA) maintains the National Registry of Evidence-Based Programs and Practices (NREPP; http://nrepp.samhsa.gov) with information on almost 400 interventions, some of which are trauma-focused.

5. In 2015 the International Society for Traumatic Stress Studies (ISTSS; www.istss.org) published the second edition of *Effective Treatments for PTSD* along with practice guidelines for a significant list of treatments: psychological debriefing for adults; acute interventions for children and adolescents; early cognitive-behavioral interventions for adults; cognitive-behavioral therapy for adults, children, and adolescents; psychopharmacotherapy for adults, children, and adolescents; eye movement desensitization and reprocessing (EMDR); group therapy; school-based treatment for children and adolescents; psychodynamic therapy for adult and child trauma; psychosocial rehabilitation; hypnosis;

couples and family therapy for adults; creative therapies for adults and children; and treatment of PTSD and comorbid disorders.

6. The International Society for the Study of Trauma and Dissociation (ISSTD; www.isst-d.org) has published guidelines on their website for the treatment of adults with dissociative identity disorder, as well as guidelines for the evaluation and treatment of children and adolescents with dissociative symptoms. The society offers courses on the treatment of complex trauma and dissociative disorders as well as two levels of certificates in the treatment of complex trauma and dissociation.

7. An international prospective treatment study named the Treatment of Patients with Dissociative Disorders (TOP DD) has provided strong evidence for specific treatment approaches in work with individuals diagnosed with dissociative disorders. More information on this longitudinal study can be found at https://topddstudy.com.

In summary, EBTTs for all disorders related to trauma are still somewhat limited. PTSD has been studied the most, and there is substantial evidence of the effectiveness of specific treatment approaches. Further research is needed to broaden the varieties of trauma-related disorders studied, the specific types of trauma studied, and the treatment approaches studied. Yet we have hope that treatment can be helpful, so for Christians this becomes a challenge and a call to respond.

> **"Whenever and wherever human beings endure suffering and humiliation, take sides. Neutrality helps the oppressor, never the victim. Silence encourages the tormentor, never the tormented."**
>
> *Nobel Laureate Elie Wiesel*

MORAL, ETHICAL, AND LEGAL DIMENSIONS OF TRAUMA TREATMENT

As with any counseling book, at some point and to some degree the moral, ethical, and legal dimensions of the topic need to be addressed. We have not included a specific chapter on ethics. This is partly due to space limitations but is more a result of our assessment that everything that has been written about ethics in the mental health professions is applicable to the treatment of trauma. In addition, much has been written on the ethics related to the use of spirituality and religious resources in counseling and psychotherapy, so it does not need to be repeated here. However, for readers interested in the topic of ethics in Christian counseling, the sidebar "Examples of References on the Moral, Ethical and Legal Aspects of Counseling" will direct you to some resources.

Examples of References on the Moral, Ethical, and Legal Aspects of Counseling

Chapelle, W. (2000). A series of progressive legal and ethical decision-making steps for using Christian spiritual interventions in psychotherapy. *Journal of Psychology & Theology, 28*(1), 43-53.

Corey, G., Corey, M. S., Corey, C., & Callanan, P. (2014). *Issues and ethics in the helping professions* (9th ed.). Stamford, CT: Cengage.

Doherty, W. J. (2009). Morality and spirituality in therapy. In F. Walsh (Ed.), *Spiritual resources in family therapy* (2nd ed.). New York, NY: Guilford Press.

Koocher, G. P., & Keith-Spiegel, P. (2016). *Ethics in psychology and the mental health professions: Standards and cases* (4th ed.). New York, NY: Oxford University Press.

Myers, J. E. B. (2016). *Legal issues in clinical practice with victims of violence.* New York, NY: Guilford Press.

Sanders, R. K. (Ed.). (2013). *Christian counseling ethics: A handbook for psychologists, counselors and pastors* (2nd ed.). Downers Grove, IL: IVP Academic.

Tan, S.-Y. (1994). Ethical considerations in religious psychotherapy: Potential pitfalls and unique resources. *Journal of Psychology & Theology, 22*(4), 389-94.

See also the codes of ethics of the American Association for Christian Counselors (www.aacc.net), the Christian Association of Psychological Studies (www.caps.net), and the North American Association of Christians in Social Work (www.nacsw.org).

We would briefly like to address what we believe to be a moral mandate, namely, that mental health professionals take a stand against the perpetration of trauma and support victims regardless of how the trauma happened. After all, mental health professionals are often the ones who most deeply interact with trauma victims. For those of us who identify as Christians, the mandate should be all the stronger if our moral convictions are based in Scripture. Value-neutral counseling has been clearly shown to be unhelpful (Corey, 2016). Mental health professionals must condemn interpersonal trauma. Of course, we do so with all the skills and sensitivity we can muster, but there is no professional rationale for avoiding taking the side of the victim whether that be in domestic violence contexts or in the aftermath of a natural disaster wherein some may argue that the disaster was God's judgment.

"Power without love is reckless and abusive, and love without power is sentimental and anemic. Power at its best is love implementing the demands of justice, and justice at its best is love correcting everything that stands against love."

Martin Luther King Jr., 1967

TRAUMA AND SPIRITUALITY

Christian counseling has a rich literature, both academic and popular, on the role of spirituality in the healing process (see sidebar "Sample of References on Spiritual Resources in Counseling"). However, only recently has literature appeared on the specific relationship between Christian spirituality and trauma counseling.

As we have combed through both the Christian and the secular literature that specifically links the concepts of spirituality and trauma, we have been pleasantly surprised to find out that quite a bit has been written. We initially set out to do a traditional literature review on the topic of trauma and spirituality. However, we decided that readers might benefit more from being exposed to specific articles and books on the topic, including a brief summary of the main focus of the content of each. To this end, the appendix at the end of the book provides a selected bibliography of much of the literature along with brief comments culled from the abstracts of these references. The appendix is categorized by topic and lists a total of 190 references, each addressing the relationship of spirituality to an aspect of trauma.

While chapter authors all discuss some aspects of Christian spirituality as they relate to particular types of traumas, they do not extend their discussion to include spirituality beyond orthodox Christian belief. However, the appendix includes a number of references that represent other faith perspectives (e.g., Buddhism and Hinduism). While it has been encouraging to see a greater openness to using spirituality and spiritual resources in treatment within the mental health professions, Christian spirituality is not always welcome. Yet the existence of publications that discuss the relevance of other religions and broader issues of spirituality to the practice of trauma therapy bolsters a sense within the field of the overall importance of spiritual dimensions of trauma. This may provide Christian counselors an increased voice with respect to the relevance of Christian spirituality to trauma survivors.

Familiarity with the literature on how broader spiritual practices from other religions can be used in counseling trauma survivors can also serve as a springboard for Christian clinicians to examine new ways of incorporating aspects of Christian spirituality into treatment. As an example, while holy name repetition as a stress management intervention (Oman & Driskill, 2003) may not be a common

Sample of References on Spiritual Resources in Counseling

Appleby, D. W., & Ohlschlager, G. (2013). *Transformative encounters: The intervention of God in Christian counseling and pastoral care.* Downers Grove, IL: InterVarsity Press.

Bade, M. K., & Cook, S. W. (2008). Functions of Christian prayer in the coping process. *Journal for the Scientific Study of Religion, 47*(1), 123-33.

Bänziger, S., Janssen, J., & Scheepers, P. (2008). Praying in a secularized society: An empirical study of praying practices and varieties. *International Journal for the Psychology of Religion, 18*(3), 256-65.

Campbell, E. (2015). Utilizing the Serenity Prayer to teach psychology students about stress management. *Journal of Psychology & Theology, 43*(1), 3-6.

Hathaway, W. L. (2009). Clinical use of explicit religious approaches: Christian role integration issues. *Journal of Psychology and Christianity, 28*(2), 105-22.

Hunter, L.A., & Yarhouse, M.A. (2009). Considerations and recommendations for the use of religiously-based interventions in a licensed setting. *Journal of Psychology and Christianity, 28*(2), 159-66.

McMinn, M. (1996). *Psychology, theology and spirituality in Christian counseling.* Wheaton, IL: Tyndale.

Moon, G. W., Bailey, J. W., Kwasny, J. C., & Willis, D. E. (1991). Training in the use of Christian disciplines as counseling techniques within religiously oriented graduate training programs. *Journal of Psychology and Christianity, 10*(2), 154-65.

Plante, T. G. (2009). *Spiritual practices in psychotherapy.* Washington, DC: American Psychological Association.

Richards, P., & Bergin, A. (1997). *A spiritual strategy for counseling and psychotherapy.* Washington, DC: American Psychological Association.

Tan, S.-Y. (2011). Mindfulness and acceptance-based cognitive-behavioral therapies: Empirical evidence and clinical applications from a Christian perspective. *Journal of Psychology and Christianity, 30*(3), 243-49.

Whittington, B. L., & Scher, S. J. (2010). Prayer and subjective well-being: An examination of six different types of prayer. *International Journal for the Psychology of Religion, 20*(1), 59-68.

Worthington, E. L., Jr., Johnson, E. L., Hook, J. N., & Aten, J. D. (Eds.). (2013). *Evidence-based practices for Christian counseling and psychotherapy.* Downers Grove, IL: IVP Academic.

Resources on the Theology of Suffering

Anderson, R. S., (2010). *Self-Care: A theology of personal empowerment and spiritual healing.* Eugene, OR: Wipf and Stock.

Boase, E., & Frechette, C. G. (Eds.). (2016). *Bible through the lens of trauma.* Atlanta, GA: SBL Press.

Cloud, H., & Townsend, J. (2001). *How people grow: What the Bible reveals about personal growth.* Grand Rapids, MI: Zondervan.

Dykstra, R. C. (2016). Meet the terrible resistance: Childhood suffering and the Christian body. *Pastoral Psychology, 65*(5), 657-68.

Eiesland, N. L. (1994). *The disabled God.* Nashville, TN: Abingdon Press.

Epstein, M. (2014). *The trauma of everyday life.* New York, NY: Viking.

Griffith, J. L. (2010). *Religion that heals, religion that harms: A guide for clinical practice.* New York, NY: Guilford Press.

Hall, M. E. L., Langer, R., & McMartin, J. (2010). The role of suffering in human flourishing: Contributions from positive psychology, theology, and philosophy. *Journal of Psychology & Theology, 38*(2), 111-21.

Hubbard, M. G. (2009). *More than an aspirin: A Christian perspective on pain and suffering.* Grand Rapids, MI: Discovery House.

Kreeft, P. (1986). *Making sense out of suffering.* Ann Arbor, MI: Servant Books.

Langberg, D. (2015). *Suffering and the heart of God: How trauma destroys and Christ restores.* Greensboro, NC: New Growth Press.

Martin, J. (2016). *Seven last words: An invitation to a deeper friendship with Jesus.* New York, NY: HarperCollins.

McGrath, A. (1995). *Suffering and God.* Grand Rapids, MI: Zondervan.

Peterman, G. W., & Schmutzer, A. J. (2016). *Between pain and grace: A biblical theology of suffering.* Chicago, IL: Moody.

Ting, R. S.-K. (2007). Is suffering good? An explorative study on the religious persecution among Chinese pastors. *Journal of Psychology & Theology, 35*(3), 202-10.

Yancey, P. (1988). *Disappointment with God.* Grand Rapids, MI: Zondervan.

Yancey, P. (1988, February 19). How not to spell relief. *Christianity Today.*

Yancey, P. (1990). *Where is God when it hurts?* Grand Rapids, MI: Zondervan.

religious practice in many Christian contexts, its use in other religions (e.g., mantra/ mantram in Hinduism and Buddhism) may encourage Christians in the use of spiritual exercises such as meditation, the Jesus Prayer, and *lectio divina*.

The literature on trauma and spirituality clearly shows that it is common for trauma survivors to be confronted with questions about life and death, spirituality, and meaning. Trauma tends to shake the foundations of survivors' spiritual belief systems, whether these beliefs are expressed in explicitly religious terms or as existential questions that are ultimately spiritual in nature. Therefore, the importance of appropriately incorporating spirituality into the treatment of trauma cannot be overstated.

CONCLUSION: A CALL FOR A MORE ROBUST THEOLOGY OF SUFFERING

We trust that this book will serve as a good summary of what is known about Christian spirituality and trauma, as well as provide a valuable resource for Christian mental health professionals who desire to be involved in responding to suffering people. We also hope that this book will challenge Christian therapists to continue to enter the dark world of human depravity and to bring the light and healing of Christ.

As we complete the process of editing this book, we are more aware than ever of the great need for a robust and realistic theology of suffering. Despite the fact that we all work with traumatized people, Christian counselors have not been quick to engage this topic theologically. Our colleagues who are biblical scholars and theologians also have not been quick to provide us with practical resources for our work in this area (Anderson, 1990; Charry, 2001). Of course, some literature does exist (see the sidebar "Resources on the Theology of Suffering" and chap. 2 in this volume), but we hope that this book will encourage other authors to develop our thinking and add to the available resources with respect to the intersection of psychology, counseling, the Bible, theology, and the human experience of suffering. This may be the primary way the church and the gospel will be able to connect to people's experience in an era that is increasingly closed to the traditional avenues of sharing our Christian faith.

REFERENCES

Anderson, R. S. (1990). *Christians who counsel: The vocation of wholistic therapy.* Grand Rapids, MI: Zondervan.

Anderson, R. S. (2010). *Self-care: A theology of personal empowerment and spiritual healing.* Eugene, OR: Wipf and Stock.

Benner, D. G. (1998). *Care of souls: Revisioning Christian nurture and counsel.* Grand Rapids, MI: Baker Books.

Boase, E., & Frechette, C. G. (Eds.). (2016). *Bible through the lens of trauma*. Atlanta, GA: SBL Press.

Bradley, R., Greene, J., Russ, E., Dutra, L., & Westen, D. (2005). Multidimensional meta-analysis of psychotherapy for PTSD. *American Journal of Psychiatry, 162*(2), 214-27.

Carter, S. L. (2016, July 24). It's no tragedy that "tragedy" is overused. *The Denver Post*, pp. D1, D6.

Chapelle, W. (2000). A series of progressive legal and ethical decision-making steps for using Christian spiritual interventions in psychotherapy. *Journal of Psychology & Theology, 28*(1), 43-53.

Charry, E. T. (2001). Theology after psychology. In M. McMinn & T. Phillips (Eds.), *Care for the soul* (pp. 118-33). Downers Grove, IL: InterVarsity Press.

Chorpita, B. F. (2003). The frontier of evidence-based practice. In A. E. Kazdin & J. R. Weisz (Eds.), *Evidence-based psychotherapies for children and adolescents* (pp. 42-59). New York, NY: Guilford Press.

Chorpita, B. F., Becker, K. D., & Daleiden, E. L. (2007). Understanding the common elements of evidence-based practice: Misconceptions and clinical examples. *Journal of the American Academy of Child and Adolescent Psychiatry, 46*(5), 647-52. doi:10.1097/chi.0b013e318033ff71

Chorpita, B. F., & Daleiden, E. L. (2010). Building evidence-based systems in children's mental health. In J. Weisz & A. Kazdin (Eds.), *Evidence-based psychotherapies for children and adolescents* (2nd ed., pp. 482-99). New York, NY: Guilford Press.

Chorpita, B. F., & Daleiden, E. L. (2013). Structuring the collaboration of science and service in pursuit of a shared vision. *Journal of Clinical Child & Adolescent Psychology, 43*(2), 323-38. doi:10.1080/15374416.2013.828297

Chorpita, B. F., & Daleiden, E. L. (2014). Doing more with what we know: Introduction to the special issue. *Journal of Clinical Child & Adolescent Psychology, 43*(2), 143-44. doi:10.1080/15374416.2013.869751

Cloud, H., & Townsend, J. (2001). *How people grow: What the Bible reveals about personal growth*. Grand Rapids, MI: Zondervan.

Cook, J. M., & Stirman, S. W. (2015). Implementation of evidence-based treatment for PTSD. *PTSD Research Quarterly, 26*(4), 1-9. Retrieved from www.ptsd.va.gov/professional/newsletters/research-quarterly/V26N4.pdf

Corey, G. (2016). *Theory and practice of counseling and psychotherapy* (10th ed.). Boston, MA: Brooks/Cole.

Corey, G., Corey, M. S., Corey, C., & Callanan, P. (2014). *Issues and ethics in the helping professions* (9th ed.). Stamford, CT: Cengage.

Doherty, W. J. (2009). Morality and spirituality in therapy. In F. Walsh (Ed.), *Spiritual resources in family therapy* (2nd ed.). New York, NY: Guilford Press.

Dykstra, R. C. (2016). Meet the terrible resistance: Childhood suffering and the Christian body. *Pastoral Psychology, 65*(5), 657-68. doi:10.1007/s11089-016-0705-5

Eiesland, N. L. (1994). *The disabled God.* Nashville, TN: Abingdon Press.

Epstein, M. (2014). *The trauma of everyday life.* New York, NY: Viking.

Frewen, P., & Lanius, R. (2015). *Healing the traumatized self: Consciousness, neuroscience, treatment.* New York, NY: Norton.

Gingrich, H. D. (2013). *Restoring the shattered self: A Christian counselor's guide to complex trauma.* Downers Grove, IL: IVP Academic.

Girguis, S. (2016, March 12). *Incorporating meaning-making into trauma therapy: An integrative adaptation to evidence-based practice.* Seminar presented at the Christian Association for Psychological Studies, Pasadena, CA.

Griffith, J. L. (2010). *Religion that heals, religion that harms: A guide for clinical practice.* New York, NY: Guilford Press.

Hajcak, G., & Starr, L. (2016). *Posttraumatic stress disorder.* Retrieved from www.div12 .org/psychological-treatments/disorders/post-traumatic-stress-disorder

Hall, M. E. L., Langer, R., & McMartin, J. (2010). The role of suffering in human flourishing: Contributions from positive psychology, theology, and philosophy. *Journal of Psychology & Theology, 38*(2), 111-21.

Hartling, L. M., & Lindner, E. G. (2016). Healing humiliation: From reaction to creative action. *Journal of Counseling & Development, 94*, 383-90. doi:10.1002/jcad.12096

Hubbard, M. G. (2009). *More than an aspirin: A Christian perspective on pain and suffering.* Grand Rapids, MI: Discovery House.

Martin, J. (2016). *Seven last words: An invitation to a deeper friendship with Jesus.* New York, NY: HarperCollins.

King, M. L., Jr. (1967). *Where do we go from here?* Annual report delivered at the 11th Convention of the Southern Christian Leadership Conference. Atlanta, GA. Retrieved from www-personal.umich.edu/~gmarkus/MLK_WhereDoWeGo.pdf

Koocher, G. P., & Keith-Spiegel, P. (2016). *Ethics in psychology and the mental health professions: Standards and cases* (4th ed.). New York, NY: Oxford University Press.

Kreeft, P. (1986). *Making sense out of suffering.* Ann Arbor, MI: Servant Books.

Langberg, D. (2015). *Suffering and the heart of God: How trauma destroys and Christ restores.* Greensboro, NC: New Growth Press.

Leach, J. (2016). Psychological factors in exceptional, extreme and torturous environments. *Extreme Physiology & Medicine, 5*(7). doi:10.1186/s13728-016-0048-y

Levine, P. (2010). *In an unspoken voice: How the body releases trauma and restores goodness.* Berkeley, CA: North Atlantic Books.

Levine, P. (2015). *Trauma and memory: Brain and body in a search for the living past: A practical guide for understanding and working with traumatic memory.* Berkeley, CA: North Atlantic Books.

McGrath, A. (1995). *Suffering and God*. Grand Rapids, MI: Zondervan.

McRay, B. W., Yarhouse, M. A., & Butman, R. E. (2016). *Modern psychopathologies: A comprehensive Christian appraisal* (2nd ed.). Downers Grove, IL: IVP Academic.

Mellody, P., Miller, A. W., & Miller J. K. (2003). *Facing codependence: What it is, where it comes from, how it sabotages our lives*. New York, NY: HarperCollins.

Myers, J. E. B. (2016). *Legal issues in clinical practice with victims of violence*. New York, NY: Guilford Press.

Oman, D., & Driskill, J. D. (2003). Holy name repetition as a spiritual exercise and therapeutic technique. *Journal of Psychology and Christianity, 22*(1), 5-19.

Park, C. L. (2013). Trauma and meaning making: Converging conceptualizations and emerging evidence. In J. A. Hicks & C. Routledge (Eds.), *The experience of meaning in life: Classical perspectives, emerging themes, and controversies* (pp. 61-76). New York, NY: Springer.

Peterman, G. W., & Schmutzer, A. J. (2016). *Between pain and grace: A biblical theology of suffering*. Chicago, IL: Moody.

Rosenthal, M. (2014, January 1). How to explain trauma to people who don't get it [Blog post]. Retrieved from www.healthyplace.com/blogs/traumaptsdblog/2014/01/01 /feeling-misunderstood-how-to-explain-trauma-to-people-who-just-dont-get-it/

Sanders, R. K. (Ed.). (2013). *Christian counseling ethics: A handbook for psychologists, counselors and pastors* (2nd ed.). Downers Grove, IL: IVP Academic.

Slattery, J. M., & Park, C. L. (2015). Spirituality and making meaning: Implications for therapy with trauma survivors. In D. F. Walker, C. A. Courtois, & J. D. Aten (Eds.), *Spiritually oriented psychotherapy for trauma* (pp. 127-46). Washington, DC: American Psychological Association. doi:10.1037/14500-007

Tan, S.-Y. (1994). Ethical considerations in religious psychotherapy: Potential pitfalls and unique resources. *Journal of Psychology & Theology, 22*(4), 389-94.

Ting, R. S.-K. (2007). Is suffering good? An explorative study on the religious persecution among Chinese pastors. *Journal of Psychology & Theology, 35*(3), 202-10.

van der Kolk, B. A. (2015). *The body keeps the score: Brain, mind, and body in the healing of trauma*. New York, NY: Penguin.

Wolterstorff, N. P. (2013). *Journey toward justice: Personal encounters in the global south*. Grand Rapids, MI: Baker Academic.

Worthington, E. L., Jr. (2010). *Coming to peace with psychology: What Christians can learn from psychological science*. Downers Grove, IL: InterVarsity Press.

Yancey, P. (1988). *Disappointment with God*. Grand Rapids, MI: Zondervan.

Yancey, P. (1988, February 19). How not to spell relief. *Christianity Today*, p. 64.

Yancey, P. (1990). *Where is God when it hurts?* Grand Rapids, MI: Zondervan.

THEOLOGICAL PERSPECTIVES ON TRAUMA:

HUMAN FLOURISHING AFTER THE FALL

RICHARD LANGER, JASON McMARTIN, AND

M. ELIZABETH LEWIS HALL

Compare two catastrophic events: the destruction of the Twin Towers in New York in 2001 and the explosion of Mount St. Helens in Washington State in 1980. Both destinations were nationally known, instantly recognizable; their iconic images were ubiquitous on postcards and calendars. Both disasters were fatal, fiery, and traumatic, captured with video and still images. Both left behind visual carnage that was almost as striking as the disaster itself. And in both cases, people wondered if the damage could ever be repaired.

Imagine you were charged with the task of restoration. What would you do? It is here where the roads diverge. In the case of the Twin Towers, the devastation was simply destructive. The first task of the restorer would be to cart away all the remnants of the old buildings; the smoldering bricks and twisted steel girders would simply be detritus that impeded restoration. But in the case of Mount St. Helens, things were different. The debris from the eruption—fallen trees, melted snow, volcanic ash, buried foliage—was actually the starting point of reforestation. These elements were not carted away; rather, they had a job to do. Their existence was not merely compatible with recovery; it was conducive to it. Within 15 years, the site of the Mount St. Helens eruption was a thriving forest whose trees were unusually tall for their age because the ash abated competing weeds and foliage in their early years. Then other plants began to grow in the now-enriched soil, and they flourished as well. This invited wildlife to return. By 1997 an Audubon Society study found more species of birds in the area than there were in the 1980 pre-eruption study of the same region (Associated Press, 1997). The final markers of restoration, for good or for ill, were the return of tourists and,

Adapted from Hall, M. E. L., Langer, R., & McMartin, J. (2010), The role of suffering in human flourishing: Contributions from positive psychology, theology, & philosophy, *Journal of Psychology and Theology*, 38, 111-121.

shortly thereafter, logging companies making plans for commercial harvesting of the newly regrown trees within the next decade.

The difference between rebuilding the Twin Towers and the Mount St. Helens forest is simple: one disaster left debris that was in the way, and the other left debris that was generative and helped the healing.

Therapists and clients alike tend to view the damage done by trauma and suffering like the debris left over from the destruction of the Twin Towers. The damage is simply in the way—it is an impediment to recovery and should be removed as soon as possible so healing can get under way. In fact, the damage from traumatic life events is more like the damage from the Mount St. Helens eruption. It can be and should be viewed as generative. Indeed, the most important task of a therapist may be not to move people as soon as possible out of the ashes of suffering but rather to help people make the ashes of their suffering generative of a new and flourishing human life.

Our suggestions for making suffering generative will begin by taking a step back. Certain aspects of our worldview must be in place in order to make our suffering generative. Therefore, we will take some time for a philosophical and theological excursus. In particular, we will examine the nature of human flourishing and the reasons for human suffering. Accurate framing of these issues enables a pathway toward understanding how suffering may be generative. Once this foundation is laid, we will examine trauma literature within the Bible, considering especially the writings of Jeremiah and the ways in which he made his traumatic suffering generative to human flourishing. Finally, we will consider some therapeutic implications of this discussion, particularly as it relates to the goals of therapy for the victims of trauma and extreme suffering.

We have no illusions that suffering is a good thing in and of itself. No one asks for trauma any more than a forest ranger would ask for a volcanic eruption. However, the badness of suffering does not mean it cannot be productive and generative, and it is our task as friends, family members, therapists, pastors, and teachers to help ourselves and others find a way to generative suffering.

PHILOSOPHICAL REFLECTIONS ON HUMAN FLOURISHING

Classical philosophical discourse on human flourishing is commonly framed under the rubric of virtue ethics, eudaimonism, or eudaimonistic ethics. To greatly condense an expansive discourse, at least three common features emerge from these discussions:

Objectivity of the good. For classical philosophy, the good was an objective notion that attached to the design or function of the object in question. The good knife was the knife that cut well because the function of a knife is to cut. This is not a statement of opinion but a statement of fact; knives are artifacts constructed with a purpose in mind, and that purpose is to cut. Furthermore, the cutting ability of a knife can be objectively assessed. Unlike personal preferences, cutting ability is a piece of public knowledge, not private knowledge (Aristotle, 1985; Pakaluk, 2005).

When it comes to human beings, of course, function or intended design is more difficult to assess. People may have different assessments of "what they were made to do." Classical philosophers were aware of these differences; nonetheless, they saw a bedrock of commonality among all people. Certain qualities are unique to individuals or cultures, but others are simply part of what it means to be human. A good human life will be characterized by successfully doing the things that all human beings must do and fully expressing the most distinctive features of human nature (Nussbaum, 1988).

What is important for our current discussion is that an objective vision of human good helps us move away from a vision of human flourishing anchored in subjective states of happiness and well-being. In other words, it avoids the conflation of pleasure and flourishing. Most important, deemphasizing emotional evaluations of the good life makes flourishing compatible with suffering. While suffering may not produce happiness directly, it might promote a long-term character change, life reorientation, or worldview change that would be contributive or constitutive of human flourishing.

Teleological understanding of human action. Classical ethics understood human action as teleological. We act in order to promote our happiness, with happiness understood in the sense of human well-being, not pleasurable sensation. Good action is conducive to flourishing or well-being; bad action is not.

The teleological understanding of human action clarifies the nature of suffering. Suffering is not the *telos* of human action, for surely no normal human being would choose to pursue suffering as a life project. However, suffering includes within it the seeds of goodness, or, to put things more precisely, there might be ingredients found in suffering that can be mixed with other parts of a person's life to make a good and meaningful story out of the whole. Indeed, the story is an apt metaphor. One might say that the point of being human is to make of one's life a story worth telling. All stories include the ingredients of both happiness and suffering. Good stories weave the two together into a narrative whole that is worthy of telling.

Importance of virtue and character. Finally, classical philosophers identified virtues as skills of human living that are particularly conducive to human flourishing. Virtues are stable dispositions to act in certain ways in response to certain life experiences and circumstances. In effect, the virtuous person consistently does the right thing well, across a broad range of human activity, even in challenging circumstances (Lewis, 1952). The possession of virtue includes performing good actions with the right motives, intentions, and attitudes (Lewis, 1952; Mattison, 2008).

Virtue, then, constitutes a bridge between flourishing and suffering. Poverty, fear, and temptation are all normal human experiences. Corresponding virtues help us navigate these experiences in ways that are conducive to human flourishing. Generosity, for example, is a virtue that helps us negotiate a world with limited material resources. Courage helps us confront a world with mortal dangers. Self-control and moderation are names for a virtue that help us avoid being harmed by excessive indulgence in things that are good in small quantities or within specific contexts.

THEOLOGICAL REFLECTIONS ON HUMAN FLOURISHING

Much of what we have just said about classical philosophy was in the minds of the early church fathers. In general, eudaimonistic approaches to ethics were welcomed by the early church and characteristic of Christian ethics until the modern era. But theology makes important additions and contributions that go well beyond the Greco-Roman philosophers from the classical tradition. Two are especially important for the current project: (a) the connection between sanctification and human flourishing and (b) the importance of the fall.

Sanctification and human flourishing. Contemporary Christians do not talk a lot about human flourishing. Instead, our doctrine of sanctification is often expressed in terms such as "spiritual growth" or "discipleship." What, then, is the relationship between sanctification and human flourishing?

New Testament thought on sanctification seems to flow along two lines. The one line is expressed in discussion of virtues and vices within the context of ordinary life activities such as work, family, and social relationships. Such talk would have been quite familiar to the Greco-Roman world. The other line of thought about sanctification is more obviously spiritual and distinctively Christian. It is expressed most commonly by phrases like "abiding in Christ," "walking in Christ," "(being) filled with Christ," or simply "living in Christ." On the surface, the explicit connection to Christ would seem to be quite different than the concepts of human flourishing based on virtues that we have been discussing. However, on closer examination, the two merge in a remarkable way.

Classical notions of human flourishing depend strongly on excellence in *distinctively human attributes*. The abilities and activities that most distinguish humans from all other animals are the abilities and activities that are most constitutive of human flourishing. In the Bible the creation narrative identifies the most distinctively human attribute as "bearing the image of God." As Berkhof (1941) notes, "According to Scripture the essence of man consists in this, that he is the image of God. As such he is distinguished from all other creatures and stands supreme as the head and crown of the entire creation" (p. 205).

When one moves to the New Testament, the image of God still contains echoes of the Old Testament notion (see Jas 3:9), but *Christ himself becomes the quintessential image bearer*. He is described as the image of the invisible God, reflecting this by his role in creation, fulfilling the law, forgiving sin, judging the world, and ultimately redeeming and recreating the cosmos. He accomplishes for the first time in human history (after the fall) the divinely ordained role of being God's regent of the created order.

Christ bears the image of God as no other human ever has. If image bearing is that which is distinctively human, then Christ is the most distinctively *human* person who has ever lived. Therefore, all of the "in Christ" language of sanctification is actually at the same time a call to fully human life—life in Christ is life in the image of God. It is a Christ-centered vision of human flourishing.

Of special note for the focus of this chapter, our union with Christ is also expressed in suffering. Apparently, both suffering itself (Phil 3:10; Col 1:24) and the attendant comfort one might receive in the context of suffering (2 Cor 1:3-7; 7:4-7) contribute to one's union and intimacy with Christ. Sanctification and suffering are both constitutive parts of the calling to abide in Christ. In other words, sanctification and suffering are both constitutive parts of the calling to live a fully human life—to flourish.

The fall and human flourishing. The second distinctive contribution of biblical revelation to our discussion of suffering and trauma is the doctrine of the fall. Fallenness in all of its manifestations is deviation from a standard established by God (Erickson, 1998; Pannenberg, 1994). In creation, God establishes God's intention, purpose, and design for the world; sin veers away from the way things ought to be and the way in which God's creatures should flourish (Plantinga, 1996). The consequences of such deviations directly result in human suffering, but a good understanding of the doctrine of sin and fallenness can go a long way to helping people process pain and suffering in generative ways.

People seek explanations of sufferings, and the assumptions of modern culture often lead a person to truncated diagnoses, which in turn incline a person toward cures that do more harm than good. For example, the Western cultural context frequently views suffering as being rooted in external circumstances. Technology, education, and other interventions are offered to eliminate the problematic circumstance and therefore the suffering. If, however, the human problem runs deeper, then the eradication of problematic circumstances will not eradicate suffering. Dallas Willard (1988) contends that the modern period has been characterized by a series of projects that have attempted to bring about utopic social conditions without seeking to change the individual persons within that societal structure at all. The result is little or no progress toward eliminating our subjective experience of suffering.

Consider a scene from the film *WALL-E*. The first time we see humans in the film, we discover that they inhabit an interstellar cruise ship called the *Axiom*, which is fleeing the garbage-infested Earth. Robotic servants on the ship cater to their every whim. The humans float around on chairs with video screens that connect them to each other and through which they engage in virtual activities with each other. What could dim this utopic vision of leisure and the absence of suffering? Every inhabitant of the *Axiom* is morbidly obese, and inhabitants fail to have genuine interactions with each other or even be cognizant of their immediate surroundings. The sequence ends with a woman who, after years aboard the *Axiom*, is knocked out of her chair and away from her video screen. She then stares in wonder and exclaims, "I didn't know we had a pool!" Clearly, eliminating external problems does not guarantee human flourishing. By realizing this fact, people may be able to avoid the trap of blaming external circumstances that are beyond their control and instead consider character formation that is within their control.

Furthermore, a well-formed doctrine of fallenness means that *there are no mere victims nor mere perpetrators.* No one is innocent of all wrongdoing, even the victim of trauma. And no perpetrator is evil merely because he or she has been a victim of sin before he or she was a perpetrator. Indeed, in far too many cases, perpetrators are acting out their victimhood by the sins they commit against others. The boundary lines between sinner and those who sin against us are not as clear as we would like. This opens the door to hope because perpetrators may still repent; it also opens the door to forgiveness because victims realize that one day they may be the violators and find themselves standing in need of grace and mercy (Rom 3:23). This understanding does not eliminate suffering, but it does give the victims of suffering additional resources for processing their trauma. It may also change their expectations about what it would mean to "set things right."

Finally, a sound understanding of fallenness may help answer or diminish the significance of certain questions that are often roadblocks to resolving suffering in generative ways. Acknowledging the previous point that there is no such thing as a "mere" victim may make a person less likely to fixate on the question "Why me?!" A variation of this question, "Why did God allow this to happen to me?" is also transformed by an understanding of fallenness.

To give a somewhat simplistic illustration, imagine a person who is the victim of a severe cut in her hand. That person might ask, "God, why did you let this happen to me?" But imagine that a person has volunteered to help clean up the devastation of Hurricane Katrina. As she is cleaning up a destroyed home, she severely cuts her hand. Of course, she may still ask why this happened, but it seems unsurprising that when one is working in the midst of wreckage, something might happen that is "not the way it is supposed to be." In a sense, all Christians who have answered the call of God have agreed to help clean up a disaster site. That is exactly what our current created order is. The fall is a disaster, and all the earth is groaning under its weight (Rom 8:22). Suffering demands less of an explanation when one is laboring in such circumstances.

LESSONS ABOUT TRAUMA FROM THE LIFE OF JEREMIAH

The theological framework for suffering summarized in the previous section can be developed by looking at a wide variety of material in Scripture that treats traumatic suffering. The Old Testament in particular has abundant narrative, prophetic, and poetic examples of people struggling to deal with trauma in a redemptive fashion. These examples include narratives of the broken and sexually scarred patriarchal families, the psalms of lament, the trauma of Job, the haunting emptiness of Ecclesiastes, and the complaints and sufferings of countless Old Testament prophets. This discussion will focus on the example of Jeremiah as found in the book that bears his name as well as the book of Lamentations.

Jeremiah as an example of dealing with trauma generatively. Jeremiah is a rich biblical source for insights into dealing with trauma in a generative way. First, Jeremiah experienced trauma throughout his life. Even his call to ministry was experienced traumatically (Thompson, 1980). Once he set about fulfilling his calling, his hearers rejected him. Even the people of his hometown betrayed him and sought to take his life. When his words came true, it only made things worse because his message was one of judgment and exile, culminating in holocaust-like images of mothers boiling their own children for food during the siege of Jerusalem.

One need not wonder how this affected Jeremiah, for he tells us explicitly, "My joy is gone; grief is upon me; / my heart is sick within me. . . . Oh that my head were waters, / and my eyes a fountain of tears, / that I might weep day and night / for the slain of the daughter of my people!" (Jer 8:18; 9:1 ESV). As this statement makes clear, Jeremiah is extremely personal, emotional, and transparent in his writing. Especially noteworthy is a series of introspective passages that have been called the "Confessions" of Jeremiah, found in 11:18-23; 12:1-6; 15:10-12, 15-21; 17:14-18; 18:18-23; and 20:7-18. These confessions contain laments, complaints, and questions. They are frank, transparent, emotional, and unguarded. They are not a glimpse into Jeremiah's soul; they are a picture window. Despite the trauma and hardship, Jeremiah is found faithful at the end. He perseveres in his call and ultimately makes peace with it, embracing it when he easily could have moved on to greener pastures. He contemplates the burning wreckage of Jerusalem and offers not only a stirring lament but also one of the most compelling reminders of God's mercy and steadfast love in all of Scripture. It would be a stretch to say that Jeremiah experienced a happy life; indeed, one might be reluctant to use the words *flourishing* or *thriving* to describe Jeremiah. However, there is no doubt that he processed his trauma in a way that was generative and that preserved his spiritual integrity.

Facing the hard questions. We mentioned in the introduction to this chapter that many people think the goal of hardship is to move through it as quickly as possible. This is not Jeremiah's response. In fact, a very helpful point of contact for those who suffer today may be to consider the questions that Jeremiah raises about his own suffering. They are strikingly familiar and up-to-date. Consider the following:

Why me? Jeremiah struggles profoundly to make sense of his life. He cannot explain why he suffers. Not unlike Job, he seems to suffer unjustly and receive no explanation from God. He bluntly exclaims, "Woe is me!" and ponders the related question "Why is my pain unceasing?" (Jer 15:10, 18 ESV). Later he asks, "Why was I ever born?" (Jer 20:18 NLT). He feels his life is pointless and incoherent. He simply cannot make sense of the chaos that engulfs him.

Where is God? When Jeremiah looks inward he asks, "Why me?" When he looks outward he asks, "Where is God?" Both questions are cries of a troubled mind speaking to a wounded heart. Jeremiah looks outward and sees devastation, sin, and destruction. Where is God in the midst of these times? Why does God not protect his chosen people? If God providentially orders the cosmos, why has it come to such a bad end? Particularly poignant is Jeremiah's statement in Lamentations 2:5 (ESV): "The Lord has become like an enemy; / he has swallowed up Israel; . . . he has multiplied in the daughter of Judah / mourning and lamentation."

Where are my friends? Jeremiah's trauma is compounded by abandonment. He is alone. When he most needs support from others, he finds none. In Jeremiah 11 the people of Anathoth, his hometown, plot to take his life. As he expresses it, "I hear many whispering. / Terror is on every side! / 'Denounce him! Let us denounce him!' / say all my close friends, / watching for my fall" (Jer 20:10 ESV). In Lamentations, passers-by, neighbors, and lovers ignore his plight and the plight of the people of Israel (Lam 1:12, 17, 19). It is common for those who are experiencing trauma to marvel that the rest of the world keeps turning, not even noticing their horrendous sufferings. Jeremiah expresses the exact same concern. Though these passers-by do nothing directly to harm him, their lack of awareness and disregard is read as an active rejection and intentional harm.

How long, O Lord? This question is by no means unique to Jeremiah. It occurs at least 20 times in Psalms alone. But Jeremiah also raises this cry against God (Jer 12:4). Similarly, he wonders when his pain will ever cease (Jer 15:18). In Lamentations 3:3 (ESV) he cries, "Surely against me he turns his hand / again and again the whole day long." His suffering takes him to the limits of his endurance. He looks ahead with anguish and fear, asking "How long?" and "What next?"

Jeremiah's questions are not to be read as a formula for processing trauma or necessary steps to growth. They are simply authentic cries of pain and confusion. We do not need to press these questions on those who suffer, but for those whose hearts resonate with Jeremiah's questions, it may be of substantial consolation to know that they are not alone. It may give people some measure of validation to know that Jeremiah has walked these roads before them.

Practical lessons from Jeremiah. Of course, some roads end badly. It is noteworthy that Jeremiah's road ended well. What guidance can be drawn from him for those who seek generativity and spiritual integrity in the midst of their traumatic suffering? Jeremiah models the following practices.

Appropriate introspection and self-reflection. In his trauma, Jeremiah does not just question God; he also questions himself. He acknowledges his own sin and his people's sin. Suffering leads him to "examine his ways," an examination that calls for a "return to the LORD" (Lam 3:40). Some wounds beggar explanation, but others are brought on ourselves by our own hardness of heart or sinful misdeeds. Jeremiah acknowledges that people sometimes place the yoke of suffering on their own necks. He knows that he is not a *mere* victim.

A discipline of "active recollection." Trauma makes one forgetful. One thought drives out another; the anguish of suffering drives out thanksgiving for God's goodness and mercy. This leads to a distorted view of both God and one's circumstances. Jeremiah resists this distortion by a discipline of active recollection. Devastating judgment is before his eyes, but he calls his mind back to the steadfast love of the Lord. He reminds himself that God's mercies never come to an end (Lam 3:21-23). He does not close up the room of his trauma but rather opens its windows and allows the morning light of God's mercy to shine in. In bitterness he makes room for hope (Lam 3:24). No matter how dark the present chapter of his life, Jeremiah realizes that it is not the final chapter. The story of the kingdom of God ends in a wedding, not a funeral. That means that if it were a Shakespearean play, it would be a comedy, not a tragedy! Jeremiah reminds himself that traumatic devastation is always penultimate, never ultimate.

Narrating his story into the broader story. Trauma is made penultimate partly by placing one's life into a larger whole. Jeremiah's story was not a self-contained narrative bounded by his own threescore and ten. His life was part of a story that would continue long after he died. Consider Jeremiah 29:11, one of the most famous (and misquoted) passages in all of his writing: "For I know the plans I have for you, declares the Lord, plans for welfare and not for evil, to give you a future and a hope" (ESV). This passage is often read as a personal assurance for a suffering individual. But the preceding verse frames this promise differently: "For thus says the Lord: When seventy years are completed for Babylon, I will visit you, and I will fulfill to you my promise and bring you back to this place" (Jer 29:10 ESV). Jeremiah's message is that the exile will not be of short duration as other prophets are promising. They will not be back in two years. In fact, they will never come back within their lifetimes.

The exile will last for 70 years. They should build houses, give their daughters in marriage, and seek the welfare of the city of their exile. They will live the rest of their years in exile and die in a foreign city.

The hope Jeremiah offers is a hope for the next generation. God's memory is long. He will restore his people from exile, but it will be accomplished only for their children and their children's children. This passage asks the people to renarrate their lives into a larger and much longer story. It is an exhortation to find meaning and purpose in the larger narrative of the kingdom of God rather than in the confined boundaries of their own personal lives.

One cannot help but wonder if contemporary Christianity has become too focused on the present and centered on the individual to embrace readily the alternative eschatological narration described above. Ultimate reconciliation and restoration are simply too remote for the microwave generation. For our society, an eschatological vision is really no vision at all. What good is a promise if it will help my children but will not help me? Who needs healing in the next world—I need it now! But for Jeremiah a hope for a better future was a real hope. Restoration for a future generation was real restoration. A story in which he was not the hero was still a good story. This may seem culturally distant to modern Americans, but the simple fact is that the eschatological nature of justice, reconciliation, and the fulfillment of divine promises is actually a central and unavoidable part of the Christian faith. Expecting it to be otherwise will only compound our disappointments.

Understanding vocation as divine appointment, not personal choice. Jeremiah's ability to press on despite his traumatic life experiences is partly attributable to his conviction that he had received a divine call. His life mission was not something he found by "looking inside himself." It was not the result of taking a strength assessment. His call was not a personal dream; it came from the outside, not the inside. Indeed, the word *calling* itself reminds us of this. We do not call ourselves; someone else has to call us. The decision to take up a call is the decision to make one's life about something outside oneself and beyond oneself. In Jeremiah's case, this was a call to speak the words of God to the people of God in the time and place that God appointed. Personal fulfillment was not the compass that directed his vocational quest.

An external notion of calling may be a helpful resource for those experiencing traumatic suffering. While trauma often shatters one's self-generated plans and dreams, an external locus of calling and meaning may prove more durable. Viktor Frankl (1985), writing of his traumatic experiences in Auschwitz, certainly found this to be the case. He stated that "the true meaning of life is to be discovered in the world rather than within man or his own psyche. . . . Being human always points . . . to something or someone, other than oneself. The more one forgets himself . . .

the more human he is and the more he actualizes himself" (p. 133). Perhaps this wisdom from Jeremiah and the Holocaust could help transform contemporary visions of suffering as well.

POTENTIAL POSITIVE OUTCOMES OF TRAUMA-RELATED SUFFERING

According to the biblical worldview, most or all suffering is the result of the entrance of sin into the world. While it is possible that some adversity accompanied the pre-fall state, it is clear from Scripture that the curse amplified the difficulties faced by human persons (Gen 3:16-19). Nevertheless, God does have ways of using the evil of the fallen world. The Bible never confuses evil with good, nor does it attempt to bleach pain from the fabric of suffering. What it does do, and do consistently, is set suffering in the broader and higher context of the providence and purposes of God. In spite of its origins in the fall, suffering is bent to the purposes of the stronger will and higher purposes of a benevolent God.

The Bible states this in global terms in Romans 8:28, reminding us that God works all things together for good to those who love God and are called according to his purpose. But it also states this in more personal terms, reminding us of both the benefits of suffering in the building of virtuous character (Rom 5:1-5; Jas 1:3-5) and the benefit that our suffering brings to others. For example, the suffering of Joseph makes possible the provision for the rest of his family during a famine (Gen 50:20). Lest we think this is unfair, Scripture also reminds us that suffering works in exactly this twofold pattern in the life of the Lord Jesus: it contributed to his character in that he learned obedience from the things he suffered, and it also contributed to the good of others because "once made perfect, he became the source of eternal salvation for all who obey him" (Heb 5:9).

According to Scripture, at least three kinds of goods can result from suffering. First, some of the pain we experience in our fallen world is the direct result of our own wrongdoing. In these cases, God's punishment for our waywardness is intended to serve a corrective function. However, much of the suffering we face, particularly in the context of trauma, is the result of the sins of others or comes from the general disorder of our world, leading to two further kinds of goods: the nurture of enduring traits of character and a reorientation toward relationship with God and others. Below we look at these kinds of goods in more depth.

Suffering and purification from sin. Sometimes suffering is a marker for the presence of sin. For those within the covenant, God's punishment is often the result of the breach of covenant requirements. Leviticus describes the escalating levels of punishment and travail that will result should the covenant partners refuse to turn back to the Lord in fidelity at each level of discipline (Lev 26:14-39). Each set of circumstances from the Lord's hand provides a new opportunity to "listen," to heed the Lord. The provision of multiple opportunities for correction extends not only to members of the covenant partnership but also to those outside it, with varying results. Pharaoh, for example, experienced brief changes of heart in the midst of the plagues; he recognized that the suffering of his nation was the result of his own sin and that of his people (Ex 9:27-28; 10:16). Sadly, Pharaoh reversed his position yet again, subjecting his people to further suffering and tragedy. In such instances, suffering and hardship are the self-caused result of sin. Yet suffering possesses potential to bring about good results by being a signpost that indicates the presence of disorder. Just as physical pain provides a marker that something is awry, so other kinds of suffering can direct one away from damaging behavior.

Suffering as character formation. The second kind of good resulting from suffering is that of virtuous character formation. As in the tradition of eudaimonism, the biblical writers affirm that the best goods for the human person are those that endure. While many such goods are unique to the Christian vision, such as those pertaining to the afterlife, others are shared in common with eudaimonistic thought. In particular, Scripture describes various character traits that can result through suffering. The virtues become stable and enduring features of the character of the person who obtains them. James, echoing the themes of Old Testament wisdom, encourages believers to rejoice because suffering can result in maturity (perfection, completion) of character (Jas 1:2-4). He contrasts the instability of the good of riches (Jas 1:10-11) with the enduring good that comes to those who withstand trial and difficulty (Jas 1:12). In various Old Testament wisdom texts, the righteous person's suffering is compared to the affluence and apparent flourishing of the wicked. The goods and pleasures of the wicked ought not to be envied, because they are fleeting. Riches and wealth, for instance, can be lost in an instant through death or disaster (Ps 37:2, 20, 36, 38; 73:18-20). The contented wicked are placed "in slippery places" (Ps 73:18 ESV). The righteous person endures through disaster and ultimately through death.

Some virtuous character traits appear only in the context of pain and suffering. Forgiveness is pointless if there is no sin. Wisdom is the skill of living well, and living well requires no skill in paradise. Maturity is often marked by the ability to overcome increasingly difficult challenges (Nash, 1988). Evils and dangers make the cultivation and employment of wisdom more necessary than it would be without them (Lactantius, 1994). Paul explains that the suffering he underwent from his "thorn" was given to help him learn humility and dependence on Christ (2 Cor 12:6-10). The author of Hebrews describes the result of hardship as "the peaceful fruit of righteousness" (Heb 12:11 ESV).

Suffering as a worldview modifier. The third set of potential positive outcomes engendered by suffering relates to the reorienting function of difficulties. Scripture consistently expounds the theme of the redirection of one's thoughts, desires, and attention toward the things of God (Col 3:1-4). Suffering and pain can help bring needed perspective. Paul encouraged the Corinthians by insisting that trials can bring about inward renewal. "So we do not lose heart. Though our outer self is wasting away, our inner self is being renewed day by day" (2 Cor 4:16 ESV).

Shifting our attention away from ourselves can be a difficult task. We naturally judge all affairs from our own point of view. We try the goodness of God in our own courts, but it seems that God at times uses suffering to accomplish a change in venue. He uses suffering to capture our full attention, and once he has our attention, he communicates in no uncertain terms a most unwelcome message: *I am God and you are not!*

There is no better example of this in Scripture than the experience of Job. Job was a righteous man who suffered much. Worse yet, he suffered for no reason—at least no reason that was apparent from his vantage point. His unwelcome counselors ironically maintained the focus on Job himself, prodding and probing his claim of righteous innocence. Throughout the discourse, the focus is on Job, on what has happened to him, on what he has done and what he has not done. The tension builds for over 30 chapters, until finally God speaks. At this point the venue of the trial of God's goodness changes dramatically. No longer is the courtroom in Job's jurisdiction. In fact, Job's entire affair is swept aside with a thrilling and frightening thunderclap of God's creative power. The only resolution to the suffering Job has endured is found when Job proves willing to change the focus of his attention from himself to God. He humbly acknowledges, "I know that you can do all things, / and that no purpose of yours can be thwarted. . . . I have uttered what I did not understand, / things too wonderful for me, which I did not know" (Job 42:2-3 ESV).

Suffering has served as Job's instructor. He has learned to know God better. He has seen his Redeemer with fresh eyes—eyes cleansed by the tears of suffering. His suffering has not been explained, but it has been set into context, and thereby it has been substantially diminished. This is a hard and theocentric sort of theodicy, but it is a theodicy that restores God and humanity back into proper relationship.

The reason suffering often contributes to flourishing is that it provides a reorientation and reevaluation of one's pursuits. Adverse events show us that we are fragile, that the future is uncertain, and that what happens to us can be random. Adverse events show us the limits of the human condition and bring into question our assumptions about ourselves and the world. They help people recognize their need for God and for other relationships. People realize they need to pursue "what really matters." Suffering is a gift, but not an intrinsic one. It is not to be sought for its own sake, nor should it be tolerated passively. At minimum, it should serve to lead us back into relationship with and dependency on God.

SUFFERING AND THE FLOURISHING LIFE: IMPLICATIONS FOR THERAPY

What are the implications for therapy of this analysis of suffering and human flourishing? In the first place, a fuller appreciation of suffering can guide our decision making in therapy. Rather than assuming that alleviation of the suffering is the immediate or primary target, attention may be paid to the role of the suffering in pointing to sin, in producing character, or in reorienting the client's worldview.

Second, a greater understanding of the role of suffering can impact the goal of treatment. A Christian view of the flourishing life sees God as the supreme Good, which leads us to align our character with God's and to a life characterized by worship. As noted above, God can use our suffering to accomplish these goals. Suffering can lead to increasing conformity to the character of Christ. It can also reorient the Christian toward the God who promises to redeem suffering and who suffered with us in the form of the cross. In this way, suffering takes on meaning in the hands of an all-knowing and loving God.

A third implication of considering suffering in light of the flourishing life is the crucial role that narrative assumes in the healing process. The connections must be drawn between suffering and one's life projects in a way that authentically reflects both the suffering one experiences and the sense that suffering makes in light of one's pursuit of a flourishing human life. "Happy is he who suffers and knows why" (Paul Claudel, as cited in Hauerwas, 1986, p. 31).

If we do not write suffering into our life stories, it remains a constant interruption or intrusion. When individuals do not engage with the significance of suffering for their worldview—when they deny the impact of the suffering—they isolate it from their "real story." They refuse to narrate their suffering into their stories, thus failing to allow it to contribute in positive ways to their lives. Stanley Hauerwas (1986) notes that "one of the problems with suffering is that it alienates us from ourselves—'this thing that is happening to me is not me.' But it is exactly the ability to make the suffering mine that is crucial if I am to be an integral self" (p. 25).

In contrast, finding a place for suffering in our narratives provides the suffering with meaning or, at a minimum, allows us to claim the suffering as ours. Every doctor can testify to the importance of indicating the causes of suffering (even if it is cancer) because the patient, knowing the cause of his or her suffering, is comforted by being able to name the affliction. Somehow it domesticates suffering if we are able to locate it in our world. A Christian perspective on the flourishing life takes this a step further in its emphasis on the teleological goal of flourishing and its understanding of calling. Our suffering can lead us to flourishing as we become increasingly conformed to the image of God, as demonstrated in the life of Christ. Suffering can also be understood as accomplishing God's purposes, as serving the divine calling on our life. We see examples of suffering that produces God-pleasing character (Rom 5:3-5; Jas 1:2-4), advances the spread of the gospel (Phil 1:12), authenticates one's calling (2 Cor 11:23-29), or confirms one's identity as a child of God (Heb 12:7). In all these situations, biblical authors narrate their suffering into the context of their callings.

CONCLUSION

In this chapter we have argued for the usefulness of considering suffering in the context of the flourishing life. When life is rightly considered as the pursuit of the objectively good life in which we live as we were intended to live, reflecting God's image, then suffering can be evaluated in light of its contributions to that *telos* or end. Considering suffering in purely hedonistic ways limits our ability to enable our clients' healing and growth and may even hinder their ability to flourish. In contrast, facilitating our clients' weaving of their suffering into the tapestry of a meaningful life can aid in healing, growth, and ultimately the pursuit of the highest Good, who suffered on the cross and was resurrected to bring us abundant life.

REFERENCES

Aristotle. (1985). *Nicomachean ethics* (T. Irwin, Trans.). Indianapolis, IN: Hackett.

Associated Press (1997, August 24). Reforestation exploding in Mount St. Helens area. *Deseret News*. Retrieved from www.deseretnews.com/article/579070/Reforestation -exploding-in-Mount-St-Helens-area.html

Berkhof, L. (1941). *Systematic theology*. Grand Rapids, MI: Eerdmans.

Erickson, M. J. (1998). *Christian theology* (2nd ed.). Grand Rapids, MI: Baker Book House.

Frankl, V. E. (1985). *Man's search for meaning* (Updated). New York, NY: Washington Square Press.

Hauerwas, S. (1986). *Suffering presence*. Notre Dame, IN: University of Notre Dame Press.

Lactantius (1994). A treatise on the anger of God addressed to Donatus. In A. Roberts, J. Donaldson, & A. C. Coxe (Eds.), *Ante-Nicene Fathers* (Vol. 7, pp. 259-80). Peabody, MA: Hendrickson.

Lewis, C. S. (1952). *Mere Christianity*. New York, NY: MacMillan.

Mattison, W. C., III. (2008). *Introducing moral theology: True happiness and the virtues*. Grand Rapids, MI: Brazos Press.

Morris, J. (Producer), & Stanton, A. (Director). (2008). *WALL-E* [Motion picture]. United States: Walt Disney Studios.

Nash, R. H. (1988). *Faith and reason: Searching for a rational faith*. Grand Rapids, MI: Zondervan.

Nussbaum, M. C. (1988). Non-relative virtues: An Aristotelian approach. *Midwest Studies in Philosophy, 13*(1), 32-53.

Pakaluk, M. (2005). *Aristotle's Nicomachean ethics: An introduction.* Cambridge, UK: Cambridge University Press.

Pannenberg, W. (1994). *Systematic theology* (Vol. 2, G. W. Bromiley, Trans.). Grand Rapids, MI: Eerdmans.

Plantinga, C. (1996). *Not the way it's supposed to be: A breviary of sin.* Grand Rapids, MI: Eerdmans.

Thompson, J. A. (1980). *The book of Jeremiah.* Grand Rapids, MI: Eerdmans.

Willard, D. (1988). *The spirit of the disciplines: Understanding how God changes lives.* San Francisco, CA: Harper & Row.

THE NEUROBIOLOGY OF STRESS AND TRAUMA

WILLIAM M. STRUTHERS,
KERRYN ANSELL, AND
ADAM WILSON

While many counselors have extensive experience in treating individuals who have suffered from what is generally referred to as trauma, studying the neurobiological aspects of trauma may appear daunting. There is a growing consensus, however, that neuroscience will play an increasingly significant role in the research and practice of counseling (Gabbard & Kay, 2001; Goss, 2015) Thus, an understanding of the neurobiological systems involved in stress response is essential for any mental health professional (King & Anderson, 2004).

What we will attempt to do in this chapter is to provide an overview of neuro-logical stress systems and address how a neuroscience-informed approach to trauma provides the clinician with additional layers of assessment and conceptu-alization (Goss, 2015). An additional goal will be to discuss how, as neuroscience increasingly informs clinical practice, it should inform psychoeducational dialogue with clients (Miller, 2016).

The subjective level of stress that an individual experiences may vary by stressor, situation, genetics (Yehuda & LeDoux, 2007), and preexisting trauma history (Frissa et al., 2016). And while experiencing acute versus chronic trauma may result in somewhat divergent consequences (Sperry, 2016), the physiological response to stress generally involves the same neurobiological systems, regardless of the nature of the traumatic event. An understanding of the nervous system, as well as the effect of trauma and trauma treatment within a neurobiological framework, is useful in the counseling process. Therefore, we will provide an overview of critical brain regions and their functions, along with a direct examination of the neurological effects of stress and trauma, before discussing the application of neuroscience to the counseling process.

OVERVIEW OF THE NERVOUS SYSTEM AND MAJOR BRAIN SYSTEMS

When considering the neurobiological factors involved in trauma, it is important to first review and locate the brain within a biopsychosocial model (McRay, Yarhouse, & Butman, 2016). Because of its complexity, many counselors avoid including the brain as part of the counseling process. However, given the brain's crucial role in processing stimuli, adapting to the environment, and coordinating responses to physical, psychological, and social stressors, an understanding of the major divisions of the brain is critical in developing a comprehensive understanding of trauma.

The brain and spinal cord are collectively referred to as the *central nervous system* (CNS). The remainder of the nervous system, a collection of neurons and nerve fibers that innervate other organ systems, is called the *peripheral nervous system* (PNS). The PNS has two major subdivisions: the *somatic nervous system* (SNS), which innervates muscles involved in voluntary movement, and the *autonomic nervous system* (ANS), which controls numerous involuntary systems such as endocrine glands, respiration, heartbeat, and digestion. The ANS has a sympathetic division involved in *fight or flight* responses and a parasympathetic division known as the *rest and digest* system.

As the brain develops in utero, it divides into three major subsections based on morphological landmarks (see Schneider, 2014, for further detail). An examination of the layers of tissue reveals that as the embryo grows, a unique tube begins to develop just under the surface. Called the neural tube, it will later become the nervous system. One end of this tube, which is hollow in the middle, will become the brain, and the other end, the posterior tip of the spinal cord. In the normal process of development, the tip of the neural tube, which is housed in the skull, develops three bumps that later form the forebrain, midbrain, and hindbrain. Within these three major subdivisions, a process of ongoing specialization and subdivision takes place throughout fetal development. This process leads to a key principle of brain function: the deeper and lower the brain region, the more primal the function; the higher up from the spinal cord, the more complex the function.

Hindbrain. Deep down in the brain, where it fuses with the spinal cord, lies the first bump on the neural tube. This region, referred to as the *hindbrain*, contains three components. The first, the *medulla* (or *medulla oblongata*), is the transition point between the spinal cord and the brain and serves as the deepest boundary of the brain. The medulla is responsible for regulating the internal processes that keep us alive, such as heart rate, breathing, and blood pressure. Its primary function is to keep involuntary systems vital for our continued survival. Because of its importance and deep position in the brain, the medulla develops early on and remains fairly unchanged. It should come as no surprise, then, that damage or disruption of this area can have life-threatening consequences.

As we move higher up into the brain, we find that the hindbrain contains two additional regions. The *pons* and *cerebellum* lie just above the medulla and form the remainder of the hindbrain. The pons assists the medulla in its life-support role, aiding in the regulation of breathing. It also takes on considerably more complex responsibilities. Involved in sleep and arousal, the pons also controls reflexive movements of the head and neck. It acts as a relay for incoming messages from the body as well as outgoing commands to the muscles. Adjacent to the pons is the cerebellum. Deriving its name from the Latin term meaning "little brain," the cerebellum is involved in motor control as well as balance and coordination. It has also been implicated in some forms of learning, memory, and attention.

Midbrain. As we continue ascending into higher brain regions, we transition from the hindbrain into the next major bump on the neural tube, known as the *midbrain.* The midbrain is the smallest of the three developmental regions but is still quite important and complex. It is subdivided into two sections, the roof and the floor. The roof, or *tectum,* sits to the right and left sides of the midline. The tectum contains several bumps called the *inferior* and *superior colliculi.* The inferior colliculi are critical to hearing and responding to auditory information. As signals come into the ear, they are rapidly sent to the inferior colliculi, which then pass them along to higher brain regions. This coordination between lower and higher regions allows hearing to be coordinated with head and neck movements in order to determine the location of a sound.

Just above the inferior colliculi are the superior colliculi, whose role is to unconsciously process visual information coming from the eyes in order to coordinate head, neck, and bodily movement. For example, reflexively moving your head out of the way of a softball or adjusting your gait as you reach the top of a set of stairs happens without much conscious thought, thanks to the superior colliculi.

Sitting under the roof of the tectum (the superior and inferior colliculi) is the floor of the midbrain. This floor is called the *tegmentum* and forms the second half of the midbrain. As noted, the brain increases in complexity in its higher regions. Thus, just as the tectum increases in its functional complexity by processing sensory signals that begin outside the organism (whereas the hindbrain is primarily involved in regulating the internal survival systems), so does the tegmentum focus on more complex tasks. For example, the tegmentum contains many specialized subsystems that are involved in arousal. It also contains regions that act as power generators for higher systems, such as voluntary movement and motivated behavior. In many ways, it acts like a manufacturing plant, where chemicals needed for complex behavior and thought are produced and then shipped up to higher brain regions.

While the tegmentum has a number of important subregions, an area especially relevant to understanding trauma is the *ventral tegmental area* (VTA). The VTA is perhaps one of the more critical regions of the midbrain because of its role in the production of the neurotransmitter dopamine. Dopamine is involved in a number of critical systems within the brain, including movement (Parkinson's disease, a movement disorder, develops as a result of the death of dopamine-producing cells near the VTA). Dopamine has also become increasingly recognized for its fundamental role in the brain's reward system.

Activation of cells within the VTA results in the release of dopamine into higher brain regions involved in the processing of significant stimuli. For example, VTA dopamine release has been linked to natural reinforcers such as food, water, and sex (Russo & Nestler, 2013). Many drugs of abuse and addiction hijack the VTA-dopamine system and cause it to activate the higher brain regions that receive this dopamine by triggering its release or mimicking dopamine (Volkow et al., 2001). This hijacking, and the resulting overuse of the reward system, ultimately results in diminished neurological functioning that may never be fully recovered.

Together the tectum and tegmentum have a considerable capability to respond to external stimuli and are able to respond with greater flexibility than a hindbrain region such as the medulla. Neurological issues involving the hindbrain or midbrain are typically life-threatening and would most likely be treated by a neurologist. Yet it is crucial for *mental* health professionals to understand the roles the hindbrain and midbrain play in the functioning of higher brain regions, where numerous mental health issues reside. For example, within the context of trauma, midbrain regions play a significant role in the detection of, processing of, and autonomic response to threatening cues.

Forebrain. Sitting atop the midbrain, and developing from the most anterior bump of the neural tube, lies the forebrain. Of the three developmental regions, the forebrain is the largest in mammals and displays a dazzling complexity. The forebrain is an especially *plastic* region of the brain. This neuroplasticity, or soft-wiring, is key to understanding the incredibly complex nature of human psychological experience. Numerous neurological processes, such as language, memory, creativity, abstract thought, and emotions, find their home in the forebrain.

As with the rest of the brain, we find that there are layers upon layers of interconnected subsections within the forebrain, each possessing a variety of functional capacities. The forebrain can be subdivided into two major subsections, the *diencephalon* and the *telencephalon*. The deepest subsection of the diencephalon is continuous with the midbrain and forms the *hypothalamus*. Connected to the pituitary gland, which sits outside the brain, the hypothalamus is involved in primary drives and motivation such as eating, drinking, temperature control, and reproduction.

The hypothalamus acts as the hormonal liaison between the body and the brain. It triggers release of its own hormones and stimulates release of pituitary hormones into the blood supply. It also detects hormones in the bloodstream released by other organs in the body. The hypothalamus and pituitary gland are critical in regulating reproductive cycles, growth hormones, and stress response. The hypothalamus detects what is going on inside the body and plays a critical role in the body's response to stress and trauma. In connection with the VTA, the hypothalamus serves as a motivation center for the brain.

Above the hypothalamus, the midbrain's tectum flows into the diencephalic region known as the *thalamus*. As the primary relay station for the senses, the thalamus takes input from the eyes, ears, mouth, and skin and sends these processed signals up to higher brain regions where our conscious perception is anchored. Sitting above the diencephalon is the *telencephalon*. The telencephalon expands outward from the midline of the brain in a symmetrical fashion. Because of this symmetrical nature, there are left and right hemispheres for each telencephalic subdivision. The telencephalon is made up of three major subregions: the *limbic system* and the *basal ganglia*, which are interconnected, and the outermost layer, the *cerebral cortex*.

Limbic system. The limbic system is a network of brain regions interconnected with other telencephalic sites, such as the cerebral cortex and diencephalon (i.e., the thalamus and hypothalamus). Yet three regions of this system are not part of the diencephalon or the cortex and deserve attention: the *hippocampus*, *amygdala*, and *septum*. While hardwired for certain prescribed responses, these three regions are remarkably flexible and thus have a greater ability to adapt to environmental changes and therefore therapeutic interventions. Here we will focus on the hippocampus and amygdala.

A major function of the hippocampus is to take information that has been identified by the brain as important (whether we are consciously aware of it or not) and to store it for later use. The procedure of processing and storing memories is called "consolidation" and is the manner in which all learning occurs. Memories may be consolidated and retrieved intentionally, such as when you are studying for an exam. However, learning may also occur unintentionally. We often remember things that we did not intentionally try to store. Memories such as a funny thing our friend did when we were little, the smell of our grandmother's house, or the details around a betrayal of a friend may have never been intentionally set to memory yet may be vividly recalled later in life. These memories may contain detailed information as well as powerful emotions and sensations. The hippocampus is directly involved in the consolidation of these unintentional, emotional, and episodic memories. As will be discussed more fully, the role of the hippocampus in memory consolidation is central to an understanding of the brain's response to stress and trauma, as well as to the recovery process (Getz, 2014).

Some have argued that the reason we do not remember many things from our early childhood is due to an immature hippocampus. Yet while we may not remember details from our early years, it does not mean that there are not significant memories consolidated by the hippocampus that may have profound effects on us (Poulos et al., 2014). Thus, the hippocampus is involved in the formation of emotional bonds, attachments, and traumatic memories that lie beneath our consciousness. These unconscious memories are critical to psychological development and have far-reaching developmental impacts (e.g., healthy sexual attitudes and behaviors).

The amygdala is an almond-shaped structure situated in the limbic system that sits toward the tip of the hippocampus. The two amygdalae (one in the right and one in the left cerebral hemisphere) are located just under the surface of the cerebral cortex, near our temples. Long known to be involved in emotion and emotional learning, the amygdala is connected to the hypothalamus and the midbrain. Negative emotions such as fear and anxiety, as well as associations with emotional events, are connected to the amygdala. During the hippocampal process of consolidation, the amygdala influences and modulates how that memory is stored. If there is a high degree of emotion associated with an event, and thus increased involvement of the amygdala, there is an increase in the likelihood of that memory being stored. Given its connections to the hypothalamus, which is involved in regulating stress hormones and survival drives, and its connections with the midbrain, which is involved in detecting significant stimuli in the environment, it should come as no surprise that the amygdala is conveniently situated alongside the hippocampus to influence the formation of emotional memories (Shin & Liberzon, 2010).

Basal ganglia. Interlaced with the limbic system are the basal ganglia. Among the several subregions, the *caudate nucleus, putamen,* and *globus pallidus* are significant for their involvement in movement, motivation, and the integration of emotions. Of particular importance to the discussion of trauma is the fact that the basal ganglia are central in setting the body's overall anxiety level (Getz, 2014). Extraordinarily intricate in their connections, these regions show a high level of plasticity compared to deeper brain regions. This plasticity allows them to learn complex goal-directed movements, as well as form nuanced layers of motivation that move beyond eating, drinking, and sex. For example, the willingness to put one's own body in harm's way in order to protect someone else requires complex levels of motivation that go well beyond basic survival instincts.

Because of their connection to the midbrain, the basal ganglia (along with the cortex) appear to be major target sites for midbrain VTA dopamine (Ikemoto, Yang, & Tan, 2015). Disruption of the basal ganglia, or their dopamine input, may result in movement disorders, motivational issues, and anxiety symptoms (Gunaydin & Kreitzer, 2016). A number of diseases are related to the basal ganglia. These diseases, such as Parkinson's and Huntington's disease, tend to display disruptions to movement. In addition, many drugs of abuse trigger the release of dopamine or activate dopamine receptors in the basal ganglia (Koob & Volkow, 2016).

Cerebral cortex. The outermost layer of the brain, which has a wrinkled and gray appearance, is the cortex. Neurologically, it is what sets humans apart from virtually every other species. The cortex enables our cognitive abilities and complex psychological experience. It is through the cortex that we exercise abstract thought, develop nuanced language, plan far into the future, and contemplate and solve complex problems. While the cortex contains numerous regions and systems, four primary cortical lobes can be identified: the *frontal, parietal, temporal,* and *occipital lobes.* These four lobes are made up of folded layers of tissue called *gyri,* which are composed of multiple layers of neurons and are involved in numerous tasks and functions. While there is a great degree of consistency between individuals in the way their gyri and lobes are formed, there is also a level of uniqueness from person to person.

While interconnected and complex in their roles, the four lobes of the brain also carry out discrete functions. For example, the occipital lobe is primarily involved in processing visual information. The temporal lobe is critical for hearing and language. The parietal lobe is involved in touch and space as well as integrating the senses. The frontal lobe is involved in higher-order thought and executive functioning. While all are important, each lobe appears to play its own part in helping us sense, integrate, process, and act on information from the world around us. It is here, in the cortex, that our conscious psychological experience emerges. The cortex is one of the last regions of the brain to finish its development and is one of the most flexible and plastic regions within the brain. Thus, it is also within the cortex that mental health interventions can have profound effects.

Additional trauma-related neurological subsystems. Early research in the physiology of stress has focused on the interconnection between the sympathetic division of the autonomic nervous system and the adrenal system located adjacent to the kidneys (Sapolsky, 2015). This *sympathetic adrenomedullary* (SAM) system is responsible for the release of the neurochemical epinephrine, also known as adrenaline. To initiate the SAM response, sympathetic neurons in the spinal cord communicate with the adrenal glands. This direct neural signal triggers the production and release of adrenaline into the bloodstream. Upon release, adrenaline binds to receptors on various target organs, causing elevated heart rate, increased blood flow to muscle tissue, and vasoconstriction in the skin and gastrointestinal area.

Incorporating hormones produced by the hypothalamus and the pituitary gland, a second hormonal stress-response system, the *hypothalamic-pituitary-adrenocortical (HPA) axis,* activates the adrenal glands via hormones released into the bloodstream. The HPA is often associated with chronic stress and the hormones cortisol and glucocorticoids (GCs; Gądek-Michalska, Spyrka, Rachwalska, Tadeusz, & Bugajski, 2013). The HPA response originates in the hypothalamus, from which neurons secrete corticotropin-releasing hormone (CRH) to stimulate the anterior pituitary to release adrenocorticotropic hormone (ACTH). ACTH is released into the bloodstream and elicits a release of GCs from the adrenal glands as long as the stressor (and ACTH) persist, affecting various organ systems throughout the body. During the HPA stress response, cortisol is released as a protective measure to manage organ damage and to promote adaptive behavior (Bale & Epperson, 2016). While the SAM and HPA systems are often understood as independent, they are in fact interconnected. The fight/flight/freeze response, originating from the SAM, functions to increase vigilance and arousal, which can activate the HPA stress response. In addition to the hypothalamus, several other brain areas show a sensitivity to these stress hormones. Neural pathways connected to the limbic system involve regions such as the amygdala, the hippocampus, and portions of the prefrontal cortex. The involvement of numerous systems allows for psychological and social stimuli to be involved in both the initiation and perpetuation of the stress response (McEwen, 2012).

HOW BRAIN SYSTEMS RESPOND TO STRESS AND TRAUMA

Now that we have completed our primer on brain regions, we can move on to a more detailed description of how the brain responds to trauma and stress. This partial overview of the brain was necessary to help the reader understand the complexity of the interrelated systems that make up the central nervous system and to help the reader more fully understand the nature and impact of trauma on the integrated neurobiological system. As with any discussion of the brain, it must be noted that, while growing rapidly, our understanding of the brain remains limited. The sheer complexity and interrelated nature of the nervous system makes a comprehensive understanding of the brain problematic. Thus, the reader will recognize that the following discussion is intended to be a summative clinical guideline that undoubtedly will be developed over time.

The neurodevelopmental impact of trauma. Trauma results when stress overwhelms an individual's existing stress-response systems, inhibiting recovery from the stressor. Often this loss of neurological equilibrium results in physical, psychological, and functional declines (Getz, 2014). In cases of severe or chronic stress, a healthy baseline may never be fully recovered, particularly without intervention. An individual who has been exposed to chronic stress may remain hindered from recovery on a neurological level, even after the cessation of the stressor (Gray, Rubin, Hunter, & McEwen, 2014). Thus, long after a traumatic experience, an individual must operate from a compromised physiological and psychological baseline.

This disrupted baseline can have a severely disruptive effect on an individual's overall behavior, self-regulation, and mental health (Carr, Martins, Stingel, Lemgruber, & Juruena, 2013). And while trauma at any age can lead to mental health issues, the brain appears to be especially vulnerable to the effects of trauma during particular developmental stages (Dunn, Nishimi, Powers, & Bradley, 2017).

It will be of no surprise to most clinicians that many instances of trauma occur during childhood. This is particularly unfortunate neurologically, as childhood contains several psychologically and neurologically critical windows. The earlier an individual experiences trauma in the lifespan, the more likely it is that he or she will suffer long-term negative effects (Ogle, Rubin, & Siegler, 2013). One of the key development periods occurs during infancy.

Trauma during these early years can pose a particularly serious threat to long-term neurobiological function. Trauma, with its neurological ramifications, is experienced differently depending on the age when the trauma occurs (Perry, 2009). This is largely due to the hierarchical nature of neural development discussed above. As in stage theories of development (e.g., Erikson, Freud), early dysregulation will be built on as development progresses, leading to subsequent dysfunction. This type of neurological dysregulation is detrimental as it significantly increases the sensitivity and duration of the stress response. This oversensitivity results in excessive use of the infant's physiological stress systems and an overexposure to excess cortisol released by the HPA axis. Researchers have found that trauma in infancy can promote long-term dysregulation of the HPA axis (Kindsvatter & Geroski, 2014; Kuhlman, Vargas, Geiss, & Lopez-Duran, 2015).

Similarly, within the first five years of life, trauma can significantly decrease brain volume, inhibit the downregulation of cortisol, and slow general recovery from acute stress (Kuhlman et al., 2015). This difficulty in regulation can lead to serious disruption in a child's overall behavior as well as his or her ability to function in social and academic settings (Kisiel et al., 2014). This developmental period of sensitivity may differ between male and female children because of the effects of gonadal hormones on HPA organization and functioning. Thus, the timing of trauma within childhood may have a significant impact on later symptomology (Bale & Epperson, 2016; Kuhlman et al., 2015).

Allostasis. One of the primary functions of the brain is to identify stressors and threats, recall and select appropriate responses to them, and then execute those responses. These functions ultimately facilitate adaptation based on the physiological and psychological consequences of past experience and allow the brain and body to return to a state of homeostasis. In the case of normal stressors, this process is adaptive and efficient. The process of seeking homeostasis in the face of stress is commonly referred to as *allostasis* (McEwen & Wingfield, 2003; McEwen et al., 2016). Regardless of whether the brain categorizes stress as good, tolerable, or toxic, stressors may alter neurobiological structure and function. As noted, this is especially true if the stress is experienced early in life (Shonkoff, Boyce, & McEwen, 2009).

Good stress, or *eustress*, can be understood as positive arousal and excitement. Eustress triggers hormonal responses but generally does not produce lasting negative physiological consequences. Tolerable stress may be caused by a stressor that contains a negative or potentially harmful component that requires an adaptive response in order to reduce potential damage to the system. An adaptive level of stress response, also known as *allostatic load*, generally occurs within a specific time-limited window and serves to protect the organism. Toxic stress, however, may be understood as the result of a massive, unmanageable stressor or the chronic presence of a stressor that cannot be properly dealt with or avoided. Toxic stressors are likely to overload an organism's ability to cope with the threat and to result in physiological, neurological, and psychological damage (Grant et al., 2014; McEwen et al., 2016).

Trauma may be understood, then, as an overwhelming of the allostatic system, which may result in long-lasting and maladaptive neurophysiological, psychological, and social outcomes. Exposure to multiple or repeated toxic stressors can result in a cumulative impact and overload and erode the protective allostatic response, causing psychological trauma and physiological damage to the brain and other organ systems (McEwen, 2013). As noted above, stressors evoke physiological, psychological, and behavioral responses. In the event of a tolerable allostatic response to stress, physiological and neurological systems will gradually return to homeostasis, whereas toxic stress is likely to result in dysregulation of these systems. This neurophysiological dysregulation is correlated with maladaptive patterns of self-regulation of emotions, thoughts, and behavior (i.e., trauma, complex trauma, posttraumatic stress disorder; Bergen-Cico, Wolf-Stanton, Filipovic, & Weisberg, 2016).

Resilience. The allostatic response and the subsequent ability to respond to stressful events may often be understood by counselors as *resilience*. Defined by Rutten et al. (2013) as "successful adaptation and swift recovery after experiencing severe adversity" (p. 4), resilience plays a central role in the clinical treatment of trauma. The impact and role of resilience in trauma can be seen throughout four phases: the initial trauma or stressor, a consequent decline in either mental or physical health, a period of recovery, and finally the establishment of a new baseline from which the individual will operate moving forward. This process of decline, recovery, and establishment of a new baseline may vary by stressor and the individual's unique susceptibility, but the general sequelae tend to follow this model. Resiliency involves the epigenetic interactions between genetics, neural functioning, and the environment (Gillespie, Phifer, Bradley, & Ressler, 2009; Rutten et al., 2013). Regarding specific neural pathways, brain systems involving both stress response and reward pathways are critically important to resilience. Systems such as the HPA axis, the sympathetic nervous system, and the mesolimbic reward pathway utilize various hormones throughout the body to activate long-term stress adaptation (Gillespie et al., 2009; Kasanova et al., 2016). While stress and trauma affect everyone, the genetic predisposition of the individual plays a significant role in the brain's baseline ability to adapt to stress and trauma.

Secure attachment is considered a significant component of resiliency (Karreman & Vingerhoets, 2012). Throughout childhood and adolescence, it is critical for an individual to develop a secure bond with his or her primary caregiver (Tost, Champagne, & Meyer-Lindenberg, 2016). This bond is first achieved through proximity and responsiveness, ultimately leading to trust. Trust allows the child to develop cognitive schemas that can adaptively integrate affective experiences. As the individual grows, this bond plays a significant role in resilience formation. Through his or her experiences with attachment in adolescence, the individual may develop emotion-regulation competencies and create an internal working model through which he or she may effectively understand and interact with the world (Rutten et al., 2013).

Similar to healthy attachment, positive emotion has also been found to provide an important source of resilience, as it may decrease pain experience and assist in psychological health recovery (Rutten et al., 2013). Researchers suggest that the presence of positive emotions may buffer against the negative effects of stress, resulting in improved physiological functioning. Positive emotion may seem a rather elusive construct, yet researchers have found tangible evidence regarding its role in resilience (Gloria & Steinhardt, 2016). Positive emotion has even been found to have a modest degree of heritability and provides a critical window during which emotional reactivity is largely determined (Roth, 2012; Straussner & Calnan, 2014). Chronic stressors often serve to decrease positive emotion during the time the stress is being experienced, yet chronic stressors such as malnutrition, adverse environmental conditions, and poverty may have a lasting impact on an individual's stress systems over time, resulting in an inability to manage stress or fear and to experience positive emotions. For example, animal studies have found that poverty negatively altered brain plasticity, reduced cortical gray matter, and impaired amygdala and hippocampal functioning (Lipina & Posner, 2012).

Memory. Any approach to trauma treatment must address not only the resulting symptomology of the trauma (e.g., anxiety, depression, maladaptive behaviors) but the memories of the trauma as well. This is evidenced by the multiple diagnostic criteria for posttraumatic stress disorder (PTSD) that address symptoms related to traumatic memories (American Psychiatric Association [APA], 2013). Thus, in order to understand and effectively treat the effects of trauma, it is necessary to further explore the manner in which traumatic memories are stored and subsequently utilized within the brain.

As mentioned, the amygdala is central to the processing of episodic memory. Yet it is also critical to the overall stress response and is often considered the primary fear-processing region of the brain. A primary functional goal of the amygdala is to assess potential threats and subsequently store those experiences for future threat assessment. These memories affect how the individual remembers and responds to similar stressors in the future (Parsons & Ressler, 2013; van der Kolk, 2002). The hippocampus, a neighboring region of the limbic system, is similarly connected to fear and threat conditioning. As the hippocampus is also involved in long-term memory processing, it too plays a crucial role in the formation and storage of traumatic memories (Tallot, Doyère, & Sullivan, 2016).

Both the amygdala and hippocampus are adept at responding to daily stressors. Yet in the face of extreme stress or trauma, the responses of and changes to these regions may diminish an individual's ability to manage future stress of any type (Bergen-Cico et al., 2016; Nalloor, Bunting & Vazdarjanova, 2014). For example, GCs in the hippocampus affect spatial and episodic memory as well as mood regulation. GCs released as a result of chronic stressors may atrophy hippocampal cells and reduce their connectivity, ultimately affecting memory storage and recall. In fact, those suffering from dissociative PTSD symptoms have been shown to have reduced gray matter volume in the hippocampus (Nardo et al., 2013).

In addition to these two fear-processing regions, the prefrontal cortex (PFC) plays a central role in managing stressors (Lanius, Bluhm, & Frewen, 2011; Lanius et al., 2001; Rinne-Albers, van der Wee, Lamers-Winkelman, & Vermeiren, 2013; Tyler, 2012). As previously discussed, this region is the center for rational thought, decision making, and higher-order cognitive processing. Yet the PFC shares connection with and is significantly affected by both the SAM and HPA. Thus the impact of stress on the SAM and the HPA can also have a significant impact on the PFC and can affect the way traumatized individuals consciously process traumatic experiences (Parsons & Ressler, 2013). Chronic stress has been shown to atrophy and reduce connections in the PFC, resulting in cognitive rigidity and increased vigilance (McEwen et al., 2016). Cognitive distortions frequently seen with PTSD (e.g., magnification and minimization) become quite understandable in light of the mediating effect fear plays on memory consolidation and cognitive functioning. Similarly, stress responses may impair a traumatized individual's ability to determine steps forward subsequent to the trauma. This impairment often leaves those suffering from PTSD with a sense of hopelessness about their future in addition to the hopelessness they may have experienced as a part of the traumatic stressor.

IMPLICATIONS FOR TREATMENT

As stated at the beginning of this discussion, exploring the neurobiological dimensions of trauma may appear overwhelming to some. Indeed, any description of the brain's role in psychological functioning should carry with it a recognition of the limitations of our current knowledge about neurobiological processes. The sheer complexity of the brain displays the wonder of God's creation (Ps 139; Rom 1:20). Yet we may increasingly glean insights from scientific observation that can guide our understanding of creation and suggest how best to intervene within that system. This is particularly true in regard to the clinical applications of neuroscience.

As noted, one of the primary roles of the brain is to sense, process, and store experience in order to develop homeostatic patterns that guide future functioning. These templates manage most common threats that present themselves in daily life (e.g., stopping quickly at a red light). Trauma occurs when the events of life move outside those homeostatic patterns and thus the brain's ability to manage the circumstance. Therefore, trauma ultimately disrupts the brain and body's ability to maintain, or return to, homeostasis. This neurophysiological dysregulation and resulting psychological distress may lead to numerous negative outcomes for the individual.

As anyone who has been in an auto accident can attest, the driver experiences an immediate loss of equilibrium (e.g., increased heart rate, shaking hands, sensation of heightened senses). Yet ideally the neurological system quickly determines that the threat has passed, and the sympathetic and parasympathetic systems begin to return to a more balanced state. However, for many, and particularly for those who seek treatment for symptoms related to trauma, an initial loss of neurological equilibrium may lead to longer-term consequences. In the case of extreme or chronic stress, the initial responses of the brain's stress-response systems (e.g., HPA, SAM) may become neurologically hardwired. In other words, what is designed to be a temporary response to threat may become established as the new homeostatic level of functioning.

While the hippocampus and amygdala are designed to determine the nature and severity of threats, they do so based on past experiences. Thus, through the overwhelming of the brain's allostatic system, a sense of threat may be sustained well after a stressful event or life circumstance has passed. Knowledge of this process is imperative for clinicians and their clients, as it displays a central tenet of neurology that informs trauma treatment: the brain changes through experience. Trauma symptoms develop through experience, and so treatment must seek to facilitate neurological change through experience. A client can no more easily "get over" their trauma than they can forget how to walk. Both were learned through experience and thus are a part of a homeostatic system.

Unfortunately, because of a lack of understanding on the part of individuals and society, trauma symptoms are often overlooked after the traumatic event. Yet as the individual continues to struggle in a state of disequilibrium, they will frequently seek some form of neurological, physiological, and psychological equilibrium.

These attempts may lead to maladaptive behaviors such as substance abuse, social isolation, and avoidance (Hammack, Cooper, & Lezak, 2012). Thus, clients presenting with a history of trauma may well display symptoms of chronic substance use as well as relational and professional difficulties.

As discussed, the brain's ability to accurately form new memories can be disrupted following trauma (Nardo et al., 2013). This is especially true in regard to memories of the traumatic event itself (Dekel & Bonanno, 2013). Thus, clinicians should avoid seeking to determine the accuracy of a traumatic memory. The subjectivity of trauma (Yehuda & LeDoux, 2007), as well as the brain's disrupted ability to process and store memories related to the stress, makes the exact details of the events less crucial than the neurological and physiological processes that maintain the traumatic state.

In addition to deficits in memory, traumatized individuals may display significant disruptions in overall cognitive functioning. Trauma has been shown to disrupt attention as well as general executive functioning (Getz, 2014). This is in large part due to the communication that takes place between the PFC and midbrain structures such as the limbic system. Ideally, the PFC maintains regulation of the limbic system and other midbrain structures. Within the typical allostatic system, the PFC becomes less active as the midbrain assesses and responds to basic threats. In the case of trauma, however, the midbrain can become dominant, limiting the individual's ability to effectively carry out executive functions such as planning or logic. Thus, clients who present with symptoms of poor executive functioning (e.g., inattention, poor decision making) should be assessed for trauma history to determine appropriate treatment.

Additional trauma symptoms described in the *Diagnostic and Statistical Manual of Mental Disorders* (APA, 2013) can also be understood in light of the neurological impact of trauma. For example, while not fully understood, the amygdala appears to play a central role in the presence of flashbacks, due to its connections to memory storage and retrieval as well as the infusion of emotion into memory (Storm, Engberg, & Balkenius, 2013). It is also important to note that the midbrain, and thus the amygdala, is not directly, or consciously, controlled by the individual. This helps to explain the intrusive nature of flashbacks and is also relevant to other common trauma symptoms such as dissociation. Research indicates that dissociation occurs in part because of the effect of trauma on the hippocampus (Ross, Goode, & Schroeder, 2015). Thus, the core symptoms of trauma generally function outside the individual's volition. While this may appear somewhat obvious to clinicians who have treated traumatized individuals, it may not be as clear to clients, who may be bewildered by the apparent hijacking of their behaviors and emotions.

Neurological impact of psychotherapy. Considerable space in this chapter has been devoted to discussing the neurological basis for trauma symptoms. Yet it is also important to discuss the manner in which the brain recovers, or is hindered from recovery, and how treatment can aid the healing process. Fortunately, research has repeatedly shown treatment to be effective in reducing trauma symptoms (Bradley, Greene, Russ, Dutra, & Westen, 2005). And while numerous treatment modalities have been used to address trauma, it is beyond the scope of this chapter to cover the various options in depth. Extensive bodies of literature explore the effectiveness of approaches such as trauma-focused cognitive behavioral therapy (Ehring et al., 2014), neurofeedback (Reiter, Andersen, & Carlsson, 2016), and eye movement desensitization and reprocessing (Watts et al., 2013).

Common to the various approaches to treatment, however, is the facilitation of the client addressing the various cognitive, behavioral, and physiological aspects of the trauma in a safe and gradual manner. This commonality begins to make sense in light of the key neurological realities discussed earlier, specifically that the brain must change through experience. In order for any treatment modality to be successful in changing the brain's homeostatic functioning, it must allow the individual to activate, and then regulate, the very neurophysiological networks underlying the trauma symptoms. Each of the above-mentioned modalities requires the client to identify, monitor, and regulate their cognitive and physiological symptoms.

For example, exposure therapy, a form of cognitive behavioral therapy, requires a client to gradually face fear-inducing stimuli while maintaining a state of relaxation. By facing the fearful stimuli, the areas of the brain affected by the trauma are activated. Yet instead of allowing himself or herself to become enveloped by their trauma response, the client learns to increase his or her own regulation, thus bringing the brain back to a more ideal state of homeostasis. This repeated process ultimately leads to lasting neurological changes.

Helpman et al. (2016) found that prolonged exposure therapy led to an overall reduction in the volume of the anterior cingulate cortex (ACC) within the midbrain as well as an overall reduction in PTSD symptoms. Similar to a reduction in the ACC, psychotherapy has been shown to reduce the overall activation of the amygdala while increasing the activation of the PFC and hippocampus (Thomaes et al., 2014). This implies that, with therapy, there is a gradual reduction in the emotional content associated with the trauma (in the amygdala) as well as increases in cognitive processing (in the PFC) and an increased ability to process and store new memories (in the hippocampus).

The role of medication in trauma treatment. While the brain can and does change, it does not change quickly or easily. The neurological effects of trauma are often hardwired. Thus, clinicians and clients must be prepared to gradually work through the treatment process, allowing the brain the time it needs to change. This patience will be all the more necessary in those who have suffered trauma early in life. As discussed, early trauma can have a far more significant impact on later neurological and psychological functioning (Kuhlman et al., 2015).

In cases of early trauma, but also with trauma experienced later in life, clients may need to determine whether medication should be incorporated into their overall treatment plan. As with other areas of mental health treatment, there is increasing evidence that the incorporation of psychotropic medication with psychotherapy can prove beneficial (Thomaes et al., 2014). In fact, the combination of psychotherapy and psychotropic medications is now considered an industry standard for the treatment of many mental health issues (Gabbard & Kay, 2001; King & Anderson, 2004). Common classes of medications used in the treatment of trauma include antidepressants (e.g., SSRIs) and anxiolytics (e.g., benzodiazepines). These medications are generally utilized to address trauma symptoms of anxiety and depression.

More recent studies show the potential benefit of pairing anxiety-reducing medication with exposure to fearful stimuli (i.e., reminders of the trauma) in order to weaken the overall neurological patterns associated with that stimuli (Parsons & Ressler, 2013). Compounds such as ecstasy, psilocybin, and other nontraditional forms of medication have also been explored as potential treatments for trauma (Mithoefer, Grob, & Brewerton, 2016). These compounds decrease amygdaloid over-excitation, resulting in decreased anxiety (Johansen & Krebs, 2009; Oehen, Traber, Widmer, & Schnyder, 2013).

The scope of the current chapter does not allow for an in-depth analysis of these or more mainstream psychopharmacological treatments of trauma. For more information, see Preston, O'Neal, and Talaga (2013). Prescription medications have become increasingly common in the treatment of mental health issues, including trauma (Olfson, Blanco, Wang, Laje, & Correll, 2014). Thus, in order to ethically carry out clinical tasks such as referring clients for medication evaluations or coordinating treatment with prescribing physicians, counselors must be able to understand and confidently utilize basic neuroscientific information in the clinical context. This is especially true in regard to the treatment of trauma.

Trauma and psychoeducation. Much of the current chapter has focused on the usefulness of neuroscientific knowledge to the counselor's conceptualization of trauma. Yet, as Miller (2016) posits, not only must counselors be educated and competent in the utilization of neuroscience in the assessment and conceptualization of cases, but they must also be able to educate their clients about treatment-relevant neuroscientific information. She explains that psychoeducation has long been an essential component of mental health treatment, and thus as neuroscience increasingly informs clinical practice, so should it inform psychoeducational dialogue with clients.

Many trauma victims struggle with their response at the time of the trauma. For example, instead of fighting back or calling for help, sexual assault victims may find themselves frozen. This freezing, otherwise known as *tonic immobility*, is a temporary state of physiological immobility brought on by an overwhelming of the allostatic system. Learning about this involuntary/reflexive response to trauma can help trauma survivors understand why they were unable to respond when the trauma was first experienced and why they continue to find themselves unable to move when they become afraid. This response is rooted in the autonomic nervous system and, as a result, is difficult to extinguish long after the traumatic event has passed. This state can become a learned response in trauma survivors that may be reexperienced when they subsequently encounter situations involving extreme fear (Abrams, Carleton, Taylor, & Asmundson, 2009). Explaining the neurological basis of this response may allow the client to view his or her reaction more accurately, rather than seeing it as a personal failure.

Psychoeducation can play a similarly normalizing role in trauma treatment in regard to explaining why clients cannot merely get over the traumatic events of the past. Explaining the hardwired nature of the neurological response to trauma not only frees clients from the shame of their ongoing symptoms but also prepares them for the long-term nature of treatment and recovery. The counselor can serve as a guide to assist clients in understanding how their brains were changed by trauma, how those changes relate to the symptoms that daily affect them, and how treatment can reduce the effect of trauma on their lives.

CONCLUSION

Scripture describes a call "to bind up the brokenhearted, to proclaim freedom for the captives and release from darkness for the prisoners" (Is 61:1). It is difficult to imagine a group more in need of this freedom and release than those who have been traumatized. Trauma is a condition of extreme complexity and severity. Stemming from a vast spectrum of acute or chronic stressors, trauma affects many facets of emotional and physical functioning, yielding serious short- and long-term neurobiological consequences for affected individuals. Having an understanding of the neurobiological systems that underlie trauma is of great importance to the mental health professional and those called on to provide support, understanding, and a framework for recovery.

While research remains somewhat limited regarding the neurobiology of stress, trauma, attachment, and resiliency, there is a growing body of literature describing the neurological impact that severe stressors, trauma, and complex trauma have on individuals. With an understanding of both the neurobiological processes involved in the formation of traumatic memories and the difficulty in managing the neurological, emotional, and psychological consequences of trauma, counselors will be better able to help clients understand their particular symptoms and to develop strategies for helping them manage and potentially overcome their traumas. By taking advantage of the plasticity of cortical systems and by understanding the more difficult-to-access subcortical regions where the emotional responses are housed, mental health professionals can be empowered to help their clients develop compensatory responses and to provide the scaffolding necessary for their clients to begin the process of recovery.

REFERENCES

Abrams, M. P., Carleton, R. N., Taylor, S., & Asmundson, G. J. (2009). Human tonic immobility: Measurement and correlates. *Depression and Anxiety, 26*(6), 550-56.

American Psychiatric Association. (2013). *Diagnostic and statistical manual of mental disorders* (5th ed.). Washington, DC: Author.

Bale, T. L., & Epperson, C. N. (2016). Sex differences and stress across the lifespan. *Nature Neuroscience, 18*(10), 1413-20.

Bergen-Cico, D., Wolf-Stanton, S., Filipovic, R., & Weisberg, J. (2016). Trauma and neurological risks of addiction. In V. R. Preedy (Ed.), *Neuropathology of drug addictions and substance misuse* (Vol. 1, pp. 61-70). Cambridge, MA: Elsevier Press.

Bradley, R., Greene, J., Russ, E., Dutra, L., & Westen, D. (2005). A multidimensional meta-analysis of psychotherapy for PTSD. *American Journal of Psychiatry, 162*(2), 214-27.

Carr, C. P., Martins, C. M. S., Stingel, A. M., Lemgruber, V. B., & Juruena, M. F. (2013). The role of early life stress in adult psychiatric disorders: A systematic review according to childhood trauma subtypes. *Journal of Nervous and Mental Disease, 201*(12), 1007-20.

Dekel, S., & Bonanno, G. A. (2013). Changes in trauma memory and patterns of posttraumatic stress. *Psychological Trauma: Theory, Research, Practice, and Policy, 5*(1), 26-34.

Dunn, E. C., Nishimi, K., Powers, A., & Bradley, B. (2017). Is developmental timing of trauma exposure associated with depressive and post-traumatic stress disorder symptoms in adulthood? *Journal of Psychiatric Research, 84*, 119-27.

Ehring, T., Welboren, R., Morina, N., Wicherts, J. M., Freitag, J., & Emmelkamp, P. M. (2014). Meta-analysis of psychological treatments for posttraumatic stress disorder in adult survivors of childhood abuse. *Clinical Psychology Review, 34*(8), 645-57.

Frissa, S., Hatch, S. L., Fear, N. T., Dorrington, S., Goodwin, L., & Hotopf, M. (2016). Challenges in the retrospective assessment of trauma: Comparing a checklist approach to a single item trauma experience screening question. *BMC Psychiatry, 16*(1), 20. doi:10.1186/s12888-016-0720-1

Gabbard, G. O., & Kay, J. (2001). The fate of integrated treatment: Whatever happened to the biopsychosocial psychiatrist? *American Journal of Psychiatry, 158*(12), 1956-63.

Gądek-Michalska, A., Spyrka, J., Rachwalska, P., Tadeusz, J., & Bugajski, J. (2013). Influence of chronic stress on brain corticosteroid receptors and HPA axis activity. *Pharmacological Reports, 65*(5), 1163-75.

Getz, G. E. (2014). *Applied biological psychology.* New York, NY: Springer.

Gillespie, C. F., Phifer, J., Bradley, B., & Ressler, K. J. (2009). Risk and resilience: Genetic and environmental influences on development of the stress response. *Depression and Anxiety, 26*(11), 984-92.

Gloria, C. T., & Steinhardt, M. A. (2016). Relationships among positive emotions, coping, resilience and mental health. *Stress and Health, 32*(2), 145-56. doi:10.1002/smi.2589

Goss, D. (2015). The importance of incorporating neuroscientific knowledge into counselling psychology: An introduction to affective neuroscience. *Counselling Psychology Review, 30*(1), 52-63.

Grant, M. M., White, D., Hadley, J., Hutcheson, N., Shelton, R., Sreenivasan, K., & Deshpande, G. (2014). Early life trauma and directional brain connectivity within major depression. *Human Brain Mapping, 35*(9), 4815-26.

Gray, J. D., Rubin, T. G., Hunter, R. G., & McEwen, B. S. (2014). Hippocampal gene expression changes underlying stress sensitization and recovery. *Molecular Psychiatry, 19*(11), 1171-78. doi:10.1038/mp.2013.175

Gunaydin, L. A., & Kreitzer, A. C. (2016). Cortico-basal ganglia circuit function in psychiatric disease. *Annual Review of Physiology, 78*, 327-50.

Hammack, S. E., Cooper, M. A., & Lezak, K. R. (2012). Overlapping neurobiology of learned helplessness and conditioned defeat: Implications for PTSD and mood disorders. *Neuropharmacology, 62*(2), 565-75.

Helpman, L., Papini, S., Chhetry, B. T., Shvil, E., Rubin, M., Sullivan, G. M., . . . Neria, Y. (2016). PTSD remission after prolonged exposure treatment is associated with anterior cingulate cortex thinning and volume reduction. *Depression and Anxiety, 33*(5), 384-91. doi:10.1002/da.22471

Ikemoto, S., Yang, C., & Tan, A. (2015). Basal ganglia circuit loops, dopamine and motivation: A review and enquiry. *Behavioural Brain Research, 290*, 17-31.

Johansen, P. Ø., & Krebs, T. S. (2009). How could MDMA (ecstasy) help anxiety disorders? A neurobiological rationale. *Journal of Psychopharmacology, 23*(4), 389-91.

Karreman, A., & Vingerhoets, A. J. (2012). Attachment and well-being: The mediating role of emotion regulation and resilience. *Personality and Individual Differences, 53*(7), 821-26.

Kasanova, Z., Hernaus, D., Vaessen, T., van Amelsvoort, T., Winz, O., Heinzel, A., . . . Myin-Germeys, I. (2016). Early-life stress affects stress-related prefrontal dopamine activity in healthy adults, but not in individuals with psychotic disorder. *PLoS ONE, 11*(3), 1-13. doi:10.1371/journal.pone.0150746

Kindsvatter, A., & Geroski, A. (2014). The impact of early life stress on the neurodevelopment of the stress response system. *Journal of Counseling & Development, 92*(4), 472-80.

King, J. H., & Anderson, S. M. (2004). Therapeutic implications of pharmacotherapy: Current trends and ethical issues. *Journal of Counseling & Development, 82*(3), 329.

Kisiel, C., Fehrenbach, T., Torgersen, E., Stolbach, B., McClelland, G., Griffin, G., & Burkman, K. (2014). Constellations of interpersonal trauma and symptoms in child welfare: Implications for a developmental trauma framework. *Journal of Family Violence, 29*(1), 1-14. doi:10.1007/s10896-013-9559-0

Koob, G. F., & Volkow, N. D. (2016). Neurobiology of addiction: A neurocircuitry analysis. *Lancet Psychiatry, 3*(8), 760-73.

Kuhlman, K. R., Vargas, I., Geiss, E. G., & Lopez-Duran, N. L. (2015). Age of trauma onset and HPA axis dysregulation among trauma-exposed youth. *Journal of Traumatic Stress, 28*(6), 572-79.

Lanius, R. A., Bluhm, R. L., & Frewen, P. A. (2011). How understanding the neurobiology of complex post-traumatic stress disorder can inform clinical practice: A social cognitive and affective neuroscience approach. *Acta Psychiatrica Scandinavica, 124*(5), 331-48.

Lanius, R. A., Williamson, P. C., Densmore, M., Boksman, K., Gupta, M. A., Neufeld, R. W., & Menon, R. S. (2001). Neural correlates of traumatic memories in posttraumatic stress disorder: A functional MRI investigation. *American Journal of Psychiatry, 158*(11), 1920-22.

Lipina, S., & Posner, M. I. (2012). The impact of poverty on the development of brain networks. *Frontiers in Human Neuroscience, 6*, 1-12.

McEwen, B. S. (1998). Protective and damaging effects of stress mediators. *New England Journal of Medicine, 338*, 171-79.

McEwen, B. S. (2006). Protective and damaging effects of stress mediators: Central role of the brain. *Dialogues in Clinical Neuroscience, 8*(4), 367-81.

McEwen, B. S. (2012). Brain on stress: How the social environment gets under the skin. *Proceedings of the National Academy of Sciences, 109* (Suppl. 2), 17180-85.

McEwen, B. S., Bowles, N. P., Gray, J. D., Hill, M. N., Hunter, R. G., Karatsoreos, I. N., & Nasca, C. (2016). Mechanisms of stress in the brain. *Nature Neuroscience, 18*(10), 1353-63.

McEwen, B. S., & Wingfield, J. C. (2003). The concept of allostasis in biology and biomedicine. *Hormones and Behavior, 42*, 2-15.

McRay, B. W., Yarhouse, M. A., & Butman, R. E. (2016). *Modern psychopathologies: A comprehensive Christian appraisal.* Downers Grove, IL: IVP Academic.

Miller, R. (2016). Neuroeducation: Integrating brain-based psychoeducation into clinical practice. *Journal of Mental Health Counseling, 38*(2), 103.

Mithoefer, M. C., Grob, C. S., & Brewerton, T. D. (2016). Novel psychopharmacological therapies for psychiatric disorders: Psilocybin and MDMA. *Lancet Psychiatry, 3*(5), 481-88.

Nalloor, R., Bunting, K. M., & Vazdarjanova, A. (2014). Altered hippocampal function before emotional trauma in rats susceptible to PTSD-like behaviors. *Neurobiology of Learning and Memory, 112*(1), 158-67.

Nardo, D., Högberg, G., Lanius, R. A., Jacobsson, H., Jonsson, C., Hällström, T., & Pagani, M. (2013). Gray matter volume alterations related to trait dissociation in PTSD and traumatized controls. *Acta Psychiatrica Scandinavica, 128*(3), 222-33.

Oehen, P., Traber, R., Widmer, V., & Schnyder, U. (2013). A randomized, controlled pilot study of MDMA (±3, 4-Methylenedioxymethamphetamine)-assisted psychotherapy for treatment of resistant, chronic Post-Traumatic Stress Disorder (PTSD). *Journal of Psychopharmacology, 27*(1), 40-52.

Ogle, C. M., Rubin, D. C., & Siegler, I. C. (2013). The impact of the developmental timing of trauma exposure on PTSD symptoms and psychosocial functioning among older adults. *Developmental Psychology, 49*(11), 2191-200.

Olfson, M., Blanco, C., Wang, S., Laje, G., & Correll, C. U. (2014). National trends in the mental health care of children, adolescents, and adults by office-based physicians. *JAMA Psychiatry, 71*(1), 81-90.

Parsons, R. G., & Ressler, K. J. (2013). Implications of memory modulation for post-traumatic stress and fear disorders. *Nature Neuroscience, 16*(2), 146-53.

Perry, B. D. (2009). Examining child maltreatment through a neurodevelopmental lens: Clinical applications of the neurosequential model of therapeutics. *Journal of Loss & Trauma, 14*(4), 240-55. doi:10.1080/15325020903004350

Poulos, A. M., Reger, M., Mehta, N., Sterlace, S. S., Gannam, C., Hovda, D. A., . . . Fanselow, M. S. (2014). Amnesia for early life stress does not preclude the adult development of posttraumatic stress disorder symptoms in rats. *Biological Psychiatry, 76*(4), 306-14.

Preston, J. D., O'Neal, J. H., & Talaga, M. C. (2013). *Handbook of clinical psychopharmacology for therapists* (7th ed.). Oakland, CA: New Harbinger.

Reiter, K., Andersen, S. B., & Carlsson, J. (2016). Neurofeedback treatment and post-traumatic stress disorder: Effectiveness of neurofeedback on posttraumatic stress disorder and the optimal choice of protocol. *Journal of Nervous and Mental Disease, 204*(2), 69-77.

Rinne-Albers, M. A. W., van der Wee, N. J. A., Lamers-Winkelman, F., & Vermeiren, R. R. (2013). Neuroimaging in children, adolescents and young adults with psychological trauma. *European Child & Adolescent Psychiatry, 22*(12), 745-55.

Ross, C., Goode, C., & Schroeder, E. (2015). Hippocampal volumes in a sample of trauma patients: A possible neuro-protective effect of dissociation. *Open Psychiatry Journal, 9*(1), 7-10.

Roth, T. L. (2012). Epigenetics of neurobiology and behavior during development and adulthood. *Developmental Psychobiology, 54*(6), 590-97.

Russo, S. J., & Nestler, E. J. (2013). The brain reward circuitry in mood disorders. *Nature Reviews Neuroscience, 14*(9), 609-25.

Rutten, B. P. F., Hammels, C., Geschwind, N., Menne-Lothmann, C., Pishva, E., Schruers, K., . . . Wichers, M. (2013). Resilience in mental health: Linking psychological and neurobiological perspectives. *Acta Psychiatrica Scandinavica, 128*, 3-20.

Sapolsky, R. M. (2015). Stress and the brain: Individual variability and the inverted-U. *Nature Neuroscience, 18*(10), 1344-46.

Schloesser, R. J., Martinowich, K., & Manji, H. K. (2012). Mood-stabilizing drugs: Mechanisms of action. *Trends in Neurosciences, 35*(1), 36-46.

Schneider, G. E. (2014). *Brain structure and its origins.* Cambridge, MA: MIT Press.

Shin, L. M., & Liberzon, I. (2010). The neurocircuitry of fear, stress, and anxiety disorders. *Neuropsychopharmacology Reviews, 35*(1), 169-91.

Shonkoff, J. P., Boyce, W. T., & McEwen, B. S. (2009). Neuroscience, molecular biology, and the childhood roots of health disparities. *Journal of the American Medical Association, 301*, 2252-59.

Sperry, L. (2016). Trauma, neurobiology, and personality dynamics: A primer. *Journal of Individual Psychology, 72*(3), 161-67.

Storm, T., Engberg, M., & Balkenius, C. (2013). Amygdala activity and flashbacks in PTSD—A review. *Lund University Cognitive Studies, 156*. Retrieved from www.lucs.lu.se/LUCS/156/LUCS156.pdf

Straussner, S. L. A., & Calnan, A. J. (2014). Trauma through the life cycle: A review of current literature. *Clinical Social Work Journal, 42*(4), 323-35.

Sullivan, R. M. (2012). The neurobiology of attachment to nurturing and abusive caregivers. *Hastings Law Journal, 63*(6), 1553-70.

Tallot, L., Doyère, V., & Sullivan, R. M. (2016). Developmental emergence of fear/threat learning: Neurobiology, associations, and timing. *Genes, Brain and Behavior, 15*(1), 144-54.

Thomaes, K., Dorrepaal, E., Draijer, N., Jansma, E. P., Veltman, D. J., & van Balkom, A. J. (2014). Can pharmacological and psychological treatment change brain structure and function in PTSD? A systematic review. *Journal of Psychiatric Research, 50*, 1-15.

Tost, H., Champagne, F. A., & Meyer-Lindenberg, A. (2016). Environmental influence in the brain, human welfare and mental health. *Nature Neuroscience, 18*(10), 4121-31.

Tyler, T. A. (2012). The limbic model of systemic trauma. *Journal of Social Work Practice, 26*(1), 125-38.

van der Kolk, B. A. (2002). Posttraumatic therapy in the age of neuroscience. *Psychoanalytic Dialogues, 12*(3), 381-92.

Volkow, N. D., Chang, L., Wang, G. J., Fowler, J. S., Franceschi, D., Sedler, M., . . . Logan, J. (2001). Loss of dopamine transporters in methamphetamine abusers recovers with protracted abstinence. *Journal of Neuroscience, 21*(23), 9414-18.

Watts, B. V., Schnurr, P. P., Mayo, L., Young-Xu, Y., Weeks, W. B., & Friedman, M. J. (2013). Meta-analysis of the efficacy of treatments for posttraumatic stress disorder. *Journal of Clinical Psychiatry, 74*(6), 541-50.

Yehuda, R., & LeDoux, J. (2007). Response variation following trauma: A translational neuroscience approach to understanding PTSD. *Neuron, 56*(1), 19-32.

TRAUMA, FAITH, AND CARE
FOR THE COUNSELOR

CYNTHIA B. ERIKSSON,
ASHLEY M. WILKINS, AND
NIKKI FREDERICK

I got into the car and immediately burst into tears.
My husband loved the mid-century modern house that the
realtor showed us, but it was built just on the edge of a high ridge of the
San Gabriel Mountains in Southern California. All I could think of was
the description of homes sliding down bluffs that I had heard as a counselor
in the aftermath of the Northridge earthquake. I could also picture the
splintered wooden homes I had seen during disaster response work
I had done in Kobe, Japan, after the earthquake in 1995. I hated
disappointing my husband, but there was no way I could feel
safe living in that home. (C. E., psychologist)[1]

Judith Herman's 1992 classic book, *Trauma and Recovery*, offers a simple yet unfortunate truth to consider: "trauma is contagious" (p. 140). That may be why Western society tends to want to put survivors in a type of quarantine; we do not really want to hear the stories, because they remind us of what could happen to us or our loved ones. But choosing the path of caregiver to trauma survivors gives us a front-row seat to the ways that life can unfold as tragedy, violence, and loss. In this chapter we will review the important work by therapists and researchers to understand more deeply the impact of trauma work on the self of the counselor. We will discuss the constructs that have been introduced to "name" the experience, and we will review research that

---

[1]This chapter will include first person narratives offered by the authors and valued colleagues.

examines factors associated with risk and resilience to the experience of traumatization for the trauma counselor. We will also ask the question of what unique risks or protective factors exist in the life of Christian faith, and we will end with specific practical suggestions that you can begin to implement in your life and work today.

DEFINING THE CONSTRUCTS

Traumatic events can significantly affect the lives of those who experience them. Individuals may develop difficulties in physical, emotional, and social functioning, as well as psychological disorders such as depression, acute stress disorder, or post-traumatic stress disorder (PTSD). Yet the effects of trauma can also extend to caregivers. In fact, the *Diagnostic and Statistical Manual of Mental Disorders* (DSM-5; American Psychiatric Association, 2013) defines exposure to traumatic events not only as personal, direct experience of events but also as "experiencing *repeated or extreme exposure to aversive details* of the traumatic event(s)" (p. 271, emphasis added). Hearing the detailed stories of trauma survivors is a sufficient stressor to create PTSD symptoms. Family, close friends, first responders, physicians, and therapists are at risk to experience symptoms related to their care of traumatized individuals.

Though many types of caregivers may be affected, therapists are in a unique role when working with trauma survivors. Therapeutic treatment often includes exposure techniques in which the trained therapist provides a safe place for clients to work through the emotions, thoughts, and beliefs regarding their traumatic events, and this can include detailed accounts of the events and their aftermath (Pearlman & Saakvitne, 1995). In addition, an important aspect of any therapy work is for the therapist to connect empathically with the client (Figley, 1995; Pearlman, 1995). This coupling of exposure to the details, emotions, and cognitions surrounding the events and an empathic connection and authentic care for clients can be extremely demanding. The Christian counselor may develop nightmares, fears, existential questions, difficulty trusting, cynicism, depression, isolation, agitation, and irritability that mirror the symptoms of their clients (McCormack & Adams, 2015). The terms *secondary traumatic stress*, *vicarious traumatization*, and *compassion fatigue* all have been used to describe such symptoms in individuals who are exposed to trauma through their helping roles.

Secondary traumatic stress. The awareness of trauma's effects on professionals began more than two decades ago. Charles R. Figley (1995) introduced the term *secondary traumatic stress* (STS), defining it as "the natural consequent behaviors and emotions resulting from knowing about a traumatizing event experienced by a significant other—the stress resulting from helping or wanting to help a traumatized or suffering person" (p. 7). He noted that individuals secondarily exposed to trauma can suffer from PTSD symptoms such as (a) recurrent distressing dreams of the event or recurrent and intrusive thoughts or images of the event; (b) efforts to avoid places, people, or events that remind one of the traumatic event; and (c) hypervigilance, difficulty concentrating, and sleep difficulties. These STS symptoms may develop quite suddenly and can be the result of hearing about one traumatic incident (Figley, 1995; Jenkins & Baird, 2002). STS symptoms may be confusing for the trauma therapist who cannot see an obvious cause (e.g., "I was not the one who experienced that trauma!"), and this may create a situation where the individual withdraws from his or her support network (Figley, 1995).

Vicarious traumatization. These shifts in relationship and self-understanding have been explored in the concept of vicarious traumatization (VT), introduced by Pearlman and her colleagues in the 1990s (McCann & Pearlman, 1990). VT is based on the constructivist self-development theory, which takes into account both the internal and the external responses to indirect trauma exposure that can affect a person's identity, worldview, and psychological development. VT is marked by profound changes in the core aspects of the therapist's self or psychological foundation, including "shifts in the therapist's identity and worldview; in the ability to manage strong feelings, to maintain a positive sense of self and connect to others; and in spirituality or sense of meaning, expectation, awareness, and connection; as well as in basic needs for and schemata about safety, esteem, trust and dependency, control, and intimacy" (Pearlman & Saakvitne, 1995, p. 152).

These existential changes in cognition and views of the self and others parallel the PTSD symptom criteria introduced in DSM-5 related to persistent negative alterations in cognitions and mood (e.g., negative beliefs about oneself or the world, a restricted range of emotions, or a feeling of detachment from others; American Psychiatric Association, 2013). VT can be understood as a transformational process occurring over time in which the counselor is significantly altered in ways that influence both work life and personal life, even sexual desire (Branson, Weigand, & Keller, 2014). The disruptions of sense of self and others can create limits on the therapist's ability to self-soothe, to be self-aware, to be empathic and compassionate, and to feel safe (Cohen & Collens, 2013; Maschi & Brown, 2010).

I have provided trauma-focused therapies to numerous veterans over the years. In venturing into the emotional pain, I have encountered a handful of narratives that I have resigned myself to never share with another person. This reluctance to disclose is not because these memories do not burden me at times or because I would not benefit from processing my responses to them with a colleague. Instead, they are so heartbreaking and grotesque that I am deeply ambivalent about alleviating my burden. (J. C., psychologist)

Compassion fatigue. Another common term used in the literature to describe the effects of trauma work on the therapist is *compassion fatigue* (CF), which was coined by Joinson (1992) when describing burnout experienced by nurses. Figley (1995) used the terms *compassion fatigue* and *secondary traumatic stress* interchangeably but felt that CF was more easily understood and less stigmatizing. His conceptualization of CF included burnout-related symptoms that highlighted the chronically stressful nature of the work: lack of energy or fatigue, hopelessness about accomplishing work goals, difficulty maintaining boundaries between work and personal life, and feeling depressed in one's occupation. In CF the burnout-related symptoms were combined with trauma-specific reactions such as nightmares or unintended thoughts about a client's trauma story, flashbacks of client material, or intrusive thoughts about a frightening experience while working with a client (Gentry, Baranowsky, & Dunning, 2002).

Relationship between constructs. Researchers have often used the three terms (*secondary traumatic stress*, *vicarious traumatization*, and *compassion fatigue*) interchangeably when describing therapist reactions. However, careful analysis has demonstrated differences and commonalities among the three. STS clarifies the nature of posttraumatic symptoms that might appear quite suddenly and cause great distress. CF acknowledges the ways that trauma material can intrude in the counselor's life but also emphasizes the ways in which exposure to client traumas can degrade the therapists' sense of efficacy, energy, hope, and boundaries in their work. Finally, VT provides a framework to understand the deep impacts of vicarious exposure as it influences the therapist's view of the world, meaning, and key constructs of self and others. STS focuses on the visible symptoms; VT emphasizes the internal experience and trauma theory. VT and CF are conceptualized as the result of an accumulation of experiences and exposures to traumatic material from clients' stories, whereas STS can result from the experience of one event or story (Jenkins & Baird, 2002).

Certain acute trauma care situations (such as the World Trade Center bombing) may create more trauma-specific (STS) symptoms than the burnout-oriented symptoms of CF, but both components are present and significantly related to emotional distress in caregivers (Adams, Figley, & Boscarino, 2008). In fact, a meta-analysis of 41 studies (including over 8,000 participants) indicated that STS and burnout symptoms are highly correlated ($r = .69$; Cieslak et al., 2014). However, a longitudinal study of two samples (in the United States and Poland) examined the relationship of STS and burnout symptoms over time. Burnout at Time 1 was a predictor of STS at Time 2, but STS at Time 1 was not related to burnout at Time 2, suggesting that while the dimensions of distress in trauma work are interrelated, the experience of burnout (emphasized in CF) may actually create risk for developing greater PTSD-related symptoms, as measured in STS (Shoji et al., 2015).

RISK AND RESILIENCE FACTORS

Figley (1995) has argued convincingly that all professionals working with trauma survivors will be affected in some way by their work. However, not all will develop severe distress, and some will even experience growth (Miller & Sprang, 2016). Certain demographic factors have been identified as risks, including gender, with women generally demonstrating more STS and VT symptoms (Baum, Rahav, & Sharon, 2014; Cornille & Meyers, 1999; Kassam-Adams, 1995). Younger trauma therapists and novice therapists have also shown to be more at risk for VT (Cerney, 1995; Way, Van Deusen, Martin, Applegate, & Jandle, 2004). Other areas that have been identified as factors of vulnerability or resilience are similar to research findings from other traumatized populations: (1) the characteristics of exposure, (2) the counselor's own trauma history, (3) the surrounding social and organizational support, and (4) the skills the counselor has to engage the traumatic material.

Characteristics of trauma exposure. The necessary, but not sufficient, cause of traumatic reactions is exposure to traumatic events. This factor has been identified in a variety of trauma-counseling settings with varied results. For example, a higher number of trauma cases on a therapist's caseload increases symptoms of VT (Brady, Guy, Poelstra, & Browkaw, 1999; Kassam-Adams, 1995; Schauben & Frazier, 1995), and the number of hours a week spent conducting trauma therapy has been significantly associated with STS (Bober & Regehr, 2006). Another study noted that longer service with war and torture survivors was a predictor of more CF in counselors (Kjellenberg, Nilsson, Daukantaité, & Cardeña, 2014). These findings emphasize the importance of the *amount or chronicity of exposure* to trauma narratives.

The *type and severity of trauma narratives* therapists are exposed to can contribute to a therapist's vulnerability to symptoms. In a sample of counselors in the United States, those working with survivors of torture, domestic violence, and sexual assault reported more STS symptoms than those working with other types of trauma (Bober & Regehr, 2006). Schauben and Frazier (1995) found that female mental health professionals who worked with survivors of sexual abuse reported significant changes in their schemata for making meaning in the world; this was especially true for those who listened to the trauma narratives of severe cases, such as repeated ritualistic abuse. When working with children who have suffered extreme hardships and trauma, a therapist may be challenged with questions about innocent suffering and the human capacity for evil (Maschi & Brown, 2010). Judith Herman (1992) writes, "Repeated exposure to stories of human rapacity and cruelty inevitably challenges the therapist's basic faith. It also heightens her sense of personal vulnerability. She may become more fearful of other people in general and more distrustful even in close relationships" (p. 141). Some narratives and presentations may increase the sense of personal threat to the therapist. Veterans Administration therapists working with veterans returning from service in Afghanistan and Iraq noted heightened clinician distress when clients presented as erratic, aggressive, impulsive, and potentially threatening to the clinician (Voss Horrell, Holohan, Didion, & Vance, 2011).

Counselor's own trauma history. Some trauma workers have gone through their own traumatic incidents in the past, and this can put them at a heightened risk to develop STS as they work as trauma counselors (Killian, 2008; Nelson-Gardell & Harris, 2003; Slattery & Goodman, 2009). When a therapist who is also a trauma survivor is exposed to the trauma narratives of clients, the images, thoughts, and emotions of past personal experiences can arise. However, research has also demonstrated that even in the midst of STS distress, being motivated to provide trauma care as a result of past trauma experiences is associated with higher levels of altruism and working through personal traumas. Therefore, this risk may also be an inspiration to do deeper personal work leading to the therapist's growth (Jenkins, Mitchell, Baird, Whitfield, & Meyer, 2011).

Social and organizational support. Healthy social interactions can be restorative and are a vital component for preventing VT, CF, and STS. Trauma and VT can often result in a breach of attachment. To combat the symptoms of isolation, mistrust, and negative views of the world, it is vital for the trauma worker to engage in social activities that can "offer feelings of hope, joy, beauty, and playfulness to counteract the more heinous aspects of human nature to which we are exposed in our work" (Yassen, 1995, p. 189). Feeling that you have people in your life you can depend on and who depend upon you and knowing that peers in your work setting are supportive are significantly related to lower STS (Rzeszutek, Partyka, & Gołąb, 2015) and VT (Cohen & Collens, 2013).

In addition, a culture of support and understanding within an organization can be a protective factor. When administrators and supervisors recognize the risks inherent in trauma counseling, they can create policies that affirm appropriate limits and support. This includes reinforcing healthy work boundaries such as taking a full hour for lunch, setting reasonable workload expectations, decreasing the number of trauma clients per day, and taking vacations (Cohen & Collens, 2013; Perry, 2014). An organizational context that allows shared power and choice for the therapist also counteracts the feelings of lack of control and powerlessness that can be part of STS and VT (Slattery & Goodman, 2009; Voss Horrell et al., 2011).

Skills to engage clients' trauma narratives. Trauma work is unique as a type of psychotherapeutic work; the importance of adequate training and education cannot be overstated. Many studies have found that those with specialized trauma training had fewer symptoms of CF, STS, and VT (Chrestman, 1995; Craig & Sprang, 2010; Hesse, 2002). In addition, Craig and Sprang (2010) found that those with specialized trauma training actually had greater satisfaction in their work than those without this type of training.

It is important for the therapist not only to possess knowledge of trauma-informed interventions but also to practice key intra- and interpersonal skills in the work context. Miller and Sprang (2016) highlight that self-care for VT and STS should not be relegated only to time outside work but that within a session, a day, or a work week, counselors can attend to five key skills to mitigate their symptoms: "experiential engagement, reducing rumination, conscious narrative, reducing emotional labor, and parasympathetic recovery" (p. 2). These skills parallel the skills related to safety, emotion regulation, and cognitive reappraisal that are often the focus of our work with clients.

Miller and Sprang (2016) emphasize the need to engage in an empathic and emotionally connected manner with clients that allows for an honest, full experience of the emotions elicited. Harrison and Westwood (2009) note that "when clinicians maintain clarity about interpersonal boundaries, when they are able to get very close without fusing or confusing the client's story, experiences, and perspective with their own, this exquisite kind of empathic attunement is nourishing for therapist and client alike" (p. 213). In addition to this healthy empathy, Miller and Sprang encourage attention to the personal narratives the therapist tells himself or herself regarding professional purpose, meaning, skills, and hope in efficacy of treatment. They also emphasize the cognitive practice of recognizing and taking active steps to reduce rumination about client material, and they challenge counselors to regularly take steps to reduce their autonomic arousal through physical activity and mindful presence.

CHRISTIAN FAITH AND CARE FOR THE COUNSELOR

The psychological literature urges practitioners to take time to develop spirituality and spiritual practice as an aspect of resilience to VT, STS, and CF (Killian, 2008; Maschi & Brown, 2010; Merlino, 2011). Baranowsky, Gentry, and Schultz (2005) state, "Develop your spirituality. . . . Spirituality is your ability to find comfort, support, and meaning from a power greater than yourself" (p. 77). The theology that clinicians hold (consciously or unconsciously) and their faith community can inform the meaning they ascribe to their work, their relationships with trauma survivors, their recognition of evil and suffering in the world, and their rhythm of rest and restoration.

Meaning and purpose. Finding meaning and purpose in one's work can contribute to resilience to VT (Cohen & Collens, 2013; Voss Horrell et al., 2011). How Christian counselors view their work and professional roles can have significant impact on their response to the demands of trauma work. Lonergan, O'Halloran, and Crane (2004) note a developmental trajectory for the trauma counselor from the "rescuer" or "savior" view to a posture of a "vulnerable human" who recognizes the vulnerability in a positive way (p. 356). A mature counselor prioritizes the care offered to clients while owning and acknowledging his or her own humanness. Christian faith and doctrine offer a framework for that developing identity. We desire to serve, but we recognize the limits of our capacity. The Christian counselor has resources that point to transcendent meaning and hope, even when confronted with human limits and the seeming meaninglessness of violence and tragedy (Cunningham, 2004).

Pearlman and Saakvitne (1995) state, "As trauma therapists and researchers, we carry the hope for the human capacity to heal from the effects of trauma" (p. 158). Our knowledge of empirically supported protocols and confidence in treatment efficacy can offer hope to clients and resilience for ourselves (Miller & Sprang, 2016). When we allow ourselves to be open to the pain and chaos of our clients' experiences, and we see their change and transformation over time, their growth can contribute to our growth (Cohen & Collens, 2013). Yet we, the authors, would add that the Christian therapist also carries a hope for transformation empowered by God's grace (Eph 2:4-5), even for the most wounded trauma survivor.

Caring for others with compassion and sacrifice. In many Christian traditions, a follower of Christ has a biblical call to compassionate, sacrificial service to others, to truly care for the brokenhearted. In fact, when asked what is the greatest commandment, Christ answers, "You must love the Lord your God with all your heart, with all your being, with all your strength, and with all your mind, and *love your neighbor as yourself*" (Luke 10:27 CEB, emphasis added). Living with compassion means being deeply moved by the pain of others, engaging at a true level of human connection, and not shying away from the complexity of pain, doubt, rage, guilt, and relief that trauma survivors can hold. This compassionate empathy can both create the risk for VT and STS and be an avenue for healthy presence (Cohen & Collens, 2013; Miller & Sprang, 2016). For Christian therapists, the source of our compassion needs to be the compassion we ourselves experience from Christ (2 Cor 1:3-7). These verses from 2 Corinthians remind us that it is the comfort we receive and the healing that we pursue that allow us to comfort others.

However, in the midst of compassion, the value of sacrificial service can be a confusing burden for Christian counselors, and a self-sacrificing posture has been associated with higher risk for VT (Adams & Riggs, 2008). There may be times when we are called in obedience to sacrifice our time, energy, or resources. However, in some Christian traditions the deep value of sacrifice creates uncertainty around physical and emotional boundaries. The needs of traumatized individuals and communities are often so great and so consistently pressing that the Christian trauma counselor may feel a sense of guilt or disobedience about saying no to a new trauma client, limiting contact outside the session time, or taking vacations. It is critical to remember that setting appropriate boundaries does have the care of the client at the center, both in terms of modeling healthy boundaries and emotion regulation and in terms of keeping the therapist healthy and whole. Unfortunately, in some situations an organizational theology of sacrifice may reinforce an unhealthy expectation of overwork and self-denial. In these settings, staff members who make choices to care for their own needs might be regarded in negative terms (e.g., lazy, selfish, or less spiritual; Maltzman, 2011). Canning (2011) suggests that the concept of stewardship may be a helpful way to note the importance of the counselor attending to both the "*use*" and the "*preservation*" of the self as a resource (p. 72).

The positive side of a theology of sacrifice is an orientation toward the needs of the client. The client benefits from the counselor's hard work of seeking peer or supervisory support, gaining new knowledge through continuing education, and pursuing expert consultation. A commitment to doing excellent work and giving time and resources to our clients reflects Christ's compassion.

Witnessing evil and a theology of suffering. Christian counseling with trauma survivors demands that we bear witness to the evil that can be part of human existence. As witnesses, we sacrifice the ability to stay unaware or ignorant of the cruelty and loss that others experience; acting as a witness to the pain of another also challenges the therapist to take a stand by voicing the injustice (Herman, 1992). The theologian Serene Jones (2009) sees this witnessing as a critical component of walking with and caring for a trauma survivor. We are called to walk in the tension of being a voice recognizing what "shouldn't be" (that is, the fact that God's ordered world should not include experiences like child abuse, violent assault, etc.) and also a voice of hope for what "will be," the hope of God's ultimate justice. Both are necessary.

> *The details of the stories, words, and images were horrific. But for me the hardest and most powerful part was imagining the emotions of the children—what they must have felt and internalized during those incidents. I had to make space for those, while also being careful not to ruminate on them. I found that countering those human evils took a combination of grieving and simultaneously seeking moments of joy, laughter, and silliness with close others in my life. This work requires me to proactively seek beauty and meaning during times of darkness or despair and to hold tightly onto the belief that evil does not get the final word.* (N.F., psychologist)

The Christian trauma counselor also has the resources of theodicy and lament. The faith community is a place where our theology of suffering (theodicy) can become a lived experience. How do we hold onto a God who is all-loving and all-powerful when there is suffering in the world? The faith community has looked to Psalms as a hymnbook of despair, disillusionment, questioning, seeking, and praise for generations. The psalms help the people of God remember what God has done for them; they witness to both the uncertainty and injustice that is in the world and the victory and rescue that God has provided. A particular source of restoration for the Judeo-Christian tradition is the act of lament. The psalms of lament and protest cry out to God that he has not yet followed through on the promises that he made to his people. In protest to God we can shake our fists and raise our voices, stating that things are not as they should be, that innocents suffer, that abuse is an intolerable evil. Our Lord hears these prayers, and we hope in the God who has made a covenant with us (Billings, 2015).

Theology of rest and restoration. The work of engaging with stories of tragedy, violence, and uncertainty can only be sustained and healed within a rhythm of sacrifice and rest. This rhythm can happen in the counseling room by taking breaks to engage the calming, parasympathetic nervous system and by spending time away from work through strategic, restful vacations (Miller & Sprang, 2016). The Christian tradition has also emphasized this rhythm in the ministry of Jesus. Disciplines of prayer, retreat, and quiet have historically provided the renewal needed for compassionate work. Bishop Tutu (2004), in the midst of reconciliation work in South Africa, describes his own rhythm as dependent on a discipline of "stillness" (p. 99). Each day he spends the early morning in quiet "to sit in the presence of the gentle and compassionate and unruffled" God of all creation (p. 100). He also includes quiet days in his weekly schedule and one day a month when he goes to a local convent to pray, read, sleep, and eat. Once a year he takes a retreat for at least three days.

The sabbath is one of the most critical components of this rhythm of rest. It may be tempting to view sabbath as a helpful reminder to take breaks from work, but many Christians seem to not really attend to the fact that keeping the sabbath is one of the Ten Commandments. A theological reflection on the importance of sabbath relates the individual to eternity (Heschel, 1951/2005). All week we are engaged in work that connects us to earthly tasks and earthly space. When we disengage from this attention and turn to sabbath, we enter a divine place: "On the Sabbath it is given us to share in the holiness that is the heart of time. *Even when the soul is seared, even when no prayer can come out of our tightened throats*, the clean, silent rest of the Sabbath leads us to a realm of endless peace, or to the beginning of an awareness of what eternity means" (Heschel, 1951/2005, p. 101, emphasis added). This taste of peace and eternity reorients us to the reality of who we are in relationship to the divine. We are not God. We are not the Savior. We are walking with others as an expression of God's love. We depend on God's comfort as we comfort others (2 Cor 1:3).

PRACTICAL STRATEGIES TO ADDRESS STS, VT, AND CF

Reflecting on the nature of trauma counseling and the possible vulnerabilities and resources available for the Christian counselor leads to the question of what to do. The following practical strategies reflect the personal choices for well-being (general self-care), the work-related options (professional care), and the resources of faith (spiritual self-care). The challenge of addressing self-care is that while everyone would agree it is a good thing to pay attention to one's health and well-being, it proves difficult to enact this belief in day-to-day life. Even in the context of STS and VT, therapists believe that things like self-care, leisure time, and supervision are important, but there is no relationship between the belief in the positive impact of these practices and the time therapists allot to do them (Bober & Regehr, 2006). Remembering that burnout can create risk for more trauma-related distress (Shoji et al., 2015), trauma counselors need to pay attention to day-to-day well-being. These strategies require intentionality and practice.

General self-care. Essential to all aspects of self-care is self-awareness—an honest assessment of personal stress levels, health, and energy. This means paying attention to cues such as tension in certain areas of the body, changes in sleep or concentration, or alterations in mood (Killian, 2008). Without this, it is easy to fool ourselves, pretending that we are without needs. Self-awareness undergirds each of the following strategies.

Prepare, plan, and prioritize. Any discipline requires practice and attention. Plan time each day for intentional time alone, allowing for emotional expression or self-encouragement (Hesse, 2002; Merlino, 2011). Set an uninterrupted time for transition away from the responsibilities of work. It may be a routine of listening to relaxing music during a commute or changing out of work clothes when you arrive home. Establish rituals and routines of care, prioritizing a rhythm of renewal and replenishment.

> *My rhythms of inspiration are essential. Each day I take off my badge, place it in a particular place in my car, and remind myself that my patients are out of my hands for the day. I relish the long drive home because it is a place where I can watch the sun on the mountains, listen to inspiring things, and remind myself that, in the midst of hearing the very worst that humanity can inflict on each other, there are still vital and beautiful and miraculous things happening.* (A. W., psychologist)

Social support. Plan time with loved ones. While the effects of VT, CF, and STS may make it tempting to withdraw or avoid relationships, it is important to prioritize connection with and social support from others (Dass-Brailsford, 2010; Pearlman & Saakvitne, 1995). Connection offers opportunities for disclosure of personal reactions and for restorative emotional support (Baranowsky et al., 2005; Norcross & Guy, 2007).

Personal therapy. Seeking personal therapy is an "explicit acknowledgement of oneself as deserving of care and of one's needs as valid and important" (Pearlman & Saakvitne, 1995, p. 62). Therapy can help identify one's unique background, wounds, and triggers in order to deepen one's capacity to work with trauma survivors. Miller and Sprang (2016) note that some trauma counselors may mistake countertransference for empathy; personal therapy focuses attention on these personal reactions.

Recreation. Clinicians should seek life balance that provides time for play away from professional duties (Hesse, 2002; Merlino, 2011; Pearlman & Saakvitne, 1995; Yassen, 1995). Specifically, recreational activities experienced as enjoyable or healing should be practiced on a regular basis (Killian, 2008). Simply put, taking care of oneself includes engaging in activities that are fun. This could include, but is not limited to, spending time in nature or with animals, creative expression (writing, art, music, etc.), gardening, or doing hobbies (Cunningham, 2004; Maltzman, 2011; Yassen, 1995). This also means being open to humor. Confronting many stories of pain may create a seriousness that can make humor seem distasteful, but joy and laughter is an important part of caring for oneself (Yassen, 1995).

Physical self-care. The body holds stress; imagine tense shoulders and sore muscles after a long day of work. Thus, it is important to both increase body awareness and care for the body (Killian, 2008).

Sleep, "down time" or resting time, and relaxation are essential in aiding recovery from physical and emotional exhaustion (Dass-Brailsford, 2010; Maltzman, 2011; Merlino, 2011). Without sleep, capacities to self soothe, monitor affect, and maintain sense of self are disrupted (Pearlman & Saakvitne, 1995). Diet and proper eating are also important aspects of caring for and "refueling" the body (Hesse, 2002; Maltzman, 2011; Merlino, 2011; Yassen, 1995). Self-care literature also exhorts clinicians to exercise (Norcross & Guy, 2007). Suggestions for (nonstressful) exercise range from taking leisurely walks and doing yoga to engaging in rigorous cardiovascular activity based on personal preference. Exercise can release muscle tension accumulated and increase endurance during work with trauma survivors (Cunningham, 2004; Yassen, 1995).

Professional care. Professional care strategies highlight the necessity of an understanding work atmosphere. The structure of a clinic or office can provide great support in trauma care by creating a culture that recognizes the impact of CF, STS, and VT, and reinforces appropriate work boundaries, supervision, and training. A culture such as this maintains respect for both therapists and clients (Harrison & Westwood, 2009; Pearlman & Saakvitne, 1995). The following strategies are meant to offer guidelines for a healthy approach to work with trauma survivors.

Limits and boundaries. Clinicians must have realistic expectations! Setting professional boundaries and limits, as well as balancing caseload with nontrauma clients is important to avoiding overwork and vicarious traumatization (Killian, 2008; Merlino, 2011; Pearlman & Saakvitne, 1995; Yassen, 1995). Additionally, there will be cases that need to be referred to other professionals. Part of limit-setting is taking breaks, vacations, and clinical sabbaticals to extend periods of rest and recovery (Cunningham, 2004; Hesse, 2002; Norcross & Guy, 2007).

Training. Remember that trauma-specific therapeutic skills are a critical component of resilience to the trauma exposure inherent in the work (Craig & Sprang, 2010; Miller & Sprang, 2016; Voss Horrell et al., 2011). Therefore, be certain to attend trainings and continuing education events designed specifically for trauma treatment. In addition, keep reading and learning about VT, STS, and CF; there are many wonderful books and websites to help counselors reflect on their experiences and normalize the challenges of trauma counseling (Lonergan et al., 2004).

Supervision. It is important to have a nonjudgmental place to process reactions and monitor responses to trauma work. Supervision and consultation can provide space in which to grow, learn, and heal with support (Cerney, 1995; Hesse, 2002; Pearlman, 1995; Yassen, 1995). Ideally, supervision would provide a shame-free space where reactions are considered normal, where clinical success can be celebrated (Cunningham, 2004; Pearlman & Saakvitne, 1995), and where existential issues such as evil and death can be discussed (Kjellenberg et al., 2014).

Teamwork. Professional peers are a primary source of support, including validation, normalizing therapist responses, preventing inappropriate responses, reframing the trauma, clarifying and providing insight, and proposing healthy patterns (Catherall, 1995; Miller & Sprang, 2016). Create policies and schedules that prioritize time for collaborating and consulting with trustworthy colleagues to monitor the effects of working with trauma survivors.

Because everyone on our care team works with people who have been traumatized, we have a practice of debriefing one another after providing care to victims. After walking with a family through the death of their 23-year-old daughter, my teammates reminded me that I would need a debriefing. I would have most likely declined if I had not been so adamant about making it a team policy. We finally set the date for my obligatory debriefing and, reluctantly, I went with very low expectations, not really seeing the need for one. After just a few gentle but pointed questions from my teammates, deep emotions pushed their way through to the surface and I began to cry. They helped me talk through my tears, and I felt an unexpected weight of anger and grief lift. I am so grateful for my teammates. I believe this debriefing practice is what enables me and them to continue giving ourselves over and over again to those who have experienced devastating tragedies. (A. G., missionary psychologist)

Workspace. Make sure that your space is safe, physically and emotionally (Pearlman & Saakvitne, 1995). Keep personally meaningful items, reminders of happiness, beauty, and peace, in your workspace. This may mean decorating your office with pictures of meaningful places or favored pieces of art or poetry (Cunningham, 2004).

Spiritual self-care. McCombs (2010) writes, "For centuries, spiritual symbols, beliefs, and spiritual practices have been used to make sense of and restore wellness after traumatic events" (p. 135). Our personal and communal spiritual formation helps sustain us in this work.

Beliefs. Consider your theology of suffering, your theology of sacrifice, and your theology of caregiving or compassion. Speak with a trusted pastor or wise friends to unravel and reflect on unconscious assumptions of responsibility, sacrifice, and suffering you encounter in order to keep those personal beliefs from limiting your work.

> *I worked with a woman who survived a brutal, premeditated sexual attack. She was a Christian and consistently spoke of her gratefulness of God's protection. I found myself interpreting her remarks as denial and tended to devalue her posture of gratefulness. I realized that I was allowing my own question—why would God allow such a thing?— to cloud my ability to truly listen and be present with her narrative.* (C. E., psychologist)

Faith community. Community can form the framework for engaging with the existential questions that arise (McCombs, 2010). Participate in religious community through worship services, smaller groups, and celebrations. Look for communities that are open to expressions of lament, doubt, and transformation.

Spiritual formation. Take time to develop specific spiritual disciplines and practices before you begin feeling the effects of your work. Such practices include prayer, participation in community life, rituals such as Communion or Eucharist, and reading Scripture. Throughout history, Christians have developed multiple forms of prayer, including Ignatian prayers and retreats, the Jesus Prayer and other breath prayers, and *lectio divina*. Do not forget the prayers of lament and protest. Join the psalmist in honestly lamenting the evil and pain you witness. Finally, our formation should also follow the command for sabbath. Practicing sabbath as a period of revival reorients us from viewing God as giving to us in limited and scarce ways to the God who provides enough (Cavanaugh, 2008).

CONCLUSION

Attending to the effects of Christian counseling with trauma survivors and prioritizing our own personal, professional, and spiritual care is a vital part of flourishing in the work. Symptoms of nightmares, intrusive thoughts, avoidance, or irritability may surprise us, but they can be a natural consequence of engaging in the trauma stories of our clients. Recognizing the symptoms of STS, VT, and CF is the first step; the next step is to honestly reflect on areas of risk or resilience that are present in our lives. Remember the call to compassion in 2 Corinthians 1:3-7; it is through the comfort we receive in our own lives that we are able to offer comfort to others. May your journey as a Christian counselor or psychotherapist for trauma survivors be a part of your own journey toward wholeness.

REFERENCES

Adams, R. E., Figley, C. R., & Boscarino, J. A. (2008). The Compassion Fatigue Scale: Its use with social workers following urban disaster. *Research on Social Work Practice, 18*, 238-50. doi:10.1177/1049731507310190

Adams, S. A., & Riggs, S. A. (2008). An exploratory study of vicarious trauma among therapist trainees. *Training and Education in Professional Psychology, 2*(1), 26-34. doi:10.1037/1931-3918.2.1.26

American Psychiatric Association. (2013). *Diagnostic and statistical manual of mental disorders* (5th ed.). Washington, DC: Author.

Baranowsky, A. B., Gentry, J. E., & Schultz, D. F. (2005). *Trauma practice: Tools for stabilization and recovery*. Cambridge, MA: Hogrefe & Huber.

Baum, N., Rahav, G., & Sharon, M. (2014). Heightened susceptibility to secondary traumatization: A meta-analysis of gender differences. *American Journal of Orthopsychiatry, 84*(2), 111-22. doi:10.1037/h0099383

Billings, J. T. (2015). *Rejoicing in lament: Wrestling with incurable cancer and life in Christ*. Grand Rapids, MI: Brazos Press.

Bober, T. & Regehr, C. (2006). Strategies for reducing secondary or vicarious trauma: Do they work? *Brief Treatment and Crisis Intervention, 6*, 1-9.

Brady, J. L., Guy, J. D., Poelstra, P. L., & Browkaw, B. (1999). Vicarious traumatization, spirituality, and treatment of sexual abuse survivors: A national survey of women psychotherapists. *Professional Psychology: Research and Practice, 30*, 386-93. doi:10.1037/0735-7028.30.4.386

Branson, D. C., Weigand, D. A., & Keller, J. E. (2014). Vicarious trauma and decreased sexual desire: A hidden hazard of helping others. *Psychological Trauma: Theory, Research, Practice, and Policy, 6*(4), 398-403. doi:10.1037/a0033113

Canning, S. S. (2011). Out of balance: Why I hesitate to practice and teach 'self-care.' *Journal of Psychology and Christianity, 30*(1), 70-74.

Catherall, D. R. (1995). Coping with secondary traumatic stress: The importance of the therapist's professional peer group. In B. H. Stamm (Ed.), *Secondary traumatic stress: Self-care issues for clinicians, researchers, and educators* (pp. 80-94). Lutherville, MD: Sidran Press.

Cavanaugh, W. T. (2008). *Being consumed: Economics and Christian desire.* Grand Rapids, MI: Eerdmans.

Cerney, M. (1995). Treating the "heroic treaters." In C. R. Figley (Ed.), *Compassion fatigue: Coping with secondary traumatic stress disorder in those who treat the traumatized* (pp. 131-49). New York, NY: Brunner/Mazel.

Chrestman, K. R. (1995). Secondary exposure to trauma and self-reported distress among therapists. In B. H. Stamm (Ed.), *Secondary traumatic stress: Self-care issues for clinicians, researchers, and educators* (pp. 29-36). Lutherville, MD: Sidran Press.

Cieslak, R., Shoji, K., Douglas, A., Melville, E., Luszczynska, A., & Benight, C. C. (2014). A meta-analysis of the relationship between job burnout and secondary traumatic stress among workers with indirect exposure to trauma. *Psychological Services, 11*(1), 75-86. doi:10.1037/a0033798

Cohen, K., & Collens, P. (2013). The impact of trauma work on trauma workers: A meta-synthesis on vicarious trauma and vicarious posttraumatic growth. *Psychological Trauma: Theory, Research, Practice, and Policy, 5*(6), 570-80. doi:10.1037/a0030388

Cornille, T. A., & Meyers, T. W. (1999). Secondary traumatic stress among child protective service workers: Prevalence, severity, and predictive factors. *Traumatology, 5*(1), 15-31. doi:10.1177/153476569900500105

Craig, C. D., & Sprang, G. (2010). Compassion satisfaction, compassion fatigue, and burnout in a national sample of trauma treatment therapists. *Anxiety, Stress, and Coping, 23,* 319-39. doi:10.1080/10615800903085818

Cunningham, M. (2004). Avoiding vicarious traumatization: Support, spirituality, and self-care. In N. B. Webb (Ed.), *Mass trauma and violence: Helping families and children cope* (pp. 327-46). New York, NY: Guilford Press.

Dass-Brailsford, P. (2010). Secondary trauma among disaster responders: The need for self-care. In P. Dass-Brailsford (Ed.), *Crisis disaster counseling: Lessons learned from Hurricane Katrina and other disasters* (pp. 213-28). Los Angeles, CA: Sage.

Figley, C. R. (1995). Compassion fatigue as secondary traumatic stress disorder: An overview. In C. R. Figley (Ed.), *Compassion fatigue: Coping with secondary traumatic stress disorder in those who treat the traumatized* (pp. 1-20). New York, NY: Brunner/Mazel.

Gentry, J. E., Baranowsky, A. B., & Dunning, K. (2002). ARP: The accelerated recovery program (ARP) for compassion fatigue. In C. R. Figley (Ed.), *Treating compassion fatigue* (pp. 123-37). New York, NY: Brunner-Routledge.

Harrison, R. L., & Westwood, M. J. (2009). Preventing vicarious traumatization of mental health therapists: Identifying protective practices. *Psychotherapy: Theory, Research, Practice, Training, 46*(2), 203-19. doi:10.1037/a0016081

Herman, J. (1992). *Trauma and recovery: The aftermath of violence—from domestic abuse to political terror.* New York, NY: Basic Books.

Heschel, A. (1951/2005). *The Sabbath*. New York, NY: Farrar, Strauss and Giroux.

Hesse, A. R. (2002). Secondary trauma: How working with trauma survivors affects therapists. *Clinical Social Work Journal, 30,* 293-309. doi:10.1023/A:1016049632545

Jenkins, S. R., & Baird, S. (2002). Secondary traumatic stress and vicarious trauma: A validational study. *Journal of Traumatic Stress, 15*(5), 423-32. doi:10.1023/A:1020193526843

Jenkins, S. R., Mitchell, J. L., Baird, S., Whitfield, S. R., & Meyer, H. L. (2011). The counselor's trauma as counseling motivation: Vulnerability or stress inoculation. *Journal of Interpersonal Violence, 26,* 2392-412. doi:10.1177/0886260510383020

Joinson, C. (1992). Coping with compassion fatigue. *Nursing, 22*(4), 116-22. doi:10.1097/00152193-199204000-00035

Jones, S. (2009). *Trauma and grace: Theology in a ruptured world*. Louisville, KY: Westminster John Knox Press.

Kassam-Adams, N. (1995). The risks of treating sexual trauma: Stress and secondary trauma in psychotherapists. In B. H. Stamm (Ed.), *Secondary traumatic stress: Selfcare issues for clinicians, researchers, and educators* (pp. 37-47). Lutherville, MD: Sidran Press.

Killian, K. D. (2008). A multimethod study of compassion fatigue, burnout, and selfcare in clinicians working with trauma survivors. *Traumatology, 14*(2), 32-44. doi:10.1177/1534765608319083

Kjellenberg, E., Nilsson, F., Daukantaité, D., & Cardeña, E. (2014). Transformative narratives: The impact of working with war and torture survivors. *Psychological Trauma: Theory, Research, Practice, and Policy, 6*(2), 120-28. doi:10.1037/a0031966

Lonergan, B. A., O'Halloran, M. S., & Crane, S. C. M. (2004). The development of the trauma therapist: A qualitative study of the child therapist's perspectives and experiences. *Brief Treatment and Crisis Intervention, 4,* 353-66. doi:10.1093/brieftreatment/mhh027

Maltzman, S. (2011). An organizational self-care model: Practical suggestions for development and implementation. *The Counseling Psychologist, 39,* 303-19. doi:10.1177/0011000010381790

Maschi, T., & Brown, D. (2010). Professional self-care and prevention of secondary trauma. In N. B. Webb (Ed.), *Helping bereaved children: A handbook for practitioners* (3rd ed., pp. 345-73). New York, NY: Guilford Press.

McCann, I. L., & Pearlman, L. A. (1990). Vicarious traumatization: A framework for understanding the psychological effects of working with victims. *Journal of Traumatic Stress, 3,* 131-49. doi:10.1002/jts.2490030110

McCombs, H. G. (2010). The spiritual dimensions of caring for people affected by disasters. In P. Dass-Brailsford (Ed.), *Crisis disaster counseling: Lessons learned from Hurricane Katrina and other disasters* (pp. 131-48). Los Angeles, CA: Sage.

McCormack, L., & Adams, E. L. (2015, March 23). Therapists, complex trauma, and the medical model: Making meaning of vicarious distress from complex trauma in the inpatient setting. *Traumatology.* Advance online publication. http://dx.doi .org/10.1037/trm0000024

Merlino, J. P. (2011). Rescuing ourselves: Self-care in the disaster response community. In F. J. Stoddard, Jr., A. Pandya, & C. L. Katz (Eds.), *Disaster psychiatry: Readiness, evaluation and treatment* (pp. 35-48). Washington, DC: American Psychiatric Publishing.

Miller, B., & Sprang, G. (2016, January 28). A components-based practice and supervision model for reducing compassion fatigue by affecting clinician experience. *Traumatology.* Advance online publication. http://dx.doi.org/10.1037/trm0000058

Nelson-Gardell, D., & Harris, D. (2003). Childhood abuse history, secondary traumatic stress, and child welfare workers. *Child Welfare, 82,* 5-26.

Norcross, J. C., & Guy, J. D. (2007). *Leaving it at the office: A guide to psychotherapist self-care.* New York, NY: Guilford Press.

Pearlman, L. A. (1995). Self-care for trauma therapists: Ameliorating vicarious traumatization. In B. H. Stamm (Ed.), *Secondary traumatic stress: Self-care issues for clinicians, researchers, and educators* (pp. 51-64). Lutherville, MD: Sidran Press.

Pearlman, L. A., & Saakvitne, K. W. (1995). Treating therapists with vicarious traumatization and secondary traumatic stress disorders. In C. R. Figley (Ed.), *Compassion fatigue: Coping with secondary traumatic stress disorder in those who treat the traumatized* (pp. 150-77). New York, NY: Brunner/Mazel.

Perry, B. D. (2014). The cost of caring: Secondary traumatic stress and the impact of working with high risk children and families. *Child Trauma Academy's Professional Series.* Retrieved from http://childtrauma.org/wp-content/uploads/2014/01/Cost _of_Caring_Secondary_Traumatic_Stress_Perry_s.pdf

Rzeszutek, M., Partyka, M., & Gołąb, A. (2015). Temperament traits, social support, and secondary traumatic stress disorder symptoms in a sample of trauma therapists. *Professional Psychology: Research and Practice, 46*(4), 213-20. doi:10.1037/pro0000024

Schauben, L. J., & Frazier, P. A. (1995). The effects on female counselors of working with sexual violence survivors. *Psychology of Women Quarterly, 19,* 49-64. doi:10.1111/j.1471 -6402.1995.tb00278.x

Shoji, K., Lesnierowska, M., Smoktunowicz, E., Bock, J., Luszczynska, A., Benight, C. C., & Cieslak, R. (2015). What comes first, job burnout or secondary traumatic stress? Findings from two longitudinal studies from the United States and Poland. *PLoS ONE, 10*(8), e0136730. doi:10.1371/journal.pone.0136730

Slattery, S. M., & Goodman, L. A. (2009). Secondary traumatic stress among domestic violence advocates: Workplace risk and protective factors. *Violence Against Women, 15,* 1358-79. http://dx.doi.org/10.1177/1077801209347469

Tutu, D. (2004). *God has a dream: A vision of hope for our time*. New York, NY: Doubleday.

Voss Horrell, S. C., Holohan, D. R., Didion, L. M., & Vance, G. T. (2011). Treating traumatized OEF/OIF veterans: How does trauma treatment affect the clinician? *Professional Psychology: Research and Practice, 42*(1), 79-86. doi:10.1037/a0022297

Way, I., Van Deusen, K. M., Martin, G., Applegate, B., & Jandle, D. (2004). Vicarious trauma: A comparison of clinicians who treat survivors of sexual abuse and sexual offenders. *Journal of Interpersonal Violence, 19*(1), 49-71. doi:10.1177/0886260503259050

Yassen, J. (1995). Preventing secondary traumatic stress disorder. In C. R. Figley (Ed.), *Compassion fatigue: Secondary traumatic stress disorder from treating the traumatized* (pp. 178-208). New York, NY: Brunner/Mazel.

PART TWO

INTERPERSONAL

CONTEXTS OF

TRAUMA

5

A DEVELOPMENTALLY APPROPRIATE
TREATMENT APPROACH FOR TRAUMATIZED
CHILDREN AND ADOLESCENTS

DANIEL S. SWEENEY AND MADELINE LOWEN

A scared child stands in the middle of your play therapy room. Her head is lowered, and she hesitates to touch the toys even with her eyes. She seems to be trying to take up as little space as possible; the world has taught her she is small. Her parents have told you about her trauma and her fears, but the words of an adult cannot portray the world of a child who has been traumatized. Despite the best intentions of the adults who care about her, this child is radically alone in a reality of fear, shame, and isolation.

An angry adolescent is compelled to come in for counseling because of his delinquent behavior. Underneath that anger, you see a desperate loneliness in him. He feels unheard and misunderstood. He has been labeled by the adults in his life and can't begin to describe the pain underlying his "diagnosis." At the outset of coming in for counseling, he sees himself as a mandated client and refuses to talk. Why should he? The counselor is just another adult who will probably label him.

The training, orientation, and experience of many of us in the helping professions are similar. Many therapists would suggest, perhaps insist, that this scared child and angry teen must *talk* about what they are feeling, what they have experienced, and what they are currently experiencing. We all know the classic counseling question: "How does that make you feel?" Naturally, these clients must verbalize their pain and frustration in order to begin the therapeutic process and experience healing. Or do they? Could it be that these two (and many other) young clients might not be able to express their stories and the accompanying pain through verbalization alone?

We suggest that therapists working with young clients who have experienced chaos, turmoil, and trauma must consider certain developmental components and trauma dynamics. Perhaps nonverbally based psychotherapeutic interventions—interventions that are play-based, expressive, and projective in nature—are not just helpful but necessary. That is the focus of this chapter: exploring the developmental fit for child and adolescent psychotherapeutic interventions.

EMPATHY AS ENTERING THE CHILD'S WORLD

As therapists, we strive to come alongside our clients in painful realities, offering them empathy and companionship on their road toward healing. Carl Rogers (Rogers & Truax, 1967) described this goal of "accurate empathy" as being "completely at home in the universe of the patient . . . sensing the client's inner world of private personal meanings 'as if' it were the therapist's own" (p. 104). Although Rogers began to advocate for the healing power of empathy many decades ago, the ultimate act of empathy occurred long before that. More than 2,000 years ago, the God of the universe made himself "completely at home in the universe" of humans, becoming a man and walking among us as Jesus Christ. Like the examples set by both the father of client-centered therapy and God the Father, it is our job as therapists to enter the reality of our clients. The young girl and adolescent boy standing in your office trying to find a safe place need this very type of empathy; they need someone to enter their worlds and meet them there.

While many therapists are well practiced in the act of empathy, as therapists we live in the reality of adulthood; the inner world of children has become far removed from our own daily experience. The challenge when working with children, especially those who have been traumatized, is to step out of our own universe and find our way into theirs. Far too often, we as therapists treat children like adults who have been zapped with a shrink ray. We expect them to enter our adult world, acting and thinking like we do, just in smaller bodies. Once again, the ultimate example of a radically different type of empathy can be seen in Jesus, who calls children to himself just as they are: "Let the little children come to me, and do not hinder them, for the kingdom of God belongs to such as these" (Mk 10:14). In fact, he takes this a step further, telling the adults that they must become more like children: "Truly I tell you, unless you change and become like little children, you will never enter the kingdom of heaven. Therefore, whoever takes the lowly position of this child is the greatest in the kingdom of heaven" (Mt 18:3-4). For a Christian therapist, entering the world of the child is not only best-practice therapy; it also reflects Christ's vision for the kingdom of heaven.

Entering into the world of a traumatized child or teenager can be particularly difficult for therapists. Not only is it emotionally difficult to witness the pain of a child and the darkness of a world that caused it, but also there are unique psychological and biological ramifications for traumatized youth. This chapter is meant as an initial guide, and we hope it will motivate therapists seeking to journey into this reality of young clients. The chapter provides signposts for this new territory, offering direction regarding the neurobiology of trauma, the unique developmental characteristics of children and teenagers, and an exploration of expressive interventions that will help the therapist enter the world of this population regardless of his or her theoretical orientation.

CHILD AND ADOLESCENT DEVELOPMENT

Adult-focused therapy often relies heavily on verbal communication skills, emotion identification, abstract conversations, and behavior management techniques. These foundational elements, however, are the very things that children and teenagers are still in the process of developing. Although Jean Piaget (1962) is often criticized for his small sample size and the conclusions he drew, his framework for cognitive development is still widely used to describe the transition that occurs from concrete to abstract thinking (Berger, 2014). According to Piaget, children younger than age 11 or 12 do not have the ability to think abstractly or reason in hypotheticals.

This means that child clients (and many teenage clients who are developmentally younger than their chronological age) are concrete thinkers, lacking the cognitive ability to explore their trauma in ways that many traditional adult therapies require. On top of this, children and teenagers do not have fully developed frontal cortices, meaning that they are still learning self-management, self-regulation, and other basic executive functioning skills (Berger, 2014). Additionally, neuroimaging studies show that the adolescent brain continues the development process (Blakemore, 2012), underscoring the need for therapeutic flexibility throughout child and teen therapy. Trauma treatments that ignore these realities unfortunately treat children like miniature adults, rather than as a unique demographic with different needs.

Because traditional therapy is often a verbal process, it is important to also understand the language development of children. Most children speak their first words around the age of one and then steadily build their vocabularies until they are able to speak in short sentences by the age of two. From this point on, their vocabularies explode, and they continue to perfect their grammar and syntax. It isn't until middle childhood that most children begin to understand puns and metaphors in language (Berger, 2014). Even for children who have large vocabularies and impressive language skills, their brains are still learning how to communicate using verbal speech. Especially when it comes to expressing strong emotions, children are frequently unable to put these feelings into words. Landreth (2012) advocates that verbal speech is not the first language of children. Instead, he believes that play is a child's language and toys are the words. Honoring this "first language" of children is one of the major distinctions between play therapy and talk therapy. Not only does this meet the language needs of children, but it also embraces the concrete thinking described above.

Another element of child development that is critical to trauma treatment is emotional development. At birth, babies exhibit primarily distress and contentment, which expands to include laughter and smiles around four months of age, followed by anger in the months immediately after. During these early stages, emotion is a relational process, with children experiencing and reciprocating emotion from their primary caregivers. The strength and security of these early attachment relationships are strongly correlated to emotional health and regulation as well as resilience throughout life. During early childhood, from age two to six, the primary emotional goal is for children to learn and master emotional regulation (Berger, 2014). By the time they reach adolescence, this emotional regulation faces significant obstacles. Adolescents experience an increase in emotional intensity leading to impulsivity, moodiness, and increased reactivity (Siegel, 2013). Therefore, we believe that psychotherapy with child and adolescent clients should take into account these fundamental developmental realities.

RATIONALE FOR PLAY AND EXPRESSIVE THERAPIES

In addition to the developmental characteristics described above, distinct characteristics of the effects of trauma (for children, adolescents, and adults) point to the benefits of using play and expressive therapies. This and the following section of the chapter will briefly explore these considerations.

To begin with, it is important and foundational to summarize our basic rationale for play and expressive therapies. Sweeney (1997), Homeyer and Sweeney (2017), and Sweeney, Baggerly, and Ray (2014) suggest several:

- Play is arguably the child's natural medium of communication, as opposed to the verbal communication that is the primary medium of adult therapy. This is often the case for adolescents as well. Adult therapy presupposes the client's ability to engage verbally, cognitively, and process abstract concepts. We consider it unfair and dishonoring to expect children (and possibly some older clients) to leave their world of expressive play and enter the adult world of verbal communication.

- This also applies to verbally precocious youth. We contend that it is an error to assume that children and youth who appear to have verbal skills are thus able to express their emotional lives in words. Their verbal abilities do not necessarily mean that words are the appropriate means of relational connection.

- Expressive therapies inherently have a unique kinesthetic quality. Play and expressive media provide an unparalleled sensory experience, which meets a basic need that people have for kinesthetic experiences. We assert that this is an extension of basic attachment needs, which convenes in both experience and relationship.

- Play and expressive therapies create the necessary therapeutic distance often needed for traumatized clients. These clients may be unable to express their pain in words but can find expression through projective media. It may well be easier for a traumatized child or adolescent to express self through a toy, a sandtray therapy miniature, or creative arts than to directly verbalize the pain.

- This therapeutic distance creates a safe environment for abreaction and catharsis to occur. All clients who have experienced trauma and crisis need a therapeutic setting in which to abreact—a place of safety where painful issues can emerge and be relived, and thus a safe place to experience the intense negative emotions that are often attached.

- Play and expressive therapies create a place for traumatized clients to experience *control*. We assert that a fundamental result of traumatizing experiences is a loss of control for those in their grip. A crucial goal for these clients must be empowerment, recognizing that the loss of control inherent in trauma and chaos is intrinsically disempowering. Words alone may be therapeutically limiting in this process.

- Expressive and play therapies provide a unique and natural setting for the emergence of therapeutic metaphors. The most powerful metaphors in therapy are those that are generated by clients themselves (as opposed to those by therapists), and expressive therapy creates an ideal environment for this to occur. Toys and expressive media serve to facilitate clients expressing their own therapeutic metaphors.

- Transference, a natural part of the therapeutic process, may be a challenge that can be effectively addressed through play and expressive therapies. This is because of the availability and use of expressive media, which create alternative object(s) of transference. Regardless of various theoretical perspectives on transference, expressive therapies provide a means for transference issues to be safely addressed if and when needed. The toys and expressive media can become objects of transference or the means by which transference issues are therapeutically addressed.

- Play and expressive therapies are effective interventions for traumatized clients. The neurobiological effects of trauma (such as prefrontal cortex dysfunction, increased activation of the limbic system, and deactivation of the Broca's area, the part of the brain responsible for speech) seem to underscore the need for nonverbal interventions. Potential neurobiological inhibitions on cognitive processing and verbalization certainly contend for the benefits of expressive intervention. We will expand on this in the next section.

- Finally, we assert that deeper intra- and interpersonal issues might be accessed more thoroughly and rapidly through play and expressive therapies. These therapeutic interventions create opportunities for nonverbal expression, which facilitate for clients a safe means of processing, and often an accelerated one.[1]

HALLMARKS OF EXPRESSIVE THERAPY

Having provided the rationale for this specific therapeutic approach in working with children and adolescents, we can now explore the nature of expressive therapies in relation to trauma. Schaefer (1994) suggested several interrelated hallmarks of expressive therapies that provide a sense of therapeutic distance and the related safety that traumatized children and adolescents need in therapy:

- *Symbolization.* Clients can use a sandtray miniature or create art to represent an abuser or victimizing situation. For example, it can be much safer for a client to select a predatory animal puppet to represent an abuser (as opposed to verbally discussing victimization). A client might create or select a building with barred windows to represent being held captive. This could represent a presenting issue that involves actual abduction or the overwhelming feeling of inescapability.

- *"As if" quality.* Clients can use the pretend quality of play/drama to act out events as if they are not real life. For example, for a young victim or witness of domestic violence, it is often challenging to process such a trauma verbally. With expressive therapies, clients can "manage the unmanageable," controlling in the *as if* element of the expressive therapy that which could not be controlled in the depths of the traumatizing situation.

- *Projection.* Clients can project intense emotions onto the expressive media, which can then be used to safely act out these strong feelings. It can feel much safer for children and adolescents to project complex and possibly frightening emotions onto animals, puppets or dolls than it would be to directly verbalize them. This therapeutic distance creates a greater sense of safety.

- *Displacement.* Clients can shift negative feelings onto the expressive media rather than expressing them directly toward an abuser or perpetrator. Play and expressive therapies not only provide the opportunity for abreaction to occur but also facilitate relational connection through the setting, the media, and the process.

---

[1]Content in list adapted from Sweeney, Baggerly, and Ray (2014).

These basic elements of expressive therapies interweave in the therapeutic process, providing the opportunity for metaphor and symbolism to facilitate access to the traumatized client's inner world. Gil (2012) summarizes these dynamics, suggesting that expressive therapy

> allows for externalized creations of internal "worlds" of affect, cognitions, perceptions, picture memories, and compartmentalized aspects of difficult life experiences. This therapy allows for mental and physical assimilation, access to symbol language and metaphor, and the possibility of both chronicling events (creating narrative scenarios), and utilizing a type of guided imagery that can promote insight and change. (p. 256)

Traumatized clients truly need the safety of expressive therapies to explore and express these "internal worlds."

NEUROBIOLOGY AND THE TREATMENT OF TRAUMATIZED CHILDREN AND ADOLESCENTS

As described above, expressive therapies provide for an experiential, sensory, and nonverbally based therapeutic experience. In contrast, more traditional talk therapies focus on the executive functioning of the cortical area of the brain, which has limited ability to process trauma (van der Kolk, 2014). When expressive therapies are used in conjunction with or as an alternative to verbally based interventions, we posit they allow clients to process deeper neurobiological issues. In this section we review the neurobiology of trauma as well as the implications for treating traumatized children and adolescents (for a more thorough exploration of the neurobiology of trauma, see chap. 3 of this book).

Physiological changes in the brain. It is well known that trauma can eventuate in significant neurobiological activity. There is an increased production of catecholamines (e.g., epinephrine and norepinephrine), which results in increased sympathetic nervous system activity—where the fight/flight/freeze response is located (De Bellis & Zisk, 2014). Initially there are often decreased levels of corticosteroids and serotonin, the most pronounced effect likely being the diminished ability to moderate the catecholamine-triggered fight/flight/freeze response. Additionally, there are increased levels of endogenous opioids, which may result in emotional blunting, memory impairment, and pain reduction (De Bellis & Zisk, 2014). It is imperative that clinicians (and clients) realize that protracted exposure to traumatic stress affects the adaptation of these chemicals. Essentially, this may permanently alter how people deal with their environment on a daily basis.

We believe that many therapists, though well trained in their areas of expertise, overlook the need to consider the neurobiological effects of trauma. Perry (2006) notes, "Simply stated, traumatic and neglectful experiences . . . cause abnormal organization and function of important neural systems in the brain, compromising the functional capacities mediated by these systems" (p. 29). Perry (2009) asserts that for traumatized clients to experience change, interventions must target under-developed and corrupted regions of the brain. Such intervention is fundamentally important for the brain regions most affected by trauma, including (but not limited to) relational connection, memory, sensory integration, executive functioning, and self-regulation. In order to resolve and reform dysfunctional neural networks, interventions must activate these systems (Gaskill & Perry, 2012, 2014; Perry, 2009), which can be done through play and expressive therapies.

One area of the brain that is particularly sensitive to trauma is the hypothalamic-pituitary-adrenal (HPA) axis, as are various noradrenergic systems. MRI scans of abused and neglected clients reveal evidence of cortical atrophy or ventricular enlargement. For example, in research of child subjects with PTSD, there is evidence of broad neuronal atrophy and diminished development (De Bellis & Zisk, 2014). This includes smaller intracranial, cerebral, prefrontal cortex areas; prefrontal cortical white matter; right temporal lobe volumes; and areas of the corpus callosum and its subregions. Research essentially demonstrates a pattern of atrophy that can be pervasive in the brain—either a deceleration of brain development or reduction of current brain volume.

A definitive example of neurobiological changes occurs in the limbic system, the part of the central nervous system that guides emotion and memory as well as behavior necessary for self-preservation (van der Kolk, 2014). Trauma may cause limbic system abnormalities in the amygdala and hippocampus. The amygdala, which readies the body for action, may get "hijacked" (Perry, 2006) by these neurobiological changes; thus the trauma victim responds before the "thinking" part of the brain (i.e., cerebral cortex) can assess threats. This results in the hypervigilance often seen in trauma victims, which can cause them to go immediately from stimulus to an arousal response without being able to make the intervening assessment of the source of their arousal. This causes them to overreact and perhaps intimidate others. We certainly see this response from traumatized children.

Verbal processing. Many of the neurobiological implications of trauma also negatively affect a client's verbal processing abilities. For instance, clients with PTSD may experience a deactivation of the prefrontal cortex, which is responsible for executive function. This interferes with their ability to measure and respond to threats in a variety of contexts; it not only makes navigating life in general challenging, but it also interferes with the therapeutic process (van der Kolk, 2003). While increased levels of physiological and emotional arousal are occurring, the ability to process these is obstructed. Van der Kolk (2002) notes, "Trauma by definition involves *speechless terror*: patients often are simply unable to put what they feel into words and are left with intense emotions simply without being able to articulate what is going on" (p. 150).

This decrease in verbal processing abilities has been demonstrated in several neuroimaging studies (Carrion, Wong, & Kletter, 2013; De Bellis & Zisk, 2014; Lanius et al., 2004). When people with PTSD relive their traumatic experience, which is what we ask them to do in therapy (usually asking that they do so in words), there is decreased activity in the Broca's area of the brain, which is related to language. At the same time, there is increased activity in the limbic system, or emotional responses (van der Kolk, 2014). When traumatized people are reliving their trauma, they have great difficulty verbalizing these experiences. This would seem to fit the definition of *speechless terror*. Malchiodi (2014) suggests that expressive therapies may provide a unique way to access these traumatic memories, which are "stored as somatic sensations and images" rather than as words (p. 11). She states that "sensory means" of therapy are a way to get around the brain's natural protective instinct, which makes the trauma "literally . . . impossible to talk about" (p. 11).

Integration of the left and right hemispheres. This juxtaposition of sensory and verbal trauma memories also supports the need for trauma interventions that work to integrate the two hemispheres of the brain. The left hemisphere is focused more on linear and verbal processing; the right hemisphere, by contrast, is focused more on the nonverbal, artistic, and metaphorical. Gil (2006) notes that evidence "suggests that trauma memories are imbedded in the right hemisphere of the brain, and thus that interventions facilitating access to and activity in the right side of the brain may be indicated" (p. 68).

Trauma appears to negatively impact the integration of the two hemispheres. Specifically, trauma causes abnormalities in the corpus callosum, the fiber tract connecting the two hemispheres (Teicher, Tomoda, & Andersen, 2006). This may explain the challenges in lateralization (accessing both hemispheres) that abused clients sometimes experience, and can certainly affect the narrative of the trauma. Siegel (2003) speaks to the inherent challenges in this:

> The linear telling of a story is driven by the left hemisphere. In order to be autobiographical, the left side must connect with the subjective emotional experience that is stored in the right hemisphere. The proposal is this: to have a coherent story, the drive of the left to tell a logical story must draw on the information from the right. If there is a blockage, as occurs in PTSD, then the narrative may be incoherent. . . . When one achieves neural integration across the hemispheres, one achieves coherent narratives. (p. 15)

Nonverbally based expressive therapies reach the metaphorically focused right hemisphere. As a result, the expression of the traumatic narrative is enhanced. We advocate that clients express trauma narratives; however, the expression does not have to be (and indeed sometimes cannot be) verbal in nature.

By focusing on the emotional experience of the right hemisphere, interventions can open a "highway for the right to offer itself to the left" (Badenoch, 2008, p. 224). Badenoch and Kestly (2015) see expressive experiences as an opportunity to access and alter "the neural nets holding implicit memory" by creating "an embodied experience of what was missing and needed at the time of the original [traumatic] event" (p. 529). With sandtray therapy, for example, Badenoch (2008) suggests that it may be beneficial to inquire about the feelings and emotions surrounding a sandtray as opposed to looking for cognitive meaning. This avoids "a leap from the right- to left-hemisphere processes" (p. 224), allowing for healing and integration between the hemispheres to occur.

Bottom-up integration. Along with lateral hemisphere integration, trauma treatment should address the integration of the lower and higher areas of the brain. Since trauma can lead to a neurobiological alarm state, where alarm reactions can overpower cortical processing (Perry, 2006; van der Kolk, 2006, 2014), cortical areas of the brain can be overwhelmed by lower regions of the brain. This is one of the reasons Perry (Gaskill & Perry, 2012, 2014; Perry, 2006, 2009) advocates that therapy with traumatized children, as well as traumatized adolescents, begin with a focus on the lower brain regions (the brainstem and diencephalon [midbrain]) and work upward. This would include moving through higher brain areas, identified by Perry as the limbic and cortical areas. Perry and Hambrick (as cited in Gaskill & Perry, 2012) emphasize that "until state regulation or healthy homeostasis is established at the brainstem level, higher brain mediated treatments will be less effective" (p. 40).

Play and expressive therapies inherently follow this evolvement. Expressive media—from toys to sand, water to paint, puppets to dress-up clothes—are fundamentally related to the brainstem and diencephalon. In sandtray therapy, for example, Badenoch (2008) asserts that arranging the sand is an experience that "encourages vertical integration, linking body, limbic region, and cortex in the right hemisphere" (p. 223). Most expressive therapy media entail the tactility, motor action, and attunement needed to engage the brainstem, as well as the rhythmic, simple narrative, and physical warmth needed to engage the diencephalon (see Perry, 2006).

The neurobiological realities discussed throughout this section are a crucial component to any developmentally appropriate trauma intervention for children and adolescents. Van der Kolk (as cited in Wylie, 2004) sums up our main points well: "Fundamentally, words can't integrate the disorganized sensations and action patterns that form the core imprint of the trauma. . . . To do effective therapy, we need to do things that change the way people regulate these core functions, which probably can't be done by words and language alone" (p. 38).

PLAY THERAPY AS A DEVELOPMENTALLY APPROPRIATE TRAUMA INTERVENTION

With our argument for developmentally appropriate interventions, we are clearly focused on play and expressive interventions. It is thus important to define play therapy. While several definitions exist, we have chosen Landreth's (2012) definition. Although Landreth does come from a specific theoretical orientation (child-centered), we believe his definition is cross-theoretical:

> Play therapy is defined as a dynamic interpersonal relationship between a child (or person of any age) and a therapist trained in play therapy procedures who provides selected play materials and facilitates the development of a safe relationship for the child (or person of any age) to fully express and explore self (feelings, thoughts, experiences, and behaviors) through play, the child's natural medium of communication, for optimal growth and development. (p. 11)

Sweeney (1997) and Sweeney, Baggerly, and Ray (2014) use this definition in their discussions of play therapy. We would adapt their work as we unpack Landreth's definition:

- We advocate that *all* therapy should be *dynamic and interpersonal.* Relationship is arguably the most curative element in psychotherapy and indeed should be a cross-theoretical therapeutic imperative.

- All play (and expressive) therapists must be *trained in play (and/or expressive) therapy procedures.* While this would appear to be an obvious factor, it is unfortunately too often overlooked. All too frequently, therapists using projective and expressive techniques such as play therapy have too little training and a lack of supervised experience.

- Play and expressive therapists must *provide selected play materials.* It is insufficient to provide a random collection of expressive media. Landreth (2012) reminds us that toys should be selected, not collected. Expressive play therapy materials should be intentionally gathered in a way that is consistent with theoretical rationale and specific therapeutic intent. Just as with the general psychotherapy process, expressive media should be congruous with therapeutic goals and objectives.

- Therapy of any kind should *facilitate the development of a safe relationship with clients*. Traumatized clients need a therapeutic experience of safety—because people do not grow or heal where they do not feel safe. Facilitation brings about this place of safety. This is true for both directive and nondirective therapeutic interventions.

- Within this context of safety, children and adolescents can indeed *fully express and explore self*, which is the basis for further therapeutic advancement. We argue that if insight and behavioral change are therapeutic goals, the ability to express and explore self is foundational.

- Play is indeed a *child's natural medium of communication*. This is a key element of play therapy. It is also, however, a key means of communication for all clients, of any age, who have a challenging time verbalizing for a variety of reasons. This is what makes expressive and projective interventions so exciting for clients of all ages.[2]

There are a wide variety of approaches to play therapy that are beyond the scope of this chapter. For a foundational text on play therapy, we recommend Garry Landreth's (2012) *Play Therapy: The Art of the Relationship*. To explore various theoretical approaches to play therapy, we recommend *Foundations of Play Therapy* (Schaefer, 2011), *Play Therapy: Comparing Theories and Techniques* (O'Connor & Braverman, 2009), and *Handbook of Play Therapy* (2nd ed.; O'Connor, Schaefer, & Braverman, 2016).

DIRECTIVE VERSUS NONDIRECTIVE APPROACHES

There is some disagreement in the play therapy field regarding which therapeutic perspective is more appropriate with children: a directive or nondirective approach. However, we are not as concerned about a therapist's specific approach as long as the child's and adolescent's best interests are kept in mind. Provided that the client's developmental level is acknowledged and honored, a wide variety of approaches can be used.

Having said this, we need to make some comments about therapeutic theory and techniques. We believe that therapeutic work with children and adolescents can and should be cross-theoretical, not atheoretical (i.e., without any theoretical foundations). Thus, play and expressive therapy approaches and techniques should always be theoretically based. Sweeney (2011) asserts that theory is always important but theory without technique is basically philosophy. At the same time, techniques may be quite valuable, but techniques without theory are reckless and could be damaging. Sweeney (2011) further asserts:

---

[2]Content in list adapted from Sweeney, Baggerly, and Ray (2014).

All therapists are encouraged to ponder some questions regarding employing techniques: (a) Is the technique developmentally appropriate? [which presupposes that developmental capabilities are a key therapeutic consideration]; (b) What theory underlies the technique? [which presupposes that techniques should be theory-based]; and (c) What is the therapeutic intent in employing a given technique? [which presupposes that having specific therapeutic intent is clinically and ethically important]. (p. 236)

We suggest taking a primarily child-centered approach with young children, more so for developmental reasons than for theoretical perspective. With a therapeutic process that is led by the child, traumatized children have the opportunity to gain mastery and control and to discover their own potential and capabilities. Additionally, as noted earlier, traumatized clients have a need for therapeutic experiences in which they can regain the control lost in the trauma event/experience; thus a case can be made for a client-led process for clients of all ages.

As children move into preadolescence and adolescence, more directive, even cognitive, expressive interventions may become possible elements of the therapeutic process. Many cognitive interventions can be adapted into expressive work, which we will comment on below.

SPECIFIC PLAY AND EXPRESSIVE INTERVENTIONS

Although we do not have the space in this chapter to explore specific interventions in detail, we offer a brief survey below. In addition to the play therapy resources noted above, readers are referred to the following: *Helping Abused and Traumatized Children: Integrating Directive and Nondirective Approaches* (Gil, 2006), *Creative Interventions with Traumatized Children* (2nd ed.; Malchiodi, 2015), and *Handbook of Child Sexual Abuse: Identification, Assessment, and Treatment* (Goodyear-Brown, 2011).

Group play/expressive therapy. The combination of expressive therapeutic work and group therapy is an exciting dynamic. There are a number of possible approaches in terms of theory, techniques, and client populations. Two resources are recommended: *Handbook of Group Play Therapy* (Sweeney & Homeyer, 1999) and *Group Play Therapy: A Dynamic Approach* (Sweeney, Baggerly, & Ray, 2014). Many standard group-therapy techniques can also be adapted for use with children and adolescents in group expressive work.

Expressive art interventions. While not many therapists are certified in art therapy, there is significant value to using art interventions with both children and adolescents (Malchiodi, 2012). These can be unstructured activities, such as scribbling, or structured activities, such as a drawing or creating a sculpture of self, family, or school settings. It is important to have adequate materials for art interventions—such as paint supplies, crayons, paper, and basic craft supplies. As always, be cautioned against interpretation.

Puppet play. Puppets can communicate things that clients are not able to. This is an example of the therapeutic distance discussed above. A wide variety of puppets is necessary so that individual or group clients can have several self-selected puppets. It is helpful to have a puppet theater, which can be a formal stage or simply a cardboard box. The clients (puppeteers) can "hide," while the puppets are the agents of expression. This can be a structured or unstructured activity.

Sandtray therapy. There is a significant history to the use of sandtray therapy with clients of all ages (see Homeyer & Sweeney, 2017). Sandtray therapy is similar to puppet play—with the sandtray being the "puppet theater" and sandtray miniatures being the "puppets." The sandtray and a large selection of sandtray miniatures create a pallet for nonverbal expression without the need for any artistic skill. This again creates a powerful means of therapeutic distance and nonverbal expression.

Drama therapy. There are numerous approaches to drama (and psychodrama), which can be powerful within the play and expressive format. Oaklander (1988) asserts that "drama is a natural means of helping children find and give expression to lost and hidden parts of themselves, and to build strength and self-hood" (p. 139). It is important to have adequate props, such as dress-up clothes and accessories.

Integrating cognitive techniques. While it is crucial to honor developmental and trauma-related issues, it is possible to incorporate cognitive techniques into expressive therapy. Another reminder: be careful not to defeat the purpose of using play and expressive therapy by jumping to the use of techniques that are beyond the developmental capabilities of a child or adolescent client. Having said this, it is possible for therapists to challenge cognitive distortions using puppets or sandtray miniatures. It is also possible to employ a solution-focused technique, such as having an adolescent client create a drawing or a sandtray in response to the "miracle question" (de Shazer, 1988).

CASE STUDIES

The following case examples illustrate how some of the techniques and principles we have discussed in this chapter can be applied. We will begin with the case of Abigail, a child client, after which we will look at the case of Peter, an adolescent client.

The case of Abigail. Abigail's case was referred to me (Daniel) by her mother. Abigail was a nine-year-old victim of sexual abuse with a PTSD diagnosis. She presented with emotional and behavioral disturbances as well as difficulties with sleeping. She had been seeing another therapist in the community, and her mother contacted me, stating that Abigail's therapy process had "stagnated."

Although Abigail was intelligent and verbally precocious, I chose to take a child-centered play therapy approach in the beginning, with the possibility of moving on to more structured activities. In the initial session, after my brief introduction to the playroom, Abigail promptly sat down on a chair and said to me, in a rather matter-of-fact manner, "I suppose you'll want to talk about the molest?"

This of course caught me off guard, since very few of my sessions begin this way! As I paused to formulate my response, I thought about what a shame it was that this child, even though she already talked like an adult, had such a concept of the counseling process. Here I was, a new therapist to her—a new *male* therapist, no less—in the first seconds of the first session, and she was disclosing a traumatic event in her life.

After a few seconds, I responded in a very child-centered manner by saying, "In here, you can decide to talk about whatever you would like, or you can choose not to talk at all." My response surprised her even more than her own initial question surprised me. After an awkward silence, because she didn't know how to answer or what to do, I said, "It's probably pretty strange being with a counselor who doesn't ask a lot of questions." With a big sigh, Abigail responded affirmatively. Although it took her a while in that first session, she began to play, and the process developed rapidly after that.

The only thing that Abigail had known about counseling was that it involved talking. After her initial surprise at my response, she was relieved not to have to process her trauma verbally. As Abigail began to work through her feelings and experiences in the playroom—through play as well as unsolicited verbalization—positive changes began to appear in her life. After three sessions, her mother reported a decrease in anxiety, increased positive relationships with family and peers, and improved sleep. It is our contention that the primary genesis of these improvements came about by allowing her to "talk" in her language and experience the understanding of a caring therapist.

The play therapy experience for Abigail was in stark contrast to her previous cognitively based counseling experience. While not eschewing verbal therapy, in light of her developmental age (slightly regressed due to the traumatic experience) as well as the neurobiological challenges of verbalization discussed earlier, I believe that an expressive therapy intervention was the most appropriate. The safety of the relational experience in play therapy needed to precede any exploration of cognitive distortions that may have developed as a result of the trauma.

The case of Peter. Peter was a 13-year-old boy who was referred for therapy because he had responded to his own sexual victimization by victimizing a younger foster girl in his home. His parents were foster parents, and he was referred to me (Daniel) for therapy because of the obvious trauma experiences but also because of his increasing behavioral disruption at home and in school.

Initially I had a conjoint session with Peter and his mother (the father and brother refused to participate). When they arrived for this first session, I asked that they create a tray together. An ongoing dynamic that occurred in this tray involved Peter either placing or asking permission to place spiders, snakes, and lizards in the tray. Each time, his mother would say no or remove the items he had placed in the tray. Near the end of the session, his mother placed a bride and groom in the tray, and Peter asked if it represented his mom and dad. When she said that they did, he promptly placed a tank in the tray and "shot" the bride and groom.

The metaphorical meaning behind this seems clear. The mother wanted Peter "fixed" (her actual words in the initial consult), and she did not want to discuss family dynamics. Peter's placement of "creepy crawly things" (as his mother described them) was a metaphor for his need to deal with some of the ugly issues in his life; the mother's removal of these things was a picture of her unwillingness to face these difficult issues. This was consistent with her verbal messages before, during, and after this session.

In Peter's subsequent sessions, following a sandtray therapy protocol (see Homeyer & Sweeney, 2017), he would create sandtray scenes, discuss the creations, respond to open-ended inquiries, and title the scenes. Many of his initial trays involved chaos and battle scenes, conflicts in which no one won. This is consistent with Allan's (1988) stages of sandplay therapy. It was also reflective of Peter's emotional perception of his own situation, which was certainly a place of great conflict from which he felt there was no escape. As the therapy continued, victories emerged from the battle, and provision was made for escape. This could be seen in later sessions by the addition of military forts and helicopters.

Another clear projection emerged in Peter's early and middle sandtray scenes and was consistently reflected in his trays. He began to use two large predatory figures—such as snakes, alligators, and bears. When clients are exploring victimization issues in the sandtray, large predatory creatures are effective metaphors for the emotionally (and physically) overwhelming experiences of being victimized. (For this reason it is helpful to have a few sandtray items that are disproportionately large [Homeyer & Sweeney, 2017]). This was Peter's way of processing the trauma of the experience of two older neighborhood adolescents molesting him—and it was typical to see two large predatory creatures in most of his early trays. Later in the therapy process, he even named the two creatures with the same names as the offenders, not knowing that I knew the names from the intake information.

As his trays progressed to reflect more order and resolution, Peter's disruptive behavior subsided. As with play therapy, in sandtray therapy (and other expressive interventions) Peter was able to manage in the fantasy of the sandtray that which was not manageable in the reality of his abuse. As an adolescent, with greater abilities to think abstractly, he was also displaying the development of insight and coping skills with which to frame his traumatizing experience. The safety of the expressive intervention enabled him to process the trauma in a unique and effective manner.

CONCLUSION

While we cannot in this chapter provide in-depth training on the use of play and expressive therapy with traumatized youth, we hope to have whetted the appetite of the reader while pointing to helpful resources. Maintaining a focus on the therapeutic relationship, as well as recognizing the importance of developmental and trauma-related issues, will form a foundation of solid clinical work with this population.

This focus on relationship has both psychological and neurobiological benefits. Perry and Pate (1994) appropriately state:

> It is the "relationship" which enables access to parts of the brain involved in social affiliation, attachment, arousal, affect, anxiety regulation and physiological hyper-reactivity. Therefore, the elements of therapy which induce positive changes will be the relationship and the ability of the child to re-experience traumatic events in the context of a safe and supportive relationship. (p. 142)

As therapists, we need to remember the importance and the dynamics of working with traumatized clients. If we focus primarily on the emotionally charged content of the trauma itself, a client's basic physiological state can actually shift. Perry (2006) suggests that this shift may lead to both the client and the therapeutic process becoming "brainstem-driven" (p. 34); brainstem-drive therapy thwarts therapeutic relationship and the processing of trauma. In response to trauma, the anxiety, along with the diminished functioning of the Broca's area, can lead the client to act in a primitive manner. This is in addition to the developmental limitations of young clients. All of these factors may well render the verbal language of therapy less accessible or perhaps useless: "No matter how much you talk to someone, the words will not easily get translated into changes in the midbrain or the brain stem" (Perry & Pate, 1994, p. 141).

The therapeutic implication becomes self-evident. That is, traditional verbal therapy may well be ineffective and perhaps detrimental. Again, this is not to eschew cognitively based interventions. Keeping in mind the concerns discussed in this chapter, therapists would do well to become cross-trained in expressive (nonverbally based) therapies in order to access trauma in clients of all ages, which is frequently based in the midbrain as opposed to the executive neurological areas.

One of the greatest human pains is the loneliness of being alone. Children and adolescents who have experienced trauma know and struggle with this routinely. These clients, already struggling for identity and autonomy in this world, are cruelly burdened when trauma strikes and are left feeling unfairly isolated. In his discussion of loneliness, pioneer play therapist Clark Moustakas (1974) poignantly stated, "It is the terror of loneliness, not loneliness itself but loneliness anxiety, the fear of being left alone, of being left out, that represents a dominant crisis in the struggle to become a person" (p. 16). It is in this lonely place that so many young victims of trauma reside and that Christian therapists must be willing to enter.

We assert that wounded children and adolescents must work through their pain through the world of play. We as Christian counselors must work against leaving a generation of hurting children to live out lives of fear and anxiety. Their survival may depend on it. Despite the popular adage, time does *not* heal wounds. Rather, it is the power of relationship that heals wounds. Yes, therapeutic relationship—but more important, relationship with God and relationship with his children. Neale (1969) wrote, "Consider the play of the child, and the nature of the Kingdom will be revealed. Christ is that fiddler who plays so sweetly that all who hear him begin to dance" (p. 174). For the sake of the children, let's join in the play.

REFERENCES

Allan, J. (1988). *Inscapes of the child's world: Jungian counseling in schools and clinics.* Dallas, TX: Spring.

Badenoch, B. (2008). *Being a brain-wise therapist: A practical guide to interpersonal neurobiology.* New York, NY: Norton.

Badenoch, B., & Kestly, T. (2015). Exploring the neuroscience of healing play at every age. In D. Crenshaw & A. Stewart (Eds.), *Play therapy: A comprehensive guide to theory and practice* (pp. 524-38). New York, NY: Guilford Press.

Berger, K. S. (2014). *The developing person through the lifespan* (9th ed.). New York, NY: Worth.

Blakemore, S.-J. (2012). Imaging brain development: The adolescent brain. *NeuroImage, 61*(2), 397-406.

Carrion, V., Wong, S., & Kletter, H. (2013). Update on neuroimaging and cognitive functioning in maltreatment-related pediatric PTSD: Treatment implications. *Journal of Family Violence, 28*(1), 53-61.

De Bellis, M., & Zisk, A. (2014). The biological effects of childhood trauma. *Child and Adolescent Psychiatric Clinics of North America, 23*(2), 185-222.

de Shazer, S. (1988). *Clues: Investigating solutions in brief therapy.* New York, NY: Norton.

Gaskill, R., & Perry, B. (2012). Child sexual abuse, traumatic experiences, and their impact on the developing brain. In P. Goodyear-Brown (Ed.), *Handbook of child sexual abuse: Identification, assessment and treatment* (pp. 29-48). Hoboken, NJ: Wiley.

Gaskill, R., & Perry, B. (2014). The neurobiological power of play: Using the neurosequential model of therapeutics to guide play in the healing process. In C. Malchiodi

& D. Crenshaw (Eds.), *Creative arts and play therapy for attachment problems* (pp. 178-96). New York, NY: Guilford Press.

Gil, E. (2006). *Helping abused and traumatized children: Integrating directive and non-directive approaches*. New York, NY: Guilford Press.

Gil, E. (2012). Trauma-focused integrated play therapy (TF-IPT). In P. Goodyear-Brown (Ed.), *Handbook of child sexual abuse: Identification, assessment, and treatment* (pp. 251-78). Hoboken, NJ: Wiley.

Goodyear-Brown, P. (Ed.). (2011). *Handbook of child sexual abuse: Identification, assessment, and treatment*. Hoboken, NJ: Wiley.

Homeyer, L., & Sweeney, D. (2017). *Sandtray therapy: A practical manual* (3rd ed.). New York, NY: Routledge.

Landreth, G. (2012). *Play therapy: The art of the relationship* (3rd ed.). New York, NY: Routledge.

Lanius, R., Williamson, P., Densmore, M., Boksman, K., Neufeld, R., Gati, J., & Menon, R. (2004). The nature of traumatic memories: A 4-T fMRI functional connectivity analysis. *Archives of General Psychiatry, 161*(1), 36-44.

Malchiodi, C. (Ed.). (2012). *Handbook of art therapy* (2nd ed.). New York, NY: Guilford Press.

Malchiodi, C. (2014). *Creative interventions with traumatized children* (2nd ed.). New York, NY: Guilford Press.

Moustakas, C. (1974). *Portraits of loneliness and love*. New York, NY: Prentice-Hall.

Neale, R. (1969). *In praise of play: Toward a psychology of religion*. New York, NY: Harper & Row.

Oaklander, V. (1988). *Windows to our children*. Highland, NY: Gestalt Journal Press.

O'Connor, K., & Braverman, L. (Eds.). (2009). *Play therapy: Comparing theories and techniques* (2nd ed.). Hoboken, NJ: Wiley.

O'Connor, K., Schaefer, C., & Braverman, L. (Eds.). (2016). *Handbook of play therapy* (2nd ed.). Hoboken, NJ: Wiley.

Perry, B. (2006). Applying principles of neurodevelopment to clinical work with maltreated and traumatized children: The neurosequential model of therapeutics. In N. B. Webb (Ed.), *Working with traumatized youth in child welfare* (pp. 27-52). New York, NY: Guilford Press.

Perry, B. (2009). Examining child maltreatment through a neurodevelopmental lens: Clinical applications of the neurosequential model of therapeutics. *Journal of Loss and Trauma, 14*, 240-55.

Perry, B., & Pate, J. (1994). Neurodevelopment and the psychobiological roots of post-traumatic stress disorder. In L. Koziol & C. Stout (Eds.), *The neuropsychology of mental disorders: A practical guide* (pp. 129-46). Springfield, IL: Charles C. Thomas.

Piaget, J. (1962). *Play, dreams, and imitation in childhood.* New York, NY: Routledge.

Rogers, C., & Truax, C. (1967). The therapeutic conditions antecedent to change: A theoretical view. In C. Rogers & E. Gendlin (Eds.), *The therapeutic relationship and its impact: A study of psychotherapy with schizophrenics.* Westport, CT: Greenwood Press.

Schaefer, C. (1994). Play therapy for psychic trauma in children. In K. O'Connor & C. Schaefer (Eds.), *Handbook of play therapy* (Vol. 2, pp. 297-318). New York, NY: Wiley.

Schaefer, C. (Ed.). (2011). *Foundations of play therapy* (2nd ed.). New York, NY: Wiley.

Siegel, D. J. (2003). An interpersonal neurobiology of psychotherapy: The developing mind and the resolution of trauma. In D. J. Siegel & M. Solomon (Eds.), *Healing trauma: Attachment, mind, body and brain* (pp. 1-56). New York, NY: Norton.

Siegel, D. J. (2013). *Brainstorm: The power and purpose of the teenage brain.* New York, NY: Penguin Putnam.

Sweeney, D. (1997). *Counseling children through the world of play.* Eugene, OR: Wipf and Stock.

Sweeney, D. (2011). Group play therapy. In C. E. Schaefer (Ed.), *Foundations of play therapy* (2nd ed., pp. 227-52). New York, NY: Wiley.

Sweeney, D., Baggerly, J., & Ray, D. (2014). *Group play therapy: A dynamic approach.* New York, NY: Routledge.

Sweeney, D., & Homeyer, L. (Eds.). (1999). *Handbook of group play therapy.* San Francisco, CA: Jossey-Bass.

Teicher, M., Tomoda, A., & Andersen, S. (2006). Neurobiological consequences of early stress and childhood maltreatment. In R. Yehuda (Ed.), *Psychobiology of posttraumatic stress disorder: A decade of progress* (pp. 313-23). Boston, MA: Blackwell.

van der Kolk, B. A. (2002). In terror's grip: Healing the ravages of trauma. *Cerebrum, 4,* 34-50. New York, NY: The Dana Foundation.

van der Kolk, B. A. (2003). The neurobiology of childhood trauma and abuse. *Child and Adolescent Psychiatric Clinics of North America, 12,* 293-317.

van der Kolk, B. A. (2006). Clinical implications of neuroscience research in PTSD. *Annals of the New York Academy of Science, 1071*(4), 277-93.

van der Kolk, B. A. (2014). *The body keeps the score: Brain, mind, and body in the healing of trauma.* New York, NY: Penguin.

Wylie, M. (2004). The limits of talk: Bessel van der Kolk wants to transform the treatment of trauma. *Psychotherapy Networker, 28,* 30-41.

TREATING SEXUAL TRAUMA
THROUGH COUPLES THERAPY

DEBRA TAYLOR

*Although it is common practice to view group or individual therapy
as the treatment of choice for CSA [childhood sexual abuse] survivors, emerging
data indicate that this may not always be the most appropriate modality.*

JACQUELINE PISTORELLO AND VICTORIA M. FOLLETTE,
"CHILDHOOD SEXUAL ABUSE AND COUPLE RELATIONSHIPS"

*Christians have the greatest motivations imaginable for grappling
with and responding to the ugly reality of sexual abuse. Christian
motivation for sexual abuse ministry can be summed up
with a single, pregnant phrase: "The gospel."*

STEVE R. TRACY, "DEFINITIONS AND
PREVALENCE RATES OF SEXUAL ABUSE"

I became a trauma therapist through a back door. I had been a marriage and family
therapist (MFT) for a few years, and gradually realized I needed to be able to help
couples with their sexuality if I was going to be an effective marital therapist, so I
began training to become a sex therapist. Once I was certified as a sex therapist, I
received many enquiries about my services from women who had been sexually
abused in childhood. Predominantly a couples therapist, I sought training on how
to help survivors of sexual abuse. I attended workshops taught by experts and rising
stars in the trauma therapy field. Throughout the 1980s and early 1990s (the era of
beepers that went off at all hours of the night and of the false memory wars, and
the era before MFTs were taught much about boundaries or about vicarious traumatization), I worked with many trauma clients.

I had been taught to do therapy from a family systems model and had been trained in couples therapy by an exceptionally gifted couples therapist. Yet I did not question when all of the "experts" were directing me to work individually with trauma victims. They were the experts; I was trying to help my clients stay alive, to heal, and to learn how to live. Who was I to question the experts' methods?

I realize now that many of the "experts" I was rushing off to learn from, or whose books I was reading, were, like myself, learning as they worked. It took me many years to understand that most therapists in that era had been trained as *individual* therapists. They did what they were trained to do—they saw their clients individually. Working with couples requires a different strategy and different skills than does working with individuals. Couple therapy is not just doing individual therapy with two people in the room. Even with nontrauma couples, it requires more structure and can escalate very quickly; couple therapy requires more active interventions from the therapist (Doherty, 2002).

Certainly for many trauma survivors, and particularly for complex trauma survivors, life, and therefore therapy, is extremely chaotic. Working in therapy with all that chaos—the chaos of the survivor, the chaos of the hurting/angry spouse, and the fragmented or rupturing marriage—demands a lot of any therapist and any couple. Despite these challenges, the therapist must maintain the therapy office as a safe environment. As Pistorello and Follette (1998) write, "The therapist must guard diligently against repeated emotional victimization of the survivor by the partner in the therapy session. Research has clearly documented the risk of revictimization for CSA [childhood sexual abuse] survivors. . . . It is incumbent on the therapist not to recreate this process in the therapy session" (p. 481). So in part to keep the trauma survivor "safe," most therapists did, and still do, work with them individually.

During my first two decades of education, training, and attempting to help trauma survivors, I felt a very distinct tension and stress. While I and many of my colleagues were working in our therapy rooms with individual survivors, the spouses (or intimate partners) were hurting, frustrated, angry, and usually pressuring the survivor for more relationship, more affection, and, especially, more sex. The partners wanted to know what was happening in therapy; was anything happening that might improve the survivor's life and therefore the couple's romantic relationship? Often, even if I tried to refer the survivor and partner to a couples therapist to work on their relationship while I worked with the survivor on the trauma, they were financially unable to do both.

In the past few years I have stumbled across a few voices in the trauma field saying there is a need to work with the *couple* in healing trauma; several of these voices have been saying this for more than a decade. For some reason I, and apparently many other helping professionals, missed these voices. This chapter takes a closer look at the rationale for and models of working with couples when one or both partners are trauma survivors.

PREVALENCE OF SEXUAL ABUSE

At least one in four children have experienced physical, emotional, or sexual abuse and/or childhood neglect. These children's brain development will be affected, and they may have impaired learning abilities, lower language development, and impaired social and emotional skills (Centers for Disease Control and Prevention [CDC], 2016). Exposure to multiple forms of trauma or exposure to repeated instances of trauma over a period of time, usually involving interpersonal betrayal, is called "complex trauma" (Cloitre, Courtois, Carapezza, Stolbach, & Green, 2011). Studies of adults indicate that over 20% of women and 4% of men have been sexually assaulted after the age of 18 (Elliot, Mok, & Briere, 2004). The most common example of complex trauma is repeated childhood sexual abuse.

The prevalence of reported sexual abuse varies widely depending on the population surveyed and the definitions, measures, and research methods used. An examination of multiple studies shows that 8%–30% of women and 2%–16% of men across all socioeconomic and ethnic groups have experienced sexual abuse involving inappropriate touch prior to age 17 (Bebbington et al., 2011). Prevalence rates are most likely underestimated due to underreporting of sexual assault and the myth that continues to pervade the culture that boys are rarely sexually abused and men are rarely raped. There is evidence that sexual-abuse rates have risen in American adolescent and young adult women. The limited data available with respect to Christians and sexual abuse suggest that rates are about the same as those of the general population (Tracy, 2011).

OVERVIEW OF TRAUMA'S EFFECTS ON THE SURVIVOR

"It is arguably one of the great miracles of our species that in the face of violation and terror, those who have been abused continue to seek out and long for connection with others."

H. B. MacIntosh and S. Johnson, 2008

A trauma survivor has to react and adapt to abnormal, disturbing, and damaging experiences. These reactions and adaptations evolve into usual functioning for the survivor, so that he or she lives in survival mode physically, mentally, and emotionally even after the danger has passed (Courtois & Ford, 2013). Over time, these survival defenses can cause psychological, relational, and physical problems.

Chapters ten and eleven discuss in greater detail the impact of complex trauma on survivors; how these effects impact the relationship are highlighted in this section.

Dysregulation of affect. One of the most profound effects of trauma is the dysregulation of affect. Many trauma survivors become imprisoned by their own emotions, flipping between being flooded with intense emotions and physiological distress and then being unable to feel or express any emotion. The survivor's brain is not able to modulate emotional arousal; he or she is not able to tolerate and contain intense emotion. Yet affect regulation is crucial for healthy, long-lasting relationships.

The "hijacked" brain. Trauma tends to cause the brain to see danger and threat everywhere. The survivor frequently misreads circumstances, facial expressions, and others' intentions, causing blowups or shutdowns in relationships, keeping the trauma survivor hypervigilant, verging on fight-flight-freeze most of the time. This makes it much more difficult to control impulses or emotions (van der Kolk, 2014). When trauma remains unprocessed, the brain gets "hijacked." The brainstem overrides inhibition, so the survivor cannot stop inappropriate reactions or refocus attention. Shifts in blood flow in the brain decrease language ability or memory and increase feelings of sorrow, sadness, and anger. The hijacked brain makes it very difficult for survivors to calm themselves down (Cohn, 2011). The impact of trauma on the brain is covered in depth in chapter three. To work with couples well, the therapist must keep in mind the tendency for trauma survivors to get hijacked.

Impact on adult attachment. All forms of abuse or neglect affect development and can drastically alter how a person forms and maintains attachments in childhood and throughout adulthood (Hecker, 2007). Sexual trauma has consistently been reported to have a severe impact on a person's ability to participate in a fulfilling couple relationship (Rellini, 2014; Zala, 2012). Many survivors of child sexual abuse report relationship problems, believe their relationships are less healthy than others' relationships, and feel unable to depend on their partners (MacIntosh & Johnson, 2008). Survivors of childhood sexual trauma experience higher rates of marital separation and divorce (Meston, Lorenz, & Stephenson, 2013; Watson & Halford, 2010) and are significantly more likely to suffer maltreatment from their partners (MacIntosh & Johnson, 2008). Couples in which a partner is diagnosed with posttraumatic stress disorder (PTSD), a common result of sexual trauma, have been shown to be three to six times more likely to divorce than those without PTSD (Monson & Fredman, 2012).

Attachment theory helps to explain why early experiences influence romantic relationships in adulthood. As Bowlby (1988), the originator of attachment theory, writes, "All of us, from the cradle to the grave, are happiest when life is organised as a series of excursions, long or short, from the secure base provided for us by our attachment figure(s)" (p. 62). Couples who are securely attached exhibit greater commitment and levels of trust as well as satisfaction within their relationship (MacIntosh & Johnson, 2008).

When early attachment relationships are disrupted by trauma, there is usually disruption in childhood attachment style that persists into adulthood. Problems within a couple's relationship are frequently about the (in)security of the bond between the partners and each partner's need for the relationship to be a safe haven and a secure base (Johnson, 2003).

Fear of abandonment. Trust issues are prevalent for survivors of sexual abuse (Courtois & Ford, 2013). The survivor may anticipate abandonment and be intensely sensitive to any distancing on the part of the spouse. The survivor may withdraw from the partner or create conditions that would cause the partner to leave. The survivor may be irritable and precipitate fights or engage in tension-reducing behaviors such as drug or alcohol use or disordered eating that may cause the partner to feel angry or alone. The survivor may be secretive about his or her previous abuse, afraid that the partner will leave if he or she knows "everything" (Courtois & Ford, 2013; Hecker, 2007).

Impact on other areas. The trauma survivor may be fearful of overburdening the partner or may dread that the partner will share the information with other people. The survivor may also believe that the partner will use the knowledge against the survivor, or that the partner will not listen or be able to empathize with the survivor. Trauma may also affect the survivor's spirituality, restricting the survivor's and the couple's ability to use shared faith as a resource for healing (Hecker, 2007).

THE ROMANTIC PARTNER AS A VICTIM OF NEGLECT

"I find the trauma literature about sexual recovery to be sorely impoverished. . . . My reading has shown partners of survivors presented as cardboard cutouts, called upon to be patient, supportive and self-sustaining through the difficult journey of trauma recovery. Certainly not my experience of them in the room."

R. Cohn, 2011

Neglect is the failure to provide for a child's basic needs—physical, emotional, medical, or educational (CDC, 2016). Cohn (2011) found in her 30 years of working with trauma survivors that it is common for the partner of the survivor to be a survivor of childhood neglect. With the focus on the trauma survivor, the child of neglect continues to be invisible—to be neglected. This partnering of trauma survivor with neglect survivor essentially locks the couple into a negative pattern of reenacting their childhood torment and triggering their attachment wounds.

Trust is not just a problem for survivors of trauma; trust is also an issue for most children of neglect. While obvious trauma is about what happened, the problem of neglect is about what did *not* happen (Cohn, 2011). People neglected as children had absent or dismissive caregivers. For these infants and children, it was pointless to cry or protest (Bowlby, 1988). They learned early that the way to survive was to become self-sufficient, to not need. Some of these children, never nurtured or mirrored by their parents, did not become aware of their feelings or needs and may not know what they want or like, even as adults. They are usually experts on their trauma partner's story, keenly focused on their partner's problems, needs, and healing (Cohn, 2011). They may not really have a story of their own. Often survivors of neglect look successful and are autonomous, and they may be high achievers. Interpersonally, however, they frequently feel powerless and mistrustful. For both trauma survivor and neglect survivor, the path to resolving issues of trust must be in the context of a relationship, ideally their marital relationship (Cohn, 2011; Feinauer, 1989).

EFFECTS OF TRAUMA ON SEXUALITY

It is common for survivors of childhood sexual trauma to report sexual difficulties: lack of sexual pleasure, sexual dysfunctions, or dissatisfaction with their sexual relationship (Barnes, 1995; Draucker & Martsolf, 2006). Some survivors are more likely to engage in risky or dangerous sexual behaviors or sexual compulsivity; others are sexually avoidant (Bouchard, Godbout, & Sabourin, 2009; Schnurr et al., 2009). Both women and men who have been sexually assaulted or raped as adults frequently develop sexual dysfunctions (de Silva, 2001). Laumann, Paik, & Rosen (1999) found that both male and female victims of unwanted sexual contact experienced sexual problems much more often than those without unwanted sexual contact. Women sexual abuse survivors describe their bodies more negatively than nonabused women. They also do not attribute positive meaning to sexual expression as frequently as women who were not abused (Colangelo & Keefe-Cooperman, 2012).

It is often mystifying and frustrating for many survivors and partners that sexual intimacy did not appear to be a problem in the early stages of their relationship. This seemingly easy sexual functioning is at least partly due to a "biochemical cocktail" that human brains and bodies produce in the early stages of a relationship. Approximately 3–18 months into the relationship, the partners' usual sexual baseline reemerges, leaving many couples, not just trauma couples, wondering what happened (Cohn, 2011). Often survivors function sexually in the early stages of romantic relationships but begin to struggle or completely break down sexually after their relationship moves into being "family," either after marriage or the birth of children (Buttenheim & Levendosky, 1994; W. Maltz, personal communication, July 23, 2015).

RATIONALE FOR THE USE OF COUPLE THERAPY IN TREATMENT

If professionals insist that trauma survivors work independently of their intimate partner until the trauma processing has been completed, what is the couple to do with their relationship distress? Is it possible to build couple therapy into the treatment model? Could couple therapy *be* the treatment model?

Importance of supportive relationships. Helping CSA survivors and their partners attain or maintain a positive marital relationship has been shown to decrease levels of depression, a very common symptom in survivors (Baucom, Whisman, & Paprocki, 2012). Research has demonstrated that survivors of sexual abuse who are able to establish healthy relationships have fewer trauma symptoms. In several studies, resiliency and overcoming abuse symptoms were associated with the survivor having supportive relationships, being married, developing self-regard, and being religious or spiritual (Feinauer, Callahan, & Hilton, 1996). The results of these studies were so compelling that these researchers concluded, "Therapists must consider conjoint therapy with abused women and their partners as part of the therapeutic regimen for survivors of sexual abuse" (p. 105).

Survivors of sexual trauma arrive at therapy in a variety of ways and with divergent presenting problems. They may present individually, directly asking for help to recover from their trauma. Alternatively, their presenting issues might be depression, anxiety, self-injury, substance abuse, migraines, or other physical ailments. Survivors frequently come to therapy because of relationship problems or sexual problems, and they are unaware that these problems may be linked to their childhood abuse or neglect (Cohn, 2011; Maltz, 2002). Many couples struggle because traumatized individuals have difficulty getting close or staying close to a partner since they careen between hyperarousal, anger, numbing, and dissociation (Greenman & Johnson, 2012).

As mentioned, most trauma therapy focuses on the individual survivor. However, disempowerment and disconnection from others are the two core experiences of psychological trauma (Herman, 1992). To recover, then, the survivor must be empowered and new connections with trustworthy people must be made. Herman (1992) states, "Recovery can take place only within the context of relationships; it cannot occur in isolation" (p. 134). Most of the trauma literature assumes that this recovery relationship applies exclusively to the therapeutic relationship and the client's experience of safety with the therapist (Briere & Scott, 2015; Zala, 2012).

Somehow healing and recovery from trauma and its effects have become the domain of mental health professionals. Yet in the middle of the night when the trauma survivor is experiencing a traumatic nightmare or flashback, it will be the intimate partner who is present, not the therapist. If the partner is told to wait on the sidelines while the trauma survivor works with the therapist on healing, what is the couple supposed to do when those inevitable trauma reactions happen outside therapy? Perhaps therapists have overlooked "the brilliance of ordinary people in healing themselves and the people they love" (Johnson, 2002, p. 7).

Needs of the spouse/romantic partner. Sexual traumatization affects not only the victim but also the survivor's spouse or intimate partner and often is expressed in ongoing conflict between partners (Barnes, 1995). Partners of survivors of sexual trauma report feeling frustrated, isolated, angry, dissatisfied, and unable to communicate well with the survivor (MacIntosh & Johnson, 2008). If and when the trauma survivor seeks help, therapy is usually conducted individually, and partners report feeling left out of the process. They also report that often both the survivor and the therapist view them like perpetrators, or at least potential perpetrators, from whom the survivor needs to be protected. Partners also feel they are forced to wait until therapy concludes—sometimes years—to have a relationship with their spouse (MacIntosh & Johnson, 2008). How can therapists best help couples who are facing the relational and sexual impacts of trauma? Should partners be expected to put their relationship and sexual needs on hold while the survivor works individually in therapy?

Maltz (2012) asserts that the survivor's partner is a "secondary victim" of the sexual abuse. As early as 1996, Reid, Wampler, and Taylor conducted in-depth interviews with the husbands of women who had been sexually abused. These survivors' partners emphasized a need for information regarding the impact of childhood sexual abuse on marriage and what to expect while the survivor is in therapy, and they wanted couple therapy as part of the healing process. Spouses of trauma survivors felt strongly that they had been kept in the dark, that the therapist did not want them in the sessions, and expressed feelings of alienation from the therapy process. The authors recommended that therapists integrate conjoint couple therapy as an adjunct to the survivor's individual or group therapy (Reid, Wampler, & Taylor, 1996).

Stigmatization of the victim. To date, most trauma therapies advocate explicitly or implicitly that the partner wait while the survivor works individually on healing the trauma before addressing relationship problems. When trauma treatment does include the partner in some way, usually the goal is to educate the partner so that the partner can be more helpful and supportive to the survivor (Hecker, 2011; Miehls & Basham, 2004). This reinforces the assumption—by the survivor, the spouse, and the therapist—that the survivor's history of abuse is the cause of all of the couple's relational difficulties and the partner is the long-suffering, deprived saint. Pistorello and Follette (1998) caution that "this process of 'benevolent blame' tends to promote the stigmatization of the survivor and may lead the couple to avoid current difficulties by focusing exclusively on historical events" (p. 480).

TREATMENT OF COUPLE ISSUES

Specific models for working with couples in which one is a survivor are described in the following section. However, whichever overall model is used, it is important first to address issues that interfere with the formation or maintenance of couple attachment and the couple's sexual relationship as well as spiritual issues, which are especially important for Christian couples.

Relational issues and attachment. Attachment theorists contend that an essential component of posttraumatic healing is the creation of loving, supportive bonds between romantic partners (Greenman & Johnson, 2012). Attachment theorists and therapists also assert that the three behavioral systems of attachment, caregiving, and sexuality must be integrated to develop a secure, healthy adult pair bond (Butzer & Campbell, 2008; Johnson, 2002). By viewing the couple through an attachment frame and helping a couple to see each other through the lens of attachment, the therapist and the partners can understand the environment in which each partner learned to relate and can value their attempts to adapt (Johnson, 2009).

Sidestepping the relational conflicts or sexual concerns between the survivor and partner, while understandable in the midst of the survivor's trauma history and symptoms, may in the long run lead to further relationship dissatisfaction and even dissolution. Without intervention, many survivors who establish a relationship with a partner who has a secure attachment style cannot believe that they deserve a healthy relationship and end up leaving or otherwise sabotaging the relationship (Courtois & Ford, 2013). Focusing on the couple and their concerns, even sexual concerns, early in trauma therapy versus waiting until the later stages of therapy may prove to be a better strategy.

Sexual healing for survivor couples. When a couple specifically comes to therapy to work together on sexual healing, emphasizing safety, deescalating the negative cycle between the couple, and establishing a secure base are primary goals (Courtois & Ford, 2013). Shifting to viewing the sexual problem as serving a function for the survivor and for the couple and exploring its function is one key to navigating this stage (Maltz, 2012). The survivor is encouraged, along with the partner, to exercise choice in the treatment goals, and the therapist uses a nonauthoritarian, collaborative style. Sexual healing should be empowering for both partners. Examining and changing sexual attitudes from abusive (e.g., "sex is an obligation") to positive (e.g., "sex is a choice") is a major aspect of sexual healing with survivors (Maltz, 2012).

In her classic book *The Sexual Healing Journey*, Maltz (2012) has designed specific exercises that survivors and their partners can practice, both individually and together, to relearn touch. These exercises are useful to help survivors stay present in the moment, relax, and communicate about their sensations, reactions, and emotions about touch. These are not typical sex therapy exercises; they are simpler and more playful and are usually done fully clothed. Maltz's exercises involve learning, sometimes for the first time for men or women who were abused as children, what gradual growth in childlike and affectionate touch is like (Maltz, 2002, 2012). Over time and with repetition of the relearning touch exercises, the couple may choose to move toward more sensual and sexual exercises such as those described by Rosenau (2002).

Spiritual issues. Depending on the individual, the partner, and their joint healing journey, working on trauma can have positive or negative effects on faith. This is an important area for the therapist to directly inquire about during assessment. Survivors may experience a greater sense of closeness to God or greater dependence on God, or they may question God and distance themselves from God or the church (National Center for PTSD, 2016b; Tracy, 2005). The spouse may feel dismay, fear, abandonment, or anger as the survivor wrestles with faith issues or seems to reject God. Modeling acceptance and openness, the therapist can maintain rapport with each partner and work collaboratively with the couple in exploring therapeutic goals that include their spiritual life individually and as a couple.

Being a part of a healthy church can have a positive impact on common trauma symptoms such as isolation, guilt, anger, and lack of meaning. However, rigid or judgmental attitudes from church leadership, Christian friendships, or the spouse can add to the survivor's sense of isolation, shame, anger, anxiety, and depression. The early phase of treatment in each of the models of couple therapy explained below focuses on stabilization, including helping the couple to develop acceptance for each other and positive communication with each other. Communication skills and education regarding trauma symptoms, the brain, emotional regulation, and attachment can be integrated into the survivor's and the partner's spiritual journey. Chapters one and four discussed trauma and faith in more depth.

MODELS OF COUPLE THERAPY FOR TRAUMA

"Sal Minuchin suggested that rather than relying on magical gurus to create change, we have to make family members healers of each other."

S. M. Johnson and A. K. Wittenborn, 2012

It is difficult to design one therapy protocol for all survivors of CSA, or to predict how long healing will take, because of the differences in abuse survivors' histories, losses, coping skills, and severity of pathology. In individual therapy, some survivors work through the three stages of trauma therapy in less than a year, some will need several years, and others decades (Courtois, 2004; Herman, 1992). What can couples and therapists expect when working on healing trauma through couple therapy?

Several resources are available to therapists to guide them as they work with couples on relational and sexual healing from the effects of sexual trauma (Basham & Miehls, 2004; Cohn, 2011; Greenman & Johnson, 2012; Maltz, 2012). No studies have definitively shown the superiority of couple therapy over individual therapy for CSA recovery or other trauma recovery. However, the findings from recent research studies reinforce the notion that "directly intervening with people's most central interpersonal relationships might result in important changes not only in the patient with psychopathology, but also in their partner and in their ongoing relationship" (Baucom, Whisman, & Paprocki, 2012, pp. 267-68). For example, studies with depressed clients comparing conjoint therapy to individual therapy indicate that both produce improvement in depression, but couple therapy results in better communication between the couple, improved relationship quality, and lower negativity between partners (Gilliam & Cottone, 2005).

There is a growing literature to encourage the use of couple therapy for the treatment of trauma, either as the primary treatment modality or as a concurrent adjunct to individual therapy. Some of these resources are manualized treatments and are intended to be followed as written. Others pull together several theories or modalities and give guidance on how to use these different views and tools in working with trauma couples. Others encourage the therapist to integrate couple therapy into the therapist's usual approach for working with trauma. Trauma therapy for couples has been and is currently being studied using emotionally focused therapy (Johnson, 2004), structural family therapy integrated with eye movement desensitization and reprocessing (Koedam, 2007), cognitive-behavioral conjoint therapy (Monson & Fredman, 2012), object-relations couples therapy (Basham & Miehls, 2004), and syntheses using aspects of trauma theory with parts of Imago Relationship Therapy and Gottman Method Couples Therapy (Cohn, 2011).

A summary of four well-formulated couple therapies for trauma follows. I strongly encourage you to determine which of these or others in the reference section appeals to you and fits with your previous training. Through further training and supervision in a treatment approach, become better equipped to help couples in which one or both partners have experienced trauma and neglect.

Cognitive-behavioral conjoint therapy for PTSD. CBCT for PTSD was designed to integrate evidence-based couple therapy interventions and individual

cognitive-behavioral PTSD treatment into a protocol that treats PTSD and enhances intimate relational functioning (Monson & Fredman, 2015). There is a very
strong association between lack of social support and PTSD. CBCT for PTSD has
been demonstrated to improve PTSD symptoms and the mental health of the
partner and to increase satisfaction within the relationship, a three-for-one benefit
for this therapy. It has also demonstrated efficacy in treating depression, panic and
anxiety, substance use, and anger (Monson & Fredman, 2012).

CBCT for PTSD is a three-phase, sequentially delivered, 15-session, manualized
treatment. It is a standalone treatment, a primary treatment for PTSD, and not an
adjunct to individual therapy. All sessions are conducted conjointly for 75 minutes
per session. Prior to beginning the treatment, the couple participates in three assessment sessions: one conjoint session and one individual session for each partner.
In these sessions the structure and requirements of the program are discussed explicitly with the partners, their motivation for full participation in the program is
assessed, and informed consent is acquired.

The first session presents the rationale for treatment and important information
about the effects of PTSD and how symptoms of reexperiencing, avoidance, emotional numbing, and hyperarousal affect relationships. In future sessions, education
and practice are designed to increase relationship satisfaction, undermine the
avoidance that maintains both the PTSD and the relationship problems, and make
meaning of the traumatic events that caused the PTSD. Specific skills that the
couple develops over the 15 sessions include communicating well, identifying and
sharing feelings, observing PTSD-related cognitions, making plans to "shrink"
PTSD in the relationship, and working as a united team to explore and change
trauma-related thoughts (Monson & Fredman, 2012). These skills are conceptualized in and remembered through the acronym "RESUME Living" (Monson &
Fredman, 2015).

In this model, both in-session and between-session skills practice are essential
(Monson & Fredman, 2012). In each therapy session the therapist and couple review
the at-home practice, new skills are taught, and the couple practices the new skills
in session. At the close of each session the next out-of-session practice is assigned.

There are at least three reasons to consider using CBCT in the treatment of
couples in which one partner is a trauma survivor. First, since it is a manualized
treatment, the therapist who has not been trained in a couples approach to working
with trauma is able to follow a detailed guide to develop competence and grow in
confidence in providing conjoint trauma therapy. Second, CBCT for PTSD has been
researched and shown effective with couples similar to the types of trauma couples
everyday clinicians see—for example, couples with substance abuse problems,
couples in which both partners have experienced trauma or neglect, couples in

which one of the partners has a major mental health diagnosis that is being treated and is stable, couples with a partner with mild cognitive impairment, and couples with a partner with non-imminent suicidality (Monson & Fredman, 2015; Monson et al., 2012). Third, many individuals and couples express reticence about participating in individual therapy yet report that they are willing to participate in couple counseling or family therapy (Monson & Fredman, 2012). Military couples in particular have reported that they are willing to participate in this type of therapy for the sake of their family but would be unwilling to attend individual therapy.

Emotionally focused couple therapy. Relationship distress often undermines healing from trauma. Survivors of complex trauma associate closeness and dependency with fear and suffering. Couple therapy is an opportunity to create a corrective emotional experience of safe connection, which can soothe and heal wounds caused by past trauma (Johnson, 2004).

The goal of emotionally focused therapy (EFT) is for the couple to create (or recreate) a safe haven of secure attachment. Securely attached individuals can regulate their emotions when facing stress, openly ask for their needs for comfort and reassurance to be met, and take in and use comfort to calm themselves. Therefore, when the couple becomes more securely attached through working in therapy, they will be able to ameliorate one of the more serious consequences of trauma, that is, affect dysregulation and the inability to self-soothe (Johnson, 2004).

Traditionally, EFT is conducted in three stages that include nine steps. In EFT trauma treatment, these stages are adapted, with Stage 1 encompassing stabilization. This includes identifying relationship cycles, patterns, and feelings; framing the negative patterns as the problem; and deescalating the negative cycles. In Stage 2 the goals are building individual and relationship capacities by retructuring the relationship into a more secure bond, acceptance of the partner and acceptance by the partner, eliciting empathic responsiveness, and asking for needs to be met. Stage 3 encompasses consolidation and integration. In Stage 3 the partners actively problem-solve and assimilate changes from therapy into their everyday lives (Johnson, 2004).

In research settings EFT is completed in 10–12 sessions. When working with trauma survivors, the pace must be slower and may take 30 sessions or more (Greenman & Johnson, 2012; MacIntosh, 2013). Unlike traditional EFT, which does not include psychoeducation, education about trauma must be included. Another difference between working in traditional EFT and EFT with trauma survivors is the need to liaise with individual therapists who may be working with the partners. Also, it is more important to assess and address possible violence and self-harming behaviors, requiring setting up safety nets or agreed-on coping behaviors (Johnson, 2002).

In working with survivors, the therapist must be even more aware than in traditional EFT of the alliance between the therapist and each partner. Rifts in the therapeutic alliance must be closely monitored and quickly mended so that the therapy session is a safe haven for each partner. Couples-specific goals, such as a survivor's need to be in control of sexuality or a spouse's disappointment with the sexual relationship, must be acknowledged and woven into therapy goals.

A preliminary research study of EFT with extremely distressed couples in which at least one member was a child sexual abuse survivor, indicates that the greatest area of challenge for CSA survivors is affect regulation. Common characteristics of survivors, such as hypervigilance, inability to trust, shame, and anger, complicate and slow down EFT treatment (MacIntosh & Johnson, 2008). This study also confirmed and highlighted several survivor themes affecting couple therapy: (a) feelings are overwhelming and dangerous; (b) I will lose control if I allow myself to feel; (c) I can't stay present in emotionally difficult situations (dissociation); (d) limited range of emotions, emotional reactivity, and being easily flooded; (e) I am wounded and unlovable; (f) I am not safe; I must be (hyper)vigilant regarding my partner because she or he will fail me; (g) sex triggers me, so I must control my and our sexuality (MacIntosh & Johnson, 2008). Studies with more couples need to be done to confirm these findings; however, the themes discovered in this qualitative study are substantiated throughout the trauma literature.

Object relations couple therapy. Basham and Miehls set out to produce an "effective culturally responsive couple therapy practice model" (2004, p. 10) for single-trauma or dual-trauma couples. They emphasize that their model is not an integration of various models but a synthesis using social theory, family theory, trauma theory, object relations theory, and attachment theory as different lenses, which are used to a greater or lesser degree according to what most benefits the unique couple with whom the therapist is working.

This couples therapy model begins with assessment and then progresses flexibly through three phases. The phases are related to classic individual trauma therapy. Phase 1 is safety, stabilization, and the establishment of an environment conducive to change. Phase 2 consists of in-depth reflection on the trauma narrative(s). Phase 3 involves the consolidation of new perspectives, attitudes, and behaviors related to the relationship.

Basham and Miehls (2004) describe couple therapy as "a challenging journey" and emphasize that a thorough biopsychosocial assessment is the compass that guides the therapy. The assessment also anchors and focuses the work. The initial assessment first determines whether the couple has food and shelter and is free from violence. Couple therapy is contraindicated in this model if physical violence between the couple is a presenting problem.

Further assessment includes "institutional factors" such as the clinician's biases and responses, the political climate, disabilities, faith-based community, extended family, ethnicity, and sexual orientation—as these all have roles in making the aftereffects of trauma either better or worse. "Interactional factors" such as intimacy, power, touch and sexuality, boundaries, communication, rituals, and the application and internalization of the victim-victimizer-bystander paradigm (see explanation below) all need to be assessed. Intrapersonal factors such as areas of resilience, PTSD symptomatology, attachment style, and object relations complete the biopsychosocial assessment (Basham & Miehls, 2004).

Phase 1 focuses a great deal on self-care, including education about PTSD and complex trauma, strategies for stress reduction, regulating affect, and self-soothing. Often during this phase the therapist needs to collaborate with other health professionals, probation officers, or the Department of Social Services (Basham & Miehls, 2004). Referrals for psychiatric consultation, medical consultation, or adjunctive activities such as yoga, meditation, hypnosis, massage, acupuncture, or neurofeedback may be given. The victim-victimizer-bystander paradigm, a key concept in this model, is introduced to the couple. Basham and Miehls posit that not only have trauma victims experienced victimization by a perpetrator, and a bystander either refused to help or dramatically rescued them, but also that survivors have internalized this template and it informs their worldview. Phase 1 encompasses a range of "psychoeducational, cognitive-behavioral, body-mind, spiritual, and ego-supportive interventions that promote adaptation and coping" (p. 136).

As is now true in individual trauma therapy, effective Phase 1 work may be the completion of therapy for many couples (Basham & Miehls, 2004; Courtois & Ford, 2013). However, if the therapist and couple agree to proceed beyond the stabilization phase, Phase 2 involves reflecting on the survivor's trauma experience(s) without full emotional reexperiencing. The goal of Phase 2 is the integration of affect, cognition, and memory. Another goal during this phase is empathic attunement as the survivor and partner share their trauma experiences. These actions are for the purpose of "restorying the narratives with a new focus on resiliency and adaptation" (Basham & Miehls, 2004, p. 136).

Phase 3 involves consolidating new perspectives, attitudes, and behaviors. This includes family of origin work, enhancing the couple's sexual relationship, and strengthening other family and community relationships. Further work at owning each of the victim-victimizer-bystander roles also happens during this phase. As in traditional individual therapy for trauma recovery, expansion and growth themes are explored in Phase 3. For example, some couples may work on their parenting roles; others may find political or social advocacy regarding trauma to be important for their growth (Basham & Miehls, 2004).

Coming Home to Passion. Cohn's (2011) therapy is a synthesis of trauma and neglect therapy, Imago Relationship Therapy, communication skills training, sex therapy, attachment theory, and brain neurobiology. *Coming Home to Passion* is written as much for clients as for therapists and could be used as bibliotherapy with the couple or by the therapist as an outline for working through the couple's communication, attachment, and sexual problems.

Cohn's approach begins with an assessment of each partner's attachment style, core wound, and primary defense strategy, and how these interact. The therapist assesses the couple's "toolbox": how they listen, empathize, and speak to each other. Are they able to access and express emotion? Are they able to repair misunderstandings and misattunements? When and how do they each get triggered?

When the assessment is complete, Cohn begins by outlining attachment theory and its application to relationships. She introduces multiple communication concepts and teaches skills in self-awareness, talking, listening, and repairing misunderstandings.

One of Cohn's biggest contributions to advancing the trauma literature and to working with survivor couples is her belief, discussed earlier, that frequently one partner is a trauma survivor and the other is a survivor of childhood neglect. From my own thirty years of working with trauma, it is enlightening to look back and see Cohn's hypothesis played out in most of the trauma couples with whom I have worked. She helps the neglect survivor to identify and own their losses and to understand how childhood neglect has shaped them. Cohn holds adamantly to the belief that both partners contribute equally to their relational difficulties and urges the couple to recognize that their relationship problems are *not* the fault of the trauma survivor, the survivor's symptoms, or their trauma history (Cohn, 2011).

Cohn also educates the couple regarding how trauma or neglect shapes the brain. She summarizes how trauma shuts down the thinking, adult brain and the speech centers and how it activates the emotions and fight or flight response. Trauma primes the brain and body to look for danger constantly. When the brain sees the environment as dangerous or a trauma memory gets activated, the brain reexperiences the trauma as if it were happening right now (van der Kolk, 2014). Cohn is realistic about the damage trauma and neglect do to the brain, but she also expresses encouragement that the brain can change. Healing is possible.

The repetitive triggering and reactivity in survivor couples is retraumatizing to both partners; it primes the brain for more fear, more stress hormones, and more depression. The cycle can lead to despair and hopelessness. However, the cycle can be stopped. To keep the cycle going both partners must participate, but either partner can use skills acquired through therapy to stop the triggering and reactivity and interrupt the cycle.

Most survivors of sexual trauma and survivors of neglect are not taught basic sexual information. Cohn provides this information and explains how trauma and neglect typically affect sexuality. Often the impasse over their sexuality has resulted in explosive or seething anger, bitterness, withdrawal, or despair. The attachment and trauma information as well as the communication and repair skills they have learned help the couple to experience empathy and warmth with each other. Then Cohn introduces "Practices," slow, gradual exercises beginning with breathing, learning to be in your own body, and being present with each other. Other practices involve remembering positive sexual times, if any, in the couple's relationship, casting a vision for the their future relationship, discussing initiation rituals, and eventually exploring each other's bodies. These exercises involve reflecting, writing, and then sharing their thoughts and feelings, using the communication tools the couple has learned in therapy.

CONCLUSION

"Jesus' earthly ministry was characterized by focused outreach to the marginalized, oppressed, and abused."

S. R. Tracy, 2011

It is my personal conviction that the field of trauma therapy needs to shift toward using couple therapy to treat couples in which one or both partners are sexual abuse survivors and that this shift is beginning to happen. Even when the survivor seeks therapy individually, both therapist and client should consider inviting the partner to join in the therapy process. Integrating the partner into the therapy could give the survivor an ally in the often difficult and lengthy process of recovery from complex trauma. Conjoint therapy can enable the partner to participate in healing rather than be left out (MacIntosh & Johnson, 2008). Johnson (2002) asserts that "couple interventions can make a crucial, and to date almost unrecognized, contribution in the treatment of traumatic stress" (p. 9).

More research on couple therapy for trauma and neglect survivors is necessary. Even more than research, though, more therapists are needed who are trained and skilled in some method of working with *couples* affected by trauma. Also, more nontrauma couples therapists must become trauma-informed. Trauma is ubiquitous; about 60% of men and 50% of women will experience at least one trauma in their lifetimes, and up to 20% of these will develop PTSD (National Center for PTSD, 2016a). Many individuals and couples are not getting the help they desperately need.

Cohn (2011) sums it up poignantly when she writes:

> I have never been able to make my peace with how long therapy, and trauma therapy
> in particular, takes. It strikes me as grossly unjust that after suffering a violent, hu-
> miliating, lonely or otherwise painful childhood, the adult might spend years of time
> and large sums of money just to be able to live with tranquility in the present. It also
> disturbed me that the therapy arrangement was such that it ends in loss: that a client
> would invest years, engaging in a profoundly intimate alliance with the therapist in
> which to heal, perhaps having a first experience of trust and safety with another
> person, and when the healing reaches its successful completion, by design the rela-
> tionship ends. It seemed an ironic booby prize: reaching one's goal means losing the
> person. . . . I wondered what it would be like if my traumatized clients could discover
> their safety, trust, and healing in relationships that they would then get to take home
> and keep. (p. xiv)

No one mode of therapy fits every person or couple. There are various reasons
that some clients will not be able to participate in couple therapy. I continue to learn
new approaches and combine aspects of multiple approaches in order to help survivors on their journey to healing. More than ever, I use couple therapy whenever
possible to help survivors who are in long-term relationships. In the middle of the
night, when a partner needs comfort, during a flashback, or when they heal and
"graduate" from therapy, my goal is that they have a secure base and a safe haven
present with them, a person they get to keep.

REFERENCES

Barnes, M. F. (1995). Sex therapy in the couples context: Therapy issues of victims of
sexual trauma. *American Journal of Family Therapy, 23*, 351-60.

Basham, K. K., & Miehls, D. (2004). *Transforming the legacy: Couple therapy with survivors of childhood trauma.* New York, NY: Columbia University Press.

Baucom, D. H., Whisman, M. A., & Paprocki, C. (2012). Couple-based interventions for
psychopathology. *Journal of Family Therapy, 34*, 250-70.

Bebbington, P. E., Jonas, S., Brugha, T., Meltzer, H., Jenkins, R., Cooper, C., & McManus,
S. (2011). Child sexual abuse reported by an English national sample: Characteristics
and demography. *Social Psychiatry and Psychiatric Epidemiology, 46*, 255-62.
doi:10.1007/200127-010-0245-8

Bouchard, S., Godbout, N., & Sabourin, S. (2009). Sexual attitudes and activities in
women with borderline personality disorder involved in romantic relationships.
Journal of Sex & Marital Therapy, 35, 106-21. doi:10.1080/00926230802712301

Bowlby, J. (1988). *A secure base.* London, England: Routledge.

Briere, J. N., & Scott, C. (2015). *Principles of trauma treatment: A guide to symptoms, evaluation, and treatment* (2nd ed.). Los Angeles, CA: Sage.

Buttenheim, M., & Levendosky, A. (1994). Couples treatment for incest survivors. *Psychotherapy, 31,* 407-14.

Butzer, B., & Campbell, L. (2008). Adult attachment, sexual satisfaction, and relationship satisfaction: A study of married couples. *Personal Relationships, 15,* 141-54. doi:10.1111/j.1475-6811.2007.00189.x

Centers for Disease Control and Prevention. (2016, April 5). *Child abuse and neglect: Consequences.* Retrieved from www.cdc.gov/ViolencePrevention/childmaltreatment/consequences.html

Cloitre, M., Courtois, C. A., Carapezza, R., Stohbach, B. C., & Green, B. L. (2011). Treatment of complex PTSD: Results of the ISTSS expert clinician survey on best practices. *Journal of Traumatic Stress, 24,* 615-27. doi:10.1002/jts.20697

Cohn, R. (2011). *Coming home to passion.* Santa Barbara, CA: Praeger.

Colangelo, J. J., & Keefe-Cooperman, K. (2012). Understanding the impact of childhood sexual abuse on women's sexuality. *Journal of Mental Health Counseling, 34,* 14-37.

Courtois, C. (2004). Complex trauma, complex reactions: Assessment and treatment. *Psychotherapy: Theory, Research, Practice, Training, 41,* 412-25. doi:10.037/0033 3204.41.412

Courtois, C. A., & Ford, J. D. (2013). *Treatment of complex trauma: A sequenced, relationship-based approach.* New York, NY: Guilford Press.

de Silva, P. (2001). Impact of trauma on sexual functioning and sexual relationships. *Sexual and Relationship Therapy, 16*(3), 269-78. doi:10.1080/14681990120064513

Doherty, W. J. (2002, November/December). Bad couples therapy: How to avoid doing it. *Psychotherapy Networker, 26*(6), 26-33.

Draucker, C. B., & Martsolf, D. S. (2006). *Counseling survivors of childhood sexual abuse* (3rd ed.). Thousand Oaks, CA: Sage.

Elliott, D. M., Mok, D. S., & Briere, J. (2004). Adult sexual assault: Prevalence, symptomatology, and sex differences in the general population. *Journal of Traumatic Stress, 17*(3), 203-11.

Feinauer, L. L. (1989). Sexual dysfunction in women sexually abused as children. *Contemporary Family Therapy, 11,* 299-309.

Feinauer, L. L., Callahan, E. H., & Hilton, H. G. (1996). Positive intimate relationships decrease depression in sexually abused women. *American Journal of Family Therapy, 24*(2), 99-106.

Gilliam, C. M., & Cottone, R. R. (2005). Couple or individual therapy for the treatment of depression? An update of the empirical literature. *American Journal of Family Therapy, 33,* 265-72. doi:10.1080/01926180590952472

Greenman, P. S., & Johnson, S. M. (2012). United we stand: Emotionally focused therapy for couples in the treatment of posttraumatic stress disorder. *Journal of Clinical Psychology: In Session, 68*(5), 561-69. doi:10.1002/jclp.21853

Hecker, L. (2007). Trauma and couple therapy. In J. L. Wetchler (Ed.), *Handbook of clinical issues in couple therapy* (pp. 83-93). New York, NY: Haworth Press.

Hecker, L. (2011). Trauma and recovery in couple therapy. In J. L. Wetchler (Ed.), *Handbook of clinical issues in couples therapy* (2nd ed., pp. 129-44). New York, NY: Routledge.

Herman, J. L. (1992). *Trauma and recovery.* New York, NY: HarperCollins.

Johnson, S. M. (2002). *Emotionally focused couple therapy with trauma survivors.* New York, NY: Guilford Press.

Johnson, S. M. (2003). Attachment theory: A guide for couple therapy. In S. M. Johnson & V. E. Whiffen (Eds.), *Attachment processes in couple and family therapy* (pp. 103-23). New York, NY: Guilford Press.

Johnson, S. M. (2004). Facing the dragon together: Emotionally focused couples therapy with trauma survivors. In D. R. Catherall (Ed.), *Handbook of stress, trauma, and the family* (pp. 493-512). New York, NY: Brunner-Routledge.

Johnson, S. M. (2009). Attachment theory and emotionally focused therapy for individuals and couples. In J. H. Obegi & E. Berant (Eds.), *Attachment theory and research in clinical work with adults* (pp. 410-33). New York, NY: Guilford Press.

Johnson, S. M., & Wittenborn, A. K. (2012). New research findings on emotionally focused therapy: Introduction to special section. *Journal of Marital and Family Therapy, 38*(s1), 18-22. doi:10.1111/j.1752-00606.2012.00292.x

Koedam, W. S. (2007). Sexual trauma in dysfunctional marriages: Integrating structural therapy and EMDR. In F. Shapiro, F. W. Kaslow, & L. Maxfield (Eds.), *Handbook of EMDR and family therapy processes* (pp. 223-42). Hoboken, NJ: Wiley.

Laumann, E. O., Paik, A., & Rosen, R. C. (1999). Sexual dysfunction in the United States: Prevalence and predictors. *Journal of the American Medical Association, 281,* 537-44.

MacIntosh, H. B. (2013). Dissociative identity disorder and the process of couple therapy. *Journal of Trauma & Dissociation, 14,* 84-96. doi:0.1080/15299732.2012.710185

MacIntosh, H. B., & Johnson, S. (2008). Emotionally focused therapy for couples and childhood sexual abuse survivors. *Journal of Marital and Family Therapy, 34,* 298-315.

Maltz, W. (2002). Treating the sexual intimacy concerns of sexual abuse survivors. *Sexual and Relationship Therapy, 17*(4), 321-27. doi:10.1080/1468199021000017173

Maltz, W. (2012). *The sexual healing journey* (3rd ed.). New York, NY: William Morrow.

Meston, C. M., Lorenz, T. A., & Stephenson, K. R. (2013). Effects of expressive writing on sexual dysfunction, depression, and PTSD in women with a history of childhood sexual abuse: Results from a randomized clinical trial. *Journal of Sexual Medicine, 10*, 2177-89. doi.org/10.1111/jsm.12247

Miehls, D., & Basham, K. (2004). Object relations couple therapy with trauma survivors. In D. R. Catherall (Ed.), *Handbook of stress, trauma, and the family* (pp. 473-91). New York, NY: Brunner-Routledge.

Monson, C. M., & Fredman, S. J. (2012). *Cognitive-behavioral conjoint therapy for PTSD: Harnessing the healing power of relationships.* New York, NY: Guilford Press.

Monson, C. M., & Fredman, S. J. (2015). Couple therapy and posttraumatic stress disorder. In A. S. Gurman, J. L. Lebow & D. K. Snyder (Eds.), *Clinical handbook of couple therapy* (5th ed., pp. 531-54). New York, NY: Guilford Press.

Monson, C. M., Fredman, S. J., Macdonald, A., Pukay-Martin, N. D., Resick, P. A., & Schnurr, P. P. (2012). Effects of cognitive-behavioral couple therapy for PTSD: A randomized controlled trial. *Journal of the American Medical Association, 308*(7), 700-709. doi:10.1001/jama.2012.9307

National Center for PTSD. (2016a). How common is PTSD? Retrieved from www.ptsd .va.gov/public/PTSD-overview/basics/how-common-is-ptsd.asp

National Center for PTSD (2016b). Spirituality and trauma: Professionals working together. Retrieved from www.ptsd.va.gov/professional/provider-type/community /fs-spirituality.asp

Pistorello, J., & Follette, V. M. (1998). Childhood sexual abuse and couple relationships: Female survivors' reports in therapy groups. *Journal of Marital and Family Therapy, 24*(4), 473-85.

Reid, K. S., Wampler, R. S., & Taylor, D. K. (1996). The "alienated" partner: Responses to traditional therapies for adult sex abuse survivors. *Journal of Marital and Family Therapy, 22*(4), 443-53.

Rellini, A. H. (2014). The treatment of sexual dysfunctions in survivors of sexual abuse. In Y. M. Binik & K. S. Hall (Eds.), *Principles and practices of sex therapy* (5th ed., pp. 375-98). New York, NY: Guilford Press.

Rosenau, D. E. (2002). *A celebration of sex: A guide to enjoying God's gift of sexual intimacy.* Nashville, TN: Thomas Nelson.

Schnurr, P. P., Lunney, C. A., Forshay, E., Thurston, V. L., Chow, B. K., Resick, P. A., & Foa, E. B. (2009). Sexual function outcomes in women treated for posttraumatic stress disorder. *Journal of Women's Health, 18*, 1549-57. doi:10.1089/jwh.2008.1165

Tracy, S. R. (2005). *Mending the soul: Understanding and healing abuse.* Grand Rapids, MI: Zondervan.

Tracy, S. R. (2011). Definitions and prevalence rates of sexual abuse. In A. J. Schmutzer (Ed.), *The long journey home* (pp. 3-12). Eugene, OR: Wipf and Stock.

van der Kolk, B. A. (2014). *The body keeps the score: Brain, mind, and body in the healing of trauma* [Kindle ed.]. New York, NY: Viking.

Watson, B., & Halford, W. K. (2010). Classes of childhood sexual abuse and women's adult couple relationships. *Violence and Victims, 25,* 518-35. doi:10.1891/0886 6708.25.4.518

Zala, S. (2012). Complex couples: Multi-theoretical couples counselling with traumatized adults who have a history of child sexual abuse. *The Australian and New Zealand Journal of Family Therapy, 33,* 219-31. doi:10.1017/aft.2012.27

ASSESSMENT AND TREATMENT OF

INTIMATE PARTNER VIOLENCE:

INTEGRATING PSYCHOLOGICAL AND

SPIRITUAL APPROACHES

TERRI S. WATSON

It is especially traumatic when acts of physical aggression are perpetrated within the family—the very place that is supposed to provide safety, sanctuary, and nurturance. As Christian counselors, we tend to underestimate the rates of violence in couple and family relationships, particularly in families of faith. However, prevalence rates demonstrate that domestic violence is as frequent in religious couples and families as in the wider population (Annis & Rice, 2001; Drumm, Popescu, & Riggs, 2009). In fact, some have suggested that religiosity is actually a higher risk factor for women in abusive relationships as a result of both internalized belief systems and external religious social structures that may pose barriers for women to leave a domestically violent situation (Popescu et al., 2009). Intimate partner violence is a significant problem in the church and in wider society.

While often used synonymously, the term *domestic violence* (DV) refers to physical, sexual, or emotional aggression used to control or dominate family members including children, partners, and the elderly, while *intimate partner violence* (IPV) is a type of DV and is most often used to describe physical aggression between partners in dating, cohabitation, marriage, or same-sex relationships (Breiding, Basile, Smith, Black, & Mahendra, 2015). Distinctions are often made between *battering* or *intimate terrorism*, a severe form of IPV that is recurrent and traumatic where physical, psychological, and often sexual abuse is utilized to dominate and control, and *situational couple violence*, where comparatively mild physical aggression, often mutual, is part of the conflict cycle of a couple (Babcock,

Canady, Graham, & Schart, 2007; Johnson & Leone, 2005). However, surveys have consistently demonstrated that women are most often the victims of IPV and sustain more significant harm from relational aggression (Jose & O'Leary, 2009). While men can also experience partner aggression, it is much more likely for women and children to be the targets of relational violence and to bear the greatest traumatic impact. Violence toward intimate partners and toward children is a crime. This chapter will primarily focus on the impact and treatment of IPV on female partners and children.

Surveys of prevalence rates in the United States found that 31.5% of women have experienced at least one incident of IPV during their lifetime; of these, 22.3% reported at least one incident of severe violence, and 8.8% reported at least one incident of rape (Breiding et al., 2014). In addition, it is estimated that nearly half of all couples seeking marital therapy have exhibited physically aggressive behavior toward each other during the previous year (Jose & O'Leary, 2009). International surveys of prevalence have found that across cultures and peoples, women have a greater risk of being injured, raped, or killed by an intimate partner than by anyone else (Garcia-Moreno, Heise, Jansen, Ellsberg, & Watts, 2005), with prevalence estimates of one in three women experiencing some form of IPV during their lifetime (World Health Organization [WHO], 2013). Worldwide, violence against women is "a pervasive and global problem that is both a human rights violation and a public health problem" (Kar & Garcia-Moreno, 2009, p. 59). Estimates of the co-occurrence of severe partner violence with severe physical aggression toward children are quite high at 92% (Slep & O'Leary, 2005).

Despite the pervasiveness of IPV in North America and around the world, most clinicians fail to inquire about IPV as part of the intake and assessment process, and many domestically abusive relationships go unidentified and therefore untreated. To address this problem of professional neglect, experts predict that by the year 2020, all 50 states will mandate specialized training in IPV as part of the licensure process for mental health professionals (O'Leary, 2008). Clearly, a Christian response to the problem of DV will require increased competency in assessment and intervention.

As Christians, we have been slow to recognize IPV as a widespread problem in the church and to develop effective faith-based approaches to intervention and treatment. Reviews of the research on IPV and religion conclude that "religion can act to both prevent and exacerbate IPV" (Levitt, Horne, Wheeler, & Wang, 2015, p. 214). Nason-Clark (2009) suggests that a "holy hush" or "sacred silence" pervades the church when it comes to actively and publicly addressing DV. It is tempting to deny the existence of DV in Christian families or to blame the victims. We hesitate to intrude into the private lives of families and marriages in our congregations.

However, our faith requires a courageous Christian response in order to provide safety and healing for those most vulnerable in society and the world through competent and effective counseling and advocacy. The church can make a difference!

This chapter explores the psychological and spiritual aspects of IPV and provides recommendations for intervention. Counseling approaches and techniques that are supported by scientific studies, clinical experience, and biblical wisdom are highlighted. Specifically, this chapter will describe the traumatic impact of IPV, provide psychological and spiritual treatment guidelines and interventions, and, finally, identify important church and community resources for prevention and intervention.

TRAUMATIC IMPACT OF INTIMATE PARTNER VIOLENCE

Maria, a survivor of severe IPV, describes her childhood home environment as "a war zone." She remembers coming home from school each day on "high alert," trying to get a sense of the mood of her parents and whether she should try to keep herself and her two younger siblings sequestered upstairs, out of the "line of fire." She wonders how growing up in this environment has affected her own struggles with depression, her choice of an abusive partner, and her difficulties finding nonviolent ways to discipline her children. She struggles to feel that God really cares for her well-being, and hesitates to tell her story to others in her church for fear they will judge her for wanting to leave her abusive husband. Maria's experience conveys the far-reaching impact of IPV on generations of family life. Without intervention, IPV becomes a recurring generational pattern for families and results in a combination of physical, psychological, and spiritual consequences.

Impact on women. IPV affects women's physical, psychological, and spiritual health in both obvious and subtle ways. In addition to the real physical danger many women experience due to IPV, women who experience partner violence also exhibit poorer general health, greater vulnerability to chronic diseases, higher substance-abuse risk, and psychological symptoms of depression and anxiety (Basile & Black, 2011). Psychologically, women who have experienced trauma in their intimate relationships will often evidence problems and symptoms in three areas: symptoms of acute stress or posttraumatic stress disorder, cognitive distortions in their views of self and others, and problematic interpersonal skills that may place them at higher risk for continued interpersonal violence (Pico-Alfonso, 2005). For women with religious commitments, IPV can lead to spiritual disengagement and withdrawal from religious communities and practices (Drumm, Popescu, & Kerstig, 2009). Consequently, effective treatment approaches must be holistic and attend to physical, psychological, relational, and spiritual concerns.

The prevalence of posttraumatic stress disorder (PTSD) among women in IPV relationships has been estimated to be between 45% and 84% (DeJonghe, Bogat,

Levendosky, & von Eye, 2008; Nathanson, Shorey, Tirone, & Rhatigan, 2012). Even after they have removed themselves from the violent home environment, many women will continue to experience debilitating trauma symptoms including intrusive reexperiencing of the traumatic events (e.g., flashbacks, nightmares, intrusive memories), avoidance (e.g., withdrawal, emotional numbing), disturbance of mood and cognition (e.g., depressive symptoms, negative thoughts of self and others), and hyperarousal (e.g., high startle reflex, difficulty concentrating, or sleep disturbance; Rodgers & Norman 2004). For some women, IPV is a continuation of the experiences of trauma and violence they experienced in childhood, which heightens the traumatic impact on all areas of functioning (DeJonghe et al., 2008). When assessing PTSD symptoms, it is important to keep in mind that some behaviors, such as hyperarousal, hypervigilance, or withdrawal, are likely adaptive for women who are still living in a psychologically or physically dangerous relationship and may not signify a psychiatric condition (Warshaw, Sullivan, & Rivera, 2013).

The impact of IPV is especially traumatic because the violence is perpetrated by an *intimate* partner, by the person who is expected to love, honor, and protect. For many victims of IPV, this reality results in a sense of despair and loss of meaning in life (Kriedler, 1995). Spiritually, women who have experienced IPV may feel abandoned by God and by the church. They may have received confusing messages about Christian marriage and women's roles. While they may work hard to give the appearance of normality, they often struggle with a negative view of themselves and feel powerless, ashamed, alone, and isolated (Nason-Clark, 2009).

While a woman's spiritual well-being can be negatively impacted by the experience of IPV, many survivors credit their faith in God as a foundational component of healing and recovery. Drawing on spiritual resources in the aftermath of a traumatic experience can be a protective factor and may moderate the development of PTSD symptoms (Pargament, Smith, Koenig, & Perez, 1998).

Impact on children. Estimates are that 30% of children who live with two parents will witness IPV (McDonald, Jouriles, Ramisetty-Mikler, Caetano, & Green, 2006), and a high percentage of these children will also be victims of physical abuse in the home, as indicated above. Children are significantly affected both by a single incident of physical aggression between parents and by living in an environment where the threat of violence is pervasive and ongoing. Similar to living in a war zone, children growing up with a chronic exposure to violence are at risk for development of *complex trauma*, a term used to describe the adverse effects of chronic, pervasive trauma on a child's development (van der Kolk, 2005). From a developmental perspective, the impact of DV on the child's emotional, cognitive, perceptual, behavioral, and interpersonal functioning interferes with the child's normal developmental processes, which results in problems in key domains of functioning (Graham-Bermann & Levendosky, 2011).

Emotionally, children may vacillate between anxious agitation and emotional numbing or withdrawal and may have difficulties controlling their emotional responses. Cognitive problems can include intrusive thoughts and flashbacks, difficulties with concentration and attention, and negative cognitions about self (Graham-Bermann & Levendosky, 2011). Perceptually, children exposed to IPV may be on high alert in their hypervigilance toward danger in the environment. As a consequence, they may over- or underestimate the potential for danger and respond accordingly. Behaviorally, they may also exhibit difficulties managing their own aggression and may exhibit self-destructive behaviors (Margolin & Vickerman, 2007).

Interpersonal difficulties such as difficulties with trust or empathy and poor social competence characteristic of insecure or disorganized attachment may also be a result of growing up in a violent home. Consequently, individuals exposed to violence as children are at greater risk for becoming victims and/or perpetrators of violence in future adult relationships (Huesmann, Dubow, & Boxer, 2011).

Impact on the family. IPV has a significant impact on family functioning. Family members feel pressure to keep the abuse hidden from others outside the family system because of fear of repercussions from the violent family member and also feelings of shame and embarrassment (McGoldrick & Ross, 2011). Often, interactions with others are carefully controlled and monitored by the abusive parent, leading to isolation and lack of social support for the family. Boundary violations such as parentification within the family are common, with children taking on a protective role with the abused parent and with younger siblings. The nonabusive parent may have limited capacity for support and connection with children because of their own struggles with emotional, behavioral, and physical symptoms. Abuse in Christian families can isolate them from the much-needed support of Christian community owing to the secrecy, shame, fear, and isolation that characterize the day-to-day life of a family living with DV (Kroeger & Nason-Clark, 2010).

ASSESSMENT AND TREATMENT OF IPV

How can the Christian counselor provide informed, effective treatment for IPV? The following overview provides clinical practice guidelines for assessment and intervention. Spiritual interventions are integrated with clinical best practice recommendations consistent with a holistic approach to the treatment of IPV-related trauma for adults, children, and families.

Assessment. Competent, ethical treatment of IPV always begins with careful assessment. Clinicians should routinely inquire about the presence of physical aggression as part of the assessment process with *all* couple and family cases.

Assessment and early intervention with IPV can play a critical role in decreasing the incidence of traumatic experiences for partners and for children. Once it is established that violence is an issue, careful assessment for other mental health symptoms, particularly trauma-related symptoms, is warranted.

Assessing for risk of violence. Routine screening for IPV utilizing both written and oral assessment questions should be included in the assessment process for couples and families. Stith, McCollum, and Rosen (2011) suggest including general questions on the intake form and oral interview to assess how conflict and anger are managed, whether partners feel safe, and so on, including the following:

- "What happens when you and your partner argue?"
- "Do you ever feel unsafe at home?"
- "Have you ever been physically hurt or felt threatened?"
- "Have you ever been or are you currently concerned about harming your partner?" (p. 23)

O'Leary (2008) recommends that each partner be asked separately and confidentially the following question, either as part of a written assessment or as part of an individual verbal interview: "In the past year, when you had a disagreement or argument with your partner, have you engaged in any acts of physical aggression against your partner such as pushing, slapping, shoving, hitting, beating, or some other acts of aggression?" (p. 485). In some clinical settings, standardized assessment tools are routinely administered to assess IPV and violence risk (see Basile, Hertz, & Back, 2007, for a review of instruments).

Partners should be asked individually and separately if they feel they are able to state their feelings and opinions without fear of retaliation from their partner. Should a partner acknowledge the presence of relational violence, clinicians should follow up with questions to assess frequency, lethality, injury, history, and risk of harm to children and intervene accordingly. The following case is an example of intake information that should raise a red flag for a careful assessment for IPV:

> During a routine screening for IPV in an initial couple's therapy session, Mr. and Mrs. Smith acknowledge that their marital conflict sometimes escalates to use of physical aggression: pushing, grabbing, and slapping each other. Further assessment reveals that verbal conflicts occur about once a week, with escalation to physical altercations occurring approximately once per month. Mr. and Mrs. Smith identify several hot topics that lead to arguments, including money, sharing of household tasks, and parenting issues.

When the initial evaluation reveals that physical aggression is present in the couple relationship, an important component of the assessment process is to determine the frequency, severity, impact, and type of IPV that is manifesting. *Situational couple violence* is a prevalent type of IPV that is evidenced by mutual physical aggression and use of physical behaviors as part of the couple's conflict cycle (Babcock et al., 2007; Johnson & Leone, 2005; Johnson, Leone, & Xu, 2014). Aggression is usually mild to moderate, and there is no pattern of fear, intimidation, and control. However, it is important to keep in mind that women are still more likely than men to sustain physical injury, even in cases of situational violence; thus ongoing assessment is warranted. The assessment process should include questions about precipitants to physical aggression, frequency, intensity, and attempts to change behavior. Despite some jurisdictions that mandate individual counseling in cases of IPV, couple therapy is increasingly being utilized as the primary intervention in cases of situational couple violence (O'Leary, 2008; Schneider & Brimhall, 2014; Stith et al., 2011).

> Scenario 1: The counselor meets with Mr. and Mrs. Smith individually to continue the IPV assessment. Mrs. Smith describes the physical altercations in detail, expressing her regret that she resorts to pushing and slapping her husband when angry. She denies any feelings of fear or being controlled and dominated by her husband and states that she can talk openly in his presence about their physically aggressive behaviors. She denies any incidents of bruises or injury resulting from their physical altercations. An individual meeting with Mr. Smith reveals a similar account of their conflict. Mr. Smith expresses remorse about the physicality of their conflicts, stating, "I promised myself I'd never lay a hand on my wife." He acknowledges that their conflicts are more volatile and less controlled when both have been drinking.
>
> The counselor agrees to continue to see the Smiths for couple counseling with the goal of cessation of aggressive behaviors during conflict. The counselor carefully monitors any ongoing violence on a weekly basis, develops a "no violence" contract with the couple, and provides alternative behaviors and skills to use during conflict.

In contrast, *battering* or *intimate terrorism* is present when there is a pervasive and reoccurring pattern of physical aggression for the purpose of domination and control (Babcock et al., 2007; Johnson & Leone, 2005; Johnson et al., 2014). Batterers often exhibit personality disorders, substance abuse or dependence, and intermittent explosive disorder. Intimate terrorism contraindicates couples therapy as a treatment focus. When battering is assessed, treatment shifts to developing a safety plan for the partner, referring the batterer to gender-specific treatment for domestic offenders, and follow-up assessment and treatment of any trauma-related symptoms with the partner and children. Treatment protocols for battering versus situational couple violence are quite different, so careful assessment is warranted.

Scenario 2. In the individual interview with Mrs. Smith, she reveals her anxiety about her husband's increasingly aggressive behavior during conflict, which has resulted in physical injury to her on several occasions in the form of bruises to her arms and face. She reluctantly reveals that he has been increasingly verbally abusive, making threats, slapping her face, and physically restraining her during altercations; demonstrating more aggression and less self-control when he is drinking. She states that the children are not present during the conflict, but worries that they can hear the fighting. Mrs. Smith reports that she is becoming increasingly fearful of her husband, who has become quite controlling of her activities. She states that she is afraid to talk about these problems in the presence of her husband and is concerned that he will refuse any further treatment if confronted. The counselor provides the wife with information about IPV, her legal rights, and works with her to develop a "safety plan" that includes calling 911 and going to a shelter with her children. The counselor offers to connect her with the local domestic violence shelter and to help her access the support of her church.

In the individual meeting with Mr. Smith, the counselor inquires about the use of physical aggression during conflict. Mr. Smith acknowledges that he may have "gotten out of hand" during conflicts with his wife but denies physical aggression. He states that his wife precipitates the conflicts with her demanding and nagging behaviors and often follows him from room to room when he is trying to get away by himself to "cool off." He denied needing help and became defensive when the counselor suggested individual treatment for substance abuse and anger issues.

Clearly, couples therapy is contraindicated for the Smiths in this scenario. Instead, Mr. Smith should be referred for treatment targeting anger management and substance abuse—ideally a gender-specific group for domestically violent men. Mrs. Smith would be referred for treatment for IPV, and she and the children would be assessed for trauma-related symptoms.

Assessing for trauma-related and mental health symptoms. Best practice guidelines recommend screening women in IPV relationships for symptoms of depression, anxiety, substance abuse, and suicidal ideation (WHO, 2013). Because of the high prevalence of PTSD among women in IPV relationships, counselors should carefully inquire about trauma-related symptoms as described above (Warshaw et al., 2013). Inquiries should be made into the client's history of abuse and neglect during childhood and adolescence, as this may exacerbate the traumatic reaction to current abuse. Assessment of client resources including social support and spiritual resources provides the Christian counselor with sources of strength and resilience that will be important during the treatment process.

Assessing children and adolescents. When IPV is known or expected, counselors should always assess the level of exposure of children in the family to violent behaviors. Children should be asked specifically about the presence of physical aggression (hitting, slapping, etc.) and verbal abuse (name calling, threatening, berating) in an open-ended and nonleading interview. Counselors should consider the child's safety when new information about family violence is revealed from the interview and should take the necessary steps for protection and child abuse reporting. Children should be assessed for trauma-related symptoms as this will determine the course of treatment (Margolin & Vickerman, 2007).

The church as first responder. Many women in IPV relationships will turn to those in spiritual authority in their lives for practical and spiritual counsel. Competent pastoral care will include believing the individual and assuring her that use of violence in the home is a violation of the marital covenant and is condemned by God and by the church (Nason-Clark, 2009). She should be assured of confidentiality and be provided with spiritual, emotional, and practical resources. Pastoral care for women in IPV relationships should include development of a safety plan (see below). If a woman chooses to stay in the abusive relationship, pastoral care should involve ongoing, confidential check-ins to monitor her safety and the safety of her children (Kroeger & Nason-Clark, 2010).

Treatment guidelines and interventions. Effective treatment of IPV incorporates client strengths, spiritual resources, and social support with sound clinical practice. As stated by Nason-Clark (2009), "Whether an abused religious woman first seeks help in a community-based agency or a church, she should be able to expect that her story of abuse is taken seriously, that she is given accurate, practical advice, that her safety and security is the top priority, and that her faith perspective is understood and respected" (p. 383). Faith-based counseling plays a key role in effective treatment of Christian IPV clients who are seeking wisdom, advice, and healing from others who respect and share their Christian worldview and values.

Effective Christian counseling and intervention with IPV include the following components: prioritizing safety, providing faith-based interventions for women, treating children, providing resources for batterers, and (possibly) considering couple and family treatment.

Safety first—social support and advocacy. The initial response to disclosure of IPV is to support disclosure and provide for the safety of the partner and her family (WHO, 2013). Disclosure of IPV can be the most dangerous time for a woman and her children, as batterers will often go to great extremes to maintain their control over their family and to discredit the disclosure. If you suspect IPV in your counseling work, ask the client directly. Assure her that you believe her, affirm her courage for disclosing the abuse, and convey that it is not her fault. Express to her that it is not God's desire that she or her children continue to experience abuse and violence. Healing for victims of IPV must begin with stopping the abuse.

Help the client develop a safety plan detailing the specific action steps she will take to protect herself and her children. Plans should include how to obtain physical protection, housing, financial resources, legal counsel, and medical and psychological care. A sample template for a comprehensive safety plan can be found at www.theraveproject.com/index.php/resources/resource_content/personalized _safety_plan. Provide the client with specific resources to implement this plan including connecting her with local DV shelters where she can receive housing in addition to legal and professional counseling. The National Domestic Violence Hotline (1-800-799-SAFE) provides information about shelters and services. Offer to facilitate collaboration between her church and community resources.

A focus on safety also requires the Christian counselor to carefully assess the IPV client for any risk of harm to self or others. Women who have experienced IPV may feel that their world is falling apart and are vulnerable to suicidal ideation, self-destructive behaviors, and substance abuse. Ensuring safety requires addressing areas of vulnerability and providing appropriate intervention.

Pastors and Christian counselors should keep in mind that domestic abusers will often attempt to maintain control of their partners and families by denying, discrediting, or dismissing the reports of violence in the home. At times, our strong desire to preserve the family can make us vulnerable to the convincing presentation of a batterer who denies or minimizes the abuse. It is important to remember that women are unlikely to lie about IPV; thus we need to err on the side of belief rather than denial and allow others such as the legal system and DV specialists to do the investigative work (Miles, 2008).

Christian counselors can often feel in a bind when working with IPV cases where marital separation is necessary to ensure safety for family members (Nason-Clark, 2009). While reconciliation and forgiveness are important Christian practices for couples, it is unethical and even dangerous to advocate for premature use of these practices in IPV cases. As Christian counselors, we need to be self-aware about the impact of our own beliefs and values on our counseling of IPV clients to ensure that our biases do not pose a barrier to advocating for safety and protection of those in need. It is important to keep in mind that it is *violence* that destroys a marriage, *not* leaving an abusive marriage to protect one's self and one's children (Nason-Clark, 2009).

Competent Christian counseling for women. Care and counsel for the abused partner should be one of the major priorities of a Christian response to IPV, as she is the most important resource for her family. The present and future well-being of children is significantly affected by their mother's psychological resilience and effective coping in the aftermath of IPV. Comprehensive treatment involves a holistic, multimodal approach that includes provision of medical, psychological, and spiritual care within a client's social context. Christian counselors should work with IPV survivors to incorporate spiritual resources in trauma treatment, deal with faulty beliefs, encourage religious coping, and promote connection with community resources.

Treatment of trauma symptoms. Most women in IPV relationships will exhibit trauma-related symptoms that are significant and debilitating and may even interfere with their ability to access and follow through on treatment recommendations (Rodgers & Norman, 2004). Thus, competent treatment of acute stress and posttraumatic stress symptoms is integral to the treatment process. While a comprehensive guide for the treatment of PTSD is beyond the scope of this chapter, an evidence-based approach includes the following components (Foa, Keane, Friedman, & Cohen, 2010): psychoeducation on PTSD and trauma symptoms, graduated exposure to and reprocessing of traumatic memories, stress inoculation training, instruction on affect regulation skills, and cognitive behavioral therapy (CBT) to address faulty belief systems. In addition, when symptoms of anxiety and depression impair functioning, a referral to a physician for a medication evaluation is warranted. Effective treatment of IPV will also address interpersonal skills to assist IPV clients in recognizing and avoiding abusive relationships, increasing assertiveness, and encouraging self-advocacy and empowerment in securing social support and resources.

Several promising, integrative approaches to treating trauma specific to IPV are emerging in the literature. Cognitive processing therapy (CPT) incorporates traditional CBT with a special focus on issues related to intimacy, control, power, and trust and is recommended for use with survivors of IPV and sexual trauma (Iverson et al., 2011; Schnicke & Resick, 1993). Cognitive trauma therapy for battered women (CTT-BW) integrates psychoeducation, CBT, and interpersonal skills training to treat symptoms and risk factors specific to IVP and has demonstrated effectiveness in randomly controlled studies (Kubany et al., 2004). One additional promising program is Helping to Overcome PTSD through Empowerment (HOPE), which integrates CBT approaches with advocacy skills (Johnson, Zlotnick, & Perez, 2011).

Incorporating spiritual coping resources. Utilization of the client's spiritual resources is especially important when treating IPV, as many survivors rely on God and their faith communities for strength, support, and guidance. Christian counselors can thereby enhance both religious and psychological coping in women who have experienced IPV to encourage healing of body, mind, soul, and spirit. Pargament, Smith, Koenig, and Perez (1998) have identified positive coping strategies that can lead to decreased PTSD symptoms among trauma survivors. Spiritual coping strategies include drawing comfort from God and the faith community, working cooperatively with one's religious community to deal with the traumatic experiences, and seeking help with specific issues through prayer.

Other important spiritual practices for Christian clients recovering from the trauma of IPV include the development of regular practices such as daily devotions, corporate worship, and fellowship with other believers that can contribute to spiritual and personal health and stability during times of crisis and turmoil. Counselors can encourage clients to practice self-care of their bodies as "living temples" (1 Cor 3:16; 6:19-20) through refraining from self-destructive behaviors, attending to medical and psychological needs, and engaging in sleep, nutrition, and exercise, which can restore a sense of normalcy to daily life. Christian practices including meditation, studying Scripture, journaling, and contemplative prayer can contribute significantly to the healing process

Spiritually, the experience of physical and psychological harm at the hands of one who is supposed to provide love, protection, and care results in a destruction of cherished beliefs and can cause feelings of spiritual anguish and despair and difficulties trusting God and Christian community. Pargament et al. (1998) have identified negative religious coping strategies that can exacerbate PTSD symptoms, including viewing the traumatic experiences as God's punishment and believing that one has been abandoned by God and the church. Domestic batterers may misuse and misquote Scripture to dominate their partners and to support and justify their actions. Consequently, Christian women in IPV relationships often experience dysfunctional beliefs about gender and their role as women. These beliefs can include assumptions that, as women, they were created by God as defective, are of less value than men, and are responsible for their own abuse and even deserving of it (Foss & Warnke, 2003). They may also feel that they are responsible for keeping their homes together at all costs and required by God to be martyrs or suffering servants for the sake of preserving their families (Kroeger & Nason-Clark, 2010).

For Christian women in IPV relationships, these beliefs may even pose a barrier for leaving the abusive relationship and moving toward safety and are one of the reasons that many in the field of DV see women of faith at greater risk for staying in abusive relationships (Foss & Warnke, 2003; Nason-Clark, 2009; Wang, Horne, Levitt, & Klesges, 2009). Women perceive that their religious community will not support separation or divorce even in cases of marital violence. Thus, receiving counseling services from a competent clinician with similar faith values can be an integral component of effective treatment.

Christian counseling can address these faulty beliefs by providing clients with a safe place to identify, explore, and correct these views of self, God, and others. Counselors can encourage their clients to review Scripture passages focusing on God's unwavering and eternal love for them (e.g., Rom 8), their immense value in God's eyes (e.g., Ps 139), and God's desire for them to dwell in safety (e.g., Mt 10:28-31;

Rom 12:18). Clients can be encouraged to journal, pray, and meditate on these passages of Scripture. In addition, reading biblical narratives of women who stood strong against violence and injustice may provide spiritual resilience and empowerment. Rebuilding a sense of trust and confidence in God's care, the goodness of others who can help, and a sense of self-efficacy and value can be an arduous task for the client and difficult to accomplish on her own.

Pastoral care. The Christian community can play an invaluable role in the protection and care of women in IPV relationships. Practical resources including housing and financial support, which may aid an individual's transition to living on her own, can be invaluable during this time of crisis. Pastors and Christian friends can provide consistent support, constant prayer, and accurate biblical teaching about God, intimate relationships, power, and suffering. As IPV survivors seek to find a sense of meaning, coherence, and purpose in their suffering, caring Christian support provides them with a safe place to wrestle with questions about God's care for them during experiences of suffering and about issues of justice including why the innocent suffer and perpetrators appear to go free.

Competent Christian counseling for children. Children who witness violence in the home are affected emotionally, behaviorally, relationally, and spiritually. Many develop trauma-related symptoms as a result of living in a chronically unpredictable, dangerous, and violent environment. Effective treatment of children who develop trauma symptoms as a result of DV includes the following components: exposure therapies that allow therapeutic retelling and reexperiencing of traumatic events, cognitive interventions to decrease intrusive thoughts and address beliefs about violence, teaching coping skills for emotions and behaviors, improving interpersonal skills, and strengthening the relationship with the nonabusive parent and in some cases the previously abusive parent (Margolin & Vickerman, 2007). Competent Christian counseling will also attend to the potential spiritual consequences of DV in children by attending to impairments in trusting God and others, addressing faulty beliefs about power and authority, and beginning to help the child develop a sense of trust, efficacy, and hope.

A handful of evidence-based programs have been developed specifically for children who experience violence in the home. Child-parent psychotherapy (CPP), developed by Lieberman and Van Horn (2005) to treat preschool children and their mothers conjointly through collaborative writing of trauma narratives, increasing maternal responsiveness, and improving parenting skills, has demonstrated good outcomes (Lieberman, Van Horn, & Ippen, 2005). The Kids Club and Preschool Kids Club programs are group therapy programs designed for use in shelters or community settings and provide psychoeducation and skills training to children who have witnessed DA (Graham-Bermann, 1992; Graham-Bermann & Edleson

2001). Specifically designed for teenagers, the Youth Relationships Project promotes nonviolent relationships through competency training, psychoeducation, and community involvement (Wolfe et al., 1996). Several other approaches that have demonstrated effectiveness in reducing trauma symptoms in children, and may also be effective when used with child victims of DV, include trauma-focused cognitive behavioral therapy (TF-CBT) and abuse-focused cognitive behavioral therapy (Vickerman & Margolin, 2007).

Competent Christian counseling for batterers. Hope for perpetrators of IPV requires the Christian community to challenge their abusive behaviors, hold them accountable to change, and provide faith-based resources for treatment. In fact, the support of faith communities may lead to better treatment outcomes for male batterers. For instance, Fisher-Townsend (2008) found that men who were referred by their pastors for IPV treatment were more likely to complete the program and attend follow-up sessions than men who were referred by a judge. The accountability provided by a Christian community may be a critical component of treatment follow-through for male batterers, who are likely to deny their use of violence in the home and attempt to blame their partners for problems.

Perpetrators of IPV should be removed from church leadership positions and be referred for professional help through involvement in a program dedicated to the treatment of DV offenders. Research suggests that religious leaders can play an important role in requiring male batterers to participate in and complete a certified program (Fisher-Townsend, Nason-Clark, Ruff, & Murphy, 2008). Such programs are offered by most communities and involve a group format to provide education on DV, encourage taking responsibility for violent behaviors, and facilitate implementation of nonviolent coping strategies. Batterers should be required to complete their treatment programs successfully, take responsibility for their abusive behaviors, demonstrate significant changes in attitudes and behaviors over a long period of time, and consent to ongoing accountability before reconciliation with the partner should be considered (Nason-Clark, 2004). Integrating the Christian language and practices of hope, forgiveness, and reconciliation can provide important spiritual resources for men during the treatment process; such faith-based treatment programs for batterers have demonstrated improved compliance and treatment outcomes with this historically treatment-resistant population (Nason-Clark, Murphy, Fisher-Townsend, & Ruff, 2004).

Couple and family therapy—when is it appropriate? As mentioned earlier, use of couple therapy in treating IPV remains somewhat controversial, but there is a growing recognition that it can be an effective approach to treatment for mutual physical aggression that is relatively minor (no bruising, injury, or risk of lethality), does not involve a pattern of intimidation or psychological abuse and control, and does not involve one partner fearing the other. Goals of treatment for IPV couples should include cessation of all physical aggression, helping the couple engage in alternative behaviors during conflict (e.g., time-outs, thinking "cool thoughts," distraction), and improving emotional connection including empathy and positive feelings of marital satisfaction (O'Leary, 2008).

Specific interventions in couple therapy for IPV include the development of a nonviolence contract with the therapist, who regularly monitors the couple for episodes of physical aggression. Individual referrals for psychological problems that pose barriers to effective self-control, including anger management training or treatment of substance abuse disorders, may be warranted; thus the couple therapist will want to work closely with community agencies. Empirically supported couple treatments such as behavioral marital therapy (Epstein & Baucom, 2002) and emotionally focused therapy for couples (Johnson, 2004) provide structured approaches to the treatment of aggressive behavior as part of the couple conflict cycle. Domestic violence–focused couple therapy (DVFCT) utilizes the couple's strengths and competencies to address IPV behaviors consistent with a solution-focused model (Stith et al., 2011).

Incorporating spiritual resources into couple therapy with IPV can increase the "power" of the interventions as couples seek to practice Christian virtues of love, patience, selflessness, forbearance, and forgiveness in their relationship, particularly during times of conflict. Pairing IPV couples with a mentor couple in the church for support and accountability can provide an important resource during times of need and provide the couple with a model of healthy marital attitudes and behaviors.

Church- and community-based interventions. Perhaps the most promising Christian response to IPV involves partnerships between churches and community agencies. Such partnerships allow families to receive competent, coordinated services that respect and utilize the client's faith commitments as part of the healing process. For Nason-Clark (2009), churches and community organizations "pave the pathway between the steeple and the shelter" (p. 389) by recognizing their need for one another in order to best serve IPV clients. An excellent example of this type of partnership is the Faith Community Domestic Violence Program in Forsyth County, North Carolina, where leaders from six Christian denominations were brought together with community DV professionals to form a Faith Leadership Training Group for mutual education, dialogue, and collaboration. The group demonstrated significant changes in knowledge, beliefs, and attitudes toward promoting victim safety (Jones & Fowler, 2009). Clearly, a Christian response to IPV involves forging creative partnerships between community resources and faith-based institutions.

STRENGTHENING THE CHURCH'S RESPONSE TO DOMESTIC ABUSE

There is no doubt that the church plays a critical role in DV prevention and intervention. In fact, research suggests that regular church attendance may be a protective factor for effects of IPV (Wang et al., 2009). Churches where condemnation of violence in relationships is preached from the pulpit can be particularly impactful (Fisher-Townsend, 2008). Other experts note that many churches offer an informal network of support for women with relationship difficulties and also offer a place of safety and support (Nason-Clark, 1997).

Many women of faith in IPV relationships seek advice from religious leaders out of a desire to receive faith-based counsel, with mixed results. Surveys of religious leaders have found that over half of them have counseled a woman who has had an experience of physical aggression at the hands of an intimate partner, and over 29% have counseled a woman in an ongoing DV relationship (Nason-Clark, 1997). Pastors often feel ill-equipped to handle the challenges of counseling DV cases but may be unaware of community resources or may be hesitant to refer to community resources out of concern that a parishioner's faith beliefs will not be respected. Ministers are likely to underestimate the prevalence of IPV in their congregations (Vedral & Esworthy, 2014), feel pressure to provide a quick fix to DV, or err on the side of saving the marriage at all costs (Miles, 2000). As a result, many women of faith experience a lack of support from religious communities; such communities can also be a barrier to their seeking safety and refuge from violent partners, as women receive explicit and implicit messages that reinforce beliefs and stereotypes that protect the abuser more than the abused.

How can churches provide a courageous Christian response to DV consistent with the biblical mandate to protect the vulnerable in society? As Christian counselors, we must advocate for change within our congregations and equip our churches to provide education, prevention, and intervention. We can encourage our spiritual leaders to condemn from the pulpit the use of physical aggression and violence in all forms and to teach that IPV is a violation of the marital covenant before God (Nason-Clark, 2009). We can provide psychoeducation to church families about healthy, nonphysical approaches to discipline and conflict resolution. Our efforts can include developing church protocols for responding to women in IPV relationships by supporting disclosure, providing safety and needed resources, and supplying ongoing pastoral care in the their journeys toward safety and healing. For perpetrators of IPV, we can challenge abusive behaviors, provide accountability and support, and refer to a treatment program that respects and incorporates issues of faith. Finally, we can take proactive steps to build bridges with DV shelters and community agencies so that Christian clients can receive both the spiritual resources and professional services that will help the abused family move away from violence and toward safety, support, and healing.

RECOMMENDED RESOURCES

For counselors:

Graham-Bermann, S. A., & Levendosky, A. A. (Eds.). (2011). *How intimate partner violence affects children: Developmental research, case studies, and evidence-based intervention.* Washington, DC: American Psychological Association.

Rubin, A. (Ed.). (2011). *Programs and interventions for maltreated children and families at risk: Clinician's guide to evidence-based practice.* Hoboken, NJ: Wiley.

Stith, S. M., McCollum, E. E., & Rosen, K. H. (2011). *Couples therapy for domestic violence: Finding safe solutions.* Washington, DC: American Psychological Association.

World Health Organization. (2013). *Responding to intimate partner violence and sexual violence against women: WHO clinical and policy guidelines.* Retrieved from www .who.int/reproductivehealth/publications/violence/9789241548595/en/

For faith communities:

Johnson, A. J. (Ed.). (2015). *Religion and men's violence against women.* New York, NY: Springer Press.

Kroeger, C. C., & Nason-Clark, N. (2010). *No place for abuse: Biblical and practical resources to counteract domestic violence* (Rev. ed.). Downers Grove, IL: InterVarsity Press.

Miles, A. (2000). *Domestic violence: What every pastor needs to know.* Minneapolis, MN: Fortress Press.

Denominational statements on domestic violence can be found at www.interfaithpartners .org/statements

Religion and Violence e-learning (RAVE): www.theraveproject.com

Faith Trust Institute: www.faithtrustinstitute.org

Faith Trust Institute. *Broken vows: Religious perspectives on domestic violence* [DVD]. Available at www.faithtrustinstitute.org

National Online Resource Center on Violence Against Women. Special collection on domestic violence and religion: http://vawnet.org/sc/domestic-violence-and-religion

National Center on Domestic and Sexual Violence publications on faith and the faith community: www.ncdsv.org/publications_religion.html

REFERENCES

Annis, A. W., & Rice, R. R. (2001). A survey of abuse prevalence in the Christian Reformed Church. *Journal of Religion and Abuse, 3*(3-4), 7-40. doi:10.1300/j154v03n03_02

Babcock, J. C., Canady, B., Graham, K. H., & Schart, L. (2007). The evolution of battering interventions: From the Dark Ages into the Scientific Age. In J. Hamel & T. Nicholls (Eds.), *Therapy for domestic violence: A practitioner's guide to gender-inclusive research and treatment* (pp. 215-46). New York, NY: Springer.

Basile, K., & Black, M. (2011). Intimate partner violence against women. In C. Renzetti, J. Edleson, & R. Bergen (Eds.), *Sourcebook on violence against women* (2nd ed.). Thousand Oaks, CA: Sage.

Basile, K. C., Hertz, M. F., & Back, S. E. (2007). Intimate partner violence and sexual violence victimization assessment instruments for use in healthcare settings. Atlanta, GA: CDC and National Center for Injury Prevention and Control. Retrieved from www.cdc.gov/violenceprevention/pdf/ipv/ipvandsvscreening.pdf

Breiding, M. J., Basile, K. C., Smith, S. G., Black, M. C., & Mahendra, R. R. (2015). *Intimate partner violence surveillance: Uniform definitions and recommended data elements, Version 2.0.* Atlanta, GA: National Center for Injury Prevention and Control, Centers for Disease Control and Prevention. Retrieved from www.cdc.gov/violenceprevention /pdf/intimatepartnerviolence.pdf

Breiding, M. J., Smith, S. G., Basile, K. C., Walters, M. L., Chen, J., & Merrick, M. T. (2014). Prevalence and characteristics of sexual violence, stalking, and intimate partner violence victimization: National Intimate Partner and Sexual Violence Survey, United States, 2011. *Morbidity and Mortality Weekly Report, 63*(8), 1-18. Retrieved from www.cdc.gov/mmwr/preview/mmwrhtml/ss6308a1.htm?s_cid=ss6308a1_e

DeJonghe, E. S., Bogat, G. A., Levendosky, A. A., & von Eye, E. (2008). Women survivors of intimate partner violence and post-traumatic stress disorder: Prediction and prevention. *Journal of Postgraduate Medicine, 54*(4), 294-300. doi:10.4103/0022-3859.41435

Drumm, R. D., Popescu, M., & Kerstig, R. (2009). Effects of intimate partner violence among Seventh-Day Adventist church attendees. *Critical Social Work, 10*(1). Retrieved from www1.uwindsor.ca/criticalsocialwork/system/files/Drumm_Popescu_Kersting.pdf

Drumm, R. D., Popescu, M., & Riggs, M. L. (2009). Gender variations in partner abuse: Findings from a conservative Christian denomination. *Affilia: Journal of Women and Social Work, 24*(1), 56-68. doi:10.1177/0886109908326737

Epstein, N. B., & Baucom, D. H. (2002). *Enhanced cognitive-behavioral therapy for couples: A contextual approach.* Washington, DC: American Psychological Association.

Fisher-Townsend, B. (2008). Searching for the missing puzzle piece: The potential of faith in changing violent behavior. In C. C. Kroeger, N. Nason-Clark, & B. Fisher-Townsend (Eds.), *Beyond abuse in the Christian home: Raising voices for change* (pp. 100-120). Eugene, OR: Wipf and Stock.

Fisher-Townsend, B., Nason-Clark, N., Ruff, L., & Murphy, N. (2008). I am not violent. In C. C. Kroeger, N. Nason-Clark, & B. Fisher-Townsend (Eds.), *Beyond abuse in the Christian home: Raising voices for change* (pp. 78-99). Eugene, OR: Wipf and Stock.

Foa, E. B., Keane, T. M., Friedman, M. J., & Cohen, J. A. (Eds.). (2010). *Effective treatments for PTSD: Practice guidelines from the International Society for Traumatic Stress Studies.* New York, NY: Guilford Press.

Foss, L., & Warnke, M. (2003). Fundamental Protestant Christian women: Recognizing cultural and gender influences on domestic violence. *Counseling and Values, 48*(1), 14-23. doi:10.1002/j.2161-007x.2003.tb00271.x

Garcia-Moreno, C., Heise, L., Jansen, H., Ellsberg, M., & Watts, C. (2005). *WHO multi-country study on women's health and domestic violence against women and initial results on prevalence, health outcomes and women's responses.* Geneva, Switzerland: World Health Organization. doi:10.1016/S0140-6736(06)69523-8

Graham-Bermann, S. A. (1992). *The Kids' Club: A preventive intervention program for children of battered women.* Ann Arbor: University of Michigan.

Graham-Bermann, S. A, & Edleson, J. (2001). *Domestic violence in the lives of children: The future of research, intervention, and social policy.* Washington, DC: American Psychological Association.

Graham-Bermann, S. A., & Levendosky, A. A. (2011). *How intimate partner violence affects children: Developmental research, case studies, and evidence-based intervention.* Washington, DC: American Psychological Association.

Huesmann, L. R., Dubow, E. F., & Boxer, P. (2011). The transmission of aggressiveness across generations: Biological, contextual, and social learning processes. In P. R. Shaver & M. Mikulincer (Eds.), *Human aggression and violence: Causes, manifestations, and consequences* (pp. 123-42). Washington, DC: American Psychological Association. doi:10.1037/12346-007

Iverson, K. M., Gradus, J. L., Resick, P. A., Suvak, M. K., Smith, K. F., & Monson, C. M. (2011). Cognitive-behavioral therapy for PTSD and depression symptoms reduces risk for future intimate partner violence among interpersonal trauma survivors. *Journal of Consulting and Clinical Psychology, 79*(2), 193-202. http://doi.org/10.1037/a0022512

Johnson, D., Zlotnick, C., & Perez, S. (2011). Cognitive behavioral treatment of PTSD in residents of battered women's shelters: Results of a randomized clinical trial. *Journal of Consulting and Clinical Psychology, 79*(4), 542-51. doi:10.1037/a0023822

Johnson, M. P., & Leone, J. M. (2005). The differential effects of intimate terrorism and situational couple violence. *Journal of Family Issues, 26*(3), 322-49. doi:10.1177/0192513X04270345

Johnson, M. P., Leone, J. M., & Xu, Y. (2014). Intimate terrorism and situational couple violence in general surveys: Ex-spouses required. *Violence Against Women, 20*(2), 186-207. doi:10.1177/1077801214521324

Johnson, S. M. (2004). *The practice of emotionally focused marital therapy: Creating connection.* New York, NY: Brunner/Routledge.

Jones, A. S., & Fowler, T. S. (2009). A faith community-domestic violence partnership. *Social Work & Christianity, 36*(4), 415-29. Retrieved from www.nacsw.org/SWCFull.pdf

Jose, A., & O'Leary, D. (2009). Prevalence of partner aggression in representative and clinic samples. In K. O'Leary & E. Woodin (Eds.), *Psychological and physical aggression in couples: Causes and interventions*. Washington, DC: APA.

Kar, H. L., & Garcia-Moreno, C. (2009). Partner aggression across cultures. In K. O'Leary & E. Woodin (Eds.), *Psychological and physical aggression in couples: Causes and interventions*. Washington, DC: APA.

Kriedler, M. C. (1995). Victims of family violence: The need for spiritual healing. *Journal of Holistic Nursing, 13*(1), 30-36. doi:10.1177/1077801206286224

Kroeger, C., & Nason-Clark, N. (2010). *No place for abuse: Biblical and practical resources to counteract domestic violence*. Downers Grove, IL: InterVarsity Press.

Kubany, E., Hill, E., Owens, J., Iannce-Spencer, C., McCaig, J., Tremayne, K., & Williams, P. (2004). Cognitive trauma therapy for battered women with PTSD (CTT-BW). *Journal of Consulting and Clinical Psychology, 72*(1), 3-18. doi:10.1037/0022-006x.72.1.3

Levitt, H. M., Horne, S. G., Wheeler, E. E., & Wang, M.-C. (2015). Addressing intimate partner violence within a religious context. In D. F. Walker, C. A. Courtois, & J. D. Aten (Eds.), *Spiritually oriented psychotherapy for trauma* (pp. 211-31). Washington, DC: American Psychological Association.

Lieberman, A. F., & Van Horn, P. (2005). *"Don't hit my mommy!" A manual for child-parent psychotherapy with young witnesses of family violence*. Washington, DC: Zero to Three.

Lieberman, A. F., Van Horn, P., & Ippen, C. G. (2005). Toward evidence based treatment: Child-parent psychotherapy with preschoolers exposed to marital violence. *Journal of the American Academy of Child and Adolescent Psychiatry, 44*, 1241-47. doi:10.1097/01.chi.0000181047.59702.58

Margolin, G., & Vickerman, K. (2007). Posttraumatic stress in children and adolescents exposed to family violence: I. Overview and issues. *Professional Psychology: Research and Practice, 38*(6), 613-19. doi:10.1037/0735-7028.38.6.613

McDonald, R., Jouriles, E. N., Ramisetty-Mikler, S., Caetano, R., & Green, C. E. (2006). Estimating the number of American children living in partner-violent families. *Journal of Family Psychology, 20*, 137-42. doi:10.1037/0893-3200.20.1.137

McGoldrick, M., & Ross, M.A. (2011). Violence and the life cycle. In M. McGoldrick, E. A. Carter, & N. Garcia-Preto (Eds.), *The expanded family life cycle: Individual, family, and social perspectives* (4th ed., pp. 384-97). Boston, MA: Allyn & Bacon.

Miles, A. (2000). *Domestic violence: What every pastor needs to know*. Minneapolis, MN: Fortress Press.

Miles, A. (2008). Calling the pastor. In C. C. Kroeger, N. Nason-Clark, & B. Fisher-Townsend (Eds.), *Beyond abuse in the Christian home: Raising voices for change* (pp. 35-46). Eugene, OR: Wipf and Stock.

Nason-Clark, N. (1997). *The battered wife: How Christians confront family violence*. Louisville, KY: Westminster John Knox Press.

Nason-Clark, N. (2004). When terror strikes at home: The interface between religion and domestic violence. *Journal for the Scientific Study of Religion, 43*(3), 303-10. doi:10.1111/j.1468-5906.2004.00236.x

Nason-Clark, N. (2009). Christianity and the experience of domestic violence: What does faith have to do with it? *Journal of Social Work and Christianity, 36*(4), 379-93. Retrieved from www.nacsw.org/SWCFull.pdf

Nason-Clark, N., Murphy, B., Fisher-Townsend, B., & Ruff, L. (2004). An overview of the characteristics of the clients at a faith-based batterers' intervention program. *Journal of Religion and Abuse, 5*(4), 51-72. doi:10.1300/J154v05n04_05

Nathanson, A. M., Shorey, R. C., Tirone, V., & Rhatigan, D. L. (2012). The prevalence of mental health disorders in a community sample of female victims of intimate partner violence. *Partner Abuse, 3*(1), 59-75. doi:10.1891/1946-6560.3.1.59

O'Leary, K. (2008). Couple therapy and physical aggression. In A. S. Gurman (Ed.), *Clinical handbook of couple therapy.* New York, NY: Guilford Press.

Pargament, K., Smith, B. W., Koenig, H. G., & Perez, L. (1998). Patterns of positive and negative religious coping with major life stressors. *Journal for the Scientific Study of Religion, 37*, 710-24. doi:10.2307/1388152

Pico-Alfonso, M. A. (2005). Psychological intimate partner violence: The major predictor of posttraumatic stress disorder in abused women. *Neuroscience and Biobehavioral Reviews, 29*, 181-93. doi:10.1016/j.neubiorev.2004.08.010

Popescu, M., Drumm, R., Mayer, S., Cooper, L., Foster, T., Seifert, M., . . . Dewan, S. (2009). "Because of my beliefs that I had acquired from the church . . .": Religious belief-based barriers for Adventist women in domestic violence relationships. *Journal of Social Work & Christianity, 36*(4), 394-414. Retrieved from www.nacsw.org/SWCFull.pdf

Rodgers, C. S., & Norman, S. B. (2004). Considering PTSD in the treatment of female victims of intimate partner violence. *Psychiatric Times, 21*(4), 1-5. Retrieved from www.psychiatrictimes.com/articles/considering-ptsd-treatment-female-victims -intimate-partner-violence

Schneider, C., & Brimhall, A. S. (2014). From scared to repaired: Using an attachment-based perspective to understand situational couple violence. *Journal of Marital and Family Therapy 40*(3), 367-79. doi:10.1111/jmft.12023

Schnicke, M., & Resick, P. A. (1993). *Cognitive processing therapy for rape victims: A treatment manual.* Newbury Park, CA: Sage.

Slep, A. M., & O'Leary, S. G. (2005). Parent and partner violence in families with young children: Rates, patterns, and connections. *Journal of Consulting and Clinical Psychology, 73*, 435-44. doi:10.1037/0022-006x.73.3.435

Stith, S. M., McCollum, E. E., & Rosen, K. (2011). *Couples therapy for domestic violence: Finding safe solutions.* Washington, DC. American Psychological Association.

van der Kolk, B. A. (2005). Developmental trauma disorder. *Psychiatric Annals, 35,* 401-8.

Vedral, J., & Esworthy, E. (2014). Broken silence: A call for churches to speak out: Protestant pastors survey on sexual and domestic violence. Commissioned by Sojourners and IMA World Health on behalf of WeWillSpeakOut.us. Retrieved from www.imaworldhealth .org/images/stories/technical-publications/PastorsSurveyReport_final.pdf

Vickerman, K., & Margolin, G. (2007). Posttraumatic stress in children and adolescents exposed to family violence: II. Treatment. *Professional Psychology: Research and Practice, 38*(6), 620-28. doi:10.1037/0735-7028.38.6.613

Wang, M., Horne, S., Levitt, H., & Klesges, L. (2009). Christian women in IPV relationships: An exploratory study of religious factors. *Journal of Psychology and Christianity, 28*(3), 224-35.

Warshaw, C., Sullivan, C. M., & Rivera, E. A. (2013). *A systematic review of trauma-focused interventions for domestic violence survivors.* National Center on Domestic Violence, Trauma & Mental Health, in collaboration with Michigan State University. doi:10.1037/e566602013-001

Wolfe, D. A., Wekerle, C., Gough, R., Reitzel-Jaffe, D., Grasley, C., Pittman, A., . . . Stumpf, J. (1996). *The youth relationships manual: A group approach with adolescents for the prevention of woman abuse and the promotion of healthy relationships.* Thousand Oaks, CA: Sage.

World Health Organization (2013). *Responding to intimate partner violence and sexual violence against women: WHO clinical and policy guidelines.* Retrieved from www .who.int/reproductivehealth/publications/violence/9789241548595/en/

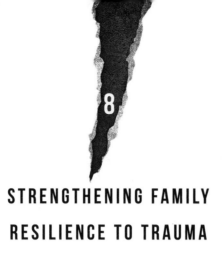

STRENGTHENING FAMILY
RESILIENCE TO TRAUMA

FRED C. GINGRICH

Much of the trauma literature emphasizes the impact of trauma on the individual. However, the literature addressing resilience supports the critical role of relational networks as a key factor in an individual's recovery from trauma. Even in an increasingly disconnected contemporary culture, family relationships, including marriages and extended family, are often a victim's primary healing community, whether they live in individualistic or collectivist cultures. The focus of this chapter is the contribution of family systems theory, assessment, and therapy to the understanding and treatment of the impact of trauma on families in general, with examples given of families with high stress and high potential for trauma (e.g., missionary and military families). The Christian mental health professional has much to offer traumatized families, rooted in a rich integration of psychological and biblical/theological resources.

For families of faith, the reality of stress, trauma, and hardship come as no surprise. Scripture details the challenges and trials that will come to people of faith (e.g., 1 Thess 3:3) and points us to the healing community that we find in the body of Christ, the church. A relational focus on resiliency, as the way people learn to cope and maintain hope in the face of trauma, is consistent with the description of the Christian life in Romans 8. The passage proclaims that in Christ "*we* are more than conquerors" (Rom 8:37, italics added), suggesting that together we are able to overcome the adversities and challenges of life.

From this foundation of the reality of family life and the hope that families have in their spiritual and community resources, in this chapter I review the concept and types of family trauma and make the case for endorsing the lens of family resilience in working with traumatized families. I then utilize concepts from family systems theory to inform our work with families in crisis.

TYPOLOGY OF FAMILY TRAUMA

Traumatic experiences and their impact on families fall into the following broad, though not distinct nor exhaustive, categories (Catherall, 2004):

- Simultaneous trauma: Family members are directly affected by a traumatic event (e.g., auto accident, home invasion, natural disaster).

- Secondary or vicarious traumatic stress: Family members witness or hear about trauma experienced by another member (e.g., rape, chronic illness, accident of another family member).

- Intergenerational trauma: Family members are affected by the trauma experienced by the previous generation (e.g., children of POWs, second generation Holocaust survivors, immigration; see Hollander-Goldfein, Isserman, & Goldenberg, 2012; Rowland-Klein, 2004; Wolynn, 2016).

- Intrafamilial trauma: Family members are traumatized by a member of the family (e.g., incest, domestic violence, alcoholism).

While distinct dynamics are associated with each type of trauma, and specific interventions are needed, these nuances are beyond the limitations of this chapter. However, I will focus on unfolding the implications of this core idea: *The healing dynamics linked to resilience are often found in the "we," not in the "I," and they arise through the process of connecting with each other in relationship* (Shem & Surrey, 1998).

INDIVIDUAL VERSUS FAMILY RESILIENCE

Southwick and Charney (2012) identify a number of resiliency factors in the literature. These include optimism (belief in a brighter future); facing fear (as an adaptive response); maintaining a moral compass, ethics, and altruism (doing what is right); religion and spirituality (drawing on faith resources); social support and role models; physical and brain fitness; cognitive and emotional flexibility; and meaning, purpose, and growth. What is missing from this list as an explicit factor supporting resilience is the crucial role of one's closest (typically family) relationships. Of course, as Boss (2016) points out, there is always a dialectic between individual and family stress and coping; both need to be considered.

However, the family systems and resilience research in support of the family resilience lens is compelling (Catherall, 2004; Hollander-Goldfein et al., 2012; Lebow & Rekart, 2004; Price, Bush, & Price, 2016; Saxe, Ellis, & Brown, 2016; Southwick & Charney, 2012). To give one example of this research evidence, Simpson (2010) found that a sense of acceptance and belonging to a family was one of the most significant protective factors for an individual in the aftermath of trauma.

CLARIFYING THE GOAL IN HELPING TRAUMATIZED FAMILIES

Boss (2016) addresses the question of whether helping a person or family in the aftermath of a traumatic experience is a matter of *coping* with stress, *adapting* to stressful circumstances, *being resilient* (or tough) in response to stress, or *managing* stress. As the name of her book implies, *management* is Boss's preferred conceptual framework, as it recognizes the implicit and ubiquitous presence of ambiguity in all traumatic situations. The ambiguities of trauma cannot be avoided and should not be simply endured; both the negative impact and the potential for posttraumatic growth and change need to be managed.

I prefer the word *resilience* when discussing a family's management of trauma. In an earlier book, Boss (2006) defines resilience as "the ability to stretch (like elastic) or flex (like a suspension bridge) in response to pressures and strains of life" (p. 48). Resilience includes one's response to "normative stress from everyday hassles, expected family transitions of entries and exits (including births and deaths) across the lifespan. It also includes the stress and trauma from unexpected crises and catastrophes" (p. 48). Resilience is the ability to bounce back to previous, or even higher, levels of functioning. It also means the ability to live relatively comfortably with ambiguity and uncertainty in the face of what are often life-changing and confusing losses.

The analogy of a bridge (Boss, 2006) suggests that *resilience* is like a bridge bending from a heavy weight but without negative effects; it can continue to absorb pressure without harm to the bridge. *Stress* is akin to the bridge absorbing the weight (pressure) and functioning as it was built to do. The bridge begins to show strain by shaking or even "groaning" but holds for now. A *crisis* results in the bridge beginning to collapse.

Another helpful conceptual perspective is used by Hollander-Goldfein, Isserman, and Goldenberg (2012) in their 20-year, in-depth qualitative study of Holocaust families. "Transcending trauma" may sound a little optimistic, but in their research they identified a number of family factors that resulted in traumatized families being able to transcend or heal and grow beyond their traumatic experiences:

- Pretrauma lives with significant attachment figures, relationships with family members; sharing of values, rituals, meaning, individual strengths prior to the war

- Mediating influence of positive parental attachment patterns (closeness–distance, empathy–self-centeredness, validation–criticalness, expressive of positive emotion–negative emotion, open–closed communication, tolerance–intolerance)

- Role of faith and ritual

- Impact of family communication and trauma narratives on children
- Intergenerational transmission of trauma from survivors to their children and grandchildren

These factors are both protective in the face of trauma and restorative in the aftermath of trauma; combined they describe what it means for a family to be resilient.

FAMILY SYSTEMS THEORY AND RESILIENCE

It is evident that experts are beginning to appreciate the value of the family systems lens in responding to trauma. The following references each support the family systems perspective of trauma: Boss (2016); Catherall (2004); Johnson (2002); Kiser (2015); Kilmer, Gil-Rivas, Tedeschi, and Calhoun (2009); Lanktree and Briere (2016); Nason-Clark, Fisher-Townsend, and Fahlberg (2013); Phillips and Kane (2008); Price, Bush, and Price (2016); Saxe, Ellis, and Brown (2016); and Walsh (2006, 2016).

Family systems theory stresses that what matters most in life is not what happens within or inside people but what happens between them. Thus, family resilience is more about *relational processes* than traits or competencies that individuals in a family either have or do not have. Resilience itself is relational, and self-repair happens better in families working together to family-repair. This perspective is highly optimistic regarding the vast resources that families possess to respond to crises and distress. In addition, thinking systemically encourages us to consider sociocultural contexts and solutions in contrast to what some consider the limiting intrapsychic perspective that predominates the therapeutic world. This perspective is poignantly illustrated in the preface to Boss's (2006) book:

> My work in New York [9/11], in Kosovo, and with people affected by the 2004 tsunami has solidified my views about including family- and resilience-based approaches in treating loss and trauma. The common focus on individual treatment and pathology after loss and trauma must be broadened to include safeguarding natural family and community struggles and rebuilding resiliency. (p. xx)

Table 8.1 summarizes the primary distinctions between a focus on healthy families, dysfunctional families, and resilient families. While each perspective has benefits, the reality is that healthy families, as described in the table, do not really exist. All families experience levels of stress and have problems. In subtle ways, our culture, often reinforced by a particular view of spirituality, suggests that there is something wrong with ordinary families who are struggling to cope with their current reality. The family systems perspective suggests that stressful events, developmental challenges, and even trauma are normal life experiences and do not constitute family dysfunction or pathology. On the other extreme, viewing families simply through the lens of dysfunction and pathology does not acknowledge the myriad of strengths and resources that families have, which are easily hidden beneath current traumatic experiences. In a similar way, a common Christian perspective is that there is a healthy, biblical model of family, and it is the ideal toward which all Christian families need to strive. The prototype of such a family is a "traditional" nuclear family with two parents (male-female married couple) and their children living in a male-led authority structure; the family is career/ministry focused, with well-behaved, authority-responsive children, and has regular (preferably daily) family devotions (cf. Clapp, 1993). So when a Christian family is struggling, the belief is that the family is not following Jesus closely, is not living in the freedom and power of the Spirit, is not utilizing their spiritual resources, is not implementing spiritual leadership appropriately, or is not a truly Christian family. A family systems perspective rooted in a biblical worldview, and taking seriously the multitude of challenged families presented in Scripture, rejects this perspective of the healthy Christian family and acknowledges the norm of highly stressed, traumatized families trying to follow God amidst their own and the world's fallenness (cf. Garland & Garland, 2007).

Table 8.1. The focus on family resilience

Healthy Families	Resilient Families	Dysfunctional Families
Assumption of success across all dimensions	Bounce-back ability in times of stress	Coping mechanisms are usually faulty
Stable over time and across situations	Trauma/problems can occur at any time	Pathological in most circumstances
Specific characteristics to emulate	Relational processes that can be learned	Specific characteristics to avoid
Ideal model of family	Real families	Negative model
No need for intervention	Targeted support and education needed	Therapy/treatment required to improve
Often desire to be like these families	Develop patterns that respond well to crises—a less lofty goal	Try to avoid being like these families

The family systems perspective also requires us to reject the view that there is one universal model of the healthy family, that there is one set of family values that all families need to adopt, that there are ways of living and being family that fit all families, and that there is one organizational structure for the healthy family. In brief, systems theory presents a focus that allows for diversity of family models, deals with the reality of family dynamics and challenges, and encourages a focus on covenant, grace, empowerment, and intimacy (Balswick & Balswick, 2014) through faith in God and the support of God's people. This highlights the contrast between ideal, God-honoring families and dysfunctional, fallen families. The focus on real families that are resilient in the face of struggles is consistent with the overarching perspectives of family presented in Scripture

UNIQUE CONTRIBUTIONS OF A FAMILY RESILIENCE PERSPECTIVE

A family resilience lens offers a number of helpful perspectives regarding the understanding and treating of families affected by trauma. Together the following points explain why a family resilience perspective distinctively adds to our appreciation of the complexity of trauma.

A relational (systemic) emphasis. As previously suggested, family systems theory is concerned about the "between" dynamics of families in contrast to the internal dynamics of individuals. In support of this perspective, research on resilience in vulnerable children has increasingly linked resilience to key protective processes in family and social relationships (Goff & Schwerdtfeger, 2004). The family system and the family's ability to function within social and cultural systems (including political, economic, and medical) contribute to augmenting or reducing the resilience of families. Family resilience is not just the presence or absence of individual hardiness or specific personality traits (e.g., easygoing temperament, higher intelligence, positive bias, or learned optimism); it is the processes themselves that families develop to cope with life. These family processes mediate the impact of stress for all members and can influence the course and outcome of many crisis events.

Ordinary and growth oriented. Families commonly demonstrate resilience. While some traumas can destroy family bonds (e.g., the death of a child; abandonment and extreme dislocation), families frequently draw on resources they were not aware of without professional intervention. Resilience refers to the ability to adapt well in the face of life's adversities, traumas, tragedies, threats, and stress. Beyond mere containment, coping, problem-solving, or crisis management, resilience points to the possibilities for positive transformation and posttraumatic growth for the family in the midst of the challenges and beyond.

The goal is not to avoid or become numb, nor to be self-sufficient and to breeze through the trauma unscathed, but rather to have the courage and hope to struggle well with suffering. Even though trauma will likely involve considerable emotional distress, which can overwhelm commonly used coping patterns, a crisis can become a positive turning point for an individual or a family. As many have discovered, resilience is forged through adversity, not despite it (Walsh, 2006, 2012a). Resilience research exactly parallels the teaching of Scripture with respect to dealing with life's challenges. For example, Joseph, after the maltreatment by his brothers, says, "You intended to harm me, but God intended it for good to accomplish what is now being done, the saving of many lives" (Gen 50:20). This and other passages affirm the biblical value of resilience as the norm for the Christian life (2 Cor 4:8-9; Rom 8:28; Jas 1:2-5).

Developmental considerations. Resilience depends on developmental factors that are at times easy to overlook. Families typically consist of children and adults, aging members and preverbal infants, each with unique developmental strengths and vulnerabilities (McGoldrick, Preto, & Carter, 2015; McGoldrick & Shibusawa, 2012). Families experience normal family transitions (e.g., the first child goes to school) accompanied by levels of stress that are usually managed effectively (Cowan & Cowan, 2012). In the presence of traumatic stress, the developmental strengths of each family member are often an underutilized resource, as well as a potential complicating factor.

In traumatic situations, the intersection of individual development and family development can also be a strength or a challenge. Developmental theorists tell us that no single coping response is invariably successful over time, and that both individual and family development is too complex to make identifying a single helpful response possible. However, events that occur out of sync with chronological or social expectations (e.g., sibling death during childhood; early widowhood) are more difficult to cope with (McGoldrick, Preto, & Carter, 2015). Furthermore, a family strength at one stage might not be considered a strength at another time. For instance, a grandmother living with a family might not be particularly stressful and may even be helpful at reducing family stress when her grandchildren are infants, but her presence in the household might become more stressful for the family when the children are adolescents.

Thus, it appears that resilience is diminished when crises are developmentally unexpected (e.g., terminal illness diagnosed in a young family), when crises are more severe or persistent than developmentally expected (e.g., lengthy separation due to employment), when stressful individual transitions collide (e.g., midlife parent and adolescent child), or when multiple stressors within a developmental time frame produce cumulative effects (e.g., a young family with a sick newborn and unemployment). Resilience is fostered when there is an expectation that some level of stress typically accompanies each stage of family life (e.g., a family with an adolescent in "trouble"). The intersection of developmental psychology, family systems theory, spirituality, and resilience to trauma provide a critical foundation for counselors' efforts to respond compassionately and competently to the impact of trauma on people's lives.

Personal and family histories do not necessarily determine the present. The widely held belief that the impact of early and severe individual or family trauma cannot be altered is being challenged by resilience research with the recognition that not only can there be recovery from some trauma, but the end result can be increased strength (Walsh, 2006). People and families with difficult pasts have the potential to improve their lives later in their development. This, of course, in no way is intended to minimize the incredible pain and long-term consequences of trauma. Complex traumatic pasts erode the coping mechanisms that healthy people assume everyone has the ability to use. It is clear that the ability to be resilient decreases with the amount, type, and chronicity of the trauma.

However, attachment theory (Bowlby, 1988; Cassidy & Shaver, 2008), while recognizing that insecure infant attachment and trauma can lead to difficulties in adulthood, suggests that attachment styles can change over the lifespan. Some more optimistic perspectives have begun to provide empirical evidence that developing secure relationships as adults (through friendship, romantic, family, or therapeutic relationships) can repair early attachment deficits (Johnson, 2002). Such perspectives acknowledge that while separation from primary contexts of safety and security is inherently traumatizing, the establishment of safety and security in primary attachment relationships can be curative. In other words, we are not lifelong victims of traumatic experiences; secure relationships in the present are an antidote.

Spirituality is an important dimension of family resilience. In addition to the explicitly Christian literature on families and faith (e.g., Balswick & Balswick, 2014), a number of secular authors have recognized the importance of spirituality in helping families (e.g., Barrett, 2009; Walsh, 2012b, 2016) and particularly the significance of religion and spirituality in terms of working with most ethnic families (McGoldrick, Giordano, & Gracia-Preto, 2005). Blume's (2006) model of family therapy describes spirituality as one of five key dimensions that affect how assessment and treatment should be conducted. Most religious systems value family, and while some distorted forms of spirituality can be toxic for individuals and families (e.g., VanVonderen, 2010), overall the consensus is that spiritual values improve individual and family functioning. This factor is probably even more significant in the face of trauma. If Boss (2006) is correct in her assertion that finding meaning after trauma is a significant part of the healing journey, then faith in a sovereign God, finding acceptance and comfort in the midst of loss, experiencing forgiveness, or finding meaning in the artistic expressions, symbols, and rituals associated with many religions can be powerfully positive dimensions of responding to trauma (Boss, 2006). For Christians, the more tangible resources of Scripture, prayer, and community provide meaning and purpose, not only for individual believers, but for families of faith.

WALSH'S MODEL OF FAMILY RESILIENCE

Walsh (2006, 2012a, 2016) provides a thorough description of the relational processes that support families during and after traumatic events. The model consists of three primary processes that overlap and intersect in more of a circular (systemic) fashion than a linear sequence. These factors focus a clinician's attention to processes that a family in crisis may not exhibit, putting the family at risk for traumatic disruption. It also provides a set of principles on which mental health professionals can base interventions in premarital counseling, parent training, and counseling in the aftermath of traumatic experiences. Table 8.2 summarizes the processes that are expanded on in succeeding subsections.

Table 8.2. Walsh's model of family resilience (2012a, p. 406)

Family Processes	Descriptors
Belief systems	• Making meaning of adversity • Positive outlook • Transcendence and spirituality
Organizational patterns	• Flexibility • Connectedness • Social and economic resources
Communication/problem solving	• Clear, consistent messages • Open emotional expression • Collaborative problem solving

Family belief systems. Families may not be aware of their implicit belief system (e.g., "we believe in God") and rarely identify, discuss, or exhibit it. Even if a family is aware of and makes explicit acknowledgments of their beliefs (e.g., "we value living as a Christian family"), they may not be able to articulate them in a way that all members of the family understand. Whatever the case, belief systems can provide relational processes and resources that help a family to be resilient in the face of trauma. Belief systems, particularly religious ones, provide meaningful explanations for the events of life and a sense of coherence, a sense that all the pieces fit together even if one does not experience it right now. Belief systems provide hope, a positive outlook (optimistic bias), and courage to do what is possible now while accepting what cannot be changed. Frequently, a belief system also includes beliefs about transcendent values and purposes far beyond the limitations of the current resources of the family, along with a spirituality that offers inspiration, faith, rituals, and spiritual resources such as prayer, Scripture, and community support.

Organizational patterns. Flexible organizational processes are necessary to handle crises. Rigid patterns of life and relationships severely limit responses and can destroy families or, at the least, intensify traumatic stress. Flexibility entails the ability to rebound, reorganize, and adapt to new challenges while maintaining a sense of stability through the disruption. This sense of stability includes the need for continuity, dependability, rituals, and routines. Strong leadership can help provide the necessary nurturance, protection, and guidance, but when the leadership is inflexible or located in only one person, the family is vulnerable if the leader experiences trauma that limits or immobilizes his or her responses. Therefore, varied family forms such as cooperative parenting, sibling caregiving, and distributed leadership functions can help a family adapt to changing and critical situations.

Organizational patterns that foster attachment, are committed and dependable, provide mutual support, are collaborative, and respect individual needs, differences, and boundaries are essential. When a family is relationally threatened, previously developed family patterns that model and encourage seeking reconnection, forgiveness, and reconciliation can sustain families through crises. Family patterns that make good use of social and economic resources in stable times are more likely to foster resilience in tumultuous times. Families that can mobilize kin, social, community, and institutional networks when in distress and who have the financial resources to continue to provide basic needs will be more resilient in the aftermath of trauma.

Communication processes. How families talk to each other matters. Clear, consistent messages (words and actions), the freedom to ask for information to clarify ambiguous and confusing experiences, and the desire to seek truth and speak truth are characteristic of communication patterns that foster family resilience. Open emotional expression, sharing the range of feelings (joy and pain, hopes and fears) with mutual empathy and respect for differences, also fosters resilience. Taking responsibility for one's own feelings and behavior and avoiding blame are key communication skills for families. Pleasurable interactions, recreation, and humor are also important. Gottman's (1999) research identifies that a five to one ratio of positive to negative expressed sentiments is as important for families as it is for couples.

Included in these communication processes are a range of ideas such as creative brainstorming, resourcefulness, collaborative problem solving, shared decision making, conflict resolution skills, negotiation skills, fairness, reciprocity, focusing on family goals, defining concrete next steps, building on success, and learning from failure. Overall, a proactive stance toward preventing problems, averting crises, and preparing for future challenges is helpful.

APPLYING WALSH'S MODEL TO FAMILIES LIVING CROSSCULTURALLY

While all families are at risk for trauma, missionary and humanitarian workers' families are a unique subset of families that illustrate high levels of chronic family stress, trauma, and resilience. In a parallel way, albeit with some differences, diplomatic families and international business families also fit this profile. A major difference between these two categories of families that live crossculturally is the degree of access to economic resources when faced with trauma. The history of missionary families is filled with stories in which economic challenges compounded the response and effects of trauma.

Another group of families, immigrant families and culturally diverse families (Gardano, 1998; Zagelbaum & Carlson, 2010), experience similar pressures and potential for trauma as a result of living in culturally unfamiliar contexts. Such families are at high risk for levels of trauma that families more connected to familiar contexts and networks of support do not often experience.

My experience with missionary families is that they have typically lived through one or more of the following incidents. None of these incidents are by themselves necessarily experienced as traumatic, but the blending of them can result in devastating trauma for missionary families.

- Extreme and frequent geographical transitions

- Bridging multicultural contexts; always being the "foreigner"

- Personal and family safety concerns related to unstable political conditions, criminal victimization, natural disasters, animosity, and suspicion

- Limited communication access and challenges even with familiar people and safe relationships

- Complex, highly unpredictable gender roles

- A sense of isolation while being in frequent contact with people

- Few indicators of success as a family and in ministry

- The challenge of repatriation

- The overwhelming significance of the task

Specifically applying Walsh's model to missionary families, it is likely that such families have strengths in the area of a belief system. More than many other types of families, the entire family's network of relationships perceives that the family shares a common purpose. Thus, in the face of crosscultural stress, educational challenges, precarious financial situations, and isolation from kinship networks, there is often a common family definition of purpose, "God's call" to missionary service. Even in the event of severe traumas such as robberies, kidnappings, car accidents, natural disasters, and political uprisings, families share a way of talking about the stress and about God's and the mission's overarching purposes being served.

Missionary families, especially from conservative religious backgrounds, tend to have fairly rigid organization with male-oriented authority structures. Flexibility in terms of interaction with the culture and openness to explore its language and values does not necessarily translate into flexibility within the family. Thus, in the event of traumatic experiences (e.g., a father's health crisis), the family may not have the adaptability within the family organization to be resilient. In the past, missionary family support and interconnectedness was considerably higher because of the "mission station" practice in which missionary families would live together on a compound, somewhat protected from the broader culture. With the trends toward urbanization and the increased focus on directly engaging the culture, mission stations are no longer the norm. My observation is that the downside of this trend is a potential isolation and loss of connection and support for missionary families.

Communication in missionary families is fostered by the religious values of responsibility, honesty, respect, and compassion. Yet other characteristics of missionary families work against communication processes that foster resilience. For example, simply because family members believe in Christ does not give them the same skills of emotional expression, empathy, and problem solving that Christ portrayed. Some aspects of missionary families, such as distance from family members, chronic stress, and isolation from extended family relationships, work against communication. Technology can help but also tends to create the illusion of connection and masks the absence of deep intimacy.

One of the tragic stories in the history of the missionary movement is the treatment of missionary children. One sad example is documented in the film *All God's Children* (Solary & Westphal, 2008). The traditional belief was that missionary children were best handled by placing them in boarding schools either in the home country or in a regional boarding school (e.g., in West Africa). This allowed both parents to devote their time to the ministry. However, because of the abuse experienced by the children in the absence of their parents, the imposed isolation of children from parents (rigid organizational patterns) with restricted and monitored contact (limited open communication), and the assumption that everyone must sacrifice for the mission (unhealthy belief system), these families experienced intense trauma without the resources to process it effectively. The consequences for individual children, their families, the mission, and the ministry were devastating. Families with members living apart from each other often find that when trauma occurs, there are few family resources to cope with it.

The member care movement (e.g., O'Donnell & O'Donnell, 2011) is responding to the unique circumstances and vulnerabilities of missionary families. Mission organizations are paying more attention and responding more specifically to families, not just individuals (Andrews, 2004; Gingrich, 2016). The family resilience literature, however, does point to the need to build resilience by fostering *relational processes* in families, not simply responding to crises after the fact.

APPLYING WALSH'S MODEL TO MILITARY FAMILIES

In a similar way, military families are at high risk for trauma. Life-giving sacrifices are required of military families. A unique constellation of stressors rarely found in other occupations results in changes to military family structures, which particularly affect children and make them even more vulnerable to stress (Castro, Adler, & Britt, 2005; Moore, 2011).

Military families particularly at risk are families who are alone (without affiliation networks), young and inexperienced families (especially pregnant couples and couples with young children), and families with a pile-up of stressors, additional challenges, or traumas (accumulation of stressors; Wiens & Boss, 2005).

Protective factors for military families include having flexible gender roles (e.g., shifting roles during deployment), actively developing coping strategies, and accessing community and social supports versus maintaining an independent, detached lifestyle both within and outside the military context (Wiens & Boss, 2005).

Military families typically do not have the strong religious belief systems of missionary families, though their commitment to the cause of defending one's country and its values does provide meaning for their sacrifice. Organizational patterns in military families may reflect the dominant patterns of authority and structure in military life and, therefore, may not promote flexibility in the face of trauma. With long deployments, connections can be tenuous for spouses and partners with each other and parents with their children. A year-long absence can be incredibly significant in the developmental growth of a young child.

Perhaps the major distinction between missionary and military families is the access military families have to economic and social resources. Military families typically live on or close to a military base with access to social support and the extensive resources of the military for all types of care (housing, familiar foods, medical services, mental health services, options for worship and spiritual support, etc.).

Given the significance of the military in the United States and in many other countries, as well as the a high percentage of military personnel returning from deployment with some diagnosable condition of acute stress disorder or posttraumatic stress disorder, it is a global concern to develop strategies and resources to assist families with the primary trauma and the secondary trauma experienced by family members. Some research is beginning to suggest particular methods for dealing with the negative effects of military-family stressors by creating systemic responses, such as training leaders to recognize and accommodate family stress, and by developing family-friendly organizational policies and practices (Everson & Figley, 2010; see also chap. 17 in this volume).

CONTRASTING FAMILY PROCESSES FOR STEREOTYPICAL MISSIONARY AND MILITARY FAMILIES

There is always a danger in generalizing to the group and losing the uniqueness of individual families. However, in order to illustrate the use of Walsh's (2006) model and how it might be used in assessment and treatment, I will risk stereotyping the characteristics of missionary and military families. Table 8.3 assesses these two groups of families in terms of the resiliency processes they might typically exhibit.

Table 8.3. Contrast between missionary and military families

Family Processes	Missionary Families	Military Families
Family belief systems	High	Mid
Making meaning of adversity	High	High
Positive outlook	Mid	Mid
Transcendence and spirituality	High	Mid
Organizational patterns	Low	Mid
Flexibility	Low	Low
Connectedness	Mid	Low
Social and economic resources	Low	High
Communication processes	Mid	Low
Clarity	Mid	Mid
Open emotional expression	Mid	Low
Collaborative problem solving	Low	Low

Characterizing family types as high, midrange, or low on each of these processes risks minimizing the uniqueness of each specific family. Yet in most cases missionary families would share a strong set of beliefs that compel them to live the way they do. This may be true of some military families but is likely not as much a family strength for all military families. The other resiliency factors could be assessed and contrasted in a similar way. Research would need to be conducted to confirm whether these hypotheses are in fact valid.

BUILDING FAMILY RESILIENCE: APPLYING THE PROCESSES

It could be argued that family systems theory is as interested in building resilience in families as it is in working with families to repair relationships in the wake of trauma. While therapy is a primary application of family systems theory, prevention is equally stressed. The problem is that so often the opportunity to work with families comes after they have realized that they are not coping well with trauma. Nevertheless, building resilience is the goal, and even in distressed families, building resilience for the future by means of interventions is as much the objective as is helping families cope with the current crisis (second-order, rather than first-order, change in systems theory). Therefore, the following recommendations lean toward second-order change, rather than focusing primarily on responding to the current stress and symptoms (the focus of first-order change).

Including trauma/crisis experiences in family assessment. Conducting *family* assessment, not only individual adult, individual child, or marital assessment, is a difficult and complex procedure. In some respects, assessment of each of the individuals, the couple dyad, the nuclear family, the extended family, and the community and culture systems is necessary (Gingrich, 2016; Heffer & Snyder, 1998; Lebow & Stroud, 2012; Williams, Edwards, Patterson, & Chamow, 2011). Family therapy itself is intimidating for many clinicians, who might fear the multiple dynamics in the room and instead prefer the one-on-one assessment procedures of individual counseling. However, with the entire family in the room, exploring how a family has experienced previous traumatic experiences is a powerful method of assessing current resources and relational processes available for coping and healing.

Techniques such as family interviews, family enactments, and experiential activities (e.g., tasks, games, projects, sandtray) are common in the family therapy literature because they can bypass rigid relational patterns that restrict free expression. Reviewing how the family has dealt with previous crises is beneficial. Taking individual inventories and compiling and contrasting individual results can also be useful.

One of the most popular assessment models of family functioning is the Circumplex Model included as part of the PREPARE/ENRICH assessment instrument (www.prepare-enrich.com). The related FACES IV is a validated instrument used to specifically assess families on the dimensions of cohesion and adaptability (Olson, 2011). A helpful use of the instrument is to compare pretrauma family functioning with posttraumatic functioning, as well as to compare current and ideal functioning. The instrument can also be used intergenerationally to assess changes or similarities over generations. Other instruments are reviewed in Lebow and Stroud (2012).

Strengthening the family's belief system. The danger in addressing belief systems is that it is difficult for caregivers, in their desire to help, not to impose their own meanings onto a crisis situation. Christian therapists may have a tendency to believe that they know God's mind in situations and then ask questions and make comments about the meaning of the family's adversity. The role of the clinician is to help the family discover what is meaningful for them in the crisis.

The following are suggested practices for strengthening family belief systems:

- Normalizing distress as a part of life, particularly as a part of the Christian's life
- Recounting generational or biblical stories of family crises and how adversity led to new possibilities

- Having developmentally and age-appropriate conversations about the family's meaning and purpose

- Cultivating transcendence and spirituality by helping the family connect to a faith community

- Teaching and modeling coping as a relational strategy, that the family coping together is better than a group of individuals each hanging on in relative isolation through difficult situations

- Focusing on the "redemptive possibilities" (Benner, 1998) in suffering and crisis, though not imposing this perspective prematurely or insensitively

- Encouraging a positive outlook by being hope-focused ("what if things were different or better?"), identifying family strengths and potential, and encouraging persistence

- Providing or encouraging families to access external resources for couples and families within their faith communities and societies

- Using religious/spiritual genograms (Frame, 2000)

- Suggesting the use of age-appropriate spiritual disciplines as a family

- Developing family rituals, symbols, or memorable objects related to the trauma that point to transcendent dimensions

- Engaging in service projects as a family related to particular trauma experiences (e.g., supporting nationals working in the area from which the family was evacuated)

Strengthening the family's organization patterns. In a society deeply committed to democratic leadership, the issue of authority in the family is complicated. In some ways, the benevolent dictator works well as a leadership model in terms of decision making and efficient operations in the family. However, regardless of the authority structure, and even in families from non-Western cultures, some collaboration and flexibility in roles can help families be more resilient in the face of crises.

The importance of social connectedness with people outside the family cannot be overestimated. The relationally isolated family is not much better off than the individual who is isolated from family and friends. Of particular significance is encouraging families to stay connected to extended families despite the high mobility of modern life. The Social Network Map (Tracy & Whittaker, 1990) is a method for helping families to explore their relationships and locations of support.

However, it is also important for families to connect with others who are themselves stable and healthy and who will provide beneficial support in the midst of a crisis. Hawkins and Manne (2004) identified three cautions regarding dependence on others during a crisis: (a) contact with victims makes people feel more vulnerable themselves (vulnerability contagion); (b) many people have little experience with trauma and are uncertain how to react to victims, which increases anxiety (helplessness anxiety); and (c) there are misconceptions, and at times somewhat contradictory information, regarding how best to react and help in times of crisis (misguided assistance). In addition, finding people who are supportive can be challenging when those around are all experiencing the same crisis, as in natural disasters and other examples of mass trauma.

Numerous other interventions and suggestions for helping families with their organizational processes exist in the family therapy and family enrichment literature. For instance, identifying and modifying family structures is one of the therapeutic skills and tasks in structural family therapy (Colapinto, 1988; Minuchin, Nichols, & Lee, 2006). This approach involves techniques such as boundary making between parts of the system, realigning power in the family, restructuring transactions, and unbalancing.

Strengthening the family's communication patterns. The massive amount of information available to help individuals, couples, and families communicate more effectively would suggest that we know a lot about what constitutes good communication, what the essential skills are, and how to resolve conflict. However, knowing how is not the same as implementing the skills in the midst of very intense, intimate, and conflictual conversations. Learning communication skills requires not only knowledge regarding how best to communicate but the ability to implement and use the skills even in the midst of crises. Speaking of marriage and family in general, Solle (2000) states, "marriage isn't at all a game of luck. The research is clear and compelling—marriage is a skill-based relationship." In support of marriage and family education rather than counseling, Solle (2006) comments that in counseling there is "too little emphasis on learning skills. [Counseling is] still more focused on 'internal constructs' . . . 'to know you is to achieve marital success.'" The value of learning skills versus knowing about healthy communication continues to be one of the significant debates in the relationship counseling field.

What is clear is that families need ways to provide safety from external threats and also safety to share pain, fears, and challenges within the family. Creating this safe context will aid families in working through the inevitable crises of life. Identifying and affirming strengths (i.e., communicating), while recognizing vulnerabilities, is a process that fosters resilience.

Contemporary families are in some ways a lot more connected than families of previous generations. Technology has allowed families to stay connected frequently and personally. Not only reading letters but hearing people's voices and seeing their faces on the screen can create a stronger bond. However, there is also an increasing awareness that technology has significant limitations in maintaining and extending attachment dimensions such as affection, touch, and sexual connection.

Berger and Hannah (1999) review a number of empirically validated communication training programs, many of which were developed as psychoeducational programs and later applied to therapeutic contexts. The skills, or "processes," as Walsh (2006) refers to them, typically involve listening, speaking, and facilitation/negotiation skills. While the research is mixed on the effectiveness of these training programs (e.g., see Gottman, 1999, for a critique), it appears that the processes by which people have conversations, especially in intimate relationships, matter immensely to building resilience in family life.

Additional considerations related to strengthening family resilience. There is a need for families to recognize and provide support for members who experience secondary trauma. While a family member may not be a primary victim of trauma, the secondary impact must be considered for anyone who witnesses, helps with, or in some way is affected vicariously by trauma. This is particularly significant for children because adults, in the midst of their efforts to cope, are not always attuned to the impact that seemingly minor components of an event can have on children. Children do not have the sophisticated cognitive abilities of adults and cannot make the distinctions adults make, such as an event being witnessed versus being experienced firsthand.

Another concern in the emerging research pertains to families who are at particularly vulnerable phases of family development. In recent years Gottman and Gottman (2007) have focused on the critical time period for a marriage surrounding the birth of the first child. The research shows that the decline of marital satisfaction commonly experienced at this time sets up patterns for couples that undermine long-term resilience.

Another consideration is the negative chain reactions that heighten risk in the aftermath of a crisis (Wimberly & Wimberly, 2007). The negative context of a crisis can produce an environment that predisposes a family to experience additional strain from further challenges. Buffering the stress effects, cushioning the impact, and overcoming obstacles produced by one crisis helps a family withstand aftershocks and rebound from setbacks.

The emphasis on family resilience may lead to a conclusion that all parts of the family are equally as pivotal in responding to crisis. However, some suggest that the couple subsystem is primary in the family system. Specifically focusing on couple resiliency in the midst of a crisis may be warranted (Phillips & Kane, 2008; Johnson & Faller, 2011). Family systems theorists have long waged this debate—should the focus be the couple or the family? A simple assessment of most families will point to the significant power, resources, and leadership located in the couple/parental subsystem that demands attention and intervention. However, on the flip side is the tendency to undervalue the role that sibling subsystems and even small children can have in helping a family cope.

BUILDING FAMILY RESILIENCE DURING A CRISIS

Opportunities to engage with families often occur during and in the aftermath of a crisis. While we might like to be able to access families prior to crises and help them build resilience, it is more common to be working with a family during a crisis and at the same time building resilience for the future. Walsh (2006) describes the concurrent processes of strengthening family resilience while responding to crisis situations in the following way (see table 8.4).

Table 8.4. The process of strengthening family resilience (Walsh, 2006, p. 162)

Create safety*	Draw on spiritual resources ▶	Introduce possibilities
▼	▲	▼
Instill hope*	Access relational support*	Problem solve together*
▼	▲	▼
Normalize family responses	Build communication*	Integrate experience into family
▼	▲	▼
De-shame ▶	Reframe blame	Stay in touch

*Major contributors to developing family resilience (Thomlison, 2010, p. 40)

The items in the first column of table 8.4 set the context for intervention by creating a safe therapeutic relationship, building positive expectations and capacities for coping, normalizing the family's crisis experience, and decreasing the embarrassment associated with having a crisis and needing to seek help. This is followed by a series of possible interventions aimed at moving beyond blame (either of self or others), developing communication competencies, detailing social-support networks, and drawing on spiritual resources. Finally, the helping process actively focuses on exploring new possibilities for ways of being family, problem solving together, pulling this together into a new experience of being family, and staying in touch both with the helper for follow-up and by checking in with each other so that gains in family functioning do not fade.

In the middle of the process is "access relational support." Of course, relational support can be found within some families and extended families, but for people of faith who have a relationship with a religious community, support can hopefully be found in these relationships. Nason-Clark et al. (2013) discuss how the church and church leaders can work toward strengthening families, as well as proactively working toward ending abuse.

Of course, the process, as with many therapeutic approaches, is a lot easier to describe than to implement. One of the most difficult aspects of this kind of work is dealing with the intense emotion generated by crisis situations both for the family and for the helper. Managing and facilitating the expression of emotion, neither denying nor fixating on the emotion, is a precarious balancing act. Another key distinction is whether the expressed emotion is a signal for further or deeper levels of distress or a part of the healing process and an indication of a beneficial change in the family system.

The emergence of emotionally focused therapy in its individual forms (e.g., Greenberg, 2002; Paivio & Pacual-Leone, 2010), its marital application (e.g., Johnson, 2004), and family variation (Johnson et al., 2005, chap. 11) provides a variety of interventions and a therapeutic process for handling the intensity and range of emotions that can be generated in crisis situations. Dealing with counter-transference and the potential for therapist burnout and vicarious traumatization are other aspects of this difficult work.

CONCLUSION

I appreciate the emphasis of Saxe et al. (2016) in their book on working with child and adolescent trauma victims. Their commitment is to do "whatever-it-takes" (p. 4). Their Trauma Systems Therapy is rooted in the belief that responders and therapists need to be "all in"—"it's about looking at the reality" rather than "averting our eyes" (p. 4). Can Christians, propelled by the love and compassion of Christ, be this for a world of traumatized families?

A systems perspective not only addresses family relationships but also looks at broader systems within society. Of particular concern is the reality that we live in a violent world in which trauma is in some ways the norm, not the exception. Mollica's (2013) *Healing a Violent World Manifesto*, in which trauma is identified as a global reality, suggests that healing is needed not only individually but at all levels of systemic interaction. In this regard I am reminded of the words of one of the grandfathers of family systems theory and therapy, Salvador Minuchin (Minuchin & Nichols, 1993):

> As I see families, I am amazed by the variety of resources people have and the ways they can change—that is, use their resources differently. This means accepting the possibilities and limitations in oneself and in others. It means tolerating

uncertainties and differences. It also means hope—for new ways of being together. This is the song our society needs to hear: the song of me-and-you, the song of the person in context, responsible to and for others. To hear it, we need the courage to renounce the illusion of the autonomous self and to accept the limitations of belonging. The survival of the species as well as the family lies in accommodation and cooperation. A society that undervalues these capacities is a society in danger—and it may well be a dangerous society. (p. 287)

While the idea of limitations in belonging, on both the individual and global levels, may not be a popular message, it is in that very acceptance of possibilities and limitations in self and in others that families find the strength and courage to develop new ways of responding to the traumatic events life brings them.

REFERENCES

Andrews, L. A. (Ed.). (2004). *The family in missions: Understanding and caring for those who serve.* Palmer Lake, CO: Mission Training International.

Balswick, J. O., & Balswick, J. K. (2014). *The family: A Christian perspective on the contemporary home* (4th ed.). Grand Rapids, MI: Baker Academic.

Barrett, M. J. (2009). Healing from relational trauma: The quest for spirituality. In F. Walsh (Ed.), *Spiritual resources in family therapy* (2nd ed., pp. 267-85). New York, NY: Guilford Press.

Benner, D. G. (1998). *Free at last! Breaking the bondage of guilt and emotional wounds.* Belleville, ON: Essence.

Berger, R., & Hannah, M. T. (Eds.). (1999). *Preventive approaches in couples therapy.* Philadelphia, PA: Brunner/Mazel.

Blume, T. W. (2006). *Becoming a family counselor.* Hoboken, NJ: John Wiley.

Boss, P. (2006). *Loss, trauma, and resilience: Therapeutic work with ambiguous loss.* New York, NY: Norton.

Boss, P. (2016). *Family stress management: A contextual approach* (3rd ed.). Thousand Oaks, CA: Sage.

Bowlby, J. (1988). *A secure base: Clinical applications of attachment theory.* New York, NY: Basic Books.

Cassidy, J., & Shaver, P. R. (Eds.). (2008). *Handbook of attachment: Theory, research, and clinical applications* (2nd ed.). New York, NY: Guilford Press.

Castro, C. A., Adler, A. B., & Britt, T. W. (2005). The military family: Common themes and future directions. In T. W. Britt (Ed.), *Military life: The psychology of serving in peace and combat: Vol. 3. The military family* (pp. 245-48). Santa Barbara, CA: Praeger Security International.

Catherall, D. R. (Ed.). (2004). *Handbook of stress, trauma, and the family.* New York, NY: Brunner-Routledge.

Clapp, R. (1993). *Families at the crossroads: Beyond traditional and modern options.* Downers Grove, IL: InterVarsity Press.

Colapinto, J. (1988). Teaching the structural way. In H. A. Liddle, D. C. Breunlin, & R. C. Schwartz (Eds.), *Handbook of family therapy training and supervision* (pp. 17-37). New York, NY: Guilford Press.

Cowan, P. A., & Cowan, C. P. (2012). Normative family transitions, couple relationship quality, and healthy child development. In F. Walsh (Ed.), *Normal family processes* (4th ed., pp. 428-51). New York, NY: Guilford Press.

Everson, R. B., & Figley, C. R. (Eds.). (2010). *Families under fire: Systemic therapy with military families.* New York, NY: Routledge.

Frame, M. W. (2000). Constructing religious/spiritual genograms. In R. E. Watts (Ed.), *Techniques in marriage and family counseling* (Vol. 1, pp. 69-74). Alexandria, VA: American Counseling Association.

Garland, D. E., & Garland, D. R. (2007). *Flawed families of the Bible: How God's grace works through imperfect relationships.* Grand Rapids, MI: Brazos.

Gardano, A. C. (1998). Risk and resiliency factors among culturally diverse families: Implications for family psychopathology. In L. L'Abate (Ed.), *Family psychopathology: The relational roots of dysfunctional behavior* (pp. 94-124). New York, NY: Guilford Press.

Gingrich, F. C. (2016). Assessing families (not just individuals) for missionary service. *Journal of Psychology & Theology, 44,* 329-47.

Goff, B. S. N., & Schwerdtfeger, K. L. (2004). The systemic impact of traumatized children. In D. R. Catherall (Ed.), *Handbook of stress, trauma, and the family* (pp. 179-202). New York, NY: Brunner-Routledge.

Gottman, J. M. (1999). *The marriage clinic: A scientifically based marital therapy.* New York, NY: Norton.

Gottman, J., & Gottman, J. S. (2007). *And baby makes three: The six-step plan for preserving marital intimacy and rekindling romance after baby arrives.* New York, NY: Crown.

Greenberg, L. S. (2002). *Emotion-focused therapy: Coaching clients to work through their feelings.* Washington, DC: American Psychological Association.

Hawkins, S. S., & Manne, S. L. (2004). Family support in the aftermath of trauma. In D. R. Catherall (Ed.), *Handbook of stress, trauma, and the family* (pp. 231-60). New York, NY: Brunner-Routledge.

Heffer, R. W., & Snyder, D. K. (1998). Comprehensive assessment of family functioning. In L. L'Abate (Ed.), *Family psychopathology: The relational roots of dysfunctional behavior* (pp. 207-33). New York, NY: Guilford Press.

Hollander-Goldfein, B., Isserman, N., & Goldenberg, J. (2012). *Transcending trauma: Survival, resilience and clinical implications in survivor families.* New York, NY: Routledge.

Johnson, S. M. (2002). *Emotionally focused couple therapy with trauma survivors: Strengthening attachment bonds.* New York, NY: Guilford Press.

Johnson, S. M. (2004). *The practice of emotionally focused couple therapy: Creating connection* (2nd ed.). New York, NY: Brunner-Routledge.

Johnson, S. M., Bradley, B., Furrow, J., Lee, A., Palmer, G., Tilley, D., & Woolley, S. (2005). *Becoming an emotionally focused therapist: The workbook.* New York, NY: Routledge.

Johnson, S. M., & Faller, G. (2011). Dancing with the dragon of trauma: EFT with couples who stand in harm's way. In J. L. Furrow, S. M. Johnson, & B. Bradley (Eds.), *The emotionally focused casebook: New directions in treating couples* (pp. 165-92). New York, NY: Routledge.

Kilmer, R. P., Gil-Rivas, V., Tedeschi, R. G., & Calhoun, L. G. (Eds.). (2009). *Helping families and communities recover from disaster: Lessons learned from Hurricane Katrina and its aftermath.* Washington, DC: American Psychological Association.

Kiser, L. (2015). *Strengthening family coping resources: Intervention for families impacted by trauma.* New York, NY: Routledge.

Lanktree, C. B., & Briere, J. N. (2016). *Treating complex trauma in children and their families: An integrative approach.* Thousand Oaks, CA: Sage.

Lebow, J., & Rekart, N. K. (2004). Research assessing couple and family therapies for posttraumatic stress disorder. In D. R. Catherall (Ed.), *Handbook of stress, trauma, and the family* (pp. 261-81). New York, NY: Brunner-Routledge.

Lebow, J., & Stroud, C. B. (2012). Assessment of effective couple and family functioning: Prevailing models and instruments. In F. Walsh (Ed.), *Normal family processes* (4th ed., pp. 501-28). New York, NY: Guilford Press.

McGoldrick, M., Giordano, J., & Gracia-Preto, N. (2005). *Ethnicity and family therapy* (3rd ed.). New York, NY: Guilford Press.

McGoldrick, M., Preto, N. A. G., & Carter, B. A. (2015). *The expanding family life cycle: Individual, family and social perspectives* (5th ed.). Upper Saddle River, NJ: Pearson.

McGoldrick, M., & Shibusawa, T. (2012). The family life cycle. In F. Walsh (Ed.), *Normal family processes* (4th ed., pp. 375-98). New York, NY: Guilford Press.

Minuchin, S., & Nichols, M. P. (1993). *Family healing: Strategies for hope and understanding.* New York, NY: Simon & Schuster.

Minuchin, S., Nichols, M. P., & Lee, W. Y. (2006). *Assessing families and couples: From symptom to system.* Boston, MA: Allyn & Bacon.

Mollica, R. F. (2013). *Healing a violent world: Manifesto.* Harvard Program in Refugee Trauma. Retrieved from http://hprt-cambridge.org/wp-content/uploads/2013/05/Manifesto-2013-Final.pdf

Moore, B. A. (Ed.). (2011). *Handbook of counseling military couples.* New York, NY: Routledge.

Nason-Clark, N., Fisher-Townsend, B., & Fahlberg, V. (Eds.). (2013). *Strengthening families and ending abuse: Churches and their leaders look to the future.* Eugene, OR: Wipf and Stock.

O'Donnell, K., & O'Donnell, M. L. (Eds.). (2011). *Global member care: The pearls and perils of good practice.* Pasadena, CA: William Carey Library.

Olson, D. (2011). FACES IV and the Circumplex Model: Validation study. *Journal of Marital and Family Therapy, 37*(1), 64-80. doi:10.1111/j.1752-0606.2009.00175.x

Paivio, S. C., & Pacual-Leone, A. (2010). *Emotion-focused therapy for complex trauma: An integrative approach.* Washington, DC: American Psychological Association.

Phillips, S. B., & Kane, D. (2008). *Healing together: A couple's guide to coping with trauma & post-traumatic stress.* Oakland, CA: New Harbinger.

Price, C. A., Bush, K. R., & Price, S. J. (Eds.). (2016). *Families & change: Coping with stressful events and transitions* (5th ed.). Thousand Oaks, CA: Sage.

Rowland-Klein, D. (2004). The transmission of trauma across generations: Identification with parental trauma in children of holocaust survivors. In D. R. Catherall (Ed.), *Handbook of stress, trauma, and the family* (pp. 117-37). New York, NY: Brunner-Routledge.

Saxe, G. N., Ellis, B. H., & Brown, A. D. (2016). *Trauma systems therapy for children and teens* (2nd ed.). New York, NY: Guilford Press.

Shem, S., & Surrey, J. (1998). *We have to talk: Healing dialogues between women and men.* New York, NY: Basic Books.

Simpson C. L. (2010). Resilience in women sexually abused as children. *Families in Society, 91*(3), 241-47. doi:10.1606/1044-3894.4001

Solary, S., & Westphal, L. (2008). *All God's children* [DVD]. Good Hard Working Productions.

Solle, D. (2000, February 17). Who wants to marry a millionaire? Retrieved from http://lists101.his.com/pipermail/smartmarriages/2000-February/000062.html

Solle, D. (2006, February 28). Rules of engagement. Retrieved from http://lists101.his.com/pipermail/smartmarriages/2006-February/002952.html

Southwick, S. M., & Charney, D. S. (2012). *Resilience: The science of mastering life's greatest challenges.* Cambridge, MA: Cambridge University Press.

Thomlison, B. (2010). *Family assessment handbook: An introduction and practical guide to family assessment* (3rd ed.). Belmont, CA: Brooks/Cole.

Tracy, E. M., & Whittaker, J. K. (1990). The social network map: Assessing social support in clinical practice. *Families in Society, 71,* 461-70.

VanVonderen, J. (2010). *Families where grace is in place: Building a home free of manipulation, legalism, and shame.* Minneapolis, MN: Bethany.

Walsh, F. (2006). *Strengthening family resilience* (2nd ed.). New York, NY: Guilford Press.

Walsh, F. (2009). Integrating spirituality in family therapy: Wellsprings for health, healing, and resilience. In F. Walsh (Ed.), *Spiritual resources in family therapy* (2nd ed., pp. 31-63). New York, NY: Guilford Press.

Walsh, F. (2012a). Family resilience: Strengths forged through adversity. In F. Walsh (Ed.), *Normal family processes* (4th ed., pp. 399-427). New York, NY: Guilford Press.

Walsh, F. (2012b). The spiritual dimension of family life. In F. Walsh (Ed.), *Normal family processes* (4th ed., pp. 347-72). New York, NY: Guilford Press.

Walsh, F. (2016). *Strengthening family resilience* (3rd ed.). New York, NY: Guilford Press.

Wiens, T. W., & Boss, P. (2005). Maintaining family resilience before, during, and after military separation. In T. W. Britt (Ed.), *Military life: The psychology of serving in peace and combat: Vol. 3. The military family* (pp. 13-38). Santa Barbara, CA: Praeger Security International.

Williams, L., Edwards, T. M., Patterson, J., & Chamow, L. (2011). *Essential assessment skills for couple and family therapists.* New York, NY: Guilford Press.

Wimberly, A. E., & Wimberly, E. P. (2007). *The winds of promise: Building and maintaining strong clergy families.* Nashville, TN: Discipleship Resources.

Wolynn, M. (2016). *It didn't start with you: How inherited family trauma shapes who we are and how to end the cycle.* New York, NY: Viking.

Zagelbaum, A., & Carlson, J. (Eds.). (2010). *Working with immigrant families: A practical guide for families.* New York, NY: Routledge.

RESPONDING TO SURVIVORS OF

CLERGY SEXUAL ABUSE

DAVID K. POOLER AND AMANDA FREY

Clergy are capable of hurting the people they are entrusted to pastor and support. While the sexual abuse of children by clergy is understood to be morally wrong, and the lasting and tragic consequences are basically understood, the sexual abuse of adults is not as well comprehended in the church and in society. This chapter will describe clergy sexual misconduct (CSM) and clergy sexual abuse (CSA) of adults, provide an overview of some of the extant literature, and explain ways to effectively work with and provide treatment to the survivor of this type of abuse. In addition, this chapter will help the reader understand the context and complex factors at play in this type of abuse; a robust understanding will help a therapist or counselor validate the experience so that rapport is built with the survivor to establish and maintain a therapeutic relationship that facilitates a healing process.

While perpetrators can be women and victims can be men, because of the patriarchal structure of most religious institutions, by far the majority of religious leaders are male and heterosexual; consequently, most victims of CSA are women, even though it is known that there are female offenders and male victims. CSA is predominantly an issue of female victimization by males in authority because of the gendered nature of religious leadership. Therefore, in this chapter we will be primarily referring to perpetrators as males and victims as females.

Unfortunately, most survivors do not receive support when they report the abuse or seek help (Garland & Argueta, 2011). Crisp (2010) examined what happens to the survivor of CSA and found a culture of silence that female victims experience from their abuser and congregation. Women who gain the courage to disclose their abuse to church authorities or others in the congregation are often further

This research was funded by Grant Me The Wisdom Foundation.

victimized when their stories are discredited. People in the church, including other leaders, can refuse to acknowledge or believe that a trusted clergyperson would violate such boundaries and sexually abuse someone (Crisp, 2010). Instead of supporting the victim by believing that the allegations are true and taking steps to hold the perpetrator accountable for his actions, the congregation essentially ignores the victim, who is often blamed for what happened and forced into silence, while the perpetrator continues performing his regular duties. Survivors report that this lack of belief and validation from the congregation is often more traumatizing than the abuse itself.

CLERGY SEXUAL MISCONDUCT AND CLERGY SEXUAL ABUSE

Clergy sexual misconduct is a term that identifies that an ethical violation occurred and acknowledges the moral dimensions of injury that happen when a clergy person uses his or her position and power to exploit, harm, and sexually abuse a congregant in a fiduciary relationship. A fiduciary relationship is one in which one person places confidence and trust in another with regard to transactions of business. This does not have to be a legally established relationship but can be one of moral or personal responsibility.

Only 13 states and the District of Columbia have in their penal codes provisions for the criminal prosecution of clergy persons who engage in sexual misconduct with adults (Renzetti & Yocum, 2013). Most of these states specify, however, that the misconduct occur specifically in a counseling relationship. One example of a broader statute is found in the Texas penal code, which states that a clergy person commits a nonconsensual sexual assault when he causes "the other person to submit or participate by exploiting the other person's emotional dependency on the clergyman in the clergyman's professional character as spiritual adviser" (Texas Penal Code, Offenses Against the Person, 22.011, Section 10). This broader definition is helpful because CSM is not isolated to formal counseling relationships.

The fact that there are states that criminalize this conduct and behavior suggests a growing awareness of CSM in the United States, but it is still often misunderstood, minimized, and dismissed as simply an affair between two consenting adults. Garland (2006) points out how sexual interaction is never consensual in cases of CSM because of the power differential between a leader and a congregant. She also notes that CSM encompasses sexual harassment, which involves sexualizing conversations with women, touching and hugging women that do not want to be hugged or touched, creating an environment of hostility, pressuring women for sexual involvement, using sexual language and jokes, pressing or rubbing up against a woman, and purposely invading personal space. Essentially, CSM includes any action, words, or behavior of a clergyperson that sexually exploits a congregant.

A related term, *clergy sexual abuse*, identifies the perpetrator's actions and captures the experience from the survivor's perspective. In many ways it is interchangeable with CSM, but CSA acknowledges what happened as abuse and identifies the potential for trauma. The term more accurately accounts for and attests to the experience between the clergyperson and the victim and identifies it not only as misconduct for the clergyperson but abuse for the victim. For the purposes of this chapter, we will use both terms but more frequently will use *clergy sexual abuse* because survivors seeking help and care may experience more validation when their experiences are identified as abuse.

MISUSE OF POWER AND EXPLOITATION OF TRUST

Rutter (1989) identifies a primary underlying component of CSA as the misuse of power. In Western society, there are power imbalances within gender, social roles, and society at large. This power is often enhanced within pastoral roles as these individuals are generally viewed as being messengers sent by God, set apart and often wholly different from congregants (Pooler, 2011). The women Rutter (1989) interviewed stated that this view of authority, coupled with cultural expectations surrounding traditional gender roles, was the reason that they felt the need to be compliant with the sexual demands of their religious leader; any type of refusal would be tantamount to disobedience to God.

Research by Grenz and Bell (2001), Flynn (2003), and Garland and Argueta (2010) supported this awareness that CSA is an abuse of power, which accurately depicts the sexual activity as abuse rather than sexual activity happening between two consenting adults. The power differential between pastor and congregant makes it impossible for a person to give consent even if the survivor reports being a willing participant. Grenz and Bell (2001) noted that pastors are symbols within society that represent trust due to the belief that God specially appoints these leaders. Because of this level of trust, recognizing patterns of behavior that are abusive is difficult, particularly for individuals who are vulnerable and looking for safety, care, and protection from a pastoral figure (Grenz & Bell, 2001).

PREVALENCE OF CSA

Clergy sexual abuse is not a rare or isolated event. Seat, Trent, and Kim (1993) examined sexual encounters that clergy have with congregants. Senior pastors from Southern Baptist churches in Tennessee, North Carolina, Mississippi, Alabama, and Georgia were asked to participate in a survey to capture the prevalence rate of sexual activity with congregants as well as to identify factors that might lead to this happening. One thousand Southern Baptist churches were randomly selected to participate, and 277 male senior pastors responded (Seat et al., 1993).

Of this number, approximately 6% indicated that they had sexual contact with either current or former congregants of their church. A limitation of this study was that perpetrators were asked to self-report, which highlights the probability of underreporting.

A decade later, Thoburn and Whitman (2004) conducted a study examining the same factors. Five hundred male Protestant pastors were randomly selected to participate in a study, and 186 responded (37% response rate). They reported that the primary reason for their sexual abuse of women resulted from marital dissatisfaction and the need to find validation and acceptance from others.

These two studies examined why perpetrators are vulnerable and what percentages of clergy were involved in CSA; however, they did not address how many people are actually abused by clergy. Also, the studies had low response rates (although these are common rates for much social-science survey research), which limits the generalizability of the findings. The following two studies attempt to address prevalence rates.

Stacey, Darnell, and Shupe (2000) and Chaves and Garland (2009) established prevalence rates of CSA by including women in the general population and using methods that are generalizable. Stacey et al. (2000) used United States census tracts in the metropolitan area of Dallas–Fort Worth in 1996 and randomly selected residents to complete a self-administered questionnaire. The researchers were interested in finding out what types of abuse they had experienced by clergy. The respondents were given questionnaires with items that asked about personal, emotional, sexual, and physical abuse by a church leader and whether they knew anyone who had experienced abuse by a church leader. Of the 1,067 participants, 47 (approximately 5%) indicated that they knew someone who personally had experienced some form of abuse by a pastor. Additionally, 29 respondents (approximately 3%) expressed that they had experienced emotional, sexual, or physical abuse by a church leader (Stacey et al., 2000). Of the victims, approximately 23% reported the abuse to religious authorities, while 11% reported the abuse to civil authorities. It is worth noting that this study did not specifically parse out sexual abuse from other forms of clergy abuse.

The best study to date with respect to the percentage of women who experience CSA in a lifetime is a methodologically sound study with results that are generalizable to the adult population of women in the United States. Chaves and Garland (2009) used the General Social Survey and determined that 2.1% of women had been the object of a sexual advance by a church leader in a congregation they were attending. To understand the current impact on congregational life the authors refined the analysis and examined only women ($n = 849$) who regularly attended church (i.e., at least once a month). They found that 3.1% had been the object of sexual advances by a church leader since they were 18. This equates to seven women in the average-size congregation of 400 (assuming that 60% are women) who have experienced clergy sexual misconduct or abuse as adults.

HOW CSA HAPPENS

There have been several theories regarding the causes of CSA. Seat et al. (1993) found that perpetrators reported that the risk that they would commit abuse was greatest at the intersection of high stress, the absence of written guidelines, and the perceived lack of adequate training about clergy sexual abuse. Of the participants who claimed sexual contact with congregants (6%), each one indicated high levels of stress, either marital or work related, and inadequate training relating to transference and countertransference that occurs in counseling sessions, which contributed to the crossing and blurring of sexual boundaries (Seat et al., 1993). Transference happens when clients direct feelings and desires (often unconscious) that are present in a family or intimate relationship toward the therapist or counselor, and countertransference occurs when the counselor directs his or her own feelings and desires (often unresolved) onto the client (Fuertes, Gelso, Owen, & Cheng, 2013). Note that transference and countertransference are not exclusively sexual in nature, but the unfulfilled desires for intimacy are often sexualized in the therapeutic relationship.

Garland and Argueta (2010) report firsthand accounts of survivors of CSA and document five salient contextual factors that contribute to an environment in which this abuse occurs. Two of these factors include congregants collectively overlooking situations that would typically call for action and a culture of "niceness" in congregational life where inappropriate behaviors are ignored or dismissed because no one wants to risk embarrassing or angering an authority figure. Lack of appropriate accountability of church leaders is the third factor, as the leaders or pastors had access to private forms of communication with congregants through cell phones, email, and informal structures in the workplace. Additionally, in 52% of these cases of CSA, the offenders not only were the victims' pastors but also provided counseling. This particular type of dual relationship is very difficult for a congregant to navigate. Lastly, victims placed implicit trust in the church and assumed that its leaders were "safe." The survivors reported that this was one reason why they continued to trust the offenders even when there was evidence that their conduct was abusive and inappropriate (Garland & Argueta, 2010).

CHARACTERISTICS OF PERPETRATORS

Friberg and Laaser (1998) interviewed 25 offenders and determined that some exhibited neurotic, psychotic, or narcissistic personality traits, while others were serial sex offenders, were impulsive professionals, or were ignorant of ethics and boundaries and did not know how to deal with power differentials. Garland and Argueta (2011) also found "features of narcissism" in perpetrators in addition to a "need for affirmation, compulsivity, and sexual and other addictions" (p. 408).

Grenz and Bell (2001) categorized offenders as being Predators, Wanderers, or Lovers. Predators are described as having no moral restrictions and using their position of power to manipulate and use others. The authors indicated that this type of leader is usually charismatic, actively seeks to abuse women, and is often a repeat or serial abuser. The Wanderer does not intentionally seek out women to abuse. For this type of perpetrator, a crisis or life transition leads him to sexualize his own needs or vulnerabilities and to sexually abuse women. Finally, the Lover views himself as being in love with a congregant, even if that woman is married. This type of relationship often begins in counseling sessions where he can offer and receive individual attention from his victim. The fact is that each of these three types exhibits predatory behavior, and there is no difference in impact on the victim. What may differentiate these three is their motivation.

Without question, there is an overlap between the personal characteristics of perpetrators and how CSA happens. The nature of the relationship between personality and the vulnerability to perpetrate, and whether there is some direction of causality, remains open to debate. For example, how a pastoral leader copes with stress, sets boundaries, and understands power may be both a function of personality and a response to environment (including training opportunities; Crisp-Han, Gabbard, & Martinez, 2011). Suffice it to say that there are complex factors that intersect when a pastoral leader abuses a congregant, which we further explore in the next section.

CONGREGATIONAL SYSTEMS AND CONTEXTS

The sexual abuse of a person in a congregation cannot happen in complete isolation; it is not wise to simply view this as only a perpetrator problem. The situation is more complex with many moving parts. Congregations function as systems and have some responsibility in the creation and solution to this problem. Some congregations create an environment that increases the likelihood of abuse happening and diminishes the ability to respond when it does. A systems approach views people as interconnected with each other as every person lives within an environment and interacts with others in that environment (Steinke, 2006). Systems regulate and use information to maintain stability or to make changes. Amplification of information may support change, and suppressing certain ideas maintains the status quo.

For example, a healthy system is one in which there is power sharing through active participation and flow of information (communication). Congregations create an environment where abuse can occur when there is little or no power sharing, communication is one-way, and all authority (and trust) is given to a leader (Pooler, 2011). Signs that such an environment potentially exists are comments from members of a congregation such as "Our pastor is above reproach," "We don't have problems of clergy sexual abuse here," or "That would never happen here"; by blindly or naively assuming that a pastor is not capable of harming someone, the conditions are set for CSA to occur (Oxford, 2012).

Additionally, a healthy congregation is able to respond appropriately when clergy sexual abuse happens by using the resources and strengths of the people within the church to address the conflict that has been created. Steinke (2006) suggests that congregations are at risk when conflict or disturbances arise because of abuse and too much focus is placed on the clergy (or victim) rather than the people of the church (and its mission) and when congregants take sides with whoever is involved in the conflict. Taking sides pits people against one another and often cultivates blame. Blame discharges pain but does little else. And congregation members need to collectively move through the aftermath of clergy-perpetrated abuse. Taking sides may feel right but will only gloss over the reality of the pain and grief that will need to be experienced by all for healing to occur.

Lastly, a congregation that is open to conversations around sex and sexuality can foster more awareness of the nature of sexual feelings or temptation, boundaries, how to have healthy connections and accountability, and how to balance appropriate closeness and distance (Grenz and Bell, 2001; Sperry, 2003; Trull and Carter, 2004). Congregations that cannot or will not have such conversations place themselves at risk to be shocked and ill-equipped when problems arise in this domain.

THE DYNAMICS OF VICTIMS' EXPERIENCES

In this section we highlight excerpts of stories from survivors to provide an understanding of the unique context of CSA. Working effectively with survivors of CSA requires a deep appreciation for the complexity of how the abuse happens in the church and how that affects the survivor's traumatic experience. For this reason we include salient experiences of survivors who participated in a research study we conducted. We interviewed 27 adult women who survived sexual abuse by a church leader. They were between the ages of 25 and 65, most were white ($n = 25$), and the abuse lasted an average of four years. Denominations represented in this sample include Eastern Orthodox, Christian Reformed, Baptist, Seventh-day Adventist, Assemblies of God, Lutheran, Episcopal, Methodist, and nondenominational. While each survivor is unique, there are some common themes that we outline in broad strokes with quotes from the interviewees as examples.

The typical process. Most often, prior to the first incident of CSA, a congregant seeks pastoral support because of a need or personal vulnerability (recent loss, marital problems, past abuse, depression, etc.). The pastoral leader identifies this vulnerability and suggests that they work on it together. They might meet in a formal counseling relationship, but many times it is an informal context and framed as discipleship, spiritual advisement, or even just friendship. As the relationship progresses and deepens, the leader sexually advances.

This abuse does not happen suddenly or quickly; it is frequently months and most often years in the making. The leader may use Bible verses, religious language, spiritual admonitions, sexual talk, and touch (e.g., frequent hugs, prolonged hugs), or make invitations to be together to break down barriers and boundaries and to persuade the victim that she is important and that sexual touch is acceptable (or even sanctioned by God) in the relationship. Many perpetrators do this even when the victim has a spouse and the spouse is aware of the time spent together. Bear in mind that for many victims this took many months and many encounters of gradual boundary crossing and blurring before any sexual activity took place. Eventually sexual activity becomes more overt, which can include any or all of the following: touching sexual organs (over or under clothing), kissing, oral sex, masturbation, intercourse, or rape. This list is not exhaustive. Even a highly erotic relationship in which there is sexual talk but no touch is abusive and damaging and is a form of CSA. The abuse may occur frequently or infrequently, but it is rare for there to be only one instance.

It is common for the victim to be blamed by the perpetrator. For a time there is no obvious talk of blame, and the victim is made to feel important and special, and the perpetrator subtly works to make the victim think she is complicit in what is happening. However, at the point at which the perpetrator begins to notice that the victim is getting uncomfortable and starts to question what is happening or to talk about it being wrong, the dynamic and conversation changes. The victim is told, "Think of the greater good," "Let's not harm the church or my reputation," or "If this becomes known and people leave the faith, it is your fault." The perpetrator uses guilt or shame to silence the victim and persuade her to not report. By using shame and persuasion to silence and pacify the victim, the perpetrator maintains access to the victim out of a pervasive need to be sexual again with her. Be aware that this cycle is enormously difficult for the victim. In her inner world she vacillates between feeling special and important to the pastor (often spiritually) and feeling confused, dazed, and perplexed, struggling to trust herself in the process. It may feel somewhat okay in the beginning but over time becomes so toxic it becomes unbearable. Eventually, the truth becomes known, either because the survivor reports it or someone else finds out. At this point the blaming and shaming come on like a torrent.

It is also at this point that the victim begins to interact with congregation members, other church leaders (denominational leaders), and even the perpetrator, but now in public with the abuse known. It is these interactions that are absolutely critical to the course and outcome of the survivor's journey. Unfortunately, a common response from the church is disbelief, invalidation, and blame.

Invalidation. Thirty-three percent of the women (9 of the 27 participants) were *not believed*, and their stories were invalidated by the congregation or other church leaders. For example, Whitney stated, "I tried to report to the different churches where he [referring to her perpetrator] was serving, but nobody wanted to hear it. Some dismissed it as, well that was a long time ago—maybe you don't remember correctly. And others were like, no, no, no; not him—he would never." Another survivor explained, "They [referring to denominational leaders] really believed the pastor on the first round until they got the second complaint, and then they realized that he had duped them and lied to them in many, many, many different ways."

Blame or punishment. Forty-four percent were blamed or punished for the abuse by their church or by other leaders within the church or denomination. For instance, one survivor said, "I was viewed as a villain. . . . They [referring to church leaders] really kept people from coming to me . . . to bridge the gap. . . . They told me I was not allowed to communicate with, like, specifically the staff and people who I was really close to." Another survivor lamented, "And they [referring to church leaders] were trying to tell me I couldn't use my voice . . . and that I was responsible for what happened to me and it was adultery. And by not accepting that it was adultery, I was being unrepentant."

Lack of support. The bystanders frequently chose the perpetrator's side (sometimes viewing the perpetrator as the victim). Painful looks, avoidance, and disgust were common responses to the victim from others in the church. The supportive community that victims once knew eventually disappeared. Most victims bought the narrative that they were at fault somehow and must have done something wrong. So there is a dual trauma at this point: invalidation and blame coming from internal cognitions (hearing the voice of the perpetrator and their own voice) and hearing the voices coming from the system around them. This is a truly infuriating and painful journey. Many survivors reported being excluded and marginalized from their church community to the point they felt compelled to leave. There was no acknowledgment of wrong, they received no support socially, and they reported an utter aloneness.

Isolation. Forty-eight percent of the women stated that they felt isolated from their church community once the abuse was reported within the church. For example, Cassandra stated:

We [referring to herself and her husband] tried to go back and restore relationships and try to, you know, have some healing but, ugh, after 18 months . . . I couldn't do it anymore because everybody was just ignoring me. People would look away. People would walk away. They would see me coming, they would go a different way so they wouldn't have to be in front of me and it was just too painful. . . . I couldn't heal because I was being ignored and not accepted. Being made to feel like I was the evil one.

Another survivor said, "By the time I told, oh I guess, four or five people, bad things started happening . . . the ostracism, the shunning, you know. It's not like I had a dead dog left on my doorstep or anything, and my house wasn't set on fire, but the ostracism started and it just, it, all of a sudden I realized I was, I was being enormously shut out."

Lucy was purposefully blamed and excluded from her community and stated:

And after ten months, um, the pastor contacted me, friendly, chipper . . . [the pastor asked], "Well, we're all wondering if you wanted to move your membership." At that point, I had gone through so much trauma, so much change, it was like this comforting thing to think, that's one root [the congregational connection] that I haven't had to . . . sever. [And I told him] I really didn't want to change my membership. I haven't found a local church out here that I wanted to move it to. And his reaction was, "Well, you know, it probably would be easier if we went ahead and did that, and, um, by the way, just to be able to do that, we probably need to put your name under church discipline." And I said, "Discipline? Why should you discipline me?" And he said, "Well, you know, so that people don't talk."

Karen was pointedly silenced: "Well the one time that they [referring to church leaders] . . . sent someone from the senate to come out and talk to me and that's when he told me I shouldn't say anything."

Relationship with God. A layer of trauma that is difficult to describe is how the victim's relationship with God is affected. One survivor wished that "people understood the, you know, the spiritual crisis, just my own work of getting to God with my own problem. You know, there was so many compounded things that it is just the grace of Jesus that I'm standing." Therefore, to aid the reader, we define two concepts that may be particularly salient to help frame the nature of relationship trauma and how relationships (including God) are affected; these are moral injury and betrayal trauma.

Certain experiences more than others cause a type of "moral" harm. Shay (2014) says moral injury happens when "1) there has been betrayal of what is right 2) by someone who holds legitimate authority 3) in a high stakes situation" (p. 183). Shay goes on to say that the physical body codes such experiences in the same way it would a physical attack. Clergy sexual abuse clearly encompasses the first two criteria, betrayal by a trusted authority. What might be argued is the stakes. We would suggest the stakes really are high because of the vulnerability or need of the person under the care of the pastor and how the pastor in his role is a representative of God. Blinka and Harris (2016) clarify that the source of this kind of injury is people's failing to prevent, bearing witness to, or participating in acts that transgress the victim's deeply held moral beliefs.

Betrayal trauma is a related concept and "occurs when the people or institutions on which a person depends for survival violate that person in a significant way" (Freyd, DePrince, & Gleaves, 2007, p. 297). Betrayal trauma is human relationship trauma. Research found that betrayal trauma is associated with posttraumatic stress disorder (PTSD) symptom severity, specifically avoidance and numbing (Kelley, Weathers, Mason, & Pruneau, 2012). A survivor of clergy-perpetrated sexual abuse has survived an individual- and institutional-level betrayal, and the impact cannot be underestimated.

Linda captures this well:

> [Speaking about the church's response:] I know that they haven't ever walked this way before, and they didn't know what they were doing, and that's been a real source of my forgiveness . . . just Father forgive them they don't know what they are doing. . . . The way they have shut me down and shut me out, relationally, and emotionally, and every other connected way . . . has been pretty devastating . . . arguably as devastating or more devastating than the actual abuse. . . . I don't believe that my church meant to re-victimize me, but that is what they did, because they didn't understand what happened.

In summary, we are suggesting that a survivor of clergy sexual abuse will have to work through the betrayal that occurred by accepting how the trauma affected their perception, experience, and ability to trust in God and others. They will need help with radical acceptance of the world as it is, because many of their fundamental assumptions about God and the church may have been undermined by the abuse and betrayal. What is also noteworthy is how resilient many survivors are and how they allow what happened to them to bring them to a place of humility and openness. Julia said it this way: "I was just ripped open. My life was in shreds. I was, you know, I had, there was nothing. I had no dignity. There was nothing left. I had nothing. I was as low as you could get and nothing left to lose. And so in that sense, I guess I was a prime candidate for therapy."

COUNSELING THE SURVIVOR OF CSA

In this section we describe best practices for working with survivors of CSA. Counseling survivors of CSA shares many of the same dynamics as counseling other trauma survivors (see chaps. 10 and 11 in this volume). However, what we have discovered to be of crucial importance when counseling a survivor of CSA is for the therapist to be able to understand and validate what actually happened and to call it abuse. While this is true for many victims of abuse, it is even more crucial in this case because of the societal and ecclesiastical resistance to believing this can happen in the church. To do this counselors need a conceptual framework for talking about the abuse of power, they should understand betrayal trauma, and they must have a robust understanding of congregational life and theological language. This awareness allows therapists to have a highly nuanced validating response that is realistic and helpful.

Engagement and assessment. Whether an event is experienced as a trauma is less about the circumstances and more about a person's attachment, coping skills, emotional regulation skills, and support system, or said simply, it is about her unique view and experience of what happened (Blaustein & Kinniburgh, 2010). People seeking help are those whose experience of abuse flooded their ability to manage it or cope with it. Therefore, in order to move into the counseling process, a survivor of CSA needs to be engaged in the process, and she will need the therapist to be grounded and present in the room.

A thorough social-history assessment should be conducted with special attention to family of origin functioning, identity development, the spiritual and religious experiences the person has had prior to the abuse (positive, helpful, damaging, etc.), and how she experiences God now. Gaining an awareness of how the person currently views self, God, and others is critical to understanding her functioning and why she came to see you. It is important to identify any previous trauma or vulnerabilities underneath or connected to the current trauma and to determine how the person copes with stress, emotional disturbance, and loss (grief). Therefore, pay attention to attachment disruptions, early childhood trauma, and any addictive or compulsive behaviors (e.g., eating, cutting) or misuse of substances. Also examine all current sources of social support and the quality and magnitude of this support especially from a congregation. In your assessment you will need to elicit all the details of the survivor's abuse story, thoroughly validating and pointing out the multiple layers of trauma that have occurred.

Believe and validate. Believe the survivor's story. An indifferent or questioning initial response is not helpful. It is critical that she is wholly believed and validated. In our study, most participants (89%) stated that having someone listen to and believe their story was instrumental to their healing. For instance, Sarah said, "We just want to be believed. We want to be believed, and while it's hard to believe that a pastor would act so selfishly, they do." Another survivor stated, "We met with the individual churches' executive committee, and they let us tell our stories and they were extremely supportive. And that was life-changing for me . . . to finally be able to say, 'This is what he did to me,' and have them respond, being supportive, believing me, [and] being angry at him . . . that was extremely supportive."

The survivor may not know how to define and describe what has happened to her or even label what happened as abuse. She may come in reporting, "I had an affair with my pastor," because that is what she has been told. It is important to name what happened as abuse and let the survivor know it was not her fault. She may need permission and help to talk about the ways the perpetrator groomed or conditioned her (e.g., sexual talk, flirting, special meetings, use of Scripture) to exploit her vulnerability. Also be aware that the survivor may have very conflicted feelings about the perpetrator. She may talk about the hurt, pain, and betrayal and at the same time identify powerful feelings of love or connection and even express loyalty to him (Carnes, 1997). Helping the survivor label, identify, and understand what has happened will start the neurobiological process of moving traumatic material from her limbic system (emotions, body) to her frontal cortex, where she can process it and start to make the cognitive shift to understand that what happened is about an abusive leader (and poorly equipped system) and not about her (Lee & Cuijpers, 2013).

Presenting problems. Types of presenting problems or complaints may consist of grief reactions, God/faith concerns, flashbacks, disturbing memories, trouble sleeping, suicidal ideation, depression or mood problems, anxiety, sexual problems, eating disorders, compulsive and addictive behavior (including sexual), relationship conflicts, marital or family problems, and vocational problems. Some common diagnoses may include PTSD, anxiety disorders, depressive disorders, or addictive disorders.

Stabilization and resource building. How quickly someone can process trauma depends on how stable they are and how many internal resources they can access during the session. Or to put it in question form, can the client modulate her affect, appropriately self-soothe, and stay present with the disturbing traumatic material without dissociating? Dissociative clients may not be able to stick with the pain, or they may figuratively fall off into the pain and be treading water. Indication that the latter is happening is rumination or "getting stuck" in overwhelming sadness or anger that is not dissipating or fading with exposure and time. Clients in this place may also be functioning out of a small or powerless ego state. It is important to remind the survivor that the abuse is over and that there is a capable adult part of her that she can access (Foa, Hembree, & Olasov, 2007).

When a client dissociates while talking about the abuse, you may need to spend some time helping her increase distress tolerance, help her identify emotions, reinforce her self-esteem, and help her enhance boundaries. In the session you can also let the client know she is not alone, or you may encourage dual attention (i.e., remembering both the abuse and that she is present in the room right now; Foa et al., 2007; see also chap. 11 of this volume). This can lower the volume or intensity of her pain. You might use mindfulness techniques to help her develop more comfort with her body, emotions, and negative thoughts—to just notice what is there, in a safe place (Luedtke, Davis, & Monson, 2015).

The quality of the therapeutic relationship is one of the most important factors in helping the client feel safe. In order for CSA survivors to start healing, they must have an experience of safety. They need a place where the defense formed by the chronic hyperarousal from the trauma can be turned off. It is important to say here that the gender of the therapist may or may not be of concern to the client. In our conversations with survivors we have found that it may indeed be helpful for a female survivor to have a male therapist with whom they can work through the abuse and betrayal they experienced by a man. To have a male therapist who believes and validates the female survivor can be very therapeutic. Other times a survivor may ask to work with a female; be sensitive and aware of these concerns. When the client can stay present with her story and the painful memories, feel emotions, calm herself, and let herself be soothed, she is ready for the trauma work (Ford, Courtois, Steele, van der Hart, & Nijenhuis, 2005).

The client must be met and accepted where she is, and the therapist will need to move at her pace. Acceptance, validation, and attenuation to shame will be crucial to the foundation of safety that is necessary for healing to happen. In each session, examine readiness and motivation to do the hard work and give her feedback about what you see. Major resistance from a client suggests that you are moving faster than she is able to go (Miller & Rollnick, 2012).

Decreasing emotional reactivity. People experience relief from trauma when there is a cognitive home for what happened or when the memories are stored and accessed in ways that are adaptive, useful, and helpful. Trauma-focused cognitive behavioral therapy, prolonged exposure therapy, and eye movement desensitization and reprocessing (Cisler et al., 2015; Kumpula et al., 2016; Lee & Cuijpers, 2013) are three effective interventions to treat a CSA survivor. These therapies are effective at moving material from the limbic system through the hippocampus and to the frontal cortex, where the disturbance is transformed and stored in existing adaptive cognitive maps (van der Kolk, 2014). If the CSA survivor is also a survivor of child abuse, and/or if they have dissociative parts, treatment approaches geared toward resolving complex trauma may be more applicable (see chaps. 10 and 11 in this volume).

Over the process of therapy, clients can lose the powerful negative emotional reactivity and the uncomfortable bodily sensations present when thinking about the memories and slowly make a shift to an undisturbed and adaptive state when recalling the memories. They can come to understand that a very sick or predatory person exploited a vulnerability to fill up something lacking in himself or to have control or power. In other words, a client can come to realize that it was about the pastor and had nothing to do with her, other than there was something about her that he exploited.

This shifting in perspective happens as the sting and pain of the trauma is decreased. Part of the sting and what causes so much pain is the negative belief that survivors have about themselves (e.g., this was my fault, I'm powerless, I did something wrong, I'm a bad person). Cognitions tend not to change until the emotional pain is relieved. When the therapist gives space for the client to experience, feel, and talk about the pain, the pain is no longer avoided and the trauma can be digested (Foa et al., 2007). Once the trauma is digested, the client tends to develop new insights, and positive cognitions often follow. The new cognitive framework develops around an understanding that the client did not do something wrong and it is not her fault. This allows the client to draw from her past experience so that she has the emotional and cognitive resources in the moment to cope with present challenges.

Meaning making. It is important to help a client make meaning of what happened and find purpose for her existence and the struggle (Marotta-Walters, 2015). A part of making meaning is finding a place for the memories of the abuse where the person can access the experience through the lens of an adaptive, resilient survivor. Working through trauma is not about forgetting it but about integrating it into one's life. Many survivors find it helpful and healing to find outlets in which to share their stories or make regular connections with other survivors. Having such conversations is important as counselees grieve, learn to live with what they have lost, and engage others in healing and helpful ways.

Part of the survivor's journey of acceptance, understanding, and eventually meaning making involves grieving. Grieving is about adjusting to what is, rather than what one wishes life would be like. This is another place where a client will need validation. The church might not feel safe anymore—that is her new reality. Church leaders might not be able to be trusted very easily—that is her new reality. In fact, a survivor of CSA may have some of the most honest and realistic views of the institution of the church. It is important to validate her perspective.

DEVELOPING HEALTHY SPIRITUALITY AND RELATIONSHIPS

Survivors are resilient; the survivors we interviewed reported getting better. However, they need others to help them grow and heal. Support from friends and family is essential to making meaning, healing, and learning to live with what happened. Survivors may need assistance navigating relationships or encouragement to make changes in how they get support. Their spiritual experiences will frequently be mediated through the relationships they have. When we asked survivors about what helped them most in their journey of healing, 30% of participants stated that family support was crucial. For instance, Mary Anne stated, "I have a . . . sister and mom that has been . . . a wonderful support." Dolores said, "My kids were all, you know, very supportive. They stuck with me. And they came to church meetings and everything that the church was having at the time. Um, you know, they supported me, but I mean, I was a wreck. Um, but I had them to support me."

In addition to family support, 59% of participants stated that they received spousal support after the abuse was reported. Sally said, "The support of my husband was, that is probably for me the biggest healing, having the support of my husband." Mary Anne said, "My husband has been a living example of how Jesus forgives us. And he's probably been the most important factor in the healing process."

Most of the women in our study (85%) indicated that they received social support within or outside their church community once the abuse was reported. One survivor shared, "And it was one of those moments where my heart just dropped, and instead what they did [referring to a specific group of friends], they basically hugged me, welcomed me. . . . It made a huge difference of that acceptance." Whitney stated, "What was most helpful was women who just recognized that I was kind of a misfit or outcast or socially awkward or whatever it was they thought about me and they just stood with me or sat with me. They allowed themselves to be physically present."

Other survivors found a support group or network helpful to their healing process. For example, Joy said:

> Within the church, what was most helpful was ending up as an adult in a group in a, basically a church-run 12-step program where they didn't focus on a specific drug or that kind of thing but more on the idea that all of us have issues in life. . . . Literally, we went through the 12 steps. We acknowledged that we were powerless over our different reactions and insecurities and hang-ups that we have in life and we went through every week meeting, and we'd meet like in a whole group first and then separate into men and women.

Affirming the power of support, Cassandra stated, "For me, just learning that you know, I'm not crazy. This wasn't my fault. Learning this stuff on the Hope of Survivors website about how this wasn't my fault and how this was a complete abuse of power and authority. That's helped me the most."

In addition to support networks and support groups, 81% of participants stated that having a professional counselor was helpful to their healing. One survivor said, "I found a Christian sexual-abuse counselor who's been phenomenal. And so that's been huge." Sarah stated, "I went to therapy. I went the more traditional route, and to talk about it was very helpful."

In the client's healing journey, she needs healthy relationships so that she can trust herself, God, and others to navigate and cope with life's stressors. As you can see from the stories, multiple sources of social support are critical, and this includes the therapist. Recovery is evident when a client has adequate functioning and effective coping strategies to navigate the dimensions of her life (e.g., relationships, church, work). A client is healing when she can make meaning of what has happened to her, has a true reservoir from which to freely give to others without demands or unrealistic expectations, and has found the space for her past abuse experience to be understood and integrated.

CONCLUSION

We know trauma happens when a situation overwhelms a person's ability to cope and leaves the person fearing great harm. The circumstances of the event often include abuse of power, betrayal of trust, entrapment, helplessness, pain, confusion, or loss. Clergy sexual abuse may include every single one of the above causes of trauma. CSA is damaging because it is often complicated by wholly inadequate institutional and societal responses; these poor responses exacerbate and confound the initial trauma. The layers of trauma are summarized as follows:

- First layer: A person seeks help from a pastoral leader out of a current vulnerability, and that vulnerability is exploited and the person is robbed and betrayed by the leader through sexual abuse.

- Second layer: The person tells the truth and is not believed.

- Third layer: The victim is blamed by the perpetrator and bystanders.

- Fourth layer: The primary social support system (the congregation) betrays the survivor.

- Fifth layer: The victim's relationship with God is affected.

- Sixth layer: Help is sought outside the church, and the professional may not be competent to address this type of abuse.

While not every survivor who seeks help is met with an incompetent professional, it does happen. It is worth noting that there are professionals who do not understand clergy sexual abuse and who inflict further harm by labeling the experience as an affair. Such previous experiences with mental health professionals may be a part of the client's story. In order to effectively treat survivors of CSA, a clinician must be aware of the multiple layers of betrayal and hurt a survivor might carry into the room.

Effectively working with a survivor of CSA is primarily about the therapist's ability to frame the experience appropriately by listening, believing, and validating. An important aspect of listening and believing involves understanding power differentials so that this type of behavior can be labeled as it truly is: abuse, not an affair. Clinicians in particular should know about resources for survivors in order to effectively support them, their families, congregations, and even church leaders (e.g., The Hope of Survivors [www.thehopeofsurvivors.com]; FaithTrust Institute [www.faithtrustinstitute.org]; Survivors Network of those Abused by Priests [SNAP; www.snapnetwork.org]; Faithful and True [www.faithfulandtrue.com]). For additional scholarly sources, there is a three-part annotated bibliography that is regularly updated (Evinger, 2016).

Be aware that the work with survivors can interface with the criminal justice system, as criminal charges may be filed against the perpetrator, and the victim may be asked to testify. As survivors heal, they may develop the courage to report to church authorities or talk to a district attorney, and they will need help navigating these processes, which can be daunting.

Survivors of CSA have much to teach all of us about how to have congregations that are safe in which people can flourish. They also are a repository of wisdom about how to heal, how to develop boundaries, and how to understand and live out the journey from victim to survivor with authenticity.

REFERENCES

Blaustein, M., & Kinniburgh, K. (2010). *Treating traumatic stress in children and adolescents: How to foster resilience through attachment, self-regulation, and competency.* New York, NY: Guilford Press.

Blinka, D., & Harris, H. W. (2016). Moral injury in warriors and veterans: The challenge to social work. *Social Work & Christianity, 43*(3), 7-27.

Carnes, P. (1997). *The betrayal bond: Breaking free of exploitative relationships.* Deerfield Beach, FL: Health Communications.

Chaves, M., & Garland, D. (2009). The prevalence of clergy sexual advances toward adults in their congregations. *Journal for the Scientific Study of Religion, 48*(4), 817-24. doi:10.1111/j.1468-5906.2009.01482.x

Cisler, J. M., Sigel, B. A., Kramer, T. L., Smitherman, S., Vanderzee, K., Pemberton, J., & Kilts, C. D. (2015). Amygdala response predicts trajectory of symptom reduction during Trauma-Focused Cognitive-Behavioral Therapy among adolescent girls with PTSD. *Journal of Psychiatric Research, 71*, 33-40. doi:10.1016/j.jpsychires.2015.09.011

Crisp, B. R. (2010). Silence and silenced: Implications for the spirituality of survivors of sexual abuse. *Feminist Theology, 18*(3), 277-92. doi:10.1177/0966735009360386

Crisp-Han, H., Gabbard, G. O., & Martinez, M. (2011). Professional boundary violations and mentalizing in the clergy. *Journal of Pastoral Care & Counseling, 65*(3), 1-11. Retrieved from http://tinyurl.com/ok6dasp

Evinger, J. S. (2016). *Annotated bibliography of clergy sexual abuse and sexual boundary violations in religious communities* (29th revision). Retrieved from www.faithtrust institute.org/resources/bibliographies/clergy-sexual-abuse

Flynn, K. A. (2003). *The sexual abuse of women by members of the clergy.* Jefferson, NC: McFarland.

Foa, E. B., Hembree, E. A., & Olasov, R. B. (2007). *Prolonged exposure therapy for PTSD: Emotional processing of traumatic experiences: Therapist guide.* New York, NY: Oxford University Press.

Ford, J. D., Courtois, C. A., Steele, K., van der Hart, O., & Nijenhuis, E. R. S. (2005). Treatment of complex posttraumatic self-dysregulation. *Journal of Traumatic Stress, 18*(5), 437-47.

Freyd, J. J., DePrince, A. P., Gleaves, D. H. (2007). The state of betrayal trauma theory: Reply to McNally—conceptual issues and future directions. *Memory, 15,* 295-311.

Friberg, N., & Laaser, M. R. (1998). *Before the fall: Preventing pastoral sexual abuse.* Collegeville, MN: Liturgical Press.

Fuertes, J. N., Gelso, C. J., Owen, J. J., & Cheng, D. (2013). Real relationship, working alliance, transference/countertransference and outcome in time-limited counseling and psychotherapy. *Counselling Psychology Quarterly, 26*(3-4), 294-312. doi:10.1080/09515070.2013.845548

Garland, D. (2006). When wolves wear shepherds' clothing: Helping women survive clergy sexual abuse. *Journal of Religion & Abuse, 8*(2), 37-70. doi:10.1300/J154v08n02_04

Garland, D. R., & Argueta, C. (2010). How clergy sexual misconduct happens: A qualitative study of first-hand accounts. *Social Work & Christianity, 37*(1), 1-27. Retrieved from www.nacsw.org.ezproxy.baylor.edu/member/Publications/49981821.pdf

Garland, D. R., & Argueta, C. A. (2011). Unholy touch: Church leaders and sexual misconduct with adults. In C. Franklin & R. Fong (Eds.), *The church leaders' counseling resource book* (pp. 405-16). New York, NY: Oxford University Press.

Grenz, S. J., & Bell, R. D. (2001). *Betrayal of trust: Confronting and preventing clergy sexual misconduct* (2nd ed.). Grand Rapids, MI: Baker Books.

Kelley, L. P, Weathers, F. W., Mason, E. A., & Pruneau, G. M. (2012). Association of life threat and betrayal with posttraumatic stress disorder symptom severity. *Journal of Traumatic Stress, 24,* 408-15.

Kumpula, M. J., Pentel, K. Z., Foa, E. B., LeBlanc, N. J., Bui, E., McSweeney, L. B., . . . Rauch, S. A. (2017). Temporal sequencing of change in posttraumatic cognitions and

PTSD symptom reduction during prolonged exposure therapy. *Behavior Therapy, 48*(2), 156-165. doi: 10.1016/j.beth.2016.02.008

Lee, C.W., & Cuijpers, P. (2013). A meta-analysis of the contribution of eye movements in processing emotional memories. *Journal of Behavior Therapy and Experimental Psychiatry, 44,* 231-39.

Luedtke, B., Davis, L., & Monson, C. (2015). Mindfulness-based cognitive-behavioral conjoint therapy for posttraumatic stress disorder: A case study. *Journal of Contemporary Psychotherapy, 45*(4), 227-34. doi:10.1007/s10879-015-9298-z

Marotta-Walters, S. (2015). Spiritual meaning making following clergy-perpetrated sexual abuse. *Traumatology, 21*(2), 64-70.

Miller, W. R., & Rollnick, S. (2012). *Motivational interviewing: Preparing people for change* (3rd ed.). New York, NY: Guilford Press.

Oxford, L. K. (2012). What healthy churches do to protect vulnerable others and prevent clergy sexual misconduct. *Family and Community Ministries, 25*(1), 81-107.

Pooler, D. K. (2011). Pastors and congregations at risk: Insights from role identity theory. *Pastoral Psychology, 60*(5), 705-12.

Renzetti, C., & Yocum, S. (2013). *Clergy sexual abuse: Social science perspectives.* Boston, MA: Northeastern University Press.

Rutter, P. (1989). *Sex in the forbidden zone: When men in power—therapists, doctors, clergy, teachers, and others—betray women's trust.* Los Angeles, CA: Jeremy P. Tarcher.

Seat, J. T., Trent, J. T., & Kim, J. K. (1993). The prevalence and contributing factors of sexual misconduct among Southern Baptist pastors in six southern states. *Journal of Pastoral Care, 47*(4), 363-70.

Shay, J. (2014). Moral injury. *Journal of Psychoanalytic Psychology, 31*(2), 182-91.

Sperry, L. (2003). *Sex, priestly ministry, and the church.* Collegeville, MN: Liturgical Press.

Stacey, W. A., Darnell, S. E., & Shupe, A. (2000). How much clergy malfeasance is really out there? A victimization survey of prevalence and perceptions. In A. Shupe, W. A. Stacey, & S. E. Darnell (Eds.), *Bad pastors: Clergy misconduct in modern America* (pp. 187-213). New York: New York University Press.

Steinke, P. L. (2006). *Healthy congregations: A systems approach* (2nd ed.). Herndon, VA: Alban Institute.

Thoburn, J., & Whitman, D. M. (2004). Clergy affairs: Emotional investment, longevity of relationship and affair partners. *Pastoral Psychology, 52*(6), 491-506. doi:10.1023/B:PASP.0000031528.62048.8b

Trull, J. E., & Carter, J. E. (2004). *Ministerial ethics: Moral formation for church leaders* (2nd ed.). Grand Rapids, MI: Baker Academic.

van der Kolk, B. A. (2014). *The body keeps the score: Brain, mind, and body in the healing of trauma.* New York, NY: Viking.

PART THREE

COMPLEX TRAUMA

AND

DISSOCIATION

BEYOND SURVIVAL:
APPLICATION OF A COMPLEX
TRAUMA TREATMENT MODEL IN
THE CHRISTIAN CONTEXT

JANA PRESSLEY AND JOSEPH SPINAZZOLA

A growing body of literature addresses trauma, spirituality, religious coping, and posttraumatic growth, with helpful delineation between adaptive and maladaptive religious coping practices (Chan & Rhodes, 2013; Gerber, Boals, & Schuettler, 2011; ter Kuile & Ehring, 2014; Thomas & Savoy, 2014). However, there is a more complicated relationship in the literature when specifically considering *complex trauma* and spirituality (Connor, Davidson, & Lee, 2003; Pargament, 2008; Walker, Reid, O'Neill, & Brown, 2009). Although research findings have identified that engagement in religious/spiritual practices can serve to insulate both acute and complex trauma survivors from negative psychological outcomes (Marriott, Hamilton-Giachritsis, & Harrop, 2014; Walker, McGregor, Quagliana, Stephens, & Knodel, 2015), other studies have found that complex trauma significantly disrupts the spiritual well-being of individuals in a way that is distinct from acute/situational trauma (Maltby & Hall, 2012; Van Deusen & Courtois, 2015). Some of the experiences noted in these studies include lower existential well-being, difficulty with belief or trust in a benevolent God or a caring community, projection of a negative parental image onto the image of God, feelings of shame and unworthiness, and religious strain. These findings lend support to the contention that "adversely affected belief systems" (Cloitre et al., 2012, p. 4) are one of the six core areas of functional disturbance occasioned by exposure to complex trauma.

Adapted from Pressley, J., & Spinazzola, J. (2015), Beyond survival, *Journal of Psychology & Theology*, 43, 8-22. Used with permission.

Given the complexities of addressing trauma within a religious context, various authors (Bryant-Davis & Wong, 2013; Walker & Aten, 2012) have encouraged the academic community to participate in collaborative scholarship combining best practice trauma-informed treatment with the psychology of religion in order to enhance clinical care that is culturally relevant for the religious community. The purpose of this chapter is to introduce and illustrate, through clinical case example, the relevance of a particular complex trauma intervention framework (i.e., Component-Based Psychotherapy [CBP]; Hopper, Grossman, Spinazzola, & Zucker, in press) in spiritually informed treatment with adult Christian clients.

UNDERSTANDING COMPLEX TRAUMA

The chronic and interpersonal context of the trauma exposure differentiates complex trauma from a more general understanding of traumatic stress or posttraumatic stress disorder (PTSD). In the *Diagnostic and Statistical Manual of Mental Disorders* (5th ed.; DSM-5; American Psychiatric Association, 2013), the criteria for posttraumatic stress disorder (PTSD) includes various stressors associated with the emergence of PTSD symptoms or diagnosis. The set of PTSD stressors identified in DSM-5, however, does not represent an exhaustive inventory of all forms of trauma exposure. In particular, it omits a number of forms of developmental trauma exposure associated with complex psychological and behavioral adaptation over the lifespan (Cook et al., 2005; D'Andrea, Ford, Stolbach, Spinazzola, & van der Kolk, 2012; van der Kolk, Roth, Pelcovitz, Sunday, & Spinazzola, 2005). For example, exposure to childhood emotional abuse and neglect is not included as an eligible stressor for PTSD in DSM-5, despite growing empirical evidence that this form of complex trauma exposure is predictive of many severe and lasting consequences in both children and adults (Norman et al., 2012; Spinazzola et al., 2014).

Defining complex trauma involves an understanding of both the nature of the trauma history and its ongoing impact. Spinazzola et al. (2005) provide the following definition:

> Complex trauma refers to a dual problem of exposure and adaptation. Complex trauma exposure is the experience of multiple or chronic and prolonged, developmentally adverse traumatic events, most often of an interpersonal nature and early-life onset. These exposures often occur within the child's caregiving system and include physical, emotional and educational neglect and child maltreatment beginning in early childhood. (p. 433)

In order to illustrate the concept of complex trauma in adult psychotherapy clients, with a particular focus on the long-term effects of childhood emotional abuse, consider the story of Tom. Tom is a Caucasian, 52-year-old married male who is living with his wife and three children in a small Midwestern city. Tom identifies as a Christian. He is successful in his work, serving as a senior partner in a respected law firm. Tom and Darlene had been married 28 years when Darlene discovered, through an envelope of misplaced receipts, that Tom had been secretly spending thousands of dollars. This discovery led to further disclosure; ultimately Tom confessed that over the past 12 years he had been secretly viewing pornography in various forms several times a week and often visiting strip clubs in a large neighboring city. In addition, Tom admitted to "escaping" to that city at least once a week to purchase marijuana and smoke in isolation. Tom described this as a place where he could "get away when I just need to stop pretending" and where he could "calm down when life gets crazy."

Over the course of the first several weeks of therapy, Tom revealed a life filled with paradox. Despite his lifelong academic and professional success, Tom's view of himself did not match his life's accomplishments. When talking about himself, Tom vacillated between self-deprecating jokes and angry, self-loathing comments. Regarding social situations, Tom admitted to being well liked by peers and colleagues because of his ability to be compliant and charming. However, he harbored a persistent fear that others would reject him "if they ever discovered my dark side." Tom reported that he has struggled with chronic depressive affect, anxiety, and feelings of emptiness. Additionally, he discussed frustration about ongoing medical issues, which reportedly included migraine headaches and chronic digestive-tract irritation.

When asked to discuss his childhood, Tom was vague and struggled to find the words to describe his family relationships. Although he attempted to characterize his family as "fine" and "typical," a more thorough assessment revealed that Tom experienced his parents as simultaneously strict and emotionally distant. In a hasty attempt to apologize for betraying his parents, however, Tom stated that he was "probably just being dramatic" and that "many other kids have it much worse . . . like the inner-city kids I work with at church."

Although it took several weeks of therapy for Tom to elaborate on his family relationships, further discussions revealed a childhood almost completely devoid of emotional connection. Tom was subject to routine verbal abuse by his father, who belittled him daily for being "too sensitive" and "not athletic enough." This maltreatment was echoed and magnified by his older brother, who, as Tom described, was more accepted by, and strongly identified with, his father. Tom disclosed that his mother, also subject to her husband's physical and verbal abuse, spent much of her time isolated from the family.

He tearfully described incidents where he would look to his mother while being berated by his father, only to find her quietly staring at the floor. Additionally, since his older brother was in high school with him, the verbal abuse Tom experienced at home often carried over to school, where his brother's friends would join in the bullying behavior. Tom admitted that he had always told himself that the stories of his life were "not bad enough to qualify as abuse," which resulted in his decision to never share his childhood experiences with his wife.

At the age of 52, Tom shared his story for the first time in his life with his therapist, and a few weeks later with his wife. Tom also admitted for the first time that despite his regular church involvement, he experiences church as a scary place. When asked further about this, Tom articulated the belief that God must look on him "with disgust" and that he "can't possibly see me as worthy of having a good life."

In view of the definition of complex trauma provided in this chapter, Tom's childhood experiences and the resulting life patterns illustrate various dynamics of trauma exposure and adaptation. During his childhood development, when emotional and social skills would normally be cultivated, Tom's experiences were defined by chronic verbal abuse, emotional neglect, domestic-violence exposure, and a pervasive lack of a protector or advocate. Tom's story reveals an adult who is coping the best that he can, but with significant gaps in his ability to regulate his emotional experience in a relationally healthy manner. Additionally, Tom's symptoms reveal chronic struggles with a negative view of himself, ongoing medical distress, spiritual fears and alienation, and a proclivity toward numbing his emotions through substance use and withdrawal into sexual fantasy. Tom's story demonstrates several ways in which complex trauma survivors learn to cope with pain; however, these trauma-driven survival skills are often significantly misunderstood by the people surrounding the survivor.

Many of the core components of the long-term impact of complex trauma overlap significantly with spiritual concerns; indeed, a history of relational trauma often leads to difficulties with meaning making and can shape and distort foundational faith beliefs. For example, a central struggle for complex trauma survivors is negative self-perception, including the experience of chronic guilt, intense shame, and feelings of being evil or unworthy. Another common experience for those with a complex trauma history is that of alterations in one's "systems of meaning," which can include hopelessness, despair, and loss of previously sustaining beliefs, including faith beliefs (Cloitre et al., 2012; Herman, 1992). Spiritually sensitive, trauma-informed therapy provides an opportunity for the therapist to connect deeply with the Christian client whose sense of hope and faith has been profoundly wounded.

COMPLEX TRAUMA: FUNDAMENTAL CONCEPTS

It is important to first note complex trauma's origins in early attachment relationships to primary caregiver(s). Attachment theory and other interpersonal theories of understanding suggest that a secure and consistent model of nurturing over time imprints on a child the belief that others can be trusted and relied on and that the world is generally a safe place (Bowlby, 1988). However, when children experience relationships as rejecting, unsafe, or tumultuous, this experience often translates into long-term negative beliefs about self and others and impairs patterns of relating. Complex trauma should also be understood in terms of its long-term biological impact on human development, with the most severe neurobiological consequences correlating with earlier abuse and/or neglect. Although an in-depth discussion of the neurobiological effects of trauma is beyond the scope of this chapter, the literature related to interpersonal neurobiology, affect regulation, and the biological impact of trauma has much to contribute to a well-formulated understanding of the traumatized client (McCrory, De Brito, & Viding, 2010; Perry, 2009; Schore, 2003; Teicher & Samson, 2016; see also chap. 3 in this volume).

When considering the effect of trauma on child development, it is important to conceptualize development as a cumulative process, with the mastery of each new task or milestone laying the groundwork for success at the next level. Experiences of relational trauma, neglect, and environmental adversity have been found to have a significant, formative impact on development (Pynoos, Steinberg, & Wrath, 1995). One of the most striking and consistent areas of developmental impact is a survivor's difficulty with regulating emotions and behavior. For a child growing up in a relatively healthy and nontraumatic environment, there are opportunities throughout development to learn to manage emotions and behaviors in ways that fit the situational demands. However, for individuals who were unable to master regulation skills in childhood because of the developmental impact of trauma, those deficits may still be functioning as the root causes of an array of functional difficulties in academic, vocational, and interpersonal situations.

Conceptualization and treatment planning in complex trauma cases are based on the premise that the majority of treatment-seeking adult survivors of complex trauma exhibit disturbances across core areas of functioning: (a) emotional and behavioral regulation difficulties; (b) disturbance in relational capacities, such as altered perceptions of self and others; (c) alterations in attention or consciousness, such as dissociation; (d) somatic distress; and (e) adversely affected belief systems (Cloitre et al., 2012). In addition, many of these clients also experience distress in one or more of the PTSD symptom clusters of hyperarousal, avoidance, and reexperiencing (van der Kolk et al., 2005).

SPIRITUALLY INFORMED TREATMENT WITH
COMPLEX TRAUMA SURVIVORS

Twenty years of research and clinical experience have substantiated that the most effective approach to treatment with complex trauma survivors involves three phases of therapy. Phase 1 focuses on facilitating physical and psychological safety, reducing symptoms, and increasing emotional and behavioral regulation capacities; Phase 2 focuses on processing and integrating traumatic memories as a part of the client's more cohesive sense of self and history; and Phase 3 focuses on connecting to and preparing for a sense of community engagement and competency beyond therapy (Cloitre et al., 2012; Gingrich, 2013; Herman, 1992).

Although these phases have distinct features, there is a necessary fluidity to treatment with complex trauma survivors, by which therapeutic work in one phase (e.g., trauma processing) will often necessitate drawing on previous work from another phase (e.g., emotional-regulation strategies). It is for this reason that the Trauma Center (www.traumacenter.org) has delineated a component-driven model of intervention with adults affected by complex trauma: Component-Based Psychotherapy (CBP; Hopper et al., in press). This model consists of four principal components—relationship, regulation, parts work, and narrative—and is predicated on the importance of client-therapist parallel process to therapeutic movement and client change. The remainder of this chapter will discuss this model, particularly in the context of working with clients from a Christian faith background.

Primary conduit of treatment change: Client-therapist parallel process. In CBP, treatment is rooted in the recognition that the client will be affected by the relationship with the therapist and, likewise, the therapist will be affected by the relationship with the client. Although a variety of relational themes will be discussed in the first of the four primary treatment components, the nature of the client-therapist connection is believed to be instrumental in the effective facilitation of all treatment components and thus will be highlighted below.

Differences in client-therapist religious beliefs. When considering client and therapist faith beliefs as a dimension of the therapeutic relationship, there is added complexity in the parallel process. For example, the client and therapist may or may not share similar spiritual beliefs or religious backgrounds. Certain religious beliefs may hold positive valence for the client and not for the therapist. In order to function in a healthy and effective manner, therapists must strive to recognize and understand their own defensive coping strategies, and they must learn how to stay attuned to the types of interactions that activate those defensive strategies (toward being either overly reactive toward a client or overly protective of a client).

In regard to the potential impact of working with trauma on the spiritual life of the therapist, there is an added consideration in knowing oneself. Do therapists have religious beliefs or traditions that leave them vulnerable to not fully hearing or witnessing a client's pain? How do therapists manage the potential cognitive dissonance between their religious beliefs and their clients' experiences and the resulting existential questions that may arise? Given the importance of therapist self-awareness when working with vulnerable clients, we highly recommend that therapists consider ongoing personal therapy for themselves and/or ongoing supervision with someone who can help navigate the psychological and spiritual reactions that may arise. Wiggins (2009) recommends a variety of spiritual self-awareness questions and exercises that may facilitate the therapist's process of self-reflection.

Maintaining an authentic therapeutic relationship. Fear of relational connection and intimacy is one of the painful legacies of exposure and adaptation to complex trauma. Clients' historical experiences commonly affect the therapeutic relationship, and therapists find themselves engaged in enactments that mirror clients' past relational struggles. Although there are countless specific ways in which a therapist can get pulled into enacting old and familiar unhealthy patterns with clients, they have the daunting task of interacting with each client in a way that embodies a new and corrective relationship. This requires therapists to be deeply mindful of their own states of attunement and self-regulation with each client in order to provide an authentic relational experience that is well paced to the client's needs and vulnerabilities.

Relational rupture and repair. The attachment theory literature describes processes by which infants and caregivers experience *ruptures* in the relationship, where infants feel momentarily abandoned or not well cared for by caregivers (Bowlby, 1988). In normative parental relationships, the primary caregiver *repairs* this temporary rupture in the relationship by tending to the child's needs. As long as the caregiver is consistently attuned and repairs are made when needed, the child learns to internalize the dynamics of a healthy relationship with another flawed human being.

This dynamic is also experienced between client and therapist in a relational treatment model (Safran & Muran, 2000) whereby therapists will inevitably intervene at times in a manner that is misattuned or dysregulated. Therapeutic ruptures and the process of acknowledgment and repair can serve as tremendous healing experiences for clients with complex trauma histories who may have rarely had the opportunity to experience relational disruption in a safe context. It is in the context of this therapeutic relationship that we will consider the four components of the CBP model.

Treatment component 1: Relationship. A client with a complex trauma history typically comes to therapy with many painful relational experiences and unhealthy definitions of relationship. One of the primary goals of this model is to assist clients in examining past relationships, drawing connections between their past and present relational patterns, and altering unhealthy relational dynamics in their present lives.

Relational component illustrated. Returning to the example of Tom and Darlene, Tom entered therapy because of marital distress related to his wife's recent discovery of his secretive financial and sexual behaviors and drug use. During the early stages of therapy, Tom and Darlene presented as a couple for treatment, and Darlene continually requested that the therapist focus on the "enforcement" of behavioral techniques to manage Tom's behavior. Although Darlene was understandably hurt and angry at the discovery of several secrets after 28 years of marriage, the ongoing intensity of her expressed emotions contributed to a cyclical communication pattern in therapy, in which Tom expressed deep shame and self-contempt related to his past behaviors and Darlene expressed ongoing anger and doubt of his sincerity and ability to change.

After a more thorough assessment of both Tom's and Darlene's histories, the therapist discovered that both individuals came from a context of childhood trauma. Both experienced varying degrees of neglect and abuse in their families of origin, and neither had disclosed this history to the other. For Tom, his behaviors and subsequent shame after being discovered by his wife paralleled the deep sense of shame and social/emotional isolation he experienced as a child. For Darlene, the relational betrayal and her experience of her husband's strip-club visits as "just another example of men viewing women as sexual objects" mirrored her own childhood experience of betrayal and sexual exploitation in her family of origin. Further, her sense of loneliness in light of Tom's withdrawal into pornography was reminiscent of her childhood memories of feeling alone in her suffering.

Both partners were continuing to live out the unique relational survival patterns originally cultivated in the context of developmental trauma. When feeling overwhelmed or defeated, Tom reverted into fantasy, which led to subsequent shame and self-loathing. When Darlene's sense of relational safety felt threatened, this fear triggered her to react angrily and aggressively in self-protection. Furthermore, this pattern overlapped with elements of spiritual struggle for both Tom and Darlene. For Tom, marital conflict elicited a further sense of shame in the eyes of God ("How can God forgive me if my wife cannot?"), while it incited a heightened sense of anger at God in Darlene's experience ("How could God allow this to happen after all I've been through?").

Tom's and Darlene's individual patterns of relating and coping made logical sense in the context of their life histories; however, their shame and secrecy had prevented them from ever disclosing, discussing, or even realizing how their histories, beliefs about themselves and others, and coping patterns had been affecting their relationship throughout their marriage. This example highlights the need for both trauma survivors to understand their relational beliefs and patterns in order to develop new and healthier relational skills and responses. The relational component of trauma therapy is well served by the use of treatment models that can empathically lead clients toward a greater range of emotional experience and safety in sitting with those emotions (e.g., Johnson, 2002). Additionally, the therapist can assist in giving language and validation to experiences in a way that helps the client understand the connection between past and present relational difficulties and patterns (Fosha, 2003).

Faith integration with the relationship treatment component. When working with a client from a Judeo-Christian religious background, an understanding of the literature both on attachment to God (Hall, Fujikawa, Halcrow, Hill, & Delaney, 2009; Kirkpatrick, 2005) and on God-image (Moriarty & Davis, 2012) can help inform the relational treatment component of CBP. Given the relevance of attachment theory to a thorough understanding of complex trauma treatment, the literature on attachment to God and God-image significantly contributes to an understanding of how one's implicit experience of God might interact with relational beliefs about self and others (i.e., in attachment theory language, "internal working models").

With some religiously oriented clients, therapeutic interventions exploring their views of God (and assumptions about God's view of them) could be beneficial in reducing a sense of spiritual shame and a negative view of self. Further, given that there is evidence to suggest that individuals' implicit experience of God is based on past relational experiences (Hall et al., 2009; Maltby & Hall, 2012), the therapeutic relationship can potentially serve as a healing agent in a client's gradual process of experiencing care and acceptance on a spiritual level.

Treatment component 2: Regulation. For individuals who have grown up in a chronically traumatic and/or rejecting environment, the issue of self-regulation is a key component of treatment (Cloitre et al., 2012). Emotional arousal and physiological arousal often serve as triggers for the fight, flight, or freeze response in the autonomic nervous system (McEwen, 1998; van der Kolk, 2006). Although this pattern of automatic response may have been adaptive and necessary for survival at one time for the client, it often becomes habitual over time and is no longer meaningfully connected to present events. For many adult clients with complex trauma histories, overwhelming emotions or high levels of arousal will automatically lead to whatever coping strategy they have learned to be most effective at emotional suppression or arousal reduction, such as self-harm, substance abuse, dissociation, or aggressive interpersonal responses to others (Ford & Courtois, 2009). The goal of addressing regulation in CBP is to enhance the client's capacity to modulate affect and arousal in a more agentic, deliberate, and adaptive manner in order to restore healthy equilibrium following dysregulation of emotions, behaviors, physiology, and thoughts. Therefore, treatment includes helping clients develop or improve awareness of arousal states and teaching clients to use tools for regulating arousal states. It is important to acknowledge, however, that the clinical presentation of emotional and behavioral dysregulation is diverse and unique to the survivor.

Regulation component illustrated. Consider distinct examples of dysregulation in what we might consider two ends of an emotional continuum for Tom and Darlene. As described above, Tom is emotionally constricted and tends to cope with his chronic shame and internalized symptoms through numbing coping patterns. Darlene, on the other hand, is emotionally reactive and tends toward overarousal and aggressive relational interactions. Tom's and Darlene's patterns, although logically connected to their past lives, are no longer functional. In the midst of their successful efforts to survive their childhoods, Tom and Darlene never learned the requisite life skills of recognizing, naming, and managing their emotions in the moment.

Darlene would benefit from the opportunity to take a step back from her reactivity and identify her emotional, cognitive, and physiological "in the moment" responses when she gets activated. In Tom's case, learning to gradually acknowledge and tolerate an emotion without numbing will be an important treatment challenge. For clients with these and other difficulties in emotional and behavioral regulation, there are several skills they can learn in order to build competence in self-regulation.

Developing capacity for self-regulation. Survivors of complex trauma often have not had the developmental opportunity to learn how to accurately understand, modulate, and verbalize their emotions, particularly in the moment of stressful interactions. Self-regulation involves first helping the client recognize both the internal and external sensory, emotional, and relational triggers that lead to affective/physiological arousal and distress.

Further, clients from a Christian faith background can be prone to experiencing guilt about expressing emotions or believing that particular emotions (e.g., anger, fear) are sinful. This is particularly true for clients who have experienced spiritual abuse or who grew up in families that professed a Christian faith and were simultaneously abusive. For these clients, permission to feel a range of emotions, assistance toward an emotional vocabulary, and empowerment to express emotions can lead to important growth and healing.

Building mindfulness skills. Survivors of complex trauma are often prone to self-criticism and shame, which can make the process of identifying and embracing emotions complicated. Through mindfulness skills training, therapists encourage clients to "sit with" feelings with the goal of increasing their self-compassion and acceptance for a range of emotional expression. Hathaway and Tan (2009) describe a religiously oriented variation of Mindfulness-Based Cognitive Therapy (MBCT) that can assist therapists in integrating aspects of prayer and meditation on God into treatment when helpful to the client.

Explicit use of spiritual resources in regulation. Various forms of prayer and meditation could be useful for some clients in the service of regulation. Contemplative prayer (Merton, 1969) and centering prayer (Keating, 1994) originate from monastic traditions and encourage quieting the mind and body while meditating on a single sacred word or phrase. Breath prayer (Barton, 2006) is a similar form of prayer that guides the individual to focus on his or her breath as the life-giving essence, while gently and rhythmically repeating a brief phrase that elicits comfort or connection to God. Additionally, religious imagery can serve as a means of self-soothing as the individual focuses on a sacred image that may evoke a sense of safety, connection, or empowerment. Clients can engage in prayer and meditation in either calm or more active states, depending on the physiological regulation needs of the individual.

One of the challenges that can arise in a Christian context is confusing dysregulated behavior with willful sin. While the concept of sin is a central component of the Christian faith, clients with emotional and behavioral regulation difficulties may be prone to survival-based coping behaviors that have served in an adaptive way, even if they are traditionally viewed as sinful (e.g., substance abuse, various sexual behaviors). For the therapist working with Christian clients, this is important to understand for various reasons. First, it is imperative to assist clients in viewing their past and present coping behaviors and relational patterns in light of trauma history. For clients who are prone to shame, it can be healing to learn how to honor their past attempts toward survival and coping. Although clients may feel motivated to change their behaviors in order to live a life consistent with faith beliefs, therapist understanding of adaptive coping behaviors is critical as clients attempt to navigate the shame associated with trauma history and subsequent coping patterns. Additionally, understanding this dynamic can assist the therapist in educating faith communities and clergy on the challenges of behavioral change for the trauma survivor.

Treatment component 3: Parts work. When working with complex trauma, it is essential to assess for dissociative symptoms given the prevalence of dissociative experience for survivors. Although it will be manifested at varying levels of severity, dissociation is a normative part of the survival experience in complexly traumatized clients (van der Kolk, McFarlane, & Weisaeth, 1996). Less severe dissociation might be experienced by trauma survivors as cognition without emotional connection or as somatic symptoms experienced without cognitive awareness (Putnam, 1997), whereas more severe dissociation might be experienced as distinct alterations in their states of consciousness (see chap. 11 in this volume).

When working within the CBP model, it is assumed that trauma survivors have "parts" of themselves, which are understood to represent split-off or unintegrated aspects of their larger identities. It is also assumed that these parts often originally helped an individual survive and endure painful experiences by containing traumatic and overwhelming memories and the associated somatic, affective, and cognitive symptoms. Trauma survivors often carry a profound burden of shame and stigma about their dissociative experiences; thus, putting these experiences into words can assist survivors in the process of feeling less alone. Relational parts work involves psychoeducation about the normalcy of experiencing aspects of self in various parts, making connections between present-day experiences of self with past trauma experience and integrating the diverse self-experiences into a more cohesive sense of self.

Parts component illustrated. In the case of Tom, therapy uncovered various ways in which he experienced different parts of himself in diverse settings and relational circumstances. For example, although Tom typically felt nervous prior to his visits to the strip clubs and profoundly guilty afterward, he reported that in that setting he felt like a "different person"—strong, attractive, sexually confident, and self-assured in a way that was not consistent with his affective experience at home. In those moments, Tom also abhorred his compliant, mild-mannered, depressive self as a "big sissy" who at home deferred to his wife and volunteered at church. As Tom explored these various self-experiences, he realized that even his mannerisms, tone of voice, and posture were different in these multiple contexts.

Tom was initially tentative in therapy when discussing parts of himself, disclosing the fear that his therapist would "think I am crazy." However, through the process of reflecting on his present-day experiences of himself in light of his past abusive context, Tom began to make connections. He was able to explore his present-day experiences in light of a childhood in which his father belittled emotional expression and his mother was disempowered. Over time, Tom developed compassion for the parts of himself that he had previously disavowed, while also beginning to integrate his affective experiences in a way that was increasingly coherent. He reported a significant level of relief in being able to acknowledge these previously confusing and disconnected states of being. Tom's treatment illustrates the manner in which relational parts work is essential to a comprehensive complex trauma treatment approach. Further treatment resources address the range of common dissociative experiences and treatment approaches (Boon, Steele, & van der Hart, 2011; Schwartz, 1995), including specific ways to incorporate Christian spirituality into work with internal parts of self (Steege & Schwartz, 2010).

Treatment component 4: Narrative. Much of the traditional trauma-treatment literature discusses the importance of memory processing for the purpose of decreasing anxiety and other psychological and physiological symptoms of PTSD (Foa, Keane, Friedman, & Cohen, 2009; Goodson, Lefkowitz, Helstrom, & Gawrysiak, 2013). In CBP, the core treatment component of narrative involves understanding, accepting, transcending, and integrating traumatic experiences into one's broader life narrative. With this understanding in mind, trauma-experience integration includes narrative processing, mourning losses, making meaning of the traumatic experiences, and moving beyond the identity of survivor to an identity of one who is engaged in a meaningful life. It is this treatment component that lends itself most naturally to the discussion of integration of faith and psychological treatment, as the larger existential questions of understanding theodicy (e.g., Who is God in the midst of my suffering?) and one's personal faith journey (e.g., How do I relate to God in light of my trauma story?) are common in trauma processing for the Christian client (see also chap. 2 in this volume).

Narrative processing. To begin with, there are several important treatment considerations when transitioning into the narrative processing. In order to safely move into this component of treatment, clients must have established adequate self-regulation capacities and have access to environmental support so that they can tolerate the anticipated distress that will likely accompany trauma processing (Cloitre et al., 2012). Additionally, therapists should help clients understand the purpose of narrative processing: to face the pain, fear, and shame of the traumatic past while remaining grounded in the present in order to integrate the traumatic memories into a more cohesive life story. When clients can tell their stories to an empathically engaged and trusted ally, the anxiety and shame begin to decrease, and the stories become less powerful and controlling over their everyday lives. Further, when clients can engage in the process of narrative processing with the aid of healthier self-regulation tools, they will begin to experience themselves as empowered and in greater control of previously chaotic arousal states.

Mourning the losses resulting from a trauma history. In the process of telling their stories, trauma survivors often come to recognize—either for the first time or at a deeper level—the many losses that resulted from the chaotic, abusive, or neglectful nature of their pasts. For some, the absence of the desired nurturing relationship with a caregiver may emerge as a profound loss to be grieved. For others, the loss of a "normal" childhood or the sense of self as damaged in ways that others do not understand may stand out as a significant injustice. There are countless losses that may emerge in the unique life of each client, and the emotionally significant process of realizing, naming, and mourning those losses can be deeply meaningful for healing. Mourning in the therapeutic process often involves sober reflection and profound sadness. At the same time, mourning can provide the opportunity for deeper self-understanding and self-compassion, due to realizing the significance of their personal pain. Mourning may also prompt some to move forward in their lives in order to advocate for healing and justice in the lives of others.

Contemporary culture often does not make space for the process of grief and mourning. This can be especially true in the Christian subculture, where some individuals and families feel the pressure to look good. Additionally, clients who identify as Christian will often report feeling guilty for a perceived lack of faith, hope, or forgiveness when they are walking through times of suffering. However, the Scriptures do not condemn or lecture those who are mourning; rather, they provide a method by which people can learn to process their pain in a spiritual context.

In his book *Raging with Compassion*, John Swinton (2007) discusses the psalms of lament as a means of expressing pain to God and others:

> A lament is a repeated cry of pain, rage, sorrow, and grief that emerges in the midst of suffering and alienation. . . . Lament, and in particular psalm-like lament, is the cry of the innocent, the one who feels treated unfairly, who feels that God has somehow not lived up to the sufferer's covenant-inspired expectations. Most importantly, lament is prayer. It is, however, a very particular form of prayer that is not content with soothing platitudes or images of a God who will listen only to voices that appease and compliment. Lament takes the brokenness of human experience into the heart of God and demands that God answer. (p. 104)

Using the language of lament, trauma survivors can begin to give voice to some of the ambivalence in their views of God and faith. The psalmist expresses intense emotions including anger, hopelessness, powerlessness, betrayal, and a sense of injustice. Psalm 13:1-2 (ESV) states:

> How long, O LORD? Will you forget me forever?
>> How long will you hide your face from me?
> How long must I take counsel in my soul
>> and have sorrow in my heart all the day?
> How long shall my enemy be exalted over me?

In this psalm, David expresses the sense of isolation and betrayal that many trauma survivors often express. Lament is engaging honestly with God in the process of meaning making, with the option of reconciliation with God despite unanswered questions about the existence of evil and suffering in the world. Additionally, the practice of lament is grounded in a framework of hope, empowerment, and future orientation.

Swinton (2007) recommends the creation of a personal lament from a pastoral perspective, but this practical treatment strategy can be adapted for use with particular Christian clients engaged in mourning and meaning-making processes in therapy. Following the sequence often reflected in sacred lament texts, clients might consider writing a lament, which could include naming the offense (e.g., "I am confused and angry that you [God] did not protect me from the suffering of my abusive and chaotic family"), along with an appeal for future justice and peace. The practice of lament can be incorporated into trauma processing with Christian clients, where they are given permission to express complex and mixed emotions to God through journaling, poetry, music, visual art, or other expressive means.

Moving through processing to meaning making. It is relatively well established that striving to make meaning of our experiences is a natural human endeavor (Frankl, 1984). Additionally, there is a growing body of literature discussing the importance of meaning making in the lives of those who have experienced trauma and adversity (Grossman, Sorsoli, & Kia-Keating, 2006; Park & Ai, 2006; Solomon, 2004). As mentioned earlier in this chapter, there is a complicated relationship in the literature between trauma, religion, and spirituality, where many of the reported outcomes of stress-related growth (Park, 2005) are focused on situational or community-based traumatic exposure, whereas complex trauma often leads to more severe disruptions in the ability to reconcile questions of suffering and faith.

Garbarino and Bedard (1996) use the term *spiritual dissonance* to describe the significant impact of complex trauma on the spiritual development of children, stating, "By 'spiritual' we refer to the inner life of children and adolescents as the cradle for the construction of meaning" (p. 467). They suggest that those who experience trauma in early stages of life are most vulnerable to lifelong struggles with meaning making. In contrast, they posit that those who experience trauma in later stages of life have greater "metaphysical momentum in the sense of the longest period of building up behaviors and beliefs to substantiate and support core belief systems" (p. 471).

In light of this, it is of the utmost importance that Christian therapists are able to sit with the deep sense of ambivalence with which many complex trauma survivors experience their faith. Sitting with this ambivalence in therapy also requires therapeutic restraint from the attempt to answer the painful "Why?" and "Where was God?" questions. Instead, the therapist should recognize that these questions "actually contain a hidden request for support in bearing the nearly intolerable feelings associated with having no answers to life's most profound questions" (Day, Vermilyea, Wilkerson, & Giller, 2006, p. 50). For the Christian therapist working with complex trauma survivors who are grappling to make sense of their faith in light of a painful history, it is of critical importance to approach the work with great humility. Making meaning of past trauma while trying to grapple with the big questions related to God's existence, God's goodness, or the benefit versus harm of religion can be a deeply confusing task for the client and the therapist.

The impact of complex trauma bears the risk of damaging or distorting one's faith system and view of self in relation to God. However, there are components of the Christian faith that both psychology and faith traditions believe to be supportive in recovery from suffering: connection (to God and community), sense of meaning, belief in something larger than oneself, observance of ritual, forgiveness, and hope. Hope, in this context, is beyond mere optimism; rather, hope "sees [dangers and heartaches] and then sees past them to possibility" (Day et al., 2006, p. 58). Although the therapeutic process can be slow and tedious, therapists should maintain the goal of helping clients move beyond the identity dichotomy of victim versus survivor to a life of meaningful engagement and fulfillment. In order for this therapeutic aspiration to become reality, however, therapists need to be able to assist their clients in embedding the trauma narratives within their greater life narratives.

Narrative component illustrated. In the latter stages of Tom's therapeutic journey, he discovered the hope that can be found in a more integrated life narrative. Although mourning the losses in his life was deeply painful (e.g., loss of a connection to his deceased parents, loss of years of authentic connection to his wife and children), Tom was surprised at the freedom that he experienced on the other side of processing his narrative with a safe and accepting therapist. Additionally, Tom allowed himself for the first time to acknowledge and verbalize the anger and confusion toward God that had previously led to further guilt and denial. The experience of sharing his ambivalent thoughts and feelings about God with someone who denied neither his faith nor his doubt led Tom to a place where he could live in the mystery and the ongoing questions of his deeply held Christian beliefs.

Finally, Tom and Darlene both learned that there was restorative hope in the process of sharing their stories with each other. Although the task of rebuilding trust was slow, Tom and Darlene learned to understand one another's vulnerabilities in the context of past abuse and neglect. It was only when Tom began to experience himself as a person of worth, through authentic relationship, that he could articulate that his life had purpose and meaning. At the end of treatment, Tom described his transformation through therapy as "waking up for the first time."

Therapist meaning making. The mere fact that one of the core areas of trauma impact is related to disrupted systems of meaning (including faith beliefs) calls for clinicians who are well trained academically and clinically and who are also spiritually sensitive and competent in the integration of faith and professional practice. Bearing witness to a client's story may be one of the most profound experiences therapists encounter. At the same time, therapists who work in treatment of complex trauma often experience vicarious traumatization (see chap. 4 in this book), which may also include altered systems of meaning making that threaten the therapists' belief systems and faith practices. Pearlman and Caringi (2009) state that "disrupted spirituality is a hallmark of both direct and indirect trauma, and rampant cynicism or despair in clients with complex trauma can challenge the helper's sense of meaning and hope" (p. 209). Perhaps the therapist working with complex trauma can benefit from heeding the words of Langberg (1997): "To sit with suffering is to be a companion to those things that will wage war on the core of your faith" (p. 241). Therefore, it is critical that therapists working with complex trauma consistently attend to their own personal, relational, and spiritual identities and nurture relationships and practices that maintain a solid sense of emotional, physical, and spiritual health.

CONCLUSION

Treating individuals affected by complex trauma is intricate, arduous work. Integrating a faith perspective into this process—while helping Christian clients contend with the challenges to their faith that inevitably arise as they grapple with the meaning and impact of the adversities they have suffered, the losses they have endured, the love and protection they were denied, and the solace that never came— is more exacting still. There remains a critical need for ongoing research on treatment outcomes with adults affected by childhood trauma, including research that takes into account the added complexities in evaluating optimal interventions with clients from a Christian faith background.

REFERENCES

American Psychiatric Association. (2013). *Diagnostic and statistical manual of mental disorders* (5th ed.). Washington, DC: Author.

Barton, R. H. (2006). *Sacred rhythms: Arranging our lives for spiritual transformation.* Downers Grove, IL: InterVarsity Press.

Boon, S., Steele, K., & van der Hart, O. (2011). *Coping with trauma-related dissociation: Skills training for patients and therapists.* New York, NY: Norton.

Bowlby, J. (1988). *A secure base: Parent-child attachment and healthy human development.* New York, NY: Basic Books.

Bryant-Davis, T., & Wong, E. C. (2013). Faith to move mountains: Religious coping, spirituality, and interpersonal trauma recovery. *American Psychologist, 68*(8), 675-84. doi:10.1037/a0034380

Chan, C. S., & Rhodes, J. E. (2013). Religious coping, posttraumatic stress, psychological distress, and posttraumatic growth among female survivors four years after Hurricane Katrina. *Journal of Traumatic Stress, 26,* 257-65. doi:10.1002/jts.21801

Cloitre, M., Courtois, C. A., Ford, J. D., Green, B. L., Alexander, P., Briere, J., . . . van der Hart, O. (2012). *The ISTSS expert consensus treatment guidelines for complex PTSD in adults*. Retrieved from www.istss.org/treating-trauma/istss-complex-ptsd-treat ment-guidelines.aspx

Connor, K. M., Davidson, J. R., & Lee, L. C. (2003). Spirituality, resilience, and anger in survivors of violent trauma: A community survey. *Journal of Traumatic Stress, 16*(5), 487-94. doi:10.1023/A:1025762512279

Cook, A., Spinazzola, J., Ford, J., Lanktree, C., Blaustein, M., . . . van der Kolk, B. A. (2005). Complex trauma in children and adolescents. *Psychiatric Annals, 35*(5), 390-98.

D'Andrea, W., Ford, J., Stolbach, B., Spinazzola, J., & van der Kolk, B. A. (2012). Understanding interpersonal trauma in children: Why we need a developmentally appropriate trauma diagnosis. *American Journal of Orthopsychiatry, 82*(2), 187-200. doi:10.1111/j.1939-0025.2012.01154.x

Day, J. H., Vermilyea, E., Wilkerson, J., & Giller, E. (2006). *Risking connection in faith communities: A training curriculum for faith leaders supporting trauma survivors.* Baltimore, MD: Sidran Institute Press.

Foa, E. B., Keane, T. M., Friedman, M. J., & Cohen, J. A. (Eds.). (2009). *Effective treatments for PTSD: Practice guidelines from the International Society for Traumatic Stress Studies* (2nd ed.). New York, NY: Guilford Press.

Ford, J. D., & Courtois, C. A. (2009). Defining and understanding complex trauma and complex traumatic stress disorders. In C. A. Courtois & J. D. Ford (Eds.), *Treating complex traumatic stress disorders: An evidence based guide* (pp. 13-30). New York, NY: Guilford Press.

Fosha, D. (2003). Dyadic regulation and experiential work with emotion and relatedness in trauma and disorganized attachment. In M. F. Solomon & D. J. Siegel (Eds.), *Healing trauma: Attachment, mind, body, and brain* (pp. 221-81). New York, NY: W. W. Norton.

Frankl, V. E. (1984). *Man's search for meaning.* New York, NY: Simon & Schuster.

Garbarino, L., & Bedard, C. (1996). Spiritual challenges to children facing violent trauma. *Childhood, 3*(4), 467-78. doi:10.1177/0907568296003004004

Gerber, M. M., Boals, A., & Schuettler, D. (2011). The unique contributions of positive and negative religious coping to posttraumatic growth and PTSD. *Psychology of Religion and Spirituality, 3*(4), 298-307. doi:10.1037/a0023016

Gingrich, H. D. (2013). *Restoring the shattered self: A Christian counselor's guide to complex trauma.* Downers Grove, IL: IVP Academic.

Goodson, J. T., Lefkowitz, C. M., Helstrom, A. W., & Gawrysiak, M. J. (2013). Outcomes of prolonged exposure therapy for veterans with posttraumatic stress disorder. *Journal of Traumatic Stress, 26*, 419-25. doi:10.1002/jts.21830

Grossman, F. K., Sorsoli, L., & Kia-Keating, M. (2006). A gale force wind: Meaning making by male survivors of childhood sexual abuse. *American Journal of Orthopsychiatry, 76*(4), 434-43. doi:10.1037/0002-9432.76.4.434

Hall, T. W., Fujikawa, A., Halcrow, S. R., Hill, P. C., & Delaney, H. (2009). Attachment to God and implicit spirituality: Clarifying correspondence and compensation models. *Journal of Psychology & Theology, 37*, 247-52.

Hathaway, W., & Tan, E. (2009). Religiously-oriented mindfulness-based cognitive therapy. *Journal of Clinical Psychology: In Session, 65*(2), 158-71. doi:10.1002/jclp.20569

Herman, J. (1992). *Trauma and recovery.* New York, NY: Basic Books.

Hopper, E., Grossman, F., Spinazzola, J., & Zucker, M. (in press). *Reaching across the abyss: Treatment of adult survivors of childhood emotional abuse and neglect.* New York, NY: Guilford Press.

Johnson, S. M. (2002). *Emotionally focused couple therapy with trauma survivors: Strengthening attachment bonds.* New York, NY: Guilford Press.

Keating, T. (1994). *Intimacy with God: An introduction to centering prayer.* New York, NY: Crossroad.

Kirkpatrick, L. A. (2005). *Attachment, evolution, and the psychology of religion.* New York, NY: Guilford Press.

Langberg, D. (1997). *Counseling survivors of sexual abuse.* Wheaton, IL: Tyndale.

Maltby, L. E., & Hall, T. W. (2012). Trauma, attachment, and spirituality: A case study. *Journal of Psychology & Theology, 40*(4), 302-12.

Marriott, C., Hamilton-Giachritsis, C., & Harrop, C. (2014). Factors promoting resilience following childhood sexual abuse: A structured, narrative review of the literature. *Child Abuse Review, 23*(1), 17-34. doi:10.1002/car.2258

McCrory, E., De Brito, S. A., & Viding, E. (2010). Research review: The neurobiology and genetics of maltreatment and adversity. *Journal of Child Psychology and Psychiatry, 51*(10), 1079-95. doi:10.1111/j.1469-7610.2010.02271.x

McEwen, B. S. (1998). Stress, adaptation, and disease: Allostasis and allostatic load. *Annals of the New York Academy of Sciences, 840*, 33-44.

Merton, T. (1969). *Contemplative prayer.* New York, NY: Image.

Moriarty, G. L., & Davis, E. B. (2012). Client God images: Theory, research, and clinical practice. In J. Aten, K. O'Grady, & E. Worthington, Jr. (Eds.), *The psychology of religion and spirituality for clinicians: Using research in your practice* (pp. 131-60). New York, NY: Routledge.

Norman, R. E., Byambaa, M., De, R., Butchart, A., Scott, J., & Vos, T. (2012). The long-term health consequences of child physical abuse, emotional abuse, and neglect: A systematic review and meta-analysis. *PLoS Medicine, 9*(11), 1-31. doi:10.1371/journal.pmed.1001349

Pargament, K. I. (2008). Problem and solution: The spiritual dimension of clergy sexual abuse and its impact on survivors. *Journal of Child Sexual Abuse, 17*, 397-420. doi:10.1080/10538710802330187

Park, C. L. (2005). Religion as a meaning-making framework in coping with life stress. *Journal of Social Issues, 61*(4), 707-29. doi:10.1111/j.1540-4560.2005.00428.x

Park, C. L., & Ai, A. L. (2006). Meaning making and growth: New directions for research on survivors of trauma. *Journal of Loss and Trauma, 11,* 389-407. doi:10.1080/15325020600685295

Pearlman, L. A., & Caringi, J. (2009). Living and working self-reflectively to address vicarious trauma. In C. A. Courtois & J. D. Ford (Eds.), *Treating complex traumatic stress disorders: An evidence-based guide* (pp. 82-103). New York, NY: Guilford Press.

Perry, B. D. (2009). Examining child maltreatment through a neurodevelopmental lens: Clinical applications of the neurosequential model of therapeutics. *Journal of Loss and Trauma, 14,* 240-55. doi:10.1080/15325020903004350

Putnam, F. (1997). *Dissociation in children and adolescents: A developmental perspective.* New York, NY: Guilford Press.

Pynoos, R., Steinberg, A., & Wraith, R. (1995). A developmental psychopathology model of childhood traumatic stress. In D. Cicchetti & D. J. Cohen (Eds.), *Manual of developmental psychopathology: Vol. 2. Risk, disorder, and adaptation* (pp. 72-95). Hoboken, NJ: Wiley.

Safran, J. D., & Muran, J. C. (2000). *Negotiating the therapeutic alliance: A relational treatment guide.* New York, NY: Guilford Press.

Schore, A. N. (2003). *Affect dysregulation and disorders of the self.* New York, NY: Norton.

Schwartz, R. C. (1995). *Internal family systems therapy.* New York, NY: Guilford Press.

Solomon, J. L. (2004). Modes of thought and meaning making: The aftermath of trauma. *Journal of Humanistic Psychology, 44*(3), 299-319. doi:10.1177/0022167804266096

Spinazzola, J., Ford, J. D., Zucker, M., van der Kolk, B. A., Silva, S., Smith, S. F., & Blaustein, M. (2005). Survey evaluates: Complex trauma exposure, outcome, and intervention among children and adolescents. *Psychiatric Annals, 35*(5), 433-39.

Spinazzola, J., Hodgdon, H., Liang, L., Ford, J. D., Layne, C. M., Pynoos, R., . . . Kisiel, C. (2014). Unseen wounds: The contribution of psychological maltreatment to child and adolescent mental health and risk outcomes. *Psychological Trauma: Theory, Research, Practice, and Policy, 6*(S1), S18-S28. doi:10.1037/a0037766

Steege, M., & Schwartz, R. C. (2010). *The spirit-led life: A Christian encounter with internal family systems.* N.p.: CreateSpace.

Swinton, J. (2007). *Raging with compassion: Pastoral responses to the problem of evil.* Grand Rapids, MI: Eerdmans.

Teicher, M. H., & Samson, J. A. (2016). Annual research review: Enduring neurobiological effects of childhood abuse and neglect. *Journal of Child Psychology and Psychiatry, 57*(3), 241-66. doi:10.1111/jcpp.12507

Thomas, E., & Savoy, S. (2014). Relationship between traumatic events, religious coping style, and posttraumatic outcomes. *Traumatology: An International Journal, 20*(2), 84-90.

ter Kuile, H., & Ehring, T. (2014). Predictors of changes in religiosity after trauma: Trauma, religiosity, and posttraumatic stress disorder. *Psychological Trauma: Theory, Research, Practice, and Policy, 6*(4), 353-60. doi:10.1037/a0034880

van der Kolk, B. A. (2006). Clinical implications of neuroscience research in PTSD. In R. Yehuda (Ed.), *Psychobiology of posttraumatic stress disorders: A decade of progress* (Vol. 1071, pp. 277-93). Hoboken, NJ: Wiley-Blackwell.

van der Kolk, B. A., McFarlane, A. C., & Weisaeth, L. (Eds.). (1996). *Traumatic stress: The effects of overwhelming experience on mind, body, and society*. New York, NY: Guilford Press.

van der Kolk, B. A., Roth, S., Pelcovitz, D., Sunday, S., & Spinazzola, J. (2005). Disorders of extreme stress: The empirical foundation of a complex adaptation to trauma. *Journal of Traumatic Stress, 18*(5), 389-99. doi:10.1002/jts.20047

Van Deusen, S., & Courtois, C. A. (2015). Spirituality, religion, and complex developmental trauma. In D. F. Walker, C. A. Courtois, & J. D. Aten (Eds.), *Spiritually oriented psychotherapy for trauma* (pp. 29-54). Washington, DC: American Psychological Association. doi:10.1037/14500-003

Walker, D., & Aten, J. D. (2012). Future directions for the study and application of religion, spirituality, and trauma research. *Journal of Psychology & Theology, 40*(4), 349-53.

Walker, D. F., McGregor, K. L., Quagliana, D., Stephens, R. L., & Knodel, K. R. (2015). Understanding and responding to changes in spirituality and religion after traumatic events. In D. F. Walker, C. A. Courtois, & J. D. Aten (Eds.), *Spiritually oriented psychotherapy for trauma* (pp. 147-68). Washington, DC: American Psychological Association. doi:10.1037/14500-008

Walker, D., Reid, H. W., O'Neill, T., & Brown, L. (2009). Changes in personal religion/spirituality during and after childhood abuse: A review and synthesis. *Psychological Trauma: Theory, Research, Practice, and Policy, 1*(2), 130-45. doi:10.1037/a0016211

Wiggins, M. I. (2009). Therapist self-awareness of spirituality. In J. D. Aten & M. M. Leach (Eds.), *Spirituality and the therapeutic process: A comprehensive resource from intake to termination* (pp. 53-74). Washington, DC: American Psychological Association. doi:10.1037/11853-003

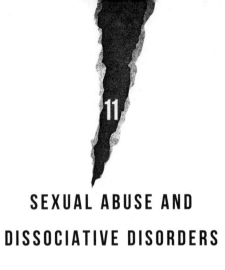

SEXUAL ABUSE AND

DISSOCIATIVE DISORDERS

HEATHER DAVEDIUK GINGRICH

How does a little girl come to grips with the fact that her father, the very person who is supposed to love and protect her, hurts her and uses her sexually? What does a pubescent boy do with his mixed feelings of guilt, shame, and excitement as his youth pastor stimulates his genitals? Unfortunately, these are not hypothetical questions. Sexual abuse (SA) of children is widespread both in the United States and throughout the world. A meta-analysis of the results of 331 studies indicated that 18% of women and 7.6% of men had been sexually abused before the age of 18 (Stoltenborgh, Van Ijzendoorn, Euser, & Bakermans-Kranenburg, 2011). In the United States, estimates of prevalence range from 24% to 40% of girls and 18% of boys, with the incidence of SA within evangelical circles appearing to be on par with rates in the general population (Tracy, 2011). Chances are high, therefore, that Christian mental health professionals will be faced with numerous clients who have experienced child SA.

WHAT IS SEXUAL ABUSE?

Legal definitions of SA vary depending on the country, state, or province. Clinically, however, it is most helpful to view SA as encompassing a broad range of activities such as Bass and Davis (2008) describe. They point out that vaginal, oral, and anal rape obviously fit within the SA category, as does genital stimulation (both giving and receiving). Less apparent may be unnecessarily intrusive medical procedures, fondling of genitals under the guise of bathing, an inappropriate kiss, or unwanted touch on any part of the body. Bass and Davis state that SA does not always have to involve physical contact. SA also includes forced nudity, being required to pose for seductive photographs, hearing comments about one's developing body, being stared at in a provocative way, being a victim of exhibitionism, or being told that all one is good for is sex.

The apparent objective severity of the abuse incident is not necessarily an accurate indicator of the subjective impact on the victim. As is the case with other types of trauma, the subjective components are usually the most salient (McFarlane & Girolamo, 2007).

HOW CHILD SEXUAL ABUSE LEADS TO ONGOING PSYCHOLOGICAL AND RELATIONAL DAMAGE[1]

Like other victims of trauma, those who have been sexually abused often struggle with the posttraumatic symptoms of intrusion (e.g., nightmares, flashbacks, intrusive thoughts and images), avoidance (e.g., constricted affect, avoidance of people or situations that could potentially trigger intrusive symptoms, dissociation), negative alterations in cognitions mood (e.g., self-blame, guilt/shame), and alterations in arousal and reactivity (e.g., hypervigilance, sleep disturbance; American Psychiatric Association, 2013). While these may be the most obvious symptoms, and those which often propel SA survivors (SASs) into counseling, SA can have even more pervasive effects.

SA, like other forms of complex trauma (see chap. 10), is a particularly devastating type of trauma in that it has a severe impact on normal developmental processes, particularly if the child is young. This is because neurological and cognitive functions are rapidly formed in early childhood, laying the necessary psychological and biological foundations crucial for subsequent healthy development (Arnold & Fisch, 2011; Ford, 2009). When these processes are blocked or interrupted as a result of trauma, the lifelong results can include impaired self-concept (Wilson, 2004), somatic dysregulation (Nijenhuis, van der Hart, Kruger, & Steele, 2004; Ogden, Minton, & Pain, 2006), disorganized attachment patterns (Lyons-Ruth, Dutra, Schuder, & Bianchi, 2006; Pearlman & Courtois, 2005), spiritual alienation (Tracy, 2005), and dissociation (DePrince & Freyd, 2007; Gingrich, 2005). In addition, SA in early childhood is associated with dissociative identity disorder (DID; Chu, 2011), for which 1.1%–1.5% of the general population meet diagnostic criteria (Brand et al., 2016).

A closer look at early developmental processes will help to shed some light on why SA in early childhood has such devastating effects. Putnam's (1997) model of Discrete Behavioral States (DBS) can be a helpful framework for understanding how such damage can have a lifelong impact (see various chapters in Dell & O'Neil, 2009). While the DBS model was developed a couple of decades ago, it

---

[1]Portions of this section and the next ("The BASK Model") were previously published in Gingrich, H. D. (2011), The role of dissociation in sexual abuse: Current research and approaches in healing. In A. J. Schmutzer (Ed.), *The long journey home: Understanding and ministering to the sexually abused* (pp. 60-73). Eugene, OR: Wipf and Stock. Used with permission.

has been supported by more recent research on attachment (e.g., Cassidy & Shaver, 2016; Lyons-Ruth et al., 2006) and psychophysiology (e.g., Shore, 2003, 2009; Siegel, 2003, 2009).

According to the DBS model, discrete, fragmented behavioral states are normative in early infancy. Newborns, for example, have no ability to regulate their emotions. When they are hungry, they may scream at the top of their lungs, their whole bodies getting into the act as they flail arms and legs with scrunched-up, red faces. But when given the breast or bottle, they immediately switch states. Their bodies instantly relax, they stop crying, and they may even make contented gurgling noises.

As children get older, they are expected to exhibit more integration between states. If, for example, a hungry five-year-old has a temper tantrum when food is not immediately available, it is likely to be seen as more problematic than if an 18-month-old exhibits the same behavior. If an adult shows such behavior, it is viewed as totally inappropriate.

With sensitive and nurturing parenting, secure attachments form which aid in the development of a more continuous, integrated sense of self and experience. For instance, if a caregiver responds to the cries of the infant, determines the reason for the crying, and takes action to alleviate the problem (e.g., by feeding, changing a diaper, or soothing), the infant learns that the parent can be counted on, which provides a sense of safety and security (Bowlby, 1988). Although the affect of infants is initially regulated externally, that is, through the responsiveness of caregivers to their needs, as children mature they develop the capacity to begin to regulate their own emotions as they learn to self-soothe (e.g., by thumb-sucking, rocking, or clutching a stuffed animal or blanket). Good parenting, therefore, not only affects attachment, and thereby the ability of individuals to function well in relationships throughout their lives, but also has a positive effect on their ability to integrate their experiences and develop a healthy sense of self.

Traumatic experiences such as SA interfere with this process of integration (Liotte, 2009). Abuse at the hands of parents, other family members, teachers, or clergy is particularly destructive because of the additional element of relational betrayal (DePrince et al., 2012; Freyd, DePrince, & Gleaves, 2007); attachment is greatly affected when the very people who are supposed to be providing a safe haven for children are the ones hurting them. Yet young children are totally dependent on their caregivers for survival. Even if the SA was not due to incest, attachment with parents may be adversely affected as children may not understand why their parents are not protecting them.

Dissociation can become an adaptive way for abused children to cope with their reality, with respect to both the trauma itself (DePrince & Freyd, 2007) and the challenges these children face in regard to attachment (Lyons-Ruth et al., 2006). For example, an incest victim who is raped in the early morning hours by her father is in the horrendous position of having to sit down at the breakfast table with her perpetrator and act as though nothing has happened. Using dissociative defenses, the child can compartmentalize the memory of being raped, effectively shutting it away, so that when she eats with her father at the breakfast table and then goes to school, she has no conscious awareness of what happened to her even minutes before. Since children dissociate easily, this process can become effortless and entirely unconscious. While nontraumatized children tend to lose their ability to dissociate as they get older (Ogawa, Sroufe, Weinfield, Carlson, & Egeland, 1997), abused children may retain that capacity out of necessity (Howell, 2011). SASs are therefore more prone to dissociation, whether at moderate levels or at the severe levels that are necessary for the development of DID.

THE BASK MODEL

As discussed above, the DBS model provides a helpful framework for understanding how early childhood trauma such as SA interferes with normal developmental processes. One such effect is that it impedes integrative processes, resulting in the ability for SASs to use dissociation as a psychological defense to a much greater extent than individuals who do not have an abuse history.

In a sense, the DBS model gives us a bird's-eye view of how and why victims of early childhood trauma dissociate. The following model, the BASK model of dissociation (Braun, 1988), further defines the components of discrete states and can be of great help when working with SA. BASK is an acronym that describes various components of experience or memory: *Behavior, Affect, Sensation,* and *Knowledge.* Any aspect of a particular experience can be dissociated from the rest. For example, an SAS may have no memory of an entire abuse incident or some aspect of it but may experience the affect (A) attached to the event. One SAS woke up regularly at 3:48 a.m. terrified but having no idea why. Eventually she recalled that her father regularly raped her around that time many nights during her childhood. Initially she had no *conscious* knowledge (K) of this series of events because the cognitive aspects were dissociated, even though she was fully aware of the emotion (A) that corresponded to it. Conversely, SASs could have full cognitive memory of an abuse incident yet display no emotion as they describe the details to you. In this case, the affect is the BASK component that is dissociated.

Sensation (S) refers to physical aspects of the experience, whether pain, pleasure, or some other aspect of somatoform dissociation. For example, SASs may experience physical pain (e.g., in the pelvic or genital area) and not know why until they make the connection to a specific abuse incident that resulted in just such pain.

Dissociated sensation is often referred to as *body memories* in the sexual abuse literature. Behavior (B) may also be dissociated from the other BASK components. For example, some female SA survivors continually run from committed, intimate relationships with men but are unaware of the connection of this to their fears of revictimization. Another illustration is a woman who vomited every time she and her husband had intercourse, but made no conscious link between that behavior and the SA she had cognitive memory (K) of as a child. Any one of these BASK components, or various combinations, can be dissociated from the others at various times for any SAS.

For survivors who dissociate to the extent of meeting diagnostic criteria for a dissociative disorder, the same principles are in operation; it is a matter of degree. For those with DID, for instance, dissociated parts of self (DPSs) may be built around clusters of events, or smaller fragments of self may compartmentalize a particular emotion or aspect of an event. For example, most of my DID clients have had a DPS whose job was to store the rage of all other parts, because to express any anger put the individual at greater risk for abuse. Amnesia, or the K component of BASK, is common among DPSs in those with DID and is also one of the dissociative symptoms identified in the *Diagnostic and Statistical Manual of Mental Disorders* (DSM-5; American Psychiatric Association [APA], 2013).

In all cases of SA, a major part of the healing process involves reintegration of these BASK components. With counselees who have DID, the dissociative splitting is more severe, involving not only fragmentation of experience but also fragmentation of a sense of self and identity (Gingrich, 2013), which means that the process of integration will generally take longer. However, the same principles apply.

THE THREE-PHASE TREATMENT MODEL

Prior to the late 1990s, the primary focus of treatment for SA was accessing and processing abuse memories. Posttraumatic reexperiencing (intrusive) symptoms such as flashbacks and nightmares were frequently triggered by attempts to work with traumatic material early on in the process of counseling and psychotherapy, resulting in further destabilization of clients. In response to these difficulties, Herman (1997) proposed a phased treatment model. This model has formed the basis of the current three-phase model that has become the standard of care for complex trauma survivors, including those with SA and DID (Brand et al., 2013; International Society for the Study of Trauma and Dissociation, 2011). This model focuses on developing safety and stabilizing symptoms (Phase 1) before attempting memory processing (Phase 2). The third phase concentrates on consolidation of therapeutic gains and healthy integration into relational networks and society. A brief summary of treatment of SA using the three-phase model is outlined below. The following summaries are based on material from my book on complex trauma (Gingrich, 2013), where more detailed descriptions of each phase of the model can also be found.

Phase 1: Safety and symptom stabilization. Paying careful attention to issues of safety both within and outside the counseling setting is crucial, as is helping such counselees to be safe from their own potential self-destructive tendencies and their posttraumatic symptoms. The full process of healing is generally long-term for SASs. Therefore, Phase 1 could potentially take many months.

Safety within the therapeutic relationship. The disruption in the formation of secure attachment relationships associated with SA not only negatively affects the development of healthy relationships in general but also makes it extremely difficult to establish a solid therapeutic relationship. Respectful, empathic reflection of content and feelings and appropriate levels of authenticity are essential skills for developing rapport.

However, safety within the therapeutic relationship goes beyond rapport in that Christian counselors must actually become safe and remain safe for their SASs. Becoming safe involves remembering that every client is unique. Therefore, what works well for one SAS may not necessarily be beneficial for a different client. SA itself is often unpredictable, with victims not knowing when they will next be assaulted. As a result, SASs can be distressed by changes for which they have not been adequately prepared. Therefore, clinicians need to give advance warning if, for example, they are going to be away, change the session time, or alter the office setting in some way.

Paying continual attention to maintaining good therapeutic boundaries is essential to remaining safe for SASs, particularly once good rapport has been established. While judicious use of touch can be a powerful tool for healing, because touch is the medium through which SA is most commonly perpetrated, it can also easily be misused with SASs. Consulting with other mental health professionals who work with SA is a good safeguard.

Safety from others. Assessing whether or not SASs are currently safe from others who have the potential to harm them is also important. SASs may not have developed the capacity to identify healthy versus unhealthy or even abusive relationships. Psychotherapists and counselors can play a role in helping SASs discern if they are in safe, healthy relationships and, if necessary, assist them in finding physical safety. Some clients with DID may have experienced ritual abuse and mind control in addition to "regular" abuse. In these cases, special attention needs to be paid to whether they are in danger of being accessed (and reabused) by their perpetrator group (see chap. 12).

Safety from self and symptoms. It is not unusual for SASs to struggle with self-destructive and suicidal tendencies that must be dealt with right from the beginning of the counseling process. Intrusive posttraumatic symptoms can also be overwhelming for both the clients who are reexperiencing the abuse and their psychotherapists who may feel caught in a losing battle of managing the associated crises. The good news is that the ability of SASs to dissociate can be harnessed by counselors to help contain both posttraumatic and self-destructive symptoms.

Use of dissociation for symptom containment. Even when SASs do not dissociate to the extent of developing DID, I have found that they respond well to techniques I originally learned in treating highly dissociative clients. I think of symptoms as cries for help, as red flags that something needs attention. SASs may not be consciously aware of the reason for particular symptoms, but I believe that some part of them is allowing symptoms to manifest. Behavioral contracting with these DPSs can result in immediate reduction of symptoms.

If Claire is a client who is experiencing intrusive visual images of SA, the negotiation around this symptom may go something like the following:

> Claire, I know that these scenes that flash through your mind are very disturbing to you and are affecting your ability to function well at work. One way to look at what's happening is that there's a part of you that is allowing the images to come as a way of trying to help you heal, without realizing that the pictures are actually making life harder for you. Would you be willing to let me communicate with that part of you so that we could come to some kind of agreement about temporarily stopping those images?

Using language such as "a part of you" may seem strange to other types of clients, but it tends to resonate with SASs who intuitively sense that they have aspects of self or experience that are not fully integrated. If Claire consents, I will go on in this fashion:

> Claire, we can do this one of two ways. I can invite all parts of you to listen in and then ask if the part of you that is allowing the images to flash through your mind is listening. You could then respond according to your internal sense of what is happening. Or, I could give the same invitation but use a short-cut way of responding through use of "yes" and "no" finger signals.

The technical name for such finger signals is *ideomotor signaling* (Shenefel, 2011). I demystify the process by explaining to clients that use of the finger signals is just a way to bypass their conscious, cognitive processes and allow a hidden part of them a safe way to communicate. If Claire chooses to go this route, we would agree on which finger means "yes" and which indicates "no." I would then describe how the relevant finger would twitch a little when responding, without Claire having to make a conscious decision about which is the right answer. Claire and I would also come up with a "stop" signal so that if for any reason she could not verbalize her desire to pause or terminate the process, she could still communicate that wish to me. Ideomotor signaling is merely a tool to allow easier initial access to a disso-ciated aspect of the self of the SAS. The negotiation process is not dependent on its use, although clients often prefer it once they have experienced its benefits.

If Claire has decided she is willing to give it a try but is concerned that it will not work, I respond, "This is just a technique that I've found to be helpful with many of my clients, Claire. If nothing happens, nothing happens! In that case we'll just try something else." This generally alleviates any pressure to perform. I then go over again what Claire can expect:

> Claire, we have already decided on "yes," "no," and "stop" signals. In a few minutes I'll invite you to relax. Many people find that it's easier to concentrate if they close their eyes, but you can decide whether to close them or not. You will be able to hear what I'm saying at all times and are free to ask questions or stop the process at any point. I will then invite all parts of you to listen in, after which I will introduce myself, go over the finger signals once more, and go from there. *[Note: I always introduce myself because I do not know how dissociative the client might be and whether or not all parts of the client have been privy to my prior discussions with Claire.]* Do you have any other questions?

If Claire is ready to proceed, I will begin. After ensuring that the finger signals are understood, I will then say, "Claire has been telling me that she has been seeing a lot of images of a little girl getting hurt. Is the part of Claire who knows about these images listening in?" If there is no response, I will wait for a minute or two. If nothing happens, I will ask if there is a reason that there is no reply in an attempt to find out whether concerns exist have not been previously expressed. If there is an initial "no" response, I will ask the rest of Claire to extend the invitation inter-nally to listen in, offering further explanation of why I am seeking contact. Some-times this alleviates any fears, and that part of the client is then willing to have contact. If the initial response is a "yes," I will also explain my reasons for wanting to communicate. For example:

> I know that the images that Claire is seeing have been allowed for a reason. I want you to know that Claire now understands that you want to get her attention. That message has been received. The problem is that this is not a good time for Claire to deal with the content of those images. Claire needs to be able to work and attend school, and the images are making it hard for her to do that. She will need some time to stabilize. However, Claire is aware that she needs to deal with those images. Would you be willing to put those images away somewhere inside where Claire can't see them until some point in the future when Claire is better able to make use of them?

Often there is a "yes" response once that part of the client understands that he or she has been heard. I then debrief the entire experience with Claire. I let her know that this type of symptom containment is a temporary measure. My experience has been that such symptoms either totally disappear for a period of time or are greatly reduced.

A similar process can be used for other intrusive, recurring symptoms such as nightmares or dissociated affect. Self-destructive or suicidal behavior can be negotiated in the same way. The key is to make the contract with "all parts of Claire" so that there is no sabotage from other DPSs.

A DPS, whether an alter personality of a DID client or a dissociated aspect (BASK component) of an SAS who does not have DID, may initially present as antagonistic or even highly destructive to the client (e.g., actively suicidal, self-harming). In the DID literature such DPSs are often referred to as *persecutor alters* for this very reason.

Most often this hostility masks fear or is a misguided attempt to protect the client. For example, if a brutally raped child is told that she will be killed if she talks to anyone about the SA, a DPS associated with that trauma may believe that revealing the SA in therapy may result in her death. Ironically, in the DID client, the DPS may not understand that all dissociated parts of the client share the same body, so that the attempt to "silence" the one revealing the "secret" in therapy will result in her own death (and the death of all the other DPSs). Psychoeducation about the process of dissociation and the client's own dissociated personality structure may, therefore, need to precede successful negotiation around safety from self or resistance to discussing the abuse. I tend to talk to clients about dissociation as being on a continuum (see Gingrich, 2013) rather than prematurely share with them a DID diagnosis, which could potentially be destabilizing.

When contracting does not work well, it may be because the negotiations have not been done with the most appropriate DPS. For example, there may be some DPSs that are very concerned about suicidal behavior and will easily negotiate a no-suicide contract. But if they are not the DPSs that are feeling suicidal, the contract may be meaningless.

Other ways of managing symptoms. Of course, there are more traditional ways of helping SASs with their symptoms. Cognitive-behavioral techniques such as systematic desensitization and relaxation training, dialectical behavior therapy, and use of mindfulness can certainly be helpful. Courtois and Ford's (2009) excellent edited book, for example, contains chapters on multiple theoretical approaches to working with SA and other forms of complex trauma, including how to manage symptoms. However, I have focused primarily on making therapeutic use of the dissociative capacities of SA clients because the positive results are so immediate and are not as well known.

Phase 2: Processing of traumatic memories. The processing of horrendous SA memories is difficult for both clients and psychotherapists. Appropriate timing is essential for entering this second phase. Clients should be stable and have a good support network in place that can help sustain them through this work.

The BASK mode is particularly helpful during Phase 2 work. As mentioned earlier, for a particular memory to be fully integrated, all four BASK components need to be addressed. It is common for SASs to not have cognitive knowledge (K) for some or all abuse incidents. However, even when clients have never had amnesia for a particular traumatic experience, the affect (A), physical sensation (S), and behavior (B) associated with that knowledge (K) may be dissociated from it. Therefore, memory processing involves not merely accessing and talking about a particular memory at the cognitive level (K) but addressing all BASK components associated with it.

Accessing memories. Symptoms are clues to accessing blocked memories. Nightmares, full or partial flashbacks, intense emotion (e.g., anxiety, depression) for no apparent reason, seemingly random physical ailments, or confusing behavior can all be evidence of dissociated BASK components. The key to accessing the memory is to access the part of the individual who knows what the symptom is about. The procedure is similar to that which I described for symptom containment. I begin by getting consent from the client, deciding whether to use verbal responses or ideomotor signaling, going over the finger signals (if applicable), asking all parts of the person to listen in, introducing myself, and then asking if the part of the person who understands the symptom is available.

Let's say that Claire presents with the same symptom as before, that is, of being disturbed by visual flashbacks. However, rather than being in Phase 1, she is now in Phase 2 of the healing process. In this situation I would go through the same steps as before, but rather than asking that the symptom be compartmentalized, I now want to seek permission to process the content of the images. I will assume that preliminary steps have been taken and that through ideomotor signaling I have confirmation that I have contact with the part of Claire who understands what the flashbacks are about. I would proceed as follows:

> It was about a year ago that you agreed to keep Claire from seeing these images and you kept them away until recently. Thank you for keeping your agreement. Not seeing those images all the time really helped Claire get stronger, and she is doing much better now. I'm wondering if you think that this might be a good time for Claire to take a closer look at those images.

If there is a "yes" response, I would continue: "It is still important for Claire not to be overwhelmed. So we would need to take a look at one image at a time and go at a pace that Claire is comfortable with. Are you OK with that?" The same kind of procedure can be used whatever the problematic symptom might be (e.g., sound, smell, full flashback, nightmare, intense emotion).

It is essential to lay appropriate groundwork for memory processing. Once the decision has been made to enter Phase 2, clients sometimes want to dive into the process in an attempt to get it done quickly. When the necessity of careful pacing is not understood by the entire person, the result can be like opening Pandora's box—that is, memories can flood to the surface leaving the client feeling totally out of control and destabilized.

Even if Claire feels that she is ready to begin processing a particular memory, and the part of her that has allowed the visual images to come indicates assent to begin memory processing, I would also ask "all of Claire" if any part of her has concerns about going forward. If any apprehension is indicated, I would ask for clarification and, on the basis of the information given, either come to the conclusion that the timing is not good after all or continue the dialogue until all parts of Claire are comfortable continuing. Ideomotor signaling can be used only when asking closed questions, so any ongoing discussion requires verbal responses. Generally, this is not a problem once initial contact has been made with the relevant DPS.

Processing the SA memory. It is important for the SAS to be able to put together a cohesive trauma narrative (Siegel, 2003; 2009). So that there are no gaps in the narrative, and in order to combat the intense shame with which SASs inevitably struggle, clients should be encouraged to share every detail of the abuse memory from beginning to end. I used to think that by allowing my clients to talk only about the key aspects of abuse incidents, I was protecting them. In retrospect, I believe I was actually defending myself from having to face the full horror of what they had experienced. However, when there have been many similar incidents over time with the same perpetrator, groups of memories can sometimes be worked through simultaneously. All DPSs that hold similar memories, or aspects of specific memories, would have to be present (i.e., coconscious), adding in any nuances that are specific to their particular memories, even if one DPS shares the primary narrative.

While all of the BASK components of the SA memories need to be reexperienced to some degree in order for integration to occur, memory processing is not the equivalent of catharsis. There will be some tension between the client being "back there" and reliving the experience, and being in the here and now with the counselor. If clients begin to get lost in their memories, psychotherapists can help to keep their clients grounded by reminding them of where they are and what is happening in the present. For example, if Claire, in the middle of describing what she sees in her visual flashbacks, suddenly stops talking and looks terrified, I would say something like the following: "Claire, focus on my voice. It's Heather. You're in my office. It's 2017. I would like you to leave where you are inside and come back to the present. Feel the fabric of the chair you're sitting on with your fingers. Open your eyes and you will see the green paint on the walls and the purple color of the shirt that you're wearing."

Sometimes encouraging the client to move their hands or feet or stand up can also help. Usually this is all that is necessary. However, if Claire is still unresponsive, I would try a different tactic. Using a firm yet gentle voice, I would state, "Claire, I'm going to count to three, and when I reach the number three, you are going to open your eyes and come back to my office. One . . . you are beginning to come back . . . two . . . you are almost here . . . and three . . . you can open your eyes." On one occasion, as a last resort I snapped my fingers to get the client's attention, but that produced a startle response that was not ideal.

Once Claire is fully back in the present, we will process what happened and decide whether we should continue with the memory or wait until the following session. If we agree that putting it on hold for a week is a better option, Claire's dissociative abilities can again be utilized to keep her from being retraumatized during the week. I could give Claire the option of temporarily "storing" the memory in my filing cabinet or placing it in an imaginary locked container inside of her. It is important that all DPSs understand that the memory needs to be compartmentalized between sessions.

If working through a particular memory feels too overwhelming for the counselee, the emotional intensity can be lowered by using distancing techniques. For example, SASs can be invited to visualize a TV screen complete with a remote control that will enable them to stop, play, rewind, fast forward, pause, and mute the action. The affective element (A) can be processed once the cognitive knowledge (K) has been gained.

While it may be tempting to extend a session if a memory is not completely processed, it is generally better to keep to the agreed-on session time so that the client knows what to expect. On occasion a longer session can be prearranged for a particular purpose. But memory processing is intense, and there is nothing to be gained by both client and psychotherapist leaving a session totally depleted. Allow sufficient time at the end of each session to debrief with clients and ensure that they are grounded enough to get home safely.

Avoiding suggestibility. Much research has been done on the nature of memory since the False Memory Syndrome Foundation, formed in 1993, made claims that therapists could implant false memories of sexual abuse, and that repressed memories, that is, amnesia for sexual abuse, were not possible (Hyman & Loftus, 1997). Research findings have shown conclusively that it is possible to have memory blocks for incidents of trauma and sexual abuse (Brown, Scheflin, & Whitfield, 1999). Results have also indicated that memory is not infallible, that it is subject to distortion (Chu, 2011).

For this reason, those working with SASs have to be particularly careful not to ask leading questions. Open, general questions that put the onus on clients to fill in the missing pieces need to be standard practice. For example, if the client says, "I see a dark figure coming through the door," potentially suggestible responses could be "Is it a man?" or "Is it your uncle?" or even "Could it be an evil spirit?" Nonsuggestive interventions could be "Tell me more about this figure" or "Can you describe what you are seeing?" or even an empathic reflection of feeling such as "You seem really scared right now."

We cannot know for sure that what our clients remember is accurate in every detail. Perpetrators sometimes use drugs, tricks, or lies, which can all distort perception (Miller, 2012). However, for healing to take place, it is the subjective experiential reality of the client that is important. This can be explained to clients in a way that does not invalidate their experience but acknowledges that the only way to know for sure what happened is if there is corroborating evidence (e.g., medical records, court documentation, or eyewitness accounts of others). The most helpful stance that the counselor or psychotherapist can take is to process SA memories as though what clients remember is true, while retaining some healthy skepticism because of the fallibility of memory.

Working through intense emotions: General guidelines. A significant aspect of Phase 2 work is helping clients process the intense emotions surrounding their SA experiences. The A component of the BASK model is one aspect of this work. However, strong emotions are not limited to occasions in which SASs are remembering how they felt at the time that they were being abused; they also arise as a result of confronting the overall impact these traumatic events have both in the past and in the present.

Some SASs have dissociated their emotions to such an extent that they are easily overwhelmed by awareness of having any degree of affective experience. At the other extreme are those who have had difficulty controlling emotional impulses. The key is to strike a balance between encouraging increased awareness of affect so that it does not remain dissociated and maintaining some control of the process.

Just as dissociation can be used to help contain posttraumatic symptoms in Phase 1, so the ability of SASs to dissociate can be useful in Phase 2 affective work. For example, if a client has expressed powerful anger during the session that has not been fully worked through, the anger can be figuratively stored away between sessions so that relationships in the outside world are not damaged through inappropriate outbursts.

My basic rule within sessions is that neither I nor the client is harmed and that my office is not damaged. Within this framework a lot is permissible in terms of emotional expression. Christian clients, in particular, may be hesitant to acknowledge the strength of what are often labeled negative emotions (e.g., hatred, anger) out of fear that they will be dishonoring God. I remind these individuals that God already knows what emotions they are harboring, so that even if they attempt to deny their existence, they are not fooling God.

I find the analogy of an infected wound helpful. Sometimes a deep cut can heal over on the surface while festering underneath. Such wounds may need to be lanced, allowing the pus to drain, after which they can be cleaned and disinfected so that proper healing can occur. Emotional wounds are similar. Intense, disturbing emotions may need to come to the surface and be worked through so that the wound can properly heal.

Christian SASs who are struggling with what a "Christian" response to their abuse could look like may also be referred to Scripture. The psalmist expresses a range of deeply felt, raw emotions such as desire for revenge (e.g., Ps 10, 28, and 55), despair, and hopelessness (Ps 42). Christ himself expressed agony in the Garden of Gethsemane as he wrestled with his imminent crucifixion (Mk 14:32-36). Individuals who have been sexually abused can often identify with such feelings.

Dealing with specific emotions. While a wide range of emotions can come up for SASs, some are commonly experienced. The following are examples of groups of emotions that are often related:

- *Mourning: denial, anger, and depression.* There are many losses for SASs to mourn: loss of childhood innocence, the recognition that they were not a loved child, loss of hope that their parents will ever love them, or coming to grips with lost relational or career opportunities because of their symptoms. For survivors who had amnesia for their abuse until later in life, there has to be readjustment of their whole sense of life history and, therefore, identity. While healing can open up new doors of possibility, nothing can take away the years, relationships, or opportunities that already have been lost. It is no wonder that SASs, even after many years of counseling, go back and forth between disavowal of the abuse and depression that accompanies the realization of the truth. These losses need to be identified and permission given to grieve them.

- *Shame.* The sexual nature of the trauma perpetrated against them makes SASs particularly vulnerable to struggling with shame. Shame is painfully apparent when clients have difficulty making eye contact. Shame can serve as a barrier to entering Phase 2 work because of the related fear of exposing oneself to someone else (i.e., the counselor). However, the nonjudgmental response of the psychotherapist can be immensely powerful in decreasing shame. After successfully testing the waters with their counselors, SASs often find it helpful to continue to "break the silence" by sharing their abuse histories with others. Sometimes they need guidance in how much to reveal and to whom, so that they do not reveal such personal information indiscriminately, with damaging consequences.

- *Self-hatred.* Related to shame is self-hatred. SASs tend to blame themselves for their abuse, believing that there is something inherently bad in them that is deserving of punishment. While it is true that we are all sinners (Rom 3:23), it is not true that SA is a legitimate form of love, affection, or discipline. Self-blame is further encouraged by perpetrators who use it as a way to keep their victims from reporting the abuse. The empathic, nonjudgmental acceptance of counselors who see their SASs as valuable creations of God will go a long way in breaking through these distorted self-perceptions. Christian clients often are aware of the Bible verses that talk about our worth as children of God. However, this truth seldom penetrates their whole beings, being relegated instead to cognitive, head knowledge. However, being in the presence of a person who knows their worst secrets and accepts them anyway is often an important step toward recognizing that Christ, too, loves and values them.

- *Fear of abandonment.* SASs were emotionally abandoned as children by those who were supposed to protect them, a relational pattern that often replays itself throughout their lives. Seldom having developed a secure attachment style, SASs bring their relational insecurities into the therapeutic relationship. As a result, these counselees are extremely sensitive to perceived rejection and tend to have deep-seated fears of being abandoned. Consistency over time, sometimes many months or years, is the primary way to combat abandonment issues. The counselor taking vacation times, going to conferences, and canceling sessions for any reason (including illness, surgery, weather, childbirth, or family crisis) and virtually any change affecting the structure of the sessions (e.g., change in office, appointment times, or fees) can be expected to stir up fears of abandonment. These should be anticipated and care should be taken to prepare clients ahead of time for any changes.

- *Anxiety, fear, and terror.* SASs have had a lot to fear. During memory processing, some of the terror that survivors felt as children in the midst of a particular abuse incident resurfaces, or the anxiety that they experienced while anticipating the next attack is relived. In their adult lives, these fear responses are commonly dissociated from their source (A of BASK). While relaxation exercises, systematic desensitization, and other behavioral or cognitive-behavioral techniques can be useful in helping to work toward alleviating these feelings, at times they are minimally helpful. In some of these instances I have found that it is a child DPS that is the one feeling the terror. A clue that the anxiety stems from dissociated affect can be to ask clients, "How old do you feel when you are so afraid?" Often they are surprised to realize that they do not feel like an adult. This can become a steppingstone for further memory processing.

Antianxiety medication can be helpful for clients whose anxiety is so high that attempts to compartmentalize it are not effective. If counselees are too overwhelmed, they will not be able to make good use of therapy. Toward the end of the therapy process, SASs will often find that they no longer need to take antianxiety medication on a regular basis.

Integration of self. When a particular memory is processed in such a way that all the BASK components are addressed, a more integrated memory is a result. When a number of memories are processed, along with the emotions that arise in reaction to these memories, integration of self is furthered. A good analogy might be a jigsaw puzzle in which many of the puzzle pieces have been cut up or torn into smaller parts. In order to complete the puzzle, one must first put each puzzle piece back together before finding its place in the puzzle as a whole. For SASs whose abuse was not chronic, or for those who were abused at an older age, the puzzle may have been relatively intact even before entering treatment. Others, whose SA resulted in DID, may have entered therapy severely fragmented, with little of the puzzle intact. In instances where there has been greater use of dissociation to keep aspects of self and experience compartmentalized, integration of self will generally take longer.

Phase 3: Consolidation and resolution. SASs may have experienced major upheaval during Phase 2. Their view of their own life history, and therefore their overall sense of identity, may have been severely challenged. This is particularly true of survivors who have DID; in fact, identity confusion is considered a DSM-5 (APA, 2013) dissociative symptom area. While much work will have been done in Phase 2 to grieve these losses as well as begin to wrestle with a new sense of who they are, consolidation of these changes is the core component of Phase 3. It is also not unusual for emotions that were supposedly worked through in Phase 2 to reappear in Phase 3 as they are examined through the eyes of a more fully integrated individual.

Learning new coping strategies. In Phases 1 and 2, the dissociative abilities of SASs were used to help them manage overwhelming emotions. However, by the end of Phase 2, integration of self and experience have progressed to the extent that counselees no longer have the same capacity to dissociate. Therefore, they need to develop new ways of dealing with their feelings. This is where counselors can draw on everything they know about helping clients regulate their affect (e.g., cognitive-behavioral techniques, relaxation training, dialectical behavior therapy, mindfulness).

Navigating changing relationships. As SASs get healthier, they will likely experience increased tension in many of their former relationships. In a marriage, for example, the SAS may have previously been in a dependent role, a position that may be challenged as the survivor gains strength, desires a more equal footing, and finds his or her voice. The spouse of a DID client may have developed relationships with various DPSs (e.g., child personalities) and may consciously or unconsciously sabotage continued growth. Similarly, parental roles may change as healthier counselees either increase their involvement or change how they relate to their children.

If similar changes can be navigated within friendships, these relationships may be strengthened. However, counselees may discover that they have emotionally outgrown their former friendships and struggle with how to develop new relationships on a different basis. This may also apply to their relationship with God as well as relationships within the body of Christ. Counselees may find themselves searching for a new place to worship, recognizing that their theology no longer fits with that of their current church, or that it no longer meets the spiritual, emotional, or relational needs it once did. The process can be particularly painful when former church congregations have invested a lot of time and energy in the SAS and have been helpful at an earlier place in the journey of healing.

Relationships with members of their family of origin may be tumultuous, particularly if incest was involved. SASs who choose to explicitly address the issue of their abuse with family members risk rejection and even rage from those who are unwilling to acknowledge the abuse or who blame the victims for it. Whether or not survivors choose to confront their perpetrators, at the point in time when the abuse is no longer kept secret, family members are forced to choose sides.

The process of forgiveness. One of the difficulties in looking at forgiveness is that it is defined in various ways by Christian authors. Sells and Hervey (2011) summarize the literature on forgiveness, particularly as it is relevant to SA. I have found Tracy's (2005) category of psychological forgiveness particularly applicable for counselors and psychotherapists. He suggests that for survivors psychological forgiveness involves both letting go of hatred and revenge and extending grace to the ones who wronged them, perhaps by praying that their perpetrators find healing. Psychological forgiveness does not necessitate reconciliation of the relationship between victim and perpetrator. Reconciliation is often not possible because the perpetrator either denies or minimizes the abuse and/or there is risk of further victimization of survivors or their children. The deep-seated dysfunction of the SA perpetrator is often not understood by Christian pastors or laypeople, who may exert undue pressure on the SAS to quickly reconcile with a perpetrator who is neither fully repentant nor safe (Anton & Fortune, 1992).

Many of my Christian SASs have expressed concern that I too will push them toward premature forgiveness, when they cannot envision extending forgiveness toward their perpetrator as even a possibility despite what is exhorted in the Bible. The approach I take is to talk about forgiveness as a process that will take time. I remind them that God knows them and loves them and will not expect the impossible.

While SASs can make a decision that they want to forgive and can begin the process early on in treatment, I do not believe that forgiveness can be complete until some point in Phase 3 work. Prior to trauma processing, SASs do not wholly understand what has been perpetrated against them and the full impact of the abuse on their lives; therefore they do not entirely comprehend what they are attempting to forgive. I have found that forgiveness is generally a natural outcome of the healing process for those who are seeking spiritual and psychological wholeness.

Ending the therapeutic relationship. Many SASs will never have experienced the healthy ending of a relationship. Terminating therapy well, therefore, can serve as a model for future good endings. The longer the counseling relationship, the greater the period of time that should be devoted to termination issues. Early on in Phase 3, the thought of ending the therapeutic relationship will likely be totally overwhelming to SASs. However, as SASs become more comfortable with who they are as people, as therapeutic gains are consolidated, and as issues of changing relationships, emotional regulation, and forgiveness are resolved, they will become more comfortable with the idea of termination.

I often space out appointments in the last few months of counseling so that SASs have a chance to gain confidence that they can cope between sessions without decompensating. If we have met once a week, I will suggest going to every other week, then every third week, and so on, with the stipulation that clients can ask for additional sessions between times if they feel the need. I also keep the door open to the possibility of future sessions. Having these options available helps to alleviate anxiety, so that extra sessions are seldom necessary.

The ending of such an intense, long-term relationship involves loss for both SASs and their therapists. It is tempting to make exceptions that counselors would not normally consider with regard to ongoing contact with SASs. While receiving updates from former clients from time to time may be appropriate, it is important to keep in mind ethical guidelines with regard to any kind of ongoing relationship. Clients will often hope that a mutual friendship can develop after the formal counseling relationship is over. However, because of the power differential between therapist and client, it is highly unlikely that a fully mutual relationship is possible after the kind of intensive counseling necessitated by SA, and it is generally considered unethical.

SPIRITUAL ISSUES AND RESOURCES

Some SASs come into therapy with a strong faith in God and an ability to benefit greatly from explicit use of spiritual resources. The challenge is to not err either on the side of being overly cautious or on the side of being overly presumptuous about what might be helpful as it relates to spirituality. Discerning the difference is a matter of developing good clinical judgment and spiritual discernment and then carefully testing the waters with informed consent from the client.

There are SASs who report full healing solely through the prayer ministries and the relational support of their church. I have no reason to doubt these testimonies. God is the source of all healing, with psychotherapy being only one vehicle. However, many survivors, both Christian and not, have distorted views of God and would not benefit from prayer ministry of any kind. They often wrestle with how God could love them yet not have rescued them from terrible abuse. It is particularly difficult for those who were abused by their own fathers to view God the Father as anything but punitive and abusive.

The most therapeutic responses toward SASs who are struggling with how God could have allowed them to suffer so much are often either empathic responses (e.g., "It just hurts so much to know that God didn't somehow stop the abuse from happening, even when you pleaded with him so desperately to rescue you") or responses that combine empathy and genuineness (e.g., "I feel so sad thinking about you as a little girl crying out to God for help and feeling so abandoned by him when the abuse didn't stop").

When counselees are not given the simplistic answers they may have come to expect of Christians, but instead are given permission to openly admit their doubts and fears with respect to their relationship with God, I have found that they can often begin to see where God was at work in their lives all along. As hostility toward God lessens, it may be more appropriate to respectfully offer to use Scripture to help confront their distortions about God or to bring comfort in times of distress.

I believe that prayer is an essential aspect of the healing process for SASs. Christian counselors should pray for their clients outside session time, as well as silently pray for wisdom and discernment as the session progresses. While in-session verbal prayer can be helpful, it needs to be used with caution and the full, meaningful consent of the client. The key is to recognize that prayer, in the context of therapy, is a specific type of intervention and needs to be processed with the client as any other intervention would be (Chapelle, 2000; McMinn, 1996; Tan, 1994,

1996). For example, discussions regarding who should pray (i.e., client, counselor, or both), what the focus of the prayer should be, and the timing of the prayer all need to be part of the decision-making process. If explicit prayer does happen, it needs to be debriefed with the client.

Specialized forms of prayer, such as inner healing prayer (e.g., Hurding, 1995) or Theophostic Prayer Ministry (Smith, 2005; now called Transformation Prayer Ministry, www.transformationprayer.org), are generally used by lay counselors or prayer ministers. However, they could potentially be used in Phase 2 by mental health professionals as part of memory processing, particularly if integrated within the fabric of the therapy process as a whole. Again, informed consent is necessary, and such an intervention must be carefully processed and debriefed.

Some SASs report ritualized abuse by Satanic cults or secret societies (see Gingrich, 2013; Miller, 2012; and chap. 12 in this volume for more information about dealing with ritual abuse as well as the demonic). While the three-phase model still applies to these clients, there are additional issues to consider, including being triggered by symbols of Christianity.

Christians in general do not understand dissociative symptoms. Therefore, in some church contexts or circles, SASs who have DID are thought to be particularly sinful or are accused of being demon possessed. Whether or not there is any validity to these charges, great damage can be done to SASs who are forced to undergo deliverance or exorcism rituals. Counselors should not be surprised when this subject is broached in therapy. Highly dissociative SASs may have already been through traumatizing attempts to rid them of evil spirits, which then become additional trauma to process in Phase 2, or they may be feeling pressured by their faith communities to undergo such procedures.

COUNSELOR SELF-CARE

Working with SASs can take a physical, emotional, and spiritual toll. Listening to horrendous abuse narratives week after week can lead to vicarious traumatization, a condition in which counselors can manifest trauma symptoms as a result of conducting psychotherapy with trauma survivors. Practitioners must, therefore, find ways to build physical, emotional, spiritual, and professional resilience against becoming traumatized themselves (see Gingrich, 2013, and chap. 4 in this volume for more details).

HOW THE CHURCH CAN HELP

While counseling or psychotherapy can be of immense help in the healing process of SASs, it is not enough. Churches play a necessary role. Outlined below are some examples of how churches can play a part in the healing process.

Education. The posttraumatic and dissociative symptoms of SASs can be easily misinterpreted and misunderstood. Therefore, it is important for pastors, lay leaders, lay counselors, life coaches, spiritual directors, and other members of church congregations to be educated about SA and DID. Counselors can offer seminars, consult with church leaders, or point individuals to books and other resources. Some organizations exist specifically to help minister to SA and highly dissociative individuals and to train those who desire to be of help to them (see Gingrich, 2013, for more information about organizations that train Christians to work with SA, as well as other resources that are available.)

Churches can help to prevent child SA from occurring in the first place through screening volunteers (including running background checks), developing protocols to reduce the possibility of abuse, and training staff and volunteers to recognize signs of child abuse. There is also Christian education curriculum that helps teach children about abuse (e.g., FaithTrust Institute, www.faithtrustinstitute.org). SA can be addressed from the pulpit as well.

Emotional and spiritual support. Support for SASs can be offered either formally or informally. Formal support can take the form of groups such as Celebrate Recovery, other modified 12-step programs, or groups specifically designed for SASs. Some churches have a lay ministry program in place in which lay counselors, mentors, prayer ministers, or life coaches are available to wounded people.

Often the best kind of support is informal. Ultimately SASs need to be surrounded by caring, safe people who will accept them wherever they are in their healing process without judgment. There can be danger for SASs from people who push too hard and fast for healing, perhaps expecting easy fixes through prayer, deliverance from demons, or application of Scripture.

HOPE

People sometimes think it is strange that my favorite course to teach is Counseling for Trauma and Abuse and that the clients I most enjoy working with are adults who have been abused as children, particularly those with DID. What has kept me in this field for over 30 years? It is the privilege of walking with such deeply wounded individuals and witnessing the miracle of healing that God performs in their lives. There is hope for even the most fragmented and damaged survivors of SA, as well as hope that those of us in helping roles can be sustained in the midst of such difficult work.

REFERENCES

American Psychiatric Association (2013). *Diagnostic and statistical manual of mental disorders* (5th ed.). Washington, DC: Author.

Anton, J., & Fortune, M. M. (Producers), & Gargiulo, M. (Director). (1992*). Hear their cries* [Video]. Available from FaithTrust Institute at www.faithtrustinstitute.org

Arnold, C., & Fisch, R. (2011). *The impact of complex trauma on development.* Lanham, MD; Jason Aronson.

Bass, E., & Davis, L. (2008). *The courage to heal: A guide for women survivors of child sexual abuse* (4th ed.). New York, NY: William Morrow Paperbacks.

Benner, D. G. (1998). *Care of souls: Revisioning Christian nurture and counsel.* Grand Rapids, MI: Baker Books.

Bowlby, J. (1988). *A secure base: Parent-child attachment and healthy human development.* London, England: Routledge.

Brand, B., McNary, S. W., Myrick, A. C., Classen, C., Lanius, R., Loewenstein, R. J., . . . Putnam, F. W. (2013). A longitudinal naturalistic study of patients with dissociative disorders treated by community clinicians. *Psychological Trauma: Theory, Research, Practice, and Policy, 5*(4), 301-8.

Brand, B. L., Sar, V., Stavropoulos, P., Krüger, C., Korzekwa, M., Martinez-Taboas, A., & Middleton, W. (2016). Separating fact from fiction: An empirical examination of six myths about dissociative identity disorder. *Harvard Review of Psychiatry, 24*(4), 257-70. doi:10.1097/HRP.0000000000000100

Braun (1988). The BASK model of dissociation: Clinical applications. *Dissociation, 1*(2), 16-23.

Brown, D., Scheflin, A. W., & Whitfield, C. L. (1999). Recovered memories: The weight of the evidence in science and in the courts. *Journal of Psychiatry & Law, 27,* 5-156.

Cassidy, J., & Shaver, P. R. (2016). *Handbook of attachment: Theory, research, and clinical application* (3rd ed.). New York, NY: Guilford Press.

Chapelle, W. (2000). A series of progressive legal and ethical decision making steps for using Christian spiritual interventions in psychotherapy. *Journal of Psychology & Theology, 28*(1), 43-53.

Chu, J. A. (2011). *Rebuilding shattered lives: Treating complex PTSD and dissociative disorders* (2nd ed.). Hoboken, NJ: John Wiley & Sons.

Courtois, C. A., & Ford, J. D. (Eds.). (2009). *Treating complex traumatic stress disorders: An evidence-based guide.* New York, NY: Guilford Press.

Dell, P. F., & O'Neil, J. A. (Eds.) (2009). *Dissociation and the dissociative disorders: DSM-V and beyond.* New York, NY: Routledge.

DePrince, A. P., Brown, L. S., Cheit, R. E., Freyd, J. J., Gold, S. N., Pezdek, K., & Quina, K. (2012). Motivated forgetting and misremembering: Perspectives from betrayal trauma theory. *Nebraska Symposium on Motivation, 58,* 193-50.

DePrince, A. P., & Freyd, J. J. (2007). Trauma-induced dissociation. In M. J. Friedman, T. M. Keane, & P. A. Resick (Eds.), *Handbook of PTSD: Science and practice* (pp. 135-50). New York, NY: Guilford Press.

Ford, J. D. (2009). Neurobiological and developmental research: Clinical implications. In C. A. Courtois & J. D. Ford (Eds.), *Treating complex traumatic stress disorders: An evidence-based guide* (pp. 31-58). New York, NY: Guilford Press.

Freyd, J. J., DePrince, A. P., & Gleaves, D. H. (2007). The state of betrayal trauma theory. *Memory, 15,* 295-311.

Gingrich, H. D. (2005). Trauma and dissociation in the Philippines. *Journal of Trauma Practice, 4*(3/4), 245-69.

Gingrich, H. D. (2013). *Restoring the shattered self: A Christian counselor's guide to working with complex trauma.* Downers Grove, IL: IVP Academic.

Herman, J. (1997). *Trauma and recovery: The aftermath of violence—from domestic abuse to political terror.* New York, NY: Basic Books.

Howell, E. F. (2011). *Understanding and treating dissociative identity disorder: A relational approach.* New York, NY: Taylor & Francis Group.

Hurding, R. (1995). Pathways to wholeness: Christian journeying in a postmodern age. *Journal of Psychology and Christianity, 14,* 293-305.

Hyman, I. E., & Loftus, E. F. (1997). Some people recover memories of childhood trauma that never really happened. In P. S. Appelbaum, L. A. Uyehara, & M. R. Elin (Eds.), *Trauma and memory: Clinical and legal controversies.* New York, NY: Oxford University Press.

International Society for the Study of Trauma and Dissociation (2011). Guidelines for treating dissociative identity disorder in adults (3rd revision). *Journal of Trauma and Dissociation, 12,* 188-212.

Liotte, G. (2009). Attachment and dissociation. In P. F. Dell & J. A. O'Neil (Eds.), *Dissociation and the dissociative disorders: DSM-V and beyond* (pp. 53-65). New York, NY: Routledge.

Lyons-Ruth, K., Dutra, L., Schuder, M., & Bianchi, I. (2006). From infant attachment disorganization to adult dissociation: Relational adaptations or traumatic experiences? *Psychiatric Clinics of North America, 29,* 63-86.

McFarlane, A. C. (2007). Resilience, vulnerability, and the course of posttraumatic reactions. In B. A. van der Kolk, A. C. McFarlane, & L. Weisaeth (Eds.), *Traumatic stress: The effects of overwhelming experience on mind, body, and society* (pp. 155-81). New York, NY: Guilford Press.

McFarlane, A. C., & Girolamo, G. (2007). The nature of traumatic stressors and the epidemiology of posttraumatic reactions. In B. A. van Der Kolk, A. C. McFarlane, & L. Weisaeth (Eds.), *Traumatic stress: The effects of overwhelming experience on mind, body, and society* (pp. 129-54). New York, NY: Guilford Press.

McMinn, M. R. (1996). *Psychology, theology, and spirituality in Christian counseling.* Wheaton, IL: Tyndale.

Miller, A. (2012). *Healing the unimaginable: Treating ritual abuse and mind control.* London, England: Karnac Books.

Nijenhuis, E. R., van der Hart, O., Kruger, K., & Steele, K. (2004). Somatoform dissociation, reported abuse, and animal defence-like reactions. *Australian and New Zealand Journal of Psychiatry, 38,* 678-86.

Ogawa, J. R., Sroufe, L. A., Weinfield, N. S., Carlson, E. A., & Egeland, B., (1997). Development and the fragmented self: Longitudinal study of dissociative symptomatology in a nonclinical sample. *Developmental Psychopathology, 9,* 855-79.

Ogden, P., Minton, K., & Pain, C. (2006). *Trauma and the body: A sensorimotor approach to psychotherapy.* New York, NY: Norton.

Pearlman, L. A., & Courtois, C. A. (2005). Clinical applications of the attachment framework: Relational treatment of complex trauma. *Journal of Traumatic Stress, 18,* 449-60.

Putnam, F. W. (1997). *Dissociation in children and adolescents: A developmental perspective.* New York, NY: Guilford Press.

Schmutzer, A. J. (Ed.). (2011). *The long journey home: Understanding and ministering to the sexually abused.* Eugene, OR: Wipf and Stock.

Sells, J., & Hervey, E. G. (2011). Forgiveness in sexual abuse: Defining our identity in the journey toward wholeness. In A. J. Schmutzer (Ed.), *The long journey home: Understanding and ministering to the sexually abused* (pp. 169-85). Eugene, OR: Wipf and Stock.

Shenefel, P. D. (2011). Ideomotor signaling: From divining spiritual messages to discerning subconscious answers during hypnosis and hypnoanalysis, a historical perspective. *American Journal of Clinical Hypnosis, 53*(3), 157-67.

Shore, A. N. (2003). Early relational trauma, disorganized attachment, and the development of a predisposition to violence. In M. F. Solomon & D. J. Siegel (Eds.), *Healing trauma* (pp. 107-67). New York, NY: Norton.

Shore, A. N. (2009). Right-brain affect regulation: An essential mechanism of development, trauma, dissociation, and psychotherapy. In D. Fosha, D. J. Siegel, & M. Solomon (Eds.), *The healing power of emotion: Affective neuroscience, development, and clinical practice* (pp. 112-44). New York, NY: Norton.

Siegel, D. J. (2003). An interpersonal neurobiology of psychotherapy: The developing mind and the resolution of trauma. In M. F. Solomon & D. J. Siegel (Eds.), *Healing trauma: Attachment, mind, body, and brain* (pp. 1-56). New York, NY: Norton.

Siegel, D. J. (2009). Emotion as integration: A possible answer to the question, What is emotion? In D. Fosha, D. J. Siegel, & M. Solomon (Eds.), *The healing power of emotion: Affective neuroscience, development, and clinical practice* (pp. 145-71). New York, NY: Norton.

Smith, E. M. (2005). *Healing life's hurts through Theophostic Prayer.* Campbellsville, KY: New Creation.

Stoltenborgh, M., Van Ijzendoorn, M. H., Euser, E. M., & Bakermans-Kranenburg, M. J. (2011). A global perspective on child sexual abuse: Meta-analysis of prevalence around the world. *Child Maltreatment, 16,* 17-101.

Tan, S.-Y. (1994). Ethical considerations in religious psychotherapy: Potential pitfalls and unique resources. *Journal of Psychology & Theology, 22*(4), 389-94.

Tan, S.-Y. (1996). Practicing the presence of God: The work of Richard J. Foster and its applications to psychotherapeutic practice. *Journal of Psychology and Christianity, 15*(1), 17-28.

Tracy, S. R. (2005). *Mending the soul: Understanding and healing abuse.* Grand Rapids, MI: Zondervan.

Tracy, S. R. (2011). Definitions and prevalence rates of sexual abuse: Quantifying, explaining, and facing a dark reality. In A. J. Schmutzer (Ed.), *The long journey home: Understanding and ministering to the sexually abused* (pp. 3-12). Eugene, OR: Wipf and Stock.

Wilson, J. P. (2004). PTSD and complex PTSD: Symptoms, syndromes, and diagnoses. In J. P. Wilson & T. M. Keane (Eds.), *Assessing psychological trauma and PTSD* (2nd ed., pp. 7-44). New York, NY: Guilford Press.

THE TREATMENT OF RITUAL
ABUSE AND MIND CONTROL

ALISON MILLER AND
HEATHER DAVEDIUK GINGRICH

Someone recently told me (Alison) that I needed a break from "studying evil." That phrase, *studying evil*, stuck with me, and as I thought about it, I realized that it is indeed what I have been doing. The people I have treated for the past 25 years, survivors of mind control (MC) and ritual abuse (RA) whom I study, learn from, write about, and hopefully help heal, have, since childhood, been traumatized by highly organized evil.

While we only need to look at news headlines to be reminded of the presence of evil in this world, and we are aware that we are all sinners, many of us are unaware of the depths of evil in which some human beings engage. It may even be easier to remain relatively oblivious to these horrible realities that can potentially threaten our sense of safety in the world. This may be part of the reason that there has been ongoing controversy about the very existence of ritual abuse and mind control (deMause, 1994). However, despite the emotional difficulty of the material, it is important to address because many Christian counselors knowingly or unknowingly have clients who have been victims of RA or MC or both. This chapter will be a challenging read.

DEFINITIONS

The terms *ritual abuse* and *mind control*, while intricately related, are not synonymous, yet unfortunately there has not been consensus about exactly how they differ. Some writers (e.g., Noblitt & Noblitt, 2014) use *RA* as a generic term and reserve *MC* for abuse by medical experts and government agencies. Others (e.g., Lacter, 2011; Miller, 2012) use *MC* as the generic term and reserve *RA* for mind control by religious groups. In any case, the goal of both is to take control of a victim's mind and behavior so that the person will engage in activities that would ordinarily run counter to the positive aspects of human nature. The way the terms are used is less important than an understanding of the actual practices and their effect on the victims.

Lacter, in her extensive website (End Ritual Abuse, http://endritualabuse.org/), describes the activities of persons or groups engaging in these practices:

- Extreme, sadistic, repetitive, physical abuse/torture, often to near-death
- Exploitation of the mind's capacity to dissociate trauma, to manipulate behavior, to create amnesia, and to prevent disclosure
- Mind-control and brainwashing techniques for the purpose of indoctrination and control
- Drugs to induce immobility, pain, confusion, hallucinations, unconscious states, depersonalization, and derealization
- Systematic abuse and rituals to coerce and indoctrinate victims into the abusers' beliefs and worldview
- Force, threats, and manipulation to coerce victims to harm others
- Sexual abuse of children and adults including rape, prostitution, pornography, snuff films, and bestiality
- Trafficking and slavery of children and adults
- Abuse beginning in infancy and childhood, with the goal of lifelong control
- Deprivation of basic needs and human contact, including confinement and isolation
- Human and animal sacrifice to appease and empower humans and their deities
- Nonconsenting medical and psychological experimentation to increase the ability to control a victim's mind and behavior
- Attempts to control or dominate the "soul," "spirit," or their equivalents crossculturally

RECENT HISTORY OF RA/MC

For millennia, and probably for all recorded history, occult religious groups have abused children in the names of their deities (Noblitt & Noblitt, 2008, 2014). For example, the Old Testament contains references to malevolent magical practices (e.g., Ezek 13) and sacrifice of children (e.g., Abraham and Isaac in Gen 22:1-13 and Heb 11:17; Jephthah and his daughter in Judg 11:29-40; the people of Judah in Jer 7:31).

More recent historical records (Lifton, 1986/2000) describe Nazi doctors who experimented in heinous ways on both children and adults in the World War II concentration camps, places where there were no ethical guidelines for research on human beings. What is not generally known is that these same Nazi doctors, along with experts of other nationalities eager to learn from them, continued their experiments after the war. The results of such appalling research served to guide international political and criminal groups who wanted to learn how to train children to participate in illegal activities their entire lives without their conscious knowledge of this participation.

Hoffman's memoirs (2014, 2016) of her personal experience of over 70 years demonstrate some of the early connections between the Nazi doctors, US and international political groups, secret societies (in her case the Illuminati and a hidden group within the Freemasons), magical religions that connected worship with sexual violence, and traditional organized crime involving child prostitution and pornography, human trafficking, and drug smuggling. She remembers her grandfather, a top-level Illuminati programmer of human minds, and his assistant swapping methods with the Nazi doctor Josef Mengele, and American and international politicians taking advantage of both these sources of mind control knowledge. She shows how, when she was still a child and an adolescent, her primary owners (i.e., her family) sold her services for prostitution and breeding to organized criminal groups that traded in child sexual victims and babies for various kinds of misuse.

STRUCTURED PERSONALITY SYSTEMS

In chapter eleven, I (Heather) contrasted the developmental processes that occur in children raised in a healthy environment with those who have suffered from chronic, relational trauma in early childhood. In healthy development the dissociated self-states that are present at birth become increasingly integrated through attuned parenting from a primary attachment figure. In cases of child abuse, such as incest or physical and emotional abuse by a parent, the normal process of integration is thwarted, the child is more likely to develop an insecure attachment style, and the ability to dissociate that exists for all young children is more likely to be used as a psychological defense mechanism to deal with the trauma. The fragmentation of the child's self and identity that accompanies such abuses thus tends to be a spontaneous occurrence to which the perpetrator may be oblivious.[1]

This is quite different from the intentional use of dissociation by mind-controlling perpetrator groups. Such groups, whether religious, political, or merely

---

[1] This chapter will be more easily understood if chap. 11 has been read previous to this one.

criminal, use their knowledge of dissociation to create highly organized, structured personality systems in their victims. Just as dissociative identity disorder (DID) is highly associated with abuse in early childhood (Carlson, Tuppett, & Sroufe, 2009) as well as the development of an insecure attachment style (Gingrich, 2013), such groups realize that for mind control to be effective it has to begin in infancy and involve life-threatening torture on top of a base of insecure or no attachment.

According to the self-reports of our clients and those of other therapists treating victims of RA/MC,[2] there appear to be commonalities with respect to how various perpetrator groups operate. Most mind-controlled clients begin life with an insecure or disorganized attachment, deliberately induced by the abuser group. Then they are trained from birth, or (if their abuse occurred only outside the home) from a very young age (three years old or younger), through drugs, torture, and life-threatening trauma to become many "people" (i.e., to develop DID). Movies, music, stories, pictures, and virtual-reality technology are all used to distort these children's perceptions of reality when they are so young that they cannot distinguish fantasy or story from objective truth.

The perpetrator's goal is to split off internal parts or alternate personalities who will remain children, and train these internal children to believe what the abusers tell them and to do jobs assigned by the abusers. The abusers then carefully store these child parts in designated internal locations in an imaginary structure or inner world, thereby imprisoning them in their traumatic situations at the original ages. These alternate personalities do not spontaneously appear in the "real" world, where they would mature, but emerge only when called out through preassigned signals by the abuser group in order to perform assigned tasks.[3] Those alters who are designated to commit evil acts such as ritual murder, assassination, torture, and other crimes are taught to perform their tasks without emotions; the emotions are stored elsewhere in the internal system. Strong barricades or walls, reinforced by torture, are constructed in the victims' internal worlds to prevent communication between various parts, in particular to separate the trained alters from the "front people" who handle everyday life. No one part, therefore, knows the entire narrative of any situation, which makes it unlikely that there will be any internal interference to prevent the victim from accomplishing the task desired by the perpetrator group.

---

[2]We belong to the Ritual Abuse/Mind Control special interest group (SIG) of the International Society for the Study of Trauma and Dissociation. The SIG currently consists of around 150 therapists who treat RA/MC, a significant number of whom have written books or book chapters on the topic.

[3]From here forward we will use the term *alter* as a short form for "alternate personality." Some other terms that could be used are *inner children*, *dissociated parts of self*, *dissociated self-states*, or *parts of self*. However, do not use the term *alter* with RA/MC clients as it can be confused with the word *altar*, which may be terrifying if memories of rituals involved sacrifices on an altar.

Each victim's personality system is typically set up as a hierarchy or a set of inter-related hierarchies. Those in charge, usually adolescent alters, give orders to those under their command. Under them are punishers or enforcers (also called *perse-cutor alters* in the DID literature) who administer punishments to disobedient alters (see the section "How the Abuser Group Protects Its Secrets" below). Survivors of these abuses usually have hundreds of alters, most of them mere fragments of personality. The front person (sometimes called the "host personality") is designed to be unaware of the internal parts and their activities. People outside the perpetrator group, such as therapists and child protection workers, are often unaware of the dissociative disorder and usually see only the front person.

IDENTIFYING RA/MC

Chapters two and four of Alison's (Miller, 2014) book for survivors contain checklists for persons who think they may be survivors of these abuses. Here are some of the most common items about which you might ask a client or listen for in his or her story:

- Having immediate, strong, unstoppable reactions to certain sights, sounds, or touches, and feeling that certain behaviors must be performed in response to these

- Having a strong impulse to return home to family or childhood places, even if they are far away, especially after making disclosures about abuse

- Suddenly falling into a strong suicidal depression without knowing why

- Feeling as if the head has a division between the right and left sides

- Flashbacks that involve technology, such as virtual reality or an electrified chair or helmet

- Memories that appear to be impossible, such as alien abductions

- Making drawings characterized by ritual-like features (e.g., lots of red and black, knives, fire, cages, robes, body parts, blood)

- Preoccupation with or needing to avoid newscasts, magazine articles, or conversations about MC or RA

- Psychiatric symptoms that worsen around the client's own birthday, family members' birthdays, Christmas, Easter, Halloween, May Day, and early September

- Cutting patterns, shapes, or letters on the client's own body

- Intrusive thoughts or impulses regarding violent sex, sex with children, or sex with animals

- Odd, ritualistic songs or chants running through the client's head, sometimes with a sexual, bizarre, or "you'd better not tell" theme
- Hearing voices giving the order not to talk or to be quiet
- Symptoms such as bodily pain, nausea, a severe headache, paranoid thoughts and fear, or flashbacks of violent events after talking about possible abuse memories
- Spontaneous spasms as if receiving an electric shock
- Feeling that there is something foreign inside the body that can do harm to the client or others or can signal the client's location or thoughts to abusers
- Worrying that he or she will harm or murder someone or has done so
- Feeling that his or her energy will poison others
- Dreams that seem to describe MC or RA experiences
- Fears, phobias, and nightmares associated with the following:

  - religion and church
  - Christmas and Easter
  - going to the doctor or the dentist
  - bodily fluids and excretions
  - injections and needles
  - weapons
  - birthdays and weddings
  - police, jails, and cages
  - baths and drowning
  - insects, snakes, spiders, and rats

  - cameras and being photographed
  - specific colors or shapes
  - ropes, being tied up, being hung
  - confined spaces, basements, crawl spaces, pits
  - death and burial
  - red meat or certain other foods
  - harm being done to loved ones or pets

No single one of these items means that your client has a history of mind control or ritual abuse. Some of the fears (like needles, insects, or the dentist) are common, so it is important to look for ordinary ways to account for them in the client's life history. Look at the entire pattern of answers. If many of the items fit, especially the uncommon ones, you might suspect RA and MC.

HOW THE ABUSER GROUP PROTECTS ITS SECRETS

All child abusers tell their victims not to tell anyone else what they have experienced. The words they say to children range from "It's our little secret" to "You don't want me to go to prison, do you?" to "I'll kill your mother if you talk to anyone about this." However, the training used by mind controllers is much more systematic and relies on the dissociative personality system for its effectiveness. Organized abuser groups, including those associated with government agencies and the military, place the highest priority on their abuse of children not being discovered. Therefore, they train the inner parts of their victims' complex personality systems to be loyal, silent, and obedient by creating very elaborate security mechanisms within each survivor's system. This ensures that the perpetrator group and handlers are notified and can take action if any alter begins to remember and/or disclose the abuse.

Warning and punishment programming. Certain alters are trained to administer warnings and punishments if the person is disobeying the abusers, in particular telling anything about the abuse memories. Warnings may come via frightening voices who sound like the abusers, saying such things as "Don't talk" or "Shut up," or via sudden unexpected pain.

If the person does not heed a warning, more severe punishments kick in, carried out by terrified child and adolescent alters who are doing their assigned jobs of punishing in the belief that any punishment given by the actual abusers, whom they believe know everything, will be worse. A common punishment is using parts of traumatic memories to retraumatize through flooding the system with feelings of despair, recalling the pain of a rape, or hallucinating the presence of the perpetrators in the therapy room. There are alters trained to cut the body's arms, sometimes with cult symbols, or to attempt suicide; the dangerously suicidal ones believe that they do not belong to the body and will not die with it. Since mental health workers are aware of self-injury as common in adolescence and as part of borderline behavior, they do not suspect ritual abuse when it occurs.

Certain alters are trained to physically return to the group so that the perpetrators can regain control of the person through use of additional torture; they will attempt this if the perpetrators' "Don't talk" rule is disobeyed. A phone call home may also activate these alters. If the individual does not return, he or she may well exhibit serious psychiatric symptoms that appear to require hospitalization. Unfortunately, admission is not a guarantee that perpetrators will not have access to the survivor while he or she is hospitalized. Like sexual offenders, members of perpetrator groups gravitate to professions where victims are available.

Access programming and the Big Lie. All the childhood training relies on what I (Alison) call the Big Lie. The powerful adult abusers emphasize to their child (and later adult) victims that they know everything their victims do or say and, in some cases, even everything they think. Trickery is used when the victims are children to make them believe this lie. There are many versions of the Big Lie—for example, "The invisible all-seeing Eye always sees you," "Satan (or God) is always watching you and will let us know about you," "Your stuffed animals (or the crows, or microchips we put in your body) report on you to us," "We have magical abilities to know what you do, say, and think." Young children do not understand the concept of deception and so believe such lies, as do child alters even after the person has reached adulthood. This is a basic strategy in mind control.

The abuser group often does know if the survivor has remembered or disclosed forbidden material. It is easy for the survivor to be observed by group-loyal family members when he or she is a child. When the survivor has grown up and moved away, information is gleaned through young reporter alters who, believing the Big Lie, have the job of contacting a designated group member if there has been disloyalty, having been taught that they had better tell the group or else the all-knowing group will punish them severely.

The reporter alters are not put under the authority of the internal leaders and may see themselves as spies, telling the abusers to whom they are loyal about the activities of the "traitor" parts of the person. The existence of reporter alters is hidden from the front (everyday) person and from those alters in charge of the personality system. The individual feels a strong urge to "phone home," contacts his or her designated family or group member, switches into a reporter alter, gives the information, and then switches back. Neither the everyday person nor the alters who are in charge of the personality system have any idea that reporting has occurred.

When a reporter alter discloses disloyalty, the group immediately goes into action to close down memories and elicit terror about the consequences of remembering and telling. Alters are trained to "come when called," that is, to respond to access triggers such as beeps over the phone or hand signals from across the street, so that perpetrator group members can abduct them and torture them into submission. At other times a mere phone call from a member of the perpetrator group, who may threaten torture or trigger programming that activates internal punisher alters, will suffice to control the client's behavior. This can severely undermine the counseling process.

Punishment of children, and later of adult survivors, for disobedience or disloyalty is swift and cruel. Beatings, imprisonment, torture, gang rape, electroshock—abuser groups do not hesitate to hurt children severely in order to get across their instructions to never disobey. There are also "object lessons" in which someone purported to be a traitor is killed painfully—for example, by being skinned alive—while other children watch. The usual consequence threatened for disobedience or disloyalty is death to the victim or his or her loved ones. Young alters of survivors remember these extreme punishments and are terrified of their recurrence. There is specific programming to make victims afraid of therapists, physicians, clergy, and law enforcement officers, all of whom abuse the children while in their professional roles. Sometimes it is just a group member in uniform; other times it is an actual physician, priest, pastor, therapist, or police officer who belongs to the group.

TREATMENT

The goal of treatment is ultimately the same as it is for other complex trauma survivors, including those with DID (see chaps. 10 and 11 in this volume). As discussed in chapter eleven, the standard of care for treatment of complex trauma is a three-phased approach. Safety is developed and symptoms stabilized (phase 1), the trauma is processed (phase 2), and the gains are consolidated, furthering greater integration of self and identity (phase 3). However, there are additional complicating factors in the treatment of survivors of RA/MC (see also Gingrich, 2013).

Phase 1: Safety and stabilization. The development of a sense of safety and stabilization of symptoms can take a long time, often many years, for survivors whose trauma has come at the hands of other people, whether or not via organized abuse. However, when RA/MC survivors are currently being accessed by a perpetrator group so that the client is continuing to be traumatized, they may eventually feel safe within the therapeutic relationship, but they are *not* actually safe in broader life.

Phase 1 with these survivors needs to focus, first and foremost, on actual physical safety. It is imperative that the counselor not press the client to disclose traumatic memories early in therapy, because any disclosure that is made may trigger reporter parts of the client to contact the perpetrator group, who will then take action to close the security leak. (This is discussed in detail below.)

Most survivors come from families in which all relatives were involved in the abuser group. Therefore, the therapist needs to gently inquire about where the client's family is and how much contact he or she has with various family members. Determining whether the client is likely to be currently safe is your first priority.

Another reason not to push for memory work in the early stages is that disclosures will set off programming designed to destabilize a client who initially appeared stable. Begin, then, by getting to know the front person and whichever members of the personality system present themselves to you. Those who put them forward will be watching you to see whether or not you are going to switch into an abuser personality and hurt them. It takes a long time to build trust with someone who has been so massively betrayed; there is no substitute for time and consistency.

Working with the personality system. As mentioned, survivors of RA/MC have many persecutor alters. Some give threats or warnings; others administer punishments. It is very important not to fight with the persecutor alters and not to encourage the other alters to engage in a "war" with them. If there is already an internal war, aim for peace rather than taking sides with "good" alters against "bad" ones. The persecutors are simply child and adolescent parts doing the jobs they were assigned by the abusers, in fear that if they do not do those jobs, something even worse will happen. It is important to befriend these alters; you will be the first kind person they have ever met. Whatever you do, do not try to oust or imprison the persecutor parts—you will need them as your allies. They have been told by the abuser group that no one outside the group will ever accept them. Prove the abusers wrong.

Earlier we discussed how the personality systems of RA/MC survivors are set up as one or more hierarchies. You as a therapist, along with the client's safe and supportive friends or spiritual community, need to pursue a strategy of establishing rapport with the dominant alter personalities (that is, those in charge of the internal hierarchies) and showing them how they have been deceived. With such help, these internal leaders can help the other parts work through their traumatic memories and achieve personal freedom. As you get to know the parts who present themselves first, notice whether or not they are hearing voices warning them not to talk or threatening them. If so, ask to talk with the voices. Express curiosity about why they are saying these things and whether it is a job they were assigned. Ask what will happen if they do not do their jobs. You can gradually work your way up the hierarchy as each alter is replaced by the one who threatens and tries to control that alter. Treat every alter with respect and curiosity. Try to get them to talk with one another in order to improve internal communication. Working with the system in this way is an important part of therapy. It is wisest not to approach the traumatic memories until those inside parts whom the abusers put in charge are cooperating with you (see Miller, 2014, chap. 14).

Phase 2: Trauma processing. Eventually your client will be ready to work with the traumatic memories, if those alters in charge of the system are cooperative and there is some degree of external safety. In order to reconstitute a traumatic memory for healing purposes, all of those parts of the person involved in that memory need to come together. This is possible in many but not all mind-controlled personality systems. If the person was mind-controlled throughout childhood, there are often parts who have been trained to locate all the other parts who are involved in a particular memory. Mind controllers want the personality systems they control to be well organized so that they can call up specific alter personalities to perform their tasks. Fortunately for therapists, it is possible to access and learn this internal organization to help clients work through their memories.

In our experience, when the important parts of a survivor client, including not just the front person but also the designated leaders of the internal personality system, are determined to recover and trust you as their therapist, you can trust those internal leaders to bring forward the different sections of the system and the most important memories (usually the ones that created the "programs") for healing in the right order.

I (Alison) prefer to work through a traumatic memory in one or more two-hour sessions. I ask the personality-system leaders to gather all the alters involved in that memory, including the ones who hold physical or emotional feelings as well as those who have the story line. I have these leaders look for alters, usually young children, who were assigned the job of hiding part of the memories to prevent the programming from being resolved and tell these children to add their parts to the memories. Then I have the client deliberately dissociate the bodily and emotional feelings into a sealed container, and all alters involved watch the "video" of the memory, with sight and sound only. After they have all seen and heard what happened, they add in the feelings gradually until all feelings have been put together with the memory, which is then put into a labeled container to prevent flashbacks or "leaking" of feelings into everyday life. I then spend some time discussing the meaning of this memory with system leaders and those involved in the event. The front people do not have to be present if the memory did not involve them. Front people have a very important job, to handle everyday life, and knowing memories prematurely can destabilize them.

Phase 3: Consolidation and resolution. For the most part, Phase 3 goals will be similar for RA/MC clients as they are for other clients with DID (see chap. 11). The biggest difference is that RA/MC clients will need to continue to be vigilant with respect to potential attempts of perpetrator groups to re-access them. There is likely to be ongoing memory work for some time, even after the bulk of the trauma processing has been completed, because these clients have had many more traumatic experiences than most abuse survivors. They may have very few skills in creating and maintaining relationships because they have not been permitted to build friendships outside the perpetrator group. Therefore, they may need considerable coaching in this area.

SPIRITUAL ABUSE

The spiritual abuse in these groups is deliberate and heinous. The Satanic and Luciferian groups in particular have the objective of destroying the soul, and they stop at nothing to achieve this. They are aware that God does not intervene directly to rescue abused children, and they take advantage of this fact to convince their victims that they are better off with Satan, since God has rejected them. Some of the specifics as to how this is done are outlined below. We need to warn you that the graphic details may be upsetting.

Desecration of sacraments, Scripture, and religious holidays. Satanic cults utilize Christian symbols and intentionally desecrate them during their rituals. Survivors report being forced to participate in black masses where they first watch a person being killed with a knife (or are forced to kill the person themselves) and then participate in ritualized cannibalism (i.e., literally drink the person's blood and eat his or her flesh). Given such an experience, it is understandable that participating in a Christian communion service could serve as a trauma trigger for an RA survivor with alters who hold such horrific memories (whether or not actual human sacrifice occurred or whether alters have been deceived into thinking that it occurred).

One survivor reported being forced to repeat the Lord's Prayer over and over again while simultaneously hurting someone or, conversely, hearing the perpetrator group chant the Lord's Prayer as the survivor is ritually gang-raped. Many variations on this theme have occurred and are reported in the literature. Counselors may unwittingly retraumatize such clients if they naively suggest that the survivor meditate on passages of Scripture that the counselors intend to bring peace and comfort when they may in fact have the reverse effect. Words have often been distorted by the perpetrator groups: peace means war, light means darkness, God means Satan, and so forth. So if you see your client wince or shudder when you use certain words, be alert that these words may have a very different meaning for the client's hidden parts.

The major Christian holidays are also holy days for Satanist groups (in addition to many other occult holidays). These are times when all survivors have programming to attend the rituals, and if they do not attend, they will experience symptoms such as nightmares, flashbacks, feelings of terror, suicide attempts, inability to sleep or eat, compulsions to return to the perpetrator group, and so on. I (Heather) have come to dread the season of Lent because so many of my RA/MC clients have decompensated as a result of programming that is conducted in connection to the church calendar. The symptoms mentioned above are exponentially exacerbated during these time periods. The additional stress these crisis situations create for counselors also can increase the chance of vicarious traumatization. I know that I have to consciously force myself to focus on the miracle of Christ's resurrection at Easter time rather than wonder how many children are being hurt or killed during Holy Week.

Simulation of God, Satan, heaven, and hell. Ritually abusive groups want to make sure that the children they abuse do not turn to the true God, so they engage in deceptions in order to make these children believe that God has rejected them. They simulate hell with fires and a man in a Satan suit coming out of the fire, while telling the children that this is where they will go when they die because of the bad things they have done. A child being tortured is told to pray to God for help, and no help arrives; then the child is told to pray to Satan, and a man in a Satan suit arrives and stops the torture. A man dressed up similar to artists' conceptions of God or Jesus rapes the children or spits on them and says they are so evil that he rejects them. The child is made to harm a man tied to a cross or to stab a baby who is supposedly the baby Jesus. Some cult leaders say they are God. "Forgiveness" may be conferred through rape by a priest of the group.

Even speaking about God or Jesus with survivors who have been exposed to these kinds of tricks may bring up memories of these events to their hidden inner alters. If you say, "Jesus loves you," it may translate to the child alters as "Jesus is going to rape you." So it is very important to be careful about what you say and to ask how alters are interpreting your words. God's love is best communicated through the therapist's own loving acceptance of all parts of the person, especially those alters who believe themselves to be evil. It may help to point out that if they were truly evil, they would not feel guilt.

Forced perpetration. In our experience, every survivor who grows up as part of such a group is forced to perpetrate abuse on others in some way. With an adult man's hand over his or her hand, a little child is made to stab or sexually abuse an animal or a vulnerable human being. Afterward the child is told that he or she is evil, and only the group and its deity can now accept him or her. Although the front person of the survivor is usually not aware of these experiences, the resulting shame can maintain the survivor's isolation from the rest of humanity and continued connection to the group. As the child gets older, pressure is put on him or her to perform the abuse without the assistance of an adult hand. This is done through forced "lesser of two evils" choices: "Kill this dog or we will kill your baby brother," or "Hurt this person or we will hurt them much more than you are able to." Again, the child or adult is shamed for having committed this evil act. It is important for therapists to understand that most survivors who come for therapy did not choose to do evil but chose only to perform the least evil alternative. Even killing can be an act of mercy toward an animal or person who would have died more painfully.

Satanic and Luciferian groups frequently pair each child with a "disposable" child, usually one whose existence is not known in the outside world. After the children form a friendship bond, perhaps the only bond the child has ever had, the chosen child's hand is used to kill the "disposable" child, and the living child is told that anyone he or she loves will die, so it is best not to love anyone. The group members tell such children that the acts that they have committed are so evil that no one but the group will ever accept them.

Unfortunately, this can sometimes be true. Some therapists as well as some potential friends of survivors find their reality so difficult to bear that they cannot listen to it. Survivors are acutely attuned to what a listener can take, and will not disclose to those who cannot handle it. It is important for survivors to know, however, that there are genuine people who will be their friends or their therapists, see them as human beings who have endured extreme suffering, and extend respect and compassion to them.

THE QUESTION OF DEMONS

Individuals vary widely when it comes to beliefs about how active a role evil spirits play in the current era. However, even for a clinician who is skeptical with respect to believing in evil entities, it is quite unsettling when one seems to be talking to a demon whose voice is dramatically changed from the client's, who states that his or her name is Beelzebub (or Lucifer, Legion, Leviathan, etc.), and who is threatening harm to the counselee, the counselor, or both! Even more perplexing is that I (Heather) believe that I have talked to actual demons in sessions, but I have also *felt* as though I was talking to a demon when, in reality, I was interacting with a perse-cutor alter. What complicates matters considerably is that perpetrator groups use deception with respect to the demonic in addition to the deceptive trickery we have already discussed.

Alters as human spirits or evil spirits. Just as they did in past centuries, the Satanic and Luciferian groups operating nowadays engage in rituals to invite demons or evil spirits to enter their victims. However, their leaders are now aware that the trauma experienced by children who are subjected to such rituals actually causes a dissociative split that results in the creation of a new alter. Little children under conditions of threat and torture often say what they are told to say, that is, that they are inviting in a demon. They may also be shown a "mirror" with a picture of a demon on it (one of the cults' favorite tricks). Therefore, when they split and produce a new alter that is told it is a demon, even though it is not, the alter believes itself to be one and is then trained how to act like one, sometimes by a "big demon," an adult in a costume.

Some practitioners (e.g., Steve Oglevie, a self-styled Christian "deprogrammer" who gives seminars for therapists) believe that discarnate "human spirits," in ad-dition to demonic spirits, can take residence in victims of RA. However, there are alternate explanations for what can appear to be a human spirit. For example, the first case of a "human spirit" that I (Alison) met initially presented as a demon, although it was actually an alter of a devout Christian young man. I asked for its name, and it said "Trevor." That was a strange name for a demon, so I asked why it had that name. It said it was the spirit of the man's dead grandfather, whose name was Trevor. I asked how old it was, and in a young child's voice it said "three." I asked what it was wearing, and it said "brown shorts and a gray T-shirt." This alter was split off when the boy was abused in his grandfather's death ritual at age three.

It is common for a leader of a perpetrator group to split off (i.e., create) an alter in the victim (often through rape) and instruct it to be an internal copy of him or someone else. It is important that therapists recognize that alters created in this fashion *are* really alters, often internal system leaders, just as Trevor was actually an alter rather than either a demon or the human spirit of his dead grandfather.

Such alters can be immensely helpful in the healing process once they are correctly identified.

Alters named "Satan." I (Heather) have a video recording of a former female client who has given me permission to use it for educational purposes. At one point in the recording, a guttural, male-sounding voice announces that he is Satan. He comes across as extremely threatening, controlling, and powerful, so the tendency is to believe that he is, in fact, Satan or at the least an evil spirit. Certainly the majority of my students seem convinced that what they are seeing is demonic as they fearfully view the recording.

In actuality "Satan" turned out to be a dissociated part of self that was created in order to hold the memories of a specific cult ritual. In essence "Satan" saved the counselee's life. Once "Satan" realized that there was no current danger, he acknowledged he wasn't the same as that "other" Satan, changed his name to Stephen, and then, upon realizing that the body of the client was female, changed it to Stephanie! Alison, too, has met many "Satans" and supposed demons that, in her experience, have all turned out to be parts of the person split off by a combination of drugs and abuse as well as training.

Distinguishing demons from alters. If one assumes a supernaturalistic explanation for the demonic (i.e., that demons can be real spiritual entities) rather than the naturalistic explanation offered by many mental health professionals (i.e., that demons are *not* actual spiritual entities but are always manifestations of psychological symptoms), the question becomes, how can counselors tell the difference between an actual demon and an alter?

Some Christians working in the field (e.g., Friesen, 1991; Hawkins, 2009) have written that you can tell a true demon from an alter by how it behaves—for example, demons are more ferociously and more strenuously opposed to God (Hawkins, 2009), or they take animal form rather than human form (Friesen, 1997). In our experience, however, alters have sometimes had very good training in how to act like evil spirits, and other alters have been trained to "be" animals by being caged with animals and forced to behave like those animals (e.g., beg for food). It is easy to feel that we are discerning spiritual reality when we are actually being deceived by alters acting on their training, or we are reacting out of our own countertransference (e.g., anxiety, fear) reactions.

I (Alison), like Heather, have had to think about this question thoroughly over my many years of work with ritual abuse survivors. My present understanding is as follows: The demonic is to be identified by the deliberate performance of what is actually evil in that it does harm to others, rather than by the trappings and popular portrayals of Satanism. As Jesus says, "By their fruit you will recognize them" (Mt 7:16). Demons are forces of evil that affect human beings through temptation to act in ways that violate other persons or animals. In other words, the demonic takes control of us when we yield to what is commonly known as "sin"—envy, cruelty, sexual perversion, and lust for power, control, material possessions, or status. This can happen to anyone regardless of whether they are exposed to Satanism.

The same temptations occur within churches, nonprofit groups, government bureaucracies, and ordinary families. One ritually abused client of mine worked through a memory of a near-death experience she had in childhood, in which an angelic being took her through a "life review" of all her actions. She discovered that behaviors of hers that she had been told were extremely evil were actually not, often because she had chosen the lesser of two evils. Other things she had not thought significant were indeed judged to be evil because they involved cruelty or pettiness—in other words, sin. Although we cannot take such a subjective experience as evidence of truth, we likely can agree that it is the motivation to do harm that constitutes evil rather than the external appearance. Little children, for example, do not yet understand the morality of motivation and believe that breaking ten plates by accident is worse than breaking one deliberately.

Hoffman's memoirs (2014, 2016) illustrate the importance of a deeper understanding of the nature of evil. As an Illuminati "queen," she was chosen to assume a high position in the international cult network. For this position, she was supposed to be possessed by myriads of demons, which were simulated through deceptions such as we have previously discussed. But to Hoffman's mind, the real evil was not in these supposed demons; it was in the temptation to power and cruelty. Throughout her life Hoffman was invited to accept and enjoy the power her position would give her if she would only become a "conscious" perpetrator and identify with the goals of the perpetrator group. Choosing to kill with her own hands was particularly important to the group, and because she steadfastly refused to do so, she was eventually discarded by the group. The boy she grew up with, who was designated to be the "king" to her "queen," yielded to the temptation of power and was given significant authority within the group.

Deliverance prayer. While Scripture does talk about the gift of "discernment of spirits" (1 Cor 12:10 NRSV), our own countertransference reactions of fear in response to what we are observing in our RA/MC clients can significantly interfere with our ability to accurately discern what is going on, even if we believe that we have been given this spiritual gift. In fact, the potential harm to survivors with DID that can result from an alter being mistaken as an evil spirit is so great that both Alison and I would strongly discourage therapists from participating in deliverance prayer or exorcisms or encouraging their clients to seek after them elsewhere.

I (Heather) had an RA/MC client tell me that the deliverance prayer that he had undergone was more traumatizing to him than the ritualistic torture he had endured, despite the care and "saneness" with which the prayer had been done. When the prayer group was commanding the "evil presences" to go "in Jesus' name," what the group did not realize is that they were actually observing terrified alters who interpreted the group as wanting to annihilate them. The resulting trauma can lead to the splitting off of additional dissociated parts (i.e., the creation of new alters). The client referred to above split off an alter who presented as the integrated, demon-free individual that the prayer warriors expected to see after a successful deliverance session. Unfortunately, when this alter could not continue to maintain the façade because other alters were not willing to stay hidden, the survivor moved to a different city as a way to keep the church group from discovering the truth. To my knowledge, those involved in the deliverance prayer never did find out what had actually taken place.

One of the other possible ramifications of attempted deliverance prayer/exorcisms is that they inadvertently confirm for survivors the lies that perpetrator groups have attempted to instill throughout their lives, that is, that they are evil and that they will be rejected by everyone except for the perpetrator group. Ironically, although the goal of deliverance teams would generally be seen as increased freedom for the survivor, when alters are mistaken for demons it can send desperate survivors back to the perpetrator groups and thereby into greater bondage.

In cases where the client insists on undergoing deliverance prayer despite the clinician's warnings as to its possible detrimental effects, I would highly recommend that all involved parties be aware of the results of the study by Bull, Ellason, and Ross (1998), who examined the experiences of individuals with DID who had undergone exorcism-like rituals. The key factors found to be necessary for a positive experience were the following: permission of the individual, noncoercion, active participation by the individual, understanding of DID dynamics by the exorcist, implementation of the exorcism within the ongoing context of psychotherapy, compatibility of the procedure with the individual's spiritual beliefs, incorporation of the individual's belief system, and instruction so that the individual can use the exorcism procedure independently (p. 191). We cannot, however, overemphasize the potential dangers involved, particularly with RA/MC survivors.

An expanded definition of spiritual warfare. I (Heather) have found it very freeing to expand my definition of spiritual warfare beyond explicit power encounters, such as those seen in exorcisms. Some authors (e.g., Bufford, 1988; Powlison, 1995) have suggested that it is more important to engage in personal, spiritual disciplines such as Bible study, prayer, confession of sin, fleeing temptation, and making ongoing righteous choices. These fit with the biblical concept of putting on the "armor of God" (Eph 6:10-17).

I find Kraft's (1993) writings particularly pertinent in this regard. He states that "the most important aspect of a deliverance ministry is never the casting out of the demons. The aim is healing. But the healing isn't complete until the deep level hurts that disrupt a person's relationship with God, self, and others are worked through under the power of the Holy Spirit" (p. 140). While Kraft does not explicitly mention therapy here, I think that this view has relevance to Christian counseling; as we help survivors to process their trauma, and as they go on to make increasingly good decisions, the power of satanic forces to influence them is greatly diminished.

Smith (2013), the developer of Theophostic Prayer Ministry (now called Transformation Prayer Ministry; www.transformationprayer.org), does not see any need to address a demon directly. Rather, he believes that "the reason for the demon's presence is rooted in that person's belief system. The person's emotion that is stirred becomes the bridge back to those beliefs. After following the emotion, identifying the beliefs and receiving Christ's perspective, the demons have no purpose, reason, or right to stay" (p. 75).

While we do not think that Smith's ministry protocol takes into account the complexity inherent in work with RA/MC survivors, the treatment approaches we have been advocating are consistent with Smith's focus on uncovering the lies that perpetrator groups have often instilled.

If Kraft (1993) and Smith (2013) are correct in their assertions, it is potentially good news for psychotherapists who work with RA/MC clients in that it can take some of the pressure off with respect to determining whether or not clients are being directly influenced by evil spirits.

ADDITIONAL SPIRITUAL CONCERNS

RA/MC survivors inevitably struggle with questions related to *meaning* ("Why was I subjected to these horrors?"; "How can I find purpose for my suffering?"), *evil* ("How could anyone do such horrendous things to a child?"; "How could I have hurt/killed something/someone else unless I were evil?"), and *survival* ("Why am I alive when others died?"), along with other difficult questions that are ultimately spiritual in nature. We and other therapists treating survivors have found ourselves asking the same questions as our clients. Some recent Christian books on the topic of pain and suffering with respect to abuse survivors (e.g., Langberg, 2015; Peterman & Schmutzer, 2016), as well as chapter two in this volume, can be helpful in sorting through a theology of suffering for ourselves as Christian therapists. However, a theological solution offered to clients will often be perceived as spiritual abuse to RA/MC survivors who need to emotionally process through their sense of abandonment by God. Fortunately, it is not necessary for us to have all the answers to these profound questions in order to help survivors. It is our demonstration of God's love in action that makes the difference, not the "answers" we offer to the profound and unanswerable questions.

Recognizing and dealing with implied spiritual issues. Benner (1988, 1998) suggests that questions related to existential concerns are ultimately spiritual in nature, whether or not an individual recognizes them as such. We encourage Christian counselors to stay attuned to the underlying spiritual nature of such questions while at the same time treading carefully when they arise. It is important to give permission for the RA/MC survivor to explore these issues without the counselor offering an "answer" that springs from his or her own religious tradition. Survivors have experienced severe mind control in which their beliefs have been forcibly manipulated into passive agreement with the perpetrators' teachings. It would be only too easy to take advantage of this to indoctrinate clients rather than setting them free from mind control so that they can truly explore the difficult questions.

Avoiding religious language can help place a moral or ethical issue outside a particular doctrinal framework. For example, using the terms *light* versus *darkness* will be more appropriate than the terms *God* versus *Satan* for someone who does not identify with a specifically Christian framework. Chapter twenty in Alison's book for survivors (Miller, 2014) addresses many such issues using secular rather than religious language.

Where was God? The question of why God allowed this suffering is addressed in most of the chapters of this volume but is focused on specifically in chapter two, with significant attention to the topic also in chapter fourteen. While the question of God and suffering comes up with most trauma survivors, it will invariably come up with RA/MC clients because of the extensiveness of the trauma and the intentionality behind the torture they have experienced. As mentioned earlier, in abuser groups that are religious in nature, perpetrators often dress up like depictions of religious figures and then rape or torture the child. Those abused by Satanic cults, for example, frequently report that Jesus raped them as part of a ritual. For these survivors the question is not only "Why did God not protect me?" but also "What did I do that was so bad that Jesus raped/tortured me?" Obviously this will have ramifications for such a survivor's relationship with God.

Guilt and forgiveness. RA/MC victims are deliberately loaded with guilt and shame by their perpetrator groups. As noted, victims of Satanic cults are made to commit evil acts when given "lesser of two evils" choices, and then are told they are condemned to hell as a result. They may have spent time in a place they were told was hell, where they were tortured by someone dressed as Satan and/or someone impersonating God. They have been programmed to be flooded with memories of atrocities they supposedly committed if they begin to remember what happened.

Any therapist, Christian or not, must address the issues of guilt and forgiveness. It is important not to minimize a survivor client's guilt. Even if a murder was simulated and the person was not actually responsible for it, the guilt is very real. Survivors, especially their child parts, frequently feel guilty for acts for which they were not actually responsible, and it is important to explain why they were not responsible for those acts. It is our acceptance of survivors, including what they have done, that will make real to them the reality of the kind of genuine love that comes from God. We must also not push survivors to forgive or even to have contact with family members who have abused them in the context of perpetrator groups. Such persons are likely to have remained involved with the group and will abuse again if given an opportunity. Premature forgiveness both violates the survivor's integrity by minimizing their wounding and exposes them to present-day danger. See Sells and Hervey (2011) and Tracy (2005) for a helpful discussion on working with sexual abuse survivors around the issue of forgiveness. While these authors do not write specifically about RA/MC survivors, what they say is applicable.

CONCLUSION

We have taken on a virtually impossible task by attempting to discuss the complicated treatment of survivors of RA/MC within the confines of a book chapter. While we realize that this chapter may have raised as many questions as it has answered, we trust that it has at least increased awareness of RA/MC as a subspecialty of complex trauma work and given you some resources for further information on the topic. Survivors badly need therapists with the courage and faith to tackle this most challenging of specialty areas. Although no one feels like an expert in this area, we can only gain expertise by taking on the challenge of working with such counselees.

REFERENCES

Benner, D. G. (1988). *Psychotherapy and the spiritual quest.* Grand Rapids, MI: Baker.

Benner, D. G. (1998). *Care of souls: Revisioning Christian nurture and counsel.* Grand Rapids, MI: Baker Books.

Bufford, R. K. (1988). *Counseling and the demonic.* Dallas, TX: Word.

Bull, D., Ellason, J., & Ross, C. (1998). Exorcism revisited: Some positive outcomes with dissociative identity disorder. *Journal of Psychology & Theology, 26,* 188-96.

Carlson, E. A., Tuppett, M. Y., & Sroufe, L. A. (2009). Dissociation and the development of the self. In P. F. Dell & J. A. O'Neil (Eds.), *Dissociation and the dissociative disorders: DSM-V and beyond* (pp. 39-52). New York, NY: Routledge.

deMause, L. (Ed.). (1994, Spring). Cult abuse of children: Witch hunt or reality? [Special issue]. *Journal of Psychohistory, 21*(4), 505-18.

Friesen, J. (1992). Ego-dystonic or ego-alien: Alternate personality or evil spirit? *Journal of Psychology & Theology, 20,* 197-200.

Friesen, J. (1997). *Uncovering the mystery of DID*. Eugene, OR: Wipf and Stock.

Gingrich, H. D. (2013). *Restoring the shattered self: A Christian counselor's guide to complex trauma*. Downers Grove, IL: IVP Academic.

Hawkins, T. R. (2009). *Dissociative identity disorder: Recognizing and restoring the severely abused*. Grottoes, VA: Restoration in Christ Ministries.

Hoffman, W. (2014). *The enslaved queen: A memoir about electricity and mind control*. London, England: Karnac Books.

Hoffman, W. (2016). *White witch in a black robe: A true story about criminal mind control*. London, England: Karnac Books.

Kraft, C. H. (1993). *Deep wounds, deep healing: Discovering the vital link between spiritual warfare and inner healing*. Ann Arbor, MI: Servant.

Lacter, E. P. (2011). Torture-based mind control: Psychological mechanisms and psychotherapeutic approaches to overcoming mind control. In O. B. Epstein, J. Schwartz, & R. W. Schwartz (Eds.), *Ritual abuse and mind control: The manipulation of attachment needs* (pp. 57-142). London, England: Karnac Books.

Langberg, D. (2015). *Suffering and the heart of God: How trauma destroys and Christ restores*. Greensboro, NC: New Growth Press.

Lifton, R. J. (1986/2000). *The Nazi doctors: Medical killing and the psychology of genocide*. New York, NY: Basic Books.

Miller, A. (2012). *Healing the unimaginable: Treating ritual abuse and mind control*. London, England: Karnac Books.

Miller, A. (2014). *Becoming yourself: Overcoming mind control and ritual abuse*. London, England: Karnac Books.

Noblitt, J. R., & Noblitt, P. P. (2014). *Cult and ritual abuse: Narratives, evidence and healing approaches* (3rd ed.). Santa Barbara, CA: Praeger.

Noblitt, R., & Noblitt, P. P. (Eds.). (2008). *Ritual abuse in the twenty-first century: Psychological, forensic, social and political considerations*. Bandon, OR: Robert D. Reed.

Peterman, G. W., & Schmutzer, A. J. (2016). *Between pain and grace: A biblical theology of suffering*. Chicago, IL: Moody.

Powlison, D. (1995). *Power encounters: Reclaiming spiritual warfare*. Grand Rapids, MI: Baker Books.

Sells, J., & Hervey, E. G. (2011). Forgiveness in sexual abuse: Defining our identity in the journey toward wholeness. In A. J. Schmutzer (Ed.), *The long journey home: Understanding and ministering to the sexually abused*. Eugene, OR: Wipf and Stock.

Smith, E. (2013). Theophostic Prayer Ministry. In D. W. Appleby & G. Ohlschlager (Eds.), *Transformative encounters: The intervention of God in Christian counseling and pastoral care* (pp. 63-76). Downers Grove, IL: IVP Academic.

Tracy, S. R. (2005). *Mending the soul: Understanding and healing abuse*. Grand Rapids, MI: Zondervan.

SEX TRAFFICKING:
A COUNSELING PERSPECTIVE

SHANNON WOLF

Becca is a quiet 13-year-old girl from a small town in the Southwest. Following the divorce of her parents, her mother moved with Becca and her two younger sisters to a larger city 40 miles away. Because her mom worked a late shift at a nearby grocery store, Becca babysat her sisters from after school to after bedtime. She missed her father, her friends, and her old school. Until a few of weeks ago when she met her boyfriend, Jack, Becca was lonely. They're going to be married soon, but she can't tell anyone because Jack is 27 and people wouldn't understand. Recently, after her sisters were asleep, Jack asked Becca to meet him at his nearby apartment where they made love for the first time—it was everything she dreamed it would be. Since then, they've met almost every night to have sex. Jack bought her clothes that made her look older and sexy.

A few nights ago, Jack asked Becca for an important favor. Jack asked her to have sex with a man that he owes a lot of money to in order to pay off his debt. They had a terrible fight that ended with him promising that this was only once and then they could afford to get married. She tearfully agreed. When Becca arrived at Jack's apartment the next night, he gave her a drink to "help her relax." She was feeling sleepy and kind of dizzy when there was a knock on the door and four men, not just one, walked in. The men took turns having sex with her even though she cried and begged to go home. Once they left, Jack told her that he was proud of her but that she couldn't tell anyone what happened or those men would kill her. He also told her that she had to come back the next night to meet more of his friends or something bad would happen to her family.

Trafficking of persons, or human trafficking, is an illegal activity that touches all nations and has long-lasting physical, social, and psychological consequences for the survivor as well as all those involved. Traffickers exploit both genders, all ethnicities, the aged and young, as well as the educated and unschooled. No people group is left untouched by this crime. Trafficking includes, but is not limited to, forced labor, forced commercial sex acts, organ trafficking, and forced child soldiering (O'Callaghan, 2012; Rakin & Kinsella, 2011). This chapter will limit its focus to forced commercial sex acts.

Currently, trafficking of persons is at epidemic proportions (Yakushko, 2009). While it is difficult to know exactly how many people are currently being trafficked, it is estimated that approximately 27 million individuals worldwide are enslaved (Belser, 2005). In fact, trafficking of persons is one of the chief global crimes, producing billions of dollars annually, and is expected to surpass, if it has not already done so, both drug and weapons trafficking in revenue within the next few years. A trafficker can sell an individual multiple times but can only sell a drug or weapon once. This fact makes trafficking people attractive to organized crime rings.

BIBLICAL CONSIDERATIONS

Although over the past few decades mental health professionals have focused their attention on the problem of human trafficking, human slavery has been around for thousands of years (see the sidebar at the end of this chapter for more information on the modern history of human trafficking). The book of Genesis recounts Jacob's sons selling their brother Joseph into slavery (Gen 37). Another example is found in the book of Hosea. Gomer, Hosea's wife, is believed by some to have been a temple prostitute when he married her (Weaver, 2006). In this ancient culture, a woman rarely offered herself as a sacred prostitute but was given by her parents as a sacrifice to fertility gods in pagan worship. Such may have been the case for Gomer. What is striking about this story is that Gomer's struggle with relationships is similar to those of some trafficking victims. Consider the difficulty Gomer apparently experienced with intimate relationships. On several occasions she left her husband to live with other men, and she even had children with these men. At one point Hosea had to purchase her out of prostitution. It seems that Gomer continued returning to a life that was familiar to her even though she had a stable family. This behavior is similar to many women who are survivors of trafficking.

Even though human trafficking is not directly mentioned in the Bible (the concept was not developed until the twentieth century), biblical principles concerning the care of those who are unable to protect or care for themselves are easily found. The Gospel of Luke contains the parable of the good Samaritan (Lk 10:29-37). In this story, Jesus gave the imperative to love your neighbor. The essential point is not to identify who is or is not your neighbor but to act with genuine concern for all people.

The well-known parable begins with a description of a man who was stripped, beaten, and rendered helpless. This man was truly at the mercy of anyone who wanted to take further advantage of him. Two religious leaders noticed him but did not offer to help. Their actions were a direct violation of the Levitical law that demanded that Israelites show mercy to all people (Lev 19:34). A Samaritan, someone who was thought by Israelites to be beneath them, saw the man, and "when he saw him, he had compassion" (Lk 10:33 ESV). This is reminiscent of Jesus' authentic empathy for people. The Samaritan not only felt pity for the man but acted benevolently toward him. This parable is a practical model for Christian conduct concerning individuals whose ability to care for themselves is compromised, such as victims of sex trafficking.

Another passage of interest is found in a different Gospel. The book of Matthew contains an account of the final judgment (Mt 25:31-46). The passage emphasizes that all the people of the earth will be judged; ultimately every person on earth will be called on to account for his or her use of the opportunities of service experienced through life. Jesus stresses the importance of assisting people who are unable to care for themselves. He lists six situations in which individuals were in positions of vulnerability and needed help. The verb "I was" indicates that Jesus himself identifies with those in need. This point is emphasized when Jesus says, "I assure you that when you have done it for one of the least of these brothers and sisters of mine, you have done it for me" (Mt 25:40 CEB). The term *least*, also found in Matthew 10:42, is a reference to "the little ones," or those who are most vulnerable (Hagner, 1995). The imperative in Matthew 25 to care for truly helpless people is underscored by its connection to the final judgment.

This passage is concerned with benevolence and kindness to the vulnerable and suffering. These acts are not calculated behaviors aimed at pleasing God but a normal response to another human being in need. In the presence of need, representatives of Christ are to respond with acts of mercy. In this way, followers of Christ offer mercy and grace that has been given to them.

The charge to be representatives of Christ to the world requires that the church address the complex topic of human trafficking. Limited knowledge of trafficking's impact on spiritual matters, accompanied by a failure to openly address this issue, makes it difficult to care for victims within the church body and surrounding communities. This lack of information necessitates the continuation of exploration in this area.

DEFINING HUMAN TRAFFICKING

Even though the term *trafficking* was included in the language of the 1949 United Nations (UN) resolution, an internationally recognized definition has only been developed in the past few years. At their meeting in Italy at the end of 2000, the United Nations signed the Protocol to Prevent, Suppress, and Punish Trafficking in

Persons. Central to this document is clarification that human trafficking is not a form of human smuggling or illegal immigration (Laczko, 2002). Also included was an attempt at defining human trafficking; however, this undertaking was fraught with challenges.

Both feminists and Christian organizations such as Restore NYC and Traffick 911 viewed all prostitution as a violation of human rights and, until the early 2000s, had significant influence in the United Nations' work toward resolutions on trafficking. Around this time, another group began to lobby for a different definition of trafficking, believing that the right to engage in prostitution was also a human right that should be protected by international recognition (Doezema, 2002). This group contended that with the linking of human trafficking, specifically sex trafficking, to human rights issues, the public would associate legal prostitution with trafficking, which would jeopardize legal prostitution. They demanded that the UN change the definition of trafficking to reflect this difference. The controversy between these two groups made negotiating the creation of the definitions very difficult. Both groups claimed human rights protection, forcing the international community to debate the issue. In addition, the group that viewed prostitution as legitimate work encouraged the inclusion of men, women, and children in the definition of trafficking and also wanted to expand the recognized forms of labor trafficking to include the areas of domestic help, sweatshops, and agriculture (Human Rights Center, 2005b).

The UN committee also debated the issue of consent. While the feminists and Christian groups contended that prostitutes do not freely consent to commercial sex acts, others argued that trafficking occurs only with the use of force or abduction. The lobbyists for legal prostitution also demanded that the UN distinguish between adults and children, claiming that women do not need the same level of protection as children. In the end, the UN protocol defined trafficking as

> the recruitment, transportation, transfer, harboring, or receipt of persons, by means of threat, or use of force or other form of coercion, of abduction, of fraud, of deception, of abuse of power or of a position of vulnerability or of the giving or receiving of payments or benefits to achieve the consent of a person having control over another person for the purpose of exploitation. (United Nations Office on Drugs and Crime, Article 3, paragraph A, 2014)

Achieving the protocol consensus was a tremendous accomplishment; however, the definition primarily focused on the trafficker and not the victim. More work was still needed to clearly define trafficking as a human rights violation linked to international crime (Hyland, 2001). Indeed, the protocol's glaring weakness is the focus on criminalizing the trafficker and omitting protective standards for the victim. While protective language is included in the document, the protocol falls short of mandating actual protection for victims.

Currently, 117 nations have signed the updated protocol. Notably, the United States chose not to sign the latest version. The reason for this decision is that the United States has developed a much more comprehensive approach to targeting and convicting traffickers as well as protecting victims; it even has a prevention element in the approach (Hyland, 2001). However, even though the United States has encompassing legislation in place, similar to the United Nations, lawmakers have continued to wrestle to define human trafficking in such a way that the protection of victims and criminalization of the act of trafficking are included in legislation.

For the United States, President Clinton's Council on Women developed the first contemporary definition of trafficking in persons as a policy definition, not a legal one. The definition, penned in the late 1990s, states:

> Trafficking is all acts involved in the recruitment, abduction, transport, harboring, transfer, sale, or receipt of persons; within national or across international borders; through force, coercion, fraud, or deception; to place persons in situations of slavery or slavery-like conditions, forced labor or services, such as prostitution or sexual service, domestic servitude, bonded sweatshop labor, or other debt bondage. (O'Neill, 2000)

Three years later, under President Bush's administration, this policy definition evolved into the legal definition of the Trafficking Victims Protection Act that is still used today (US Department of State, 2003). Trafficking in persons was defined as

- sex trafficking in which a commercial sex act is induced by force, fraud, and coercion, or in which the person induced to perform such act has not attained 18 years of age; or

- the recruitment, harboring, transportation, provision, or obtaining of a person for labor or services, the use of force, fraud, or coercion for the purpose of subjection to involuntary servitude, or slavery (US Department of State, 2003).

In this definition, three key ideas guide the interpretation of trafficking in persons:

- Both labor and sexual exploitation are recognized as trafficking.

- Force, fraud, or coercion is used to ensnare the victim.

- Human trafficking is clearly distinguishable from human smuggling. The primary difference between the two is the element of slave-like conditions for the trafficking victim and that trafficking can happen without crossing international lines.

DOMESTIC MINOR SEX TRAFFICKING

The United States refers to the trafficking of anyone under the age of 18 as domestic minor sex trafficking (DMST). Just how many children and adolescents are victimized annually is impossible to establish. As with all forms of trafficking, victims can be misidentified, and because of the dynamics between traffickers and victims, even the victims may not perceive themselves as being trafficked (Jordan, Patel, & Rapp, 2013). However, the estimates range from as few as 15,000 to as many as 400,000 victims under the age of 18 each year (Jordan et al., 2013; Willis & Levy, 2002).

By examining arrest cases involving prostitution by adolescents, Mitchell, Finkelhor, and Wolak (2010) learned that these adolescents were paid to perform sex acts in the range of $50–$150 per act. It appears that traffickers prefer children and younger teens as they are more desirable to those who purchase prostitutes. Additional research cited by these authors uncovered that in 98% of these cases, money was given for sex acts; however, in other cases sex was exchanged for food, shelter, and drugs.

Mitchell et al. (2010) state that child traffickers set an amount of income that must be generated by their victims. The authors go on to say that for the victims to reach this amount of money, they had to perform multiple commercial sex acts daily, with the average number of clients seen per week varying from 6 to 40. These acts included sexual intercourse, oral sex, anal sex, and group sex. Some of those interviewed also described stripping and being subjected to humiliation or pain during sex.

It appears that the trend in the United States and around the world is that the younger the victim is, the more money a trafficker can charge. In fact, over half of all sex trafficking victims in the United States are American-born children, and the average age a child enters into trafficking has decreased to 12 years old. These children are often taught to dress and speak as if they are much older, and they are told to claim to be 18 years of age if they are caught. One might wonder why traffickers choose victims who are so young. The market seems to demand "clean" girls, and the perception is that the younger a child, the cleaner she or he is.

DIFFICULTIES IN RESEARCHING TRAFFICKING

The difficulties in defining trafficking are partially due to the problems found in researching the phenomenon. However, the most difficult problem of producing quality research on trafficking and thus providing much-needed information is due to not being able to locate and interview trafficked individuals. Because trafficking is a clandestine activity, it is impossible to accurately and systematically gather much-needed data. In the past, this problem has led to mixing the data on smuggling, trafficking, and illegal immigration (Gordy, 2000; Laczko, 2002). In addition, some studies defined human trafficking as sex trafficking and failed to list incidences of labor trafficking (Chapkis, 2003). In other documents, illegal immigrants and migrant sex workers were included in trafficking data even though there was no force, fraud, or coercion involved in their decisions. Still other reports limited their focus to abusive conditions in the sex trade and ignored all other forms of trafficking. The result was information that was unreliable and confusing. The findings did not produce the answers that therapists so desperately needed and looked to the research to provide.

An example of unreliable information is found in the oft-quoted approximation of the prevalence of trafficking produced by the US Department of State, which is 800,000–900,000 each year with 14,000–18,000 occurring inside the United States. The United Nations even quotes these numbers as they form their policies (United Nations Office on Drugs and Crime [UNODC], 2014). Problematically, no one knows where these numbers came from or how the government came by them.

These numbers produced by the US government have been revised several times, with each revision citing past difficulties with reliable methodology (O'Neill, 2000). In 2000 the number of victims was estimated at 45,000–50,000, and then in 2003 it was believed that 18,000–20,000 people were being trafficked, and finally in 2004 the current numbers of 14,000–17,000 were cited. The academic community has questioned these numbers and the way they were produced. But without reliable data, the best any government can do is guess at the scope of the trafficking problem.

Estimating data is not limited to the United States. The United Nations Educational, Scientific, and Cultural Organization (UNESCO) has attempted to examine the statistics used in a number of sources of data. So far, in each case, the validity is questionable, because the numbers cannot be supported. Because of the difficulty in gaining accurate and systematic data on trafficking, it is impossible to fully understand the scope of the problem or produce reliable research on the numerous sub-issues surrounding trafficking. Without this research, the mental health community will continue to have their questions unanswered and struggle with developing trusted treatment models.

RISK FACTORS FOR VICTIMIZATION

In identifying risk factors for trafficking victimization, one truth is glaringly evident—anyone can be a victim of trafficking. However, specific tendencies increase the risk of ensnarement with the primary risk factor being a nonprotective family system. Trafficking victims typically do not come from stable homes with devoted parents and the stereotypical white-picket-fenced house. In fact, these victims tend to belong to single-parent homes that are chaotic and fail to provide secure attachment for family members. Perhaps the most prevalent risk factor is the lack of a secure bond between the parent and child. It is this lack of a secure, loving, and protective family for children and adolescents that puts them at the greatest risk of being trafficked. In a recent study, all of the participants described a distinct lack of belonging in their families (Wolf & Floyd, 2015). A few of the participants reported being involved in their local churches' youth groups but always felt as if they didn't fit in. It was the promise of belonging that first attracted them to their traffickers.

Those who run away or are removed from their families due to neglect or abuse by their parents are also vulnerable (Lloyd, 2005). In addition, physical and emotional abandonment by parents and other family members are powerful predictors of victimization. When abandonment is combined with neglect and other forms of abuse, the risk of victimization rises exponentially (Norton-Hawk, 2002; Rabinovitch, 2003; Raphael & Shapiro, 2002; Reid, 2010). Children who are removed from their families and placed in foster care typically experience strong feelings of isolation, abandonment (Coy, 2008; Rabinovitch, 2003), anxiety, grief, depression, stress, fear, and confusion (Bruskas, 2008). In this state of emotional and mental turmoil, a child may run away from the foster family or group home, which leads to homelessness (Norton-Hawk, 2002; Raphael & Shapiro, 2002). According to the National Center for Missing and Exploited Children (NCMEC, 2014), of the children and adolescents who run away from foster care, 59% will be trafficked—many of them within the first 36 hours they are on the street. Traffickers commonly prey on the homeless and runaways, as they are particularly emotionally and physically vulnerable (Lloyd, 2005).

Childhood sexual assault is another strong predictor of trafficking victimization (American Psychological Association [APA], 2014; Van Dorn et al., 2005). In fact, sexual abuse in childhood was a common experience of children and young women caught in trafficking. One consequence of molestation is the breakdown of normal self-protection responses. These children mature without the ability to adequately protect themselves or correctly assess situations as risky. Another consequence of childhood sexual abuse concerns developed attitudes toward sex and self-image in relationship to sexual activity that may make a life of sexual exploitation seem normal (APA, 2014). Still another consequence of child sexual abuse centers on self-concept, particularly self-denigration (Reid, 2010). Examples of denigrating thoughts include "The only way someone will care for me is if I have sex with him" and "Good people don't want anything to do with me" (APA, 2014). This type of self-talk was the strongest predictor of sexual exploitation in children and adolescents (Reid, 2010).

PORTRAIT OF A TRAFFICKER

A trafficker of persons, better known as simply a trafficker, is one who exploits another person for personal gain. However, traffickers may limit their actions to the recruitment of victims or the transport of them, thereby aiding in victimization. Other traffickers may be tasked with training the victim to perform certain functions, whether it is teaching a task for a sweatshop or instructing the victim in commercial sex work such as prostitution, stripping, or pornography (APA, 2014). The manner in which these roles are accomplished vary greatly, from a well-organized network to an individual trafficker managing it all.

Perpetrators are highly diverse (APA, 2014). Traffickers may be the victim's family member, coach, boyfriend, or Sunday school teacher. They may be well known to the victim and the community or be complete strangers. Traffickers include people in authority, such as police officers and school principals, and those who do not involve themselves in the community. Some traffickers are engaged in other forms of criminal behaviors—for example, drug dealing—while others choose to limit their activities to only trafficking.

In a 2009 report, the United Nations Office on Drugs and Crime noted that women are just as likely to be traffickers as men. Of the data that was available to the UN committee, in 14 countries, more than 50% of convicted traffickers were female. In the United States, that number is quite a bit lower; federal convictions of traffickers show that 23% of the sex traffickers were female (Kyckelhahn, Beck, & Cohen, 2009). Whether they are part of a larger network or operating as individuals, women play a lead role in exploiting victims (Shelley, 2010). Some of these women were once victims of trafficking who then became traffickers.

For a recruiter to be effective, he or she must be able to readily identify a susceptible victim and quickly gain the victim's trust. According to the Human Rights Center (2005a), perpetrators often know their victims. They may be from the same neighborhood, may have gone to church together, or may even be members of the same family. By choosing victims from among individuals who are already known to them, traffickers are able to recognize potentially easy victims and develop relationships with them.

Another trend noted by the Human Rights Center (2005a) is that traffickers tend to choose victims who are of the same nationality or ethnicity as they are. This is seen most clearly in the trend of US citizens and recently naturalized citizens to prey on immigrants from their own countries of origin. When trafficking involves victims who lack legal status, the perpetrator has more leverage with which to threaten and create fear in the victim (Free the Slaves & Human Rights Center, 2004).

It seems to be the public perception that trafficking is most often part of a larger organized crime ring. However, researchers and practitioners have exposed just how complex the act of trafficking actually is (Bruckert & Parent, 2002). One recent study revealed that 90% of federally prosecuted trafficking cases had only one defendant (Small, Adams, Owen, & Roland, 2008). This does not necessarily mean that 90% of trafficking is perpetrated by an individual. It is possible that it is easier for law enforcement to identify and prosecute a single defendant than it is a larger, better-organized network.

CONTROLLING THE VICTIM

Traffickers gain control and exploit their victims by using force, fraud, and coercion; however, how this happens differs between traffickers. Some traffickers cause their victims to become addicted to substances, and others may choose victims who are already addicts. Controlling the supply of drugs then becomes a means for controlling the victim. Other forms of coercion may include promising employment or marriage to ensnare the victim. Still other traffickers use threats of deportation of or harm to family members. Those who are homeless, addicts, disabled, and mentally ill are all common and easy targets for traffickers (Hynes, 2002; Pierce, 2009).

Coercion and manipulation. Manipulation and coercion are common methods used to control victims (Bauer, 2007). Coercion, a primary method of controlling victims, can be defined as mental force or mental violence (Hopper & Hidalgo, 2006). Examples of coercion include threats of death or rape, selling the victims' children, and telling victims that they will go to hell if they do not submit to the wishes of the trafficker. Coercion is often used alongside physical violence, which makes the threats more believable to the victim.

Coercion is so common that in 2008 the United States clarified the term in the reauthorization of the Victims of Trafficking and Violence Protection Act (APA, 2014). Rep. Howard Berman (D-CA, 2008) stated, "A scheme, plan, or pattern intended to inculcate a belief of serious harm may refer to nonviolent and psychological coercion, including but not limited to isolation, denial of sleep, and punishments, or preying on mental illness, infirmity, drug use, or addictions (whether pre-existing or developed by the trafficker)" (APA, 2014, p. 36). To further clarify coercion, Raphael & Ashley (2008) published the findings of their interviews with former victims. The women described coercion in the recruiting process: they were told that they owed the trafficker for their clothes and shelter and were indebted to their kindness; later, the coercive comments were more abusive and included threats of physical harm or being ousted from the "family."

The psychological violence has been likened to torture (Kurtz, Surratt, Inciardi, & Kiley, 2004). Trafficked victims have been neglected, forced to witness acts of violence toward other victims, shamed, and separated from children (APA, 2014). In addition, traffickers may force victims to sell personal belongings and control eating, sleeping, and toilet habits. Sometimes bodily functions are used as a means of punishing the victim. Shared Hope International recorded one victim's account of such abuse (Smith, 2009). To punish one young victim, a trafficker hung her by her hands in a dark closet for three days. The girl was not allowed to drink, eat, or use the toilet. When she defecated on herself, she was taunted and shamed.

Physical violence. Physical and sexual violence are commonly used to assure the ongoing submission of a victim (Dalla, 2000). Violence ranges from slapping to rape to gunshot and knife wounds. One study found that two-thirds of trafficking victims had been raped, with one-third having been raped more than five times (Farley, Baral, Kiremire, & Sezgin, 1998). Studies indicate that up to 90% of trafficking victims experience violence (Farley et al., 1998; Dalla, 2000; Raphael & Shapiro, 2002). International research supports these findings, indicating similar trends of violence in the Middle East, Asia, Africa, Europe, and Central America (Acharya, 2008; APA, 2014). Physical violence against trafficking victims can be extreme and life threatening. In fact, homicide is the leading cause of death in these victims.

Frequent relocation. Moving victims from place to place is another method used by traffickers to maintain control. These moves are designed to keep victims from becoming familiar and thus comfortable with their surrounding (Hynes, 2002). Relocation also makes identifying potential sources of help more difficult, and victims remain isolated from society.

Creating a sense of family. The yearning for a loving and stable family is so strong in children, teens, and young adults that creating an illusion of family is not difficult for those who seek to entrap victims. Traffickers take full advantage of this easily exploited longing. Many traffickers craft a quasi-family, offering affection and attention to victims who are hungry for positive attention. Familiar terms for family members are also used, such as calling the trafficker "Daddy" and other victims in the home "sisters" or "wives-in-law" (Lloyd, 2005; see table 13.1). Dependence on the new family is fostered, and loyalty is demanded. These pseudofamilies provide a sense of belonging, identity, and structure that appeals to many victims, and it is easy to understand how victims form strong bonds to the trafficker and fellow victims in the home (Wolf & Floyd, 2015).

As an illustration of how these pseudofamilies manipulate their victims, consider the story of Heidi, a 14-year-old incarcerated in a juvenile detention center. When Heidi first arrived at the detention center, she was frantic to return to her baby, saying that she was afraid for her life. It was quickly determined that Heidi had never given birth, but her anxiety for this child was very real. Her counselor uncovered the full story. Heidi had been trafficked for the past two years and was recently given an 11-year-old to both care for and groom for the sex trade. Her trafficker explained that this younger girl was now Heidi's daughter and that the girl's well-being was in Heidi's hands. Notice that Heidi was only 12 when she herself first became trafficked. She was also given to a "mother" when she first arrived—the only mother who showed any affection and loyalty toward Heidi, a relationship that aided in trauma bonding.

Table 13.1. Common sex trafficking terms (adapted from Smith, 2009)

Facilitator	A person or organization who provides the means for trafficking to occur. This may include a hotel clerk, taxi driver, or online server where victims are advertised.
Daddy	The name many victims are required to call their trafficker.
Family	The people under the control of the trafficker. The trafficker plays the role of father or (if the trafficker is female) mother. Other victims are referred to as "sisters" or "wives-in-law."
Bottom	A female (usually older) who is in charge or responsible for the other victims and is in charge while the trafficker is away. She can inflict punishment.
Buyer	(Also known as a "john.") A person who trades money, shelter, or something of value for sex acts.
Madam	An older female trafficker who manages a brothel.
Finesse pimp	A trafficker who uses psychological manipulation instead of physical violence; however, the threat of violence is always present.
Gorilla pimp	A trafficker who uses extreme violence to maintain control of the victim.
Stable	Victims of the same trafficker that normally live together.
Survival sex	The act of exchanging sex acts for basic needs such as food and shelter.
Automatic	The behavior of the victim who follows the trafficker's instructions even when he/she is not close by.
Choosing up	The process of changing pimps (traffickers). Typically, this very dangerous process is done by making eye contact with another trafficker. If the original pimp wants the victim back, he must pay for the victim, which often leads to violence toward her.
Date	The act of prostitution.
Kiddie stroll	An area where young victims are displayed for prostitution.
Lot lizard	A term reserved for victims who perform sex acts at truck stops.
Seasoning	A combination of psychological and physical intimidation and manipulation designed to remove a victim's resistance and ensure she will obey the trafficker. Tactics often include gang rape, sodomy, beatings, starvation, sleep deprivation, isolation, and threats.
Turn out	A victim's first time as a prostitute.

The placing of this new child with Heidi further tied Heidi to this family by creating another important relationship, one that Heidi took very seriously. At this point, Heidi's trauma bond expanded to include this child. Heidi also increased her standing in the family. With her added responsibilities as a mother, she did not have to serve as many customers. Also notice the use of common family terms. For a child who never knew what a healthy family looked like, this pseudofamily offered the promise of belonging she had been starving for. Finally, by being given a younger child to groom, Heidi had now taken a step toward becoming a victimizer.

TRAUMA BONDS

In their effort to better understand the powerful emotional connection between the trafficker and victim, Wolf and Floyd (2015) researched the phenomena known as "trauma bonds." They found that traffickers typically provide affection and feign love for their victims as a way of gaining their cooperation in the early stages of victimization. Violence and cruelty, or the threat of it, is then introduced and alternated with affection. The randomness of cruelty and affection creates the powerful dynamic for the phenomenon of trauma bonding to develop. Trauma bonds are powerful emotional attachments of a victim to a perpetrator, such as a trafficker, that are mitigated by numerous traumatic events. The victim feels strong emotional ties to the trafficker and to the other victims that are in the same family or group. These bonds appear to be an adaptive response to extreme trauma and tend to occur when all other attempts at coping have been exhausted. Therefore, trauma bonds are a type of defense mechanism that has connections to attachment theory and learned helplessness. At its core, trauma bonds can be understood as an attachment issue wrapped with worldview and identity confusion and topped off with trauma, loss, and grief.

The process of creating a functioning trafficking victim is referred to as "grooming" and includes a combination of reward and punishment, freedom and bondage, affection and degradation, all of which aid in the development of trauma bonds (APA, 2014; Wolf & Floyd, 2015). Thus the stronger the attachment to the trafficker, the more control over the victim the trafficker has, so that even when the trafficker is not present the victim will follow his or her instructions to the letter. In addition, when given the chance to escape, most will not leave due to this powerful bond. Likewise, many who are rescued from trafficking do not want to leave their trafficker and will do everything in their power to return to the family. Breaking this bond is the most difficult task counselors face when working with victims.

THERAPEUTIC CONSIDERATIONS

Beginning in the 1990s the mental health community slowly began to recognize the need for information on trafficking, specifically treatment interventions (Wolf & Floyd, 2015). Therapists adapted sexual-assault treatment plans to use with survivors of trafficking. They quickly realized that the problem was much more complex than sexual assault alone and are only recently beginning to understand the profound impact trafficking has on its victims.

The effects of trafficking on the victim are numerous and profound. Exposure to chronic victimization increases the risk of physical and psychological difficulties. In fact, routine abuse results in a wide range of expected symptoms from impaired cognitive functioning to attachment disorders (Floyd, 2008). The primary symptoms that are often seen are depression, posttraumatic stress disorder (PTSD), anxiety, shame, attachment disorders, addiction, and behavioral problems.

Relationship difficulties. Among the expected difficulties is the stunted ability to develop healthy relationships. According to Herman (1992), traumatic events have far-reaching effects. Not only do these events target psychological structures and worldviews; they attack attachment systems and the way the individual interacts with his or her community. These events destroy foundational assumptions about the value of the self and of society. Victims are commonly exposed to oppressive traumatic relationships where they submit to the demands of the trafficker to avoid violence (Cantor & Price, 2007). Future relationships may be challenging for former victims as a consequence of the dynamics experienced while under the control of the trafficker.

When traffickers randomly alternate kindness and affection with cruelty and violence, while at the same time isolating the victim from those who would oppose the abuse, victims tend to believe that they cannot escape the trafficker. In fact, as mentioned earlier, victims normally do not attempt to escape, and instead form a traumatic attachment, or trauma bond, to the trafficker. It may even appear that a victim chooses to be with the trafficker. This trauma bond is commonly very difficult to break even when the victim is no longer under the care of the abuser. It is typical for rescued victims to attempt to reconnect with the trafficker even after some time has passed since captivity. In interviews with former victims of trafficking, when asked what would have helped the individual try to escape from the trafficker, several stated that had someone convinced them that the trafficker lied about loving them, they would have left sooner (Wolf & Floyd, 2015).

Mental disorders. Given the traumatic environment in which many victims live, it is understandable that mental disorders are common among this population, with complex posttraumatic stress disorder being the most common diagnosis (Hossain, Zimmerman, Abas, Light, & Watts, 2010). Another expected mental health problem in victims is depression, which also encompasses suicidal ideation and behaviors as well as self-inflicted injuries (APA, 2014). In addition, feelings of guilt and shame are common, and in some cases victims believed that they deserved to be trafficked (Rafferty, 2008).

At the time of this writing, a specific treatment for survivors of trafficking has not been developed. Practitioners borrow from therapies used for PTSD, domestic violence, and other such issues (Jordan et al., 2013). A model is sorely needed to provide for the unique needs of the survivors. One reason for the difficulty in developing a treatment protocol for this population is the complexity of this issue. Trauma counseling is a sophisticated form of therapy. Counseling trafficking victims is even more so. Not only is the counselor required to have a working knowledge of trauma; he or she must also have knowledge of family systems, attachment theory, development issues, culture, spiritual concerns, personality development, pathology, and matters pertaining to identity.

Collins and Collins (2005) recommend a holistic approach that includes cognitive and affective stability, behavioral adjustments, and integration into society. Jordan et al. (2013) note that survivors of trafficking typically do not have the education or skills needed to function well in broader society. Full recovery for this population is slow and arduous due to the combination of lack of knowledge, complex PTSD symptoms, and the absence of specific treatment modalities for trafficking.

COUNSELING FOCI

Counselors must be mindful to move slowly and have realistic expectations for progress. Should the individual enter therapy shortly after he or she was rescued from the trafficker, the client may still be peri-trauma, the mental and emotional state of ongoing trauma. In other words, the victim is functioning as if the trauma is currently happening. To begin therapy as if the person was posttrauma and ready to work toward health would be a mistake. It may even appear as if the person is resistant to counseling, when the client just needs more time to realize that they are safe and the abuse has ended. Therapists may choose to focus on self-care and safety concerns at this time.

Building a strong therapeutic bond is foundational to all forms of counseling. This is even more important when counseling this population. For many of these clients, forming a close relationship with someone who does not want to exploit them or abuse them is a foreign idea. It may take time for this bond to develop. Without it, deep disclosure is unlikely to occur. In addition, the client may terminate prematurely. Through the therapeutic relationship, Christian counselors are able to demonstrate a genuine Christlike concern for trafficking survivors, many of whom may have never experienced this kind of unconditional acceptance. Through this avenue, counselors are able to demonstrate God's grace—a powerful balm for a wounded soul.

The assessment phase of counseling can begin while the therapeutic bond is being forged. Completing a thorough assessment prior to using interventions is vital. The wise therapist remembers that clients and their stories are unique and will tailor treatment to the individual. No matter how common the expected symptom or experience, it is never wise to make assumptions about what the individual client's life was like. As with the development of the therapeutic bond, the assessment should not be rushed and should be allowed to happen slowly. Clients must be guided in revealing the information the counselor seeks. In addition to the areas normally included in trauma assessment (such as sleep disturbances and intrusive memories), therapists need to focus on potential trauma bonding. Does this attachment still exist? Do strong feelings for her trafficker remain intact? Limited questions and increased discussion prompts will assist in this process. For example, a therapist may say, "You haven't mentioned your relationship with your boyfriend [the term the client uses for her trafficker]. Tell me about him."

Counseling this population includes managing and then dissolving trauma bonds. Because these attachments can be so powerful, vigilance is needed to predict and then intervene when the client is at risk for returning to the trafficking relationship. As noted, many former victims truly believe that their traffickers love them, referring to them as husband, boyfriend, daddy, and so on. At times, the trafficker-victim relationship is the vehicle for the only affection that some of these girls have ever known, and giving up that relationship is painful and frightening. Feelings of loss, confusion, anxiety, and grief are common responses.

While many of the treatment objectives will be similar to other complex trauma cases (see chaps. 10 and 11), there are some areas where additional attention must be given. These areas include attachment work, self-identity, family systems, foundational assumptions of how the world works and the individual's place in the world, problem solving, and methods to self-soothe.

Careful development of the treatment plan is vital. Because of the nature of trafficking, great effort should be made to build a trusting relationship between the client and the therapist before working through treatment objectives. In order to survive, most victims became proficient at gauging what people want and giving it to them. Counselors might find this survival skill used in sessions as the individual will often play the part of who they believe the counselor wants them to be

Table 13.2. Sample treatment plan for former trafficking client

Early Phase	Middle Phase	Final Phase
1. Establish a strong bond with client	1. Self-safety work	1. Establish healthy support network
2. Thorough assessment	2. Trauma bond work	2. Crystalize therapeutic changes
3. Establish healthy coping and self-soothing skills	3. Complex trauma work	
	4. Challenge worldview and replace with accurate view of self and society	
	5. Attachment work (family systems may be a part of this)	
	6. Introduce God as an attachment figure	
	7. Grief work	
	8. Establish social and educational skills	

The Modern History of Human Trafficking

In the United States, the anti-trafficking movement can be traced back to the end of the 1800s when Josephine Butler, a leader in the feminist movement, termed involuntary prostitution the *white slave trade* (Derks, 2000). This term referred to the kidnapping and transporting of white women for the purpose of forced commercial sex. Because of Butler's efforts, sex trafficking received wide media coverage that led to a public outcry against this crime. The outcome included national legislation aimed at ending the white slave trade. Her campaign brought the issue of involuntary prostitution onto the international stage. Prompted by the force of outraged Christian groups, the United Kingdom, and other European countries joined the United States in regulating against all prostitution (Bullough & Bullough, 1987).

In 1902 the first draft of an agreement to end white slavery was penned in Paris. By 1904, 16 countries signed the document, The International Agreement for the Suppression of the White Slave Trade (Doezema, 2002). This original document focused on fraudulent or violent recruitment of women for prostitution. Central to the description of the crime was transporting the victim across international lines. Less than six years later, the agreement was changed to include women and girls who were forced into prostitution in their country of origin (Wijers & Lap-Chew, 1997). In 1921 the League of Nations, a precursor to the United Nations, broadened its definition of white slavery to include boys as possible victims.

The International Convention for the Suppression of the Traffic of Women was signed in Geneva, Switzerland, in 1933 and condemned all recruitment for commercial sex outside one's own country (Wijers & Lap-Chew, 1997). Much of the language used in the document was consistent with the US abolitionist movement, a movement that had its roots in the evangelical church. Not only did this document move toward a condemnation of all prostitution, it also re-termed white slavery as trafficking. Many of the abolitionist standards found in the 1933 document were reiterated in the United Nations Convention for the Suppression of Traffic in Persons and the Exploitation of Prostitution of Others, signed in 1949. The chief difference between the 1933 and 1949 documents was the statement that all prostitution was inconsistent with the dignity and value of a human being, a belief that is still held today. It further stated that prostitution actually endangered the well-being of the person, her family, and the community in which she lived (Wijers & Lap-Chew, 1997). This language was the strongest seen to date. In essence, the document was stating that trafficking was a crime against all humanity and the trafficked victim in particular.

Over the next four decades, little attention was given to trafficking. Unfortunately, during this time the prevalence of this crime grew to staggering proportions. Traffickers became more sophisticated in their methods of recruiting and selling their product. Additionally, the Western world's acceptance of recreational sex decreased the outrage toward all prostitution that once led the way in criminalizing sex trafficking. Tragically, the zeal to protect and rescue victims once seen in the Christian church was no more.

Prompted by reports of child sex trafficking, sex tourism, and the AIDS epidemic, the international community took a renewed interest in trafficking of persons during the 1980s (Doezema, 2002). A decade later, trafficking of persons was again brought before the United Nations. The World Conference on Human Rights, held in Vienna, Austria, in 1993 and the World Conference on Women in China two years later focused on the problem of sex trafficking. More than 70 members of the United Nations ratified the 1949 document, and by November 2000 the General Assembly adopted the Protocol to Prevent, Suppress, and Punish Trafficking in Persons, Especially Women and Children (Kelly & Regan, 2000). Individual nations strengthened the UN document as the public outcry against trafficking increased again, with the Christian community leading the charge. In the United States, the general consensus was that these activities happened in other countries and that if trafficking occurred inside our borders, it was an isolated incident.

Not all were pleased with the direction of the international coalition to end sex trafficking. The Network of Sex Work Projects (NSWP), along with other international organizations, demanded a distinction between sex trafficking and those who freely choose to work in the sex trade (Doezema, 2002; Murphy & Ringheim, 2002). They argued that by focusing on the violation of human rights in the sex trade, the public would view all sex work as a violation. Feminists and Christian groups joined together and countered that all sex work devalues the individual, and they questioned whether those who offer sex acts for payment truly do so of a free will.

While this debate was at its peak, the United States passed the Victims of Trafficking and Violence Protection Act (TVPA, 2000), signed into law by President Clinton and reauthorized by President Bush in 2003. TVPA is central in fighting trafficking within the United States. The act allowed for the creation of a federal office that organized and monitored various federal and state anti-trafficking efforts. TVPA also allowed for the creation of a task force to assist the office and aid in efforts to eradicate trafficking of persons within the US borders. Both the federal office and state-level task forces focused on creating legislation and aiding in prosecution of traffickers and the protection of victims of trafficking. The TVPA also influences the standards of anti-trafficking efforts in other countries.

and give information that they believe the counselor wants to hear. At times, clients may change the details of the story or change their stories entirely in an attempt to please the counselor or protect the trafficker or both. Wise therapists will recognize this as a coping mechanism and not manipulation. One former victim described daily training where her trafficker would give her a scenario and she would have to create an identity and background story on the spot and present it to the trafficker as if it were the truth. If she hesitated or failed to be convincing, she would be beaten.

Working with this population is stressful but rewarding. Realistic expectations for the time it will take for a client to reach goals will save the clinician much frustration. The adage that this is a marathon and not a sprint applies here. Indeed, some people may take years for their wounds to heal. While some remain in counseling until they complete their counseling goals, others are in and out of counseling throughout their lifetimes.

CONCLUDING THOUGHTS

There is a great effort by the United States as well as other countries to end human trafficking. Laws have been put in place to criminalize the traffickers and those who assist in the trafficking process. Assistance programs for victims have been funded to aid in everything from medical needs to career training. Nonprofit organizations have opened shelters to provide resources for rescued victims. Mental health professionals are diligently working to develop treatment modalities to address the unique difficulties of these victims.

Even though advancements have been made in battling trafficking during the past few decades, it remains a thriving enterprise. Traffickers are skilled at finding inventive methods for eluding law enforcement. The nature of this crime is generally so well hidden that trafficking is at times conducted in the open and citizens are not even aware that they are observing trafficking activities.

The question of what needs to be done to end this heinous activity remains. The efforts that are ongoing must be continued. It is essential that researchers forge ahead in working to describe the problem and suggest possible solutions. Laws must be adapted so that traffickers are punished while victims are protected, and it is imperative that those who work with victims persist in the important work of providing effective treatment options. Two fundamental areas that should be more thoroughly explored are the breakdown of the family and the demand for modern slaves. A primary risk factor for potential trafficking victimization is family dysfunction. By helping build healthier families, the potential pool of possible victims dwindles. Strengthening families includes promoting individual health, thriving marriages, and strong parent-child relationships.

There will always be individuals who prey on others for their own gain. If the demand for the goods provided by trafficked individuals lessens, then the use of trafficked persons will also decrease. This type of change is a major undertaking. The public must be educated on what trafficking is and how to recognize the products of trafficking, whether it be domestic servitude, items made in a sweatshop, or a person being sold for sex. Attitudes toward the trafficker and the trafficked must be changed. When the public refuses to purchase items that are produced by modern slaves or to use the services of labor traffickers, the lessening demand for victims will lead to fewer trafficked individuals. Similarly, when the public's mindset of normal, healthy sexuality does not include commercial sex work and instead embraces sex within a committed intimate relationship as found only in marriage, the demand for sex trafficking will decrease. Until then, societies around the globe will continue to battle human trafficking.

REFERENCES

Acharya, A. K. (2008). Sexual violence and proximate risks: A study on trafficked women in Mexico City. *Gender, Technology and Development, 12,* 77-99.

American Psychological Association. (2014). *Report of the task force on trafficking of women and girls.* Retrieved from www.apa.org/pi/women/programs/trafficking/report.pdf

Bauer, M. (2007). *Close to slavery: Guestworker programs in the United States.* Montgomery, AL: Southern Poverty Law Center. Retrieved from www.splcenter.org

Belser, P. (2005). *Forced labor and human trafficking: Estimating the profits.* Geneva, Switzerland: International Labour Office.

Bravo, L. (2011). The role of the transatlantic slave trade in contemporary anti-human trafficking discourse. *Seattle Journal for Social Justice, 9*(2), 555-59.

Bruckert, C., & Parent, C. (2002). *Trafficking in human beings and organized crime: A literature review.* Ottawa, Canada: Royal Canadian Mounted Police. Retrieved from https://childhub.org/en/system/tdf/library/attachments/bruckert_02_crime_0708.pdf?file=1&type=node&id=18277

Bruskas, D. (2008). Children in foster care: A vulnerable population at risk. *Journal of Child and Adolescent Psychiatric Nursing, 21*(2), 70-77.

Bullough, V., & Bullough, B. (1987). *Women and prostitution: A social history.* Buffalo, NY: Prometheus.

Cantor, C., & Price, J. (2007). Traumatic entrapment, appeasement and complex post-traumatic stress disorder. Evolutionary perspectives on hostage reactions, domestic abuse and the Stockholm Syndrome. *Australian and New Zealand Journal of Psychiatry, 41,* 377-84.

Chapkis, W. (2003). Trafficking, migration, and the law. *Gender & Society, 17*(6), 923-37.

Collins, G. C., & Collins, T. M. (2005). *Crisis and trauma: Developmental-ecological intervention.* Boston, MA: Houghton Mifflin.

Coy, M. (2008). Young women, local authority, care and selling sex. *British Journal of Social Work, 38*(7), 1408-24.

Dalla, R. L. (2000). Exposing the "pretty woman" myth: A qualitative examination of the lives of female streetwalking prostitutes. *Journal of Sex Research, 37,* 344-53.

Derks, A. (2000). *Combating trafficking in Southeast Asia: A review of policy and programme responses.* International Organization for Migration. Retrieved from https://childhub.org/en/system/tdf/library/attachments/derks_iom_2000_combating_t.pdf?file=1&type=node&id=16308

Doezema, J. (2002). Who gets to choose? Coercion, consent and the UN Trafficking Protocol. *Gender and Development, 10*(1), 20-27,

Farley, M., Baral, I., Kiremire, M., & Sezgin, U. (1998). Prostitution in five countries: Violence and post-traumatic stress disorder. *Feminism and Psychology, 8,* 405-26.

Floyd, S. (2008). *Crisis Counseling.* Grand Rapids, MI: Kregel.

Free the Slaves & Human Rights Center. (2004). *Hidden slaves: Forced labor in the United States.* Washington, DC: Free the Slaves; Berkeley, CA: Human Rights Center. Retrieved from www.law.berkeley.edu/files/hiddenslaves_report.pdf

Gordy, M. (2000). A call to fight forced labor. *Parade, 20,* 4-5.

Hagner, D. (1995). *Word Biblical Commentary: Vol. 33b. Matthew 14–28.* Dallas, TX: Word Books.

Herman, J. L. (1992). *Trauma and recovery.* New York, NY: Basic Books.

Hopper, E., & Hidalgo, J. (2006). Invisible chains: Psychological coercion of human trafficking victims. *Intercultural Human Rights Review, 1,* 185-209.

Hossain, M., Zimmerman, C., Abas, M., Light, M., & Watts, C. (2010). The relationship of trauma to mental disorders among trafficked and sexually exploited girls and women. *American Journal of Public Health, 100*(12), 2442-49.

Human Rights Center. (2005a). *Hidden slaves: Forced labor in the United States.* Berkeley: University of California. Retrieved from http://digitalcommons.ilr.cornell.edu/cgi/viewcontent.cgi?article=1007&context=forcedlabor

Human Rights Center. (2005b). *Freedom denied: Forced labor in California.* Berkeley: University of California. Retrieved from www.oas.org/atip//country%20specific/Forced%20Labor%20in%20California.pdf

Hyland, K. E. (2001). The impact of the Protocol to Prevent, Suppress and Punish Trafficking in Persons, Especially Women and Children. *American University Washington College of Law Human Rights Brief, 8*(2), 30-38.

Hynes, H. P. (2002). The United States: Migration and trafficking in women. In J. G.

Raymond et al. (Eds.), *A comparative study of women trafficked in the migration process: Patterns, profiles and health consequences of sexual exploitation in five countries (Indonesia, the Philippines, Thailand, Venezuela and the United States)* (pp. 47-52). North Amherst, MA: Coalition Against Trafficking in Women. Retrieved from www.oas.org/atip/Migration/Comparative%20study%20of%20women%20trafficked%20in%20migration%20process.pdf

Jordan, J., Patel, B., & Rapp, L. (2013). Domestic minor sex trafficking: A social work perspective on misidentification, victims, buyers, traffickers, treatment, and reform of current practice. *Journal of Human Behavior in the Social Environment, 23*(3), 356-69.

Kelly, L., & Regan, L. (2000). *Stopping traffic: Exploring the extent of, and responses to, trafficking in women for sexual exploitation in the UK*. Policing and Reducing Crimes Unit, Research, Development, and Statistics Directorate. Retrieved from https://childhub.org/en/child-protection-online-library/policing-and-reducing-crime-unit-police-research-series-2000

Kurtz, S. P., Surratt, H. L., Inciardi, J. A., & Kiley, M. C. (2004). Sex work and "date" violence. *Violence Against Women, 10*, 357-85.

Kyckelhahn, T., Beck, A., & Cohen, T. (2009). *Characteristics of suspected human trafficking incidents 2007–2008* [Bureau of Justice Statistics special report]. Washington, DC: US Department of Justice. Retrieved from www.bjs.gov/content/pub/pdf/cshti08.pdf

Laczko, F. (2002) Human trafficking: The need for better data. Migration Policy Institute. Retrieved from www.migrationpolicy.org/article/human-trafficking-need-better-data

Lloyd, R. (2005). Acceptable victims? Sexually exploited youth in the U.S. *Encounter: Education for Meaning and Social Justice, 18*(3), 6-18.

Mitchell, K. J., Finkelhor, D., & Wolak, J. (2010). Conceptualizing juvenile prostitution as child maltreatment: Findings from the National Juvenile Prostitution Study. *Child Maltreatment, 15*(1), 18-36.

Murphy, M., & Ringheim, K. (2002). Violence against women. *Outlook, 20*(1), 1-8.

National Center for Missing and Exploited Children. (2014, August). *Foster care, runaways, homelessness and child trafficking*. Lecture presented at the Texas Attorney General's Anti-Trafficking Taskforce Meeting, Austin, Texas.

Norton-Hawk, M. (2002). The lifecourse of prostitution. *Women, Girls & Criminal Justice, 3*(1), 1, 7-9.

O'Callaghan, M. (2012). The health care professional as a modern abolitionist. *Permanente Journal, 16*(2), 67-69.

O'Neill, R. A. (2000). *International trafficking in women to the United States: A contemporary manifestation of slavery and organized crime*. Washington, DC: US Department of State, Bureau of Intelligence & Research, DCI Exceptional Intelligence

Analyst Program. Retrieved from https://www.cia.gov/library/center-for-the-study
-of-intelligence/csi-publications/books-and-monographs/trafficking.pdf

Pierce, A. (2009). *Shattered hearts: The commercial sexual exploitation of American Indian women and girls in Minnesota*. Minneapolis: Minnesota Indian Women's Resource Center. Retrieved from www.miwrc.org/graphics/reports/Shattered-Hearts -Full.pdf

Rabinovitch, J. (2003). The Prostitutes' Empowerment, Education and Resource Society. In M. Farley (Ed.), *Prostitution, trafficking, and traumatic stress* (pp. 255-66). Binghamton, NY: Haworth.

Rafferty, Y. (2008). The impact of trafficking on children: Psychological and social policy perspectives. *Child Development Perspectives 2*(1), 13-18.

Rakin, G., & Kinsella, N. (2011). *Human trafficking: The importance of knowledge information exchange*. London, England: Springer.

Raphael, J., & Ashley, J. (2008). *Domestic sex trafficking of Chicago women and girls*. Illinois Criminal Justice Information Authority. Retrieved from www.icjia.state.il.us/ assets/pdf/ResearchReports/Sex%20Trafficking%20Report%20May%202008.pdf

Raphael, J., & Shapiro, D. (2002). *Sisters speak out: The lives and needs of prostituted women in Chicago—A research study*. Chicago, IL: Center for Impact Research. Retrieved from www.healthtrust.net/sites/default/files/publications/sistersspeakout.pdf

Reid, J. A. (2010). Doors wide shut: Barriers to the successful delivery of victim services for domestically trafficked minors in a southern U.S. metropolitan area. *Women & Criminal Justice, 20*(1), 147-66.

Shelley, L. (2010). *Human trafficking: A global perspective*. Cambridge, England: Cambridge University Press.

Small, K., Adams, W., Owen, C., & Roland, K. (2008). *An analysis of federally prosecuted CSEC cases since the passage of the Victims of Trafficking and Violence Prevention Act of 2000*. Washington, DC: Urban Institute Justice Policy Center. Retrieved from www. ncjrs.gov/pdffiles1/ojjdp/grants/222023.pdf

Smith, L. (2009). *Renting lacy*. Vancouver, WA: Shared Hope International.

United Nations Office on Drugs and Crime (UNODC). (2009). *Global report on trafficking in persons*. Retrieved from www.unodc.org/documents/Global_Report_on_ TIP.pdf

United Nations Office on Drugs and Crime (UNODC). (2014). UNODC report on human trafficking exposes modern form of slavery. Retrieved on March 2, 2016 from www.unodc.org/unodc/en/human-trafficking/global-report-on-trafficking-in-persons.html

US Department of State. (2000, October 28). Victims of trafficking and violence protection act of 2000. Retrieved from www.state.gov/j/tip/laws/61124.htm

US Department of State. (2003, January 7). Trafficking victims protection reauthorization act of 2003. Retrieved from www.state.gov/j/tip/laws/61130.htm

Van Dorn, R., Mustillo, S., Elbogen, E., Dorsey, S., Swanson, J., & Swartz, M. (2005). The effects of early sexual abuse on adult risky sexual behaviors among persons with severe mental illness. *Child Abuse & Neglect, 29*, 1265-79.

Weaver, S. (2006, July 5). The prophet and the prostitute: Exposition of Hosea [Blog post]. Retrieved from https://pastorhistorian.com/2006/07/05/the-prophet-and-the-prostitute-exposition-of-hosea-11-21

Wijers, M., & Lap-Chew, L. (1997). *Trafficking in women, forced labour and slavery-like practices.* Utrecht, Netherlands: Foundation Against Trafficking in Women.

Willis, B., & Levy, B. (2002). Child prostitution: Global health burden, research needs, and interventions. *Lancet, 359*, 1417-22.

Wolf, S., & Floyd, S. (2015, September). *The development of trauma bonds in victims of human trafficking.* Paper presented at the world conference of the American Association of Christian Counselors, Nashville, TN.

Yakushko, O. (2009). Human trafficking: A review for mental health professionals. *International Journal for the Advancement of Counseling, 31*(3), 158-67.

PART FOUR

GLOBAL

CONTEXTS OF

TRAUMA

FAITH AND DISASTER MENTAL HEALTH:
RESEARCH, THEOLOGY, AND PRACTICE

JAMIE D. ATEN, ALICE SCHRUBA,
DAVID N. ENTWISTLE, EDWARD B. DAVIS,
JENN RANTER, JENNY HWANG, JOSHUA N. HOOK,
DAVID C. WANG, DON E. DAVIS, AND
DARYL R. VAN TONGEREN

Across the globe, natural disasters (e.g., floods, storms, and earthquakes) and human-caused disasters (e.g., technological disasters, terrorist incidents, and mass shootings) have increased in their frequency, scope, and human impact. For example, from 1985 to 1994, there were 2,334 natural disasters and 34,112 terrorist incidents worldwide, while from 2005 to 2014, there were almost twice as many: 4,050 natural disasters and 64,708 terrorist incidents. Since 1995 there have been nearly 18,000 natural and technological disasters worldwide, collectively affecting 6 billion people and causing 2.2 million deaths, injuring another 6.4 million people, and leaving 128.8 million people homeless (Guha-Sapir, Below, & Hoyois, n.d.; START, 2015). Also, in the United States alone, from 1983 to 2012 there were 78 mass shootings, causing 547 deaths and injuring another 476 people (Bjelopera, Bagalman, Caldwell, Finklea, & McCallion, 2013). The economic impact of disasters has also increased. Since 1995 natural and technological disasters have collectively caused $2.7 trillion in damage (Guha-Sapir et al., n.d.), and the United Nations Office for Disaster Risk Reduction (UNISDR) estimates that the worldwide annual economic losses from disasters is between $250 billion and $300 billion (UNISDR, 2015).

This chapter was made possible through the support of a grant from the John Templeton Foundation (Grant #44040). The opinions expressed in this publication are those of the author(s) and do not necessarily reflect the views of the John Templeton Foundation.

The psychological impact of disasters can be tremendous too. Adult disaster survivors often experience mental health difficulties such as depression, anxiety disorders, general/nonspecific psychological distress, suicidality, substance use disorders, or posttraumatic stress symptoms (PTSSs) or disorder (PTSD; Galea, Nandi, & Vlahov, 2005; Norris et al., 2002). For instance, among directly affected adult survivors of human-caused disasters, the prevalence rate of disaster-related PTSD ranges from 30% to 60%, and for adult survivors of natural disasters, the prevalence rate of disaster-related PTSD ranges from 5% to 60% but usually falls in the lower half of that range (Galea et al., 2005). Alternatively, natural and human-caused disasters can catalyze perceived posttraumatic growth, such as increased personal resilience (e.g., life satisfaction, meaning and purpose in life, self-efficacy, and coping skills) and enhanced social and community resilience (e.g., family connectedness, perceived social support, prosocial behavior, and civic engagement; Cook, Aten, Moore, Hook, & Davis, 2013).

Disasters can also significantly affect survivors' religious/spiritual (R/S) lives, both for good or ill (e.g., Aten & Boan, 2016). On the one hand, religion/spirituality can serve as a potent resilience factor (Pargament & Cummings, 2010), helping survivors successfully cope, make meaning, adapt, and even grow following a disaster (e.g., Chan & Rhodes, 2014). On the other hand, disasters can lead to the loss or decline of survivors' faith (Sibley & Bulbulia, 2012; Stratta et al., 2013), and they can lead survivors to experience R/S struggles that can fuel the aforementioned disaster-related mental health difficulties (e.g., Park, 2016).

Thus, in this chapter, we seek to equip Christian mental health providers to help disaster survivors navigate issues of faith. First, we review the empirical literature on faith and disaster mental health. Then we explore Christian theological perspectives on suffering. Finally, we offer recommendations for providing disaster spiritual and emotional care in clinical practice.

EMPIRICAL LITERATURE ON FAITH AND DISASTER MENTAL HEALTH[1]

Over the last two decades, a growing number of researchers have examined the intersections of faith and mental health in disaster contexts. In this section, we summarize this empirical literature, focusing first on the impact of disasters on faith and next on the impact of faith on postdisaster well-being.

Influence of religious/spiritual appraisal. Research has demonstrated relationships between religious and spiritual appraisal and disaster reactions. Kroll-Smith and Couch (1987) examined religious attributions and coping in a community affected by a 23-year-long mine fire that eventually led to calamity. They found that

---

[1]Adapted with permission from Aten, O'Grady, Milstein, Boan, Smigelsky, Schruba, and Weaver (2014).

most participants attributed this technical disaster to human failure rather than to God. Ai, Cascio, Santangelo, and Evans-Campbell (2005) found similar reactions to human-made disasters in their study of survivors of 9/11. However, their data revealed additional insight into another possible difference in how people respond across disasters, noting that negative coping was associated with defense or retaliation patterns of reaction to 9/11, in effect creating an "in-group" versus "out-group" difference based on religious ideology.

Likewise, Pargament et al. (1994) conducted a longitudinal study of the Gulf War crisis in which they learned that negative religious coping was significantly tied to psychological distress. Conversely, survivors of natural disasters (sometimes referred to as "acts of God"), appear to more readily incorporate spiritual and religious meaning into their interpretation of the disaster, as well as their responses and coping mechanisms. For instance, survivors of the 2010 Haiti earthquake referenced God as the author of the earthquake and cited prophetic references from the Bible to make sense of the event (O'Grady, Rollison, Hanna, Schreiber-Pan, & Ruiz, 2012). Additionally, Smith, Pargament, Brant, and Oliver (2000) found that positive religious coping strategies had a positive effect on postflood spiritual growth, in addition to leading to the reduction of psychological distress for survivors of a Midwest flood.

How survivors view and experience God. The way people view the Divine is influenced by a number of factors including traumatic life experiences. Likewise, certain views of God or the Divine have been demonstrated in the research to affect psychological functioning during and after trauma events, including large-scale disasters (Moriarty & Davies, 2012; Richards & O'Grady, 2007). After 9/11 Briggs, Apple, and Aydlett (2004) found that this tragic event appeared to increase participants' connection with transcendence. O'Grady et al. (2012) found that 80% of earthquake survivors agreed or strongly agreed with the statement "My faith in a God/a higher power has grown since the earthquake." However, 23% of participants agreed or strongly agreed that they felt more distant from God/a higher power since the earthquake, and 20% indicated that they were less spiritual since the earthquake. Overall, people's daily spiritual experiences with God, their perceptions of God's awareness of them, and their sense of "specialness" to God predicted their degree of spiritual transformation above and beyond the amount of loss they experienced in the earthquake.

Aten, Madison, Rice, and Chamberlain (2008) found that Hurricane Katrina survivors often held a multifaceted view of God that existed on a continuum from a loving and caring parental figure to a judging and even punishing figure. Newton and McIntosh (2009) found that Jewish survivors of Hurricane Katrina held more positive and benevolent views of God than Christian survivors, who were more apt to report feeling as though God was sending punishment. According to the Conservation of Resources (COR) stress theory, "loss is the primary operating mechanism driving stress reactions" (Hobfoll, Freedy, Green, & Solomon, 1996, p. 324). After Hurricane Katrina, Aten, Bennett, Davis, Hill, and Hook (2012) found that increased levels of resource loss were related to a more negative God concept, as well as viewing God as less in control.

Survivor religion/spirituality and well-being. Religion and spirituality may moderate the impact of disaster on individuals' well-being. Research suggests that religion and spirituality serve as a buffer for the potential deleterious effects of disasters and/or a contributor to psychological distress following disasters. After 9/11, Ai et al. (2005) discovered stronger faith, hope, and spirituality to be inversely correlated with depression and anxiety related to the exposure of direct and indirect 9/11 trauma. Further, researchers found that religious comfort helped to protect participants from negative emotional and physical health outcomes commonly associated with resource loss and was also associated with posttraumatic growth.

Religious strain, however, was linked to poorer emotional and physical health outcomes following disaster resource loss (Cook et al., 2013). Likewise, Johnson, Aten, Madson, and Bennett (2006) surveyed approximately 600 residents of Mississippi who survived Hurricane Katrina. In this study, those individuals who possessed positive religious and spiritual beliefs (e.g., God concept, religious coping strategies, religious support, meaning making) were shown to be less affected by the effects of exposure to hurricanes as well as the degree of resource loss (i.e., material and interpersonal). These individuals also experienced reduced rates of PTSD symptoms, depression, and alcohol use.

Taken as a whole, this body of burgeoning research may indicate that it is not so much how religious or spiritual one is but rather how one uses one's faith (i.e., positive religious coping versus negative religious coping strategies) that appears to have the most significant impact on well-being outcomes. Of course, the reader must be cautious in drawing conclusions since much of this research is correlational in nature. It is equally likely, for example, that there is an underlying mental health or personality factor at work in both faith and response to significant life events.

Spirituality/religion and posttraumatic transformation. Disasters can create psychological and spiritual transformation in individuals. Depending on the resources in place in people's lives, the transformation can be toward decline, such as (but not limited to) PTSD, or toward growth (Calhoun & Tedeschi, 2006; Roberts & Ashley, 2008). For example, a study of Haitian earthquake survivors found that those who relied on their spirituality for meaning making and coping evidenced greater resilience during and after the trauma than those who did not do so. Participants also attributed their description of posttraumatic growth to positive framing—a sense of a larger purpose or of order amidst disaster. Some saw the disaster as a potentially growth-stimulating experience for Haiti (e.g., a chance to rebuild a better country; O'Grady et al., 2012). Jang and LaMendola (2007) studied 607 survivors of a major earthquake in Taiwan and found that survivors' spirituality had a direct link with posttraumatic growth, and that the community's collective spiritual narratives about suffering contributed to the psychological growth following the earthquake.

CHRISTIAN RESPONSES TO SUFFERING

Now that we have surveyed some of the psychological research on spiritual appraisals of disasters and how they may affect mental health symptoms after a disaster, we now turn to perspectives of suffering within Christianity that are relevant for people helping disaster survivors. Theodicy (i.e., the problem of evil in the world) is a complex theological concept (see chap. 2 in this volume). Our goal in this section is to draw some practical principles from the Bible, starting first with the book of Job.

Within the broad testimony of Christian Scripture, one can scarcely think of suffering without considering the story of Job. In the biblical account, Job was a righteous man whom God allowed to suffer greatly at the hand of Satan. In a single day, marauders stole Job's donkeys and oxen and killed all but one of the servants that oversaw them. All his sheep and more servants were then killed by fire from heaven. All his camels were stolen by another raiding party who killed more of his servants. Moreover, his seven sons and three daughters were killed when a windstorm caused a house to collapse on them.

Here we have two major categories of suffering illustrated: natural disasters and disasters produced by human activity. In both cases, God is characterized as allowing these tragedies to occur. On yet another day, God allows Satan himself to strike Job: "So Satan went out from the presence of the LORD and afflicted Job with painful sores from the soles of his feet to the crown of his head" (Job 2:7).

Although Job's story is a classic example of events that raise questions regarding theodicy, it is also an interesting study in disaster response. Job is visited by three friends (and a fourth character who appears later in the book). Their initial response to Job is one of shared grief and a ministry of presence:

> When Job's three friends . . . heard about all the troubles that had come upon him, they
> set out from their homes and met together by agreement to go and sympathize with
> him and comfort him. When they saw him from a distance, they could hardly rec-
> ognize him; they began to weep aloud, and they tore their robes and sprinkled dust
> on their heads. Then they sat on the ground with him for seven days and seven nights.
> No one said a word to him, because they saw how great his suffering was. (Job 2:11-13)

This scripture passage reveals a lesson: our first task in responding to suffering is to enter into relationship with survivors and to be present in their suffering. But suffering inevitably raises questions such as "Where is God?" Another common question that is raised is "Do those who suffer somehow bring it upon themselves?" Recall the disciples' question when they encountered a man who was born blind: "Rabbi, who sinned, this man or his parents, that he was born blind?" (Jn 9:2). It is all too easy to blame the victim (Ryan, 1976), but we see that Christ rebukes this type of response and instead points to the natural order of living in a fallen world.

As Job's friends shift from a ministry of presence to debating the source of Job's suffering, they increasingly point their fingers at Job. Chapter by chapter, Job's frustration grows. In chapter 16 he retorts:

> I have heard many things like these;
>> you are miserable comforters, all of you!
> Will your long-winded speeches never end?
>> What ails you that you keep on arguing?
> I also could speak like you,
>> if you were in my place;
> I could make fine speeches against you
>> and shake my head at you.
> But my mouth would encourage you;
>> comfort from my lips would bring you relief. (Job 16:1-5)

Job himself recognized that it is easy to "make fine speeches" against those who suffer, but he instead commends bringing comforting words. As it is, his friends have become "miserable comforters"—something, no doubt, that Christian mental health professionals ought to avoid doing. Unfortunately, Job's friends still failed to learn that it was not their place to assign blame, leading Job to cry out:

> How long will you torment me
>> and crush me with words?
> Ten times now you have reproached me;
>> shamelessly you attack me.
> If it is true that I have gone astray,
>> my error remains my concern alone.
> If indeed you would exalt yourselves above me
>> and use my humiliation against me,
> then know that God has wronged me
>> and drawn his net around me. (Job 19:2-6)

Here we see another subtle risk to those who seek to help crisis-affected persons: exalting ourselves above those who suffer. Humility, along with the knowledge that our situations could easily be reversed, is a necessary posture for effective disaster response. Indeed, the Gospels provide examples of self-sacrifice to help people in need: "Greater love has no one than this: to lay down one's life for one's friends" (Jn 15:13).

But why respond to disaster at all? In some ways, the response of Job's friends seems reasonable. Of the 124 times the Bible uses the word *disaster* (all, incidentally, in the Old Testament), the vast majority are in the context of prophecies about God bringing disaster on the unrighteous. Yet even here there are hints that a personal or societal crisis is not always to be seen as the judgment of God. When Haman hatched a plot to kill all the Jews, Mordecai told Esther that her royal position could not protect her: "And who knows but that you have come to your royal position for such a time as this?" (Esther 4:14). When David was pursued by Saul and hiding in caves, he cried out to God, "Have mercy on me, my God, have mercy on me, / for in you I take refuge. / I will take refuge in the shadow of your wings / until the disaster has passed" (Ps 57:1). Crying out to God in the midst of suffering is a common theme scattered throughout the Psalms and the Prophets (e.g., Jer 17:17). Thus, there is good precedent for Christian mental health professionals to support spiritually oriented disaster survivors in turning their pleas of suffering to God instead of stifling such cries (or condemning them, as Job's friends did).

But what about those biblical occasions when the Bible depicts suffering as a clear consequence of spiritual rebellion? Even in those instances we are warned against delighting in adversities. For example, Edom was chastised for its haughtiness in the face of the suffering of its Jewish brothers (Obad 1:10). The Bible also warns against reveling in the misfortunes of others: "Whoever mocks the poor shows contempt for their Maker; / whoever gloats over disaster will not go unpunished" (Prov 17:5). Condemnation, ridicule, delight, and the naive assumption that we are immune from suffering not only are unhelpful but typically reflect poorly on the state of our own souls. It is clear that we must reject our tendency toward judgment and instead embrace humility. This does not mean hearing about tragedy and only expressing concern by praying—at least not when we are in a position to do more. Throughout the Scriptures, we are pictured as responsible for one another. We see this very early in the creation story: "It is not good for the man to be alone. I will make a helper suitable for him" (Gen 2:18). Part of the design of creation is that we are to help one another.

Families, of course, can be expected to pull together in times of crisis—"A friend loves at all times, and a brother is born for a time of adversity" (Prov 17:17)—but they do not always do this well. Even when families pitch in to the best of their ability, distance and lack of resources may render such efforts impotent. Hence, the author of Proverbs tells us, "Do not forsake your friend or a friend of your family, / and do not go to your relative's house when disaster strikes you— / better a neighbor nearby than a relative far away" (Prov 27:10).

Throughout the biblical narrative, we see the theme of God's active work of redemption, as God repeatedly demonstrates that God is not the kind of being who just brought creation into existence and then was uninvolved. Rather, we see repeated examples of a God who is capable of, interested in, and committed to intervening. We see a God who promises in Revelation 21:4 that "God shall wipe away all tears" (KJV) from those who suffer—if not in this life, then in the new creation.

Thus, when considering how to respond to disasters, we must ensure that our theology of disasters is coherent with the larger biblical narrative and with scriptural truths. In contrast to the Old Testament, examples of disasters in the New Testament suggest that disasters are not so much manifestations of divine wrath sent to a particular group of persons; rather, disasters are evidence of the creation moaning for liberation from the effects of humanity's sin (Rom 8:18-23). Moreover, we see the example of God's ultimate sacrifice, love, and commitment, reflected in God's choice to enter human suffering and suffer personally even to the point of death, yet with the promise of new life and redemption. Thus, we are challenged to see beyond the present suffering to the world as God intended it to be—a redeemed and restored new creation that reflects and glorifies the Creator.

In fact, in themselves disasters often reflect the four-phase biblical metanarrative of creation, sin, salvation, and redemption. Throughout the Bible, God promises to be with us and to walk with us through times of suffering. As Christians, we too are called to minister to and with those people who suffer, including disaster survivors.

PRACTICING DISASTER SPIRITUAL AND EMOTIONAL CARE[2]

Christian mental health professionals are in a unique position to help disaster survivors address both mental health and spiritual issues, as well as to collaborate with the church during times of disaster. In this section we build on the psychological research and biblical framework above by offering examples of both microlevel (person focused) and macrolevel (community focused) interventions that are key to successful disaster spiritual and emotional care. We conclude the section by considering the ways in which having Christian mental health professionals involved in disaster spiritual and emotional care may help shape future Christian integrative efforts.

---

[2]Adapted with permission from Aten, O'Grady, Milstein, Boan, Smigelsky, Schruba, and Weaver (2014).

Disaster church-psychology collaboration. Christian mental health professionals should take steps to engage key gatekeepers within faith communities to build collaborative relationships that can be leveraged in response to disasters. Church leaders often act as gatekeepers in their respective faith communities, and they are more willing to refer members to professionals when they have an established relationship (e.g., Aten, 2004). Therefore, Christian mental health professionals should make a strategic effort to build partnerships with church leaders in their community *prior to* disasters so that a relationship is already in place if and when a disaster strikes (Evans, Kromm, & Sturgis, 2008; Roberts & Ashley, 2008). These partnerships will help pave the way for greater church-psychology collaboration in response to disasters.

Church leaders are the experts about their communities, so Christian mental health professionals should use a dialogical (i.e., two-way) rather than didactic (i.e., one-way) approach to collaboration. When meeting with such gatekeepers, Christian mental health professionals should seek to maintain a humble, learning posture, especially as it applies to the dynamics of specific faith communities and cultural contexts, so that church leaders and mental health practitioners together can create a community-specific and culturally sensitive approach to disaster preparedness and response (O'Grady et al., 2012).

Psychological First Aid (PFA) for community religious professionals. When disaster strikes, the impact may be moderated by early intervention. Prior to 2002, Critical Incident Stress Debriefing (CISD) was the modal intervention strategy employed internationally in the immediate aftermath of trauma (Litz, 2008). CISD is a specific, seven-phase, small-group, supportive crisis intervention process. However, subsequent empirical research has cast doubt on some of the supposed benefits of CISD and even demonstrated a potential for it to cause more harm than good (Emmerik, Kamphuis, Hulsbosch, & Emmelkamp, 2002). Because of these controversies, CISD became part of a more comprehensive intervention protocol known as Critical Incident Stress Management (CISM; Everly & Mitchell, 1999, 2011). Currently, CISM involves seven core components: (1) pre-crisis preparation, (2) demobilization and staff consult, (3) defusing, (4) CISD, (5) individual crisis intervention, (6) family CISM, and (7) follow-up referral (Everly & Mitchell, 1999). Despite these revisions, the debriefing component of CISM continues to raise concerns about its effectiveness as a flexible and adaptable tool for early intervention. In light of such concerns, most practice guidelines (such as the Center for Mental Health Services of the Substance Abuse and Mental Health Services Administration and the Departments of Veterans Affairs and Defense) now recommend Psychological First Aid (Litz, 2008).

The purpose of PFA is to provide children, adults, and families with support that decreases risk factors and increases resilience factors to trauma (Vernberg et al.,

2008). PFA is an evidence-informed intervention for survivors of natural and human-caused disasters. Compared to traditional psychotherapy, it is less clinically oriented in nature and primarily focuses on addressing the immediate mental health needs of disaster survivors. PFA consists of nine core actions: (1) contact and engagement, (2) safety and comfort, (3) stabilization, (4) information gathering, (5) current needs and concerns, (6) practical assistance, (7) connection with social supports, (8) information on coping, and (9) linkage with collaborative services (Forbes et al., 2011). PFA has more of a triage focus, with the goal of helping to enhance and stabilize the psychological well-being of disaster survivors. As a result, PFA has been adapted for a wide range of community professionals to be able to deliver this intervention.

Of particular relevance to the current chapter, PFA has also been contextualized for community religious professionals. In *Psychological First Aid: Field Operations Guide for Community Religious Professionals* (Brymer et al., 2006), the authors introduce a variation of Psychological First Aid that addresses religious and spiritual themes, including (a) clarifying religious, spiritual, and existential terminology; (b) how to worship with someone of a different faith; and (c) talking to children and adolescents about their spiritual/religious concerns and involving them in religious activities. Christian mental health professionals could use this resource to train clergy and church leaders in this intervention, thereby increasing a community's capacity to provide disaster spiritual and emotional care. Christian mental health professionals are encouraged to acquire this spiritually focused resource to enhance their own clinical practice.

Consultation, outreach, and advocacy. Christian mental health professionals can also promote disaster spiritual and emotional care through consultation, outreach, and advocacy efforts. Aten, Topping, Denney, and Hosey (2011) developed a three-tier consultation and outreach model to provide mental health training for clergy and churches. In tier one, Christian mental health professionals provide basic disaster mental health information to local clergy. In tier two, Christian mental health professionals and church leaders work together to help educate their congregation members. In tier three, congregation members reach out to their local communities to provide information on topics such as common reactions and problems, as well as information on when and where help can be found locally.

Similarly, on behalf of churches, Christian mental health professionals can advocate for resources by applying the best science and information available to address disaster needs and policy. In this role, Christian mental health professionals can work with local churches and organizations to identify needs and gaps in services and help them bring those needs to light (Aten et al., 2008). For example, after Hurricane Katrina, several churches were concerned that local authorities were planning to use relief dollars to expand a local port used for industry rather than fund low-income housing. In this case, several local Christian psychologists collaborated with churches to help them develop a policy-influencing "voice" and refine their message. Empirical data were provided to faith leaders to help support their arguments and thereby enhance their ability to influence policy. Overall, successful consultation, outreach, and advocacy interventions are characterized by (a) establishing relationships with local community and religious leaders, (b) striving to be culturally appropriate, (c) fostering bidirectional collaboration, (d) promoting a cyclical approach (e.g., implementation, evaluation, and refinement), (e) being contextualized to the community, and (f) helping organize resources (Aten et al., 2013; Milstein, Manierre, & Yali, 2010).

Clinical services. In addition to preparedness and community-level interventions, Christian mental health professionals may have the opportunity to develop psychotherapeutic relationships with individuals and families affected by a disaster. As noted earlier, support interventions like PFA are recommended for early response. However, there is a general consensus suggesting that traditional psychotherapy may be better suited for helping survivors at intermediate and long-term phases of disaster recover (e.g., six weeks to several months or longer after the disaster) following proper clinical assessment (Raphael & Wooding, 2006). Post-disaster therapy interventions include exploring and understanding how survivors' ways of thinking, feeling, and behaving are affecting their acute postdisaster adjustment. In many cases, these interventions are more change-oriented than support-oriented and are intended to help people either change or accept their postdisaster circumstances.

For example, research evidence strongly supports the usefulness and effectiveness of cognitive behavioral therapy (CBT) to treat disaster survivors (Aten, 2012a, 2012b). Specifically, symptoms of distress, posttraumatic stress, depression, and anxiety decrease following the implementation of CBT techniques (Hamblen, Gibson, Mueser, & Norris, 2006; Hamblen et al., 2009; Taylor & Weems, 2011). Common CBT techniques used with disaster survivors include psychoeducation concerning potential trauma responses to disasters, deep breathing techniques, muscle relaxation techniques, and prolonged imaginal or in vivo exposure (Bryant, Moulds, & Nixon, 2003; Hamblen et al., 2009; Stein et al., 2003; Taylor & Weems, 2011).

Researchers from the National Center for PTSD (2015) developed CBT for Post-Disaster Distress utilizing many of the aforementioned techniques, which are designed to challenge maladaptive disaster-related beliefs (Hamblen et al., 2009). This intervention seeks to mitigate "cognitive, emotional, and behavioral reactions to disaster, including symptoms of PTSD, depression, stress vulnerability, and functional difficulties" (Hamblen et al., 2009, p. 207). For children and adolescents, programs such as StArT (Taylor & Weems, 2011) and Cognitive Behavioral Intervention for Trauma in Schools (CBITS; Stein et al., 2003) have similarly adapted cognitive behavioral techniques in order to reduce children's and teens' symptoms of trauma, depression, and anxiety through the use of games, presentations, workbooks, and developmentally appropriate examples.

Although not yet empirically supported for use within a disaster context, there is strong empirical support for Christian accommodative adaptations of CBT (Aten, 2012a, 2012b). In working with survivors' long-term situations, the integration of spiritual and religious themes into treatment has been found to be helpful in enhancing treatment effectiveness. Thus, when religious and existential issues present in the context of psychotherapy for disaster survivors, Christian mental health professionals may find it useful to merge elements from CBT for Post-Disaster Distress and Christian accommodative CBT (Aten, 2012a, 2012b).

According to Worthington, Johnson, Hook, and Aten (2013), Christian accommodative CBT for disaster survivors might involve 8–12 sessions consisting of three parts or phases: psychoeducation, anxiety management techniques, and cognitive restructuring. During the psychoeducation phase, the psychotherapist would discuss common postdisaster psychological problems (e.g., depression, anxiety, substance abuse, PTSD) and R/S problems such as R/S struggles (e.g., anger toward God) and discrepancies between how people view God theologically and how they are experiencing God emotionally (e.g., I believe God is loving and powerful, but I am experiencing God as distant and unable or unwilling to protect me; Moriarty & Davis, 2012).

In the next phase, anxiety management techniques can be used to enhance survivors' disaster-related coping efforts. Here, in addition to encouraging the use of traditional anxiety management methods such as breathing techniques, muscle relaxation, and positive self-talk, the psychotherapist might also discuss the use of positive religious coping methods (Worthington et al., 2013). Such coping methods might involve seeking R/S support (e.g., from clergy and congregational members), religious purification/forgiveness, collaborative religious coping, spiritual connection, benevolent religious reappraisal, religious direction/conversion, religious helping, religious focus, active religious surrender, and marking religious boundaries (Pargament, Koenig, & Perez, 2000). Lastly, during the cognitive restructuring phase, the psychotherapist can challenge faith-relevant cognitive distortions (e.g., between survivors' beliefs and biblical truths), reinforce adaptive thinking, and assign homework utilizing religious practices such as journaling, Christian imagery, healing prayer, and other religious coping strategies. To determine if such an approach might be psychotherapeutically beneficial to clients, Christian mental health professionals may do a thorough assessment that includes inquiring about clients' religious and spiritual history and commitments (Worthington et al., 2013).

Other scholars encourage the use of pastoral counseling to help disaster survivors. For example, Harris et al. (2008) recommended that survivors utilize pastoral counseling and related services following a disaster. Harris et al. (2008) emphasized that such services are needed to provide disaster survivors with additional strategies and guidance on the utilization of R/S resources before, during, and after a disaster.

CONCLUSION

Research has shown that for many disaster survivors, religion and spirituality play an important role in the recovery process. The purpose of this chapter has been to review the current research on the psychology of religion/spirituality and disasters, provide an overview of Christian responses to suffering, introduce examples of disaster interventions, and highlight how disaster psychology might affect the future of Christian integrative efforts in psychology.

Overall, Christian mental health professionals working with disaster survivors have the potential to facilitate individual and community healing in the aftermath of disasters by integrating spiritual care with the best of what professional psychology and counseling have to offer. When Christian mental health professionals build their work on a strong theological foundation coupled with both micro- and macrolevel approaches to their work, they will be better positioned to provide holistic spiritual and emotional care to disaster survivors.

Furthermore, Christian mental health professionals who integrate spiritual care into their disaster mental health services will also be better positioned to encourage adaptive church preparedness activities and responses that will promote effective disaster spiritual and emotional care. Our hope is that, within the fields of professional psychology and counseling, this chapter will help raise interest in pursuing the practice and research of disaster spiritual and emotional care and will help inform the practice of such care from a uniquely Christian perspective.

REFERENCES

Ai, A. L., Cascio, T., Santangelo, L. K., & Evans-Campbell, T. (2005). Hope, meaning, and growth following the September 11, 2001, terrorist attacks. *Journal of Interpersonal Violence, 20*(5), 523-48.

Aten, J. D. (2004). Improving understanding and collaboration between campus ministers and college counseling center personnel. *Journal of College Counseling, 7,* 90-96. doi:10.1002/j.2161-1882.2004.tb00263.x

Aten, J. D. (2012a). Disaster spiritual and emotional care in professional psychology: A Christian integrative approach. *Journal of Psychology & Theology, 40,* 131-35.

Aten, J. D. (2012b). More than research and rubble: How community research can change lives (including yours and your students'). *Journal of Psychology and Christianity, 31,* 314-19.

Aten, J. D., Bennett, P. R., Davis, D., Hill, P. C., & Hook, J. N. (2012). Predictors of God concept and God control after Hurricane Katrina. *Psychology of Religion and Spirituality, 4,* 182-92.

Aten, J. D., & Boan, D. (2016). *Disaster ministry handbook.* Downers Grove, IL: InterVarsity Press.

Aten, J. D., Boan, D. M., Hosey, J. M., Topping, S., Graham, A., & Im, H. (2013). Building capacity for responding to disaster emotional and spiritual needs: A clergy, academic, and mental health partnership model (CAMP). *Psychological Trauma: Theory, Research, Practice, & Policy, 10,* 1-10.

Aten, J. D., Madison, M. B., Rice, A., & Chamberlain, A. K. (2008). Postdisaster supervisor strategies for promoting supervisee self-care: Lessons learned from Hurricane Katrina. *Training and Education in Professional Psychology, 2,* 75-82.

Aten, J. D., O'Grady, K. A., Milstein, G., Boan, D., Smigelsky, M., Schruba, A., & Weaver, I. (2014). Providing spiritual and emotional care in response to disaster. In D. F. Walker, C. A. Courtois, & J. D. Aten (Eds.), *Spiritually oriented psychotherapy for trauma* (pp. 189-210). Washington, DC: American Psychological Association.

Aten, J. D., Topping, S., Denney, R., & Hosey, J. (2011). Helping African American clergy and churches address minority disaster mental health disparities: Training needs, model, and example. *Psychology of Religion and Spirituality, 3,* 15-23.

Bjelopera, J. P., Bagalman, E., Caldwell, S. W., Finklea, K. M., & McCallion, G. (2013). *Public mass shootings in the United States: Selected implications for federal public health and safety policy.* CRS Report for Congress No. R43004. Congressional Research Service 7-5700. Retrieved from www.crs.gov

Briggs, M. K., Apple, K. J., & Aydlett, A. E. (2004). Spirituality and the events of September 11: A preliminary study. *Counseling and Values, 48*(3), 174-82.

Bryant, R. A., Moulds, M. L., & Nixon, R. V. D. (2003). Cognitive behavior therapy of acute stress disorder: A four-year follow-up. *Behavior Research and Therapy, 41,* 489-94.

Brymer, M., Jacobs, A., Layne, C., Pynoos, R., Ruzek, J., Steinberg, A., . . . Watson, P. (2006). *Psychological First Aid: Field operations guide for community religious professionals.* National Child Traumatic Stress Network and National Center for PTSD. Retrieved from www.nctsnet.org/nctsn_assets/pdfs/pfa/CRP-PFA_Guide.pdf

Calhoun, L. G., & Tedeschi, R. G. (2006). The foundations of post-traumatic growth: An expanded framework. In L. G. Calhoun & R. G. Tedeschi (Eds.), *Handbook of posttraumatic growth: Research and practice* (pp. 1-23). Mahwah, NJ: Lawrence Erlbaum.

Chan, C. S., & Rhodes, J. E. (2014). Measuring exposure in Hurricane Katrina: A meta-analysis and an integrative data analysis. *PLoS ONE, 9,* 1-15.

Cook, S., Aten, J., Moore, M., Hook, J., & Davis, D. (2013). Resource loss, religiousness, health, and posttraumatic growth following Hurricane Katrina. *Mental Health, Religion & Culture, 16,* 352-66.

Emmerik, A. A., Kamphuis, J. H., Hulsbosch, A. M., & Emmelkamp, P. M. (2002). Single session debriefing after psychological trauma: A meta-analysis. *Lancet, 360,* 766-71. doi:10.1016/S0140-6736(02)09897-5

Evans, D., Kromm, C., & Sturgis, S. (2008, August). *Faith in the Gulf: Lessons from the religious response to Hurricane Katrina.* Retrieved from www.southernstudies.org/sites/default/files/Gulf%20Report-Faith.pdf

Everly, G. S., Jr., & Mitchell, J. T. (1999). *Critical Incident Stress Management (CISM): A new era and standard of care in crisis intervention* (2nd ed.). Ellicott City, MD: Chevron.

Everly, G. S., Jr., & Mitchell, J. T. (2011). *A primer on Critical Incident Stress Management.* Retrieved from www.icisf.org/a-primer-on-critical-incident-stress-management-cism/

Forbes, D., Lewis, V., Varker, T., Phelps, A., O'Donnell, M., Wade, D., . . . Creamer, M. (2011). Psychological First Aid following trauma: Implementation and evaluation framework for high-risk organizations. *Psychiatry, 74,* 224-39.

Galea, S., Nandi, A., & Vlahov, D. (2005). The epidemiology of post-traumatic stress disorder after disasters. *Epidemiologic Reviews, 27,* 78-91.

Guha-Sapir, D., Below, R., & Hoyois, P. (n.d.). *EM-DAT: The CRED/OFDA international disaster database* [Data file]. Université Catholique de Louvain, Brussels, Belgium. Retrieved from www.emdat.be

Hamblen, J. L., Gibson, L. E., Mueser, K. T., & Norris, F. H. (2006). Cognitive behavioral therapy for prolonged postdisaster distress. *Journal of Clinical Psychology, 62,* 1043-52.

Hamblen, J. L., Norris, F. H., Pietruszkiewicz, S., Gibson, L. E., Naturale, A., & Louis, C. (2009). Cognitive behavioral therapy for postdisaster distress: A community based treatment program for survivors of Hurricane Katrina. *Administration and Policy in Mental Health and Mental Health Services Research, 36,* 206-14.

Harris, J. I., Erbes, C. R., Engdahl, B. E., Olson, R. H., Winskowski, A. M., & McMahill, J. (2008). Christian religious functioning and trauma outcomes. *Journal of Clinical Psychology, 64,* 17-29. doi:10.1002/jclp.20427

Hobfoll, S. E., Freedy, J. R., Green, B. L., & Solomon, S. D. (1996). Coping in reaction to extreme stress: The roles of resource loss and resource availability. In M. Zeidner & N. S. Endler (Eds.), *The handbook of coping: Theory, research, applications* (pp. 322-49). New York, NY: John Wiley & Sons.

Jang, L., & LaMendola, W. (2007). Social work in natural disasters: The case of spirituality and post-traumatic growth. *Advances in Social Work, 8*(2), 305-16.

Johnson, T. J., Aten, J., Madson, M., & Bennett, P. (2006). *Alcohol use and meaning in life among survivors of hurricane Katrina.* Paper presented at the 4th Biennial International Conference on Personal Meaning: Addiction, Meaning, & Spirituality, Vancouver, British Columbia.

Kroll-Smith, J. S., & Couch, S. R. (1987). A chronic technical disaster and the irrelevance of religious meaning: The case of Centralia, Pennsylvania. *Journal for the Scientific Study of Religion, 26*(1), 25-37.

Litz, B. T. (2008). Early intervention for trauma: Where are we and where do we need to go? A commentary. *Journal of Traumatic Stress, 21*, 503-6. doi:10.1002/jts.20373

Milstein, G., Manierre, A., & Yali, A. M. (2010). Psychological care for persons of diverse religions: A collaborative continuum. *Professional Psychology: Research and Practice, 41*, 371-81.

Moriarty, G. L., & Davis, E. B. (2012). Client God images: Theory, research, and clinical practice. In J. Aten, K. O'Grady, & E. Worthington, Jr. (Eds.), *The psychology of religion and spirituality for clinicians* (pp. 131-60). New York, NY: Routledge.

National Center for Posttraumatic Stress Disorder. (2015, August 14). Disaster mental health treatment. Retrieved from www.ptsd.va.gov/public/treatment/therapy-med/disaster_mental_health_treatment.asp

Newton, A. T., & McIntosh, D. N. (2009). Associations of general religiousness and specific religious beliefs with coping appraisals in response to hurricanes Katrina and Rita. *Mental Health, Religion & Culture, 12*(2), 129-46.

Norris, F. H., Friedman, M. J., Watson, P. J., Byrne, C. M., Diaz, E., & Kaniasty, K. (2002). 60,000 disaster victims speak: Part I, an empirical review of the empirical literature, 1981–2001. *Psychiatry: Interpersonal and Biological Processes, 65*, 207-39.

O'Grady, K. A., Rollison, D. G., Hanna, T. S., Schreiber-Pan, H., & Ruiz, M. A. (2012). Earthquake in Haiti: Relationship with the sacred in times of trauma. *Journal of Psychology & Theology, 40*, 289-301.

Pargament, K. I., & Cummings, J. (2010). Anchored by faith: Religion as a resilience factor. In J. W. Reich, A. J. Zautra, & J. S. Hall (Eds.), *Handbook of adult resilience* (pp. 193-210). New York, NY: Guilford Press.

Pargament, K. I., Ishler, K., Dubow, E., Stanik, P., Rouiller, R., Crowe, P., . . . Royster, B. J. (1994). Methods of religious coping with the Gulf War: Cross-sectional and longitudinal analyses. *Journal for the Scientific Study of Religion, 33*, 347-61.

Pargament, K. I., Koenig, H. G., & Perez, L. (2000). The many methods of religious coping: Development and initial validation of the RCOPE. *Journal of Clinical Psychology, 56*, 519-43.

Park, C. L. (2016). Meaning making in the context of disasters. *Journal of Clinical Psychology.* doi:10.1002/jclp.22270

Raphael, B., & Wooding, S. (2006). Longer-term mental health interventions for adults following disasters and mass violence. In E. C. Ritchie, P. J. Watson, & M. J. Friedman (Eds.), *Interventions following mass violence and disasters: Strategies for mental health practice* (pp. 174-92). New York, NY: Guilford Press.

Richards, P. S., & O'Grady, K. A. (2007). Theistic counseling and psychotherapy: Conceptual framework application to counselling practice. *Counseling and Spirituality, 26*(2), 79-102.

Roberts, S. B., & Ashley, W. C., Sr. (Eds.). (2008). *Disaster spiritual care: Practical clergy responses to community, regional, and national tragedy.* Woodstock, VT: SkyLight Paths.

Ryan, W. (1976). *Blaming the victim* (2nd ed). New York, NY: Vintage Books.

Sibley, C. S., & Bulbulia, J. (2012). Faith after an earthquake: A longitudinal study of religion and perceived health before and after the 2011 Christchurch New Zealand earthquake. *PLOS ONE, 7*(12): e49648. doi:10.1371/journal.pone.0049648

Smith, B., Pargament, K., Brant, C., & Oliver, J. (2000). Noah revisited: Religious coping by church members and the impact of the 1993 midwest flood. *Journal of Community Psychology, 28,* 168-86.

START (National Consortium for the Study of Terrorism and Responses to Terrorism; 2015). *Global Terrorism Database* [Data file]. Retrieved from www.start.umd.edu/gtd

Stein, B. D., Jaycox, L. H., Kataoka, S. H., Wong, M., Tu, W., Elliott, M. N., & Fink, A. (2003). A mental health intervention for schoolchildren exposed to violence: A randomized controlled trial. *Journal of the American Medical Association, 290,* 603-11.

Stratta, P., Capanna, C., Riccardi, I., Perugi, G., Toni, C., Dell'Osso, L., & Rossi, A. (2013). Spirituality and religiosity in the aftermath of a natural catastrophe in Italy. *Journal of Religious Health, 52,* 1029-37.

Taylor, L. K., & Weems, C. F. (2011). Cognitive-behavior therapy for disaster-exposed youth with posttraumatic stress: Results from a multiple-baseline examination. *Behavior Therapy, 42,* 349-63.

United Nations Office for Disaster Risk Reduction. (2015). *The human cost of weather related disasters: 1995–2015.* Geneva, Switzerland: Author. Retrieved from www.unisdr.org/2015/docs/climatechange/COP21_WeatherDisastersReport_2015_FINAL.pdf

Vernberg, E., Steinberg, A., Jacobs, A., Brymer, M., Watson, P., Osofsky, J., . . . Ruzek, J. I. (2008). Innovations in disaster mental health: Psychological first aid. *Professional Psychology: Research and Practice, 39,* 381-88.

Worthington, E. L., Johnson, E. L., Hook, J. N., & Aten, J. D. (Eds.). (2013). *Evidence-based practices for Christian counseling and psychotherapy.* Downers Grove, IL: IVP Academic.

IMPROVING TRAUMA CARE
IN DEVELOPING NATIONS:
PARTNERSHIPS OVER PROJECTS

PHILIP G. MONROE AND DIANE LANGBERG

Tsunamis in Asia; earthquakes in Central and South America; genocides in Bosnia, Rwanda, and Syria; child soldiers fighting wars around the world; failed states and religious wars leading to massive refugee crises in the Middle East and Europe; human trafficking for sex and servitude; relentless, systemic violence in the world's inner cities—all of these events produce traumatized individuals and communities. In addition to these news-making stories we have the hidden daily scourge of gender-based violence. The United Nations Statistics Division (2015) reports that one out of three females is a victim of beatings, rape, or coerced sex or is otherwise abused in their lifetime. But this oft-quoted global statistic mutes the daily experience of vast numbers of girls and women who face the threat of rape and other forms of sexual violence. Sadly, many threats to their personhood—incest, child marriage, genital mutilation—are approved by the local community. Violence is a major health and development issue for girls *and boys* worldwide, and only a fraction obtain help from law and justice systems (United Nations Statistics Division, 2015).

The epidemic of psychosocial trauma around the world numbs the minds of both the victim and the onlooker. Symptoms include, but are not limited to, the minimum diagnostic criteria for posttraumatic stress disorder. Many individuals experience life-altering subclinical symptoms even when they do not meet criteria for a diagnosis. Trauma, by definition, overwhelms the individual. However, it also tends to overwhelm entire systems, including those who hear about such traumas. The usual response to atrocity is to try to remove it from the mind, to flee the memory. Those who hear about atrocities also wish to flee by way of distraction and forgetfulness. Such stories threaten comfort, social status, and the integrity of a social or organizational system. They disrupt and demand attention, and so individuals, communities, and nations find it tempting to deny these stories or their life-altering consequences.

Yet "silence is no virtue; it is vice twice-compounded: indifference toward the victims, complicity with the executioners" (Brown, 1989, p. 36). Thus, both victim and onlooker experience a dialectic tension between the need to forget trauma and the need to speak about trauma so that it is acknowledged and validated.

Trauma is the mission field of the twenty-first century, in need of well-trained mental health professionals prepared to deploy around the world. In this chapter we explore the personal, cultural, clinical, theological, and ethical requisites for those desiring to initiate trauma care work in developing nations. We conclude with a case study of an extended partnership between American Christian counselors and Rwandan counselors and caregivers highlighting lessons learned over a seven-year period.

TRAUMA AS MISSION

Despite the primal urge to forget trauma, many missional Christian counselors find themselves moved by their faith to use their expertise through direct care experiences in international settings. These caregivers believe that they are called to follow Jesus Christ into his suffering for the world in order to bear witness to his character and participate in the work of healing and reconciling the world to God. For many counselors, trauma care is a place of service and mission (Langberg, 2015).

But are counselors ready for such a mission? As with any mission, the work of trauma care is neither simple nor efficient since much of the work unfolds little by little. One helper helps another who, in turn, helps another. Thus it is essential that there exists an army of well-trained, competent mental health practitioners able to respond to the need. Yet compassion and calling are not enough. Good intentions will not protect vulnerable populations from cultural missteps by counselors that undermine local leadership, create economic dependency, and ultimately lead to inoculating victims against future hope and efforts to recover from their injuries.

Those filled with a sense of calling to "bind up the brokenhearted" (Is 61:1) need to be equipped to serve in settings outside their own if they are going to provide help and avoid harm to self and others. Competencies must extend beyond knowledge about psychosocial trauma and effective clinical interventions.

REQUISITES FOR CROSSCULTURAL COUNSELORS

If more than training in trauma intervention is necessary to be effective in doing crosscultural education and clinical care, what is required to ensure that work completed is actually helpful and not harmful? In this section we will discuss the necessary character and cultural competencies, as well as competencies in treatment intervention.

Character competencies. The Christian virtue of *humility* is an essential foundation for any mental health practitioner but is even more crucial in crosscultural contexts. We obey the first and second greatest commandments (love of God and love of neighbor as self) when we approach others with the recognition that our neighbors whom we want to help may have much to teach us about loving God. One of the great dangers of the helping professions is the capacity to seduce the helper into thinking he or she is somehow above or better than the helped. Even when aware of this temptation, the helper can easily see himself or herself as the one with more and the helped as the one with less, resulting in a sense of superiority or greater value. This attitude leads to seeing the giving of help as a one-way street where practitioners unintentionally expect that their dispensed services will fill up oppressed and needy victims who lack what they have to offer (Friere, 2000). Valuing Western mental health resources, clinicians are often blinded from seeing a wealth of relational and intellectual capital within an indigenous community (Smith et al., 2011). This blindness can make it difficult to listen first, to receive from them, and to walk together as partners.

In contrast, genuine humility leads to assuming the *posture of a student*—that of listener and learner. We often think of listening as a basic skill in any helping relationship. And while it is a learned skill, listening across and through cultures (including one's own) requires a maturing interpersonal "I-Thou" capacity where others become more than stereotypes or bit characters in one's own narrative (Buber, 1958). This attitude of listening and learning emanates from a deep motivation to understand the person and their rich, enculturated story (Goh, Koch, & Sanger, 2008).

The true student also possesses a desire to study culture, family and community norms, rituals, faith traditions, power structures, and social and historical contexts. Such drive often emanates from a strong belief that God's creational and missional character is more deeply understood in strengths-based assessments than in merely looking for what appears to be the result of the fall. Exploring strengths in individuals, society, churches, and culture helps outsiders notice what God is doing within local communities through the resources divinely given to them. In addition, acknowledging strengths within other cultures and communities provides the opportunity for personal growth. Entering another culture with eyes open invites a student to see his or her own failings (as well as his or her embedded societal failings—materialism, entitlement, lack of community, busyness, and self-absorption) more clearly. In short, if God is already at work in every community, then it is the mental health practitioner's job to see what God is already doing in that region and join in to note, encourage, and build on that foundation (Smith et al., 2015).

Time and economic pressures work against this listening and learning posture. The outside expert is sometimes present for only a short time and is encouraged to deliver as much content as possible so as to justify the expenses incurred. If one does not resist them, these pressures will curtail some of the most important learnings that happen during quiet conversations when answers to the following questions can potentially emerge:

- How are psychological issues dealt with?
- How are emotions held, understood, and experienced?
- Is there a psychological vocabulary?
- What does healing look like?
- How do people grieve?
- What is daily life like?
- What resources exist for dealing with trauma?
- What are the roots of faith in the culture?
- How are "outsiders" viewed?
- What other causes of trauma exist in the country?
- What is the role of the church in the country?
- How are gender roles understood?
- What cultural norms govern family, church, village, and nation?
- How is suffering understood?

This student-learner position enables an outsider to pause to learn these important truths before diagnosing problems or offering solutions, thereby avoiding simplistic translations of mainstream, Western, mental health diagnoses and interventions into other settings. The result of creating learning space prepares local and international partners to find flexible, creative, and strengths-oriented responses rather than canned and poorly contextualized interventions.

Consider the following short vignette. A Christian therapist travels to a developing nation to provide trauma care for those widowed after a genocide. There she meets one widow. She hears the woman's story of seeing her husband and three children brutally murdered by two men in the village. The widow had known these men all her life. She had attended school and church with them. Her husband had helped one of the men build his house. Now, after the genocide, she encounters them daily as she goes to a nearby lake for water. The perpetrators were briefly imprisoned for their crimes, but the country is not able to punish all who murdered; thus she must meet them on the street and in the markets each day. She notices that their families are intact.

Such a complex story must be well understood before any intervention is suggested to help the widow deal with her insomnia, racing heart, and deep despair. She cannot leave her situation. Her trauma is ongoing and continuous. The social pressure to simply accept her reality and forget is massive. In addition, the meaning behind her symptoms runs counter to common Western mental health depictions (e.g., Hagengimana & Hinton, 2009).

Many of the current mental health interventions utilized in the West assume the presence of certain societal infrastructures (e.g., justice, privacy, adequate policing, access to medical and mental health services) and the capacity to remove oneself from daily reminders of trauma. The therapist will serve the widow best by first understanding not only the extent of her trauma experiences but also what local and natural resources are being used to help her survive, even if she does not thrive. Most important, the student-listener will incarnate (put flesh on) God providing an opportunity for both listener and widow to connect to the one who creates and sustains them.

Cultural competencies. Effective trauma care in international settings requires more than good character. It also requires a set of cultural intelligence competencies that flesh out the meaning of being incarnational (Elmer, 2006; Livermore, 2011). Goh, Koch, and Sanger (2008) summarize these competencies in four types of cultural intelligence: metacognitive (the ability to monitor self regarding assumptions, thoughts, and reactions), cognitive (cultural knowledge base), motivational (developed intrinsic satisfaction in crosscultural interactions), and behavioral (capacity for flexible responses as an outsider). Of these four types, it appears that drive (motivation) and self-awareness (metacognition) form the basis of being able to acquire knowledge of cultural complexities as well as develop strategies of engagement. The culturally competent Christian counselor engages in an endless loop of observation, action, and reappraisal in order to avoid foreclosed (premature) assumptions about a particular community.

Cultural competencies naturally lead therapists to consider how to best contextualize trauma knowledge and practices into the culture of a local community (Dawson, 2007). For example, therapists seeking to provide counseling services in a cooperative community would likely seek group-oriented rather than individual-oriented interventions (e.g., corporate lament expressions). In addition, technical clinical language (e.g., flashbacks) would not be merely transliterated into the local language; rather, existing words would be chosen to convey the core meaning (e.g., nightmare while awake). Optimal contextualization requires the presence and leadership of a cultural bridge person—someone with local knowledge, expertise, and respect, as well as courage to understand and teach outsiders.

Cultural adaptation takes time and is rarely linear in process. However, mental health practitioners who invite "pushback" can avoid common cultural errors. According to Shah (2012), "pushback describes the modes (active or passive, noticeable or covert) by which a group expresses its resistance and/or provides redirection to any intervention" (p. 444). Inviting pushback is necessary, argues Shah, given the power (i.e., social, cultural, economic, educational) asymmetries between helper and the helped. Trauma therapists recognize the importance of encouraging resistance as part of the recovery process where traumatized individuals begin to reclaim God-given agency—dominion and voice. In the act of resistance, outside helpers need not feel rejected but rather enriched by new perspectives of human flourishing. Where history and culture make overt pushback difficult, outsiders can encourage forms of resistance and collaboration by creative third person questions such as "If someone from outside were causing unintended problems, how would the community respond?"

Sometimes pushback comes in unexpected moments. In one situation, a Western clinician wishing to avoid the appearance of colonialism refused to allow an African peer to carry his bag from the car to the guesthouse. The African initially felt that he was not trusted. But what could have been a relational breach was avoided when the peer explained that carrying the bag was an important act of honor in that particular society. The ensuing discussion between the two new friends resulted in deepening mutual understanding and prepared both to resolve training challenges the next week.

Dialogue education or participatory learning is one powerful intervention known to be useful in ensuring that training done by external helpers is of use (culturally and practically) to participants. Dialogue education (Vella, 2002) has as its primary principle the engagement of learner and teacher in developing mutually agreed-on learning content *and* outcomes. For example, a group of Western educators planned domestic-violence training in a developing country. Prior to the group's arrival, leaders from both countries met via web conference to discuss desired training activities. While the Western leaders had initially filled most of the training with content delivery and subsequent discussion, the local leaders noted the need for small-group discussion as well as the use of traditional means of learning new material. In addition, singing and time for games were seen not as fillers but as integral to the development of new knowledge and skills.

Trauma intervention competencies. Competent Christian mental health professionals ensure that the trauma interventions they teach to local caregivers are supported in the current psychological and religious literatures. While creativity, adaptation, and contextualization are necessary in crosscultural applications of mental health interventions, therapists must begin their preparation on a solid knowledge base. Typical understandings of posttraumatic stress disorder and complex trauma reactions can be found in the works of Herman (1997) and Langberg (2003). More recent work by Gingrich (2013) provides a Christian perspective on complex trauma and dissociation. These publications offer information on the three-part trajectory of recovery—safety/stabilization, memory processing, and reconnection—that is the current standard of care in the West.

When working with complex trauma crossculturally, it is necessary to build on this base, especially in settings where trauma is ongoing and continuous and where few trained providers exist. In recent years there has been a proliferation of interventions designed to be delivered in such settings where providers, time, and costs are of primary concern. Perusing the literature, a Christian counselor might begin examining those interventions with empirical support (Schauer & Schauer, 2010). For example, those interested in the region of sub-Saharan Africa would do well to start with Smigelsky et al's (2014) review of the causes, costs, and interventions that have been employed in that region. Those interested in lay-led interventions used in refugee and asylum-seeking populations might explore the data regarding narrative exposure therapy (Neuner, Onyut, Ertl, Odenwald, Schauer, & Elbert, 2008). Still others may wish to start with the well-known trauma-focused cognitive behavior therapy modified for regions of continuous trauma exposure (Kira, Ashby, Omidy, & Lewandowski, 2015).

Other forms of brief interventions (psychoeducation, ritual, movement, art, resilience training, etc.) have a nascent literature as well. These are used widely but lack robust empirical evidence to date—usually due to being utilized by individuals and institutions not yet prepared to undertake the rigors of a scientific study.

For example, *Healing the Wounds of Trauma* (Hill, Hill, Bagge, & Miersma, 2014) has been widely used for more than a decade around the globe with strong anecdotal support. This training program utilizes a "train-the-trainer" model to expose participants (often clergy and lay leaders) to new understandings of faith and trauma through story and Scripture engagement. The experiential program, described in more detail later in this chapter, seeks not only to educate attendees but also to provide them with skills to pass on their understanding to others. Only now is this model receiving attention from those able to complete effectiveness research.

Early adoption of untested interventions should not be viewed entirely in a suspicious light. After consulting in more than a dozen countries, it is clear to us that interventions that bring together communities by means of integrating facts (past and present traumas and resiliencies) and faith (communal worship through lament practices) with a future hope orientation lead the way in positive reception over interventions that focus only on education and coping skills.

It is important to keep in mind that we clinicians bear the responsibility to ensure the safety of those who receive treatment from us. Quality clinical practice includes informing partners of intervention limitations and possible negative outcomes (e.g., increasing trauma symptoms, increasing social rejection or physical attack after disclosing sexual trauma in a group setting). From our own experience, much harm has been done when counselors become wedded to one particular model over others, promise results beyond what is possible, and resist the use of other interventions. As an example, once at a conference, one of us was confronted by a clinician who insisted that any clinical work in Rwanda not using eye movement desensitization and reprocessing (EMDR) was a waste of time and money. Such an opinion reveals an unhealthy allegiance to one model and a failure to adopt local healing practices known to help with recovery.

Theological competencies. When natural disasters occur and people are traumatized, there are many questions and struggles related to God, his sovereignty, and his protection. These questions grow exponentially in response to human-caused traumas such as war, genocide, or rape. Trauma of any kind challenges and sometimes distorts faith. The competent Christian mental health practitioner understands the complex relationship between trauma and faith, as well as best practices to encourage reestablishing faith practices that support recovery. The competent therapist chooses to be a student of a theology of trauma (Ganzevoort, 2008).

Why does God allow evil acts and suffering? What does suffering say about God and me? Such questions during and after trauma illustrate a common response—discontent with previously embraced beliefs and experiences (Wortmann, Park, & Edmondson, 2011). As one Rwandan said, "I used to think God was the God of the Hutus; then I decided he was the God of the Tutsis. Now when I look at my devastated family and country I am not certain he exists at all." Another voiced a similar loss: "I used to see the church as a healing place, a sanctuary; now I see it as a cemetery." When, as in the case of Rwanda, leaders of faith communities conspire to do evil, moral injury occurs, leaving victims with no place to ask their questions. In addition, those who have been involved in combat or those forced to commit atrocities may also experience intense shame and thus greater spiritual struggle (Currier, Drescher, & Harris, 2014).

As with Job, theodicy experiences almost universally lead to reappraising what we formerly thought about ourselves, the world, and God. The competent counselor recognizes that a verbalized lament (especially in corporate worship) provides opportunity for intimacy with God and community to be strengthened (Snow, 2012). Such acts of worship have the possibility of building resiliency, improving hope, and reestablishing purpose and meaning (Walker, Reid, O'Neill, & Brown, 2009). A Rwandan caregiver once said, "My faith is stronger. Surviving itself is a sign that

God exists. God is the father of the fatherless and husband of the widows. When your brother is no longer there, God sends other brothers—visibly, practically. I am being that to my fellow Rwandans."

Unfortunately, religion can be used to abuse, to support evil, to teach lies about the character of God, and to further crush those who have been battered and oppressed by their trauma. Victims are blamed and ostracized for their own rapes; those with trauma symptoms are accused of demon possession or evil and are told they are being punished by God. Scripture texts have been used in the service of domestic abuse, clergy sexual abuse, child sexual abuse, and oppression of many kinds.

Since faith has the potential to raise hard questions and difficult struggles, to strengthen and build up as well as confuse and oppress, it is critically important to understand the ways in which Scripture is distorted by faith communities in a given culture and used to support ongoing traumas such as the battering of women and children, sexual assault, mutilation of bodies, and crushing of spirits.

Speaking truth into such deceptions requires carefulness, respect, and gentleness with local ministry leaders just as it does with victims. The competent therapist uses the previously discussed contextualization skills to talk to pastors and leaders in language they understand. For example, instead of using sociological data to convince a pastor that female rape victims are not responsible for their condition, a therapist might follow theologian Steven Tracy's (2013) lead and explore biblical texts supporting the care and protection of women.

Ethical competencies. Those desiring to engage in trauma recovery in developing nations, *without causing harm*, need to consider a special set of ethical concerns and ideals in addition to what has previously been discussed.

Over the last 15 years the psychological community has paid increasing attention to the need for guidelines for those providing global mental health services and education. Weine et al. (2002) identified a significant deficit in most trauma-related training curricula, stating that "the literature on international trauma work demonstrates neither a comprehensive nor serious attempt to address the values, framework, techniques, challenges and outcomes of international training" (p. 157). While their essay encouraged trauma-education trainers to pay attention to values and contextualization, almost nothing was said about local faith and spiritual values other than an exhortation to respect clergy as essential community gatekeepers.

In 2007 the World Health Organization's Inter-Agency Standing Committee produced a valuable set of guidelines for trauma and disaster responders. These guidelines pointed to preparatory work to ensure that any mental health service provided would avoid harm, protect human rights, avoid discrimination, ensure local participation in delivery of services, and be integrated into other humanitarian and economic supports. This document encouraged outsiders to "facilitate conditions for appropriate communal, cultural, spiritual, and religious healing practices" (p. 25).

While both of the preceding documents had as their core the goal of "do no harm," international trauma facilitators can easily do harm without knowing it. Wessells (2009) examined a number of subtle forms of harm to avoid: approaching others with a deficits orientation, parachuting in without consideration of entrance and exit, lack of sensitivity to culture, failing to consider holistic interventions, and, possibly the worst, creating a dependency culture unable to continue care without outside help.

Finally, and most recently, the American Psychological Association (APA, 2015) has adopted a set of competencies (formerly known as the *New Haven Competencies for Trauma Psychology Training and Practice*) designed to articulate the minimal requirements for those providing international trauma education. These guidelines emphasize the need to know the current scientific literature regarding the diagnosis, assessment, and intervention of trauma along with trauma-informed professionalism and understanding of relationships and systems.

Each of these documents gives ample opportunity for interested therapists to do the necessary preparation to "do no harm" and to pursue capacity building in developing nations. For example, the international trauma literature points to using cost-effective intervention strategies utilizing trained lay counselors with refugees rather than attempting to replicate professional therapy models (e.g., Lambert & Alhassoon, 2015). Or consider another more potent example. Rather than continuing to provide psychological debriefing services to an entire community after a disaster, the competent therapist recognizes that such an intervention may harm individuals or undermine natural defenses that could protect against chronic trauma (APA, n.d.).

TRAINING AND BEING TRAINED: A PARTNERSHIP MODEL IN RWANDA

If the above competencies are pursued, partnerships between international mental health professionals, local institutions, and lay counselors will naturally (though not always easily) occur. Strengths among partners can be shared, weaknesses can be supported, and solutions can emerge when different perspectives and ideas are brought to bear on a problem (Aten et al., 2013). Learning takes place for both groups. Clinicians go to help and find they are also helped. They go to teach and are taught. They go to give but receive in abundance. The following is a brief case study that describes such a partnership formed in Rwanda between American Christian therapists and Rwandan church leaders, local professionals, and lay counselors.

A brief history of Rwanda. Most of the world is aware that in 1994 Rwanda suffered a cataclysm of human tragedy while much of the world watched from a safe distance. For most outsiders, this genocide seemed to appear out of nowhere. In reality the genocide had its roots as far back as European colonial manipulation of tribal and class differences to promote disunity and retain power. For a chronology and an extensive report of the 100 days of genocide, see PBS (1999). In short, upward of one million Tutsis and moderate Hutus lost their lives, many at the hands of their neighbors. After the genocide stopped, approximately 1.5 million people fled to neighboring countries, mingling victims and genocidaires in massive refugee camps. Now, some 22 years later, the country appears to be stable and prospering, in large part because of Rwandan leadership supported by international donors.

Step one: listening and learning. This case study begins some years ago when one of us (Diane) had a providential meeting with a Rwandan master's level counselor at a conference. Later, on a trip to Rwanda, they met again and began a friendship shaped by mutual learning. Not long afterward, a small group of Christian clinicians were invited by Anglican clergy to "come over and help us." During this trip, no formal teaching was provided; rather, the trip consisted of meetings with ministries of the government, clergy, institutions (e.g., hospitals and schools), humanitarian organizations, along with victims and perpetrators—all designed to identify resources and challenges to addressing the massive trauma needs in the country. Conversations and discussions continued after the trip, including in-depth reading to better understand the history, culture, and traditions of the region. The result of this engagement concluded with a memorandum of understanding signed by the American Association of Christian Counselors (AACC) and the Rwandan government to work on building up local professional and lay counselors already deeply involved in trauma work, many of whom were dealing with personal as well as secondary trauma histories. All parties involved believed strongly that while international resources existed that could advance local counseling capacity, the best use of resources would not include direct trauma care to Rwandan clients.

Step two: establishing bridge persons. During Dr. Langberg's initial trip to Rwanda and the later initial "listening and learning" tour, two key Rwandan women provided important insights into the state of the country vis-à-vis counseling, trauma needs, and current local resources. Over and over again these individuals sacrificed time and energy to help outsiders understand the country's history and cultural complexities. Conversations took place during trips, on their visits to the United States, and via teleconferences. Learning gained from previous intervention efforts by other organizations was a primary focus. Through the collaborate work, dreams and ideas turned into plans for an initial training in late 2011.

Step three: initial training and dialogue conferences. Funded by AACC members, a team of four Americans and two Rwandans led a conference of approximately 45 lay and professional counselors representing 11 humanitarian organizations. Participants represented religious and secular service organizations, ranging in age and experience from recent university graduates to those who had been involved in caring ministries for decades. Didactic presentations on trauma symptoms and interventions and core listening skills were made in English and Kinyarwandan languages. One of the presentations exploring "talking, tears, and time" can be found in chapter nine of Langberg (2015). However, the bulk of the conference was set aside for discussion, skill observation and practice, and other forms of experiential learning (e.g., group art, music, and the recitation of local proverbs) appreciated by nonindividualistic cultures.

Using dialogue education principles, the participants voiced their strong desire for (a) the creation of an ongoing association of counselors for support and (b) more training with specific trauma counseling interventions. One seasoned Rwandan counselor reported that it was the first time anyone had taken the time to hear her story, while another experienced counselor reported that it was the first time she had observed counseling done by others. Communication and learning continued after the training by way of email and teleconference once the American team returned home.

One and half years later, a larger group of American mental health practitioners met again with many of the same participants to continue participatory learning of additional trauma-related topics such as domestic abuse, child sexual abuse, and rape. In a country such as Rwanda, all traumas tend to be viewed through the lens of genocide, thereby minimizing the more common experiences of abuse in daily life. Participants engaged in lively discussions of whether marital rape is even possible (in a country where a dowry is paid for the wife) while considering biblical texts. Those returning noted how much growth had taken place among the Rwandan caregivers, in their own trauma processing and their clinical skills.

In each of the first two trainings, as well as the trainings that followed, emphasis was placed on care for the caregiver. As in most contexts, these resilient caregivers had been afforded little time to grieve personal and corporate losses. Together local and international participants utilized songs, symbols, drawings, rituals, and dance to grieve, lament, and seek comfort, thus deepening bonds and building resilience.

Step four: assessing and responding to challenges. As with any new venture, roadblocks and challenges were present. Following the 2013 trip, the Rwandan/American leadership team noted that three important issues needed to be addressed: deficient cultural training of international mental health trainers, minimal consultations between American and local caregivers in between the short-term trips, and lack of partnership with a stable Rwandan organization with deep roots in the country, able to reach lay and ministry leaders.

Training mental health practitioners. Highly qualified mental health practitioners capable of advanced clinical skills may not necessarily have the competency in treating trauma in order to effectively train counseling providers in developing nations. Most clinicians receive only a cursory understanding of posttraumatic stress disorder, and even fewer have been trained to engage others in diverse cultural settings as co-learners.

To address this problem, Biblical Seminary launched the Global Trauma Recovery Institute (GTRI), a 140-clock-hour, postgraduate continuing education training program to enhance competencies in the areas of neurobiology of psychosocial trauma, advanced crosscultural listening skills, strengths-based clinical and spiritual interventions, global mental health ethics, faith and trauma, and dialogue education principles. Content and engagement components are delivered in four hybrid courses culminating in a final immersion experience for those desiring it. A group of 24 clinicians began the training program with 10 choosing to travel to Rwanda for a joint learning experience in 2014. This trip culminated in the official launch of the Rwandan Association of Christian Counselors. The GTRI program continues at present with participants from Europe, Africa, India, and Australia.

Ongoing consultations. On several occasions Rwandan counselors asked for support, encouragement, and advice in between the annual trips. Such engagement had happened in the past between key leaders, but local counselors rarely had the opportunity to engage at this level. Following the 2014 trip, several of the immersion students began weekly text and voice communications with Rwandan participants. These interactions served to advance the American understanding of Rwandan life as well as to improve the Rwandans' counseling intervention skills. The connections built during 2014 led several Americans to return again in 2015 and 2016 to train and observe Rwandan clinical practice in action.

Partnership with Rwandan institutions. Financing trips and trainings is one of the central challenges of work in developing nations. Donors and nongovernmental organizations come and go even if the need remains. As a result, local service providers may bounce from organization to organization, following the grant money, in order to support their families. Even strong humanitarian organizations may either change their focus or leave altogether when they have changes in leadership. In contrast, a partnership with an indigenous institution provides the possibility of a more stable foundation for long-term engagement as outsiders.

Soon after the 2013 training trip, we engaged in conversations with both the American and the Rwandan Bible societies regarding their Scripture-engaged trauma healing programs. The Bible Society in Rwanda serves all denominations and is well respected by Roman Catholics and Protestants alike. As mentioned earlier, one of the society's core programs trains trauma-healing facilitators to lead healing groups using a contextualized version of *Healing the Wounds of Trauma*, a story-based curriculum produced by the Trauma Healing Institute of the American Bible Society (http://thi.americanbible.org/; see also Hill et al., 2014). This curriculum is being used in many language groups around the world. The program establishes training facilitators throughout the country, often embedded in existing churches, thereby offering greater stability of resources over time.

During the summers of 2014 through 2016, GTRI-trained clinicians joined with Bible society facilitators and the newly birthed Rwandan Association of Christian Counselors for a community of practice conference designed to improve the knowledge and skill base of both groups, as well as to advance local and international collaborations. Evidence of success included reports of new collaborations between counselors and Bible society staff, joint trainings on the topic of domestic abuse, plus ongoing supervision regarding difficult cases. Most recently, GTRI fellows and Rwandan leaders discussed possibilities of providing joint trainings for another Bible society in a nearby country.

The cycle continues with incremental growth. The process of listening, learning, planning, assessing, and taking action continues. New challenges and opportunities must be faced. Several GTRI graduates have begun their own partnering ministries in Rwanda, expanding ministry outreach possibilities. One such graduate partnered with the Bible Society of Rwanda to support a "three-legged stool" of recovery in a United Nations camp housing 18,000 Congolese refugees (Evans, Gatwaza, & King, 2016). With funds from American Christians, the Bible society provided holistic support: faith (Bibles in their own language), trauma healing programs, and financial stability (sewing machines and training in order to be able to make a living). Recent plans have led another GTRI graduate, at the request of the Rwandan Bible Society, to embark on a research program assessing the effectiveness of *Healing the Wounds of Trauma*.

CONCLUSION

Trauma is a vast mission field. It is the mission field of the twenty-first century. In this field, as in every other field of service, Jesus calls helpers to follow him into "the fellowship of His sufferings" (Phil 3:10 NASB). In doing so we hallow—honor or make holy—the name of God. To hallow the name of God is to reverence his character, defend his honor, and obey his authority. One of the major tests of hallowing the divine name is Christ-followers' attitudes toward fellow human beings. Injustice on the part of human beings toward other human beings profanes the name of God. Complicity—silence—is the most common form of profanation. Workers in the trauma mission field begin by finding ways to bear witness to the pain of the oppressed. In the words of Wiesel (1986), the first line of help is to "never be silent wherever and whenever human beings endure suffering and humiliation. We must always take sides. Neutrality helps the oppressor, never the victim. Silence encourages the tormentor, never the tormented. Sometimes we must interfere" (para. 8).

While bearing witness is the clinician's greatest tool in the process of recovery, competent trauma care providers and educators recognize that actions completed on behalf of others without their consent, approval, and planning may not deliver the desired result. Historically, the Western world has gone to the rest of the world as the knowers, teachers, and doers. We have often assumed the superior position with our resources, knowledge, skills, and the *supposed* right understanding of problems. We have assumed that if we can just instruct and give what we have, then everything will get better. Such approaches have been both arrogant and ignorant.

A better model, one seasoned with great respect, mutuality, and assumption of personal need, is required. Such work, if done well and respectfully, is far more like putting a multicultural group of people in a kitchen to cook a large meal. Each will bring something different in terms of knowledge and skill, each will bring creative ideas and traditions, and each will end up ultimately bringing something unique to the table. As a result, a fine, diverse, and creative meal will be presented; respect and understanding will have grown; joy will be shared; and we daresay some laughter will have occurred along the way.

Thus, the first lesson learned is that of being a student from the outset. Those who want to provide trauma care and training in developing-nation settings must be willing to maintain the role of a student, bearing witness to the rich tapestry of local life and experiences. Further, they must be more interested in listening to local leaders express their own assessments of local opportunities and challenges. Failure to take a learning stance on the part of the individuals delivering trainings can result in well-intentioned mental health practitioners being more likely to harm than to help.

In addition to taking on the role of a student, the most successful help offered comes in the form of mutually beneficial partnerships. Too often our partnerships look more like agreements where outsiders get permission from key gatekeepers to control the decisions made and deliver the services. This is not a partnership. Western mental health professionals schooled in individualism and scientism have much to learn from much less educated caregivers. We benefit greatly from learning community-based care founded on rich faith practices.

Navigating true partnerships takes time and is rather expensive and inefficient because true relationships are not born overnight. It takes time to find and engage locally respected stakeholders, to listen, and to consider solutions as well as a plan for implementation that does not create dependency, neuter the power structures of local leadership, or always require outside resources. Plans drawn with good intentions will frequently change. Temptations abound to move quickly in order to circumvent the time it takes to contextualize materials or obtain stakeholder agreements. However, it is wise to remember an African proverb often quoted in Rwanda: "If you want to go fast, go alone, but if you want to go far, go together."

REFERENCES

American Psychological Association. (2015). *Guidelines on trauma competencies for education and training.* Retrieved from www.apa.org/ed/resources/trauma-compe tencies-training.pdf

American Psychological Association, Society of Clinical Psychology. (n.d.). *Psychological debriefing for post-traumatic stress disorder. Status: No research support/ treatment is potentially harmful.* Retrieved from www.div12.org/psychological-treat ments/treatments/psychological-debriefing-for-post-traumatic-stress-disorder/

Aten, J. D., Boan, D. M., Hosey, J. M., Topping, S., Graham, A., & Im, H. (2013). Building capacity for responding to disaster emotional and spiritual needs: A clergy, academic, and mental health partnership model (CAMP). *Psychological Trauma: Theory, Research, Practice, and Policy, 5,* 591-600.

Brown, R. M. (1989). *Elie Wiesel: Messenger to all humanity* (Rev. ed.). Notre Dame, IN: University of Notre Dame Press.

Buber, M. (1958). *I and thou.* New York, NY: Scribner.

Currier, J. M., Drescher, K. D., & Harris, J. (2014). Spiritual functioning among veterans seeking residential treatment for PTSD: A matched control group study. *Spirituality in Clinical Practice, 1*(1), 3-15.

Dawson, J. (2007). African conceptualizations of posttraumatic stress disorder and the impact of introducing Western concepts. *Psychology, Psychiatry, and Mental Health Monographs, 2,* 101-12.

Elmer, D. (2006). *Cross-cultural servanthood: Serving the world in Christlike humility.* Downers Grove, IL: InterVarsity Press.

Evans, H., Gatwaza, Z. C., & King, C. (2016, March). *Voices of refugees in Africa: Case studies in Rwanda and Louisville, Kentucky: Three-part model supporting refugees.* Presentation made at the 2016 Global Community of Practice, Philadelphia, PA.

Friere, P. (2000). *Pedagogy of the oppressed* (30th anniversary ed.). New York, NY: Continuum.

Ganzevoort, R. R. (2008). Teaching that matters: A course on trauma and theology. *Journal of Adult Theological Education, 5*(1), 8-19.

Gingrich, H. D. (2013). *Restoring the shattered self: A Christian counselor's guide to complex trauma.* Downers Grove, IL: IVP Academic.

Goh, M., Koch, J. M., & Sanger, S. (2008). Cultural intelligence in counseling psychology: Applications for multicultural competence. In S. Ang & L. N. Dyne (Eds.), *Handbook of cultural intelligence: Theory, meaning, and application* (pp. 257-70). New York, NY: M. E. Sharpe.

Hagengimana, A., & Hinton, D. E. (2009). "Ihahamuka," a Rwandan syndrome of response to the genocide: Blocked flow, spirit assault, and shortness of breath. In D. E. Hinton & B. J. Good (Eds.), *Culture and panic disorder* (pp. 205-29). Stanford, CA: Stanford University Press.

Herman, J. (1997). *Trauma and recovery: The aftermath of violence: From domestic violence to political terror.* New York, NY: Basic Books.

Hill, H., Hill, M., Bagge, R., & Miersma, P. (2014). *Healing the wounds of trauma: How the church can help.* New York, NY: American Bible Society.

Inter-Agency Standing Committee. (2007). *IASC guidelines on mental health and psychosocial support in emergency settings.* Geneva, Switzerland. Retrieved from www .who.int/mental_health/emergencies/guidelines_iasc_mental_health_psycho social_june_2007.pdf

Kira, I. A., Ashby, J. S., Omidy, A. Z., & Lewandowski, L. (2015). Current, continuous, and cumulative Trauma-Focused Cognitive Behavior Therapy: A new model for trauma counseling. *Journal of Mental Health Counseling, 37,* 323-40.

Lambert, J. E., & Alhassoon, O. M. (2015). Trauma-focused therapy for refugees: Meta-analytic findings. *Journal of Counseling Psychology, 62,* 28-37.

Langberg, D. M. (2003). *Counseling survivors of sexual abuse.* Maitland, FL: Xulon Press.

Langberg, D. M. (2015). *Suffering and the heart of God: How trauma destroys and Christ restores.* Greensboro, NC: New Growth Press.

Livermore, D. (2011). *The cultural intelligence difference: Master the one skill you can't do without in today's global economy.* New York, NY: ANACOM.

Neuner, F., Onyut, P., Ertl, V., Odenwald, M., Schauer, E., & Elbert, T. (2008). Treatment of posttraumatic stress disorder by trained lay counselors in an African refugee settlement: A randomized controlled trial. *Journal of Consulting and Clinical Psychology, 76,* 686-94.

PBS (1999, March). The triumph of evil: 100 days of slaughter. A chronology of U.S./U.N. actions. *Frontline.* Retrieved from www.pbs.org/wgbh/pages/frontline/shows/evil/ etc/slaughter.html

Schauer, M., & Schauer, E. (2010). Trauma-focused public mental-health interventions: A paradigm shift in humanitarian assistance and aid work. In E. Martz (Ed.), *Trauma rehabilitation after war and conflict: Community and individual perspectives.* New York, NY: Springer.

Shah, S. A. (2012). Ethical standards for transnational mental health and psychosocial support (MHPSS): Do no harm, preventing cross-cultural errors and inviting pushback. *Clinical Social Work Journal, 40*, 438-49.

Smigelsky, M. A., Aten, J. D., Gerberich, S., Sanders, M., Post, R., Hook, K., . . . Monroe, P. (2014). Trauma in sub-Saharan Africa: Review of cost, estimation methods, and interventions. *International Journal of Emergency Mental Health, 16*(2), 127-36.

Smith, B., Collins, G. R., Cruz, E., Cruz, P., Cruz, S., Cruz S., Jr., . . . Warlow, J. (2011). *The Cape Town declaration on care and counsel as mission.* Retrieved from www.belhaven.edu/careandcounsel/declaration.htm

Snow, K. N. (2012). Resolving anger toward God: Lament as an avenue toward attachment. *Dissertation Abstracts International, 73*, 1269.

Tracy, S. R. (2013). Concepts of gender and the global abuse of women. *Cultural Encounters 9*(1), 4-22. Retrieved from www.joomag.com/magazine/mag/0019233001475705277?feature=archive

United Nations Statistics Division (2015). The world's women 2015: Trends and statistics. Retrieved from http://unstats.un.org/unsd/gender/worldswomen.html

Vella, J. K. (2002). *Learning to listen, learning to teach: The power of dialogue in educating adults* (Rev. ed.). New York, NY: Jossey Bass.

Walker, D., Reid, H. W., O'Neill, T., & Brown, L. (2009). Changes in personal religion/spirituality during and after childhood abuse: A review and synthesis. *Psychological Trauma: Theory, Research, Practice, and Policy, 1*(2), 130-45.

Weine, S., Danieli, Y., Silove, D., Van Ommeren, M., Fairbank, J. A., & Saul, J. (2002). Guidelines for international training in mental health and psychosocial interventions for trauma exposed populations in clinical and community settings. *Psychiatry: Interpersonal and Biological Processes, 65*(2), 156-64.

Wessells, M. G. (2009). Do no harm: Toward contextually appropriate psychosocial support in international emergencies. *American Psychologist, 64*(8), 842-54.

Wiesel, E. (1986, December 10). Nobel Peace Prize Acceptance Speech. Oslo, Norway. Retrieved from www.nobelprize.org/nobel_prizes/peace/laureates/1986/wiesel-acceptance_en.html

Wortmann, J. H., Park, C. L., & Edmondson, D. (2011). Trauma and PTSD symptoms: Does spiritual struggle mediate the link? *Psychological Trauma: Theory, Research, Practice, and Policy, 3*(4), 442-52.

TRAUMA COUNSELING FOR MISSIONARIES:
HOW TO SUPPORT RESILIENCE

KAREN F. CARR

Those who serve in dangerous places are neither giants nor flawless heroes.
Instead we are our church's living letters, demonstrating the grace, love and
power of God through our willingness to give our lives in service to others.

KATE MCCORD, *WHY GOD CALLS US TO DANGEROUS PLACES*

"Today is the day you die" were the first words heard by Phyllis Sortor (2015) just after she was seized by armed men in central Nigeria. She was struck in the face, dragged, taken to an isolated place, and threatened with death multiple times. She was held hostage for 11 days and was finally released after a dramatic series of promises and delays. During her captivity Phyllis experienced fear, exhaustion, despair, and certainty of death. For some, this would be reason to end their missionary career.

Trauma was not new to this 71-year-old woman. She was the daughter of missionaries in Mozambique, where she was born and raised. Her grandparents were missionaries in Korea during the Japanese occupation, and she often heard spiritually formative stories about her grandfather's arrest and subsequent death in a prison camp. She had been on the mission field for 16 years and knew how to live in the bush and "rough it." She had experienced two home invasions, one involving physical assault. She had suffered through the illness and death of her husband, a deep grief. Some might have been marked by these experiences with increased vulnerability, but Phyllis said these traumas made her stronger and more resilient.

In the midst of her exhaustion, fear, and despair, Phyllis started praying to God, "Save me, save me, save me." She began to talk with one of her captors, motivating him to shift from threatening to kill her to vowing to protect her. She spoke forcefully to herself: "Take control of yourself and show these captors what kind of person you are—a strong woman, a leader, a missionary." She wanted her captors to see her as a person to be respected, not reviled. She sang hymns, prayed, and reflected on the suffering experienced by Jesus. She held on to the belief that God was keeping her, despite continued threats and dangers. She had an underlying joy and assurance that held steadfast despite her bleak external circumstances.

While not all missionaries experience the particular traumas that Phyllis did, trauma is often a part of the lives of missionaries. In this chapter I explore the types of crises that many missionaries experience. I examine unique aspects of counseling missionaries and ways to contribute to their resilience.

INCIDENCE AND TYPES OF TRAUMA EXPERIENCED BY MISSIONARIES

A study (Schaefer et al., 2007) comparing missionaries with the US population found that missionaries in West Africa and Europe had encountered more severe trauma than the general US population. In West Africa, 92% of male and 85% of female missionaries reported one or more severe traumas in their lives. In Europe, 82% of male and 73% of female missionaries reported one or more severe traumas. In comparison, in a sample of the general population of the United States, 61% of men and 51% of women reported one or more severe traumas. The differences were more pronounced when comparing these three populations with those who had experienced three or more severe traumas (see table 16.1).

Table 16.1. Percentage of population with at least three traumas

% of population with at least three traumas	Men	Women
US general population*	10%	5%
Missionaries in Europe[†]	47%	30%
Missionaries in West Africa[†]	71%	64%

*Data from the National Comorbidity Survey (Kessler, Sonnega, Bromet, Hughes, & Nelson, 1995)
[†]Missionary study results (Schaefer et al., 2007); *N* = 250

Schaefer et al. (2007) reported that the most common traumas for West Africa missionaries were serious illness (61%); car, train, or plane accidents (56%); unexpected death of family member or close friend (51%); immediate exposure to fighting, civil unrest, or war (48%); burglary (41%); serious threat or harm to family member or close friend (38%); seeing another person seriously injured or dying as a result of accident or violence (34%); and evacuation (31%). For missionaries from Europe, the most common traumas were car, train, or plane accidents (66%); unexpected death of a family member or close friend (54%); and burglary (38%).

Since the time of this study, missionaries serving in sub-Saharan Africa have seen a rise in terrorist threats, including burning of churches, kidnappings, and bombings and shootings in public locations targeting Westerners. Recent events with missionary victims include mass shootings by al-Qaeda affiliates in Mali, Burkina Faso, and Cote d'Ivoire as well as kidnappings in Burkina Faso and Nigeria.

IMPACT OF TRAUMA

Reactions to trauma are varied and dependent on many factors, including the nature of the trauma, personality, pretrauma experiences, belief systems, support networks, and culture. While there may be a tendency to assume that those experiencing trauma will have long-term negative reactions, posttraumatic adaptation is a more common response, with many aspects of resilience being manifested (Bonanno, 2004; McMackin, Newman, Fogler, & Keane, 2012).

Many of the initial responses to trauma are common and understandable reactions to abnormal events. Lists of common reactions to trauma for adults, adolescents, and children can be a helpful resource for those clients who would benefit from normalizing their responses to trauma. However, some may develop more pathological responses to trauma, including acute stress disorder, posttraumatic stress disorder, generalized anxiety, depression, or other complications warranting referral to trained mental health professionals.

Despite the high rate of exposure to trauma for missionaries in the Schaefer et al. (2007) study, the rate of posttraumatic stress disorder (PTSD) was surprisingly low. Overall only 4.8% of missionaries fulfilled the criteria for PTSD (5.4% in West Africa and 2.2% in Europe; p. 536).

RECOVERY FROM TRAUMA

Dolan (1998) articulates a common progression for those who suffer trauma. She describes a movement from victim self-identification to survivor to celebrant. She points out that many people assume that being a survivor is the final stage of trauma recovery. Her research and experience reveal that those who remain in the survivor stage experience a low-grade depression and general pessimism about life. However, it is possible to experience genuine joy despite experiences of horrible suffering. For various reasons, some people may linger or remain in the victim or survivor stages. Therapeutic interventions may be needed to assist further recovery.

In Dolan's (1998) paradigm, the purpose of the victim stage is to acknowledge that something terrible has happened. Movement begins when the victim acknowledges that a bad thing has happened and begins to identify or express the associated feelings. The task of this stage is for counselees to find the courage to tell someone else what has happened to them, to honestly and fairly assess what was their responsibility and what was not, and to let go of shame.

This leads to the survivor stage, in which counselees develop an understanding that they have lived beyond the time at which the traumatic experience occurred. The tasks are to acknowledge and appreciate the strengths and resources that have allowed their survival and eventual well-being, and to forgive and be forgiven for any wrongdoing associated with the trauma.

Finally, in the celebrant stage, counselees are able to more genuinely express gratitude and joy. The celebrant has found a capacity to embrace life in its fullness. Being a celebrant does not mean that one celebrates the suffering or the trauma itself, although some may come to a place of being able to say they are grateful for the experience because of the character change it has produced. The purpose of the celebrant stage is to live a life characterized by fullness, joy, and authenticity. The tasks or challenges are to continue to take risks and choose life despite discomfort and unfamiliar territory, and to devote time and energy to positive, healthy choices.

Dolan's (1998) description of victims, survivors, and celebrants has some similarities to Mancini and Bonanno's (2012) descriptions of responses to potentially traumatic events. Possible trajectory outcomes include chronic distress (victim), recovery (survivor), and resilience (celebrant). Chronic distress is characterized by the presence of posttraumatic symptoms and functional impairment, which may be long-term. The recovery trajectory includes milder symptoms and functional difficulties but gradually subsides as the person returns to normal pre-crisis functioning. The resilience trajectory includes mild symptoms, minimal impairment, healthy coping, and positive emotions such as enjoyment of life. Mancini and Bonanno state, "Indeed, a hallmark characteristic of resilient persons is their capacity for generative experiences despite adversity" (p. 82).

RESILIENCE IN THE FACE OF ADVERSITY

McCord (2015) states, "It's in these places of disappointment where we develop patience, obedience, and a deepening sensitivity to God's spirit.... We would prefer a sense of competence, the strength of our own agency, yet Christ calls us to follow Him and trust that He, the Good Shepherd, will lead us well" (p. 118).

Sometimes when I read the list of traumas most often experienced by missionaries, it washes over me in an academic and theoretical haze. However, when I stop to reflect on my personal experience as a missionary serving with the Mobile Member Care Team (MMCT; www.mmct.org) in West Africa, I realize that in a 15-year timespan I personally experienced seven of the eight most common traumas listed.

While serving as clinical director for the MMCT West Africa team and living in Cote d'Ivoire and Ghana, I was diagnosed with ovarian cancer, was trapped in the middle of fighting, witnessed a child being killed in a car accident, lost missionary friends to malaria, knew a missionary friend who was beaten and shot at, woke up to discover thieves had robbed us in the middle of the night, and was evacuated from a civil-war situation to another part of the country. Each of these traumas had significant impact on me, shaping and stretching me and taking me on a winding path.

What often felt like setbacks turned out to be openings for new aspects of ministry direction or character formation. Though I had often questioned whether I had the strength or perseverance to serve long-term in the face of personal trauma, none of these things had the power to remove me from the place of God's call. However, my perspective and reactions to those traumas (strongly related to my theology of suffering) shifted as I listened to and reflected on transformational words from the Bible and influential words from leaders and friends.

As a missionary psychologist, both experiencing trauma and caring for traumatized missionaries, the most powerful lesson and most challenging command from Scripture for me to implement was to forgive. I could hold on to the righteous rage directed toward rapists who attacked a young missionary girl I knew and had shared a meal with the night before, or I could release the poisonous rage back to God, knowing that I would never know this perpetrator or hear him ask for forgiveness. This was my choice. And that choice determined how the traumas I experienced or heard about ultimately affected me.

Spiritual resilience. In *Trauma and Resilience*, Frauke and Charlie Schaefer (2012) describe four pretrauma spiritual characteristics that make missionaries more resilient:

1. An acquired healthy biblical theology of suffering provides a sturdy framework of support through inevitable struggles after trauma.

2. A practiced ability to forgive will facilitate letting go of debilitating anger, hurt, bitterness, and resentment.

3. Familiarity with accepting and expressing strong feelings in relationship with God and others will allow for connecting, healing, and regaining of hope more quickly after adversity.

4. Security and openness in a few relationships, particularly with other believers, will provide a much needed safe place to help sustain missionaries in vulnerable times. (p. 36)

Schaefer and Schaefer (2012) then describe four posttrauma spiritual resources that positively affect the recovery process:

1. Experiencing God's presence in "the valley of the shadows," however weak or veiled, is key to assuring Christian believers of the enduring relationship with the author and sustainer of their lives.

2. Expressing strong feelings in lament to God is a way to reconnect with him.

3. Finding a path from anger and bitterness to true forgiveness frees the person from being trapped in an ongoing, self-destructive bond to the painful past.

4. Experiencing God's grace can help someone rebound from the self-condemnation that trauma can cause. (pp. 136-37)

Schaefer and Schaefer (2012) have also developed a Spiritual Resilience Checklist that can be found in appendix A of their book (reproduced in table 16.2 below).

Pretrauma resilience. Phyllis Sortor, the missionary kidnapped and held hostage in Nigeria, was asked to reflect on what contributed to her resilience in the midst of and following her traumatic experiences (P. Sortor, personal communication, May 26, 2016). Her first response was *commitment.* She had a determined, deeply held conviction that God had called her to serve in Nigeria, and she was fully committed to that call no matter what happened to her. She also reminded herself of the examples of Paul and Jesus, meditating on what they had been through, and recognizing that although they had been through even more than she had, they had kept going in their ministry. Despite being certain at times that she was going to die, Sortor always had hope. In fact, this was one of several seemingly contradictory feelings that harmonized in her heart—certainty of death paired with abiding hope, terror in companionship with peace, despondency laced with joy, guilt coupled with assurance. And a never-ending certainty that God was keeping her.

Her words are familiar. Brown (2007) conducted a study of 30 missionaries who had experienced traumas such as robberies, evacuation, rape, carjackings, and war. He only interviewed those who had stayed or returned to their field of service, curious to know what had contributed to their resilience.

First, Brown examined which factors were present in the missionaries before their traumatic experiences. He discovered four themes, which he described as a strong personal "call" to be where they were, preparedness from birth, words from God, and sturdy relationships. These four themes warrant further unpacking to better understand what might contribute to the trauma trajectories and resilience of missionaries.

Clear sense of call. The notion of having a call comes up repeatedly in conversations with missionaries who reflect on what contributes most to their resilience (Brown, 2007; Carr, 2012). A biblical example of this can be found in the commissioning of Barnabas and Saul in Acts 13:2-3: "One day as these men [prophets and teachers of the church of Antioch] were worshiping the Lord and fasting, the Holy Spirit said, 'Appoint Barnabas and Saul for the special work to which I have called them.' So after more fasting and prayer, the men laid their hands on them and sent them on their way" (NLT). It is interesting to note that the call came directly from the Holy Spirit and yet was received, affirmed, and implemented in the context of prayer, fasting, and Christian community.

Receiving a call may sometimes be confused with having a passion. Certainly identifying our passion can be an important part of the discernment process. Passion motivates, inspires, delights, and energizes. A call without passion may become a grim, teeth-gritting, works-oriented duty that lacks grace. However, a passion without a call is often an emotional response that may be unstable and may fail the missionary in the difficult or traumatic times. Passions may or may not be founded on realistic expectations of self or others. Ultimately, resilience is affected by one's motivation for serving. Those who feel that they are fulfilling God's purpose for their lives are better able to endure loss, hardship, and disappointments than those who came for other motivations, such as attraction to the job, a sense of adventure, or pressure from a spouse or family. The problem with these motivations is that one may not end up in the job one came for, the setting may not be adventurous or romantic at all, and coming because of pressure from a family member often leads to a sense of resentment later on.

Henri Nouwen (1988), a priest and author, spent some time gazing at a statue called *Christus auf Palmesel* (Christ on a palm-donkey) and wrote:

> As he rides into Jerusalem surrounded by people shouting "hosanna," cutting branches from the trees and spreading them in his path (Matthew 21:8), Jesus appears completely concentrated on something else. He does not look at the excited crowd. He does not wave. He sees beyond all the noise and movement to what is ahead of him: an agonizing journey of betrayal, torture, crucifixion, and death. His unfocused eyes see what nobody around him can see. . . . There is melancholy, but also peaceful acceptance. There is insight into the fickleness of the human heart, but also immense compassion. There is a deep awareness of the unspeakable pain to be suffered, but also a strong determination to do God's will. Above all, there is love, an endless, deep and far-reaching love born from an unbreakable intimacy with God and reaching out to all people, wherever they are, were, or will be. There is nothing that he does not fully know. There is nobody whom he does not fully love. (p. 135)

The ultimate example we have of following a personal call from God is Christ himself, whose call is rooted in his acceptance by the Father and intimate relationships in the Trinity. Counselees can be encouraged with the truth that they are invited into this relational dialogue to seek out and listen to God's voice as they make decisions about their future.

Preparedness from birth. This is what we sometimes jokingly refer to as coming from "hardy stock." In essence this refers to the kind of family background, life experiences, and cultural influences that shape one's work ethic, attitude toward hardship, and response to suffering. Those who are strangers to hard work and setbacks seem to struggle more with the daily stresses of missionary life such as heat, humidity, power cuts, traffic, pollution, language learning, corruption, lack of water, inefficient infrastructure, and exposure to poverty. The steady eroding of coping mechanisms that may occur with the constant daily pounding of environmental and cultural stressors creates a vulnerability affecting the ability to manage a traumatic situation. In contrast, those who have learned to roll with the punches and endure minor setbacks with humor and perspective will be better situated to enter a traumatic situation with personal determination that is rooted in constant surrender of their will to God's.

Words from God. The ability to discern what God is saying relates to the condition of one's spiritual formation. For example, one missionary was held hostage for many weeks in a small cage. After he was released, he expressed gratitude that he had memorized so much Scripture, because he was able to recall verses that were a source of comfort and strength to him during his captivity. Scripture memorization or access to Scripture during traumatic events is often cited by missionaries as an invaluable resource and source of encouragement and strength. Some may also feel that God is speaking to them in the midst of crisis situations or afterward, bringing words of healing and perspective. Those who have given priority to spiritual formation will have access to powerful words of healing and nourishment as they enter times of dryness and spiritual darkness.

Sturdy relationships. A strong social-support system provides the backbone of trauma recovery. Two key areas of support contributing to resilience are team cohesion and a consultative leadership style (J. Fawcett, 2002, 2003). The level of social support as well as the perception of organizational support during and after a crisis affects one's ability to cope with it and one's overall resilience (Forbes & Roger, 1999; Keane, Scott, Cavoya, Lamparski, & Fairbank, 1985).

Posttrauma resilience. Brown (2007) described four self-identified posttrauma factors that most contributed to missionary resilience: being part of a supportive network, having supportive and directive leadership, quickly finding a new ministry focus, and experiencing the closeness and protection of God.

Being part of a supportive network. Just as having sturdy relationships prior to trauma contributes to resilience, being part of a strong support system during and after the crisis is associated with many aspects of posttrauma recovery; conversely, low levels of social support are correlated with low emotional well-being (Watson & Brymer, 2012). While professional support is important, it cannot take the place of supportive community. One role of a counselor may be to encourage clients to explore or discover their natural networks and to strengthen existing supports (Mukherjee & Alpert, 2006). Ultimately, recovery can only happen in the context of relationships (Cohen, 2006).

Having supportive and directive leadership. Many crosscultural workers reference the presence and attitude of their leaders as being a critical factor in how they coped with various traumas and stressors. For example, a missionary doctor was driving when a young person suddenly ran in front of his vehicle. Though he tried to swerve to miss him, the child was hit and died. The car rolled, and the passengers were seriously injured. The doctor was filled with guilt, although there was nothing he could have done. After doing all he could for the family and answering questions from the police, he returned home. Soon after arriving home, his field leader called, listened to him, and communicated assurance and support. The next day, when I met with him for crisis counseling, his description of his leader's support, profound in its simplicity, became a central theme because it offered hope and stability to him in an otherwise overwhelming and horror-inducing experience. The significance of this contact was also formative for the leader who had initially resisted the idea of directly contacting the driver, feeling that others were more qualified to help him and his input was not needed.

Conversely, there are examples of missionaries who experienced trauma and lament but whose leaders did not contact them, did not show up, or did not acknowledge what happened to them. Research shows a negative association between expressions of bitterness or disappointment in leadership during times of crisis and ability to adapt successfully to the losses of the trauma (G. Fawcett, 2003). This may be related to the actual support given by the leadership as well as the person's perception of, and trust in, his or her leadership in general.

Quickly finding a new ministry focus. Brown (2007) found that, particularly for missionaries who had to evacuate from their places of service, having the option to invest in new ministry opportunities contributed to their longevity and well-being. Those who were in limbo and experienced inactivity had more struggles. Strategies employed during chronically dangerous situations that are associated with resilient outcomes include actively seeking information, shifting expectations and focus, creating specific routines related to life's necessities, and maintaining an attraction for life (Watson & Brymer, 2012). It stands to reason that those who are able to participate in goal-directed activities where they can find meaning and purpose beyond their own needs will flourish.

Experiencing the closeness and protection of God. Many missionaries I have worked with in crisis counseling have talked about an incarnational experience of the "peace that passes understanding" when going through a traumatic event. This has not meant that they did not experience physical harm. In fact, many were beaten or threatened or robbed or nearly killed, but there was a strong sense of God's presence and protection nonetheless. Phyllis Sortor (personal communication, May 26, 2016) found herself going back to an old familiar hymn, the words resonating with strengthening force: "Oh Jesus, I have promised to serve thee to the end. Be thou forever near me, my Master and my Friend. I shall not fear the battle if thou art by my side." Once again we find a blending of contrasts. The soul is crying out for what it needs—God's protection and closeness—and feeling the comfort of that, while potentially also being in the midst of a reality that is crushing and extremely painful.

HOW COUNSELORS CAN CONTRIBUTE TO MISSIONARY RESILIENCE

Counselors may sometimes take a somewhat narrow view of the ways they can contribute to helping missionaries, thinking primarily of assessment and counseling interventions. There are, however, many ways that those trained in counseling skills can contribute by sharing their knowledge and skills with those in unique positions to be primary supports to traumatized missionaries. The Spiritual Resilience Checklist in table 16.2 provides a list of considerations.

Consultation to mission leaders. Counselors are in a unique role to encourage the development of priorities that will promote staff care. Some of the key areas to reinforce are related to encouraging relational support, developing a theology of suffering, developing a theology of risk, and affirming or clarifying the call. It is possible that the counselor will have opportunity to address these things in the context of a counseling session, but more likely the counselor's role will be as a consultant to mission organizational leaders, helping them to develop resilience by encouraging development in these areas.

Encourage relational support. Counselors are often told by peer caregivers that they do not know what to say or do when they are in the presence of someone who is suffering. A counselor can coach the supportive community to use the power of their comforting presence to give the person a supportive space from which to find clarity and meaning in the midst of their suffering. Although the one who is suffering is often asking questions, the comforter may find that any answers they try to provide fall flat and do not actually address what is behind the questions. These questions are often forms of lament rather than an intellectual pursuit. Suffering is often expressed in agonized questions that do not have an answer. As Pat Russell stated, "It is not a problem that demands a solution. Suffering is a mystery that demands a presence" (as cited by Shaum, 2012, p. 15).

Many agencies may think primarily of building and strengthening relationships from within their own organization. However, networks formed across organizations and cultural groupings will bring additional resources, skills, and practical help to crisis situations. Relationships that are broken or riddled with unresolved conflicts will be less than adequate in the midst of a crisis. Proactive nurturance of a loving Christian community will strengthen the resilience of the agency and individuals as they face traumatic events.

Table 16.2. Spiritual resilience checklist (Schaefer & Schaefer, 2012, pp. 146-47)

Sound Theology of Suffering

- ☐ Has the person (have I) grappled with his or her (my) theology of suffering, and are the resulting assumptions biblical?

- ☐ Does our (my) organization encourage and promote a sound theology of suffering?

Intrinsic Religious Motivation

- ☐ Does the person (do I) have a habit of attending community worship and prayer?

- ☐ Does the person (do I) have at least two close Christian friends for mutual support and sharing openly and deeply?

- ☐ Does the person (do I) have a regular habit of personal prayer and studying the Bible?

- ☐ Does the person (do I) have a regular practice of participating in spiritual retreats, contemplative prayer, and receiving spiritual direction?

Ability to Face and Share Uncomfortable Feelings

- ☐ Is the person (am I) authentically and honestly talking about difficult life experiences and surrounding feelings?

- ☐ Does our (my) organization support honest sharing of uncomfortable feelings, or are there indirectly communicated messages that "good Christians" should not have certain feelings?

Knowing and Extending Forgiveness

- ☐ Does the person (do I) have experiential knowledge of receiving forgiveness from God and from others?

- ☐ Is the person (am I) aware of the forgiveness process and able to distinguish forgiving from excusing or glossing over injuries?

- ☐ Does our (my) organization encourage and promote giving, experiencing, and knowing forgiveness?

Knowing and Receiving Grace

- ☐ Does the person (do I) have a deep experience of being loved and valued by God?

- ☐ Is the person (am I) accepting of human brokenness as a common experience and able to love others (myself) when the brokenness is visible, rather than being overly condemning?

- ☐ Does our (my) organization encourage a culture of openness, vulnerability, and support as its members deal with their brokenness?

Supportive Relationships with Other Believers

- ☐ Does this person (do I) have at least two close Christian friends?

- ☐ Does this person (do I) give growing and maintaining close relationships a measure of priority over ministry work?

Agencies can work proactively to strengthen interpersonal relationships. This may translate to encouraging participation in workshops focused on interpersonal skills. It may involve sending mediators to service areas to address conflicts before opposing sides become intransigent.

In addition to coaching leaders to reinforce relational networks in the ministry locations, counselors should pay special attention to the relationships between leaders and their staff. Regular and frequent communication from leadership will build trust. Following a crisis, communication from the leader that acknowledges the impact and significance of the trauma is essential. If at all possible, traveling to visit the traumatized missionary and providing onsite supportive presence will be highly significant and may be more remembered than any professional trauma intervention. Sadly, perhaps even more memorable will be the absence of a phone call or visit following a trauma (Brown, 2007).

Encourage development of a theology of suffering. If missionaries are encouraged to work toward developing and embracing a biblical theology of suffering, it will pave the way for them to respond to inevitable crises in resilient ways. It will also foster the hard work and arduous journey required for growth and recovery in the aftermath of crises. All too often, a North American posture toward pain is to avoid it completely or to move through it as rapidly as possible. A biblical view of suffering acknowledges that suffering is sometimes God's path to accomplish the greatest good for the kingdom of God (e.g., Ps 119:67; Rom 5:3-5; 2 Cor 1:9; 4:8-11, 17; 12:7-10; Phil 3:8-11; 2 Tim 2:10; Heb 12:10-11; Jas 1:2-4; 1 Pet 1:6-7; 4:1). Shaum (2012) states, "If I were to help the person find a solution to his or her pain as quickly as possible, I *might* be undermining the redemptive work God wants to do through a prolonged period of endurance" (p. 17).

In Brown's study, 74% of those interviewed mentioned that they had advanced in the development of a biblical view of suffering following their traumatic experience. A theology of suffering is organic. It requires an intentional, ongoing commitment to examine our highly influential cultural beliefs in light of scriptural truth. Christians may have stated beliefs such as "As a Christian, I will suffer" (a biblically based truth), while harboring an underlying core belief that God will spare them from certain types of suffering. This core belief will be challenged and perhaps shattered when the suffering one hoped would never happen becomes reality. Christians may begin to wonder if they are being punished or abandoned by God and may struggle with feelings of anger and rejection because of the sacrifices they have made.

Traumatic experiences give us opportunity to reexamine our personal beliefs about suffering and to go deeper in our reflections about who God is, what it means to experience the fellowship of Christ's suffering, and what grace is in the midst of suffering. This is why we as counselors cannot just give someone a prewritten theology of suffering, but we can facilitate a process whereby his or her theology of suffering is shaped by pain and the Holy Spirit's counsel and wisdom in response to those experiences.

Develop a theology of risk. Sanders (2007) observed, "The greatest achievements in the history of missions have come from leaders close to God who took courageous, calculated risks" (p. 12). Mission leaders are in a unique and often very difficult position as they wrestle with making decisions about sending staff into high-risk areas. Frank discussions about theology of risk might include decision-making criteria for field assignments, ongoing care, evacuation, and follow-up care. Tolerance for risk varies individually and is highly subjective, and yet the impact of individual decisions on the wider community is profound. Attitudes and decisions about risk are spiritually relevant with many practical implications.

For example, a team is based in a country with increasing terrorist attacks and threats. Does the decision to stay or leave depend on the home office leadership, or should it be made by the team? What if some team members want to stay and others want to leave? What should be the criteria for staying or leaving? What if one person is determined to be a martyr for questionable motives? What if another is ready to die for Christ for pure reasons? What if some want to leave because they are afraid or because they are being pressured by or want to respect the wishes of their home church or family? What if the national leadership is asking the team to leave because they are creating more danger for national believers by staying? These are some questions that leaders and missionary workers can start to discuss prior to traumatic events. A thorough examination of the decision-making process and choices made by early believers in the book of Acts will reveal that there is no one way prescribed in Scripture for how Christians should respond to risk. Sometimes believers flee from danger, and other times they move directly into it.

Facilitated discussions about theology of risk may expose some beliefs that are not actually biblically correct. Hampton (2016) describes 12 myths about risk that are common to Christian workers living overseas. For example, one myth is that "we are always safe in the center of God's will." While this may refer to a kind of "spiritual safety" as described in verses related to God's protection and care, it may translate erroneously to a belief that those who are following God's purposes will never be harmed. Confusion, crisis of faith, and anger are common for those who live by this myth and then experience traumatic events. Christian workers can be helped to identify risk myths and, in the context of discussion, begin to rework their beliefs into a more scriptural foundation that will contribute to their long-term well-being when going into high-risk situations.

Training programs. As counselors, we cannot respond directly to every traumatic situation that missionaries will face. One way to replicate our skills is to focus on training missionaries and leaders in how to care for one another.

Training that focuses on further developing relational skills is an essential component of pre- and post-crisis resilience. One example of this is Sharpening Your Interpersonal Skills (SYIS; www.itpartners.org), a week-long training program that enhances listening, grief management, and conflict resolution skills (Williams, 2002).

The Mobile Member Care Team (MMCT; www.mmct.org), an organization I was privileged to be a part of, served Africa from 2000 to 2017, primarily through providing member care training. Sharing of resources was one of the distinctives of this organization. A key goal of MMCT was to build a network of trained peer caregivers who would support each other in crises (Jerome, 2001; Jerome & Carr, 2002). Ideally, networks of peer responders are multicultural and from many different mission organizations, facilitating more diverse and deeper relationships as well as strengthening community supports. In response to crises, our belief is that more people are served and the community is strengthened if care is provided inter-organizationally.

Training programs that develop crisis response skills in leaders will contribute to pre- and post-crisis resilience. The content of a crisis response training program might include the typical impact of crises, the potential pathological effects, how to make initial contact, and how to provide one-on-one psychological first aid. The workshop might also include personal assessment of attitudes toward suffering and risk. Other possible topics are when and how to make referrals and ethical issues such as confidentiality and boundaries. The following recommendations will help to ensure quality control in peer-to-peer crisis training:

- Develop an application process that requires participants to explain why they want to take the training.

- Ask for leader and peer references providing endorsement of participants' skills and the community's willingness to engage with them as crisis responders.

- Provide a 1:4 staff-to-participant ratio to ensure adequate attention to personalized coaching and mentoring.

- Provide training that is highly skills based and that models skills, allows for practice, and provides feedback.

- Commit to ongoing, qualified mentoring and coaching after the formal training program is completed.

Following an MMCT Crisis Response Training, there was a renewed eruption of fighting in Côte d'Ivoire, and about 200 missionaries were evacuated from the country (some of them for the third time). They were scattered to at least four surrounding West African countries. In each of these locations, peer responders who had been trained by MMCT were involved in providing practical help in housing, food, and childcare as well as emotional and social support and the opportunity to talk about the crisis the missionaries had just experienced. MMCT staff provided coaching and mentoring from a distance. The feedback we received from the recipients of the peer debriefing affirmed that the care they received contributed to their perception that they were well cared for and ultimately enhanced their resilience and ability to recover from this trauma of war and evacuation.

With support and input from trained counselors, missionary peers can be equipped to serve each other in effective ways. Because counselors cannot be in every place that missionaries are serving, and because peers can better identify with the unique situations that missionaries face, it makes sense to invest our skills and energies in this kind of replication model.

Counseling traumatized missionaries. Phyllis Sortor (personal communication, May 26, 2016) was released 11 days after she was taken hostage. For some, this symbolized the end of her crisis. However, what happens in the aftermath of a crisis has a critical bearing on the recovery process.

Phyllis Sortor described how she was joyfully greeted by those who had been intimately involved in the negotiation process. She returned to the United States and was reunited with family members and friends and her home church. She was given opportunity to debrief, and she met with a counselor to talk about what had happened to her. A group debriefing that included all those who had been involved in her release brought a sense of stability and normalcy into her life. This was done in a familiar and safe location, and each person shared what their experience had been for each of the 11 days. This helped Phyllis to feel that her experience was a shared one, as opposed to her feeling scrutinized and on the hot seat. It was instrumental in breaking through her isolation.

Yet she also had unmet longings. When she was first released, she asked if she could go back to Hope Academy, where she had lived and worked for years, to let her friends know she was safe. She was not allowed to do that, possibly for safety reasons. When she was sent back to the United States, it was presumed that she would never return to Nigeria. From a logical standpoint, and for reasons of safety, many would likely endorse that choice. But Phyllis was driven by something more than logic and freedom from risk. She keenly felt the Lord's call on her life to return to Nigeria. Her leaders wisely asked her to do additional work related to the healing process. She journaled about her experience and was gripped with a horrible fear of going back. God spoke to her in the midst of that time through an African American preacher who spoke about the resurrection and God's power to roll away any stone that blocks us from peace and joy. She experienced a deeply cleansing healing combined with a clear call to return to Nigeria. More conversations with her leadership led them to support her return. Phyllis Sortor's story brings home some unique issues for missionaries entering into a counseling or trauma recovery process.

Sorting out God's call, personal risk, and the expectations of others. Bonhoeffer (1997) wrote:

> Who stands fast? Only the man whose final standard is not his reason, his principles, his conscience, his freedom, or his virtue, but who is ready to sacrifice all this when he is called to obedient and responsible action in faith and in exclusive allegiance to God—the responsible man, who tries to make his whole life an answer to the question and call of God. Where are these responsible people? (p. 5)

Depending on our own theology of suffering and risk, as well as our cultural values related to comfort and happiness, it may be difficult to understand why a person would choose to return to a high-risk situation. For some, looking from the outside, the sacrifices made by missionaries are too great or are unnecessary. To be an effective counselor for missionaries, personal biases must be examined. Consider the following questions: What is your own tolerance for risk and pain? Do you feel it is always in a person's best interests to be in the safest place he or she can be? How do you understand and talk with someone about the call he or she has received from God?

When a missionary is exploring whether or not to return to a high-risk location, a number of factors can be explored in the counseling context. To what extent has the person worked through the trauma? What is the person's current resilience level, and how might he or she respond to future exposure to trauma? What support system will the individual have upon returning to the location? What level of support does the individual have from leadership to return? How much support does the individual have from his or her home sending church? How does the family feel about the person's return? How are the reactions of others affecting the person?

In some cases missionaries may choose to return to high-risk situations despite the objection of their family members. This creates additional stress for these missionaries but is only one factor among many for them to consider, especially if they have a strong sense that God is calling them to a particular place and this call has been affirmed by trusted and competent members of their organization and Christian community. In other cases missionaries may feel called to high-risk areas, but external factors may overrule this sense of call. Examples include a lack of support from their mission leadership, disagreement by their support system, or closed doors because of war, deportation, or visa refusal from the country in question.

A family prepared for years to go to a particular country. They sold their house, raised support, and did language learning and further education to prepare for fulfilling God's call for them to go to this country. Just months before they were scheduled to go, war erupted in the country, closing all doors to their entry. As they waited for some kind of clarity and direction, they had questions such as "Did we hear God correctly?" "Why is this happening?" and "What do we do now?" In these situations, missionaries may feel confused, angry, and hurt. These are all understandable reactions and are important to process for effective trauma recovery.

In our independent cultures in the West, we often do not think about the role of the extended family or home church in the trauma recovery process. In many cases, the home church leadership has an important role in ongoing decisions related to the well-being of missionaries; therefore they should be involved in the recovery process along with the leadership of the sending organization. Extended family may include parents and adult children of missionaries. For example, parents of a missionary couple may strongly object to their grandchildren being taken into a high-risk area. Although this objection may not stop the family from going, the impact of the parents' disapproval may have ongoing ripple effects that surface quite significantly during and after a traumatic event. Counselors might consider offering family sessions to work through these complicated reactions.

Common issues in missionary posttrauma counseling. Several themes may come up when counseling missionaries who have experienced trauma. While these are not exclusive to missionaries, they may be particularly weighty given the nature of living crossculturally and in high-risk settings. It may be helpful to initiate discussion in these areas, whether the missionary brings them up or not. Common issues in missionary posttrauma counseling include anger, anxiety/fear, grief, guilt/self-blame, and meaning making.

Anger. Wangerin (1992) wisely observes, "When those who are grieving ask passionate questions, remember that their questions do not come from an inquisitive mind but from a disappointed soul. Questions asked in anger often don't have answers because they aren't questions, they are accusations" (pp. 216-17). Anger, rage, and fury can all be elements of the missionary's response to trauma. The anger might be at a person responsible for the trauma, a teammate who did not respond well after or during the trauma, leaders who have failed to respond adequately, a corrupt or failed government, or God.

All of these anger responses are natural and common, and yet the victim may need to receive permission to acknowledge and express these feelings. The anger may be more intense than the situation merits, indicating perhaps a buildup from historical issues. Gentle exploration of the anger in the context of an umbrella of grace that ultimately leads to forgiveness will bring a cleansing of emotions that may become toxic if suppressed. One must resist the temptation to give answers to the "why" questions and instead listen with the purposeful intention of responding in ways that facilitate the person choosing pathways of healing. If the person is choosing self-destructive paths or behavior that is damaging to his or her relationships, gentle but firm redirection is needed.

Anxiety and fear. Intense fear is a common aspect of many traumatic experiences. There will be lingering fear and anxiety following the traumatic experience. That is just a biochemical reality! Missionaries may feel guilty that they have felt fear, quoting passages that admonish us to "fear not." I have not had much success in stopping fear by telling myself to stop feeling that way. As I look at 1 Peter 5:7, it seems that the Lord is acknowledging that we will feel fear, and then he is giving us an option for what to do with it: "Give all your worries and cares to God, for he cares about you" (NLT). It is his love, kindness, and massive competence in carrying our burdens that gives us the courage to surrender something we can never control. Yes, fear will be a common occurrence after trauma, and counselees will need practical help for how to respond to it. Deep breathing, muscle relaxation, mindfulness, grounding, imagery techniques, and centering prayer are all ways for the person to experience freedom from paralyzing anxiety (see Schaefer & Schaefer, 2012, pp. 118-33). In some cases, referral to a psychiatrist for medication evaluation may also be appropriate if the fear has become debilitating and recurrent.

Grief. McCord (2015) writes:

> Many of us initially follow Christ to dangerous lands full of zeal, convinced of our own strength, commitment, and ideals. We know, cognitively, theologically, that Christ is with us. Along the way, we lose our earthly foundations. We experience failure, loss, and suffering. We come to the end of ourselves and find that Christ is still with us. We learn to walk with Jesus in humility, limping as it were, trusting His presence to accompany and guide us. We learn that Christ alone is sufficient and our souls rest in his light even while the darkness swirls around us. (p. 202)

Oftentimes counselors working with missionaries will discover that the trauma they have just experienced is only one of many crises. If a counselor asks missionaries to list the losses they have endured, both tangible and existential, he or she may be astonished at the volume they will produce. Counseling received after a trauma may be a missionary's first opportunity to actually process and begin to grieve losses sustained both pre- and postcrisis. Because grief is most commonly associated with death, individuals may be surprised to realize that they are grieving multiple losses but have not had a name for the sadness they have been experiencing. When our team left Cote d'Ivoire during the war and relocated to Ghana, we lost our home, our friends, our sense of safety and security, our ministry momentum, our local advisory council, and a sense of familiarity. These were all losses associated with the trauma of war that also needed to be processed.

The way we process grief has the potential to lead us to greater intimacy with God or to isolation from him. Counseling looks at how a person is choosing to self-soothe. Is a person choosing things that draw him or her closer to God, such as quality times with friends, time in the Psalms, music, rest, and journaling? Or is he or she choosing comforts that give temporary relief but contribute to isolation from God, such as pornography, social isolation, workaholism, or alcohol abuse? An important aspect of Christian trauma counseling will involve helping the person to choose an individualized practice of grieving that ultimately leads him or her into deeper intimacy with the one true Comforter.

Guilt/self-blame. Many trauma survivors struggle with guilt or self-blame when they recount the story of what happened to them. This may be even more prevalent for missionaries who often have an acute sense of responsibility and a tendency to judge themselves. An important aspect of trauma counseling is to *acknowledge and reframe* (Carr, 2012). This comes from the original model of cognitive restructuring developed by Aaron Beck, a technique designed to help depressed patients see the inaccuracy of their negative thinking (Beck, Rush, Shaw, & Emery, 1979).

In 2002 our team was caught in the middle of civil war in Cote d'Ivoire. We were allowed to evacuate in our own cars. As we drove out of Bouaké, the streets were lined with Africans who were unable to leave. The silence was damning, the expressions hopeless, and our guilt acute. Missionaries who have to evacuate often wonder what will happen to the ones left behind. There is a sense of abandoning others. This feeling may be more intense after missionaries leave and then realize that they did not leave adequate resources behind (e.g., advance pay for any employees who had to stay). Guilt may be enhanced or diminished according to what national colleagues said to their expatriate friends before they left—whether it was a message encouraging them to leave or a plea to stay. Leaders may be particularly prone to guilt depending on how they made the decision for themselves and others to leave and how their followers or national colleagues have responded to them (e.g., with compliance or with resentment, criticism, and anger).

To acknowledge and reframe the above situation would mean giving space to recognize that feelings of guilt and abandonment are understandable and natural. Acknowledging the feelings gives room for the necessary grief. Reframing builds perspective and context. Reframing comments are more readily received and processed if the feelings of guilt have already been acknowledged. The counselor may make comments such as "It sure is natural to feel this way about having to leave behind people who are suffering." This statement can be followed by a pause and then followed by "This was not your fault, and you could not control what happened." Reframing might also include assurances that the decision to leave was not reflective of a lack of caring or commitment. Redirection of focus may help individuals see ways that they are still able to express care and support of those affected by their decision.

Sometimes a person's guilt and shame might be based on actions or choices made in the midst of a trauma that were wrong, hurtful, or mistakes. An important aspect of the acknowledge-and-reframe intervention is assisting the survivor in gaining perspective. Mistakes may have been made and regrets inevitable, but learning and growth springs from those mistakes. Mistakes or missteps that seemed large in the midst of the crisis may now seem smaller in light of more important factors.

The counseling process can allow the person to identify areas of remorse and perhaps a need for repentance and forgiveness. The counselor can be an agent of grace, helping the person to receive forgiveness and release shame in order to progress in their healing.

Meaning making. As the intensity of emotions diminishes and the struggle for survival is past, a trauma survivor may be able to cognitively go to a place of extracting meaning from the traumatic event. If a question about significance or meaning is asked too soon, it will likely fall flat or seem pushy and insensitive. Careful timing and sensitivity to the person's recovery process is crucial. Asking questions tentatively and respectfully, the counselor might explore such areas as the following:

- What did you take away from this event?
- What kinds of things did you learn from this time?
- How has this event shaped or changed you?
- What do you feel the Lord is showing you from this crisis?
- In hindsight, what are some of the things you've gained from having gone through this trauma?

As Christians, we are sometimes able to see the ways God has redeemed suffering and used it for good purposes. It might be our own growth or the encouragement of another or our ability to help others. In some cases, however, we may never see a redemptive purpose of a trauma in our lifetime. By nature, God is a redeemer. Even Job who suffered more than most encourages us with his exclamation of this truth:

But as for me, I know that my Redeemer lives,

and he will stand upon the earth at last.

And after my body has decayed,

yet in my body I will see God!

I will see him for myself.

Yes, I will see him with my own eyes.

I am overwhelmed at the thought! (Job 19:25-27 NLT)

CONCLUSION

Bishop Ken Untener (1979), in a prayer titled "A Future Not Our Own," wrote:

> This is what we are about. We plant the seeds that one day will grow. We water the seeds already planted knowing that they hold future promise. We lay foundations that will need further development. We provide yeast that produces effects far beyond our capabilities.
>
> We cannot do everything, and there is a sense of liberation in realizing this. This enables us to do something, and to do it very well. It may be incomplete, but it is a beginning, a step along the way, an opportunity for the Lord's grace to enter and do the rest. We may never see the end results, but that is the difference between the master builder and the worker.

May we all have the grace and courage to invest in God's kingdom by using our gifts in a spirit of humility. May we never lose the deep awe and respect for the sacred trust that has been given us to be companions to the wounded. For we ourselves are broken and inadequate, yet we are given the privilege to be instruments of God's healing.

REFERENCES

Beck, A., Rush, J., Shaw, B., & Emery, G. (1979). *Cognitive therapy of depression.* New York, NY: Guilford Press.

Bonanno, G. A. (2004). Loss, trauma, and human resilience: Have we underestimated the human capacity to thrive after extremely aversive events? *American Psychologist, 59,* 20-28.

Bonhoeffer, D. (1997). *Letters and papers from prison.* New York, NY: Touchstone.

Brown, R. (2007). Resilience in ministry despite trauma. In R. Hay, V. Lim, D. Blocher, J. Ketelaar, & S. Hay (Eds.), *Worth keeping: Global perspectives on best practice in missionary retention* (pp. 315-18). Pasadena, CA: William Carey Library.

Carr, K. F. (1997, October). Crisis intervention for missionaries. *Evangelical Missions Quarterly, 33,* 451-58.

Carr, K. F. (2005). The Mobile Member Care Team as a means of responding to crises: West Africa. In L. Barbanel & B. Sternberg (Eds.), *Psychological interventions in times of crisis* (pp. 75-98). New York, NY: Springer.

Carr, K. F. (2012). Personal resilience. In C. Schaefer & F. Schaefer (Eds.), *Trauma and resilience: A handbook; Effectively supporting those who serve God* (pp. 93-104). Condeo Press.

Cohen, E. (2006). Play and adaptation in traumatized young children and their caregivers. In L. Barbanel & B. Sternberg (Eds.), *Psychological interventions in times of crisis* (pp. 151-79). New York, NY: Springer.

Dolan, Y. (1998). *One small step: Moving beyond trauma and therapy to a life of joy.* Watsonville, CA: Papier-Mache Press.

Fawcett, G. (2003). Preventing trauma in traumatic environments. In J. Fawcett (Ed.), *Stress and trauma handbook: Strategies for flourishing in demanding environments* (pp. 40-67). Monrovia, CA: World Vision International.

Fawcett, J. (2002). Preventing broken hearts, healing broken minds. In Y. Danieli (Ed.), *Sharing the front line and the back hills* (pp. 223-32). Amityville, NY: Baywood.

Fawcett, J. (Ed.). (2003). *Stress and trauma handbook: Strategies for flourishing in demanding environments.* Monrovia, CA: World Vision International.

Forbes, A., & Roger, D. (1999). Stress, social support and fear of disclosure. *British Journal of Health Psychology, 4,* 165-79.

Hampton, A. (2016). *Facing danger: A guide through risk.* New Prague, MN: Zendagi Press.

Jerome, D. (2001). Mobile Member Care Team—West Africa: Our journey and direction. In K. O'Donnell (Ed.), *Doing member care well: Perspectives and practices from around the world* (pp. 117-26). Pasadena, CA: William Carey Library.

Jerome, D., & Carr, K. (2002). Mobile member care teams. In J. R. Powell & J. M. Bowers (Eds.), *Enhancing missionary vitality* (pp. 399-407). Palmer Lake, CO: Mission Training International.

Keane, T. M., Scott, W. O., Cavoya, G. A., Lamparski, D. M., & Fairbank, J. A. (1985). Social support in Vietnam veterans with posttraumatic stress disorder: A comparative analysis. *Journal of Consulting and Clinical Psychology, 53,* 95-102.

Kessler, R. C., Sonnega, A., Bromet, E., Hughes, M., & Nelson, C. B. (1995). Posttraumatic stress disorder in the national comorbidity survey. *Archives of General Psychiatry, 12,* 1048-60.

Mancini, A. D., & Bonanno, G. A. (2012). Differential pathways to resilience after loss and trauma. In R. A. McMackin, E. Newman, J. M. Fogler, & T. M. Keane (Eds.), *Trauma therapy in context: The art and craft of evidence-based practice* (pp. 79-98). Washington, DC: American Psychological Association.

McCord, K. (2015). *Why God calls us to dangerous places.* Chicago, IL: Moody.

McMackin, R. A., Newman, E., Fogler, J. M., & Keane, T. M. (Eds.). (2012). *Trauma therapy in context: The art and craft of evidence-based practice.* Washington, DC: American Psychological Association.

Mukherjee, P., & Alpert, J. (2006). Overview of psychological interventions in the acute aftermath of disaster. In L. Barbanel & B. Sternberg (Eds.), *Psychological interventions in times of crisis* (pp. 3-35). New York, NY: Springer.

Nouwen, H. (1988). *The road to daybreak.* New York, NY: Doubleday.

Sanders, O. (2007). *Spiritual leadership.* Chicago, IL: Moody.

Schaefer, F. C., Blazer, D., Carr, K., Burchett, B., Schaefer, C. A., & Davidson, J. (2007). Traumatic events and posttraumatic stress in cross-cultural mission assignments. *Journal of Traumatic Stress, 20*(4), 529-39.

Schaefer, F. C., & Schaefer, C. A. (Eds.). (2012). *Trauma and resilience: A handbook; Effectively supporting those who serve God.* Condeo Press.

Shaum, S. E. (2012). Reflections on a theology of suffering. In F. C. Schaefer & C. A. Schaefer (Eds.), *Trauma and resilience: A handbook; Effectively supporting those who serve God* (pp. 1-23). Condeo Press.

Sortor, P. (2015). Phyllis Sortor's interview at First Free Methodist Church. Retrieved from https://vimeo.com/123905200

Untener, K. (1979, November). A future not our own. Retrieved from www.journey withjesus.net/PoemsAndPrayers/Ken_Untener_A_Future_Not_Our_Own.shtml

Wangerin, W. (1992). *From mourning into dancing.* Grand Rapids, MI: Zondervan.

Watson, P., & Brymer, M. (2012). Promoting resilience through early intervention. In R. A. McMackin, E. Newman, J. M. Fogler, & T. M. Keane (2012). *Trauma therapy in context: The art and craft of evidence-based practice* (pp. 141-63). Washington, DC: American Psychological Association.

Williams, K. (2002). *Sharpening your interpersonal skills.* Colorado Springs, CO: International Training Partners.

PREVENTING AND TREATING COMBAT

TRAUMA AND SPIRITUAL INJURY

LAURA SCHWENT SHULTZ,
JESSE D. MALOTT,
AND ROBERT J. GREGORY

With over three million service members having deployed as a result of the lengthy conflicts in Iraq and Afghanistan and a shortage in available Veterans Administration (VA) services, there is an urgent need for community-based care for our veterans. The goals of this chapter are to provide Christian therapists with a brief overview of the wounds sustained by service members in the recent conflicts in the Middle East, to illustrate the psychological and spiritual consequences of the deployment cycle for service members and their families, to describe community-based approaches to care, and to provide guidance to Christian therapists caring for these veterans.

GLOBAL WAR ON TERRORISM AND THE IRAQ/
AFGHANISTAN/SYRIAN CONFLICTS

The Global War on Terror (GWOT) began as a response to the terrorist attacks on the United States on September 11, 2001. Operation Iraqi Freedom (OIF), Operation New Dawn (OND) in Iraq, Operation Enduring Freedom (OEF) in Afghanistan, and Operation Inherent Resolve (OIR) in Iraq and Syria have resulted in the deployment of almost three million US service members over the course of almost two decades of conflict.

Because of the extended nature of the conflicts in Iraq and Afghanistan and the smaller, volunteer force, troops frequently deploy more than once, have longer deployments than initially intended, and spend much less time stateside between deployments than in previous conflicts (Tanielian & Jaycox, 2008). According to a 2017 report, approximately 7,000 service members had died, and 53,000 had been wounded in action (Department of Defense, 2017). The number of long-term physical and psychological injuries is staggering. Improvements in medical technology and health care have resulted in much better survival rates than in previous conflicts, but frequently the survivors carry the psychological, moral, and spiritual wounds of war. In the first quarter of 2015, over 660,000 veterans who sought treatment were diagnosed with a mental illness, with countless others yet to seek help (Epidemiology Program, Post-Deployment Health Group, Office of Public Health, Veterans Health Administration, & Department of Veterans Affairs, 2015).

WHAT IS COMBAT TRAUMA?

Deployment to a combat zone inevitably results in repeated and chronic exposure to many stressors and potentially traumatic experiences. Potentially traumatic experiences can include exposure to firing a weapon, being attacked by the enemy, witnessing injury or death, or proximity to explosions. The aftermath of direct combat (e.g., handling of bodies or remains, dealing with prisoners of war, or witnessing the destruction of homes and villages) can be potentially equally traumatic and may contribute more to spiritual/existential injuries (National Center for Post-Traumatic Stress Disorder & Department of Veterans Affairs, 2004).

Sammons and Batten (2008) assert that in addition to witnessing potentially traumatizing events, service members deployed to Iraq and Afghanistan experience significant psychological stress as a result of the unconventional nature of the recent conflicts. The enemies often are indistinguishable from civilians, and they commonly use improvised explosive devices (IEDs) that are difficult to detect and are highly lethal. La Bash, Vogt, King, and King (2009) report that US troops are, therefore, exposed to the atrocities of insurgency-style warfare where they may be forced to decide between killing potentially innocent civilians and risking the safety of themselves or their units. Because there is no distinct front line, troops are constantly at risk for personal injury. Deployment to the conflicts in Iraq and Afghanistan often means having to maintain a perpetual state of vigilance in order to survive (La Bash et al., 2009). The combination of the acute stressors of combat and the chronic stressors of deployment, such as sleep deprivation, heat, hunger, separation from family, and concerns about the home front, often result in psychological and spiritual injuries for those serving.

PSYCHOLOGICAL SEQUELAE OF COMBAT STRESS

The psychological sequelae of combat stress appear to begin during deployment. Felker, Hawkins, Dobie, Gutierrez, and McFall (2008) screened service members who presented for initial mental health care between May and July of 2005 while they were still in theater[1] at a US military hospital in Kuwait. The researchers found that 34% of their sample (*N* = 296) suffered from adjustment disorders, 32% from depressive disorders, 12% from posttraumatic stress disorder (PTSD), and another 13% suffered from other anxiety disorders including acute stress disorder. Additionally, 18% of the sample participants screened positive for two or more Axis I disorders as defined by the DSM-IV-TR (American Psychiatric Association, 2000).

Other studies have attempted to estimate the number of service members with diagnosable psychological injuries postdeployment. One large mental health screening (*N* = 88,235) conducted by the Department of Defense indicated that over 20% of active-duty soldiers and over 42% of reserve soldiers required mental health treatment on return from Iraq (Milliken, Auchterlonie, & Hoge, 2007). Specifically, the study found that service members were returning from combat with positive screens for PTSD, major depression, alcohol misuse, and other mental health problems. Lapierre, Schwegler, and LaBauve (2007) found that 44% of the soldiers who returned from the OIF and OEF conflicts reported clinically significant levels of posttraumatic stress symptoms, depressive symptoms, or both. McDevitt-Murphy et al. (2010) found that 39.1% of OIF/OEF veterans screened positive for PTSD and 26.5% screened positive for hazardous drinking. Another large study of OIF/OEF veterans who were seen at VA health care facilities found that 25% received mental health diagnoses with 56% of those patients being diagnosed with two or more distinct comorbid conditions (Seal, Bertenthal, Miner, Sen, & Marmar, 2007).

PREDICTORS OF PSYCHOLOGICAL SEQUELAE FOLLOWING DEPLOYMENT

In addition to the location of the deployment, several other factors are likely to influence the extent and timing of the development of mental health symptoms—specifically, reservist/National Guard status, concerns about the home front during deployment, and relational stressors experienced during reintegration.

Reservist/National Guard status. National Guard and Reserve members have comprised approximately 40% of the US OIF/OEF troops (Shea, Vujanovic, Mansfield, Sevin, & Liu, 2010), and several studies have suggested that they are at higher risk than active-duty service members for developing mental health problems following deployment (Lane, Hourani, Bray, & Williams, 2012; Browne et al., 2007; Schwartz, Doebbeling, Merchant, & Barret, 1997; Stretch, Marlowe, Wright, & Bliese, 1996).

While the exact reason why reservists and National Guard members seem to return with greater psychological symptoms is speculative, Friedman (2005) asserts

---

[1]The term *theater* is a commonly used abbreviation for the "theater of war," which is defined by Schading (2007, p. 246) as being "the area of air, land, and water that is, or may become, directly involved in the conduct of war."

that the difference may be, in part, due to the many ways reservists and National Guard members are distinct from active-duty troops. Unlike active-duty troops, members of the National Guard and reservists are civilians and therefore are not immersed in military culture. They do not live on military bases and therefore often have less access to the support and family services than active-duty troops have (Friedman, 2006). Additionally, their expectations surrounding their terms of service differ from that of active-duty troops; they did not volunteer for full-time military service, and they may not have expected they would be deployed to a war zone. Their training is less intensive than that of their active-duty counterparts and may not equip them as well for the stressors of combat (La Bash et al., 2009). They also may be less equipped than active-duty personnel to deal with the stress of being separated from their families, because they typically experience fewer military commitments (Vogt, Samper, King, King, & Martin, 2008). Browne et al. (2007) also assert that the contexts in which reserve forces deploy are different from active-duty forces; they often deploy as individuals and have limited prior knowledge of or relationship to their comrades, resulting in decreased unit cohesion. Because of the limited amount of time they are given to prepare to deploy, reserve troops also may be more likely to be asked to serve in various capacities within theater for which they have not received specific training (Browne et al., 2007).

National Guard members and reservists also often report greater problems at home during deployment and greater difficulty with reintegration than do active-duty troops (Browne et al., 2007; Vogt et al., 2008). This may be due to the differing stressors that National Guardsmen and reservists face because of both demographic differences and differences that result from being civilians with occupational commitments other than the military. Demographically, guardsmen/reservists are often older (Browne et al., 2007; Kehle et al., 2010; Vasterling et al., 2010) and more likely to be married (Vasterling et al., 2010), resulting in the potential for greater disturbance within the family unit. Additionally, many may have lost their civilian jobs or may fear a pending job loss following return from deployment (Doyle & Peterson, 2005; La Bash et al., 2009). Because they often return home to communities that are not immersed in military culture, their family, friends, and coworkers may have little understanding of what the reservists/guardsmen may have faced while deployed (Browne et al., 2007), which can result in an increased sense of isolation for the service member (Doyle & Peterson, 2005).

Home front concerns. Concerns about finances, parenting issues, and other worries about loved ones back home have always been a priority for service members during deployments. During the recent conflicts, however, communication with families and friends has dramatically increased as a result of improved technology such as email and cellular phones. Although increased communication can be uplifting, this may also increase the service member's concern and worry about home front issues while concurrently increasing their sense of helplessness because of the distance of deployment (La Bash et al., 2009).

Not only are home front issues a risk factor for stress during a deployment; they may also be a predictor of postdeployment adjustment issues. Vogt et al. (2008) found that concerns about family/relationship disruptions significantly predicted posttraumatic stress symptomatology in Gulf War I combat veterans ($ES = .42$, $p < .05$). Similarly, home front concerns also appear to be associated with negative outcomes in OIF/OEF veterans. Booth-Kewley, Larson, Highfill-McRoy, Garland, and Gaskin (2010) conducted a large ($N = 1,569$) study of Marines who deployed to Iraq or Afghanistan from 2002 to 2007 and found that deployment-related stressors such as family concerns resulted in a stronger association with screening positive for PTSD than did combat exposure. Vasterling et al. (2010) also showed a positive correlation between the home front concerns experienced during deployment and the severity of PTSD symptomatology. Additionally, postdeployment life stressors such as reintegration issues were correlated with the PTSD severity of National Guard soldiers in this sample (Vasterling et al., 2010).

Relational concerns. Upon return home, service members frequently encounter various reintegration problems. Sayer et al. (2010) surveyed 1,226 OIF/OEF veterans who were receiving VA medical services and found that an estimated 40% of combat veterans in their sample reported "some" to "extreme" difficulty in social functioning, productivity, community involvement, and self-care domains within the 30 days prior to completing the survey. Difficulties in social relationships, such as getting along with family members and friends, were particularly common. This finding is not surprising in light of other publications that have suggested that military deployment and exposure to combat trauma can have significant adverse consequences for family intimacy and nurturance of children (McFarlane, 2009) and marital relationships (Goff, Crow, Reisbig, & Hamilton, 2007; Solomon, Dekel, & Zerach, 2008).

Not only do the service members have difficulty in familial relationships during reintegration, but frequently their family members also experience similar challenges. During deployment, it is often necessary for family members to shift roles and take on new responsibilities, such as managing the household finances. Upon their return, the service members may expect familial duties to resume "as normal," whereas their partners may or may not want to relinquish the roles they acquired during their loved ones' deployments. This renegotiation of familial roles is necessary following a deployment and can cause relational discord if not managed well.

MORAL AND SPIRITUAL SEQUELAE OF COMBAT STRESS

The moral and spiritual consequences of war have garnered increasing attention in recent years. Faith and spirituality can provide resilience to psychological distress in combat veterans (Bormann, Liu, Thorp, & Lang, 2012) and an interpretive framework with which to make meaning of suffering (Fontana & Rosenheck, 2005; Park, 2010). However, witnessing or perpetrating human suffering, injustice, death, and morally ambiguous scenarios can fracture service members' moral and spiritual frameworks and hinder their abilities to make meaning following deployment (Drescher, Foy, Kelly, & Leshner, 2011; Litz et al., 2009). Moral injury has been explained as an array of possible symptoms, including anger, demoralization, poor self-care, shame, and guilt (Gray et al., 2012; Maguen et al., 2011), associated with activity or inactivity that violates a service member's core values and beliefs (Litz et al., 2009). These experiences can include killing, atrocities, disproportionate violence, betrayal by leadership, harm to civilians, and the inability to prevent harm. These moral injuries have been shown to be better predictors of PTSD than more conventional life-threat stressors (Litz et al., 2009). Further, as many espouse faith in God as their primary source of meaning, one's faith can also become a casualty of traumatic experiences of war (Fontana & Rosenheck, 2004).

Guilt and shame. As veterans struggle to make meaning of traumatic experiences, particularly those that violate their consciences, they may feel guilt and/or shame over their actual or perceived roles. In the psychological literature, guilt has often been associated with postdeployment psychopathology and therefore viewed as dysfunctional (Resick, Nishith, Weaver, Astin, & Feuer, 2002). Often guilt can be misplaced, such as feeling guilty for surviving an attack from enemy forces when other members of the unit were not so fortunate (termed "survivor guilt"). However, guilt also promotes prosocial behaviors, reparative actions, reintegration, and posttraumatic growth (Dekel, Mamon, Solomon, Lanman, & Dishy, 2016). Although *guilt* and *shame* are often used interchangeably, there seems to be a major distinction: with guilt the veteran feels remorse for the action, whereas with shame the veteran makes global and stable negative attributions about the self (e.g., "I am unworthy of love"; Nazarov et al., 2015). Often veterans return home from deployment feeling ashamed and isolate from the communities and people that once provided them with a pathway toward reintegration and self-worth.

Grief. Significant loss also often occurs during combat deployments, both for service members and for their families. Service members may experience intense grief over the loss of a comrade, as the relationships within a unit often become some of the closest social relationships in the service member's life. Upon returning home, service members may experience grief over the many things they have missed while they were away, such as children growing up, significant events in the lives of their loved ones, loss of civilian employment, friends moving away, and transitions within familial roles and relationships. Family members also experience significant grief throughout the deployment cycle because they often feel abandoned by their military family member during difficult life circumstances. Reintegration presents additional sources of grief for family members as they adjust to the physical and emotional injuries that are now a part of their loved ones' lives.

Implications for faith. An aphorism is that "faith is found or lost in a foxhole," and it is true that combat presents many situations that frequently challenge a service member's previously held beliefs or expose a lack of spiritual development. Whereas some service members may turn to religion for support, others may begin to doubt how a loving God could allow such atrocities. Significant trauma can also lead to negative consequences if veterans are unable to make sense of their experiences within the context of their spiritual beliefs and instead feel abandoned or punished by God. Combat trauma may thus result in a loss of core spiritual values, or veterans may feel a sense of estrangement from God (Underwood & Teresi, 2002). On the other hand, veterans may also describe that although they believe in a forgiving and loving God, the only way for them to atone for their wrongdoings is to reject forgiveness and to punish themselves.

In Sayer et al.'s (2010) large survey, which sought to assess the reintegration needs of Iraq and Afghanistan veterans, 42% of OIF/OEF veterans reported that they had lost touch with their spirituality or were experiencing difficulty in their religious life. This disruption in spirituality was common both in veterans who met the criteria for PTSD (67%) and in those with negative PTSD screens (25%). Existential difficulty, such as having trouble finding meaning or a sense of purpose in life, was also reported by 42% of this group. In the same study, Sayer et al. (2010) also sought to understand the treatment interests of OIF/OEF combat veterans, and 32% of those surveyed indicated that they would be interested in receiving spiritual counseling during reintegration. In addition, in a large study of Vietnam veterans, Fontana and Rosenheck (2004) concluded that many of the veterans seeking mental health services were doing so out of guilt and spiritual distress, not PTSD.

CURRENT APPROACH TO MILITARY MENTAL HEALTH CARE

Currently, OIF/OEF veterans have two primary options through which they may receive care. First, the Department of Defense (DoD) operates a military health system that provides care for active-duty military and their family members, eligible military retirees, and some reserve-component members (Burnam, Meredith, Tanielian, & Jaycox, 2009). Primarily, these services are delivered on military bases and in clinics where active-duty members are given priority in receiving treatment. DoD services are supplemented through partnerships with civilian providers who accept TRICARE, the medical insurance plan offered by the military (Burnam et al., 2009). Additionally, the Veterans Health Administration (VHA) operates 1,233 hospitals and outpatient clinics nationwide to serve eligible veterans and some active-duty service members (U.S. Department of Veterans Affairs, 2017).

VETERANS AFFAIRS INTERVENTIONS FOR PTSD AND MORAL INJURY

Although PTSD became an official diagnostic label in 1980, the VA began to emphasize its treatment during the Global War on Terror because of increasing rates of suicide. Two primary evidence-based therapies that have been strongly endorsed by the VA for PTSD treatment are prolonged exposure (PE) and cognitive processing therapy (CPT). PE (Foa, Hembree, & Rothbaum, 2007) is primarily a behavioral intervention that targets both the intrusive memories of the traumatic event through repeated imaginal exposures and the learned avoidant responses through in vivo exposure homework assignments. CPT (Resick & Schnicke, 1993) is a 12-week manualized treatment focused on the maladaptive beliefs experienced during and after traumatic experiences that affect emotions and behaviors. Although it was originally developed for sexual abuse survivors, it has been adapted for military trauma. Despite widespread dissemination and a mandate that veterans have access to these therapies, some VA researchers and clinicians have questioned whether this may be premature. They have criticized high dropout rates, limited research, doubts about real improvement in function, and limited flexibility to address the variability and complexity of posttraumatic responses (Steenkamp & Litz, 2014).

Eye movement desensitization and reprocessing (EMDR; Carlson, Chemtob, Rusnak, Hedlund, & Muraoka, 1998) has been strongly recommended and is being used by many providers within the VA (Department of Veterans Affairs & Department of Defense, 2010). It has demonstrated effectiveness for treatment of PTSD in soldiers (Carlson et al., 1998) and involves less focus on homework, often a deterrent for veterans seeking treatment. The VA continues to research new areas of treatment, including mindfulness and interpersonal interventions, and has placed increasing emphasis on using chaplains in PTSD treatment, signifying recognition of the spiritual injuries that often accompany PTSD.

With this increasing emphasis on the spiritual impact of war, new interventions and programs are being developed in an attempt to assess and treat moral injuries and build spiritual resilience. One step taken was the creation of a research and education center for Mental Health Integration for Chaplain Services. The purpose of this program was to fund research targeting best clinical practices for integrating faith and mental health for veterans and to provide training and certifications for chaplains to better embed them into mental health teams across the VA.

In addition, since the construct of moral injury surfaced, researchers and clinicians have been developing a variety of interventions, a few of which are gaining supportive data. Adaptive Disclosure (Litz, Lebowitz, Gray, & Nash, 2015), an eight-session manualized therapy for PTSD, was designed to target not only life-threat but also moral injury and traumatic loss. Combining imaginal exposure with a variety of cognitive and experiential interventions, the goal of the therapy is to identify unhelpful beliefs so that they may be examined, to accept emotional experience, and to reclaim one's own sense of goodness. Another cognitive behavioral intervention, Impact of Killing in War (Maguen & Burkman, 2014), is a six-session module to be used after completing trauma-focused therapy and provides the veteran opportunity to identify his or her beliefs about killing others in combat, to work toward self-forgiveness, and to create an action plan for making amends.

These therapies emphasize changing cognitions about one's personal wrongdoings. To promote further healing, self-forgiveness, restoration of a sense of community belonging and self-worth, and development of one's faith are likely to be critical elements for many veterans with PTSD. Unfortunately, many of these goals fall outside the scope of typical targets of VA-sponsored interventions. Therefore, it is essential that community-based interventions seek to address these unmet needs.

FAITH-BASED COMMUNITY INTERVENTIONS

In addition to targeting aspects of reintegration such as self-forgiveness, community-based interventions are optimal for addressing some of the barriers that often result in underutilization of DoD and VA mental health services by our veterans. One possible barrier is the concern of stigma associated with mental health diagnosis/treatment for military members. Many service members are hesitant to seek treatment through the traditional military venues because they fear consequences that may come as a result of having a mental-health-related problem on their military record. For example, they could fear that their ability to be promoted would be affected (Burnam et al., 2009). The military culture so greatly esteems strength that it may perpetuate the belief that any symptom is a sign of weakness; thus, service members may also fear judgment from their peers if they seek mental health treatment (Hoge et al., 2004).

Another significant barrier to veterans receiving mental health care is geographic distance from treatment facilities (Druss & Rosenheck, 1997; Seal et al., 2010). Many service members live too far from a VA hospital to be able to receive the necessary mental health care. Reservists and National Guard members are especially likely to reside in remote locations and to have difficulty accessing services (Doyle & Peterson, 2005).

Faith-based organizations (FBOs) are uniquely suited to address these barriers because they are distinct from the military system and they are ubiquitous in most communities, rural and urban. In 2004, by executive order, the VA Center for Faith-Based and Community Initiatives was established to minimize regulatory obstacles to those providing care for returning veterans. Understanding the need for community reintegration, especially in regard to communities of faith, 27% of religious congregations have reported hosting a group that supported veterans and their families within the last 12 months (Werber, Derose, Rudnick, Harrell, & Naranjo, 2015).

Hometown Support Program. One example of a program seeking to maximize community-based support for service members and their families throughout the deployment cycle is the Hometown Support Program through HEROES Care. Because it is outside the military system, the program has special relevance for those service members who are hesitant to pursue mental health care because of stigma. Additionally, because the Hometown Support Program is community-based, it is ideal for the National Guard and reserve service members who generally have less access to military resources and who may depend more heavily on community resources due to geographic proximity. Finally, because the program includes a faith-based component, any spiritual needs that may arise during the deployment cycle can be addressed.

The Hometown Support Program is the result of the combined efforts of several nonprofit civilian organizations committed to meeting the growing needs of service members and their families. They have sought to raise up "an army to serve an army"—hundreds of Hometown Support Volunteers who serve military families with the hopes of preventing, mitigating, and alleviating symptoms of psychological, moral, and spiritual injury.

In order to become a Hometown Support Volunteer, an individual must first become a Stephen Minister (www.stephenministries.org) by satisfactorily completing 50 hours of Stephen Ministry training for lay caregivers in areas such as the art of listening, relating gently and firmly, maintaining boundaries, confidentiality, making referrals, working with individuals who are suicidal, and ministering to those experiencing divorce, grief, or other family crises. The extensive network of Stephen Ministry congregations (over 10,000 congregations across all 50 states) provides the core volunteers who are eligible to become Hometown Support Volunteers.

In addition to the 50 hour Stephen Ministry training, a Hometown Support Volunteer must then complete eight hours of training offered by HEROES Care (http://heroescare.org/), which serves as the administrative agency for the Hometown Support Program. The goal of this secondary training is to provide the

Stephen Minister with information regarding the unique nature of providing lay care to a military service member and his or her family. Topics covered include the structure and composition of US Forces, emotional consequences of the deployment cycle, how children may respond to the deployment cycle, posttraumatic stress disorder, traumatic grief, alcohol and drug abuse, sexual trauma, and secondary trauma to family members (Shultz, 2008).

Once a Stephen Minister has completed the required training to become a Hometown Support Volunteer (HSV), he or she is assigned a military family to serve. In compliance with the requirements of Stephen Ministries, the HSV is always matched by gender to the care receiver, who could be the service member or the service member's spouse. The HSV will address the family's physical, emotional, and spiritual needs by contacting the care receiver on a weekly, biweekly, or monthly basis, depending on the preference of the service member and family. HSVs are encouraged to provide face-to-face care or communicate with the care receiver electronically through telephone, email, or Skype based on the care receiver's preference and geographic proximity.

The responsibilities and duties of an HSV are distinctly different from that of a Stephen Minister. In addition to demonstrating human compassion and understanding, which is a standard part of the Stephen Ministry training, the HSV serves as a conduit to resources that can assist the care receiver and family in various hardships that may be encountered throughout the deployment cycle. For example, through regular contact with the care receiver, the HSV may learn of financial needs, home repairs that need to be completed, issues with childcare, or other tangible needs that the family has as a result of the service member's deployment. Through collaboration with the local church congregation that has commissioned the HSV and HEROES Care, these tangible needs often can be met. Additionally, because the HSV is supported by a local church congregation, if the care receiver is amenable, he or she can receive assistance from the HSV's congregation in the form of friendship, letters of encouragement, prayer, or more tangible forms of support such as yard work, minor home repairs, or babysitting.

HSVs also clearly differ from Stephen Ministers in that they must agree to respect and promote the free exercise of whatever religious beliefs the military service member and his or her family members hold. HSVs are serving members of the US Armed Forces; therefore, they cannot proselytize. Specifically, HSVs cannot try to convert the person to the HSV's own religion or try to induce the person to participate in or join the HSV's faith congregation. If the military service member freely expresses interest in spiritual ministry from the HSV, then the HSV is free to provide prayer or coordinate transportation to worship services, but these requests must be fully initiated by the care receiver.

HSVs are trained to be aware of when their lay caregiving skills may need professional bolstering. Through a partnership with Give an Hour (www.giveanhour.org), the Hometown Support Program offers free, professional counseling to care receivers and their family members once a mental health need is identified. Give an Hour is a network of over 7,000 licensed mental health professionals located throughout the country—including psychologists, counselors, marriage and family therapists, psychiatrists, psychiatric nurse practitioners, and social workers—who have agreed to volunteer one hour each week to serve veterans and their families. Providers offer free care for individuals, couples, and families and treat a variety of presenting concerns, such as PTSD, depression, anxiety, substance abuse, traumatic brain injuries, bereavement, and relationship or intimacy concerns. Because these are private therapists who are not affiliated with the military in any way, service members and their families can receive services without any fear of negative effects on their military career.

With the wide-reaching presence of Stephen Ministry and Give an Hour, the Hometown Support Program was developed as a national strategy with the intention of the program being launched in every state. Currently, the Hometown Support Program has expanded to 25 states. A total of 2,843 HSVs have been trained in 579 "Outposts" or local congregations. To our knowledge, at least 115 family members or single soldiers have taken advantage of referrals through the Hometown Support Program to Give an Hour mental health providers, and 30 suicides have been averted.

The following are some examples of other programs that have been developed to support returning veterans and the unique spiritual and relational obstacles that face them today:

- *Coming Home Project.* This California-based program with Zen Buddhist roots offers multi-day family retreats, workshops, and a network of psychotherapists and chaplains to provide psychological, relational, and spiritual support throughout deployment and reintegration. http://coming homeproject.net/

- *Cru Military.* Cru (formerly Campus Crusade for Christ) has developed a ministry to veterans and their families with particular emphasis on providing resources for military families and helping them to connect with Christian communities. As with Cru, much of the focus is on the development and resilience of one's faith during and after deployment. http://crumilitary.org/

- *MilitaryBeliever.com.* This connection-hub website offers service members, veterans, and families the ability to search for churches and ministries that have advertised a specific emphasis on ministry for veterans and families.

The site also offers various social-networking options for connecting with other like-minded veterans. http://militarybeliever.com/

- *Military Outreach USA.* This FBO has created a network of congregations and organizations that have committed to caring for the military community. It offers resources and training for these FBOs to offer assistance with particular concerns of moral injury and homelessness. http://militaryoutreachusa.org/

- *Soul Repair Center.* Based out of Brite Divinity School, the Soul Repair Center is a formal research and educational center focused solely on assisting veterans with PTSD and moral injuries. They have produced their own publications, training conferences, and a full-length film, *Honoring the Code*, a documentary about the development and healing of moral injury. www.brite .edu/programs/soul-repair/

- *Samaritan's Purse: Operation Heal Our Patriots.* This FBO has narrowed its focus to primarily offering marital support for wounded veterans and their spouses in the form of a week-long marriage enrichment retreat. The retreat is biblically based, offers the services of chaplains, and provides opportunities for refreshment and reconnection for partners. www.samaritanspurse. org/what-we-do/about-operation-heal-our-patriots/

- *Soldier's Heart.* This unique organization offers clear spiritual perspective on PTSD and moral injury in training clinicians, clergy, and caregivers around the country. In addition, it provides domestic and international "healing retreats" and "reconciliation journeys" in attempts to heal participants from spiritually injurious military experiences. Emphasis is placed on storytelling, and civilians are invited to "witness" the stories of these veterans so that the community shares the burdens of one another with the ultimate goal of community forgiveness and restoration. www.soldiersheart.net/

TIPS FOR PRACTICING CHRISTIAN COUNSELORS AND PSYCHOTHERAPISTS

For those who may be in situations where you are currently able to provide community support, spiritual counseling, and/or mental health services to service members or their family members throughout the deployment cycle, please consider the following key points:

- *Each service member and each deployment is unique.* Although some experiences and emotions are common among combat veterans and their families, each service member is unique. Therefore, each one will respond to combat stress in different ways. Each family member also will respond differently depending on the nature of his or her relationship to the service member and developmental level. Additionally, the service member or family member likely will experience each deployment differently; what a person felt during the first deployment may not be indicative of his or her experience during a second deployment. Therefore, do not assume that you understand the service member's experience or the experience of the family members. Instead, ask open-ended questions and seek understanding.

- *Encourage the family to seek social support.* Community support from extended family members, neighbors, friends, and churches is crucial for family members during a deployment, especially for reservists and National Guard members who are not embedded in a military community. This will decrease isolation and will help foster the meeting of physical, emotional, and spiritual needs during the service member's absence. Additionally, during reintegration, support from the Christian community is essential if service members are to heal from their moral and spiritual injuries.

- *It takes time to rebuild familial relationships following a deployment.* During a deployment, both the service member and the family members left behind will change. Encourage military families to go slowly and intentionally spend time getting to know each other again and reconnect in ways that acknowledge the new roles established within the family system. Families should be open to service members talking about their combat experience; however, they should also understand if their loved one is not initially willing to do so. While most service members and their families are able to establish a new equilibrium eventually, others may have difficulty and need to seek professional help. Encourage the family to be patient; this process may take time.

- *Spend time establishing the relationship before encouraging the service member to share traumatic experiences.* Deployments develop intensely close bonds within units that are difficult to replicate in the civilian world. Often upon discharge from military or end of deployment, service members can feel disconnected, isolated, and mistrustful of those who have not shared their experiences. Further, talking about traumatic experiences with others can feel particularly vulnerable and shaming. It is critical that the clinician honor this vulnerability by allowing the therapeutic relationship to develop and prioritizing it over any structure or particular intervention.

- *Assess for changes in faith.* For any work with returning service members, it will be important to assess for their perceptions of God, place in their congregation, or changes in beliefs. Although these crises of faith may engender a growth and a deepening of faith, they may also lead to hopelessness, depression, loss of meaning, and even self-harming or handicapping. Allowing service members to explore these changes without correction or criticism may be an especially helpful service that the clinician can provide in lieu of home congregations, where they may be met with some perceived judgment.

- *An appropriate level of guilt can facilitate healing.* Especially for Christian service members, guilt serves to make meaning of personal wrongdoing, to build empathy for others, and to move them toward redemption and their faith communities. It may be helpful to assist service members in determining whether they are shouldering an accurate level of responsibility. However, minimizing or challenging someone's level of guilt will often serve to make it stronger and keep the person from naturally working through it.

- *Encourage service members to invite others into their stories.* Sociologist Brené Brown (2012) defines shame as "the intensely painful feeling or experience of believing that we are flawed and therefore unworthy of love and belonging" (p. 69). This shame leads service members toward isolation and disconnection unless trusted others are there to witness their stories with honor and acceptance. However, being vulnerable and disclosing combat experiences is difficult for most service members. It may be easier for them to share these stories initially with a mental health professional, with clergy, or with another service member.

CONCLUSION

As Christian counselors and psychotherapists, we are uniquely suited to provide hope to families coping with the emotional and spiritual injuries that often result from combat stress and trauma. Veterans' stories of suffering, violation, and shame are heavily defended because for them they represent weakness and failure. Yet as Paul encouraged in 2 Corinthians 12:9: "But he said to me, 'My grace is sufficient for you, for my power is made perfect in weakness.' Therefore, I will boast all the more gladly of my weaknesses, so that the power of Christ may rest upon me" (ESV). Sharing in these stories is an honor as we contribute to veterans' pathways to healing and community.

REFERENCES

American Psychiatric Association (2000). *Diagnostic and statistical manual of mental disorders* (4th ed., text rev.). Washington, DC: Author.

Booth-Kewley, S., Larson, G., Highfill-McRoy, R. M., Garland, C., & Gaskin, T. (2010). Correlates of posttraumatic stress disorder symptoms in Marines back from war. *Journal of Traumatic Stress, 23*(1), 69-77.

Bormann, J. E., Liu, L., Thorp, S. R., & Lang, A. J. (2012) Spiritual wellbeing mediates PTSD change in veterans with military-related PTSD. *International Journal of Behavioral Medicine, 19*, 496-502.

Brown, B. (2012). *Daring greatly: How the courage to be vulnerable transforms the way we live, love, parent, and lead.* New York, NY: Gotham Books.

Browne, T., Hull, L., Horn, O., Jones, M., Murphy, D., Fear, N., . . . Hotopf, M. (2007). Explanations for the increase in mental health problems in UK reserve forces who have served in Iraq. *British Journal of Psychiatry, 190*, 484-89.

Burnam, M., Meredith, L., Tanielian, T., & Jaycox, L. (2009). Mental health care for Iraq and Afghanistan war veterans. *Health Affairs, 28*(3), 771-82.

Carlson, J. G., Chemtob, C. M., Rusnak, K., Hedlund, N. L., & Muraoka, M. Y. (1998). Eye movement desensitization and reprocessing (EMDR) treatment for combat-related posttraumatic stress disorder. *Journal of Traumatic Stress, 11*, 3-24.

Dekel, S., Mamon, D., Solomon, Z., Lanman, O., & Dishy, G. (2016). Can guilt lead to psychological growth following trauma exposure? *Psychiatry Research, 236*, 196-98.

Department of Defense. (2017). *U.S. Casualty Status.* Retrieved from www.defense.gov/casualty.pdf

Department of Veterans Affairs & Department of Defense (2010). *VA/DoD clinical practice guideline for management of post-traumatic stress.* Retrieved from www.healthquality.va.gov/guidelines/MH/ptsd/cpg_PTSD-full-201011612.PDF

Doyle, M. E., & Peterson, K.A. (2005). Re-entry and reintegration: Returning home after combat. *Psychiatric Quarterly, 76*(4), 361-70.

Drescher, K., Foy, D., Kelly, C., & Leshner, A. (2011). An exploration of the viability and usefulness of the construct of moral injury in war veterans. *Traumatology, 17*, 8-13.

Druss, B., & Rosenheck, R. (1997). Use of medical services by veterans with mental disorders. *Psychosomatics: Journal of Consultation Liaison Psychiatry, 38*(5), 451-58.

Epidemiology Program, Post-Deployment Health Group, Office of Public Health, Veterans Health Administration, & Department of Veterans Affairs (2014, March). *Analysis of VA healthcare utilization among Operation Enduring Freedom (OEF), Operation Iraqi Freedom (OIF), and Operation New Dawn (OND) veterans: Cumulative from 1st Qtr FY 2002 through 1st Qtr FY 2014.* Retrieved from www.publichealth.va.gov/docs/epidemiology/healthcare-utilization-report-fy2014-qtr1.pdf

Felker, B., Hawkins, E., Dobie, D., Gutierrez, J., & McFall, M. (2008). Characteristics of deployed Operation Iraqi Freedom military personnel who seek mental health care. *Military Medicine, 173*(2), 155-58.

Foa, E. B., Hembree, E. A., & Rothbaum, B. O. (2007). *Prolonged exposure therapy for PTSD: Emotional processing of traumatic experiences.* New York, NY: Oxford University Press.

Fontana, A., & Rosenheck, R. (2004). Trauma, change in strength of religious faith, and mental health service use among veterans treated for PTSD. *Journal of Nervous and Mental Disease, 192*, 579-84.

Fontana, A., & Rosenheck, R. (2005). The role of loss of meaning in the pursuit of treatment for posttraumatic stress disorder. *Journal of Traumatic Stress, 18*, 133-36.

Friedman, M. (2005). Veterans' mental health in the wake of war. *New England Journal of Medicine, 352*(13), 1287-90.

Friedman, M. J. (2006). Posttraumatic stress disorder among military returnees from Afghanistan and Iraq. *American Journal of Psychiatry, 163*, 586-93.

Goff, B. N., Crow, J., Reisbig, A., & Hamilton, S. (2007). The impact of individual trauma symptoms of deployed soldiers on relationship satisfaction. *Journal of Family Psychology, 21*(3), 344-53.

Gray, M. J., Schorr, Y., Nash, W., Lebowitz, L., Amidon, A., Lansing, A., . . . Litz, B. T. (2012). Adaptive disclosure: An open trial of a novel exposure-based intervention for service members with combat-related psychological stress injuries. *Behavior Therapy, 43*, 407-15.

Hoge, C. W., Castro, C. A., Messer, S. C., McGurk, D., Cotting, D. I., & Koffman, R. L. (2004). Combat duty in Iraq and Afghanistan, mental health problems, and barriers to care. *New England Journal of Medicine, 351*, 13-22.

Kehle, S. M., Polusny, M. A., Murdoch, M., Erbes, C. R., Arbisi, P. A., Thuras, P., & Meis, L. A. (2010). Early mental health treatment-seeking among U.S. National Guard soldiers deployed to Iraq. *Journal of Traumatic Stress, 23*(1), 33-40.

La Bash, H., Vogt, D., King, L., & King, D. (2009). Deployment stressors of the Iraq war: Insights from the mainstream media. *Journal of Interpersonal Violence, 24*(2), 231-58.

Lane, M. E., Hourani, L. L., Bray, R. M., & Williams, J. (2012). Prevalence of perceived stress and mental health indicators among reserve-component and active-duty military personnel. *American Journal of Public Health, 102*(6), 1213-20.

Lapierre, C., Schwegler, A., & LaBauve, B. (2007). Posttraumatic stress and depression symptoms in soldiers returning from combat operations in Iraq and Afghanistan. *Journal of Traumatic Stress, 20*(6), 933-43.

Litz, B. T., Lebowitz, L., Gray, M. J., & Nash, W. P. (2016). *Adaptive disclosure: A new treatment for military trauma, loss, and moral injury.* New York, NY: Guilford Press.

Litz, B. T., Stein, N., Delaney, E., Lebowitz, L., Nash, W. P., Silva, C., & Maguen, S. (2009). Moral injury and moral repair in war veterans: A preliminary model and intervention strategy. *Clinical Psychology Review, 29*, 695-706.

Maguen, S., & Burkman, K. (2014). *Killing in war and moral injury: Research and clinical implications.* Invited lecture presented at the 17th Annual VA Psychology Leadership Conference, San Antonio, TX.

Maguen, S., Vogt, D. S., King, L. A., King, D. W., Litz, B. T., Knight, S. J., & Marmar, C. R. (2011). The impact of killing on mental health symptoms in Gulf War veterans. *Psychological Trauma: Theory, Research, Practice, and Policy, 3*, 21-26.

McDevitt-Murphy, M., Williams, J., Bracken, K., Fields, J., Monahan, C., & Murphy, J. (2010). PTSD symptoms, hazardous drinking, and health functioning among U.S. OEF and OIF veterans presenting to primary care. *Journal of Traumatic Stress, 23*(1), 108-11.

McFarlane, A. (2009). Military deployment: The impact on children and family adjustment and the need for care. *Current Opinion in Psychiatry, 22*(4), 369-73.

Milliken, C., Auchterlonie, J., & Hoge, C. (2007). Longitudinal assessment of mental health problems among active and reserve component soldiers returning from the Iraq war. *Journal of the American Medical Association, 298*(18), 2141-48.

National Center for Post-Traumatic Stress Disorder & Department of Veterans Affairs (2004). *Iraq War clinician guide* (2nd ed.). Retrieved from www.ptsd.va.gov/profes sional/manuals/manual-pdf/iwcg/iraq_clinician_guide_v2.pdf

Nazarov, A., Jetly, R., McNeely, H., Kiang, M., Lanius, R., & McKinnon, M. C. (2015). Role of morality in the experience of guilt and shame within the armed forces. *Acta Psychiatrica Scandinavica, 132*, 4-19.

Park, C. L. (2010). Making sense of the meaning literature: An integrative review of meaning making and its effects on adjustment to stressful life events. *Psychological Bulletin, 136*, 257-301.

Ramchand, R., Schell, T., Karney, B., Osilla, K., Burns, R., & Caldarone, L. (2010). Disparate prevalence estimates of PTSD among service members who served in Iraq and Afghanistan: Possible explanations. *Journal of Traumatic Stress, 23*(1), 59-68.

Resick, P. A., Nishith, P., Weaver, T. L., Astin, M. C., & Feuer, C. A. (2002). A comparison of cognitive-processing therapy with prolonged exposure and a waiting condition for the treatment of chronic posttraumatic stress disorder in female rape victims. *Journal of Consulting and Clinical Psychology, 70*, 867-79.

Resick, P. A., & Schnicke, M. K. (1993). *Cognitive processing therapy for rape victims: A treatment manual*. Newbury Park, CA: Sage.

Sammons, M., & Batten, S. (2008). Psychological services for returning veterans and their families: Evolving conceptualizations of the sequelae of war-zone experiences. *Journal of Clinical Psychology, 64*(8), 921-27.

Sayer, N.A., Noorbaloochi, S., Frazier, P., Carlson, K., Gravely, A., & Murdoch, M. (2010). Reintegration problems and treatment interests among Iraq and Afghanistan combat veterans receiving VA medical care. *Psychiatric Services, 61*(6), 589-97.

Schading, B. (2007). *A civilian's guide to the U.S. military: A comprehensive reference to the customs, language, and structure of the armed forces*. Cincinnati, OH: Writer's Digest Books.

Schwartz, D., Doebbeling, B., Merchant, J., & Barret, D. (1997). Self-reported illness and health status among Gulf War veterans: A population-based study. *Journal of the American Medical Association, 277*(3), 238-45. doi:10.1001/jama.277.3.238.

Seal, K. H., Bertenthal, D., Miner, C. R., Sen, S., & Marmar, C. (2007). Bringing the war back home: Mental health disorders among 103,788 US veterans returning from Iraq and Afghanistan seen at Department of Veterans Affairs facilities. *Archives of Internal Medicine, 167,* 476-82.

Seal, K. H., Maguen, S., Cohen, B., Gima, K. S., Metzler, T. J., Ren, L., Bertenthal, D., & Marmar, C. R. (2010). VA mental health services utilization in Iraq and Afghanistan veterans in the first year of receiving new mental health diagnoses. *Journal of Traumatic Stress, 23*(1), 5-16.

Shea, M., Vujanovic, A., Mansfield, A., Sevin, E., & Liu, F. (2010). Posttraumatic stress disorder symptoms and functional impairment among OEF and OIF National Guard and Reserve veterans. *Journal of Traumatic Stress, 23*(1), 100-107.

Shultz, L. S. (2008). *Caring for service members and their families: A guide for Hometown Support Volunteers.* High Ridge, MO: Operation Homefront.

Solomon, Z., Dekel, R., & Zerach, G. (2008). The relationships between posttraumatic stress symptom clusters and marital intimacy among war veterans. *Journal of Family Psychology, 22*(5), 659-66.

Steenkamp, M. M., & Litz, B. T. (2014). One-size-fits-all approach to PTSD in the VA not supported by the evidence. *American Psychologist, 69,* 706-7.

Stretch, R., Marlowe, D., Wright, K., & Bliese, P. (1996). Post-traumatic stress disorder symptoms among Gulf War veterans. *Military Medicine, 161*(7), 407-10. Retrieved from PsycINFO database

Tanielian, T. & Jaycox, L. H. (Eds.). (2008). *Invisible wounds of war: Psychological and cognitive injuries, their consequences, and services to assist recovery.* Santa Monica, CA: RAND.

Underwood, L. G., & Teresi, J. A. (2002). The Daily Spiritual Experiences Scale: Development, theoretical description, reliability, exploratory factor analysis, and preliminary construct validity using health-related data. *Annals of Behavioral Medicine, 24,* 22-33.

U.S. Department of Veterans Affairs. (2017). Veterans Health Administration: About VHA. Retrieved from www.va.gov/health/aboutVHA.asp

Vasterling, J. J., Proctor, S. P., Friedman, M. J., Hoge, C. W., Heeren, T., King, L. A., & King, D. W. (2010). PTSD symptom increases in Iraq-deployed soldiers: Comparison with nondeployed soldiers and associations with baseline symptoms, deployment experiences, and postdeployment stress. *Journal of Traumatic Stress, 23*(1), 41-51.

Vogt, D. S., Samper, R. E., King, D. W., King, L. A., & Martin, J. A. (2008). Deployment stressors and posttraumatic stress symptomatology: Comparing active duty and National Guard/Reserve personnel from Gulf War I. *Journal of Traumatic Stress, 21*(1), 66-74.

Werber, L., Derose, K. P., Rudnick, M., Harrell, M. H., & Naranjo, D. (2015). Faith-based organizations and veteran reintegration: Enriching the web of support. *RAND Corporation.* Retrieved from www.rand.org/pubs/research_reports/RR931.html

PART FIVE

CONCLUSION

AND APPENDIX

REFLECTIONS ON CHRISTIAN COUNSELING'S
ENGAGEMENT WITH TRAUMA

HEATHER DAVEDIUK GINGRICH AND FRED C. GINGRICH

He turned the desert into pools of water.
He turned the dry and cracked ground into flowing springs
PSALM 107:35 NIRV

Jesus said to her, "I am the resurrection and the life."
JOHN 11:25 NIRV

The course on trauma and abuse that I (Heather) teach is still an elective at our educational institution, as is a course on crisis and disaster counseling. Trauma courses are not usually required parts of the curriculum of APA-accredited psychology programs, nor are they compulsory for CACREP-accredited counseling programs. Why is this when the majority of clinicians' caseloads involve stories of traumatic experiences that drastically affect whatever the clients' presenting problems may be?

WHY IS TRAUMA OFTEN UNRECOGNIZED?

If mental health professionals are not trained to recognize the pervasiveness of trauma or to identify potential trauma symptoms in particular clients, they may remain unaware of the trauma histories of their counselees. If a thorough trauma assessment is not carried out, and it often is not, counselees may not share their trauma with their therapists. Perhaps there is too much shame attached to being a victim for a client to risk revealing what has happened to them. In some cases, clients may be amnestic regarding their trauma so that even if asked, they would deny having experienced trauma. It is also not uncommon for clients who have cognitive awareness of traumatic events to not connect their trauma background to their current emotional, behavioral, and relational symptoms, particularly if the symptoms are not extreme forms of the more familiar DSM-5 posttraumatic symptoms of intrusion, avoidance, or alterations in arousal (American Psychiatric Association [APA], 2013).

In addition, complex trauma survivors (CTSs) may be easily missed, because while the above-mentioned posttraumatic symptoms are inevitably present, other symptoms may be more obvious (Gold, 2000). For example, CTSs often have difficulty regulating affect, which can result in diagnoses of anxiety disorders, depressive disorders, bipolar disorders, impulse control disorders, or personality disorders. They may experience relational difficulties that are expressed as problems with family of origin, parent-child conflict, distress within romantic relationships including sexual dysfunction, or problems with interpersonal and career contexts. Any of the above can contribute to difficulties with day-to-day functioning, which may be evidenced in difficulty obtaining or maintaining employment, problems with time management, and so on. If one of these above symptom areas is what initially brings a trauma survivor into therapy, and the clinician is not aware of the relationship of such symptoms to a history of childhood or other severe trauma, the counselee is unlikely to receive adequate treatment.

THE TRAUMA LENS

Some people within the trauma field have offered alternatives to the current DSM (APA, 2013) and predominant conceptualizations of psychopathology. Ross (2007), for example, has long suggested the usefulness of a trauma lens. In order to develop this perspective, I (Heather) have a colleague who is in the process of examining the relationship of trauma to each of the DSM-5 diagnostic categories.

Another example from the literature makes a similar point. Bradley (2000) identified trauma as one of six factors that explain the development of psychopathology (trauma, abuse, and loss; high anxiety; stress reactivity/temperament; brain dysfunction; attachment difficulties; and sensitivity to expressed emotion and conflict within family contexts). What is striking about this list is that many of these factors, including brain dysfunction, could be rooted in traumatic experience. We know from the brain research that the plasticity of the brain (e.g., Siegel, 2015) means that trauma can damage brain structure and functioning (see chap. 3 in this volume). However, we also know that trauma treatment can positively alter brain morphology. Likewise, other factors mentioned by Bradley such as attachment, anxiety, and familial conflict also are closely tied to a history of trauma. While the trauma lens is increasingly seen as a valuable addition to mental health care, it is difficult to predict how much impact this approach will have on the mental health fields as a whole.

TRAUMA AND TRAUMA-INFORMED FAITH COMMUNITIES

As we reflect on the overall trajectory of this book, we are again drawn to the centrality of the Christian community as a core aspect of Christian faith and counseling. We wonder what the role of the church is in both our faith and our work as counselors, and more specifically the role of the spiritual community in trauma treatment. Blanch (2015) introduced to us the concept of "trauma-informed faith communities." She states, "A *trauma-informed* congregation responds by providing moral leadership, supportive relationships, compassionate presence, and tools for spiritual healing," all qualities that the church has aspired to have throughout history. When members of congregations are educated with respect to trauma symptoms and the process of recovery, Blanch suggests they are better able to provide appropriate care for hurting people. For example, if the root causes of specific behaviors are understood, church members are less likely to be judgmental and better able to listen, which is often what trauma survivors need.

According to Blanch (2015), faith-based communities can play an important role not only in educating their own congregations but also in representing a moral voice to the broader community. She mentions resources that are available for educational purposes, including a special interest group on trauma-informed congregations that is part of the broader ACEs Connection Network (www.acesconnection.com; ACEs is an acronym referring to "adverse childhood experiences"). The goal of this network is to connect people regarding trauma-informed, resilience-building practices.

As Christian counselors we believe that we can play an important advocacy role within our own churches and community networks. Even if our primary calling is to conduct therapy, a broader educational role can potentially have broad ripple effects and have a positive impact on many more people than through our clinical work alone. What spheres of influence could you potentially make use of in this regard?

OUR PLEA AND OUR CHALLENGE

Our hope is that this book has served to open your eyes to the many ways that trauma symptoms can manifest, both those that are typically thought of as trauma-related and those where the trauma connection is less obvious. We trust that you have learned new approaches to treatment that you can apply with your own clients. We also hope that you have a better sense of what the Bible has to offer to you as a Christian counselor as well as to your trauma clients in terms of a more robust view of theodicy and suffering, scriptural precedent for looking at trauma, and ideas for how to incorporate spirituality into trauma counseling.

The following Celtic prayer seems an appropriate way to end a book on trauma treatment, particularly with the expressed desire to be a part of the world's healing.

It is with this aspiration that we press on to respond more compassionately, more knowledgably, and more skillfully to the traumatized people we encounter.

> O Sun behind all suns
> O Soul within all souls
> grant me the grace of the dawn's glory
> grant me the strength of the sun's rays
> that I may be well in my own soul
> and part of the world's healing this day
> that I may be well in my own soul
> and part of the world's healing this day.
> (Newell, 2000, p. 41)

REFERENCES

American Psychiatric Association (2013). *Diagnostic and statistics manual of mental disorders* (5th ed.). Washington, DC: Author.

Blanch, A. (2015, October 23). Growing hope: The healing potential of trauma-informed faith communities. *Church Health Reader*. Retrieved from http://chreader.org/growing-hope/

Bradley, S. J. (2000). *Affect regulation and the development of psychopathology.* New York, NY: Guilford Press.

Gold, S. N. (2000). *Not trauma alone: Therapy for child abuse survivors in family and social context.* Philadelphia, PA: Taylor and Francis.

Newell, J. P. (2000). *Celtic benediction: Morning and night prayer.* Grand Rapids, MI: Eerdmans.

Ross, C. (2007). *The trauma model: A solution to the problem of comorbidity in psychiatry.* Richardson, TX: Manitou Communications.

Siegel, D. J. (2015). *The developing mind: How relationships and the brain interact to shape who we are* (2nd ed.). New York, NY: Guilford Press.

APPENDIX

RELIGION, SPIRITUALITY, AND TRAUMA: AN ANNOTATED BIBLIOGRAPHY

FRED C. GINGRICH

This appendix is an extensive annotated bibliography referred to in the introduction and in chapter one. The references include both conceptual and empirical studies. Please note that this is not a bibliography on trauma and trauma treatment but rather includes literature that specifically incorporates the dimensions of religion and spirituality as they relate to trauma.

The references are organized into categories as follows:

- R/S and Trauma (390-97)

- R/S Resources for Coping, Resilience, and Posttraumatic Growth (PTG) (398-404)

- R/S and Trauma Treatment (404-8)

- R/S and Specific Strategies and Techniques for Trauma Treatment (408-15)

- R/S Related to Specific Types of Trauma and Populations (416-53)
    - Military personnel and veteran trauma (416-22)
    - Interpersonal trauma (422-32)
    - Disasters and trauma (432-40)
    - Violent and collective trauma (440-43)
    - Additional types and populations (444-53)

Note: "R/S" refers to religious/spiritual (or religion/spirituality); "MHP" to mental health professional; "tx" to treatment; "PTSD" to posttraumatic stress disorder; "PTG" to posttraumatic growth; "CSA" to child(hood) sexual abuse; "IPV" to interpersonal violence. Assume that the referenced documents are from academic journals unless otherwise indicated.

Thanks to Steffi Joslin, MA, for her assistance in the compilation of this research.

R/S AND TRAUMA

Author (date)	Abi Hashem (2012)
Focus	Religious and pastoral responses to trauma
Type of document	Book chapter; conceptual
Abstract highlights	• A brief encyclopedia article in a secular publication.

Author (date)	Aten & Walker (2012); Walker & Aten (2012)
Focus	Introduction and conclusion to a special journal issue on R/S and trauma
Type of document	Conceptual
Abstract highlights	• Shares lessons learned from the research and clinical practice in area of trauma, as well as future directions for study and research. • Refers to child-abuse prevention and tx, intimate partner violence, responding to survivors of natural disasters, and theological and theoretical integrative approaches to trauma tx.

Author (date)	Bowland (2015)
Focus	R/S issues in psychotherapy with trauma survivors
Type of document	Review
Abstract highlights	• Review of Walker, Courtois, and Aten (2015).

Author (date)	Doehring (1993)
Focus	R/S during and after trauma
Type of document	Book; conceptual
Abstract highlights	• Trauma results in the internal experience of "desecration" and changes one's representations of God.

Author (date)	Gostečnik, Slavič, Lukek, & Cvetek (2014)
Focus	R/S and trauma
Type of document	Conceptual
Abstract highlights	• Retraumatization often develops a highly ambivalent relationship to God, and all religiosity can be extremely conflictual. • People blame God either for not having protected them, for having left them to feel so alone, or for having been indifferent to them, or they may even turn their wrath on God as the source of cruelty. • Frequently trauma prompts people to turn to God and religion in search of help. • Need for research to answer why some turn to religion while others turn away.

Author (date)	Grame, Tortorici, Healey, Dillingham, & Winklebaur (1999)
Focus	R/S issues for those who have a history of trauma
Type of document	Conceptual
Abstract highlights	• MHPs and clergy need to collaborate in tx; need for cross-professional training for both MHPs and clergy; R/S assessment and tx plans needed. • Body-soul connection is well-established in trauma. • Implications of (1) attachment theory, (2) self-psychology theory, (3) Thomas Aquinas's theology of embodiment, and (4) object relations theory.

Author (date)	Grand (2015)
Focus	Responding to the problem of evil and suffering
Type of document	Book chapter; conceptual, case study
Abstract highlights	• Cruelty perpetrated by one human being on another in war, genocide, terrorism, torture, mass rape, and mass shootings occurred throughout history; so the question that has been posed from time immemorial, without adequate answer, is, Do we as humans possess an innate propensity for evil? Can goodness somehow contain and heal? • Humans can be conceptualized as having multiple self-states with each state presenting an ethical marker; sometimes people behave as perpetrators and sometimes as rescuers. • Encouraging dialogue between victim self-states and perpetrator self-states creates potential for new life.

Author (date)	Grant (1999)
Focus	R/S and trauma
Type of document	Conceptual
Abstract highlights	• Trauma presents psychological and spiritual challenges that are unfamiliar to the average person. • MHPs need to recognize that organizations of self and God are often thrown into question or destroyed by experiences of trauma. • Deconstructive power of trauma exposes the lack of substance and cohesiveness that comprises identity and images of God.

Author (date)	Hall & Johnson (2001)
Focus	Theodicy, therapy, and the problem of suffering
Type of document	Conceptual
Abstract highlights	• Theodicies are philosophical/theological attempts to reconcile the presence of evil and suffering in the world with the idea of an all-powerful and good creator God. • Evaluates the usefulness of theodicies in responding to the suffering person's needs. • Epstein's CEST theory and Stolorow's theory of trauma are discussed to clarify the needs of the sufferer. • It is concluded that theodicy, particularly in some forms, can be helpful in changing the sufferer's theory of reality through an experiential encounter with God.

Author (date)	Harper & Pargament (2015)
Focus	Trauma and R/S pathways to healing
Type of document	Book chapter; conceptual
Abstract highlights	• Explores the complex and dynamic ways in which R/S is embedded in the posttraumatic recovery process. • R/S affects people's understandings of traumatic events, the selection of methods to cope with adversity and the coping methods themselves, and the short- and long-term outcomes of trauma. • Provides summary of ways in which R/S can be integrated into the posttraumatic recovery process, accompanied by promising outcome data from spiritually integrated intervention studies.

Author (date)	Harris, Erbes, Winskowski, Engdahl, & Nguyen (2014)
Focus	Social support and trauma symptoms
Type of document	Empirical (quantitative)
Abstract highlights	• Variables: social support, religious comfort, and trauma symptoms. • Tested theory that R/S variables serve as a proxy for social support because individuals in spiritual communities access higher levels of social support than those with no such community. • Social support, religious comfort, and religious fear and guilt make independent contributions to posttraumatic adjustment, whereas social support partially mediates the relationship between alienation from one's higher power, religious rifts, and trauma symptoms.

Author (date)	Harris, Leak, Dubke, & Voecks (2015)
Focus	Religious strain and postconventional religiousness in trauma survivors
Type of document	Empirical (quantitative)
Abstract highlights	• Postconventional religious reasoning has been one of the best defined indicators of R/S development in the literature. • Attempted to identify the types of religious challenges most relevant to the development of postconventional religiousness. • Participants who reported higher levels of postconventional religiousness included those who had experienced (a) more total trauma exposure, (b) more religious rifts with others in their faith group or family, (c) lower levels of religious fear and guilt, and (d) lower levels of religious comfort.

Author (date)	Hipolito et al. (2014)
Focus	R/S and empowerment in trauma informed care
Type of document	Empirical (quantitative)
Abstract highlights	• R/S may serve a protective function in the posttrauma period, but few studies have systematically examined the process through which this occurs.
	• Tested a theoretical model that examines the protective roles of R/S and personal empowerment in the relationship between childhood and adulthood experiences of violence and mental health/well-being.
	• Need to develop trauma-informed practice protocols that incorporate spirituality.

Author (date)	Kalsched (2013)
Focus	R/S and developmental interruptions due to trauma
Type of document	Book; conceptual; case studies
Abstract highlights	• Delves into the mystical or spiritual moments that often occur around the intimacies of psychoanalytic work in the area of trauma.
	• Includes stories of ordinary patients and ordinary psychotherapists who, through working together, glimpse the reality of the human soul and the depth of the spirit and are changed by the experience.

Author (date)	Kusner, & Pargament (2012)
Focus	R/S and trauma
Type of document	Book chapter; conceptual
Abstract highlights	• R/S struggles, doubts, and uncertainties can be triggered by trauma.
	• Support, solace, and peace can be gained from spiritual resources after trauma.
	• Explores spiritual character of trauma, spiritual ways of coping with trauma, and the spiritual outcomes of trauma.
	• How can spirituality be addressed in the context of tx to promote growth and resilience and to prevent the development of serious problems?

Author (date)	Park & Gutierrez (2013)
Focus	Psychological well-being and global and situational meanings in the context of trauma
Type of document	Empirical (quantitative)
Abstract highlights	• Examined the relationship between global and appraised meaning and well-being in a sample of 189 college students who had experienced a highly stressful event in the past five years. • Elements of both global meaning (especially self-esteem beliefs) and situational meaning (especially appraisals of the event as violating one's goals) were independently related to a range of well-being outcomes, including depression, anxiety, stress, subjective happiness, and life satisfaction. • Demonstrates the importance of both global and situational meanings in adjusting to life stress.

Author (date)	Rambo (2015)
Focus	R/S and trauma
Type of document	Conceptual
Abstract highlights	• Life following an overwhelming event of violence is fundamentally changed; survivors struggle to reconcile their present experience of life (including the trauma) with their experience of faith. • When individuals and religious communities try to put the events behind them and proclaim the good news before it's time, they fail to attend to the ongoing realities of a death that does not go away. • Explores a theology that witnesses to what remains after the trauma.

Author (date)	Reinert, Campbell, Bandeen-Roche, Sharps, & Lee (2015)
Focus	Gender and race variations in religious involvement, early trauma, and adult health
Type of document	Empirical (quantitative)
Abstract highlights	• Sought to determine gender and race variations in regard to the influence of religious involvement as a moderator of the effects of early traumatic stress on health-related quality of life among adult survivors of child abuse. • Cross-sectional predictive design used to study Seventh-day Adventist adults in North America ($N = 10{,}283$). • Findings suggest gender and racial differences must be considered when devising holistic interventions for improving health outcomes of early trauma survivors.

Author (date)	Severson, Becker, & Goodman (2016)
Focus	Psychological and philosophical reflections on trauma and suffering
Type of document	Conceptual; edited book
Abstract highlights	• Trauma is difficult to understand and to deal with, yet the process of wrestling with it can be transformative. • Interdisciplinary essays discuss influential thinkers such as Augustine, Foucault, Freud, Heidegger, and Lacan, along with literature from Homer, the book of Job, and Shakespeare.

Author (date)	Smith (2004)
Focus	R/S and trauma
Type of document	Conceptual
Abstract highlights	• Positive and negative impact of R/S on coping. • Inconsistent results in the literature concerning the relationship between trauma and R/S. • Different roles clergy and MHPs can play in tx.

Author (date)	Starnino (2016)
Focus	R/S, trauma, and mental illness
Type of document	Empirical (qualitative, case study)
Abstract highlights	• Identifies spirituality as a helpful resource for dealing with various types of trauma experiences and encourages the role of spirituality within trauma-related theory (e.g., spiritual coping, meaning making, and PTG). • Little is known about the relationship between trauma and spirituality among people with severe psychiatric disorders, yet a high percentage of those with psychiatric disabilities are known to have trauma histories, and a majority self-identify as R/S. • Provides a hermeneutic, phenomenological, qualitative study of two cases with co-occurring psychiatric disabilities and trauma histories. • Offers useful examples of how spirituality and trauma can affect one another and how people with psychiatric disabilities draw on spirituality to cope as they strive for recovery.

Author (date)	van den Blink (2010)
Focus	R/S and trauma
Type of document	Conceptual
Abstract highlights	• Offers an account of how an appreciation of theology and practice of Christian spirituality can benefit victims. • Summarizes the contributions of neuroscience to understanding the physiology and psychology of trauma. • Provides an explanation of the important contribution that contemplative prayer can make to those who have suffered trauma and abuse and those who want to help them.

Author (date)	Van Deusen & Courtois (2015)
Focus	R/S and complex developmental trauma
Type of document	Book chapter; conceptual; case study
Abstract highlights	• Observes the effects of multiple, repetitive traumas occurring primarily over the course of childhood on an individual's spiritual development. • Using the work of Erik Erikson and James Fowler, assesses how and when experiences of complex trauma affect standard developmental trajectories. • Looks at how the five primary domains of complex PTSD (CPTSD) influence a survivor's ability to develop a healthy sense of faith that fosters positive identity and hope. • Includes case of a client with dissociative identity disorder to illustrate how extreme emotional dysregulation and trauma-related expectations of relationships affect spirituality, attachment to God, and faith development; specific strategies for integrating issues of spirituality into each of the three main phases of tx for CPTSD.

Author (date)	Van Hook (2016)
Focus	R/S as a resource for coping with trauma
Type of document	Conceptual
Abstract highlights	• Addresses ways in which trauma is experienced, potential interactions between trauma and spirituality, and possibilities for promoting healing.

Author (date)	Van Hook, Furman, & Benson (2016)
Focus	R/S and trauma
Type of document	Special issue; conceptual
Abstract highlights	• Role of trauma in the lives of individuals, families, and communities and pathways to healing. • Articles address a wide range of life experiences, cultural aspects, and contexts and highlight the potential interaction between trauma and spirituality or religion.

Author (date)	Whitmire (2015)
Focus	R/S and self-care for counselors working with trauma
Type of document	Dissertation; empirical (qualitative)
Abstract highlights	• Addresses the trauma counselor's perspective on spirituality and self-care using a phenomenological perspective of 10 practicing, professional trauma counselors working in six trauma settings to determine (1) their understanding of spirituality and (2) whether or not spirituality is a viable tool in self-care for alleviating vicarious traumatization • Six major themes were identified across the interviews: current self-care practices, core beliefs and values, influence of core beliefs and values, individual spirituality, spirituality and self-care, and trauma's affect on spirituality, personally and professionally.

Abstract highlights (continued)	• Individual spirituality ameliorated vicarious traumatization for trauma counselors. • Implications for clinical practice include specialized training, education, supervision, and implementation of strategies and techniques for ongoing adjustment and recovery. • Recommendations for future research include effectiveness of existing training on R/S topics and current competencies of counselors working with R/S diversity.

Author (date)	Woodcock (2001)
Focus	R/S and trauma
Type of document	Book chapter; conceptual
Abstract highlights	• Existential change frequently makes sense from within an R/S framework, but beliefs and practices with respect to trauma, suffering, and change vary depending on the religious tradition. • Therapists can maintain their capacity for effective practice by making good use of their current experience and working across the boundaries of spiritual and cultural differences.

Author (date)	Wortmann, Park, & Edmondson (2011)
Focus	R/S struggles, PTSD symptoms, and trauma
Type of document	Empirical (quantitative)
Abstract highlights	• Among the mechanisms that may predict PTSD symptoms is R/S struggle, a set of negative religious cognitions related to understanding or responding to stressful events. • Assessed exposure to trauma and nontrauma events during the first year of college, R/S due to the most stressful event, and PTSD symptoms resulting from the index event. • R/S struggle partially mediated the relationship between trauma and PTSD symptoms. • Some individual subscales of R/S (specifically, punishing God reappraisal, reappraisal of God's powers, and spiritual discontent) partially mediated the relationship between trauma and PTSD symptoms; however, reappraisal of the event to evil forces did not relate to PTSD symptoms. • Results suggest that R/S struggle is an important cognitive mechanism for many trauma victims and may have relevance for cognitive therapy for PTSD.

Author (date)	Zenkert, Brabender, & Slater (2014)
Focus	MHP and R/S perspectives on trauma clients
Type of document	Mixed methods
Abstract highlights	• As compared to working with nontrauma clients, therapists view attention to R/S in trauma therapy as necessary. • Emphasis on R/S within a traumatized population possesses distinctive qualities in comparison to other populations.

R/S RESOURCES FOR COPING, RESILIENCE, AND POSTTRAUMATIC GROWTH (PTG)

Author (date)	Boehnlein (2007)
Focus	R/S after trauma
Type of document	Book chapter; conceptual; case studies
Abstract highlights	• Trauma raises R/S questions, challenges a person's core belief systems, involves an examination of previously stable cultural and religious assumptions that were the foundations of a person's life. • Clinical issues arise such as healing in the context of R/S belief systems, psychotherapy for PTSD, and interpersonal and social reintegration. • Discusses psychological challenges after trauma related to R/S, the role of the healing process in restructuring values and meaning after trauma, and the therapeutic relationship.

Author (date)	Bonanno (2004)
Focus	Resilience after extremely aversive events
Type of document	Conceptual
Abstract highlights	• Trauma theorists have often viewed resilience as either rare or even pathological. • Many people are exposed to loss or potentially traumatic events at some point in their lives, and yet they continue to have positive emotional experiences and show only minor and transient disruptions in their ability to function. • Resilience represents a distinct trajectory for recovery; resilience in the face of loss or potential trauma is more common than is often believed; there are multiple and sometimes unexpected pathways to resilience.

Author (date)	Brewer-Smyth & Koenig (2014)
Focus	R/S and resilience in survivors of childhood trauma
Type of document	Conceptual
Abstract highlights	• Examines the neurobiological, behavioral, and health outcomes for survivors. • R/S can promote emotional, neurotic, and psychotic consequences. • R/S can be a powerful source of hope, meaning, peace, comfort, and forgiveness for the self and others. • Faith-based communities can promote forgiveness rather than retaliation, opportunities for cathartic emotional release, and social support.

Author (date)	Brooks (2012)
Focus	R/S and PTG
Type of document	Dissertation; empirical (qualitative)
Abstract highlights	• Used Tedeschi and Calhoun's (1996) Posttraumatic Growth Inventory (PTGI) with five dimensions. • Assessed for relating to others, new possibilities, personal strength, spiritual change, and appreciation of life. • Traumatic life experiences can be identified as spiritual marker events. • For MHPs, seek training, increase knowledge and understanding of the PTG process; assess individuals' strengths along the five PTG factors; take trauma and R/S histories; incorporate personal strengths and spirituality as resources in the recovery process.

Author (date)	de Castella & Simmonds (2013)
Focus	R/S growth following trauma
Type of document	Empirical (qualitative)
Abstract highlights	• Some survivors of trauma report experiencing beneficial changes in self-perception, relationships, and philosophy of life, as well as positive changes in existential or R/S matters. • Ten Christian women who experienced R/S growth following trauma were analyzed using Interpretative Phenomenological Analysis. • Religion provided a framework that assisted participants to incorporate life changes and to find meaning in their suffering. • Trauma prompted a process of questioning and meaning making that facilitated deeply experienced personal and spiritual growth and was related to intrinsic religiosity.

Author (date)	Eriksson & Yeh (2012)
Focus	Resilience to trauma
Type of document	Book chapter; conceptual
Abstract highlights	• Discusses R/S aspects of abuse, interpersonal violence, cancer, and combat exposure. • Offers framework of spiritual development as a guide to tx; resources to encourage thriving, meaning making, and coping. • Explores religious coping, the importance of the religio-cultural context, the reality of spiritual crisis, and potential for PTG and transformation.

Author (date)	Farley (2007)
Focus	Connection between R/S, trauma, and resiliency
Type of document	Conceptual; case studies
Abstract highlights	• A model of individual resiliency from family-based trauma; characteristics are explored for their compatibility with spiritual practices. • Case examples from various practice settings are given to exemplify application of R/S practices to the development of resiliency traits. • Implications for practice include increased understanding of the use of spirituality as a tool to enhance adaptability and coping.

Author (date)	Gear Haugen (2012)
Focus	Effects of traumatic events on R/S
Type of document	Dissertation; empirical (longitudinal)
Abstract highlights	• Investigation of 85 emerging adults' experiences of adversity, religiousness, and spirituality. • About half of all participants reported at least some level of negative spiritual appraisals (desecration and sacred loss) of events that had occurred to them. • Significant PTG for five of eight factors of R/S and posttraumatic R/S change among those with high levels of trauma.

Author (date)	Gerber, Boals, & Schuettler (2011)
Focus	Positive and negative R/S coping, PTG, and PTSD
Type of document	Empirical (quantitative)
Abstract highlights	• Assessed relationships between religious coping, gender, PTSD, and PTG with a sample of 1,016 participants. • Positive religious coping was more strongly related to PTG, and negative religious coping was more strongly related to PTSD; remained significant after controlling for traditional coping methods, gender, and race. • Positive religious coping partially mediated the relationship between gender and PTG, and positive correlations were also observed between negative religious coping and PTG and between positive religious coping and PTSD.

Author (date)	Harris et al. (2008)
Focus	Christian R/S functioning and trauma outcomes
Type of document	Empirical (quantitative)
Abstract highlights	• Some trauma survivors find their faith helpful in recovery, others find it a source of distress, and still others abandon their faith. • Used measures of religious action and behaviors in a community sample of 327 church-going, self-identified trauma survivors. • Principal components analysis of positive and negative religious coping, religious comforts and strains, and prayer functions identified two dimensions: seeking spiritual support, which was positively related to PTG, and religious strain, which was positively related to posttraumatic symptoms.

Author (date)	Harris et al. (2010)
Focus	Coping functions of prayer and PTG
Type of document	Empirical (quantitative)
Abstract highlights	• Those who pray more report more PTG. • Which types of prayer may be operating with which types of trauma experienced. • Participants (*N* = 327) completed questionnaires assessing trauma history, prayer coping functions, and PTG. • Praying for calm and focus was independently related to higher levels of PTG; however, the relationship between prayer for calm and focus and PTG was not significant for those whose most significant trauma was interpersonal in nature, but was significant for those with non-interpersonal trauma.

Author (date)	Mijares (2005)
Focus	Trauma and transformed identities within a psychospiritual paradigm
Type of document	Book chapter; conceptual; case studies
Abstract highlights	• Alternative methods for treating posttraumatic reactions to violence and sexual abuse. • Trauma can open doors to transformation when treated within an integrative, psychospiritual paradigm. • Examples from tx based on the work of Jung, Campbell, Gilligan, Assagioli, and mystical teachings from religious traditions. • Client narratives are presented to illustrate how trauma and psychospiritual tx can lead to transformed identities.

Author (date)	Pargament (2001)
Focus	Psychology of religion and coping
Type of document	Book; conceptual
Abstract highlights	• An overview of the theoretical underpinnings and research regarding the benefits and dangers of R/S in psychological coping. • Religion helps some people cope, while for others it does not. • Religious belief can serve as a defense or a form of denial, but faith can also help people in crisis and in times of stress.

Author (date)	Pargament (2007)
Focus	Spiritually integrated model of counseling
Type of document	Book; conceptual
Abstract highlights	• Resources for creating a spiritual dialogue with clients, assessing spirituality as a part of their problems and solutions, and helping them draw on spiritual resources in times of stress. • R/S can serve as a foundation to help cope, and it can serve to transform life and produce growth.

Author (date)	Pargament & Cummings (2010)
Focus	Religion as a resilience factor
Type of document	Book chapter; conceptual
Abstract highlights	• Religiousness can play a significant role in response to major life stressors; challenges stereotypes of religiousness as a defense or source of pathology; religiousness is a significant resilience factor for many people.
	• There is evidence that religiousness can help people move beyond prior levels of adjustment to achieve fundamental positive transformation; however, some forms of religiousness may exacerbate rather than mitigate the effects of major life stressors.

Author (date)	Pargament, Desai, & McConnell (2006)
Focus	R/S as a pathway to PTG or decline
Type of document	Book chapter; conceptual
Abstract highlights	• Spirituality can play a critical role in how traumas are understood, how they are managed, and how they are ultimately resolved; however, spirituality can be potentially helpful (PTG) or harmful (decline).
	• Considers factors that may determine whether spirituality leads ultimately to growth or decline.
	• Discusses practical implications of this body of theory and research for efforts to help people cope with major trauma including the meaning of R/S and its place in the context of coping with life traumas.

Author (date)	Peres, Moreira-Almeida, Nasello, & Koenig (2007)
Focus	R/S and resilience in trauma victims
Type of document	Conceptual
Abstract highlights	• The way people process stressors is critical in determining whether or not trauma will be experienced.
	• Clinical and neuroimaging findings suggest that PTSD patients experience difficulty in synthesizing the traumatic experience in a comprehensive personal narrative.
	• Building narratives based on healthy R/S beliefs may facilitate the integration of traumatic sensorial fragments in a new cognitive synthesis, thus working to decrease posttraumatic symptoms.
	• The role of spirituality in fostering resilience in trauma survivors advances our understanding of human adaptation to trauma.

Author (date)	Schultz, Tallman, & Altmaier (2010)
Focus	R/S factors such as forgiveness in coping with interpersonal trauma
Type of document	Empirical (quantitative)
Abstract highlights	• Examined the roles of forgiveness and the importance of religion and spirituality in PTG after a significant interpersonal transgression among a diverse sample of 146 adults. • PTG may follow the experience of being significantly hurt by another person. • Transgression severity was negatively related to forgiveness; the more distressing the event, the more revenge and avoidance were endorsed in response to the offender; benevolence toward the offender predicted growth in the area of relating to others; positive relationship between forgiveness and PTG was mediated by the importance of religion and spirituality; however, the relationship between unforgiveness and lack of growth was not similarly mediated. • R/S variables may influence how individuals respond to significant interpersonal transgressions through positive processes.

Author (date)	Shaw, Joseph, & Linley (2005)
Focus	R/S and PTG
Type of document	Research review
Abstract highlights	• Reviewed 11 studies that reported links between R/S and PTG. • These studies show that R/S is usually, though not always, beneficial to people in dealing with the aftermath of trauma; traumatic experiences can lead to a deepening of R/S; positive religious coping, religious openness, readiness to face existential questions, religious participation, and intrinsic religiousness are typically associated with PTG.

Author (date)	Tan (2013)
Focus	Christian R/S factors, resilience, and PTG
Type of document	Conceptual
Abstract highlights	• There are various pathways to resilience, and the factors influence how effectively people deal with trauma and adversities in their lives. • Research literature shows evidence (a) for resilience in returning service members and their families, (b) for resilience in civilian populations, and (c) that the majority of individuals who have gone through a traumatic event, in whatever form, end up exhibiting resilience. • Resilience can be enhanced or increased by a number of clinical strategies or applications gleaned from research that can be used in practice in the following six major areas of fitness: physical fitness, interpersonal fitness, emotional fitness, thinking fitness, behavioral fitness and spiritual fitness. • The world's major religions, such as Christianity, Judaism, Islam, Buddhism, and Hinduism, all teach that suffering is part and parcel of life and that growth or transformation can be the eventual outcome.

Author (date)	ter Kuile & Ehring (2014)
Focus	Changes in R/S after trauma
Type of document	Empirical (quantitative)
Abstract highlights	• After a traumatic experience, religious beliefs and activities can either increase or decrease. • 293 trauma survivors responded to questionnaires related to traumatic experiences and religiosity. • Nearly half of the sample reported changes in religious beliefs and activities as a consequence of the trauma; as hypothesized, shattered assumptions and prior religiosity interacted to predict a decrease in religious beliefs and activities; increases in religiosity were related to the use of religion as a coping mechanism and to currently living in a religious environment; a decrease in religious beliefs was related to higher levels of PTSD.

Author (date)	Werdel, Dy-Liacco, Ciarrocchi, Wicks, & Breslford (2014)
Focus	Positive affect, personality, gender, perceived stress, social support, faith maturity, and spiritual struggle in PTG
Type of document	Empirical (quantitative)
Abstract highlights	• 109 male and 320 female volunteers were investigated as to the unique contributions and moderating effects of positive and negative experiences of spirituality in predicting variance in stress-related growth. • Examined whether there was a positive effect over and above the variance explained by social support, perceived stress, gender, and the domains of the Five-Factor Model of Personality. • Faith maturity predicted variance in stress-related growth after controlling for the influence of personality and gender. • Faith maturity and spiritual struggle predicted significant unique additional variance in positive affect over and above the variance predicted by personality, social support, and stress-related growth. • Spiritual struggle moderated the relationship between stress-related growth and positive affect. • Results are discussed in light of Park's model of religion as a meaning-making framework.

R/S AND TRAUMA TREATMENT

Author (date)	Bennet (1999)
Focus	Training model
Type of document	Dissertation; training model
Abstract highlights	• Clinical training model on religious, spiritual, and exceptional experiences in the tx of trauma and dissociation.

Author (date)	Berrett, Hardman, O'Grady, & Richards (2007)
Focus	R/S in the tx of trauma and eating disorders
Type of document	Conceptual
Abstract highlights	• Both trauma and eating disorders can distance women from their own spirituality, which undermines a potentially important tx resource. • Suggestions based on the authors' clinical experience for helping eating disorder patients who have suffered trauma to rediscover their faith and spirituality. • How spirituality can be used as a resource to assist women throughout tx and in recovery.

Author (date)	Brown (2008)
Focus	Cultural competence in trauma psychotherapy
Type of document	Book; conceptual; case studies
Abstract highlights	• Tx of trauma survivors must take into account the complexity of an individual's unique background and multilayered identities. • Identity includes age, social class, ethnicity, religious faith, sexual orientation, and immigrant status. • Multiple strategies are given for treating patients with awareness of both dominant group privilege and one's own identity and culture.

Author (date)	Bryant-Davis et al. (2012)
Focus	R/S in trauma recovery for children and adolescents
Type of document	Conceptual
Abstract highlights	• Much of the research in R/S and trauma refers to adults and has less emphasis on children and adolescents. • Delineates ways to incorporate and acknowledge R/S in tx for children and adolescents who are trauma survivors.

Author (date)	Brymer et al. (2006)
Focus	Psychological First Aid (PFA) field operations guide for community religious professionals
Type of document	Conceptual
Abstract highlights	• PFA is an evidence-informed modular approach to help children, adolescents, adults, and families in the immediate aftermath of disaster and terrorism. • Designed to reduce the initial distress caused by traumatic events and to foster short- and long-term adaptive functioning and coping. • Principles and techniques meet four basic standards: (1) consistent with research evidence on risk and resilience following trauma, (2) applicable and practical in field settings, (3) appropriate for developmental levels across the lifespan, and (4) culturally informed and delivered in a flexible manner.

Author (date)	Courtois (2015)
Focus	Ethics of attending to R/S issues in trauma tx
Type of document	Conceptual
Abstract highlights	• Healing from trauma is fundamentally a spiritual process or a quest for spirituality involving a deep need for meaning and value.
	• Some traumatized individuals are assaulted and/or neglected by perpetrators who are related to them as parents or through other blood ties or kinship, friendship, or professional and fiduciary associations, including clergy and other representatives of faith traditions, teachers, coaches, therapists, doctors, military commanders, and supervisors.
	• Attention to how their R/S beliefs were altered by the trauma is within the domain of psychotherapy and is in the interest of healing, renewal, and transformation.
	• Evidence-based strategies are now available for the tx of trauma symptoms, and trauma-informed care overtly includes attention to spiritual issues.
	• R/S intervention guidelines and tx guidance for symptoms of classic and complex PTSD include attention to R/S factors.
	• Discusses ethical imperative to "do no more harm" and to include within tx attention to R/S.
	• Discusses ethical risks and dilemmas that are relatively unique in trauma tx and can challenge the psychotherapist's competence and personal worldview, including faith and spiritual beliefs.

Author (date)	Frawley-O'Dea (2015)
Focus	God image and sexual abuse survivors
Type of document	Book chapter; conceptual
Abstract highlights	• To the extent that one's image of God is a relationally and experientially constructed phenomenon, it is organic and can be cast and recast throughout the life cycle.
	• When people have been subject to developmental betrayal trauma (e.g., sexual abuse), and perhaps especially sexual abuse by a member of the clergy, their internalized relationships with the divine can be harnessed to the trauma for the rest of their lives.
	• Offers a relational paradigm of an individual's development of a God image, then discusses the potential impact of sexual abuse on the victim's relationship with the divine.
	• Focuses particularly on the role of the therapist as a transformational or transitional figure.

Author (date)	Kalayjian (2002)
Focus	Biopsychosocial impact and R/S factors in tx
Type of document	Book chapter; case studies
Abstract highlights	• Discusses biological, psychosocial, and spiritual impact of trauma on communities, families, and individuals, including the intergenerational impact.
	• Offers six-step model for tx of current trauma.

Author (date)	Richards, Hardman, Lea, & Berrett (2015)
Focus	R/S assessment of trauma survivors
Type of document	Book chapter; conceptual; case study
Abstract highlights	• Discusses why the assessment of the spiritual dimension of trauma survivors' lives is crucial for effective tx.
	• Describes a multilevel, multidimensional approach to assessment and offers some process suggestions and clinical questions that can facilitate a spiritual assessment.
	• Discusses R/S issues that may be relevant in the tx of trauma survivors, as well as several standardized R/S measures that can be helpful in assessment and outcome research.

Author (date)	Sigmund (2003)
Focus	Clergy and the tx of PTSD
Type of document	Conceptual; case studies
Abstract highlights	• There is a dearth of controlled scientific studies evaluating the effectiveness of spiritual interventions; need for controlled studies to verify the usefulness of spiritual assessment and intervention in patients with PTSD.
	• A more rigorous analysis of how clergy can best serve this population is needed.

Author (date)	Stone (2013)
Focus	Treating religious trauma and spiritual harm
Type of document	Conceptual
Abstract highlights	• Religion can be a source of harm and trauma, yet this fact is underreported in the literature; spirituality can negatively affect mental health when it is used to bypass problems, feelings, and needs.
	• Addresses need to explore the potentially harmful effects of religion and spirituality.
	• Looks at role of secure attachment and the combination of individual and group therapy to treat religious trauma and spiritual struggles.

Author (date)	Walker, Courtois, & Aten (2015)
Focus	R/S and traumatized clients
Type of document	Book chapter; conceptual
Abstract highlights	• Spirituality is a diversity variable that should be addressed in case conceptualization and tx.
	• Particular types of damage to relational spirituality are a consequence of complex interpersonal trauma.
	• Gives models for addressing spiritual issues in psychotherapy.
	• Provides overview of spiritually oriented trauma-focused cognitive behavior therapy (SO-TF-CBT), an example of a secular trauma tx that has been adapted to include spiritual content.

Author (date)	Wilson & Moran (1998)
Focus	R/S and PTSD tx
Type of document	Conceptual
Abstract highlights	• Traumatic life events affect the body, self-structure, and soul of the survivor, including the psychological dimension of the self and the faith systems and spirituality that give meaning to one's life.
	• Psychological trauma caused by natural disasters, accidental disasters, disasters of human origin, and violence often leave the spiritual domain in disarray.
	• Offers practical considerations for mental health practitioners and pastoral counselors from whom the victims of severe trauma seek help.
	• Various religions and belief systems can facilitate recovery from significant psychological trauma and PTSD.
	• Encourages those who respond to victims of trauma to develop a holistic model of tx designed to revitalize, transform, and heal their clients.

R/S AND SPECIFIC STRATEGIES AND TECHNIQUES FOR TRAUMA TREATMENT

Author (date)	Abdul-Hamid & Hughes, (2015)
Focus	R/S (Sufism), EMDR, and trauma psychotherapy
Type of document	Conceptual
Abstract highlights	• Eye movements seem to be the most effective form of bilateral stimulation (BLS) in EMDR.
	• Summarizes the cultural applicability of EMDR as well as the value of incorporating R/S into psychotherapy.
	• Islamic Sufism, in common with other traditional religions, has long been known to have a psychotherapeutic perspective and has been used over time to help people to overcome trauma and stress.
	• The ritual movements associated with the Sufi Dhikr may involve a form of BLS, and this might underline some of the therapeutic effectiveness of it.
	• This could give EMDR an even wider and more popular acceptance in the Middle East and the Muslim world.

Author (date)	Agger, Igreja, Kiehle, & Polatin (2012)
Focus	R/S and testimonial therapy for torture survivors in Asian countries
Type of document	Conceptual
Abstract highlights	• Considers the therapeutic impact of including culturally and religiously adapted ceremonies within testimonial therapy with torture survivors.
	• Discusses the development of testimonial therapy, Asian healing practice and interception, and embodied spirituality and healing.
	• Suggests a need to study the potential benefit of including mindfulness, an embodied approach facilitating interception, and other spiritual practices into trauma tx.

Author (date)	Altmaier (2013)
Focus	Meaning making in response to trauma
Type of document	Conceptual
Abstract highlights	• Meaning-making is an intentional process whereby the use of stories and similar narrative forms of communication with others and with oneself create the context in which meaning can develop. • Various R/S beliefs, such as those pertaining to the ultimate purpose in life, contribute to development of meaning after trauma. • R/S provides a holding context in which to experience deep and frightening emotions. • Developing meaning is a primary way in which individuals respond to traumatic events that allow them to achieve a deep assimilation of previously unacceptable events and to experience emotional and behavioral resolution.

Author (date)	Ballaban (2014)
Focus	Traumatic biblical narratives and spiritual recovery from trauma
Type of document	Case study
Abstract highlights	• Identity is tied to the narratives we create more than to the events that occur in life. • Traumatic events in life can create discontinuities in that narrative that interfere with functioning. • Traumatic biblical narratives in pastoral counseling assist clients in articulating personal traumatic episodes and beginning the process of integrating traumatic experiences and initiating growth.

Author (date)	Chopko & Schwartz (2009)
Focus	Mindfulness and PTG
Type of document	Empirical (quantitative)
Abstract highlights	• Research on the reactions of first responders (e.g., police officers, firefighters) to traumatic incidents has largely focused on negative symptoms (e.g., PTSD) rather than aspects promoting mental health. • Studied the relationship between mindfulness (using the Kentucky Inventory of Mindfulness Skills) and PTG (using the Post-Traumatic Growth Inventory) among 183 police officers. • Effort toward spiritual growth was positively correlated, and accepting events without judgment was negatively correlated, with PTG.

Author (date)	Dagmang (2012)
Focus	God-talk as a means of healing through novel writing and auto-analysis
Type of document	Conceptual
Abstract highlights	• Examines communication with divine presence and creativity through the trauma/PTSD described in the novel *Candlelights: Memories of a Former Religious Brother Seminarian*. • Describes the author's remembrance, reenactment, disclosure, and domestication of the original but hidden sources of trauma and their psychic and somatic effects. • Illustrates the significance of the novel as an art that facilitated the discovery of trauma's truth; led the author to realign his personal history via the classic stories of Teresa de Ávila, Juan de la Cruz, and Thérèse de Lisieux, and toward a salvific regard for Jesus of Nazareth, whose own narrative of suffering theologically is integrated into every story of suffering.

Author (date)	Follette, Briere, Rozelle, Hopper, & Rome (2015)
Focus	Mindfulness-oriented and contemplative interventions for trauma
Type of document	Edited book; case studies
Abstract highlights	• Elements of the contemplative traditions may sharpen the effectiveness of existing empirically based therapies and how to apply them safely; integrates mindfulness and other contemplative practices into clinical work with trauma survivors. • Discusses specific tx approaches, including mindfulness-based stress reduction, acceptance and commitment therapy, dialectical behavior therapy, mindfulness-based cognitive therapy, and mindful self-compassion. • Addresses the neurobiological foundations of mindfulness-oriented work and the fundamental physiological processes as they relate to trauma and recovery. • Describes innovative tx applications for different trauma populations, such as clients with chronic pain, military veterans, underserved communities, and children and adolescents.

Author (date)	Kick & McNitt (2016)
Focus	Trauma, spirituality, mindfulness, and hope
Type of document	Conceptual
Abstract highlights	• Discusses how the use of terror management theory can assist the trauma victim in conceptualizing the world as a "just place" and helps create a space for the person's spiritual views and belief system. • In military contexts, duty to country and one's battle buddies (service before self) results in shame and guilt when the military member is unable to manage fear and anxiety upon returning to civilian life.

Author (date)	Maltby & Hall (2012)
Focus	Trauma, attachment, and R/S
Type of document	Case study
Abstract highlights	• How to address the interaction of trauma, R/S, and attachment in long-term attachment-based psychoanalysis. • Summarizes the convergence of attachment theory and psychoanalysis, and reviews literature on attachment to God and trauma, including complex traumatic stress. • Recommendations are made about dealing with trauma and R/S issues from an attachment-based perspective.

Author (date)	Mayer (2013)
Focus	EMDR, R/S, and healing in children
Type of document	Conceptual
Abstract highlights	• EMDR is an integrative approach shown to be effective in dealing with posttrauma symptoms in children, adolescents, and adults. • The process can move clients to R/S meaning making that fosters more positive emotional states and adaptive behaviors. • Theoretical support from theologians, religious educators, and EMDR specialists is presented especially in regard to clients' self-transcendent experiences.

Author (date)	Montes (2015)
Focus	Tx approaches to R/S issues in trauma therapy
Type of document	Dissertation; empirical (qualitative)
Abstract highlights	• Childhood abuse can have positive, negative, or both positive and negative effects on R/S. • R/S often provides both positive and negative forms of coping. • Explores therapist-reported approaches to addressing faith issues in trauma therapy in light of previously published recommendations and protocols.

Author (date)	C. L. Park (2009)
Focus	Overview of theoretical perspectives in tx of trauma
Type of document	Book chapter; conceptual
Abstract highlights	• People report positive changes through their struggles with adversity and often claim to experience improved relationships with family and friends, a clearer sense of their own strengths and resilience, changed priorities about what is important in life, and various other positive changes after struggling with stressful or traumatic events. • What factors influence personal growth, and what effect does growth have on physical and mental health? • Focuses on how positive life change might be fostered in the context of medical illness.

Author (date)	C. L. Park (2013)
Focus	Trauma and meaning making
Type of document	Book chapter; conceptual
Abstract highlights	• Includes cognitive, emotional, motivation, philosophical, social, and cultural perspectives on meaning making in the aftermath of trauma. • Meaning is particularly important when individuals confront highly stressful and traumatic life experiences. • Provides an overview of current conceptual and empirical work on meaning in the context of trauma, as well as suggestions for future research.

Author (date)	C. L. Park, Cohen, & Murch (1996)
Focus	Assessment and prediction of stress-related growth
Type of document	Empirical (quantitative)
Abstract highlights	• Development of the Stress-Related Growth Scale (SRGS) and its use in a study examining determinants of stress-related positive outcomes for college students. • The SRGS has acceptable internal and test-retest reliability, and scores are not influenced by social desirability. • Showed that college students' SRGS responses were significantly related to those provided by friends and relatives on their behalf. • Tested the determinants of stress-related growth longitudinally. • Significant predictors of the SRGS were (a) intrinsic religiousness, (b) social support satisfaction, (c) stressfulness of the negative event, (d) positive reinterpretation and acceptance coping, and (e) number of recent positive life events.

Author (date)	C. L. Park, Edmondson, & Mills (2010)
Focus	R/S worldviews and stressful encounters
Type of document	Book chapter; conceptual
Abstract highlights	• R/S is a central part of the meaning-making framework for many people; influences people's appraisal of, and coping with, both normative transitions and unexpected crises. • The meaning-making framework is broad enough to encompass the coping challenges that are considered within both the stressful life events approach and the developmental or normative transition approach. • The interaction of R/S meaning systems and stressful life events is best conceptualized as an ongoing and recursive process of mutual influence.

Author (date)	E. A. Park (2014)
Focus	Creative and expressive therapies to explore R/S themes with traumatized children
Type of document	Dissertation; conceptual
Abstract highlights	• Explores the conceptual relationship between trauma, spirituality, and the use of art therapy within a family psychology framework in the tx of traumatized children and their families.
	• Because of the developmental limitations of children's language capability to articulate their experiences, artistic expression may be a viable way of accessing and exploring children's spirituality.
	• Fits within a broader systems framework that is holistic, nonreductionist, and culturally sensitive.

Author (date)	Partridge & Walker (2015)
Focus	R/S struggles using spiritually oriented trauma-focused cognitive behavioral therapy
Type of document	Case study
Abstract highlights	• Demonstrates the struggles experienced by a child with complex trauma involving child abuse who later became a Christian.
	• Examines the cultural backdrop, client demographics, history of the trauma, and the client's spiritual functioning.
	• Considerations for using spiritually oriented interventions within the context of trauma-focused cognitive behavioral therapy (TF-CBT).

Author (date)	Pressley & Spinazzola (2015)
Focus	Complex trauma tx model in a Christian context
Type of document	Conceptual; case study
Abstract highlights	• Disrupted systems of meaning are a core domain in which adults with a complex trauma history are affected, often leading to adversely affected belief systems.
	• For adult survivors of childhood trauma, experiences related to shame, betrayal, meaning making, and mourning often complicate their R/S beliefs.
	• Introduces and illustrates the relevance of a complex trauma intervention (Component-Based Psychotherapy) framework in the context of spiritually informed tx with adult Christian clients.
	• Particular focus on the ways in which clients' faith beliefs and practices can serve as a potential resource and/or barrier in tx.

Author (date)	Slattery & Park (2015)
Focus	R/S and meaning making with trauma survivors
Type of document	Book chapter; conceptual
Abstract highlights	• Outlines the meaning-making framework and meaning response styles of people exposed to trauma.
	• Systems of meaning help people interpret and label experiences (e.g., good/bad, fair/unfair, dangerous/desirable), which then creates the emotional and behavioral impact of these experiences as well as later encounters.
	• Trauma is an event so discrepant from a person's meaning system that it alters or damages that person's meaning system (and sometimes those of their family and friends).
	• Trauma damages or even "shatters" meaning, whereas focusing on meaning and creating an adaptive and growth-promoting sense of meaning can be part of healing from trauma.

Author (date)	Verbeck et al. (2015)
Focus	R/S and the working alliance with trauma survivors
Type of document	Book chapter; conceptual; case material
Abstract highlights	• After a traumatic event, clients often attempt to use their R/S knowledge to try to make meaning out of their experiences, and the conclusions they reach in these circumstances can profoundly affect mood and decisions about future action.
	• Likewise, psychotherapists sometimes struggle with their own reactions to clients' religious interpretations of an event; they may also struggle to use interventions tailored to their clients' beliefs.
	• R/S issues are difficult to negotiate in trauma tx, especially when clinicians are expected to be adept enough to juggle counter-transference.
	• Both research and case vignettes are used to illustrate the authors' professional experience, including approaches to the more common choice points in the therapy working alliance, such as interventions and disclosure of beliefs.

Author (date)	Walker, Reese, Hughes, & Troskie (2010)
Focus	R/S issues in trauma-focused cognitive behavior therapy (TF-CBT) for children and adolescents
Type of document	Conceptual; case studies
Abstract highlights	• TF-CBT has emerged as a leading tx for trauma recovery.
	• Examines role of R/S in TF-CBT for children and teens; development of a model for assessing and treating R/S in TF-CBT.
	• Focuses on the client's preexisting R/S functioning, as well as on changes in R/S after abuse.
	• Model will assist clients from various R/S affiliations to process childhood abuse.

Author (date)	Wimberly (2011)
Focus	Narrative approaches to treating trauma
Type of document	Conceptual
Abstract highlights	• Presents a narrative or storytelling approach to managing trauma. • Helping R/S caregivers, as first responders, to manage the impact of trauma on victims as well as on their own lives as caregivers. • Caregivers come from a wide range of traditions that draw on creation spirituality. • Reviews the literature supporting evidenced-based trauma intervention and its importance to narrative intervention.

Author (date)	Zimmermann (2011)
Focus	Eastern spirituality and recovery from childhood trauma
Type of document	Dissertation; empirical (qualitative)
Abstract highlights	• Informed by constructivist, humanistic, transpersonal perspectives, and meditation and other Eastern pathways, examined the trajectory of 10 female childhood trauma survivors' journeys of psychological healing and spiritual awakening. • Participants had engaged in Eastern spiritual practices aiming at self-realization as well as in Western psychotherapeutic approaches aiming at ego integration. • All interviewees portrayed ways in which psychological healing and spiritual awakening interfaced to promote PTG. • Six key themes emerged: (1) untiring aspiration, (2) opening to the mystery, (3) undoing the story, (4) healing connections, (5) repairing the split, and (6) reclaiming the body. • Narratives revealed significant psychological and spiritual transformation even after severe child abuse. • Discusses the clinical implications of East/West integration in tx.

R/S RELATED TO SPECIFIC TYPES OF TRAUMA AND POPULATIONS

Military personnel and veteran trauma

Author (date)	Baroody (2011)
Focus	R/S and trauma among veterans
Type of document	Book chapter; conceptual
Abstract highlights	• Redefines the nature of the religious experiences of combat veterans; explores the religious nature of the personality changes within the soldiers; seeks to provide alternative interventions that may assist them in recovering a renewed sense of self, reintegrating back into the family system, and normalizing life within their home culture.
	• Seeks to infuse hope into the therapeutic process, which can lead to resilience and a greater sense of well-being (shalom).
	• Of 10 therapists working with Iraq veterans, none could recall when the subject of religion became a therapeutic issue or when clients talked about their faith in relationship to either primary or secondary trauma experienced as a result of deployments; typically, therapy centers on the effects of traumatic stress on their lives and the lives of their families.
	• Explores why and how talk of or about religion in these sessions would be beneficial.

Author (date)	Bormann, Hurst, & Kelly (2013)
Focus	Mantram (sacred word) repetition and veterans with PTSD
Type of document	Empirical (qualitative)
Abstract highlights	• Describes ways in which a Mantram Repetition Program (MRP) was used for managing PTSD symptoms in 65 outpatient veterans with PTSD who reported a total of 268 triggering events.
	• Program included six weekly group sessions (90 min/wk) on how to (1) choose and use a mantram, (2) slow down thoughts and behaviors, and (3) develop one-pointed attention for emotional self-regulation.
	• Interviews were conducted at three months post intervention as part of a larger randomized clinical trial; results indicated that the MRP was helpful in managing a wide range of emotional reactions.
	• Content analysis of the reported outcomes resulted in 12 discreet categories, including relaxing and calming down, letting go of negative feelings, thinking clearly and rationally, diverting attention away from triggering events, focusing attention, refining mantram skills, dealing with sleep disturbances, coming back from flashbacks, slowing down, communicating thoughts and feelings more effectively, feeling in touch spiritually, and letting go of physical pain.

Author (date)	Bormann, Thorp, Wetherell, Golshan, & Lang (2013)
Focus	Meditation-based mantram intervention for veterans with PTSD
Type of document	Empirical (quantitative)
Abstract highlights	• Explored the efficacy of a portable, private, meditation-based mantram intervention for veterans with chronic PTSD. • Prospective, single-blind randomized clinical trial was conducted with 146 outpatient veterans diagnosed with military-related PTSD. • Randomly assigned to either (a) medication and case management alone (i.e., tx-as-usual [TAU]), or (b) TAU augmented by a six-week group mantram repetition program (MRP + TAU). • Total of 136 veterans (66 in MRP + TAU; 70 in TAU) completed posttreatment assessments; indicated significantly greater symptom reductions in self-reported and clinician-rated PTSD symptoms in the MRP + TAU compared with TAU alone; also reported significant improvements in depression, mental health status, and existential spiritual well-being. • This is a nonpharmacological treatment that does not focus on trauma and has potential as a facilitator of exposure-based therapy or to enhance spiritual well-being.

Author (date)	Currier, Drescher, & Harris (2014)
Focus	Spiritual functioning among veterans seeking residential tx for PTSD
Type of document	Empirical (quantitative)
Abstract highlights	• 788 persons (194 Vietnam veterans in the VA; 194 matched men; 200 Iraq/Afghanistan veterans with PTSD; 200 younger but demographically matched controls) completed the Brief Multidimensional Measure of Religiousness and Spirituality (BMMRS). • Compared to their control group counterparts, veterans from the two clinical samples endorsed weaker spirituality across nearly all dimensions assessed in the study (daily spiritual experiences, forgiveness, private practices, religious coping, organizational religiousness, values); veterans from these two eras largely did not differ from one another in their spiritual functioning. • Spirituality factors were also generally correlated with PTSD symptom severity at the start of tx; greater forgiveness problems were uniquely linked with more symptomatology across both eras.

Author (date)	Currier, Kuhlman, & Smith (2015)
Focus	R/S and risk for suicide among veterans and other military populations
Type of document	Conceptual
Abstract highlights	• Given the troubling suicide rates among military veterans and active-duty personnel and the potential for inclusion of R/S in treatment, there has been limited research and discussion of ethical challenges involved in integrating spirituality into preventive and tx interventions. • Briefly summarizes supporting evidence for addressing spirituality in preventive and tx interventions with military populations, and introduces several ethical concerns that providers may need to consider as they attend to spiritual concerns among veterans and other military personnel who might be at risk for prematurely ending their lives.

Author (date)	Decker (2007)
Focus	Tx for combat trauma from a mystical/spiritual perspective
Type of document	Conceptual
Abstract highlights	• Recovery from combat trauma may depend on discovering a personal meaning in the traumatic experience, in the war, and in civilian life. • The term *spirituality* is traditionally reserved for the experience of prayer and worship but can be understood more broadly. • Presents a rationale for the integration of the spirituality of combat and civilian life into the clinical tx of traumatic sequelae via a mystical perspective; spirituality may be viewed as either immanent or transcendent.

Author (date)	Flowers (2015)
Focus	Christian spirituality, PTG, and veterans
Type of document	Dissertation; empirical (qualitative)
Abstract highlights	• Discusses the research question "What is it like for veterans who experience PTG in the aftermath of trauma through Christian spirituality?" • Interviews with 10 war veterans focused on 7 patterns and 16 subpatterns as part of the process of PTG through Christian spirituality. • Describes PTG as a continuous process, in which it took deliberate effort to move forward in positive ways; participants were self-directed and in constant search of complete wholeness and holistic healing; stated they needed the inclusion of Christian spirituality as part of the PTG process, and it was the key element in their moving forward.

Author (date)	Foy & Drescher (2015)
Focus	R/S, honor, moral injury, and trauma tx for military personnel and their families
Type of document	Conceptual; case study
Abstract highlights	• When faced with combat experiences involving personal injury or the deaths of fellow soldiers and civilians, warriors may experience spiritual struggles about their combat traumas even while turning to God or a higher power for support.
	• R/S can serve an important resource for making meaning of their own war experiences, as well as honoring fallen friends who made the ultimate personal sacrifice; however, for others R/S will become a casualty of their war experiences when morally injurious events are encountered in combat; moral injury refers to the psychosocial-spiritual consequence of involvement in events that violate deeply held moral beliefs.
	• The concept of moral injury is useful in improving understanding of the negative spiritual consequences of combat and in tailoring spiritually based interventions to address them; identifies key R/S issues, both positive and negative; describes a spirituality and trauma group therapy module followed by a case study illustrating an approach to addressing combat-related changes in R/S.

Author (date)	Gubkin (2016)
Focus	R/S and the traumatizing experiences of combat
Type of document	Conceptual; case study
Abstract highlights	• Combat demands significant levels of adaptation and resilience.
	• Spirituality may be challenged by these experiences, and the soldier may be left both psychologically and spiritually wounded as a result.
	• Incorporating spirituality into the healing process may help mend the wounds of combat soldiers, especially within an integrative tx framework.
	• Spirituality and the impact of traumatizing combat experiences are discussed from a cultural perspective using the experiences of an Israeli soldier as an example.

Author (date)	Harris et al. (2011)
Focus	Spiritually integrated intervention for veterans exposed to trauma
Type of document	Empirical (quantitative)
Abstract highlights	• *Building Spiritual Strength* (BSS) is an eight-session, spiritually integrated group intervention designed to address religious strain and enhance religious meaning making for military trauma survivors.
	• Assesses the intervention's effectiveness with veterans who have histories of trauma; participants were randomly assigned to a BSS group ($n = 26$) or a waitlist control group ($n = 28$).
	• BSS participants showed statistically significant reductions in PTSD symptoms based on self-report measures.

Author (date)	Hasanović & Pajević (2015)
Focus	Religious moral beliefs (RMB), trauma severity, and PTSD among Bosnia and Herzegovina war veterans
Type of document	Empirical (quantitative)
Abstract highlights	• Sought to determine the correlation of the level of RMB with trauma experiences and PTSD severity. • 120 Bosnian war veterans divided into two equal groups, one with and one without PTSD. • Religious moral beliefs were inversely related to trauma severity and presented PTSD symptoms. • RMB may have a protective role in the mental health stability of severely traumatized war veterans.

Author (date)	Lanham & Pelletier (2013)
Focus	Christian R/S and healing from war trauma
Type of document	Book chapter; conceptual
Abstract highlights	• Explores emotional healing from trauma, utilizing the application of spiritual interventions, positive coping strategies, and specific approaches for engaging the often emotionally guarded veteran; includes quotes from those who have made the conscious decision to add spiritual interventions into their healing experience. • Discusses the benefit of reconnecting with "spiritual roots" and integrating one's renewed spirituality with the reality of the past, resulting in a "new normal" for emotional stability and improvement in quality of life.

Author (date)	Oman & Bormann (2015)
Focus	PTSD, mantram repetition, and self-efficacy in veterans
Type of document	Empirical (quantitative)
Abstract highlights	• Many military veterans with PTSD refuse or drop out of commonly used trauma-focused, evidence-based txs; research supports the value of spiritual components in diverse types of health care interventions. • Investigated the effects of the Mantram Repetition Program (MRP) on self-efficacy for managing PTSD symptoms with 132 veterans with PTSD who were randomly assigned to case management plus MRP or to case management alone. • MRP participants chose a short, sacred phrase from a spiritual tradition (e.g., "Jesus," "Barukh attah Adonai," "Om mani padme hum"), repeating the phrase silently throughout the day to interrupt unwanted thoughts and behaviors and to improve concentration and attention. • MRP group self-efficacy means as well as tx effects showed linear weekly increases from baseline to post-intervention; tx effects on self-efficacy were significant and mediated tx effects on depression, mental health, spiritual well-being, satisfaction with physical health, and both self-reported and clinician-assessed PTSD symptoms.

Author (date)	Sherman, Harris, & Erbes (2015)
Focus	R/S, PTSD symptoms, and assessment of veterans
Type of document	Conceptual; case study
Abstract highlights	• Many clinicians do not routinely assess or incorporate the R/S domain of functioning in psychological services. • Describes a model for conceptualizing how trauma can affect spirituality by reviewing the possible consequences of each PTSD symptom cluster on clients' belief systems and spiritual practices; specific implications for tx are described for each symptom cluster.

Author (date)	Tait, Currier, & Harris (2016)
Focus	Prayer, coping, and trauma disclosure in deployed US veterans of the Iraq and Afghanistan conflicts
Type of document	Empirical (quantitative)
Abstract highlights	• Within six months of returning from combat zones, 110 veterans (80% men, average age 31, 93% Caucasian white, 53% Protestant and 29% Catholic, with an average 14.2 years of education) were assessed in terms of the ways in which the veterans utilized prayer as a means of coping with difficulties in life. • Indicated that prayer for assistance was associated with fewer PTSD symptoms; prayer for calm and focus was inversely related to depressive symptoms; defer/avoid prayer was positively associated with depressive symptoms. • Supports emerging ideas about prayer as a form of trauma disclosure and highlights the relevance of this approach in coping for veterans as they readjust to civilian life.

Author (date)	Tran, Kuhn, Walser, & Drescher (2012)
Focus	R/S, PTSD, and depressive symptoms in veterans
Type of document	Empirical (quantitative)
Abstract highlights	• Community samples have identified positive and negative associations between R/S and depression; however, research on religiosity is lacking in the area of PTSD. • Significant associations between religiosity, PTSD, and depressive symptoms were observed in veterans enrolled in PTSD residential treatment; contrary to the hypothesis, higher levels of extrinsic-social religious motivation were associated with lower severity of PTSD and depressive symptoms. • A more negative concept of God was associated with higher severity of PTSD and depressive symptoms, whereas a more positive concept of God was associated with lower severity of depressive symptoms and was not significantly associated with PTSD symptoms.

Author (date)	Vujanovic, Niles, Pietrefesa, Schmertz, & Potter (2013)
Focus	Mindfulness, PTSD, and the tx of military veterans
Type of document	Conceptual
Abstract highlights	• How might a practice that has its roots in contemplative traditions, seeking heightened awareness through meditation, apply to trauma-related mental health struggles among military veterans?
	• Clinicians and researchers are increasingly using mindfulness in Western mental health tx programs; mindfulness is about bringing an attitude of curiosity and compassion to present experience.
	• Discusses the integration of mindfulness with current empirically supported txs for PTSD.

Author (date)	Worthington & Langberg (2012)
Focus	Self-forgiveness in treating complex trauma and moral injury in former soldiers
Type of document	Conceptual
Abstract highlights	• Being in the military, especially if deployed in combat or combat-potential settings, can create opportunities for self-condemnation occurring through moral injury or apart from and within the context of complex trauma.
	• Moral injury is internal conflict due to doing or witnessing acts not in line with one's morals.
	• Complex trauma involves a prolonged history of subjection to totalitarian control and involves danger, stress, and inability to escape from the situation (e.g. combat situations).
	• Military deployment might lead to self-condemnation due to moral failures by wrongdoing or when soldiers let down their peers and themselves.
	• Active wrongdoing, moral failure, and failures of church- and culture-created religious expectations contribute.
	• Soldiers need the skill of self-forgiveness through secular and religiously tailored programs delivered via psychoeducational groups, workbooks, or online.

Interpersonal trauma

Author (date)	Ahrens, Abeling, Ahmad, & Himman (2010)
Focus	R/S coping, well-being, and recovery from sexual assault
Type of document	Empirical (quantitative)
Abstract highlights	• Examines predictors and outcomes of positive and negative religious coping among 100 sexual assault survivors who believed in God.
	• African American survivors were more likely to use both forms of religious coping than were survivors from other ethnicities.
	• Suggested that positive religious coping is related to higher levels of psychological well-being and lower levels of depression, whereas negative religious coping is related to higher levels of depression regardless of ethnicity.
	• Only outcome where ethnicity makes a difference is PTG with a stronger relationship between positive religious coping and PTG among Caucasian survivors.

Author (date)	Barrett (2009)
Focus	Healing and relational trauma
Type of document	Book chapter; empirical (qualitative; longitudinal)
Abstract highlights	• Exit and follow-up interviews of participants in a tx program based on the Collaborative Stage Model.
	• Asked what they believed had changed in their lives and to what they attributed this change.
	• Followed up six months and one year later, again asking whether they had maintained their changes and, if so, to what they attributed their changes.
	• Some participants have been interviewed as long as 20 years after they left the program.

Author (date)	Baty (2012)
Focus	R/S in PTG of sexual trauma survivors
Type of document	Dissertation; empirical (qualitative)
Abstract highlights	• Spirituality has been influential in the achievement of PTG for some survivors through meaning-making processes.
	• A hermeneutic phenomenological method was used to gain understanding of how and why spirituality is helpful for some female CSA survivors and not others, and to gain knowledge about how spirituality is experienced as a key-contributing factor of PTG.
	• 8 female CSA survivors (ages 30–70) participated in 30 days of daily prayer/meditation, journaling, and weekly focus group attendance (for 4 weeks) using the *Being Delivered* spirituality framework.
	• All participants experienced spirituality-influenced PTG; 25% experienced most spirituality-related growth in the domain of connection with others; 25% experienced most growth in the domain of personal strength; 12.5% experienced growth in appreciation of life; 37.5% experienced most growth in spiritual change.

Author (date)	Bowland, Edmond, & Fallot (2013)
Focus	R/S coping and trauma symptoms in older survivors
Type of document	Empirical (quantitative)
Abstract highlights	• 43 spiritually distressed older women (ages 55–83) who had survived multiple types of interpersonal trauma participated in a spiritually focused group intervention designed to address spiritual struggles related to earlier abuse and to enhance spiritual coping.
	• Hypothesized that the intervention would increase spiritual well-being and that R/S coping would mediate the relationship between the intervention and the outcomes of depression, posttraumatic stress, anxiety, somatic symptoms, and spiritual well-being.
	• Results provide strong initial support for the importance of understanding the effect of negative R/S coping on depression and anxiety symptoms.

Author (date)	Bryant-Davis, Ullman, Tsong, & Gobin (2011)
Focus	Sexual assault, social support, and R/S coping in the recovery of African American women
Type of document	Empirical (quantitative)
Abstract highlights	• Investigates the relationship between social support and R/S coping strategies and posttrauma symptoms in a sample of 413 African American female sexual assault survivors. • Indicated that survivors with greater social support were less likely to endorse the symptoms of depression and PTSD; conversely, increased use of religious coping was related to greater endorsement of depression and PTSD symptoms.

Author (date)	Bryant-Davis & Wong (2013)
Focus	R/S coping and interpersonal trauma recovery
Type of document	Conceptual
Abstract highlights	• Religious coping, spirituality, and faith-based approaches to trauma recovery include endorsement of beliefs, engagement in behaviors, and access to support from faith communities. • Compared with negative religious coping, spirituality and positive religious coping have been associated with decreased psychological distress for survivors of child abuse, sexual violence, intimate partner violence, community violence, and war; research demonstrates increased use of positive religious coping among some survivors with higher rates of PTSD.

Author (date)	Elliott (1994)
Focus	Christian faith and the prevalence and sequelae of sexual abuse
Type of document	Empirical (quantitative)
Abstract highlights	• Examines the impact of religious faith on the prevalence and long-term sequelae of CSA in a sample of 2,964 professional women. • Examines impact of parents' religious faith on prevalence rate; impact of sexual abuse on adult religious practices; religion as a mediating factor related to adult symptomatology.

Author (date)	Fallot & Blanch (2013)
Focus	R/S dimensions of IPV
Type of document	Conceptual
Abstract highlights	• Explores a definition of trauma in the context of interpersonal violence and the impact of interpersonal trauma on psychological well-being. • Explores R/S in the aftermath of trauma, including the place of R/S resources in trauma recovery and healing. • Considers relationships between religious contexts and interpersonal violence, including the impact of religious abuse and the role of religious involvement in violence prevention. • Recommendations are given for developing trauma-informed services and communities that reflect knowledge about religion, spirituality, violence, and trauma recovery.

Author (date)	Fowler & Hill (2004)
Focus	Social support, R/S, and coping among African American women survivors of IPV
Type of document	Empirical (quantitative)
Abstract highlights	• Examines partner abuse, mental health, and coping in a sample of African American women survivors of partner abuse (*N* = 126).
	• Investigates mediating effects of social support and spirituality, as culturally relevant factors in coping, on the relationships between partner abuse and both depression and PTSD symptoms.
	• PTSD symptoms are significantly related to partner abuse after controlling for the effects of social support and spirituality.

Author (date)	Gall (2006)
Focus	R/S coping and life stress among adult survivors of CSA
Type of document	Empirical (quantitative)
Abstract highlights	• 101 adult survivors of CSA participated.
	• Data on abuse descriptions, coping resources of social support, and general cognitive appraisal, spiritual coping, and current distress; spiritual coping was assessed in relation to a current negative life event.
	• Spiritual coping predicted the current distress of adult survivors beyond the contribution of demographics, severity of abuse, cognitive appraisal, and support satisfaction; self-directed, active surrender and passive deferral significantly contributed to the prediction of anxious mood, while only spiritual discontent predicted depressive mood beyond the contribution of other factors.
	• Negative forms of spiritual coping (e.g., spiritual discontent) tend to be related to greater distress, while more positive forms of spiritual coping (e.g., spiritual support) were related to less distress.
	• Highlights the importance of making a distinction between negative and positive forms of spiritual coping when investigating the role of spirituality in current life functioning.

Author (date)	Gall, Basque, Damasceno-Scott, & Vardy (2007)
Focus	R/S and current adjustment of adult survivors of CSA
Type of document	Empirical (quantitative)
Abstract highlights	• Sample of 101 men and women survivors of CSA completed questionnaires on spirituality (relationship with God or higher power), person factors (blame attributions, self-acceptance, hope), and current adjustment (mood, personal growth, resolution of the abuse).
	• Indicated that relationship with a benevolent God or higher power is related to the experience of less negative mood and a greater sense of personal growth and resolution of the abuse.
	• Relationship with a higher power is related to other person factors such as self-acceptance and hope.
	• Relationship with a benevolent God appears to have an indirect link to depressive mood and resolution of abuse through the mediating pathways of hope and self-acceptance; in contrast, relationship with God appears to have a more direct association to the outcome of personal growth for these survivors.

Author (date)	Ganje-Fling, Veach, Kuang, & Houg (2000)
Focus	CSA and spiritual well-being
Type of document	Empirical (quantitative)
Abstract highlights	• 43 individuals receiving psychotherapy for CSA and 34 clients who sought psychotherapy for other reasons were compared on several aspects of spiritual functioning.
	• The two groups did not differ significantly in spiritual well-being; both groups scored lower than samples of medical outpatients and hospice workers.
	• Most participants reported initiating and discussing spiritual issues during therapy, were satisfied and comfortable with these discussions, rated spirituality as important to problem resolution, and listed several obstacles to spiritual development.

Author (date)	Glenn & Trice (2014)
Focus	R/S and resilience with adult childhood trauma survivors
Type of document	Conceptual
Abstract highlights	• Identifies gaps in resilience research as it relates to spiritual meaning making and childhood trauma survivor development.
	• Explores the influence of sacred text interpretations on resilience.
	• Addresses contextual considerations for pastoral counseling with emerging adult childhood trauma survivors.
	• Discussion of the complex relationship between spiritual coping, theological conflict, and survivor adjustment.

Author (date)	Grossman, Sorsoli, & Kia-Keating (2006)
Focus	Meaning making by male survivors of CSA
Type of document	Empirical (qualitative)
Abstract highlights	• How 16 resilient male survivors of serious CSA, representing a range of racial, ethnic, and socioeconomic backgrounds, made meaning from their abuse experiences.
	• Three types of meaning-making styles were identified in the narratives: meaning making through action (e.g., helping others), using cognitive strategies (e.g., developing a psychological framework for understanding the abuser), and engaging spirituality.
	• The more experience these men had with specialized trauma therapy, the more likely they were to make meaning by attempting to understand their perpetrators.

Author (date)	Hall (1995)
Focus	Spiritual effects of CSA in adult Christian women
Type of document	Empirical (quantitative)
Abstract highlights	• Religious Status Inventory was completed by 75 women divided into three groups: 33 abused clinical subjects, 20 nonabused clinical subjects, and 22 nonabused nonclinical subjects. • Abused group demonstrated significantly lower spiritual functioning than both of the other groups on the total score as well as on four of eight subscales; no significant differences were found between the nonabused clinical group and the nonclinical control group. • Sexual abuse adversely affects spiritual functioning in three broad areas: a sense of being loved and accepted by God, a sense of community with others, and trust in God's plan and purpose for the future.

Author (date)	Jacobs (2015)
Focus	R/S and depression in young adult survivors of CSA
Type of document	Dissertation; empirical (quantitative)
Abstract highlights	• Investigates the relationship between religiosity and depression in adult survivors of childhood physical and sexual abuse across several religious and spiritual dimensions. • Suggests that high religious event attendance and high religious faith importance are protective against a diagnosis of depression, while high spiritual life importance, having a religious experience, childhood physical abuse, and childhood sexual abuse are associated with a depression diagnosis.

Author (date)	Kennedy & Drebing (2002)
Focus	Abuse and religious experience in religiously committed evangelical adults
Type of document	Empirical (quantitative)
Abstract highlights	• Two hypotheses were tested: (1) experience of abuse is related to more frequent (a) religious behavior, such as prayer, church attendance, and Bible reading, and (b) religious experiences, such as religious visions, healings, and speaking in tongues; (2) abuse is also associated with evidence of alienation from God, as noted in more frequent reports of God as distant and more frequent religious doubting. • Survey data from 3,424 adults attending one of four new evangelical-movement churches was controlled for socioeconomic and religious socialization variables. • Self-report of the frequency of abuse was positively associated with frequency of reported transcendent religious experiences and with feelings of distance from God; a significant relationship between abuse and more conventional religious behavior was not found. • Provides mixed support for the idea that abuse results in ambivalent responses toward religion and God.

Author (date)	Krejci et al. (2004)
Focus	Sexual trauma, spirituality, and psychopathology
Type of document	Empirical (quantitative)
Abstract highlights	• 71 sexual trauma victims were compared to 25 control subjects on spiritual well-being, the Eating Disorder Examination, the PTSD Symptom Scale, and the SCID-I/P. • Groups did not differ in terms of spiritual well-being; sexual trauma status was associated with most of the psychopathology outcomes; however, its impact on psychopathology was largely unmoderated by spirituality; the level of spiritual well-being did not alter the probability of current psychopathology; however, increased spiritual well-being was generally associated with lower psychopathology for the entire sample.

Author (date)	Levitt, Horne, Wheeler, & Wang (2015)
Focus	IPV within religious contexts
Type of document	Book chapter; conceptual; case studies
Abstract highlights	• Focuses on the personal and community interactions and messages that reinforce IPV in faith-based families, and explores the psychological literature on the role of R/S in the experience of survivors of IPV. • Case studies are used to describe ways to address the potentially destructive aspects of religion that perpetuate IPV against women.

Author (date)	Marotta-Walters (2015)
Focus	R/S meaning making and clergy-perpetrated sexual abuse
Type of document	Conceptual; case material
Abstract highlights	• Meaning making is a cognitive and affective change in the way an individual perceives a painful experience; following exposure to trauma, meaning making is a psychotherapeutic factor that promotes adaptation, as well as a process that is closely related to R/S. • Explores how psychospiritual development of an adult is shaped by exposure to clergy-perpetrated sexual abuse in childhood, how the trauma might be processed through current empirically informed tx models for adults, and how tx strategies and techniques vary depending on the stage of tx at which meaning making might occur.

Author (date)	Murray-Swank & Pargament (2005)
Focus	Spiritually-integrated intervention for sexual abuse
Type of document	Empirical (case studies)
Abstract highlights	• An eight-session, spiritually integrated, manualized individual intervention for two female survivors of sexual abuse with spiritual struggles (*Solace for the Soul: A Journey Towards Wholeness*).
	• An interrupted time-series design included daily measurements of positive and negative religious coping, spiritual distress, and spiritual self-worth, as well as comprehensive measures of spiritual well-being, religious coping, and images of God pre- and post-intervention and one to two months later.
	• Both clients showed an increase in positive religious coping, spiritual well-being, and positive images of God. In addition, ARIMA intervention analyses revealed significant changes during the course of the intervention (e.g., increased daily use of positive religious coping).

Author (date)	Murray-Swank & Waelde (2013)
Focus	R/S and sexual trauma
Type of document	Book chapter; conceptual, case material
Abstract highlights	• Considers both Western and Eastern spiritual perspectives.
	• Empirical review of the relationships between spirituality, religion, and sexual trauma.
	• Highlights research on a manualized, spiritually integrative program for sexual abuse survivors.
	• Considers theoretical frameworks and various strategies for integrating spirituality in sexual trauma work.
	• Focuses on meditation and mindfulness in sexual trauma work.

Author (date)	Rardin (2014)
Focus	Recovery process of second-generation adult cult survivors
Type of document	Dissertation; empirical study
Abstract highlights	• Narrative study of the role of spirituality in the healing journey and integration into the mainstream of second-generation adult survivors of cults or fundamentalist religions.
	• Participants were asked about their attitude toward spirituality and, if spirituality was present, whether it was positive, negative, or neutral during their recovery process.
	• For survivors of religious cults, spirituality is the source of their trauma, a unique circumstance where the trauma is rooted in what would otherwise be a coping mechanism.
	• Examines cult survivors' methods for reclaiming their spirituality.

Author (date)	Reinert & Edwards (2009)
Focus	Attachment theory, childhood mistreatment, and religiosity
Type of document	Empirical (quantitative)
Abstract highlights	• Explores the relationship of verbal, physical, and sexual mistreatment to attachment to God as well as to concepts of God. • Each form of mistreatment was related adversely to the religiosity measures. • Attachment to parents mediated the relationship between two maltreatment variables (verbal and physical) and attachment to God, as well as the concept of God as loving and as distant; however, attachment to parents did not mediate the relationship between attachment to God and the sexual abuse variable. • Sexual abuse was strongly related to difficulties with attachment to God and one's concept of God; secure attachment to parents provided the necessary context for socialization into religion.

Author (date)	Rossetti (1995)
Focus	Clergy-perpetrated CSA and attitudes toward God and the Catholic Church
Type of document	Empirical (quantitative)
Abstract highlights	• Explores the effects of CSA by priests and other perpetrators on victims' trust in the Catholic Church, the priesthood, and their relationship to God. • Adult Catholics in the United States and Canada were separated into three groups: those who reported no CSA ($n = 1,376$), those who had been sexually abused as children but not by a priest ($n = 307$), and those who had been sexually abused by priests ($n = 40$). • Found a significant decline from those "not abused" to those "abused by a priest"; slight decline in trust for those "abused but not by a priest"; however, the results were statistically inconclusive. • 347 victims were then separated into two groups based on their having received psychotherapy; the "tx" group ($n = 152$) reported significantly less trust in the priesthood, the church, and their relationship to God than the "no tx" group ($n = 194$). • Highlights the possible spiritual damage caused by CSA, particularly if the perpetrator was a religious leader, and supported the need to assess the religious impact of the victim's abuse and to include a process of spiritual healing.

Author (date)	Sinha & Rosenberg (2013)
Focus	Trauma interventions and religion among youth exposed to community violence
Type of document	Research review
Abstract highlights	• 13 studies focused on R/S factors and were reviewed to explore the promise of school- and community-based solutions in reducing the impact of exposure to violence and chronic traumatic events. • Included five intervention studies, five cross-sectional studies, and three nonexperimental studies; six of the studies included R/S as a measured variable. • Review confirmed significant associations between rates of exposure to chronic community violence and presence of PTSD symptoms; five intervention studies confirmed the effectiveness of cognitive behavioral therapy or group therapy in reducing trauma symptoms; two cross-sectional studies identified R/S factors as moderating the impact of chronic community violence; one study revealed higher rates of spirituality/creativity among adolescents with more exposure to traumatic events.

Author (date)	Thanh-Tu, Bellehumeur, & Malette (2014)
Focus	R/S in a trauma and recovery model for women survivors of sex trafficking
Type of document	Conceptual
Abstract highlights	• It is crucial to understand the pain underlying the journeys of survivors, who undergo helplessness, meaninglessness, and disconnection as a result of their traumatic experiences. • Used Herman's (1992, 1997) model of safety, remembrance/mourning, and reconnection to respond to survivors' experiences. • In addition, R/S can be included as part of the meaning-making process; survivors can use spirituality to cope in a manner that contributes to their recovery.

Author (date)	Walker, McGregor, Quagliana, Stephens, & Knodel (2015)
Focus	Changes in R/S after child abuse
Type of document	Book chapter; conceptual; case studies
Abstract highlights	• Considers ways of responding to child abuse survivors' changes in faith after trauma; reviews research that relates various forms of traumas to spiritual outcomes. • Differentiates individuals who use their spirituality to cope with and make meaning of their faith, those who experience damage to specific aspects of faith, and those who experience simultaneous increases and damage to different aspects of faith. • Includes clinical recommendations for responding in psychotherapy to changes in faith after traumatic events; case studies demonstrating psychotherapeutic responses to changes in faith among trauma survivors.

Author (date)	Walker, Reid, O'Neill, & Brown (2009)
Focus	Changes in R/S during and after childhood abuse
Type of document	Literature review
Abstract highlights	• Identified 34 studies of child abuse as they relate to R/S; included information on a total of 19,090 participants.
	• Studies were classified according to both the form of abuse and the form of R/S.
	• Majority of studies indicated either some decline in R/S ($n = 14$) or a combination of both growth and decline ($n = 12$).
	• Seven studies gave preliminary indications that R/S can moderate the development of posttraumatic symptoms or symptoms associated with other disorders.

Disasters and trauma

Author (date)	Aten (2012)
Focus	Disaster spiritual and emotional care in professional psychology
Type of document	Conceptual
Abstract highlights	• A Christian integrative approach to disaster spiritual and emotional care in professional psychology.
	• Practice guidelines are offered, as well as diverse examples of faith-based disaster interventions.
	• Theological and integrative implications are discussed, as well as thoughts on how disaster spiritual and emotional care will contribute to the future of integration.

Author (date)	Aten, Bennett, Davis, Hill, & Hook (2012)
Focus	Predictors of God concept and God control after Hurricane Katrina
Type of document	Empirical (quantitative)
Abstract highlights	• Examined hurricane-related resource loss predictors on God concepts and God control among Hurricane Katrina survivors ($N = 142$) from Mississippi Gulf Coast communities approximately five months after the storm.
	• Increased levels of resource loss predicted a more negative conceptual portrayal of God; greater object resource loss predicted perceptions of less God control over the outcome of events.
	• Strongest individual predictor of a God concept that was more negative and in less control of event outcomes was the loss of food and water, suggesting the importance of critical resource loss on how one conceives of God.
	• For many people who self-identify as R/S, resources may be the one explanatory system that is uniquely capable of helping disaster survivors to understand traumatic events, to have a sense of control of such events, and, in the process, to still maintain a healthy picture of one's self.

Author (date)	Aten & Boan (2016)
Focus	Church-based disaster ministry handbook
Type of document	Book; conceptual
Abstract highlights	• When disasters happen, people turn to local churches as centers for response and assistance; in such cases, knowing what to do can be the difference between calm and chaos, courage and fear, life and death; however, few churches plan in advance for what they should do when the storm hits. • Provides a practical guide for disaster preparedness and suggests that disaster ministry is a critically important work of the church: preparing for the unthinkable, providing relief to survivors, caring for the vulnerable, and helping communities recover.

Author (date)	Aten et al. (2013)
Focus	Clergy, academic, and MHP partnerships in disaster emotional and spiritual care
Type of document	Conceptual
Abstract highlights	• Introduces a clergy, academic, and mental health partnership (CAMP) model that has been used to respond to emotional and spiritual needs that developed in the wake of several disasters affecting the southeast Gulf Coast region. • Intended to build capacity and infrastructure for facilitating (a) disaster emotional and spiritual care training, (b) a clergy and MHP network, (c) emotional support/resiliency experiences for clergy and MHPs, (d) community outreach, and (e) direct services to vulnerable populations.

Author (date)	Aten et al. (2015)
Focus	Spiritual and emotional care in disasters
Type of document	Book chapter; conceptual
Abstract highlights	• Reviews current research on R/S and disasters. • Disaster trauma is unique in its collective dimension (as opposed to individual trauma). • Offers practice guidelines for MHPs regarding spiritual and emotional care in response to disaster. • R/S helps buffer disaster survivors from negative emotional and physical consequences commonly experienced in the aftermath of a disaster (e.g., depression, psychosomatic symptoms). • MHPs need to focus on the loss of community and resources and activate resilience capacities within the client. • MHPs can serve as consultants to religious organizations.

Author (date)	Aten, Topping, Denney, & Hosey (2011)
Focus	African American clergy and churches and minority disaster mental health disparities
Type of document	Empirical (qualitative)
Abstract highlights	• Conducted participatory action research by interviewing 41 African American clergy one year after Hurricane Katrina in severely affected areas of southern Mississippi. • How can MHPs work with African American clergy and their churches by providing training that targets minority disaster mental health disparities? • Offers a three-tier training model for equipping African American clergy and churches to respond to disasters in hopes of reducing minority disaster mental health disparities. • Provides sample outreach and educational training project designed to equip African American clergy and churches in their response to minority disaster mental health disparities.

Author (date)	Cook, Aten, Moore, Hook, & Davis (2013)
Focus	Resource loss, religiousness, health, and PTG following Hurricane Katrina
Type of document	Empirical (quantitative)
Abstract highlights	• Examined associations among resource loss, religiousness (including general religiousness, religious comfort, and religious strain), PTG, and physical and mental health among a sample of Mississippi university students. • Resource loss was negatively associated with health but positively associated with PTG; religious comfort was associated with positive outcomes, and religious strain was associated with negative outcomes; religious comfort buffered the negative effects of resource loss on emotional health; ancillary analyses indicated that associations between resource loss and health were mediated by religious strain.

Author (date)	Drescher et al. (2012)
Focus	Perceived meaning in life and self-efficacy after the Gulf oil spill
Type of document	Empirical (qualitative)
Abstract highlights	• In 2010 the Deepwater Horizon oil platform exploded, releasing five billion barrels of oil into the Gulf of Mexico over five months, affecting Gulf Coast communities, harming both sea and land wildlife, damaging the fishing industry, and destroying natural resources. • Following the spill, 361 individuals seeking clinical services on the Mississippi Gulf Coast revealed that the perceived effects of the spill were only weakly related to life satisfaction; perceived meaning in life and self-efficacy were much more predictive of satisfaction with life, with perceived meaning in life serving as the most important predictor. • Provides initial support for models that emphasize the role of coping mechanisms in the wake of ecological disasters.

Author (date)	Evans, Kromm, & Sturgis (2008)
Focus	Religious responses to Hurricane Katrina
Type of document	Empirical (qualitative)
Abstract highlights	• Examines associations among resource loss, religiousness (including general religiousness, religious comfort, and religious strain), PTG, and physical and mental health among a sample of Mississippi university students soon after Hurricane Katrina in 2005. • Resource loss was negatively associated with health but positively associated with PTG; religious comfort was associated with positive outcomes, and religious strain was associated with negative outcomes; religious comfort appeared to buffer the negative effects of resource loss on emotional health.

Author (date)	Feder et al. (2013)
Focus	Coping and PTSD symptoms after the 2005 Pakistani earthquake
Type of document	Empirical (quantitative)
Abstract highlights	• Conducted three years after the 2005 Pakistan earthquake; goal was to identify potentially protective psychosocial factors associated with lower PTSD and depressive symptom levels. • Adult earthquake survivors ($N = 200$) completed self-report questionnaires measuring PTSD and depressive symptoms, positive and negative affect, and four psychosocial variables (purpose in life, positive and negative religious coping, and social support). • 65% of participants met criteria for PTSD; purpose in life was associated with lower symptom levels and higher positive emotions. • A form of negative religious coping (feeling punished by God for one's sins or lack of spirituality) was associated with higher symptom levels and negative emotions; higher perceived social support was associated with higher positive emotions.

Author (date)	Furman et al. (2016)
Focus	Collective trauma, faith, and service delivery to victims of terrorism and natural disaster
Type of document	Conceptual
Abstract highlights	• Spiritual assessment and helping activities in work with victims of natural disasters and terrorism. • Based on international survey research and the authors' own experiences as victims of natural disaster and terrorism regarding the topics of R/S in the helping relationship. • Discusses the appropriateness of 21 generic, spiritually based helping strategies for potential use in the helping relationship following a disaster.

Author (date)	McIntosh, Poulin, Silver, & Holman (2011)
Focus	R/S and physical and mental health after collective trauma
Type of document	Empirical (quantitative, longitudinal)
Abstract highlights	• Associations of R/S with physical and mental health were examined in a national sample ($N = 890$) after the September 11, 2001, terrorist attacks (9/11).
	• Health information was collected before 9/11, and health, religiosity, and spirituality were assessed longitudinally during six waves of data collection over the next three years.
	• Religiosity (i.e., participation in religious social structures) predicted higher positive affect, fewer cognitive intrusions, and lower odds of new onset mental and musculoskeletal ailments.
	• Spirituality (i.e., subjective commitment to spiritual or religious beliefs) predicted higher positive affect, lower odds of new onset infectious ailments, more intrusions, and a more rapid decline in intrusions over time.
	• Religion and spirituality independently predict health after a collective trauma, controlling for pre-event health status; they are not interchangeable indices.

Author (date)	O'Grady, Rollison, Hanna, Schreiber-Pan, & Ruiz (2012)
Focus	Relationship with the sacred after the Haiti earthquake
Type of document	Empirical (quantitative)
Abstract highlights	• Investigates the impact of the Haitian people's relationship with the divine on their psychospiritual transformation following the Haiti earthquake in 2010.
	• Frequency of R/S factors and predictors of PTG and spiritual transformation are described.

Author (date)	Park (2016)
Focus	Meaning making in disasters
Type of document	Conceptual
Abstract highlights	• Little attention has been paid to successful coping processes in recovering from natural and technological disasters.
	• Factors underlying adaptive psychological responses and recovery after disasters have important implications for intervention and prevention efforts.
	• A meaning-making perspective can help survivors successfully adapt after disasters.

Author (date)	Ramsay & Manderson (2011)
Focus	R/S, resilience, PTG, and extreme weather events
Type of document	Book chapter; conceptual
Abstract highlights	• Faith-based communities are among the first on the ground at times of sudden disaster. • Need to consider R/S factors in managing suffering and supporting resilience. • Discusses the principles of positive psychology, Frankl's work on logotherapy, and the more recent work of psychologists Tedeschi, Calhoun, and Janoff-Bulman regarding PTG, meaning making, and resilience. • Examines the role of religious communities in providing care, along with the current humanitarian guidelines on religion in disasters, specifically extreme weather events.

Author (date)	Ren (2012)
Focus	R/S and community in indigenous trauma therapy following the 2008 China earthquake
Type of document	Case report
Abstract highlights	• Focuses on survivors of the 2008 earthquake in China in order to understand how Chinese spirituality may be involved in the process of psychological rehabilitation. • MHPs tend to view an individual who has experienced tremendous trauma as simply suffering from PTSD, depression, or grief. • Encourages MHPs to appreciate the deeply personal and cultural spiritual resonances that clients present with in the aftermath of trauma. • Understands the meaning of spirituality in the context of Chinese culture, a culture in which spirituality in community serves as a deep bond between the family system and the culture and faith system.

Author (date)	Roberts & Ashley (2008)
Focus	Clergy responses to community, regional, and national tragedy
Type of document	Book; conceptual
Abstract highlights	• Integrates the classic foundations of pastoral care with the unique challenges of disaster response on community, regional, and national levels. • Offers the latest theological perspectives and tools, along with basic theory and skills from the best disaster-response literature, research, and concepts. • A comprehensive explanation of a disaster's life cycle and how spiritual care changes following a disaster.

Author (date)	Sibley & Bulbulia (2012)
Focus	R/S and perceived health after the 2011 Christchurch, New Zealand, earthquake
Type of document	Empirical (quantitative, longitudinal)
Abstract highlights	• Explores how a natural disaster of this magnitude affected deeply held commitments and global ratings of personal health depending on earthquake exposure. • Consistent with the Religious Comfort Hypothesis, religious faith increased among the earthquake-affected, despite an overall decline in religious faith elsewhere in the country; offers the first population-level demonstration that secular people turn to religion at times of natural crisis. • Found no evidence for superior buffering regarding subjective ratings of personal health from having religious faith. • Among those affected by the earthquake, a loss of faith was associated with significant subjective health declines, whereas those who lost faith elsewhere in the country did not experience similar health declines. • Suggests that religious conversion after a natural disaster is unlikely to improve subjective well-being, yet upholding faith might be an important step on the road to recovery.

Author (date)	Smith, Pargament, Brant, & Oliver (2000)
Focus	R/S coping by church members after the 1993 Midwest flood
Type of document	Empirical (quantitative)
Abstract highlights	• Questionnaires were distributed through churches in flood-affected communities in Missouri and Illinois; questionnaire was completed by 209 adults six weeks after the flood, and a follow-up was completed by 131 respondents six months after the flood. • Religious dispositions, attributions, and coping activities were related to psychological and religious outcomes; religious attributions and coping activities predicted psychological and religious outcomes at both six weeks and six months after controlling for flood exposure and demographics. • Positive religious coping may mediate the relationship between religious dispositions and psychological and religious outcomes.

Author (date)	Stratta et al. (2013)
Focus	R/S in the aftermath of a natural catastrophe in Italy
Type of document	Empirical (quantitative)
Abstract highlights	• Assesses the influence of R/S and psychological traumatic effects on a population that had been exposed to an earthquake compared with a control population that had not been exposed.
	• 901 people were evaluated, and their self-perceptions of R/S were used to distinguish between spiritual and religious, spiritual-only, religious-only, and neither spiritual nor religious dimensions.
	• Sample that experienced the earthquake showed lower scores on the spiritual dimension; a weakening of spiritual religiosity in people having difficulty coping with trauma is a consistent finding.
	• Religious-only sample of those who were exposed to the earthquake demonstrated reexperiencing and arousal domain scores similar to the population that was not exposed; religious dimension helped to buffer the community against psychological distress caused by the earthquake; religiosity dimension can positively affect the ability to cope with traumatic experiences.

Author (date)	Taylor (2001)
Focus	R/S and personal values as neglected components of trauma tx
Type of document	Conceptual
Abstract highlights	• Experiences with disaster casualties raise questions about the neglect of spiritual factors in the appraisal of victims.
	• The WHO definition of health and well-being takes patterns of belief/value systems into account.
	• The outcome, it is argued, should more closely approximate the reality of human reactions seen after catastrophe, indicate more of the support systems available sometimes to assist in the recovery of casualties, and encourage academic psychologists to reconsider the place of values in human behavior.

Author (date)	Ting (2016)
Focus	Resiliency among post-earthquake Tibetans' religious community
Type of document	Case report
Abstract highlights	• More awareness of a culturally sensitive approach to psychological relief work during emergencies and disasters has been raised locally and internationally.
	• In the aftermath of the 2010 earthquake that shook the Tibetan community of Yushu in Qinghai, China, anthropological data was gathered on the survivors' healing process as they dealt with loss and poverty.
	• Four vignettes are narrated to highlight the Tibetan "openhearted" attitude as a way to celebrate life and embrace grief.
	• Suggests that modern psychologists have much to learn from the life-celebrating and resilience of this ethnic community in China.
	• When providing psychological relief aid, a new paradigm of care is needed, and religion could play a pivotal role in recovering the strengths of the suffering individuals.

Author (date)	Worthington et al. (2016)
Focus	Forgiveness and psychological, physical, and spiritual resilience in disasters
Type of document	Conceptual
Abstract highlights	• Resilience may necessitate forgiveness—of perpetrators of interpersonal harms (e.g., Rwandan Genocide in 1994), of inadequate responder assistance (e.g., Hurricane Katrina), or in situations where community members perceive themselves as victims of offense by virtue of their group affiliation (e.g., survivors of school shootings); victims may experience unforgiveness toward others in human-caused disasters and may deal with unforgiveness toward God in natural disasters. • A meta-analysis of forgiveness interventions and an empirical study of awareness-raising campaigns on college campuses are utilized to estimate the effects of forgiveness on public health, public mental health, relationships, and spirituality across society after disasters.

Violent and collective trauma

Author (date)	Connor, Davidson, & Li-Ching (2003)
Focus	R/S, resilience, and anger in survivors of violent trauma
Type of document	Empirical (quantitative)
Abstract highlights	• Evaluates the relationship between R/S, resilience, anger and health status, and posttraumatic symptom severity in trauma survivors. • Community sample ($N = 1,200$) completed an online survey that included measures of resilience, spirituality (general beliefs and reincarnation), anger, forgiveness, and hatred. • Survivors of violent trauma ($n = 648$) measures were evaluated with respect to their relationship to physical and mental health, trauma-related distress, and posttraumatic symptom severity. • General spiritual beliefs and anger emerged in association with each outcome, whereas resilience was associated with health status and posttraumatic symptom severity only. • Forgiveness, hatred, and beliefs in reincarnation were not associated with outcome.

Author (date)	Gone (2009)
Focus	Community-based tx for Native American historical trauma
Type of document	Empirical (qualitative)
Abstract highlights	• 19 staff and clients in a Native American healing lodge were interviewed regarding the therapeutic approach used to address the legacy of Native American historical trauma. • Interviewees believe that such pain must be confessed in order to purge its deleterious influence and neutralize the pathogenic effects of colonization; cathartic expression of such pain was said to inaugurate lifelong habits of introspection and self-improvement, including a reclamation of indigenous heritage, identity, and spirituality. • Need to partner with indigenous programs in the exploration of locally determined therapeutic outcomes for existing culturally sensitive interventions that are maximally responsive to community needs and interests.

Author (date)	Grayshield, Rutherford, Salazar, Mihecoby, & Luna (2015)
Focus	Historical trauma of Native American elders
Type of document	Empirical (qualitative)
Abstract highlights	• Phenomenological study of 11 Native American elders addressed three research questions: (a) the effect of historical trauma on self, family, and community; (b) how historical trauma currently affects Native people and their communities; and (c) what they would recommend that counselors and therapists do in addressing issues of historical trauma for native and tribal people. • Participants spoke of historical trauma in terms of loss of tribal language and culture; Native people themselves have the answers to healing and wellness for their own people. • Recommendations for nontribal people who work with Native people and communities.

Author (date)	Hecker, Barnewitz, Stenmark, & Iversen (2016)
Focus	Pathological spirit possession and trauma-related symptoms
Type of document	Empirical (qualitative)
Abstract highlights	• Spirit possession is considered an idiom of distress entailing dissociative symptoms and frequently associated with trauma exposure and trauma-related disorders; study explored subjective disease models and the relationship between spirit possession and trauma-related disorders.
	• 73 (formerly) possessed persons in the Eastern Democratic Republic of the Congo, referred by traditional and spiritual healers, were interviewed about their experiences of pathological spirit possession, trauma exposure, PTSD symptoms, depressive symptoms, shame and guilt, psychotic symptoms, somatic complaints, and the impairment of psychosocial functioning.
	• Significant correlations were found between spirit possession over the lifetime and PTSD symptom severity, feelings of shame and guilt, depressive symptoms, somatic complaints, and psychotic symptoms; spirit possession during the preceding four weeks was associated with PTSD symptom severity, impairment of psycho-social functioning, and psychotic symptom severity.
	• Pathological spirit possession is a broad explanatory framework for various subjectively unexplainable mental and physical health problems including but not limited to trauma-related disorders.

Author (date)	Lee, Connor, & Davidson (2008)
Focus	Eastern and Western spiritual beliefs and violent trauma
Type of document	Empirical (quantitative)
Abstract highlights	• Examined the associations between R/S beliefs and trauma history, and R/S beliefs and PTSD symptoms.
	• Online survey in 2001 from community samples that were representative of the US adult population ($N = 1,969$).
	• Measured R/S concepts and beliefs familiar to both Western and Eastern cultures; Eastern R/S beliefs, but not Western R/S beliefs, were associated with a history of violent trauma.
	• Among those who had experienced violent traumas, agreement with both types of R/S beliefs were related to more severe PTSD symptoms; however, the mechanism of acquisition and effects of beliefs remain unknown.
	• If inquiry into the R/S beliefs of a client is indicated, it may be of value to keep in mind that differences between belief types may exist and to take these differences into account in tx.

Author (date)	Maeland (2010)
Focus	Reintegration of female child soldiers in Northern Uganda
Type of document	Book; conceptual
Abstract highlights	• The reintegration of thousands of formerly abducted children from the Lord's Resistance Army back to their families and communities in northern Uganda represents tremendous challenges. • Cultural and religious complexities that surround young females, often accompanied by their own children, is examined through an understanding of the religious and ritually rich Acholi and Northern Ugandan context and culture. • Consists of contributions from diverse fields such as anthropology, psychology, moral philosophy, religious studies, and theology.

Author (date)	Neuner et al. (2012)
Focus	Spirit possession experiences among former child soldiers and war-affected civilians in Northern Uganda
Type of document	Empirical (quantitative)
Abstract highlights	• Phenomena of spirit possession have been documented in many cultures, but quantitative studies that report the prevalence of spirit possession and provide evidence for its validity as a psychopathological entity are lacking. • Epidemiological study was conducted in 2007–2008 with $N = 1113$ youths and young adults aged between 12 and 25 years in war-affected regions of Northern Uganda. • Participants were interviewed using a scale of *cen* (local equivalent of spirit possession), measures of psychopathology (PTSD and depression), as well as indicators of functional outcome on suicide risk, daily activities, perceived discrimination, physical complaints, and aggression. • *Cen* was more common among former child soldiers than among subjects without a history of abduction; *cen* was related to extreme levels of traumatic events and uniquely predicted functional outcome even when the effects of PTSD and depression were controlled for. • Long-lasting war that is accompanied by the proliferation of spiritual and magical beliefs and propaganda can lead to high levels of harmful spirit possession; provides evidence for the incremental validity of spirit possession as a trauma-related psychological disorder in this context.

Additional types and populations

Author (date)	Adedoyin et al. (2016)
Focus	R/S coping strategies among traumatized African refugees in the United States
Type of document	Conceptual
Abstract highlights	• Most African refugees are from war-torn or natural disaster–affected countries with ethnic, religious, and political conflict. • Religious coping strategies are often utilized by traumatized African refugees; attending religious activities and membership in religious congregations are common. • Such strategies result in marked improvements in overcoming traumatic experiences; in addition, personalized religious undertakings empowered African refugees to effectively address traumatic memories and acculturation stressors.

Author (date)	Bell, Jacobson, Zeligman, Fox, & Hundley (2015)
Focus	R/S coping and resilience in individuals with dissociative identity disorder
Type of document	Empirical (quantitative)
Abstract highlights	• Review of existing literature related to R/S, resilience, and dissociative identity disorder (DID). • Study examined the relationships between these constructs and individuals with DID ($N = 52$). • Implications of the findings for counselors treating individuals with DID.

Author (date)	Blakey (2016)
Focus	R/S in helping African American women with histories of trauma and substance abuse
Type of document	Empirical (case study)
Abstract highlights	• Discusses how 26 African American women with histories of trauma and substance abuse used R/S during the recovery process. • Components include (1) reclaiming spirituality, (2) finding meaning, (3) trusting the process, and (4) active faith. • R/S can be an effective tool that promotes and facilitates recovery, but MHPs need to recognize that not all women want to develop and nurture a spiritual life and that they must take their lead from them.

Author (date)	Bowland, Edmond, & Fallot (2012)
Focus	Spiritually focused intervention with older trauma survivors
Type of document	Empirical (quantitative)
Abstract highlights	• Evaluated the effectiveness of an 11-session, spiritually focused group intervention with older women survivors (age 55 years and older) of interpersonal trauma (child abuse, sexual assault, or domestic violence) in reducing trauma-related depressive symptoms, posttraumatic stress, and anxiety. • 43 women survivors of interpersonal trauma were randomized into tx ($n = 21$) or control ($n = 22$) groups and participated in group psychotherapy. • Tx group had significantly lower depressive symptoms, anxiety, and physical symptoms at posttest compared to the control group; posttraumatic stress symptoms also dropped significantly in the tx group, and gains were maintained at three-month follow-up.

Author (date)	Denney, Aten, & Leavell (2011)
Focus	PTG and R/S growth among cancer survivors
Type of document	Empirical (qualitative)
Abstract highlights	• How does having cancer affect the spiritual growth of cancer survivors across a multidimensional conceptualization of spirituality? • The posttraumatic spiritual growth of 13 cancer survivors was examined using phenomenological data analysis. • Participants reported experiencing spiritual growth across the following domains of spirituality: (a) general spirituality, (b) spiritual development, (c) spiritual social participation, (d) spiritual private practices, (e) spiritual support, (f) spiritual coping, (g) spirituality as a motivating force, (h) spiritual experiences, and (i) spiritual commitment. • Growth was not endorsed in the following three domains of spirituality outlined in the model: (a) spiritual history, (b) spiritual beliefs and values, and (c) spiritual techniques for regulating and reconciling relationships.

Author (date)	Fallot (2007)
Focus	R/S in recovery from serious mental health problems
Type of document	Empirical (qualitative)
Abstract highlights	• Reviews a variety of discussion groups and consultations, published literature, consumer perceptions, and MHPs and religious professionals. • Both potentially supportive and burdensome roles of R/S in recovery were noted; MHPs report both hope for and discomfort with these domains in the context of mental health services. • Recommendations regarding the appropriate place of R/S in psychiatric rehabilitation and related supports.

Author (date)	Gall, Charbonneau, & Florack (2011)
Focus	R/S factors and perceived growth following breast cancer diagnosis
Type of document	Empirical (quantitative)
Abstract highlights	• Investigates the role of religious salience, God image, and religious coping in relation to perceived growth following a diagnosis of breast cancer. • 87 breast cancer patients were followed from prediagnosis up to 24 months post surgery. • Provided limited support for the role of positive aspects of spirituality in relation to perceived growth. • While some forms of positive religious coping demonstrated positive associations, others evidenced no relationship or negative relationships with growth. • Underscores the need to attend to negative aspects of spirituality from early on in the process of cancer adjustment, for such expressions may have implications for women's ability to develop and maintain a positive perspective in their coping over the long-term.

Author (date)	Hoover (2016)
Focus	R/S among adolescents and young adults affected by trauma
Type of document	Dissertation; empirical (qualitative)
Abstract highlights	• Examined the moderating effects of R/S coping based on two types of religious coping: positive and negative. • Also examined subjective experiences of religious coping in response to traumatic events in a sample of 23 adolescents and young adults (ages 18–26 years) • Indicated that participants used both positive and negative religious coping and that more methods of positive religious coping were reported; both positive and negative religious coping were associated with more trauma symptoms, but neither association was significant. • Negative religious coping explained greater variance in trauma symptoms than did positive religious coping.

Author (date)	Janas (2012)
Focus	R/S beliefs and trauma symptoms in firefighters
Type of document	Empirical (quantitative)
Abstract highlights	• Firefighters cope with chronic stress, but do those with R/S beliefs report fewer symptoms of trauma? • 60 participants revealed that spirituality does not act as a protective factor in the reduction of trauma symptoms; however, the number of traumatic events experienced was a predictor for spiritual beliefs, suggesting that the firefighters can experience PTG. • Following trauma, firefighters can experience a change in philosophy of life involving a deepening existential, or R/S, dimension.

Author (date)	Langman & Chung (2013)
Focus	Forgiveness, R/S, traumatic guilt, and PTSD among people with addiction
Type of document	Empirical (quantitative)
Abstract highlights	• Spirituality and forgiveness have been shown to be associated with psychological well-being, whereas guilt has been associated with poor health; however, little is known about the relationship between forgiveness, spirituality, guilt, PTSD, and psychological comorbidity among people in recovery from addiction.
	• Studied 81 people in recovery from addiction and 83 non-addicts from a city in the United Kingdom.
	• 54% of the addiction group met the criteria for full PTSD and reported anxiety, somatic problems, and depression; they described themselves as spiritual, had strong feelings of guilt associated with their addiction, and had difficulty forgiving themselves.
	• Spirituality predicted psychological comorbidity, and feelings of guilt predicted PTSD symptoms and psychological comorbidity; unexpectedly, forgiveness did not predict outcomes.
	• People with drug and alcohol addiction tend to have experienced significant past trauma and PTSD symptoms; posttraumatic stress reactions and associated psychological difficulties can be better understood in the light of guilt and spirituality.

Author (date)	Lev (2015)
Focus	Transpersonal experiences and improved well-being in trauma-based dissociative disorders
Type of document	Dissertation; empirical (quantitative)
Abstract highlights	• Spirituality is generally considered protective to mental health, but there is limited research measuring the effect spirituality has on individuals with more severe mental health diagnoses.
	• Examined the relationship between transpersonal experiences and psychological well-being in 79 individuals diagnosed with trauma-based dissociative disorders.
	• Showed a significant positive correlation between transpersonal experiences and psychological well-being.
	• Recognizing the value of transpersonal experiences for well-being in those with dissociative disorders may prove beneficial for clinical tx.

Author (date)	Luna Pendleton (2013)
Focus	Ecuadorian shamanic perspectives on trauma and spirituality
Type of document	Dissertation; empirical (qualitative)
Abstract highlights	• The broader topic of trauma, spirituality, and healing was explored through the narratives of two indigenous Ecuadorian shamans and two North American women who had experienced indigenous shamanic healing. • A shamanic understanding of trauma is embedded within a profound and sacred cosmological context. • The shaman's understanding of trauma is intrinsically tied to spirituality, and thus the relationship between the experience of trauma and of the numinous is entwined. • It offers psychology an expansive perspective that supports the inclusion of complementary approaches to the clinical tx of trauma; this includes therapeutic modalities such as spiritual stories, metaphors, ritual, and ceremony.

Author (date)	Miller (2002)
Focus	Integrated approach to addictions and trauma recovery
Type of document	Conceptual
Abstract highlights	• Co-occurrence of addiction with trauma-based mental health problems forms a toxic feedback loop, creating assessment and tx challenges. • Traditional separation of addiction and mental health tx has contributed to a high level of recidivism among clients challenged by trauma and addiction problems. • ATRIUM, a tx model rooted in an understanding of trauma reenactment, integrates cognitive behavioral and relational tx through an approach that stresses mind, body, and spiritual health.

Author (date)	Morgan (2009)
Focus	Trauma, addiction, and spirituality
Type of document	Conceptual
Abstract highlights	• Discusses prevalence of trauma, substance use disorders, and their co-occurrence in both clinical and community populations. • Deeper understanding of these phenomena is providing new and promising tx modalities. • Spiritual development and growth complement these emerging txs.

Author (date)	Newmeyer et al. (2016)
Focus	R/S and compassion fatigue among trauma therapists in Romania
Type of document	Empirical (qualitative)
Abstract highlights	• Among trauma therapists, R/S may (a) buffer against compassion fatigue, secondary traumatic stress, and burnout, as well as (b) bolster spiritual growth and compassion satisfaction.
	• Replicated a previous finding in which trauma therapists who endorsed a strong spiritual orientation reported increased compassion satisfaction when engaged in short-term, cross-cultural trauma work.
	• Short-term (one to two weeks) trauma therapists were compared to equally trained professionals working in the same context for two to five months (intermediate-term) and six months to one year (long-term).
	• Statistically significant increases in secondary trauma in both the intermediate- and long-term trauma therapists were observed.
	• However, on pre- and post-measures the long-term trauma therapists reported statistically significant increases in resilience, which implies that the presence of the short-term therapists was beneficial to the long-term therapists.

Author (date)	Park, Edmondson, & Blank (2009)
Focus	R/S pathways to stress-related growth in cancer survivors
Type of document	Empirical (qualitative)
Abstract highlights	• Examined the linkages between personal religiousness, religious control appraisals for the cancer, and religious coping with subsequent stress-related growth, and compared them with a parallel secular pathway defined as hope, self-control appraisals, and active coping.
	• 172 young to middle-aged adult survivors of a variety of types of cancer who had been diagnosed approximately 2.5 years prior were assessed twice across a one-year period.
	• Both pathways predicted stress-related growth, but the religious pathway was a much stronger predictor of subsequent stress-related growth than was the secular pathway.
	• More attention should be given to the influence of multiple dimensions of R/S on growth to better understand the transformative processes reported by many survivors.

Author (date)	Prout, Gerber, & Gottdiener (2015)
Focus	Trauma, defenses, religious engagement, and substance use
Type of document	Empirical (quantitative)
Abstract highlights	• Evaluated the potential moderating roles of defense mechanisms and religious coping on the already-established relationship between trauma symptoms and substance abuse. • Sample of 340 college students; trauma symptoms were associated with increased substance use and abuse. • Use of immature defenses was significantly associated with trauma and substance use; increased substance abuse was also associated with higher rates of negative religious coping; individuals who endorsed trauma symptoms were also more likely to use positive and negative religious coping; defenses and coping did not moderate the relationship between trauma and substance use.

Author (date)	Roland (2016)
Focus	Meaning, PTG, and PTSD symptoms among teachers in El Salvador
Type of document	Dissertation; empirical (quantitative)
Abstract highlights	• Studied 257 violence-exposed teachers from educational departments throughout El Salvador (a highly religious country) and the roles of theistic and nontheistic spiritual experiences, as well as meaning made of salient stressors from their lives, perceptions of PTG, and PTSD symptomatology. • (1) Nontheistic spiritual experiences uniquely predicted greater meaning made in the presence of control variables; (2) theistic and nontheistic experiences jointly explained variance in perceived PTG, with neither approach emerging as a unique predictor; and (3) nontheistic experiences predicted lower PTSD symptom severity, and theistic experiences were uniquely linked with more trauma-related symptomatology. • Supports the importance of spirituality as a protective factor in persons exposed to pervasive trauma and the importance of developing interventions for this population.

Author (date)	Santoro, Suchday, Benkhoukha, Ramanayake, & Kapur (2016)
Focus	Adverse childhood experiences and R/S in emerging adolescents in India
Type of document	Empirical (quantitative)
Abstract highlights	• Examined childhood adversity and R/S in a sample of adolescents from Hyderabad, India. • 139 adolescents reported that adversity and existential well-being were significantly and inversely related; boys endorsed a greater number of adverse childhood experiences, except physical abuse, which was endorsed at comparable rates by gender; girls reported greater degrees of well-being and religiosity; however, no gender differences were found on daily spiritual experiences and religious coping. • Well-being was significantly associated with religiosity, daily spiritual experiences, and religious coping for girls; adversity was associated with greater desire to connect with a higher power in boys and increased religious coping in girls.

Author (date)	Shinall & Guillamondegui (2015)
Focus	R/S and end-of-life care among trauma patients
Type of document	Empirical (quantitative)
Abstract highlights	• Evidence suggests that religiousness is associated with more aggressive end-of-life (EOL) care among terminally ill patients. • Offers retrospective review of all trauma patients surviving at least two days but dying within 30 days of injury over a three-year period at a major academic trauma center. • Examines the association of religious affiliation and request for chaplain visit with aggressive EOL care among critically injured trauma patients. • Controlling for social factors, severity of injury, and medical comorbidities, religious affiliation was associated with a 43% increase in days until death; controlling for these same variables, chaplain request was associated with a 24% decrease in time until death.

Author (date)	Smedley (2016)
Focus	Negative spiritual responses to trauma from urban ministry workers
Type of document	Dissertation; empirical (qualitative)
Abstract highlights	• Urban community settings are often filled with community violence, including violence in the home or school; urban settings are often composed of minority groups who live near the poverty line and experience issues of social and racial oppression; minority groups are often religious and utilize R/S as a means to cope with stress. • Utilized the literature and data taken from focus groups with urban ministry workers to better understand themes of why people distance themselves from their R/S upon experiencing trauma. • Three major themes, several subthemes, and additional community descriptions were all coded for the purpose of describing the experience of families in the urban setting.

Author (date)	Ting & Watson (2007)
Focus	Religious persecution among Chinese pastors
Type of document	Empirical (qualitative)
Abstract highlights	• Nine Chinese pastors were interviewed about their experiences during persecution using a hermeneutic phenomenology method. • Eight themes emerged as unique ways to respond and cope during the suffering: experiencing God's presence, letting go and surrender to God, identification with the passion of Christ and his disciples, preparing to suffer, normalizing their suffering, worshiping and reciting Scriptures, fellowship and family support, and believing in a greater purpose. • Four themes regarding posttraumatic transformation emerged. • Christian counselors are encouraged to explore the meaning and emotion of suffering in therapy, as well as to use culturally sensitive coping mechanisms.

Author (date)	Vis & Battistone (2014)
Focus	Trauma and spiritual-based strategies for adolescent students
Type of document	Conceptual
Abstract highlights	• Review of the trauma literature identifies the significance of both community and faith-based intervention in positive posttraumatic recovery. • While a link has been identified between the use of Christian strategies and a decreased risk of posttraumatic symptoms, the literature suggests that adolescents may avoid the use of Christian strategies during their recovery. • Spiritually based strategies are discussed in an effort to effectively respond to the spiritual and psychological needs of adolescents in faith-based schools on the occasion of a traumatic event.

Author (date)	Weiss-Ogden (2014)
Focus	Trauma and spiritual well-being of women with substance use disorders
Type of document	Dissertation; empirical (quantitative)
Abstract highlights	• Trauma experiences are often at the core of co-occurring substance abuse and mental health disorders, and spirituality is a mitigating factor in recovery from co-occurring trauma and substance use disorders. • Study examined the relationship between trauma and the spiritual well-being of women with substance use disorders. • Participants included 108 adult female residents of a two-year modified therapeutic community who met DSM-IV criteria for a substance use disorder and reported a lifetime history of at least one traumatic occurrence. • Women who experienced sexual molestation had significantly lower Spiritual Well-Being scores than those who had not experienced this trauma. • As the age at first occurrence increased, so did Spiritual Well-Being scores; or the younger the participant was at the age of each of these trauma occurrences, the lower her Spiritual Well-Being scores. • No significant relationship was found between the total number of traumatic occurrences and Spiritual Well-Being scores of women with substance use disorders.

Author (date)	Wilson (2015)
Focus	Trauma, coping, and pregnant couples' biopsychosocial-spiritual health
Type of document	Dissertation; empirical (quantitative)
Abstract highlights	• Pregnancy and trauma are each complex biopsychosocial-spiritual processes with implications for the couple relationship. • Includes a systematic review of literature published on the impact of traumatic stress on obstetric, neonatal, and postnatal outcomes, and a study of couples' experiences with traumatic stress, pregnancy coping, and the couple relationship. • Maternal trauma can affect obstetric physical and mental health, fetal prenatal health, and maternal postnatal outcomes. • Maternal and partner pregnancy stress, trauma, and relationship report are related; discusses patterns of moderation and indirect effects between the variables; recommendations are made for medical family therapy researchers and practitioners.

Author (date)	Yedlin (2012)
Focus	R/S, trauma exposure, PTSD, and alcohol use in emerging adults
Type of document	Dissertation; empirical (quantitative)
Abstract highlights	• Study of 1,660 college students between the ages of 18 and 25. • Explored the role of R/S in relation to interpersonal trauma frequency, PTSD, and alcohol use in emerging adults. • Religious identity, frequency of prayer, and spiritual beliefs moderated the relation between interpersonal trauma frequency and PTSD. • No significant moderational role of R/S in the relation between PTSD and alcohol use. • Slight mediation by PTSD of the relation between interpersonal trauma frequency and alcohol use. • Use of R/S in interventions and txs following interpersonal trauma.

REFERENCES

Abdul-Hamid, W. K., & Hughes, J. H. (2015). Integration of religion and spirituality into trauma psychotherapy: An example in Sufism? *Journal of EMDR Practice and Research, 9*(3), 150-56. doi:10.1891/1933-3196.9.3.150

Abi Hashem, N. (2012). Religious and pastoral responses to trauma. In C. R. Figley (Ed.), *Encyclopedia of trauma: An interdisciplinary guide* (pp. 542-44). Thousand Oaks, CA: Sage.

Adedoyin, A. C., Bobbie, C., Griffin, M., Adedoyin, O. O., Ahmad, M., Nobles, C., & Neeland, K. (2016). Religious coping strategies among traumatized African refugees in the United States: A systematic review. *Social Work and Christianity, 43*, 95-107.

Agger, I., Igreja, V., Kiehle, R., & Polatin, P. (2012). Testimony ceremonies in Asia: Integrating spirituality in testimonial therapy for torture survivors in India, Sri Lanka, Cambodia, and the Philippines. *Transcultural Psychiatry, 49*(3/4), 568-89. doi:10.1177/1363461512447138

Ahrens, C., Abeling, S., Ahmad, S., & Himman, J. (2010). Spirituality and well-being: The relationship between religious coping and recovery from sexual assault. *Journal of Interpersonal Violence, 25*(7), 1242-63.

Altmaier, E. M. (2013). Through a glass darkly: Personal reflections on the role of meaning in response to trauma. *Counselling Psychology Quarterly, 26*(1), 106-13. doi:10.1080/09515070.2012.728760

Aten, J. (2012). Disaster spiritual and emotional care in professional psychology: A Christian integrative approach. *Journal of Psychology & Theology, 40*(2), 131-35.

Aten, J., Bennett, P. R., Davis, D., Hill, P. C., & Hook, J. N. (2012). Predictors of God concept and God control after Hurricane Katrina. *Psychology of Religion and Spirituality, 4*(3), 182-92.

Aten, J., & Boan, D. (2016). *Disaster ministry handbook*. Downers Grove, IL: InterVarsity Press.

Aten, J., Boan, D. M., Hosey, J. M., Topping, S., Graham, A., & Im, H. (2013). Building capacity for responding to disaster emotional and spiritual needs: A clergy, academic, and mental health partnership model (CAMP). *Psychological Trauma: Theory, Research, Practice, & Policy, 5*(6), 591-600.

Aten, J. D., O'Grady, K. A., Milstein, G., Boan, D., Smigelsky, M. A., Schruba, A., & Weaver, I. (2015). Providing spiritual and emotional care in response to disaster. In D. F. Walker, C. A. Courtois, & J. D. Aten (Eds.), *Spiritually oriented psychotherapy for trauma* (pp. 189-210). Washington, DC: American Psychological Association. doi:10.1037/14500-010

Aten, J., Topping, S., Denney, R., & Hosey, J. (2011). Helping African American clergy and churches address minority disaster mental health disparities: Training needs, model, and example. *Psychology of Religion, and Spirituality, 3*(1), 15-23.

Aten, J. D., & Walker, D. F. (2012). Religion, spirituality, and trauma: An introduction. *Journal of Psychology & Theology, 40*(4), 255-56.

Ballaban, S. (2014). The use of traumatic biblical narratives in spiritual recovery from trauma: Theory and case study. *Journal of Pastoral Care & Counseling (Online), 68*(4), 1-11.

Baroody, A. N. (2011). Spirituality and trauma during a time of war: A systemic approach to pastoral care and counseling. In R. B. Everson & C. R. Figley (Eds.), *Families under fire: Systemic therapy with military families* (pp. 165-90). New York, NY: Routledge.

Barrett, M. J. (2009). Healing from relational trauma: The quest for spirituality. In F. Walsh (Ed.), *Spiritual resources in family therapy* (2nd ed., pp. 267-85). New York, NY: Guilford Press.

Baty, S. D. (2012). *Healing the invisible wound: Examining spirituality in the posttraumatic growth of sexual trauma survivors* (Doctoral dissertation). Retrieved from http://gradworks.umi.com/35/16/3516060.html

Bell, H., Jacobson, L., Zeligman, M., Fox, J., & Hundley, G. (2015). The role of religious coping and resilience in individuals with dissociative identity disorder. *Counseling and Values, 60*(2), 151-63. doi:10.1002/cvj.12011

Bennet, M. E. (1999). *Religious, spiritual, and exceptional experiences in trauma treatment: A clinical training model* (Doctoral dissertation). Ann Arbor, MI: Antioch New England Graduate School.

Berrett, M. E., Hardman, R. K., O'Grady, K. A., & Richards, P. S. (2007). The role of spirituality in the treatment of trauma and eating disorders: Recommendations for clinical practice. *Eating Disorders, 15*(4), 373-89. doi:10.1080/10640260701454394

Blakey, J. M. (2016). Role of spirituality in helping African American women with histories of trauma and substance abuse heal and recover. *Social Work and Christianity, 43*(1), 40-59.

Boehnlein, J. K. (2007). Religion and spirituality after trauma. In L. J. Kirmayer, R. Lemelson, & M. Barad (Eds.), *Understanding trauma: Integrating biological, clinical, and cultural perspectives* (pp. 259-74). New York, NY: Cambridge University Press. doi:10.1017/CBO9780511500008.018

Bonanno, G. A. (2004). Loss, trauma, and human resilience: Have we underestimated the human capacity to thrive after extremely aversive events? *American Psychologist, 59*(1), 20-28. doi:10.1037/0003-066X.59.1.20

Bormann, J. E., Hurst, S., & Kelly, A. (2013). Responses to mantram repetition program from veterans with posttraumatic stress disorder: A qualitative analysis. *Journal of Rehabilitation Research & Development, 50*(6), 769-84. doi:10.1682/JRRD.2012.06.0118

Bormann, J. E., Thorp, S. R., Wetherell, J. L., Golshan, S., & Lang, A. J. (2013). Meditation-based mantram intervention for veterans with posttraumatic stress disorder: A randomized trial. *Psychological Trauma: Theory, Research, Practice, and Policy, 5*(3), 259-67. doi:10.1037/a0027522

Bowland, S. (2015). What kind of God is that? Religious/spiritual issues in psychotherapy with trauma survivors. *PsycCRITIQUES, 60*(20). doi:10.1037/a0039113

Bowland, S., Edmond, T., & Fallot, R. D. (2012). Evaluation of a spiritually focused intervention with older trauma survivors. *Social Work, 57*(1), 73-82. doi:10.1093/sw/swr001

Bowland, S., Edmond, T., & Fallot, R. D. (2013). Negative religious coping as a mediator of trauma symptoms in older survivors. *Journal of Religion, Spirituality & Aging, 25*(4), 326-43. doi:10.1080/15528030.2012.739989

Brewer-Smyth, K., & Koenig, H. G. (2014). Could spirituality and religion promote stress resilience in survivors of childhood trauma? *Issues in Mental Health Nursing, 35*(4), 251-56. doi:10.3109/01612840.2013.873101

Brooks, K. N. (2012). *The lived experience of posttraumatic growth and the influence of spirituality* (Doctoral dissertation). Retrieved from http://gradworks.umi.com/35/77/3577654.html

Brown, L. S. (2008). *Cultural competence in trauma psychotherapy: Beyond the flashback.* Washington, DC: American Psychological Association. doi:10.1037/11752-000

Bryant-Davis, T., Ellis, M. U., Burke-Maynard, E., Moon, N., Counts, P. A., & Anderson, G. (2012). Religiosity, spirituality, and trauma recovery in the lives of children and adolescents. *Professional Psychology: Research and Practice, 43*(4), 306-14. doi:10.1037/a0029282

Bryant-Davis, T., Ullman, S. E., Tsong, Y., & Gobin, R. (2011). Surviving the storm of sexual assault: The role of social support and religious coping in the recovery of African American women. *Violence against Women, 17*(12), 1601-18.

Bryant-Davis, T., & Wong, E. C. (2013). Faith to move mountains: Religious coping, spirituality, and interpersonal trauma recovery. *American Psychologist, 68*(8), 675-84. doi:10.1037/a0034380

Brymer, M., Jacobs, A., Layne, C., Pynoos, R., Ruzek, J., Steinberg, A., . . . Watson, P. (2006). *Psychological First Aid: Field operations guide for community religious professionals* (2nd ed.). National Child Traumatic Stress Network and National Center for PTSD. Retrieved from www.nctsnet.org/nctsn_assets/pdfs/pfa/CRP-PFA_Guide.pdf

Chopko, B. A., & Schwartz, R. C. (2009). The relation between mindfulness and posttraumatic growth: A study of first responders to trauma-inducing incidents. *Journal of Mental Health Counseling, 31*(4), 363-76.

Connor, K. M., Davidson, J. T., & Li-Ching, L. (2003). Spirituality, resilience, and anger in survivors of violent trauma: A community survey. *Journal of Traumatic Stress, 16*(5), 487.

Cook, S., Aten, J., Moore, M., Hook, J., & Davis, D. (2013). Resource loss, religiousness, health, and posttraumatic growth following Hurricane Katrina. *Mental Health, Religion & Culture, 16,* 352-66.

Courtois, C. A. (2015). First, do no more harm: Ethics of attending to spiritual issues in trauma treatment. In D. F. Walker, C. A. Courtois, & J. D. Aten (Eds.), *Spiritually oriented psychotherapy for trauma* (pp. 55-75). Washington, DC: American Psychological Association. doi:10.1037/14500-004

Currier, J. M., Drescher, K. D., & Harris, J. I. (2014). Spiritual functioning among veterans seeking residential treatment for PTSD: A matched control group study. *Spirituality in Clinical Practice, 1*(1), 3-15. doi:10.1037/scp0000004

Currier, J. M., Kuhlman, S., & Smith, P. N. (2015). Empirical and ethical considerations for addressing spirituality among veterans and other military populations at risk for suicide. *Spirituality in Clinical Practice, 2,* 68-73. doi:10.1037/scp0000057

Dagmang, F. D. (2012). God-talk as a means of healing: A spiritual rebirth through novel writing and auto-analysis. *Journal of Dharma, 37*(3), 325-38.

de Castella, R., & Simmonds, J. G. (2013). "There's a deeper level of meaning as to what suffering's all about": Experiences of religious and spiritual growth following trauma. *Mental Health, Religion & Culture, 16*(5), 536-56.

Decker, L. R. (2007). Combat trauma: Treatment from a mystical/spiritual perspective. *Journal of Humanistic Psychology, 47,* 30-53. doi:10.1177/0022167806293000

Denney, R. M., Aten, J. D., & Leavell, K. (2011). Posttraumatic spiritual growth: A phenomenological study of cancer survivors. *Mental Health, Religion & Culture, 14*(4), 371-91.

Doehring, C. (1993). *Internal desecration: Traumatization and representations of God.* Lanham, MD: University Press of America.

Drescher, C. F., Baczwaski, B. J., Walters, A. B., Aiena, B. J., Schulenberg, S. E., & Johnson L. R. (2012). Coping with an ecological disaster: The role of perceived meaning in life and self-efficacy after the Gulf oil spill. *Ecopsychology, 4,* 56-63.

Elliott, D. M. (1994). The impact of Christian faith on the prevalence and sequelae of sexual abuse. *Journal of Interpersonal Violence, 9*(1), 95-108. doi:10.1177/0886260 94009001006

Eriksson, C. B., & Yeh, D.-A. (2012). Grounded transcendence: Resilience to trauma through spirituality and religion. In K. Gow & M. J. Celinski (Eds.), *Individual trauma: Recovering from deep wounds and exploring the potential for renewal* (pp. 53-71). Hauppauge, NY: Nova Science Publishers.

Evans, D., Kromm, C., & Sturgis, S. (2008). *Faith in the Gulf: Lessons from the religious response to Hurricane Katrina.* Institute for Southern Studies. Retrieved from www .facingsouth.org/sites/default/files/Gulf%20Report-Faith.pdf

Fallot, R. D. (2007). Spirituality and religion in recovery: Some current issues. *Psychiatric Rehabilitation Journal, 30*(4), 261-70. doi:10.2975/30.4.2007.261.270

Fallot, R. D., & Blanch, A. K. (2013). Religious and spiritual dimensions of traumatic violence. In K. I. Pargament, A. Mahoney, & E. P. Shafranske (Eds.), *APA handbook of psychology, religion, and spirituality: Vol. 2. An applied psychology of religion and spirituality* (pp. 371-87). Washington, DC: American Psychological Association. doi:10.1037/14046-019

Farley, Y. R. (2007). Making the connection: Spirituality, trauma and resiliency. *Journal of Religion & Spirituality in Social Work: Social Thought, 26*(1), 1-15. doi:10.1300 /J377v26n01_01

Feder, A., Ahmad, S., Lee, E. J., Morgan, J. E., Singh, R., Smith, B. W., . . . Charney, D. S. (2013). Coping and PTSD symptoms in Pakistani earthquake survivors: Purpose in life, religious coping and social support. *Journal of Affective Disorders, 147,* 156-63.

Flowers, S. E. (2015). *Veterans' experience of posttraumatic growth through Christian spirituality: A heuristics study* (Doctoral dissertation). Retrieved from http://grad works.umi.com/36/69/3669371.html

Follette, V. M., Briere, J., Rozelle, D., Hopper, J. W., & Rome, D. I. (2015). *Mindfulness-oriented interventions for trauma: Integrating contemplative practices.* New York, NY: Guilford Press.

Fowler, D. N., & Hill, H. M. (2004). Social support sources and spirituality as culturally relevant factors in coping among African American women survivors of partner abuse. *Violence Against Women, 10,* 1267-82.

Foy, D. W., & Drescher, K. D. (2015). Faith and honor in trauma treatment for military personnel and their families. In D. F. Walker, C. A. Courtois, & J. D. Aten (Eds.), *Spiritually oriented psychotherapy for trauma* (pp. 233-52). Washington, DC: American Psychological Association. doi:10.1037/14500-012

Frawley-O'Dea, M. G. (2015). God images in clinical work with sexual abuse survivors: A relational psychodynamic paradigm. In D. F. Walker, C. A. Courtois, & J. D. Aten (Eds.), *Spiritually oriented psychotherapy for trauma* (pp. 169-88). Washington, DC: American Psychological Association.

Furman, L. D., Benson, P. W., Moss, B., Danbolt, T., Vetvik, E., & Canda, E. (2016). Reflections on collective trauma, faith, and service delivery to victims of terrorism and natural disaster: Insights from six national studies. *Social Work and Christianity, 43,* 74-94.

Gall, T. L. (2006). Spirituality and coping with life stress among adult survivors of childhood sexual abuse. *Child Abuse & Neglect, 30*(7), 829-44. doi:10.1016/j.chiabu .2006.01.003

Gall, T. L., Basque, V., Damasceno-Scott, M., & Vardy, G. (2007). Spirituality and the current adjustment of adult survivors of childhood sexual abuse. *Journal for the Scientific Study of Religion, 46*(1), 101-17. doi:10.1111/j.1468-5906.2007.00343.x.

Gall, T. L., Charbonneau, C., & Florack, P. (2011). The relationship between religious/spiritual factors and perceived growth following a diagnosis of breast cancer. *Psychology and Health, 26*(3), 287-305.

Ganje-Fling, M., Veach, P. M., Kuang, H., & Houg, B. (2000). Effects of childhood sexual abuse on client spiritual well-being. *Counseling and Values, 44*(2), 84-91.

Gear Haugen, M. R. (2012). *Does trauma lead to religiousness? A longitudinal study of the effects of traumatic events on religiousness and spirituality during the first three years at university* (Doctoral dissertation). Retrieved from https://etd.ohiolink.edu/

Gerber, M. M., Boals, A., & Schuettler, D. (2011). The unique contributions of positive and negative religious coping to posttraumatic growth and PTSD. *Psychology of Religion and Spirituality, 3*(4), 298-307. doi:10.1037/a0023016

Glenn, C. B., & Trice, B. (2014). A bridge over troubled waters: Spirituality and resilience with emerging adult childhood trauma survivors. *Journal of Spirituality in Mental Health, 16*, 37-50. doi:10.1080/19349637.2014.864543

Gone, J. P. (2009). A community-based treatment for Native American historical trauma: Prospects for evidence-based practice. *Journal of Consulting and Clinical Psychology, 77*(4), 751-62. doi:10.1037/a0015390

Gostečnik, C., Slavič, T., Lukek, S., & Cvetek, R. (2014). Trauma and religiousness. *Journal of Religion & Health, 53*(3), 690-701. doi:10.1007/s10943-012-9665-y

Grame, C. J., Tortorici, J. S., Healey, B. J., Dillingham, J. H., & Winklebaur, P. (1999). Addressing spiritual and religious issues of clients with a history of psychological trauma. *Bulletin of the Menninger Clinic, 63*(2), 223-39.

Grand, S. (2015). Responding to the problem of evil and suffering. In D. F. Walker, C. A. Courtois, & J. D. Aten (Eds.), *Spiritually oriented psychotherapy for trauma* (pp. 253-71). Washington, DC: American Psychological Association.

Grant, R. (1999). Spirituality and trauma: An essay. *Traumatology, 5*(1). doi:10.1177/153476569900500103

Grayshield, L., Rutherford, J. J., Salazar, S. B., Mihecoby, A. L., & Luna, L. L. (2015). Understanding and healing historical trauma: The perspectives of Native American elders. *Journal of Mental Health Counseling, 37*(4), 295-307. doi:10.17744/mehc.37.4.02

Grossman, F. K., Sorsoli, L., & Kia-Keating, M. (2006). A gale force wind: Meaning making by male survivors of childhood sexual abuse. *American Journal of Orthopsychiatry, 76*(4), 434-43.

Gubkin, R. (2016). An exploration of spirituality and the traumatizing experiences of combat. *Journal of Humanistic Psychology, 56*(4), 311-30. doi:10.1177/0022167814563142

Hall, M. E. L., & Johnson, E. (2001). Theodicy and therapy: Theological/philosophical contributions to the problem of suffering. *Journal of Psychology and Christianity, 20*(1), 5-17.

Hall, T. A. (1995). Spiritual effects of childhood sexual abuse in adult Christian women. *Journal of Psychology & Theology, 23*(2), 129-34.

Harper, A. R., & Pargament, K. I. (2015). Trauma, religion, and spirituality: Pathways to healing. In K. E. Cherry (Ed.), *Traumatic stress and long-term recovery: Coping with disasters and other negative life events* (pp. 349-67). Cham, Switzerland: Springer International.

Harris, J. I., Erbes, C. R., Engdahl, B. E., Olson, R. A., Winskowski, A. M., & McMahill, J. (2008). Christian religious functioning and trauma outcomes. *Journal of Clinical Psychology, 64*(1), 17-29. doi:10.1002/jclp.20427

Harris, J. I., Erbes, C. R., Engdahl, B. E., Tedeschi, R. G., Olson, R. H., Winskowski, A. M. M., & McMahill, J. (2010). Coping functions of prayer and posttraumatic growth. *International Journal for the Psychology of Religion, 20,* 26-38.

Harris, J. I., Erbes, C. R., Engdahl, B. E., Thuras, P., Murray-Swank, N., Grace, D., . . . TuVan, L. (2011). The effectiveness of a trauma focused spiritually integrated intervention for veterans exposed to trauma. *Journal of Clinical Psychology, 67*(4), 425-38. doi:10.1002/jclp.20777

Harris, J. I., Erbes, C. R., Winskowski, A. M., Engdahl, B. E., & Nguyen, X. V. (2014). Social support as a mediator in the relationship between religious comforts and strains and trauma symptoms. *Psychology of Religion and Spirituality, 6*(3), 223-29. doi:10.1037/a0036421

Harris, J. I., Leak, G. K., Dubke, R., & Voecks, C. (2015). Religious strain and postconventional religiousness in trauma survivors. *Psychology of Religion and Spirituality, 7*(2), 173-78. doi:10.1037/rel0000026

Hasanović, M., & Pajević, I. (2015). Religious moral beliefs inversely related to trauma experiences severity and presented posttraumatic stress disorder among Bosnia and Herzegovina war veterans. *Journal of Religion & Health, 54*(4), 1403-15. doi:10.1007/s10943-014-9954-8

Hecker, T., Barnewitz, E., Stenmark, H., & Iversen, V. (2016). Pathological spirit possession as a cultural interpretation of trauma-related symptoms. *Psychological Trauma: Theory, Research, Practice, and Policy, 8*(4), 468-76.

Hipolito, E., Samuels-Dennis, J. A., Shanmuganandapala, B., Maddoux, J., Paulson, R., Saugh, D., & Carnahan, B. (2014). Trauma-informed care: Accounting for the interconnected role of spirituality and empowerment in mental health promotion. *Journal of Spirituality in Mental Health, 16*(3), 193-217. doi:10.1080/19349637.2014.925368

Hoover, S. C. (2016). An examination of the moderating effects of religious coping among adolescents and young adults affected by trauma. *Dissertation Abstracts International, 76,* (12-B)(E).

Jacobs, M. (2015). Spirituality and depression in young adult survivors of childhood physical and sexual abuse. *Dissertation Abstracts International, 76*, (2-B)(E).

Janas, D. M. (2012). *Impact of spiritual/religious beliefs on incidents of trauma symptoms in firefighters* (Doctoral dissertation). Retrieved from http://gradworks.umi .com/35/33/3533089.html

Kalayjian, A. (2002). Biopsychosocial and spiritual treatment of trauma. In F. W. Kaslow (Ed.), *Comprehensive handbook of psychotherapy: Vol. 3. Interpersonal/humanistic/ existential* (pp. 615-37). Hoboken, NJ: John Wiley & Sons.

Kalsched, D. (2013). *Trauma and the soul: A psycho-spiritual approach to human development and its interruption.* New York, NY: Routledge.

Kennedy, P., & Drebing, C. E. (2002). Abuse and religious experience: A study of religiously committed evangelical adults. *Mental Health, Religion & Culture, 5*(3), 225-37. doi:10.1080/13674670110112695

Kick, K. A., & McNitt, M. (2016). Trauma, spirituality, and mindfulness: Finding hope. *Social Work & Christianity, 43*(3), 97-108.

Krejci, M. J., Thompson, K. M., Simonich, H., Crosby, R. D., Donaldson, M. A., Wonderlich, S. A., & Mitchell, J. E. (2004). Sexual trauma, spirituality, and psychopathology. *Journal of Child Sexual Abuse, 13*(2), 85-103. doi:10.1300/J070v13n02_05

Kusner, K., & Pargament, K. I. (2012). Shaken to the core: Understanding and addressing the spiritual dimension of trauma. In R. A. McMackin, E. Newman, J. M. Fogler, & T. M. Keane (Eds.), *Trauma therapy in context: The science and craft of evidence-based practice* (pp. 211-30). Washington, DC: American Psychological Association. doi:10.1037/13746-010

Langman, L., & Chung, M. (2013). The relationship between forgiveness, spirituality, traumatic guilt and posttraumatic stress disorder (PTSD) among people with addiction. *Psychiatric Quarterly, 84*(1), 11-26. doi:10.1007/s11126-012-9223-5

Lanham, S. L., & Pelletier, J. H. (2013). Spirituality in facilitating healing from war trauma. In R. M. Scurfield & K. T. Platoni (Eds.), *Healing war trauma: A handbook of creative approaches* (pp. 287-302). New York, NY: Routledge.

Lee, L., Connor, K. M., & Davidson, J. T. (2008). Eastern and Western spiritual beliefs and violent trauma: A U.S. national community survey. *Traumatology, 14*(3), 68-76. doi:10.1177/1534765608320328

Lev, S. N. (2015). *Spirit unbroken: Transpersonal experiences and improved well-being in those diagnosed with trauma-based dissociative disorders* (Doctoral dissertation). Retrieved from http://gradworks.umi.com/36/68/3668368.html

Levitt, H. M., Horne, S. G., Wheeler, E. E., & Wang, M.-C. (2015). Addressing intimate partner violence within a religious context. In D. F. Walker, C. A. Courtois, & J. D. Aten (Eds.), *Spiritually oriented psychotherapy for trauma* (pp. 211-31). Washington, DC: American Psychological Association.

Luna Pendleton, B. (2013). *Narratives of trauma, spirituality, and healing: An Ecuadorian shamanic perspective* (Doctoral dissertation). Retrieved from http://pqdtopen.proquest .com/doc/1500558545.html?FMT=ABS

Maeland, B. (Ed.). (2010). *Culture, religion, and the reintegration of female child soldiers in Northern Uganda.* New York, NY: Peter Lang.

Maltby, L. E., & Hall, T. W. (2012). Trauma, attachment, and spirituality: A case study. *Journal of Psychology & Theology, 40*(4), 302-12.

Marotta-Walters, S. A. (2015). Spiritual meaning making following clergy-perpetrated sexual abuse. *Traumatology, 21*(2), 64-70. doi:10.1037/trm0000022

Mayer, S. (2013). EMDR, spirituality, and healing in children. *Counseling et Spiritualité, 32,* 27-36.

McIntosh, D. N., Poulin, M. J., Silver, R. C., & Holman, E. A. (2011). The distinct roles of spirituality and religiosity in physical and mental health after collective trauma: A national longitudinal study of responses to the 9/11 attacks. *Journal of Behavioral Medicine, 34*(6), 497-507. doi:10.1007/s10865-011-9331-y

Mijares, S. G. (2005). Sacred wounding: Traumatic openings to the larger self. In S. G. Mijares & G. S. Khalsa (Eds.), *The psychospiritual clinician's handbook: Alternative methods for understanding and treating mental disorders* (pp. 75-95). New York, NY: Haworth Press.

Miller, D. (2002). Addictions and trauma recovery: An integrated approach. *Psychiatric Quarterly, 73*(2), 157.

Montes, B. L. (2015). Psychotherapist approaches to spiritual issues in trauma therapy. *Dissertation Abstracts International, 75,* (7-B)(E).

Morgan, O. J. (2009). Thoughts on the interaction of trauma, addiction, and spirituality. *Journal of Addictions & Offender Counseling, 30,* 5-15.

Murray-Swank, N. A., & Pargament, K. I. (2005). God, where are you? Evaluating a spiritually-integrated intervention for sexual abuse. *Mental Health, Religion & Culture, 8*(3), 191-203.

Murray-Swank, N. A., & Waelde, L. C. (2013). Spirituality, religion, and sexual trauma: Integrating research, theory, and clinical practice. In K. I. Pargament, A. Mahoney, & E. P. Shafranske (Eds.), *APA handbook of psychology, religion, and spirituality: Vol. 2. An applied psychology of religion and spirituality* (pp. 335-54). Washington, DC: American Psychological Association. doi:10.1037/14046-017

Neuner, F., Pfeiffer, A., Schauer-Kaiser, E., Odenwald, M., Elbert, T., & Ertl, V. (2012). Haunted by ghosts: Prevalence, predictors and outcomes of spirit possession experiences among former child soldiers and war-affected civilians in Northern Uganda. *Social Science & Medicine, 75*(3), 548-54. doi:10.1016/j.socscimed .2012.03.028

Newmeyer, M., Keyes, B., Palmer, K., Kent, V., Spong, S., Stephen, F., & Troy, M. (2016). Spirituality and religion as mitigating factors in compassion fatigue among trauma therapists in Romania. *Journal of Psychology & Theology, 44*(2), 142-51.

O'Grady, K. A., Rollison, D. G., Hanna, T. S., Schreiber-Pan, H., & Ruiz, M. A. (2012). Earthquake in Haiti: Relationship with the sacred in times of trauma. *Journal of Psychology & Theology, 40*(4), 289-301.

Oman, D., & Bormann, J. E. (2015). Mantram repetition fosters self-efficacy in veterans for managing PTSD: A randomized trial. *Psychology of Religion and Spirituality, 7*(1), 34-45. doi:10.1037/a0037994

Pargament, K. I. (2001). *The psychology of religion and coping: Theory, research, practice* (Rev. ed.). New York, NY: Guilford Press.

Pargament, K. I. (2007). *Spiritually integrated psychotherapy: Understanding and addressing the sacred.* New York, NY: Guilford Press.

Pargament, K. I., & Cummings, J. (2010). Anchored by faith: Religion as a resilience factor. In J. W. Reich, A. J. Zautra, & J. S. Hall (Eds.), *Handbook of adult resilience* (pp. 193-210). New York, NY: Guilford Press.

Pargament, K. I., Desai, K. M., & McConnell, K. M. (2006). Spirituality: A pathway to posttraumatic growth or decline? In L. G. Calhour & R. G. Tedeschi (Eds.), *Handbook of posttraumatic growth* (pp. 121-37). Mahwah, NJ: Erlbaum.

Park, C. L. (2009). Overview of theoretical perspectives. In C. L. Park, S. C. Lechner, M. H. Antoni, & A. L. Stanton (Eds.), *Medical illness and positive life change: Can crisis lead to personal transformation?* (pp. 11-30). Washington, DC: American Psychological Association.

Park, C. L. (2013). Trauma and meaning making: Converging conceptualizations and emerging evidence. In J. A. Hicks & C. Routledge (Eds.), *The experience of meaning in life: Classical perspectives, emerging themes, and controversies* (pp. 61-76). New York, NY: Springer.

Park, C. L. (2016). Meaning making in the context of disasters. *Journal of Clinical Psychology, 72*(12), 1234-46. doi:10.1002/jclp.22270

Park, C. L., Cohen, L. H., & Murch, R. L. (1996). Assessment and prediction of stress-related growth. *Journal of Personality, 64*(1), 71-105.

Park, C. L., Edmondson, D., & Blank, T. O. (2009). Religious and non-religious pathways to stress-related growth in cancer survivors. *Applied Psychology: Health and Well-Being, 1*(3), 321-35.

Park, C. L., Edmondson, D., & Mills, M. A. (2010). Religious worldviews and stressful encounters: Reciprocal influence from a meaning-making perspective. In T. W. Miller (Ed.), *Handbook of stressful transitions across the lifespan* (pp. 485-501). doi:10.1007/978-1-4419-0748-6_25

Park, C. L., & Gutierrez, I. A. (2013). Global and situational meanings in the context of trauma: Relations with psychological well-being. *Counselling Psychology Quarterly, 26*(1), 8-25.

Park, E. A. (2014). *Utilizing creative and expressive therapies to explore spiritual themes with traumatized children: A family psychology perspective and theoretical formulation* (Doctoral dissertation). Retrieved from http://gradworks.umi.com/36 /06/3606080.html

Partridge, K. J., & Walker, D. F. (2015). Addressing spiritual struggles using spiritually oriented trauma-focused cognitive behavioral therapy: An international case study. *Journal of Psychology and Christianity, 34*(1), 84-88.

Peres, J. P., Moreira-Almeida, A., Nasello, A. G., & Koenig, H. G. (2007). Spirituality and resilience in trauma victims. *Journal of Religion & Health, 46*(3), 343-50. doi:10.1007 /s10943-006-9103-0

Pressley, J. D., & Spinazzola, J. (2015). Beyond survival: Application of a complex trauma treatment model in the Christian context. *Journal of Psychology & Theology, 43*(1), 8-22.

Prout, T. A., Gerber, L. E., & Gottdiener, W. H. (2015). Trauma and substance use: The role of defenses and religious engagement. *Mental Health, Religion & Culture, 18*(2), 123-33.

Rambo, S. (2015). Spirit and trauma. *Interpretation, 69*(1), 7-19. doi:10.1177/0020964314552625

Ramsay, T., & Manderson, L. (2011). Resilience, spirituality and posttraumatic growth: Reshaping the effects of climate change. In I. Weissbecker (Ed.), *Climate change and human well-being: Global challenges and opportunities* (pp. 165-84). New York, NY: Springer. doi:10.1007/978-1-4419-9742-5

Rardin, M. A. (2014). *Psychospiritual trauma and integration: A narrative study of the recovery process of second-generation adult cult survivors* (Doctoral dissertation). Retrieved from http://gradworks.umi.com/36/06/3606933.html

Reinert, D. F., & Edwards, C. E. (2009). Attachment theory, childhood mistreatment, and religiosity. *Psychology of Religion and Spirituality, 1*(1), 25-34. doi:10.1037 /a0014894

Reinert, K. G., Campbell, J. C., Bandeen-Roche, K., Sharps, P., & Lee, J. (2015). Gender and race variations in the intersection of religious involvement, early trauma, and adult health. *Journal of Nursing Scholarship, 47*(4), 318-27. doi:10.1111/jnu.12144

Ren, Z. (2012). Spirituality and community in times of crisis: Encountering spirituality in indigenous trauma therapy. *Pastoral Psychology, 61*(5/6), 975-91. doi:10.1007 /s11089-012-0440-5

Richards, P. S., Hardman, R. K., Lea, T., & Berrett, M. E. (2015). Religious and spiritual assessment of trauma survivors. In D. F. Walker, C. A. Courtois & J. D. Aten (Eds.), *Spiritually oriented psychotherapy for trauma* (pp. 77-102). Washington, DC: American Psychological Association. doi:10.1037/14500-005

Roberts, S. B., & Ashley, W. C., Sr. (Eds.). (2008). *Disaster spiritual care: Practical clergy responses to community, regional, and national tragedy.* Woodstock, VT: SkyLight Paths.

Roland, A. G. (2016). Meaning, perceived growth, and posttraumatic stress among teachers in El Salvador: Assessing the impact of theistic and non-theistic experiences of spirituality. *Dissertation Abstracts International, 76,* (9-B)(E).

Rossetti, S. J. (1995). The impact of child sexual abuse on attitudes toward God and the Catholic church. *Child Abuse & Neglect, 19*(12), 1469-81. doi:10.1016/01452134 (95)00100-1

Santoro, A. F., Suchday, S., Benkhoukha, A., Ramanayake, N., & Kapur, S. (2016). Adverse childhood experiences and religiosity/spirituality in emerging adolescents in India. *Psychology of Religion and Spirituality, 8*(3), 185-94. doi:10.1037/rel0000038

Schultz, J. M., Tallman, B. A., & Altmaier, E. M. (2010). Pathways to posttraumatic growth: The contributions of forgiveness and importance of religion and spirituality. *Psychology of Religion and Spirituality, 2*(2), 104-14. doi:10.1037/a0018454

Severson, E., Becker, B., & Goodman, D. M. (Eds.). (2016). *In the wake of trauma: Psychology and philosophy for the suffering other.* Pittsburgh, PA: Duquesne University Press.

Shaw, A., Joseph, S., & Linley, P. A. (2005). Religion, spirituality, and posttraumatic growth: A systematic review. *Mental Health, Religion, & Culture, 8,* 1-11.

Sherman, M. D., Harris, J. I., & Erbes, C. (2015). Clinical approaches to addressing spiritual struggle in veterans with PTSD. *Professional Psychology: Research and Practice, 46*(4), 203-12. doi:10.1037/pro0000020

Shinall, M. J., & Guillamondegui, O. D. (2015). Effect of religion on end-of-life care among trauma patients. *Journal of Religion and Health, 54*(3), 977-83. doi:10.1007/s10943-014-9869-4

Sibley, C. S., & Bulbulia, J. (2012). Faith after an earthquake: A longitudinal study of religion and perceived health before and after the 2011 Christchurch New Zealand earthquake. *PLOS ONE, 7*(12): e49648. doi:10.1371/journal.pone.0049648

Sigmund, J. A. (2003). Spirituality and trauma: The role of clergy in the treatment of posttraumatic stress disorder. *Journal of Religion & Health, 42*(3), 221.

Sinha, J. W., & Rosenberg, L. B. (2013). A critical review of trauma interventions and religion among youth exposed to community violence. *Journal of Social Service Research, 39*(4), 436-54. doi:10.1080/01488376.2012.730907

Slattery, J. M., & Park, C. L. (2015). Spirituality and making meaning: Implications for therapy with trauma survivors. In D. F. Walker, C. A. Courtois, & J. D. Aten (Eds.), *Spiritually oriented psychotherapy for trauma* (pp. 127-46). Washington, DC: American Psychological Association. doi:10.1037/14500-007

Smedley, J. M. (2016). Negative spiritual responses to trauma: Lessons from urban ministry workers. *Dissertation Abstracts International, 76,* (9-B)(E).

Smith, S. (2004). Exploring the interaction of trauma and spirituality. *Traumatology, 10*(4), 231-43.

Smith, B., Pargament, K., Brant, C., & Oliver, J. (2000). Noah revisited: Religious coping by church members and the impact of the 1993 Midwest flood. *Journal of Community Psychology, 28*, 168-86.

Starnino, V. R. (2016). When trauma, spirituality, and mental illness intersect: A qualitative case study. *Psychological Trauma: Theory, Research, Practice, and Policy, 8*(3), 375-83. doi:10.1037/tra0000105

Stone, A. M. (2013). Thou shalt not: Treating religious trauma and spiritual harm with combined therapy. *Group, 37*(4), 323-37.

Stratta, P., Capanna, C., Riccardi, I., Perugi, G., Toni, C., Dell'Osso, L., & Rossi, A. (2013). Spirituality and religiosity in the aftermath of a natural catastrophe in Italy. *Journal of Religion & Health, 52*(3), 1029-37. doi:10.1007/s10943-012-9591-z

Tait, R., Currier, J. M., & Harris, J. I. (2016). Prayer, coping, disclosure of trauma, and mental health symptoms among recently deployed United States veterans of the Iraq and Afghanistan conflicts. *International Journal for the Psychology of Religion, 26*(1), 31-45.

Tan, S.-Y. (2013). Resilience and posttraumatic growth: Empirical evidence and clinical applications from a Christian perspective. *Journal of Psychology and Christianity, 32*(4), 358-64.

Taylor, A. W. (2001). Spirituality and personal values: Neglected components of trauma treatment. *Traumatology, 7*(3), 111-19. doi:10.1177/153476560100700303

ter Kuile, H., & Ehring, T. (2014). Predictors of changes in religiosity after trauma: Trauma, religiosity, and posttraumatic stress disorder. *Psychological Trauma: Theory, Research, Practice, and Policy, 6*(4), 353-60. doi:10.1037/a0034880

Thanh-Tu, N., Bellehumeur, C. R., & Malette, J. (2014). Women survivors of sex trafficking: A trauma and recovery model integrating spirituality. *Counseling et Spiritualité, 33*, 111-33. doi:10.2143/CS.33.1.3044833

Ting, R. S.-K. (2016). Celebrating life and death: Resiliency among post-earthquake Tibetans' religious community. *Journal of Psychology & Theology, 44*(2), 124-32.

Ting, R. S.-K., & Watson, T. (2007). Is suffering good? An explorative study on the religious persecution among Chinese pastors. *Journal of Psychology & Theology, 35*(3), 202-10.

Tran, C. T., Kuhn, E., Walser, R. D., & Drescher, K. (2012). The relationship between religiosity, PTSD, and depressive symptoms in Veterans in PTSD residential treatment. *Journal of Psychology & Theology, 40*(4), 313-22.

van den Blink, H. (2010). Traumaverwerking en spiritualiteit [Trauma and spirituality]. *Psyche En Geloof, 21*, 20-32.

Van Deusen, S., & Courtois, C. A. (2015). Spirituality, religion, and complex developmental trauma. In D. F. Walker, C. A. Courtois, & J. D. Aten (Eds.), *Spiritually oriented psychotherapy for trauma* (pp. 29-54). Washington, DC: American Psychological Association. doi:10.1037/14500-003

Van Hook, M. P. (2016). Spirituality as a potential resource for coping with trauma. *Social Work and Christianity, 43*(1), 7-25.

Van Hook, M., Furman, L. D., & Benson, P. W. (2016). Introduction: Special issue on spirituality and trauma. *Social Work and Christianity 43*(1), 1-5.

Verbeck, E. G., Arzoumanian, M. A., Estrellado, J. E., DeLorme, J., Dahlin, K., Hennrich, E., . . . Dalenberg, C. (2015). Religion, spirituality, and the working alliance with trauma survivors. In D. F. Walker, C. A. Courtois, & J. D. Aten (Eds.), *Spiritually oriented psychotherapy for trauma* (pp. 103-26). Washington, DC: American Psychological Association. doi:10.1037/14500-006

Vis, J., & Battistone, A. (2014). Faith-based trauma intervention: Spiritual-based strategies for adolescent students in faith-based schools. *Journal of Religion & Spirituality in Social Work: Social Thought, 33*(3-4), 218-35. doi:10.1080/15426432 .2014.930636

Vujanovic, A. A., Niles, B., Pietrefesa, A., Schmertz, S. K., & Potter, C. M. (2013). Mindfulness in the treatment of posttraumatic stress disorder among military veterans. *Spirituality in Clinical Practice, 1*(S), 15-25. doi:10.1037/2326-4500.1.S.15

Walker, D. F., & Aten, J. D. (2012). Future directions for the study and application of religion, spirituality, and trauma research. *Journal of Psychology & Theology, 40*(4), 349-53.

Walker, D. F., Courtois, C. A., & Aten, J. D. (2015). Basics of working on spiritual matters with traumatized individuals. In D. F. Walker, C. A. Courtois, & J. D. Aten (Eds.), *Spiritually oriented psychotherapy for trauma* (pp. 15-28). Washington, DC: American Psychological Association. doi:10.1037/14500-002

Walker, D. F., McGregor, K. L., Quagliana, D., Stephens, R. L., & Knodel, K. R. (2015). Understanding and responding to changes in spirituality and religion after traumatic events. In D. F. Walker, C. A. Courtois, & J. D. Aten (Eds.), *Spiritually oriented psychotherapy for trauma* (pp. 147-68). Washington, DC: American Psychological Association. doi:10.1037/14500-008

Walker, D. F., Reese, J. B., Hughes, J. P., & Troskie, M. J. (2010). Addressing religious and spiritual issues in trauma-focused cognitive behavior therapy for children and adolescents. *Professional Psychology: Research and Practice, 41*(2), 174-80. doi:10.1037 /a0017782

Walker, D. F., Reid, H. W., O'Neill, T., & Brown, L. (2009). Changes in personal religion/ spirituality during and after childhood abuse: A review and synthesis. *Psychological Trauma: Theory, Research, Practice, and Policy, 1*(2), 130-45. doi:10.1037/a0016211

Weiss-Ogden, K. R. (2014). *The relationship between trauma and spiritual well-being of women with substance use disorders* (Doctoral dissertation). Retrieved from http://pqdtopen.proquest.com/doc/1554346673.html?FMT=ABS

Werdel, M., Dy-Liacco, G., Ciarrocchi, J., Wicks, R., & Breslford, G. (2014). The unique role of spirituality in the process of growth following stress and trauma. *Pastoral Psychology, 63*, 57-71. doi:10.1007/s11089-013-0538-4

Whitmire, C. H. (2015). The role of spirituality in self-care for counselors working with trauma. *Dissertation Abstracts International, 76*, (1-B)(E).

Wilson, G. A. (2015). Trauma, coping, and the couple relationship: An investigation of pregnant couples' biopsychosocial-spiritual health. *Dissertation Abstracts International, 75*, (10-B)(E).

Wilson, J. P., & Moran, T. A. (1998). Psychological trauma: Posttraumatic stress disorder and spirituality. *Journal of Psychology & Theology, 26*(2), 168-78.

Wimberly, E. P. (2011). Storytelling and managing trauma: Health and spirituality at work. *Journal of Health Care for the poor and underserved, 22*(3, Suppl.), 48-57. doi:10.1353/hpu.2011.0103

Woodcock, J. (2001). Trauma and spirituality. In T. Spiers (Ed.), *Trauma: A practitioner's guide to counselling* (pp. 131-56). New York, NY: Routledge.

Worthington, E. L., Jr., Griffin, B., Toussaint, L., Nonterah, C., Utsey, S., & Garthe, R. (2016). Forgiveness as a catalyst for psychological, physical, and spiritual resilience in disasters and crises. *Journal of Psychology & Theology, 44*(2), 152-65.

Worthington, E. L., Jr., & Langberg, D. M. (2012). Religious considerations and self-forgiveness in treating complex trauma and moral injury in present and former soldiers. *Journal of Psychology & Theology, 40*(4), 274-88.

Wortmann, J. H., Park, C. L., & Edmondson, D. (2011). Trauma and PTSD symptoms: Does spiritual struggle mediate the link? *Psychological Trauma: Theory, Research, Practice, and Policy, 3*(4), 442-52. doi:10.1037/a0021413

Yedlin, J. I. (2012). *The role of religion and spirituality in the relation between trauma exposure, posttraumatic stress disorder, and alcohol use in emerging adults* (Doctoral dissertation). Retrieved from http://gradworks.umi.com/35/07/3507088.html

Zenkert, R. L., Brabender, V., & Slater, C. (2014). Therapists' responses to religious/spiritual discussions with trauma versus non-trauma clients. *Journal of Contemporary Psychotherapy, 44*(3), 213-21. doi:10.1007/s10879-014-9264-1

Zimmermann, E. A. (2011). *A narrative inquiry of women practitioners of eastern spirituality in recovery from childhood trauma* (Doctoral dissertation). Retrieved from http://gradworks.umi.com/34/90/3490158.html

CONTRIBUTORS

Kerryn Ansell, BA, is an alumna of Wheaton College and a graduate student at Northwestern University (IL). She is studying clinical mental health counseling, specializing in child and adolescent development. She has contributed to published research in neuropsychology and health psychology while at the Mayo Clinic (Rochester) and University of Newcastle (New South Wales).

Jamie Aten, PhD, is the Dr. Arthur P. Rech and Mrs. Jean May Rech Associate Professor of Psychology and founder and executive director of the Humanitarian Disaster Institute at Wheaton College (IL). His primary professional interests focus on the integration of psychological science and theology, with an emphasis on disaster mental health and trauma.

Karen F. Carr, PhD, is a clinical psychologist serving with Barnabas International. She has served in full-time missionary care since 2000. She lived in West Africa for nearly 15 years, providing training and crisis response with the Mobile Member Care Team (mmct.org). She has written several chapters and articles focusing on trauma care for missionaries.

Don E. Davis, PhD, is assistant professor of counseling and psychological services at Georgia State University. His research focuses on humility and other related virtues (e.g., forgiveness and gratitude) that help strengthen and repair relationships. He is also interested in the integration of spirituality into therapy and psychological interventions.

Edward B. Davis, PsyD, is associate professor of psychology at Wheaton College (IL). He is a licensed clinical psychologist and a core faculty member in the Wheaton PsyD program. His professional interests include assessment psychology, positive psychology, multicultural psychology, and the psychology of religion and spirituality, particularly people's relational spirituality (how they view and relate to God).

David N. Entwistle, PsyD, is professor of psychology at Malone University in Canton, Ohio. His interests include the integration of psychology and Christianity, coping, religious coping, and psychosocial issues in chronic illnesses.

Cynthia Blomquist Eriksson, PhD, is associate professor of psychology at Fuller Theological Seminary, Graduate School of Psychology. She is a clinical psychologist specializing in trauma, spirituality, and stress in ministry. Her teaching and publications focus on the needs of aid workers, missionaries, and pastors as they care for trauma survivors and recognize trauma in their own lives. She has received grant funding to create programs that facilitate collaboration between psychologists and ministry leaders.

Nikki Frederick, PhD, is a psychologist resident in Portland, Oregon. She currently has a private practice where she sees adolescents, adults, and couples for psychotherapy services. She emphasizes relational and existential approaches to therapy and specializes in treating depression, anxiety, trauma, and interpersonal difficulties.

Amanda Frey, LMSW, originally from Pennsylvania, now calls Texas home. The move was prompted by pursuing her MSW at the Diana R. Garland School of Social Work at Baylor University. During her academic career she collaborated with David Pooler, PhD, on research capturing experiences of female survivors of clergy sexual abuse across denominations. After graduating, Amanda began working as a behavioral health counselor and program director for geriatric populations at Providence DePaul Center in Waco.

Fred C. Gingrich, DMin, is professor of counseling at Denver Seminary. He is an approved supervisor with the American Association of Marriage and Family Therapy. In 2005 he returned to North America after eight years of service as professor of counseling at Alliance Graduate School in the Philippines, where he directed the MA programs in Christian counseling and marriage and family ministry. While in the Philippines he developed and directed the EdD counseling program offered by the Asia Graduate School of Theology. He has written a number of articles on marriage and family counseling, member care, and global mental health, and he coauthored the book *Skills for Effective Counseling: A Faith-Based Integration* with Elisabeth Nesbit Sbanotto and Heather Davediuk Gingrich (IVP).

Heather Davediuk Gingrich, PhD, is professor of counseling at Denver Seminary. She specializes in the treatment of complex trauma, including adult survivors of abuse, and has done research, writing, and clinical work in the area of dissociative disorders and trauma, as well as crosscultural counseling and research. Her books include *Restoring the Shattered Self: A Christian Counselor's Guide to Complex Trauma* (IVP) and *Skills for Effective Counseling: A Faith-Based Integration*, coauthored with Elisabeth Nesbit Sbanotto and Fred Gingrich (IVP).

Robert James Gregory, PhD, is professor emeritus at Wheaton College in Illinois, where he served as department chair for seven years until his retirement in 2012. He is the author of *Foundations of Intellectual Assessment* (1999) and *Psychological Testing: History, Principles, and Applications* (2016), now in its seventh edition. He lives near Seattle, Washington, where he pursues his artistic side as a prolific acrylics painter.

M. Elizabeth Lewis Hall, PhD, is professor of psychology at Rosemead School of Psychology, Biola University. Her current research focuses on women's issues in the evangelical subculture, meaning making in suffering, and the integration of psychology and theology. In addition to publications in evangelical journals such as *JPT*, *JPC*, and *Christian Scholars Review*, she has contributed a Christian voice in secular venues such as *Mental Health, Religion and Culture, Sex Roles*, and *Psychology of Women Quarterly*. She serves as associate editor for *Psychology of Religion and Spirituality* and as contributing editor for the *Journal of Psychology & Theology*.

Joshua N. Hook, PhD, is associate professor of psychology at the University of North Texas and is a licensed clinical psychologist in the state of Texas. His research interests focus on humility, religion/spirituality, and multicultural counseling. He blogs regularly at JoshuaNHook.com.

Jenny Hwang, MA, is the project manager for the Humanitarian Disaster Institute at Wheaton College. She received her master's degree in international disaster psychology from the University of Denver. Her research interests focus on global mental health in the context of disasters, social justice, crosscultural communication, and the psychological impact of forced migration.

Diane Langberg, PhD, is a practicing psychologist in Jenkintown, Pennsylvania, and is globally recognized for her work with trauma victims. She has trained caregivers the world over in responding to trauma and to the abuse of power. She is clinical faculty at Biblical Theological Seminary and directs a group counseling practice in Jenkintown. Her books include *Counsel for Pastors' Wives, On the Threshold of Hope, In Our Lives First: Meditations for Counselors*, and *Suffering and the Heart of God: How Trauma Destroys and Christ Restores*.

Richard Langer, PhD, is professor of biblical studies and theology at Talbot School of Theology, Biola University. He serves as the director of the Office of Faith and Learning. He specializes in the integration of faith and learning and has also published in the areas of bioethics, theology, and philosophy.

Madeline Lowen, MA, is a graduate of George Fox University's master of marriage, couples, and family counseling program. Her clinical experience focuses on working with children and families in high-risk populations. She has presented on trauma-sensitive education and has collaborated on several manuscripts in the areas of trauma and attachment.

Jesse David Malott, MDiv, PsyD, is a former minister and now clinical psychologist for Christ Community Health Services in Memphis, Tennessee. He specialized in combat trauma and traumatic brain injury as the PTSD fellow at the Memphis VA, where he also led the development of a novel group treatment for moral injury in veterans. He has done research and clinical work in the areas of trauma, grief, and spiritual injury.

Jason McMartin, PhD, is associate professor of theology at Rosemead School of Psychology and Talbot School of Theology, Biola University. He researches theological anthropology, sin, and flourishing. He has published in areas such as the integration of psychology and theology, philosophical theology, and spiritual formation.

Alison Miller, PhD, is a clinical psychologist in private practice in Victoria, Canada. She worked for many years in child and youth mental health services, treating children, parents, and families. She has worked with survivors of ritual abuse and mind control since 1990. Her two books on this subject break new ground in understanding these atrocities. *Healing the Unimaginable* (2012) sets out a road map for therapists treating survivors, and *Becoming Yourself* (2014) gives survivors an understanding of their condition and the way to find true healing.

Philip G. Monroe, PsyD, is director of training and mentoring with the American Bible Society in their Mission: Trauma Healing program. He is the Taylor Visiting Professor of Counseling and Psychology at Biblical Seminary, where he directed the graduate school of counseling for seventeen years. He maintains a private practice with Diane Langberg & Associates. His areas of specialty include crosscultural mental health and trauma recovery.

David Pooler, PhD, LCSW, is associate dean for academic affairs in the Diana R. Garland School of Social Work at Baylor University. He studies how social workers and other helping professionals flourish in their work and focuses on making safe spaces and places. In his practice he works with trauma survivors, people with dissociative disorders, and addictions. He has authored or coauthored more than 15 journal articles and book chapters.

Jana Pressley, PsyD, is director of training and professional development at the Trauma Center in Massachusetts. She is an adjunct associate professor at Richmont Graduate University in Atlanta, Georgia, and was formerly the clinical training and associate professor in the clinical psychology doctoral program at Wheaton College Graduate School. Her research interests are focused on the experience of court-involved young adults who have suffered relational trauma in the midst of chronic poverty and community violence, as well as the impact of complex trauma history on adult spirituality and meaning making.

Jenn Ranter, MA, is the managing director of the Humanitarian Disaster Institute, Wheaton College. She received her master's degree in clinical psychology from

Wheaton College in 2011. Her primary research interests include the psychology of religion and spirituality, with an emphasis on disaster mental health and trauma.

Alice Schruba, MA, is a doctorate of psychology candidate at Wheaton College and research assistant at the Humanitarian Disaster Institute at Wheaton College. Her primary research interests focus on the integration of psychological science within a disaster context, specifically the impact of disaster on spiritual and mental health.

Laura Schwent Shultz, PsyD, is a clinical neuropsychologist and the chief behavioral health officer at Christ Community Health Services in Memphis, Tennessee. She previously served as the director of the development team for the HEROES Care Program, a community-based program for service members and their families, providing support throughout the deployment cycle. She has done research, writing, and clinical work in the areas of combat trauma, neuropsychology, and health psychology.

Joseph Spinazzola, PhD, is the executive director of the Trauma Center and vice president of behavioral health and trauma services at Justice Resource Institute. He is a research professor of clinical practice in the department of psychology at Suffolk University and an adjunct professor at Richmont Graduate University. He is the director of the Complex Trauma Treatment Network of the SAMHSA-funded National Child Traumatic Stress Network, a national initiative to transform large regional and statewide systems of care, and is co-principal investigator of the Developmental Trauma Disorder National Field Trial. He specializes in the assessment, diagnosis, prevention, and treatment of complex trauma in children and adults.

William M. Struthers, PhD, is professor of psychology and neuroscience coordinator at Wheaton College (IL). He specializes in psychopharmacology, the biological bases of addiction, sexual compulsivity, neuroethics, and science/faith dialogue. He has conducted research, writing, and advocacy work in the area of pornography and sexual exploitation and is author of *Wired for Intimacy: How Pornography Hijacks the Male Brain* (IVP).

Daniel Sweeney, PhD, LMFT, RPT-S, is professor of counseling, director of the clinical mental health counseling program, and director of the NW Center for Play Therapy Studies at George Fox University. He is an international presenter on the topics of play and sandtray therapy and other expressive interventions for trauma. Daniel has authored or coauthored several books, including *Group Play Therapy: A Dynamic Approach* and *Sandtray Therapy: A Practical Manual*.

Debra L. Taylor, MA, is a marriage and family therapist and a certified sex therapist. She has taught sex therapy graduate courses at Richmont Graduate University, Dallas Theological Seminary, Fuller Theological Seminary, and Azusa

Pacific University. She has conducted research on female sexuality and is coauthor with Archibald Hart and Catherine Hart-Weber of *Secrets of Eve: Understanding the Mystery of Female Sexuality*.

Daryl R. Van Tongeren, PhD, is assistant professor of psychology at Hope College in Holland, Michigan. His research focuses on the social motivation for meaning and its relation to virtues and morality. He was named a 2016 Rising Star by the Association for Psychological Science. His research has been funded by generous grants from the John Templeton Foundation.

David C. Wang, PhD, is assistant professor of psychology at Rosemead School of Psychology in California. His areas of research interest include trauma and traumatic stress, spiritual formation and character/virtue development, mindfulness and self-compassion, spiritual theology (with special interest in the English Puritans), and various topics related to multicultural psychology and social justice.

Terri S. Watson, PsyD, ABPP, is associate dean and associate professor of psychology at Wheaton College (IL). She is a board certified clinical psychologist, an approved clinical supervisor with the Center for Credentialing and Education, and an approved supervisor with the American Association for Marriage and Family Therapy. Her clinical and scholarship interests include Christian faith and clinical psychology integration, clinical supervision, and crosscultural applications of psychology.

Ashley Wilkins, PhD, is a staff psychologist at the Jerry L. Pettis Memorial VA Medical Center. She specializes in the treatment of adults with trauma and PTSD, addressing complex and recent trauma related to combat and war zones as well as survivors of childhood and adult sexual traumas. Her clinical work, research, and writing have focused on trauma, attachment, self-care, and culture. She has contributed to *Health, Healing and Shalom: Frontiers and Challenges in Christian Health Care Missions*.

Adam Wilson, PhD, is assistant professor of counseling at Denver Seminary. He is also a licensed professional counselor with a part-time practice at Southwest Counseling Associates in Littleton, Colorado, where he specializes in the treatment of children and adolescents. His research interests are in the areas of neuropsychology, psychopharmacology, and human development.

Shannon M. Wolf, PhD, is the associate director for counseling programs as well as professor of counseling and psychology at B. H. Carroll Theological Institute. She specializes in complex trauma and domestic minor sex trafficking. She writes, researches, and speaks on issues of human trafficking. In addition, she directs a counseling center in Fort Worth, Texas.

SUBJECT INDEX

CAPS

An Association for Christian Psychologists,
Therapists, Counselors and Academicians

CAPS is a vibrant Christian organization with a rich tradition. Founded in 1956 by a small group of Christian mental health professionals, chaplains and pastors, CAPS has grown to more than 2,100 members in the U.S., Canada and more than 25 other countries.

CAPS encourages in-depth consideration of therapeutic, research, theoretical and theological issues. The association is a forum for creative new ideas. In fact, their publications and conferences are the birthplace for many of the formative concepts in our field today.

CAPS members represent a variety of denominations, professional groups and theoretical orientations; yet all are united in their commitment to Christ and to professional excellence.

CAPS is a non-profit, member-supported organization. It is led by a fully functioning board of directors, and the membership has a voice in the direction of CAPS.

CAPS is more than a professional association. It is a fellowship, and in addition to national and international activities, the organization strongly encourages regional, local and area activities which provide networking and fellowship opportunities as well as professional enrichment.

To learn more about CAPS, visit www.caps.net.

CAPS BOOKS
from IVP Academic

The joint publishing venture between IVP Academic and CAPS aims to promote the understanding of the relationship between Christianity and the behavioral sciences at both the clinical/counseling and the theoretical/research levels. These books will be of particular value for students and practitioners, teachers and researchers.

For more information about CAPS Books, visit InterVarsity Press's website at www.ivpress.com/cgi-ivpress/book.pl/code=2801.